Introduction to Brands

Tan Xinzheng

Zhu Zerong

Yang Jinfei

I Wing Press

 I Wing Press

Introduction to Brands

Copyright © 2017
by Tan Xinzheng, Zhu Zerong, Yang Jinfei
All rights reserved
Printed in the United States of America
No part of The book may be used or produced in any manner whatsoever without written permission except in the case of brief quotations embodied in critical articles or reviews. For information, address I Wing Press:
admin@iwingpress.com
http://www.iwingpress.com

Printed by UADCNY Inc. http://www.printandmat.com

Designed by Wang Changhua

ISBN 9781940742113

First Edition, February 2017
First Printing, February 2017

Brand and Marketing Expert Tan Xinzheng

Tan Xinzheng.
Pen Name: Seeking for the truth comes from Jinshan
Profession:
A researcher of Renmin University of China, an Expert Member of the Standardization Administration of the People's Republic of China (brand evaluation, wholesales and retails), the Director of the China General Chamber of Commerce, the Vice-chairman of the China Foundation of Consumer Protection, the Vice-chairman of the China Association of Small &Medium Commercial Enterprise, the Vice-chairman and Secretary-general of the Chinese Vocal Institute for Chinese Ethnic Minorities, the Director of the Beijing Sky Certification Center, and the President of the Wuzhou Creativity Marketing and Planning Co., Ltd.

Career and Achievement:

For more than 30 years, Tan Xinzheng has made great achievements in the fields of journalist industry, marketing planning, setting standardization, brand and service certification, and the works of the national industry association.

1. The field of journalist industry

He has made great achievements as a journalist by issuing more than 3,000 pieces of messages, press releases, feature article, reportages, thesis and poetries, which have won more than 10 Good News Prizes at the provincial level, including a Special Prize for the *First Exploration for Newspaper Visual News*.

2. The field of marketing planning

10 years of marketing planning and large exhibition projects with national wide influence. In 2000, he won the titles of the Top 10 Planning Experts in China, and the Top 10 Planning Celebrities of China. He planned more than 100 large projects such as:

the Best Advertising Combination of the National Sugar and Wine Expo,
the Spring Action of the Green Hope Project,
the China Real Estate Planning Contest,
the China Hairdressing Contest,
the China Planning Conference,
the China Integrity Evaluation Activity,
the China Enterprise Brand Evaluation Activity,
the National After-Sales Service Evaluation Activity,
the China Alcohol Industry Evaluation Activity,
the China Jewelries and Accessories Evaluation Activity,
and the China Furniture Industry Evaluation Activity.

3. The field of setting standardization

10 years of setting standardization to make up the national standards for brands and services. Tan Xinzheng has launched, organized, drafted, implemented and promoted more than 10 national and national industrial standards, including:

the first *Evaluation of Business Enterprise Brand and Guide of Enterprise Culture Construction*,
the *Evaluation System for After-sales Service of Commodity*,
the *Standard of Circulation and Service for Alcohol Industry*,
the *Standard of Business & Service for Household Industry*,
the *Service Standard of Jewelry Accessories Business*,
the *Behavior Rules for Retailers and Suppliers in Fair Transaction*,
the *Appraisal Criteria for Business Devise*,
and the *Service Standard of Operation on Imported Wines*.

4. The field of brand and service certification

He has established the first brand and after-sales service certification authority, pioneering in Service Certification and Brand Certification. Beijing Sky Certification Center is a professional certification authority focusing on certifications of brands, after-sales services and intangible assets, which is recommended by the Ministry of Commerce of the People's Republic of China and approved by Certification and Accreditation Administration of the People's Republic of China (CNCA). Tan Xinzheng is the legal representative of the center.

5. Published works:

Taste of Life,
Cases of Real Estate Planning in China (3 Volumes),
Moving the God – Guide to Use the Commodity After-Sales Services (6 Volumes),
Introduction to Brands,
Introduction to Services,
Training Course of After-Sales Service Management Professional,
Training Course of Certification and Review Professional for After-Sales Services,
Best Combination Code for Media Promotion.

2001-2015: he has served as an expert judge for marketing, planning, standard promotion, integrity and social responsibility.

2015-now: he has served an expert judge in Chinese Hongmu professionals.

Beliefs:
1. General life target:
Fight for the best and plan for the worst.
2. Two Things that will never be done:
No guilty deeds or wicked things.
3. Two things didn't debt to others
No monetary debt and emotional debt.
4. Thee directions:
Lightening others, making personal achievements and wining honors for China.
5. Codes of conducts

Making targets in the view of the world, and doing works in a practical way;
Learning from good teachers and establishing my own style;
Be successful by selecting correct starting points and making constant efforts;
Be patient and tolerant to everyone.

E-mail: 13911159899@139.com

Introduction to Zhu Zerong

Zhu Zerong (formerly known as Zhu Xiaohui)

Profession: A management scientist

Work: *Introduction to Brands* Life

Experience: Zhu Zerong was born in 1976 in a worker's family and was brought up by his parents in an automobile factory. Therefore, he is very familiar with large enterprises since he was little.

Career:
1. Initial stage

When he was in school, he was interested in the actual management of the factory and worked as a worker of the production line after he graduated and then began to conduct basic management work of the enterprise.

2. Research direction

During his learning and work, Zhu Zerong has met the managements at all levels, and was determined to spend his life conducting the scientific researches of the management science. He gradually handled the ability to identify management issues on the site, summarize management methods, and find out the rules of scientific management, summarized and developed scientific management rules, and invented the management technical systems from the practices of enterprise management.

3. Development and achievement

He spent 22 years on the high intensity learning and research and various scientific management experiments invested and conducted by himself. Finally, he established the scientific management methods by developing advanced brand theories, designing management system, constructing management subjects and inventing management methods, and made great contributions to the establishment of the brand science. At present, he is dedicated to the research and development of the theories of brand science and management science, and has entered into a high yield period of theoretical researches.

Introduction to Yang Jinfei

Yang Jinfei
Profession: A major pioneering figure in China's service and brand certification sector; A lecturer and course developer for registered certifiers; A brilliant expert in the fields of Chinese branding, service research and certification.

Main Achievement:
1. He initiated the certification technique for "After-sale Service of Goods" and "Brand of Commercial Enterprises".
2. He designed the processes, management documents, technical standards and scoring rules for certification regarding the after-sales service of goods and brands. The following examples are:

The Evaluation System for After-sales Service of Commodity (GB/T27922-2011),

Evaluation of Business Enterprise Brand and Guide of Enterprise Culture Construction (GB/T27925-2011),

The Service Standard of Jewelry Accessories Business (SB/T10653-2012)

The Standard of Circulation and Service for Alcohol Industry (SB/T11000-2013),

Operational Service Standards of Furniture (SB/T10903-2013).

3. He has helped hundreds of large and medium-sized enterprises to build and improve their after-sales service, branding and standard systems.

Publications:
Introduction to Brands,
Touching God – A Practical Guide to After-sales Service of Goods,
Modern Vocational Education (reversed): Training of After-sales Managers,
Construction and Review of Elements for Corporate Branding and After-sales Service System,
An Evaluation Guide to Corporate Capacity in After-sales Service.

Contents

Authors Profile ··· I
Preface ·· II
Brief Introduction ··· III

Section I General Introduction

Chapter 1   Brand Introduction ·· 01
Chapter 2   Brand Definition ·· 12
Chapter 3   Brand Standardization ·· 23
Chapter 4   Brand Power ··· 31
Chapter 5   Brand User Groups ··· 40
Chapter 6   Brand Performance ··· 48
Chapter 7   Leading Position ·· 57
Chapter 8   Deciding Competitiveness ···································· 69
Chapter 9   Internet + Brand ·· 78

Section II Brand Subjects

Chapter 1   Brand History ·· 91
Chapter 2   Brand Principles ··· 105
Chapter 3   Brand Pathology ··· 116
Chapter 4   Brand Strategy ·· 124
Chapter 5   Brand Organization ·· 136
Chapter 6   Brand Consumption ··· 148
Chapter 7   Brand Products ··· 157
Chapter 8   Brand Service ··· 166
Chapter 9   Brand Quality ··· 175
Chapter 10   Brand Experience ·· 183
Chapter 11   Brand Planning ·· 191
Chapter 12   Brand News ··· 200

Section III　Brand Technology

    Chapter 1　Brand Technical System ·················· 207

    Chapter 2　Brand Technology Preparation ·················· 219

    Chapter 3　Brand Construction Technology ··················227

    Chapter 4　Brand Classification Technology ·················· 247

    Chapter 5　Brand Recognition Technology ·················· 262

    Chapter 6　Brand Management Technology ·················· 276

    Chapter 7　Brand Marketing Technology ·················· 292

    Chapter 8　Brand Communication Technology ·················· 309

    Chapter 9　Brand Collaboration Technology ·················· 324

Section IV　Brand Culture

    Chapter 1　World Brand Pattern ·················· 335

    Chapter 2　Brand and Enterprise Culture ·················· 345

    Chapter 3　Brand Artistic Conception ·················· 355

    Chapter 4　Brand Aesthetics ·················· 363

    Chapter 5　Brand Culture Consumption ·················· 371

    Chapter 6　Brand Culture Connotation ·················· 379

    Chapter 7　Brand Image Upgrading ·················· 391

    Chapter 8　Brand Artistic Expression ·················· 404

Section V　Brand Reengineering

    Chapter 1　DID Brand Reengineering Principles ·················· 415

    Chapter 2　Brand Organizations Reengineering ·················· 438

    Chapter 3　Reengineering of Brand Management System ······· 449

Questions for Review and Answers ·················· 460

Answers to the Exercises ·················· 471

Learning Methods ·················· 481

Postscript ·················· 483

Categories of Brand ·················· 487

Sino-American Multicultural Alliance Profile ·················· 489

Preface: Future-oriented Brand Subjects

We have been thinking about a key issue in the view of human beings' development: what's the future of brand science?

No matter on the level of the global brand competition or the brand economic development of any country or even the economies of industrial cluster brands, we have to think about and solve the problem of developing international brands in a large-scale. Undoubtedly, the revitalization of the brand economy depends on the establishment of a series of new brand theories, the clarification of the brand subjects' structure and the invention and development of brand technology. This lies on the systematic studies and scientific designing of the brand subjects from theories to practices in general as well as the detailed brand practices promoting international enterprises in the form of complete brand subjects.

The future-oriented attribute lays a foundation for brand science. The scientific nature of brand science can be officially defined only through substantially enhancing the proportion of science in it and creating a great of brand science principles. The birth of a new brand or the revival of an old brand entails supports of the systematic brand principles and technology. Therefore, the human beings must step into a new era–an era of the scientific brand subjects.

The profound exploration process from brand phenomena to scientific brand subjects not only means a cognitional thought, but more importantly, defines the solid scientific researches as the developing direction of brand management. We have devoted over a decade to testing, researching and studying the development of international brands both at home and abroad to systematically propose the new brand concepts, thoughts, principles and tools.

Not only us, leaders of the global brand economies and industrial cluster brand economies, leaders dreaming of creating brands, but also all the persons currently learning about brands and practitioners improving brand management need to try exploring, thinking, creating and clarifying a structure for "what's the future of brands".

From the international rule-making of brands, national, local or industrial cluster's brand economies, emerging enterprises cherishing dreams to the established enterprises planning for brand reengineering, the question of "what's the future of brands" must be answered for relative enterprises, investors and the whole brand organization.

People are eager to know about the brand future of the organizations, enterprises they work for. All organizations and enterprises have to answer this question clearly. In fact, all people will ask this question, be they the members of brand economic organization, brand investors, key members, employees or brand users. They all would like to know its answer. After repeatedly asking and pondering over this question, they turn to think about the future and prospect of a brand by virtue of the obtained explanations and understanding so as to further decide whether to continue investing and developing with the brand or leave away.

We always deem the future-oriented brand science as a perspective, anticipating and an advanced way of thinking and as anticipation thinking. Brand science needs to explain the future of a country, organization or enterprise. The future of a brand shall create a grand prospect, light up all people's dreams and influence all brand users. The brand founders, brand leaders, brand officers, brand investors and enterprise managers shall also understand how to realize the future of brands in an orderly, systematic and scientific way, so as to resolve the problems related to brand development in real terms.

In the 21st, 22nd and 23rd centuries or even a farther future of human beings, the brand science must develop based on various subjects, principles, instruments and technology. Despite the complicated brand economic phenomena and start from the essence of science, the brand science will secure significant development. And the theory and technology of the brand science will be further used in countries, economies and enterprises dedicated to developing brands.

Brand economic phenomena, brand concepts, brand designing thoughts, brand planning methods and brand practice cases will witness profound changes as time goes by whereas the systematic and scientific brand science theories, solid brand philosophy and practical brand technology and instruments will remain stable despite of time lapse, which is the essence of the *Introduction to Brands* and our original intention of studying and developing these theories for years. We believe that the proposal of the scientific brand theories is the essence of the brand science's development and we hereby hope that more achievements will be made in this field.

The progress of brand science in enterprise practice includes not only proposing some important brand thoughts, but also exploring advanced important management methods for brand organizations going through brand reengineering repeatedly. Every several years the brand reengineering of an enterprise will be conducted in the form of starting a new undertaking for the second, third or even forth time, so as to enable the brand organization to keep pace with the time, maintain its vigor and realize the eternal operation and evergreen future of the enterprise.

With years' efforts, from the view of department and subject construction we have initially established the brand theoretical system by designing structural brand theories of brand introduction, subjects, technology, cultures and reengineering. A series of rules, principle, theories, thoughts and methods have been proposed to help enterprises deepen their understanding of the brand competition patterns from the perspective of professional brand science, master the key elements of the future brand competition and help entrepreneurs, brand officers and brand practitioners as well as teachers and students of the brand major in higher education institutes to look into the future of the brands.

Introduction to Brands not only initiates the brand subjects, but also will become a popular management thought in the world, as well as an open source knowledge procedure. We have proposed the basic structure framework of brand subjects, some scientific principles, development orientations, technologies and instruments of brand science, aiming at encouraging all brand economies, enterprises, management researchers, brand technology users and brand learners to supplement new brand principles, technology and instruments through practices and sum up the problems encountered in brand researches and practices to develop a more complete, advanced and practical brand subjects for the progress of human beings so as to create brand miracles, promote the national economies of all countries, increase incomes of and provide a better life for all people.

Brief Introduction

Introduction to Brands, as the fundamental work of the brands subjects, marks a great breakthrough in the brand theoretical research system of the world. It has entered the theory promotion phase where the systematic brand theoretical research methods and advanced brand technology are being established gradually, providing powerful theoretical support for the development of brands in all countries, industries, cities and enterprises.

Reputed as the first systematic and complete work of brand science theory, the Introduction to Brands is composed of five sections including brand introduction, brand subjects, brand technology, brand culture and brand reengineering, which contain 41 articles. In the future, another 10 sub-theories will be added. The authors, Tan Xinzheng, Zhu Zerong and Yang Jinfei, are senior experts in brand science and they have devoted more than 10 years to completing the Introduction to Brands with over 500,000 Chinese characters, which has a guiding role to play in the global brand practice and development against an age of economic structure transformation and consumption up grading.

Introduction to Brands is a practical achievement in terms of brand theoretical researches and practices, which has revealed the development pattern and prospect of future brand science: it has not only officially defined brand for the first time, but also confirmed the brand position in future social and economic development and predicated that brand would dominate the economic trends of various industries.

Chapter 1

Brand Introduction

Brand is the general term for development of activities of human beings for creating, using, developing and consuming brands. Brands are the core capacity for human beings' social and economic development, the representation of the pursuit to mental and physical creations and the marks for the improvement of the civilization of human beings. Brands are the engines for the development of sciences, technologies and arts of human beings, the future-oriented frontier science for human beings, the top stage for the development of consumption power and productivity of human beings, and the inevitable achievements made by human beings in creating high-level civilizations. Brands include three structural development levels, namely, the brand economy of human beings, national branding strategies and the brand ecological organization of enterprises. Brands are the strategic knowledge reserves, capacity reserves and the development level of comprehensive utilization level for human beings, countries, enterprises and individuals, and the development method for human beings to determine productivity with consumption power. Brands have changed the basic understanding and utilization method of human beings in terms of labor division, labors and fortunes.

Where do brands come from? How do we develop brands? What's the future of brands?

Through the complicated issues related to the social patterns of brands, economic phenomena of brands and brand development, we have seen the essence of brands, and further understood the scientific development laws of brands to develop our brand ideologies, establish our systematic brand science and identify clearer practical guides and routes for the development of brands.

The human society is heading to the well-developed brand economy age rapidly, and the features of brand economy will become the basic social and economic development structure for human being to pursue cutting edge and look ahead. The population, sciences, technologies, societies, economy, cultures, capital and national actions in the future will be based on the highly developed brand social foundations through unprecedented scientific patterns and cultural and environmental frames.

The early developed countries, such as the United States, the UK, France, Germany and Italy, have already established the basic economic structure featuring the brand output countries as early as in the 20th century. Some other countries, such as Japan and South Korea, made great efforts in this aspect in the second half of the 20th century, and become developed countries through the national brand activities. Developing countries, such as China and India, are still trying to become strong brand countries in the first half of the 21st century. During the deep and rapid development of global brand economy in the 21st century, and human higher grade civilization development structure centering at brand ecology, the brand output country competition between countries and the international brand competition between enterprises are undergoing throughout the world. Today and in the far future, the meanings, values and fortunes of brands to countries, enterprises and everyone will be changed rapidly.

1 Introduction to brand science

Brands are the leading factor of society and economy that may occur at certain development degree of commodity exchange and labor division of human beings. Four basic conditions shall be met for the prosperity and development of brand economy in the history of human beings or in a country:

Section I General Introduction

(1) oversupply of commodities, or the commodities available for exchange are more than those demanded by people;

(2) commodities in higher-level forms appeared, or the supplies and demands of additional attributes of commodities, such as qualities, performance and services, have surpassed the values of the commodities as production means, and non-entity transaction varieties such as virtual products have been greatly developed as the features of new consumer demands of human beings;

(3) the labor value has been fully reflected, the initial labor divisions of human beings have developed to a high form, and the labor value assignment could be effectively reflected in the purchasing value;

(4) human beings have entered into the high-level civilization development stage, the comprehensive combination of cultures, arts and commodities have led to the systematic high-level perception demands and the consumption patterns with new brand cultures have been formed.

When the four conditions named above are met, brands will replace commodities and become the new supply-and-demand pattern of human beings. Society will be effectively connected and operated as super brand ecological chain, meaning that all human beings have entered into the age of brand economy. The developments can vary from country to country, and if any country could meet the four conditions, this means that this country has entered into the brand economy age and has the initial capacity of breeding, creating and developing brands.

Brands have two-way functions, which are a synchronous development relationship between the consumers and manufacturers, and the orders used by human beings in the brand economy age to balance social and economic development conflicts – the main core elements required in the social and economic operation structure are the most important parts in national economic capacities, social wealth, monetary assets, financial capitals and family assets.

In the long history of human beings, super social and economic development medium, such as brands, have never appeared until the 19th century. In the 20th century, brands have appeared and started playing the leading role in social economy by powerful consumption power and productivity, and playing important frontier roles in the development patterns of national strategic capitals, national wealth growth and family assets. Brands will finally substitute all competition patterns and become the most important determining competitiveness for the social stability, economic construction, enterprise development and organization patterns in a country.

1.1 Instinct of human beings to develop brands

The instinct of human beings to develop brands is completed through five stages, namely:

(1) development of survival instinct to development instinct;

(2) the civilization instinct of human beings has created the genes of brand civilization;

(3) the oversupply and booming competition of commodities have promoted the shift function of brands for brand cultures;

(4) the inherit instinct of important ideologies during civilization renaissance has officially bred brands and given the birth of brands intensely;

(5) the continuous driving force for the high level development of future brand economy comes from the instinct of human beings for branding.

Brands are not the demand instinct for the primitive survival of human beings. The primitive survival demands of human beings include food, water, clothes, shelters, and traffic tools. These basic demands will evolve with the development of human beings into the physical and mental demands of human beings for food processing, liquors, garments, precious metals, construction materials and artistic patterns. Therefore, the labor divisions of human beings will be further developed, and the demand levels will be improved constantly. When the primitive survival demands have separated from the essence of survival, the social capacity of commodity exchange will be updated to the trading attribute of commodity exchange, and the basic forms of brands and brand economy will be further developed. Human beings have spent more than 30 million years to complete the transition from the primitive survival age of fossil anthropoid to the age of civilization demand development of human beings.

However, this doesn't mean the creation of brands. In the following 6000 years' civilization improvement of human beings, brands have just been bred from prototypes and original forms. The parent of brands is the systematic civilization production process of human beings. When a specific civilization is formed and expressed through certain style, the civilization genes for breed by brands are born. Then, a long period shall be used for the birth of brands. Only when the commodities have developed to the moment of oversupply in terms of types and quantities, can the economic development of human beings be matched with the instinct expectation for civilization renaissance, and the moment of birth of brands will come.

Brands could not be created only with the genes of brand civilization. In the age without sufficient commodities, people only needed survival and the society only needed to produce commodities. Consumers did not have too many options. Brands could only be seen in case of over demand, and people did not have the concept of brands. When the supply has surpassed the demand, the diversified options of consumers will be developed, and the manufacturers shall consider the diversified competition with their competitors, so as to make consumers find them among similar options. Therefore, the word "brand" became an English word with the origin of "smear", brand acts have been established and the instinct of manufacturers to seed for market protection has developed.

The longer the age of commodity shortage of a country is in, the later the moment for the country to enter into the brand economy will be. We have noticed that it is a basic condition to create brands when commodities of a country become saturated and highly prosperous. The collective birth of brands could occur at the same time with the moment of a country to become a developed country. The reason that a country is still a developing country is that the country is still developing its commodity economy and has not entered into the brand economy age.

Brands are the final products of high-level market competition. The intensifying competition will urge the brand founders and organizers to increase the input in R&D, and pay attention to the continuous improvements in terms of raw materials, quality, equipment, production technologies and other brand performance links. The brand supporting service fields such as advertising, public relationship, marketing management, market survey, management consulting, consumer research, logistics and warehouses will be developed. The brand operation system focusing on brand business modes and operation modes are developed. The social and economic development of modern human society is the process for brands to spread throughout the world to create a giant brand ecological chain in the world.

In fact, this is the improvement of the instinct selection of human beings. Selections are occurring constantly, and the diversified brand world is formed in this way. The most basic selection is survival or development. Some enterprises are pursuing survival, and their capacities in terms of market and sales are developed. Such enterprises mainly focus on the ratio of input to output and will use the WYSIWYG economic return method to realize the improvement of the enterprises. The enterprises pursuing survival can never develop their own brands. When the enterprises of a country are developing in the survival mode, this country can never develop brands.

Some other enterprises will pursue development by giving up temporary benefits. Such enterprises would like to create the best brands by seeking for best waters, raw materials, crafts and processes. Thus, the brands are developing. In this process, the brand civilization genes inherited from the early civilization of human beings have generated surprising catalyst influence on the first international brands in the world, and the initial brands of the world were created in this way.

According to the researches on the origins of international brands, the Celtic civilization generated in the Ireland, Scotland and Gaul areas are the major origin of the brand civilization of the world. More than half of the brands and national brand symbols that are familiar to the people are from this civilization. The founders of these brands are mainly the descendants of the civilization or come from the countries and areas significantly influenced by this civilization. The fully renaissance of the craftsman spirits, natural ecological ideologies, order network and cultural and art creation styles of the Celtic civilization is the main origin of the brands in the world. The common brand civilization genes can be found from Uncle Sam or founders of P&G, Ford, IBM, Microsoft and XO, as well as modern brands of the Hollywood movie styles and music, the Italian designs, the English styles, the German automobile manufacturing industry and the Swiss watch industry.

The pursuit for brands by human beings is not limited. With the increase of incomes, people will select better brands. With the intensifying competition, enterprises will constantly select the better brand development methods. When the balanced development relationship is built between the demand selections of consumption capacity and the creation, the brand ecology with benign operation of a country will be established, and the brands of this country or enterprise will be integrated into the global brand ecological chain and become an active brand branch.

1.2 Development laws of brand economy of human beings

In general, the development of the brand economy of human beings is the process for us to constantly improve ourselves and change the world and the future, the process for human beings to pursue the perfect self-expressions, the process of constantly improving the natural ecological development laws, and the process of optimizing the social networking service functions. During this process, great brand wealth has been created, and the better civilization forms have been established. This process is the perfect and unified consistent progress process integrating theories and practices, sciences and philosophy, images and facts, mental and physical values.

Theories and practices: The development of any civilization of human beings depends on the improvements of the theoretical and practical functions. The development of brands is the process of exploring brand theories. During this process, we would find, identify and summarize the scientific laws of brands, which will be used in the brand practices, and the development routes of brands will be finally professionalized and systematized. If the births of the first brands of human beings are the self-exploration without consciousness, then the development of brands in the future will be subject to the practices guided by theories. The active brand creation during practices shall match with the brand practice guiding theories. The development of human beings has proposed higher requirements for the brand theories in the future. The theories shall deeply understand the brands in the view of human progress, and shall be closely integrated with the long-term development practices in the future. Only in this way can the brand science be developed, so as to promote the countries, societies, enterprises and families to create brand wealth, and make active contributions to the development of human beings.

Science and philosophy: The development of the dual values of brands in science and philosophy is the major difference between the brands and the ordinary commodity, commodity economy, labor or labor divisions. In science, the aim of the development of brands is not only to provide research samples for the developments of the scientific principles and technologies of brands through explorations, but it is also a process to follow the scientific laws of brand development. During the formation of a brand, philosophy has developed the brand designing thought, operation philosophy, ideology, and artistic representation. The dual value development structure of brand science and philosophy is the source of the thoughts, consciousness, missions, ideologies, creativities and creations to complete the high-level development of brand economy and the deep competition. Both science and philosophy have important sense of mission, which could further improve the efforts made by human beings to develop high-level civilizations, promote the development of human beings, improve the social and economic development of countries and are the basic conditions for the improvement of human thoughts and actions.

Imagination and facts: The brands are the process of creation and expression, the process of scientific development from images to facts, and the necessary results of synchronous development of imagination science and fact science. Imagination science has accounted for a large proportion in the brand development. The processes that brand founders conceive a brand outline or brand development prospect, enterprises depict future of brand business mode to investors, partners and employees, or designers carried out various artistic creation for brand in an abstract way are the creation processes proposing, using and developing imagination. The management executives and professional talents could translate the imaginations to actual brands, and the brand operation network could translate the brand prospect into the actual references for operation benefits, so as to complete the repeated and progressive development process from imagination to facts. The circular developments from brand imaginations to facts, the replacement of brand works and the continuous brand investments could provide sufficient spaces for imaginations and the development capacities that could be verified. Thus brands could fully grow, be mature and developed.

Mental and physical values: Brands have created the mental and physical values. The physical values are developed from the mental values and the mental values are derived from the physical values. These are the necessary results of the pursuit of human beings for good things, and the two-way development process of creating the mental and physical wealth. The human essences at the spiritual and conscious levels such as the craftsman spirit, national spirit, undertaking spirit, professional ethics, civilization development consciousness, social service consciousness, labor value consciousness, brand value consciousness and ecological environmental consciousness are integrated into the creation, production and formation of physical wealth, laying a solid foundation for the physical creation method for human beings to constantly create the expressions with more spirits, cultures and impressions. In turn, when using the branding matters, people could obtain the spirit resonance and consciousness that are consistent with the brands, so as to improve and develop the spiritual needs beyond the physical needs. This has given lives, souls and values to physical values, and make the physical matters get rid of the original physical forms and become a physical enjoying and experience process of high-level civilization. This has further stimulated the spiritual and mental expression aspirations of the physical creators to give their best effort to create better physical forms and mental states. Brands will get sufficient development space during the circulation of creation and application.

2 Birth of the brand science

The development of brands appeared as a social phenomenon and economic tendency in the first place, leading to the theoretical explanations to the brand concepts and phenomena. However, the complete and systematic brand science has not developed. This has involved the scientific explanations to the essence of brands, which is a long-term process of identifying, drawing, summarizing, inventing and developing brand scientific roles from the complicated brand phenomena, issues and tendencies. This process is a long term scientific exploration for brands, and the complete improvement process of independently developing the brand science, systematically establishing the theoretical basis of the brand science and creating the structural framework of the brand science.

The astronomy has been widely developed during the construction of pyramids and Stonehenge, and in the inscriptions on bones or tortoise shells of the Shang Dynasty. However, when the heliocentric theory was proposed by Copernicus, the observation by Galileo of the stars and the law of universal gravitation was proposed by Newton, the official system of the astronomy was established, which has become one of the most important basic sciences of modern human beings.

The formation of a science is a process of identifying scientific principles, developing academic theories and guiding practices with theories based on the summarization of experiences, which may last for hundreds or thousands years. Before the formation of a science, the explanations for complicated and confusing phenomena, the analysis of the discoveries, the exploration of theories and the proposal of concepts are the necessary steps for the birth of the science. Science can only be officially formed until the establishment of the systematic and complete scientific structure, and that the scientific laws have been identified, summarized and derived to certain extent. The proposal of scientific principles is an important part of a science, which is the most mark indicating if a science could become one of the most important basic sciences of human beings.

SECTION I GENERAL INTRODUCTION

The natural laws for the birth and development of the brand science are same as those of any sciences of human beings, which could not go beyond the development forms of sciences. The contributions of such process belong to all human beings, and the summarization of all wisdoms of human beings. The future of the development of the brand science is also the precious knowledge summary generated by interactive, complementary and alternative theories and practices of human beings. The generation of knowledge has never been easy. Respecting and cherishing knowledge is the pre-condition for the effective utilization and development of knowledge. The importance and contributions of the knowledge system of a science depend on if the knowledge could play an important role in the practices and applications of human beings.

2.1 Form of the brand science – a science focusing on development objects

The management science focusing on the brand science is different from other sciences of human beings in terms of development method, which is not focusing on the research subjects. The brand science and management science are focusing on the development subjects with the imagination science, frontier exploration and real-time dynamics as the main bodies, aiming at resolving issues in terms of future direction, structural governance, strategic development prospect and real-time dynamic management.

Generally, the ordinary development mode of sciences is built based on the previous knowledge of human beings, focusing on the documents, historical processes, historical facts, occurred cases, and references. However, the essence of the development of the brand science is different. The brand science is guiding the development and practices of human beings in the future, which is not based on the theoretical and practical researches on the histories, facts and cases in the past. The brand science aims to provide a series of knowledge ideas, knowledge structures, capacity frames, scientific rules and frontier supports to future development structure, development mode, and forms of products and services of human beings or in certain country, organization and enterprise

The brand science or the whole management science is future-oriented. At first, the brand science shall indicate the development directions for human beings, countries or enterprises, and the long-term and stable governance structure for operation. The brand science has determined the brand strategic directions of enterprises, the brand concepts used by enterprises to obtain market advantages, the brand performances to be developed to obtain determining market competitiveness, and the brand fields to be developed to promote the industrial revolutions and the scientific revolutions. The brand science could determine the brand dreams of the enterprises to gather human resource, the brand behaviors used to create new business models, the brand products used to change the consumption patterns, the brand technologies developed to avoid management issued during the development, the brand artistic forms developed to create the new fashions and the brand ecological features developed to improve the living standards of human beings.

This is a science with the imagination, creation and establishment of development capacities as pre-conditions, and the brands are based on and developed from this. The development subjects of the brand science include the great exploration of the social and economic reforms of human beings in the future and the improvement methods, the general consideration, designing and theoretical determination of the balance development of all ecological systems, consumption capacities and productivities such as the daily lives, working methods, health, social orders, employment and natural environmental protection. The foretastes, exploration practices and improvement of each brand ecological unit are the active elements of the brand development power.

The results of the development of the brand science are the diversified civilizations and life styles of human beings in the future, which is a great process of creating diversified consumption forms and physical wealth. The births and developments of all brands and the formations and developments of the brand economies of all countries have started from dreams and blueprints, as well as diversified brand creation modes according to the actual conditions and demands. The definitions, missions, models, methods and users of different brands are not identical, and will be subject to certain creative changes during the development. The brand science preferentially encourages the original and creative brands. The development nature of brand science has determined that histories, facts and cases could not become the main forces for the development of the brand science.

The development subjects of the brand science: the general structural changes of social economy, and the changes of the consuming productivities featuring the development of enterprise brand organizations. The research and development methods: determining the anchor during the dynamic changes of the brand world and summarizing and researching the scientific rules based on the anchor so as to invent and develop new patterns and academic theories to guide practices. Therefore, the essence of the brand science is to establish an open system for the dynamic knowledge development with structural distribution, which is the most advanced and developed frontier science in the world.

2.2 Nature of the brand science – the brand science as a frontier science

The brand science is a frontier science, covering the development of most frontier science fields, which has fundamental difference with the ordinary scientific development methods. The ordinary scientific researches are based on the experiment verification researches, and a long process of scientific researches, discovery and application is required from research to application.

However, the brand science is the application science field with direct reactions and reflections in the global market competition. It is ranked 1st in terms of development speed, driving fields, radiation areas and application efficiency. The violent market competition could promote the development of scientific researches and policies focusing on enterprises. The main bodies of brand development power have been placed on the product-oriented research and development links. The knowledge, such as inventions and patents, will be concentrated. The scientific activities for the long-term development of human beings, such as laboratory researches and non-profit research funding, are stimulated, making people invest more money to support the basic scientific researches in all aspects.

While promoting scientific inventions, the branding could further develop various modern management modes such as production technologies, information technologies, logistic technologies, network technologies, service technologies and new material development. The researching, development and promotion activities in the technical field are concentrated on the modern management, making the management science beyond the traditional scope of person governance and law governance to the tomorrow's management stage with the perfect combination of the management science and modern sciences. Enterprises shall constantly update the management technologies and equipment, and actively explore the methods of reforming the management links in the emerging social networks, so as to make the contents and forms of the management science focus on the tomorrow in an unprecedented method, and establish advanced management science with the modern meaning. The high level demands to the brands, systems and networks in the tomorrow's management could promote the rapid development of sciences and technologies, as well as the changes of the social and economic developments in terms of society, information, professions and industries.

To complete the targets of brand development, various brand supporting and service fields have witnessed significant development, such as industrial designing, packaging, aesthetics, music, movies, cartoons, advertising, news, public relationship and transmission, driving the diversified and rapid development of various business styles such as TV, internet, mobile internet, e-commerce, cultural industry and outsourcing services, forming the brand industry and branding derivative industry with great scales. The industries of hotels, tourisms, banking, medical care, sports and home services have been developed with the increase of the needs and improvement of incomes of human beings. The new brands created in each field have entered into a new wave of branding development.

Let's go back to the starting point of the social and economic development of human beings – brands. We could deeply feel the unique improvement role, development methods and creation patterns of brands in the development of human beings. Brands, as the important engine for the economic development of human beings, will establish a bridge connecting the past, the present and the future and lay a solid foundation for the civilization activities of modern humans by abundant, vivid and dynamic development. The development process of each brand has created right mental and physical wealth for the future of human beings. As a frontier science, the brand science will create a wider dreaming spaces, more dreaming elements and excellent life experiences, as well as the fundamental development values for the income improvement, happiness and joy in everyone.

2.3 Functions of the brand science – sciences, technologies and cultures of brands

The brand science could fully use sciences, technologies and art for development. The sciences have determined the development structure of brands, technologies have determined the practical methods of brands, and cultures could determine the expressions of brands. The harmonious development of sciences, technologies and cultures of brands could determine the guiding position of brands in the human world, and the functions of the brand science in various fields. It is an ecological system for synchronous progress of the brand science to generate functions, develop functions and promote the development and important role of the sciences, technologies and cultures of human beings.

Brands have developed into a great and advanced subject with various deep brand subjects that are supporting each other. The brand structures include the subject composition structure, the development structure of brand economy and the composition structure of the brands in detailed practices. Till today, the brand science has developed into a complicated and comprehensive subject field, covering brand history, brand strategies, brand designs, brand quality, brand advertising, brand communication, and brand experiences. Such development structure could provide the development foundation for the theoretical researches and practices for the deep development of the brand science in the future, so as to promote the knowledge of the brand science. The brand economy includes the researches and developments in the social and economic fields such as human brand economy, brand export countries, brand economic bodies, brand productivity, social brands, relationship between human and brands, brand and population development and brand labor income. The brand organizations include the frontier positions of the enterprise brands in the frontier sciences and modern social network development and the determining competitiveness, such as the required brand elements, performances and capacities. The structural brand academic researches, branding applications and brand development levels could support the development of the brand science.

Brand technologies are the processes of implementing the branding, which are the summary of the scientific preparation, technical methods, tools and all brand practices in brand development of enterprises. The development of brand technologies firstly comes from the development of brand thoughts and theories as well as the scientific summaries, rule researches and technical inventions of the brand phenomena, accidents, and activities in the societies of human beings. Especially, the brand issues encountered in the dynamic enterprise management shall be collected and analyzed to determine the latest brand scientific principles and key points for technical implementation, so as to scientifically prevent and avoid potential brand issues, effectively improve the brand performance and give full play to the technologies with effective brand effects. In practices, brand technologies could be divided into the brand order layer, brand technical layer and brand departments, which could provide the brand scientific formulas for the enterprise strategies, the implementation of brand technologies, and the daily operation of enterprise departments. According to the demands for the social network development in the future, the enterprise brands shall be updated to the brand ecological organization pattern with dynamic management to realize the multi-network developments in the chain form and flow form in the future.

Brand cultures are the methods of expressing brand cultures and arts, and the process for the brands to attract users, move brand users and develop the brand ecological organizations. The brand cultures could be reflected in many aspects, such as brand image designing, the industrial designing of brand ideologies, the brand package designing, the designing of brand identification and arts, and the brand advertising design. The brand cultures could comprehensively use the expressions of cultural arts, and various designing thought and expression methods in terms of literatures, designing aesthetics, music,

TV, shooting, and environment space art as well as the expressions with images, sounds, pictures, shapes and 3D methods. Brands have natural creativity and creation inspiration in terms of conception, aesthetics and souls of human beings. The artistic expressions of brands are the interacting development process among designing aesthetics, artistic expressions and transmission, and are the soul interaction between the brand designers and the users.

3 From brandish to brand ecology

During the development of human beings, the brands are developed in the way of brand proposition – brandish – brand ecology. Every enterprise and every nation have their own brand propositions, to determine the brand development directions, brand patterns, brand missions, brand ideologies, brand artistic expresses, and brand expression methods, which could be considered, explained, practiced, understood and used in brand propositions.

Some countries could develop into powerful brand countries, some brands could develop into world-famous international brands, some brands could have developed into legendary brands and some brands will become popular in the capital market, all of these are closely related to the firm, independent and inherited brand propositions. Although during the development of the brand propositions, that may not be welcomed in early stages, the brand founders and leaders may suffer many difficulties, but their adventure spirits, firm wills and the constant pursuit have played important roles in the development of brands, which will make the brand propositions into souls and believes. Such wills and determinations are the precious spirits of the brand legends. The brand propositions are the basic genes for the births and developments of brands.

In brand propositions, when the ideas pursued by some brands tend to be consistent, the brand propositions will become a shared brandism. If the similar pursuers have found the common brand styles and expressions in the diversified brand thoughts and brand designing tendencies, the diversified brandism will be developed, and become the important brand styles of human beings to pursue individual cultures. Therefore, diversified brand propositions have become the endless development methods of brands, such as minimalism, fashion, naturalism, blue series, purple series, green purple series, classic reminiscence styles, oriental traditional styles, future styles, modern scientific styles, the US styles, the Korean styles, the Japanese styles, the English styles, and the Chinese styles. The brandism is the method to express brand propositions through brand sciences and cultures based on the brand civilization of human beings, and is the detailed development expression in terms of brand philosophy, providing the brands with excellent physical patterns, designing ideas with perfect conception and the theme expression direction with artistic perceptions.

The development of any brandism or brand proposition could not be realized without their stable operations in the super brand ecological chain of human beings. This is the return to the natural ecology, the development of the social networks, and the common value for the sustainable social and economic development of human beings. The countries pursuing different concepts, the enterprises pursuing different development methods, and the persons pursuing different styles will be organized into different organic ecologic bodies in the shared ecological network of human beings, and form different ecological organization bodies for the creation, production, operation and consumption of brands. Countries and enterprises as social groups and person as social individuals would constantly create the ecological branches of brands in the general brand ecological chain of human beings according to their own understandings, consciousness's, spirits, pursuits, missions, hobbies and interests. The nature of human beings is an ecological body with orderly operation. All brands in the world are returning to the nature. Just like the natural developments of species and living creatures, this process has followed the development rules of the nature for the independent, combined, separate and coordinated development.

3.1 Brand development structure in social networks

Social networks include socialization, social development relationship, the civil society shared by human beings and national citizens, the non-profit social brand organization and the social network organization forms consisting of Internet, mobile internet, and logistic network. The basic feature of such networks is the basic framework based on the interpersonal networks. Society, communities, families, social services or various networks are all following the consistent social network development method. With the development of modern technologies, the social networks will be integrated and developed into an overall system network structure of human beings, which will be the coordinated development relationship between individuals and various social groups. Therefore, we should understand the human societies or network developments at the same level and in the same space.

Brands are developed based on social networks. With the modern and future developments of social networks, the organization structures, operation methods and development ways in social networks will be changed significantly. The branding social revolution is occurring quietly, developing in breeding and gradually becomes distinct and mature. Such revolution is a preparation for key strategic brand performances determining the future development capacity of human brands, the development structure of the national brand economy and the brand operation models of enterprises.

In general, the brand ecological chain of brands of human beings is a self-adapted circling system with multiple branches and independent and coordinated development. Social networks are the intercrossing networks for the organic production, deep development and distributed operation of brands. Brand ecological chain + social networks = high-level brand ecological organization, which is the future form of the branding of human beings in real term. The simplest example is that the enterprises are abandoning TV advertising and paper media reporting, focusing on the brand transmission methods based on Internet and mobile internet, and developing the social networks, social services and networking technologies based on various networking forms. Finally, the social activities of human beings, communities, groups and the interconnecting relationships among persons are moved to various network Medias. The high-level social networking development will be the pre-condition of the future development of human beings.

We should note that the understanding of human beings of networks shall not only be based on the development based on the networking thoughts or technologies. This is a misunderstanding of the development of social networks. This thought will lead to the unemployment of the practitioners of the Internet industry in 10 years, since the Internet is only a technical and application branch of the network development of human beings. The development of human society is based on the social networks, and families, enterprises, communities, countries and human societies are the products in the organizational development process based on the social networks. From the order networks 3500 years earlier, to the road networks 2000 years earlier, and then to the wire nets, TV networks and the internet space in the future, they are all the original or improved forms of social networks, which will be existing and developed at a high rate. Only in this way can a brand or brand organizer be developed effectively in the social networks, and maintain the development advantages to become brands forever.

3.2 Pursuit of human beings to brands

The pursuit of human beings to brands is the continuous power for humans to rapidly use, develop and consume brands, and the comprehensive civilization achievement made through the diversified pursuits for lives, productions, improvements and development. Pursuits are unlimited, could generate the latest and top demands of humans for brands, and have stimulated the creativities of human beings to create, produce and develop brands. The pursuits of humans to brands have significantly promoted the prosperity in the financial capital and commercial activity fields, and greatly improved the development of sciences, technologies, cultures, arts and lifestyles. The pursuits for brands have maintained high-level development of the pursuits for mental and physical demands, forming powerful countries, booming markets, happy families, rich lifestyles, excellent spirit enjoyments and various brand materials.

Thanks to the pursuit of human beings for brands, the development of human beings has played important promotion role in the past 100 years and the future 100 years. The understanding of this role could help the human beings to develop brands in a better way, experience the values of brands in a clearer way, and highlight the future brands in the development of human beings in more accurate way, so as to further create, use and develop brands, and improve the national economic construction, the affluence of people and the enterprise development.

As the structural social economic reforming force of human begins in the 21st century, branding will be further developed in the human society with unprecedented strength and depth. The high-level branding will promote the completion of the comprehensive branding in the 21st century. Brands are the social and economic development field without boundaries and angles and the thorough market coverage. The highly developed branding will perfectly store energies for a country, an enterprise and an individual, so as to fully release the creation potential at the best level.

There has never been a social development method, economic wonder or social development topics just like the brands that can stimulate the creation of the world, all people and societies, and generate the high-level development for human economies. Yesterday, today and tomorrow, the brand development of human beings will have more splendid tendency, and the legend made by each brand will be recorded in the history of human beings. All consumptions of human beings in the future, and the changes of all development powers, are composed of brands.

Exercises

1. Fill in the blanks: Brands include three structural development levels, namely, _____, national branding strategies and _____ of enterprises.

2. True and False Question: The brand science and management science are focusing on the research subjects with the imagination science, frontier exploration and real-time dynamics as the main bodies, aiming at resolving issues in terms of future direction, structural governance, strategic development prospect ad real-time dynamic management. (   )

3. Essay Question: Why are brands the excellent pursuit of human beings.

SECTION I GENERAL INTRODUCTION

Chapter 2

Brand Definition

It is difficult to define "brand" because brand keeps developing, and its functions and values to humans are getting larger. Hence the definition of brand is under continuous evolution. There are over several hundred definitions for brand around the worldwide, from the initial "identification" to the level of "product" and "marketing", and next to the level of "economy", "value" and "society". Different people will understand "brand" in their own unique way, people from different social stratums and groups viewed "brand" from their perspective and formed their own unique understanding.

The investigation on brand definition starts from brand etymology, property and development of brand definition, this is to help people know, recognize and apply brands more directly. Different understandings of brand by people from all over the world lead to multi-level brand awareness, as a result various kinds of brand awareness generated diversified brand practices. Brand definition, cognition and awareness cannot be judged right and wrong. There is no unified standard for brand definition in the world. The nature of education and learning lies in variation with each individual. Out of these many definitions of brand, we will only confirm the basic concepts of brand, but we will not make a definite definition. Like what we have expected, people shall establish their understanding of brand individually for brand development, and develop individual brand practices by one's cognition and correct brand definition or brand awareness. This is the consensus rules for brand, which is developed by the various kinds of brand awareness in humans.

1 Etymology of brand

The Chinese phrase "品牌" is the literal translation of English word "Brand". The word "Brand" derives from the Old Norse word "brandr" (Old Norse is the old Scandinavian of Germanic group, Indo-European, and ancestor of Northern European languages such as Icelandic, Danish, Swedish and Norwegian). The meaning is "burn" and "sear", and it once means to sear on livestock such as horses to display ownership.

Formation process of etymology of brand:

From 4000 years ago to 1st Century AD, the aborigines of the entire Britain were Celtics. Even during the time of Roman ruling, the native Celtic language prevailed in the entire Britain. Although the Celtic civilization is a known genome for brand civilization, brand ideas and the major civilization for entity breeding and generating human brand, but it is not where the word "brand" originated from. English was officially developed from Celtic at 700B.C, but it underwent major changes thereafter.

From 450A.D to 1066A.D, the Old English underwent the first great revolution. As recorded in *Anglo-Saxon Chronicle*, in about 449A.D, Vortigern, the King of the British Isles invited the "Anglo relatives" to help him fight against Picts. Therefore, he bestowed territory in southeast of the Angles as return, and later further sought for support. The early Germanic tribes (Angles, Saxon, and Jutes) migrated from Northern Germany and Jutland to England, governed local Celtic language and gradually formed the official "Old English".

In the 9th Century A.D, the Scandinavian entered North Britain massively, and almost occupied the East part of Britain by the end of the 9th Century. The Scandinavian spoke Northern Germanic so that Old English included large amount of Scandinavian words (represented by Old Norse). The Old Norse and Old English share many synonymous words. Thus, the Old Norse words often replace the Old English words in many English words. The world "brand" enters English as a borrowed word.

During 1066, English underwent the second great revolution, represented by Norman Conquest. Within the 300 years after William, the Duke of Normandy in 1066, the King of England could only speak French, and a large amount of French words entered Old English. In the Renaissance in the 16th Century, English absorbed and borrowed massive words from Ancient Greek and Latin, and later evolved into today's modern English, which is the product integrating multiple languages.

During formation process of English, the Old Norse "brandr" is evolved to "Brand" as a borrowed word, and becomes a major word used currently by human being. It is greatly different from the true meaning of brand. It will create difference in brand cognition if "brand" is purely understood through its literal meaning.

2 Part-of-speech of brand

Brand is a developing word, not invariable. Analysis on etymology of brand shows "Brand" is a borrowed word of English rather than the true meaning of brand from the original sense. With this in mind, people always generate misconception, and believe brand is identification, LOGO or VI. Therefore, many people only understand brand on the level of "identification". The deeper understanding is to "sear" on consumer's mind or set up expanded understanding in the aspect of "mental impression" of consumers.

As a matter of a fact, none of those is the true meaning of brand. Through the study on source of brand incubation and generation in *Brand History*, we know clearly that brand is actually the product of Celtic civilization entity, and is a higher civilization form developed in Ireland, Scotland, America, France, and Italy with migration of aboriginal Celtic and their descendants in the entire Britain in ancient and modern history. It is closely bound up with Celtic brand system habits of "symbol - token -cultural interpretation (poem, troubadour, music, film and TV) -repeated and strengthened recognition".

The civilization entity is a kind of civilization form that comprised of civilization order, social structure, working rules, national will, spiritual heritage, moral restraint, development concept and labor value. Such common civilization form finally leads human being to develop the brand economy. This competitive characteristic of brand civilization entity can be found in the brand development in Japan and Korea, the rising stars of brand economy in the second half of 20th century.

Brand cannot be generated if overall understanding of civilization form is deviated by only understanding brand literally rather than analyzing the etymology of brand. The thought consciousness of brand understanding can accurately judge matters developed by brand only under valid cognition and deep understanding of essence of things. It is unable to develop brand simply by understanding it through individual view or through a single word.

Just like the development of craftsman spirit, which has been proven to be an important link of brand ideas, the nature is to set up civilization form of craftsmanship system and basic social ethics structure, and form the basic environment for human development such that everyone respects workers and values artisans. The artisans are willing to make progression in skills, strive to be a better artisans, work hard to make the most exquisite products so as to grow their income   through labor value. However if the hope of being an artisan is the not the mainstream ideology in the society and people are unwilling to be workers, it is unable to develop unified, systematic and highly developed industrial brand civilization. The civilization can derive high level and powerful industrial brand economic strength. The essence of brand manufactured by one country begins with the basic cognition of universal meaning.

The investigation on brand nature reflects brand competition is not the competition between one brand and another, or the game between one business elite and another, and certainly not the battlefield between one enterprise and other similar enterprises. It is the competition between human civilization entities, and between social civilization order, structure and ideology. The nature is a joint development of consistent and harmonious structural competition between countries and nations, societies and enterprises, and producers and consumers. A consistent structural competition is definitely the end result for rational society and initiative ideology development.

Changes may be made by positive attitudes and actual actions of certain people, certain enterprises, certain organizations or certain countries. Brand, brand cluster and brand exporters will develop naturally in the overall formation of mainstream ideology of a country, national aspiration and willpower, as well as social development and human progress.

3 Development of brand definition

Due to the different understandings of "brand", five kinds of cognitions including identification theory, function theory, economy theory, value theory and society theory are developed for definition of brand. This is to generate different official or non-official definitions of brand. The stepped brand recognition view takes shape with human progression, social economy development especial brand economy development process, continuously improvement of brand roles in social economy, and continuously improving brand cognition during human development. It greatly enriches connotation of brand definition, and makes brand definition develop ceaselessly. From the initial Old Scandinavian "sear" to the increasingly rich understanding of brand currently, the definition of brand is expanding constantly, and becomes a significant economic term under ceaseless development and evolution. Some typical brand definitions that emerged during human development process will be studied here to seek for the common development rules:

3.1 Identification theory

In *Dictionary of Marketing Terms* (1960) of American Marketing Association (AMA), A brand is a "Name, term, design, symbol, or any other features that distinguished one seller's product or service from those of other sellers."

Philip Kotler says brand is a "name, term, symbol, design or their combined application".

William ·D· Perot & McCarthy: brand means the use of a name, term, symbol or design, or their combination to know certain product. It contains brand name, trademark and all means which can help in product cognition from the practical angle.

3.2 Function theory

Oxford Dictionary: "A brand is used to prove ownership, as a symbol of quality or for other purposes".

Ogilvy: brand is a complex symbol, and intangible combination of brand attribute, name, packaging, price, history, reputation and advertising style. Meanwhile brand is defined by impression and experiences of consumer. Brand is a media formed during marketing or communication process, linking product and interest group of consumers and bringing new value.

Lin Junming, former President of DMB & B China: a brand is a name, term, design, symbol, or any other features that distinguished one seller's product or service from those of other sellers. For a consumer, brand marks the source of the product, and protects profits of manufacturer and consumers, it can prevent imitation by competitors.

3.3 Economy theory

Baidu Baike: Brand is a kind of recognition mark, spirit symbol, value idea, and core expression of good quality.

Baidu Baike: Brand refers to trademark of a company name, product or service, and other intangible assets constituting unique market image of the Company such as symbol and advertising which can be distinct from competitors.

Alexander Bell: brand equity is a phrase invented by financial personnel to show financial value of a brand. The concepts such as brand franchise and brand loyalty are behind brand equity (financial value).

3.4 Value theory

Michael Treschow, President of Unilever: brand means how consumers feel the product. It represents the sum of trusts, relevance and significance by consumers' feeling about products and services.

Ai Feng: the direct explanation of brand is the mark of commodity. However, during actual application, the connotation and denotation of brand is far beyond range of literal interpretation. Brand contains three marks: the first is mark of commodity, i.e. trademark; the second is name of enterprise, i.e. trade name; and the third is the mark which can be used as commodity. All of the three kinds constitute the understanding of brand that is known by people.

He Jun & Li Ji: brand is not only an identification that distinguishes products from different enterprises, but also a carrier of marketing value information. Specific brand always represents information of product quality, product style, popular fashion and service level. The information is gradually understood and accepted by market, and become a representation of specific consumption value and feeling in the mind of consumers.

3.5 Society theory

Levi: the final result of brand is to become the public image, reputation or individual of commodities. These characteristics of the brand are more important than technical factors of products.

Leslie De Chernatony: in essence brands are clusters of functional and emotional values, and can guarantee customers rapidly connect brand with certain functional profits, or connect few functional benefits.

3.6 Definition in national standards about brand

In 2011, the definition of brand in Evaluation of Business Enterprise Brand and Guide of Enterprise Culture Construction (GB/T 27925-2011):

Enterprise brand

Enterprise brand is the comprehensive image jointly formed by the ability, quality, value, reputation, influence and enterprise culture (including commodities and services), and is shown by management and activities such as name, symbol and image design.

4 Conclusion of brand definition

The development history of brand definition is the development history from identification theory, function theory, economy theory and value theory to society theory, and is the development and evolution process by human beings' deepening impression on and understanding of brand in social and economic activities. In the early stage, the understanding of brand only focused on identification, it subsequently expanded to brand function, financial perspectives and value awareness, and finally to the cognition of social and human progress. The expansion of brand definition also symbolized that the understanding of brands has gradually deepened.

The definition cannot be judged from right to wrong. It is the human's true understanding of brand in different historical periods, in different countries, under different current statuses of brand economy, common opinions on brand matters, specific representation of brand's role in human and social progress and development, and in-depth change process of a series of brand practices expanding toward different fields and depths caused herewith.

The brand definition is generally proposed by four kinds of people. The first type is scientists. They analyzed and summarized brand definition from the angle of human development and scientific and natural development rules. The definition is the most accurate, and is the accurate judgment on brand discipline direction during human progress and development process. Scientists are the founder for unifying important concept of brand science cognition. The second type is researchers and scholars in social economy field. They proposed opinions on brand from social economic activities such as

SECTION I GENERAL INTRODUCTION

management and marketing, and the definition is relatively accurate. They are the major presenters of brand definition, and need to develop and perfect their academic research and papers based on brand definition. However, they may have also observed brands from phenomenon. Therefore, they can only solve brand definition that is required by one stage and the definition will vanish as time goes by.

The third type is analysts. They will judge a brand from one specific angle such as economy, securities, banking and finance, advertising and marketing so that brand definition has obvious characteristics in certain field or in certain country. Sometimes, the brand definition is only applicable to certain field in certain time frame. The fourth type is entrepreneurs. They may define brands differently according to enterprise development strategy, organizational structure and production and operation characteristics. Since their definitions will be used as a guidance on brand practices to make enterprises predisposed to business operation and business activities. However, they may be the star entrepreneurs who frequently appeared on media; hence they will form great influence on brand definition to a certain degree, and will become the figure that more entrepreneurs and pioneers look up to and follow in

Understandings of brand are diversified due to different explanations of aforesaid by four kinds of people on brand, and then different understandings of brand by different types of people with different social roles are formed. By 2015, the human's understanding of brand definition is generally shown in:

(1) One brand may adopt multiple forms, including name, mark, symbol and color combination or slogan to represent different products and market characteristics. Brand tells people the name of one or several products of a company and help to distinguish from similar products in the market. For instance, McDonald's is the joint name of an enterprise and a brand, and Head & Shoulders and Rejoice are two different brands of Procter & Gamble in the Shampoo market.

(2) Brand definition changes during continuous development, including people's cognition of identification, influence on enterprises, identification change generated by product or service characteristics, and understanding of social communication.

(3) Brand may form a kind of direct opinions. From initial customers to users, brands may let your users or potential users recognize the quality of product or service.

(4) Brand is an abstract concept, and is used to distinguish specific product form or service. For instance, milk is not a specific product. The service, business or environmental protection characteristics cannot be displayed. When people need to buy milk, they need to distinguish different brands and generate association with the brand characteristics.

Hence, we finally make a structural definition on brand according to scientific and natural laws, and economic progress and development of social economy:

Brand is the product formed by people or organization with development ability during labor value assignment and cultural value assignment process, and the final reflection of consumption desire of human being.

The structural expansion of aforesaid definition is that brand is the instinct of people with development ability to change oneself and reform nature and society, and the spiritual and material results developed during labor value and cultural value assignment process. It completes the expression process by specific product and service form, performance, identifying feature and sensual experience, and is a symbol for human beings to step to higher civilization. In market, brand is the fast recognition method to trigger consumption desire, and the ability for users to make decision on safety consumption immediately or later.

The expanded definition further emphasizes significance in two levels of human progress and market development, emphasizes contribution and labor value of brand owner especially creators, as well as embodiment during brand creation and practical development process, emphasizes the scientific mode shift rules of cultural connotation during materialization process by cultural meme and modal mode, and confirms special role of brand in human civilization development. Finally, all brand results of human being will be implemented on the level of market, and brand is a reflection of human for higher and more complete level of consumption desires in regards to consumption ability and purchasing power. This definition is based on the respect for human creation distinct, human labor value, human labor process and human civilization development process.

The definition is only the conceptualized structural definition formed during our research and development on brand discipline, and is not the final scientific definition of brand. The development of scientific term definition is a kind of human distinct to ceaselessly understand and cognize society and matters during progress and development process. We believe in the future more accurate definition will emerge. Therefore, brand definition belongs to all mankind, and is the collective contribution and the most precious spiritual wealth and materials of human beings.

5 Definition of enterprise brand

Brand definition is a kind of special bidirectional structural definition. In human ideology about brand, the brand definition is used to define what is brand and how to understand and apply brands; in enterprise brand, brand definition is an important constituent of enterprise brand concept, and a comprehensive concentrated definition representing vitality, soul and development direction of a business model. The brand definition of enterprise is used to define who it is, what it is used for, and what the future development direction is.

Brand definition is generally presented on the first sentence of brand concept in the first paragraph of business model to confirm, clarify and clearly tell what a brand is and what it is doing. And definition always appeared in the first sentence on news report of enterprise brand too. It is the core description that summarizes and presents an overview of the market role and development direction of a brand, and for social public and potential users to rapidly and accurately identify.

We have investigated major international brands with high influence in market. They can acquire investment, development and trusts from users because they can directly tell users, who they are so that brand user and all potential users can rapidly find, recognize and memorize them.

We also find the main characteristic of unnoticed enterprises or enterprises with mediocre performance in the market. The main characteristic among them is, they cannot tell who they are and what they are doing within one sentence, and this is especially true among many new companies. They have no distinctive brand description, and even no literal data such as brand description and brand introduction which can let users know them quickly. Thus, their development is not clear from the beginning. With aimless development, they thoroughly lost their direction when they are developed to certain degree, and either disappeared or maintained the status quo. The companies cannot expand, while initiators and employees gradually lost motivation and passion.

Brand definition is the reclassification of human demands to define by brand in certain field or when solving certain problem, or developing certain consumption preference so as to complete cognition of human for demands. Enterprise brand, by virtue of expansion of brand cognition, can acquire brand development opportunity while the consumption demand increases.

The specific practices of brand definition in enterprises contain three aspects:

The first is to refer to certain demand of human being by brands, such as Coca Cola for carbonated beverage, Microsoft Windows for computer operating system, Intel for CPU chip, Facebook for social network, Google for search engine, Bondi for band-aid. Brands invented and developed human demands in those application fields, and became leaders in the professional market or these areas of demand.. Their brand definitions have become the conventional representative words of demands.

Secondly brands represent certain level, brand style claim or specific needs of certain demand type. For instance, Tesla, Ferrari, Rolls-Royce and Land Rover are all automobile brands, but they are obviously different in application fields and brand claims. For cosmetics, Shampoo, oral care or Internet brands, different brands and even brands belonging to the same enterprise brand cluster try to redefine brands to effectively distinguish from existing competitive brands, and break down the professional brand market into a more unique one.

SECTION I GENERAL INTRODUCTION

The third is to define brands under business model in the commercial investment field. In order to gain continuous attention from brand investors and finish effective brand investment, brand founders need to effectively use brand concept to describe its unique value claims, market prospects, development directions, development opportunities and possible development space, with brand definition as orientation, in *Business Plan*, especially *Business Model* introduction and road show. In that way, the brand definition is prepositioned from former definition of products or services, evolved to the first thing for venture of many emerging enterprises, and become a key development line for an enterprise from foundation to future. The brand definition decides the direction, investment value and brand value of a brand.

6 Diversification theory of brand

During brand practice, consumption and usage, people have developed understandings and opinions on brands from different angles and in different ways. These understandings and opinions are accumulated by all sectors of the society during long-term practices, and varied with different social strata and life styles so as to form the diversification theory of brand. This is the worldview of people for direct understanding, feeling and experiences of brands.

6.1 Consumers' opinion on brand

(1) In terms of countries, brands are close to development level, quality assurance model, and consistent performance and characteristics of products and services in one country, and related to security, popularity and hygiene standards of brand consumption. In trustful countries, trust degree of first-time customer is positively correlated to the brand's premium level only when the premium level is high. On the contrary, when the brand premium level is low, trust degree of first-time customer will be low.

(2) In terms of users, no one knows better than the users about brands. Before purchase, users will make decisions after listening to or learning the opinions of other users. Consumers exchanged the most about purchase and use experiences of various brands. About 90% consumers in Europe are reluctant to buy brands that they have never heard of, and about 76% consumers in China are doubtful for after-sales services of brands that they have never heard of.

(3) Consumers feel assured for products of famous brands, and hesitate to buy products from small brand. Therefore, they prefer big or famous familiar brands when shopping or consuming.

6.2 Opinions of enterprise and investors on brand

Opinions of large enterprises on brand: brand is the unified external image of enterprise, and the target of all staff of an enterprise. The brand shall be guaranteed from links of purchase, R&D, production, quality, equipment, service and channel marketing. Nothing should go wrong in any of the link. The crisis PR should be on the lookout.

Opinions of large enterprises' staff on brand: It is honorable to work in a famous enterprise. Thus, staff can fully devote to the brand organization, and make every possible contribution.

Opinions of small business owners on brand: brand is concerned by large enterprises, while we focus on stable sales and balance of input-output ratio. We try to input limited funds and resources in aspects which can transform to marketing effect.

Opinions of small business staff on brand: we do not know the development prospect of the Company and opportunity for personal development here. We can only tell others what the businesses are, for instance, our company engages in e-business, garment making, and logistics. We will tell the name of our company only when asked, because our company is not a brand.

Entrepreneurs' opinions on brand: we are confident to challenge any brand in the world. We will surely have opportunities to surpass the most popular brands in current market of the field that we engage in. However, we do not know clearly about what is brand and how to develop a brand. We think that it is related to the investment limit and market expansion rate. Large scale equals to brand.

INTRODUCTION TO BRANDS

Opinions of potential international brand founder on brand: the first thing we do every day is to think of ways to provide better products and services to users. We are capable of changing the world. Even if we only improve insignificant details, we wish to better serve the society.

Opinions of investors in developed countries on brand: we want to know how big the ambition of the entrepreneur is, whether the project owns enough development prospects, whether it is a new thing, and what the brand can develop into.

Opinions of investors in developing countries on brand: we need to know how many competitors does the brand has, how the competitors are doing, whether the demand of the market is centralized, and what the successful cases are so that we can take the opportunity to succeed.

Designers' opinions on brand: we have many ideas and originalities to apply to brand so as to show the most beautiful side of the brand. I think people will certainly love them, but will people love them eventually? It seems that I will still need to improve my design level and creative capability continuously.

Workers' opinions on brand: What brands are selected by people nowadays, we actually wanted to say that our products are good even though it is not in the high-end fields in terms of brand design and core technology. We hope that people can treat brands more rationally, and have more choices. In that way, our hard work will become more valuable.

Technicians' opinions on brand: we have spent many years to be a top technician. We wish our technologies can be applied to new products and our technologies can be more extensively acknowledged and approved. However, we wish more our clients can appreciate the value of our hard-won technology, and cherish and respect fruits of our labor. We pursue better skills and technologies, and wish to bring better market return in the future by our technologies.

6.3 Opinions of all sectors of society on brand

Politicians' opinions on brand: brand represents economic strength of a country (region), and directly shows the image of the country (region). The core representative brand is the key point to carry out global cultural and economic diplomacy, and international and domestic commercial trade activities.

Socialists' opinions on brand: brand is the important symbol for social development level of the world and one country (region), embodiment of national cultural confidence, and the research focuses on national income growth, urban development mode and social purchasing power.

Economists' opinions on brand: brand is the important symbol for economic development of the world and one country (region), measurement standard for global economic activities (economic trend, economic hot spot, and economic growth level), and the research focus on economic structure.

Artists' opinions on brand: brand is the perfect expression of artistic pursuit; brand image promotion shall be created and expressed by various artistic forms such as artistic design, literature, music, dancing, film and TV art.

Scholars' opinions on brand: the brand phenomenon is worth studying, and laws of brand science are worth summarizing. As brand development prosperity, it becomes more important in current social economy, more scholars transferred their research field as well as emphasis of problem assumption, interpretation and research to brands.

Civil servants' opinions on brand: a portion of our family expenses are spent on brand, but we actually hope for good locally produced brands. We support and prefer local brands.

Soldiers' opinions on brand: we are away from the society due to life in military camps. In this period we do not need brands. Except daily demands, sometimes we will consider buying some local characteristic brands for our family members. So we are more concern on the brand in the area we serve.

Farmers' opinions on brand: our life is relatively simple since we are far from cities. Thus, most of the times, we can self-fulfilled our demands. If economic condition allows, we will buy some brands whenever possible. Actually, we wish our crops, agricultural products or farms and farmland are branded so as to improve our income level to allow us to buy and use more brands.

Opinions of lawyers and financial personnel on brand: brand is an important intangible assets of enterprise, and the constituent part of important evaluable and estimable capital.

Opinions of high-income family on brand: we enjoy life and live happily. Life pursuit is the journey to pursue extreme brands. We do not think luxury brand represents something. The brands are only normal part of our elegant life.

Opinions of medium-income family on brand: we can afford a better life. We eat, wear and use products of international brands to better show our living standard and way of enjoyment.

Opinions of low-income family on brand: we wish to afford those brands, but with limited income, we will try to cut expenditure on this aspect. In order to make our children grow happily like other kids, we will purchase some popular brands for them. We hope that they can change their life, and live a better life. Of course, our favorites are the brands with cheap price and good quality. They make our life easy and happy.

Youths' opinions on brand: we live from paycheck to paycheck. We spend our salaries and all incomes on brands that we like. Although we cannot afford many international brands, we must be familiar with them and love them so that we can talk with young friends. We are young, and someday we will surely afford those luxurious brands.

Urban white-collar workers' opinions on brand: our dream is to own all international brands. We will pay attention to the latest fashion style and more elegant life brands so that we can have enough graceful life and elegant living style. We love such atmosphere and environment.

University students' opinions on brand: we are about to work in the society, and need to know some brands. Although now we cannot afford international brands, we will work hard to buy them. If my classmates have the most popular cell phone or backpacks, I will try to buy one so that I can blend into them. I wish to be admired among classmates.

Middle school and primary school students' opinions on brand: I like this brand and I want eat that. Can we use certain brand of cloths and backpacks?

Opinions of people over 60 years old on brand: we are about to retire or have retired. We spend most of our time in leisurely. What are the nostalgic brands? I still remember the taste of a certain brand when I was young. Does that brand still survive? I grew up with that brand. I have used it for 50 years and I will continue to use it. Is this brand suitable for the aged? I may have a try.

Opinions of people at 45 on brand: through endeavors for over 20 years, finally I have some financial freedom. Now, we can start enjoying brands. We will pay more money to buy brands to make myself and my family's life better.

Opinions of people at 30 on brand: currently we need to work hard to develop our careers, and improve our incomes so as to own a better life. We can moderately know international brands and buy if condition allows. But the premise is we should follow certain expenditure plan to preferentially guarantee daily needs of our family.

6.4 Daily life concerning brand

The demands from different angles show people's in depth understanding of brands. Brands are closer to daily demands, and comprehensive branding is approached. If a brand is expressed by a family diagram, in a room of the family, almost everything, including foods, books, cloths, tables, chairs, tableware and electric appliances, is brand. We are familiar every day. In home or office, or for transportation tools, all links of life, work and entertainment are surrounded by more brands. The diversified demands of people for brands and diversified supply of brands by enterprises jointly constitute every day of human life.

Human brand supply and demands, cognition, opinions and behaviors of brands are decided by consumption desire, consumption ability and consumption governing ways. The basic desire of human on brand consumption is the source power forming brand premium level and brand development. When the medium annual income per capita reaches USD 10000, one country or region will transfer from productivity development to consumption ability development. The demands of people enter the age of brand consumption while brand consumption ability starts developing. The consumption governing way is the final real purchasing power deciding brand consumption demands. The more important role of brand economy is to show the stable income growth of working population. The income growth means people have enough consumption power to buy various brands in decision making for payment. Otherwise, when excessive brand desire cannot be satisfied, various social contradiction and social problems will occur.

7 Nine levels of brand awareness

Brand awareness is mainly shown in basic cognition of brand owner for brand. Different from cognitions of other various brands, when limited companies formed the most basic business model of human being, the brand awareness adopted by one enterprise to develop products, services and organization, and decides the key development force of the enterprise when moving forward. All productive resources, no matter talents-centered human resources, or overall awareness level of staff, quality grade of original means of production, application of production equipment, or development of operating network, are decided by brand awareness of enterprise leader (or business owner). Brand awareness is divided to nine levels to investigate development model and limitation of different brands.

Economic awareness: enterprise leaders with economic awareness have no or few brand awareness. The first purpose to develop enterprises is to acquire obvious economic income, rather than engaging in brand development. Under special circumstance, brand may occur as stunts when enterprise leader with economic awareness attracts attention of investors or take investment attraction form as main economic income, but only limited to such special circumstance. They understand the brand only as more opportunities for exposure, which make operating results better so as to successfully acquire investment or franchise incomes.

Product awareness: enterprise leaders with product awareness have preliminary brand awareness, but they are easy to deem products as brands. This is the instinct of human's cognition for brands. They lay emphasis on quality guarantee model of R&D and production link, and never or rarely carry out work on brand level. Such brands may generate two extremes: firstly, products become local established brand finally, but cannot become a national or international brand; the products are operating continuously by model of family; secondly after acquiring certain development opportunities, brands may become international brand, but only cover a small specific market field. It is good to produce quality products. It is the main method to improve family income, going concern and minority brand development.

Marketing awareness: enterprise leaders with marketing awareness have preliminary brand ability; however, generally the brand development is focus on marketing activities and sales links. The entrepreneurs, Chief Brand Officer or brand directors are generally from marketing field. These brands, due to the expanded market concept, are easy to become short-term hot brands and brands with rapid income growth in market, but more easily become extensive brand in market. Moreover, those brands will exist in a short time and disappear soon. These brands concern little about brand, service and management so they lack enduring vitality.

Service awareness: enterprise leaders with service awareness are the main force for modern brand development. Although they engage in manufacture, scientific technology R&D or trade, they characterize themselves as service enterprises. They prominently develop brand image in service field and may create image of quality service brand. These brand enterprises can acquire considerable development. Especially in the 21st century when modern service develops rapidly, the enterprise brands with service awareness will be the leader in modern market competition.

Social awareness: enterprise leaders with social awareness pay attention to embodiment of social value and make active contribution to society during brand development process. They regard serving civil society as own duty. Many brands they created are non-profit, or pursue value development except

Section I General Introduction

money. These brands are easy to acquire common social respect and public trusts, and may form enough social prestige. The brand development is endurable.

Organization awareness: enterprise leaders with organization awareness pay attention to establishment and development of brand belief. These brand enterprises will upgrade to brand ecological organization, and lay emphasis on self-applicable propagation and diffusion in user network. They are consistent with future human network development. Even if these brands do not package themselves with modern technology, the own development of brand ecological chain is enough to make the brand expand steadily so as to develop to the most popular international brand and own sustainable operation ability.

National awareness: enterprise leaders with national awareness concerns national and ethnical characteristics. In country and region with incentive and strong national awareness, these brands may own favorable development opportunity and become the respectful and popular brands. Due to high national brand premium level, these brands are easily accepted worldwide and have favorable development space. However, in countries and region with scanty national awareness, the development of these brands will be difficult as affected by de-nationalization of population awareness. Besides, the population awareness is easily affected by low national brand premium level, it goes against brand development. Insisting on developing national brand is their previous spirits for endeavor. No matter good or bad, the virtue and spirits of brand shall be respected by the universe.

Global awareness: enterprise leaders with global awareness have the world value of changing the world, and aim to develop brands to the world. Enterprises with global awareness develop by characteristics of global horizon, international style and diversified civilization. They will be concern on popularity of the brand in the world, global communication mode, and global adaptability of product and service. They will pay particular attention to world leading awareness, development of world advanced technology and trend, as well as cultivation of reserved leaders. Therefore, they need many potential talents with the same vision to guarantee the international talents pool required by global operation of the brand. The global awareness is the main power to develop international brands.

Human awareness: enterprise leaders with human awareness are driven by their vision to create everything that is deemed impossible. They aim to create next generation product, create new change in the future and even overturn the existing cognitive level of people. The brand with the largest influence in the world are generally from the native creative spirits, wild venture spirits and overturn force to change the world of brand founders or brand rebuilders. They generally can create brand new product form, and change industrial development level. Since the awareness of human beings they owned is based on human progress and development, the brands they developed are of special brand value ahead of time, thinking and reality. Thus, they will become the leader of new world brand cycle. The brands they created mostly become important milestone driving progress and development of human being.

No matter what level of brand awareness one has, the nature is to develop better products and services, and to make life better. An enterprise can go far as long as the vision is large enough. Regardless of brand awareness to be developed and brand to be created, enterprises shall think carefully and develop forwardly along the current road.

Exercises

1. Fill in the blanks: It is because of different understandings of "brand" that five kinds of cognitions including _____, _____, _____, _____, _____ are developed for definition of brand.

2. Fill in the blanks: In 2011, the definition of brand in Evaluation of Business Enterprise Brand and Guide of Enterprise Culture Construction (GB/T 27925-2011): Enterprise brand is the comprehensive image jointly formed by enterprise (including commodities and services) _____, _____, _____, _____, _____ and _____, and shown by management and activities such as _____, _____, _____.

3. Essay Question: State the nine levels of brand awareness.

Chapter 3

Brand Standardization

Brand standardization is a process of establishing, promoting and developing brand standards, which are the eventual standards for human beings to practice and develop various standards, covering the standard practices in many fields. No matter what type of standards or standardization work they represent, the eventual target is to establish the processes of standard establishment, promotion and application with the development of brands as social and economic features.

Brand standardization is an integral part of the branding process of human beings, and the purpose is to unify all production means, production sources, enterprise development patterns and consumption methods through standardized methods, and promote various resources, thoughts and behaviors in order to intensively develop important human activities more effectively.

Among the brand standardization practices of human beings, international brand standards and national brand standards have become the major standard development methods with great social influences, large transmission area and high application level thanks to their authorities, social nature and universality.

1 Structure of standardization of human beings

The development of standardization of human beings is a process of summarization, thinking, experimenting and re-summarization during the social and economic practices of human beings. The standardization marks the transition of human beings from savages to civilizations. The earliest existing form of human beings was not a country, but civilizations represented through ethnic groups with different names. During its development, each civilization has witnessed civilization consolidations in the form of wars and the warfare history displayed civilizations eliminating savages and inferior civilizations being defeated by superior ones.

The development of early civilizations of human beings was established from 2000 years BC to the 1st century A.D. During this period of time, the human civilizations in the Europe, Asia and Africa developed prosperously. Order became the earliest standardization that has played the most important dominating role in the societies and economies of human beings. This is regarded as the starting of the age of civilization.

1.1 Standardization focusing on orders

The progress made by human beings was mainly in the form of a civilization body. This is a process for social groups to evolve into civilization bodies. Different countries (as smaller units) got attached to the major civilization bodies. At that time, establishing civilization orders was more important than building a country. For example, the Codex Hammurabi, The Ancient Egypt Law, the first druid in the Celtic myths, and the rules and systems made by Zhou Gong of China, standardization processes aiming at establishing civilization orders, governance structures, social operation rules, classifications, laws and international relationships. At that time, the scope of the civilization body was obviously larger than that of a country. Country is the legal unit with free development spaces under the civilization body. The world view was the common development concept of human beings at that stage.

SECTION I GENERAL INTRODUCTION

With the development of human beings and the highlighting of state sovereignty, countries emerged in the 19th and 20th centuries as the sovereignty units of the human world, these countries were distributed all over the world and the role of civilization bodies disappeared. During the process of establishing countries, the establishment of orders became a key point after the development of the civilization of human world. However, at the current stage, we have used the concept of country to replace the concept of civilization body, and used the sense of nation to replace the world view. Therefore, the orders have been weakened as the development method of standardization, which limited the development speed of new civilizations to some extent, and the established orders based on countries were in minority, further reducing the strengths and speeds of civilization renaissance of countries. On the contrary, the countries existing as civilization bodies could be able to cooperate and co-exist through the civilization bodies to increase the development speed and accept the world, appreciate its surroundings and lay foundations of their positions in the world in a short time.

1.2 Standardization focusing on optimization

From the 2nd century B.C. to the 1st century A.D., the standardization of human beings developed into the second stage, transitioning into the standardization with the optimized development of temporary development methods as the basic form, represented by the standardizations of the Qin Dynasty of China and the Roman civilization in Europe, and both civilizations were called Daqin, one in the West and one in the East.

Unfortunately, the development of these two strict standardization got hindered. The destructions of the Qin Dynasty and Rome led to the disappearance of a great amount of historical heritages of standardizations in the history of human beings. The recording of standardization had been interrupted by the history, and we have even forgotten the existence of such standardizations.

Till 1974, we found about the truth about the standardizations from the archaeological sites, the historical relics and the preserved texts. The standardization of the Qin Dynasty was earlier than that of the Rome, and was finally accepted by the world as the official origin of the standardization of human beings today. These standardizations were conducted through repeated experiments and practice researches, during which many matters were optimized to their best conditions and then fixed. The standardized production is the major method for standardization, and the legal and digital requirements are used for the development of standardization.

1.3 Standardization focusing on codes

The standardization focusing on codes is an important standardization development stage of the history of human beings in the 20th century, represented by the first international standardization organization IEC (International Electro Technical Commission) established in 1906, the American National Standards Institute established in 1918, and the ISO (International Standardization Organization) established in 1947. The main goal of standardization is to standardize the management systems in terms of production, operation, services, safety and environment, and the integrated supply supporting service relationship in certain fields focusing on manufacturing standards and working interfaces.

With its development, the International Civil Aviation Organization, the International Maritime Organization, the standardization commissions in different countries and the standardization technical commissions, technical alliances and enterprise standardization organizations have been established. The standardization in the global scope has been fully promoted and developed, leading to the comprehensive development tendency of standardization in various fields such as the rapidly developed economic activities, the booming markets and lifestyles, and generating positive influences on the improvement of living standards and enterprise development.

A simple example of standardization is that even the batteries used in our daily lives are classified, as No.5 and No.7 batteries, determined by the standard made by IEC. For many years, the air safety standards made by the International Civil Aviation Organization have effectively ensured the safety of civil aviation, making airplanes one of the main safety transport methods in the world.

1.4 Standardization focusing on rating

The Standard & Poor Rating developed by Poor from the Railway History and the American Canals in 1860 and the stock relative credit quality rating system established by John Moody for investors in 1909 have generally made the rating systems an important part of the global standardization, and promoted the development of standardization activities focusing on evaluation, rating and indexes.

The purpose of rating is to make the levels according to rating elements such as quality, level, or credits in different fields, to determine the actual level of a country, enterprise or individual through industrial organization or a third party.

In daily lives, the evaluations we are familiar with include the ratings of the French wine producing areas and the film ratings made by the Motion Picture Association of America. In the field of qualification, the qualifications of various evaluations and ratings could effectively improve the enterprise management level. In terms of products and services, enterprises could obtain higher ranking by improving their actual development levels according to their own conditions, providing better products and services to the society.

1.5 Standardization focusing on system networks

The standardization focusing on system networks would be built between persons, countries and matters in its early stage. People only realized the standardization tendency represented by systems and Internet until the appearance of computer software systems and Internet, and then focused on the civil and social development practices composed of systems and networks.

Systems are characterized through operation structures organized by a series of self-adapted rules, which were initially used in the botany field, and then appeared in the medical field, physics, weapons and equipment, such as respiratory system, electrical system, optoelectronic system, voice control system and computer operation system, making systems the key point for the modern scientific development as well as the key point for human beings to develop unmanned technologies and natural ecology in the future. The networks have engaged in the networking development of human activities from the order network, interpersonal network, road network, wire network, telegram network, broadcasting network, TV network, distribution network, Internet, mobile Internet and vehicle network, making the networks the most familiar living and working methods for human beings.

The future of human beings must be built on the high-level development of systems and networks. Humans' deep understanding of networks and systems will comprehensively improve the significant changes to the combinations of daily lives and works, products and services, and organizations and users, which will be the main route for human beings leading them to the future lives with high intelligence, high science and comprehensive natural ecology. The development of systems and networks will greatly expand the contents of the modern standardization.

2 Formation of the thoughts of brand standardization

The brand standardization thought is an important labor division method developed by human beings in development practices, and a basic development thought used in all links such as production and operation.

According to an archaeological discovery, the standardized weapons and armed forces appeared in the Qin Dynasty of China as early as the 2nd century B.C., and the quantities, shapes, sizes and tolerances of which could meet the strict standardized replacement requirement. The pulp filling production method developed by Coca-Cola in 1900, the T-model production line developed by Ford in 1908, and the franchise chain operation mode developed by McDonald's in 1940 are the of the main inventions in the modern standardized production and operation methods, making standardization an important unit for enterprise brand development and the necessary precondition for the scaled production and the scaled development of social services.

SECTION I GENERAL INTRODUCTION

Industrial persons are those with thoughts for scaled production, services and commercial mode operations. The industrial persons are the main force for the development of modern brands. They would use the scaled development method to change the brand operation structure to the brand standardization focusing on standards, and also research and develop various standards to constantly improve the brand performance, increase the brand capacity and supply and develop new brand operation modes. With the future of the industrial persons and the brand standardization thoughts developed by industrial persons themselves, standards have been widely used in markets, becoming an important part of brands, and significantly improving the comprehensive development of brands of human beings.

Not everyone is an industrial person. The development of brands of human beings is in fact a process of brand improvement marked by three standardization thoughts, namely the handicraft persons, the industrial persons and the individualized industrial persons. The first aspect is the handicraft industry, which has the longest development period. From the potteries and precious metal products made manually in the past to the bench workers or musical instruments, the wisdoms of craftsmen cannot be substituted by machines. The key points of brand standardization are presented in terms of raw materials usage, design thinking, and manufacturing means. The modern handicraft industry is developed by optimizing the standards in all details, which will occupy an important position in the development of brands. The renaissance of handicraft brands is an important development method that is somewhat different from the development of modern industry. Industry could never fully replace the handicraft industry. By contrast, the handicraft industry will have an important labor value in employment and especially the development of the brand economy of a country.

With the industrial revolution and the scaled development of standardization, the industrial person will appear, and then the individualized industrial persons will have developed. The individualized industrial persons portrays the brand standardization thought covering the handicraft thought and the industrial person thought, which is the necessary result of the development of the diversified and individualized demands for modern brands. Industrial brands will be covered by the public brands. The individualized demands of human beings for brands will promote the development of industry towards the agile manufacturing, user-defined orders, and need-oriented production, leading to other major changes in the industrialization structure of human beings. Scientists always want to find out the secret of the manufacturing of the Terra-Cotta Warriors of the Qin Dynasty. Why were the Terra-Cotta Warriors made by volume production, but each one has its own appearance? This is a typical brand standardization case of the individualized industrial persons in terms of production method. According to the latest researches, the Terra-Cotta Warriors were completed with special production organization method, and this discovery could improve the development of the brand standardization of individualized industrial persons.

3 Development of brand standards

On the level of global enterprise competition, the brand standardization conducted by developing standards has become the major method for global enterprises to compete. McDonald's is famous for its standards and has finally developed into one of the standardized international brands that have implemented and developed brand standardization.

In the 21st century, the enterprise brand standards have been actively developed, but the standards at the national level have not been widely developed, because the global economic activities are mainly concentrated at the trading level, and no breakthrough has been made in terms of the development of the national brand standards. In 2014, the secretary office of the ISO brand evaluation international standardization technical commission was established in China, marking the starting point of the international development of brand standards among countries.

On December 31, 2011, the AQSIQ and the National Standard Commission of China issued the *Evaluation of Business Enterprise Brand and Guide of Enterprise Culture Construction* (GB/T 27925-2011), which is the first national enterprise brand evaluation standard both in China and the world. The establishment of national brand standards could guide the implementation of enterprise brands.

In China, a series of national standards and domestic trading standards with the national brand standards as the main focus, covering the service industry, enterprise cultures, business planning, liquor circulating industry, construction material industry and jewelry industry, and supported by the industry operational codes have formed a complete national brand standard family, and the drafting, issuance and implementation of such standards have generated positive influence on the social and economic development of China. Such national brand standard development program with great scale and complete series is a rare occurrence in the history of world brand development and in the world, which has laid solid foundation for the branding development of the global enterprises and the standard references and using.

GB/T 27925-2011 is an evaluation rating standard, which has broken down the evaluation indexes in terms of the brand capacities, qualities, reputations, enterprise culture and brand influences, providing multiple class evaluation guidance for the implementation works of enterprise brands as well as the suggestions, steps and basic requirements for operation. The standard is developing into international standard, so as to adapt to the developments of the brands in different countries throughout the world. The latest tendencies, advanced technologies, leading concepts and branding activities are also promoting the periodical updating of the brand standards.

The development of brand standards and the development of human matters have the same natural development principles, with the development pattern from spontaneity to chaos and from orderly reengineering to the orderly multielement open system. During the development of the informatization of the United States, the standards, interfaces and technologies were inconsistent due to the free development, and huge funds were provided in order to solve this problem until the unified standards were established. Only the informatization conducted in accordance with the consistency requirements of the standard structure order could improve the national informatization. The development of the enterprise brands of the world also depends on the consistency requirements of standardization. The development in terms of interoperability, intercommunity and compatibility is the basis to resolve the differences in terms of the brand concepts, technologies and capacities in different countries and industries, and the solution to potential economic losses caused by the irregular, repeated or failed brand development methods.

During the actual development of global brands, 70% of projects funded by investors throughout the world fail. More than 50% of the emerging enterprises exist only for two years. More than 50% of the 50 million of dollars invested by global enterprises for brand promotion each year have low efficiency. These failures and economic losses are related to the correct brand development thoughts, as well as to the service levels of the brand service providers. The development brand standards have provided a new opportunity to reduce invalid brand actions and improve the brand development efficiency, and have also provided important references for the further development of the global brands.

4 Development of brand certification

In 2014, the Chinese government officially approved the implementation of the third-party enterprise brand certification for the first time. The national certification and accreditation supervision commission approved the Beijing Wuzhou Tianyu Certification Center to expand "the Business Enterprise Brand Certification unit".

Brand certification has become the new certification item in the certification family thanks to third party certifications in the world. The main certification reference is the *Evaluation of Business Enterprise Brand and Guide of Enterprise Culture Construction* (GB/T 27925-2011). The certified enterprises could obtain the brand ratings of 2-star, 3-star, 4-star and 5-star.

The brand certification has significantly promoted the promotion and implementation of the national brand standards, and is the important milestone in the development of the global brands, which has established new development patterns for the brand standards among enterprises.

SECTION I GENERAL INTRODUCTION

As of December 31, 2015, after more than 186 large- and mid-sized enterprises, including Haier, China Salt Industry Corporation, Angang, Wuliangye, Delixi, China Nanche, Xinjiang Guotong Pipe, Xinjiang Xiangdu, Mengjinyuan, New Age, Jiangling Motors, Aucma, Ande Logistics, and Longma Environment have obtained the third party certificates, the brand certification has entered into its full development stage in China.

At the key period for global brand competition, the cross brand certifications will be gradually conducted in China, the United States, the EU and other countries. The development from brand standards to brand certification symbolizes an important mark indicating the comprehensive implementation of brand standardization from the enterprise brand development structures to development levels, representing the latest tendencies, development features, international levels and world tendencies of the standardization of global brands.

Both brand standards and certifications are the important measures to protect consumers, and the effective evidences representing the brand development level during the brand development of enterprises. Brands will not be limited by geographical boundaries. No matter where the headquarters or origins of the global brands are, they will face the same global consumers, and serve the same global brand users. Therefore, the brand standards and certifications are universal throughout the world.

The United States are the country which is in control of the most international brands, and the major market center for the competition of enterprise brands in the world. The achievements made in China in terms of brand standards and certification will accelerate the progress of the United States to become a new global brand certification center, promote the comprehensive development of the third-party brand certifications in the United States, the North America and the Europe, and make active contributions for the brands of different countries to obtain international brand certifications and explore global markets.

Brands are an important frontier development power, and the advanced competition strengths of the enterprise brands of different countries in the world. Brand value evaluation, one of the hot spots of global competition, is currently based on financial data, which has certain limitation. From the birth of brands, the development of brands was never based on financial data. The more important development mechanism is represented by the utilization of brand thoughts, the original brand creativity, the development value of brand science and philosophy, brand performance, brand management flow, the social contributions of brands, and other non-financial levers. This has made the confirmation method of brand values and the functions of brand certifications focus on the labor values, cultural values and consumer cognition. Such changes of the brand value cognition relationship will change the further understanding of human beings to brand values, and combine the brand certification with the brand practice demands to provide the certification and evaluation methods with wider development spaces, active advanced meanings and higher value.

5 Standardization of enterprise brands

With the development of brand standards and brand certification, the enterprise brand standardization has developed into a new stage to form a consistent brand development common sense with effective brand rules, brand capacity scopes, brand user services, brand pioneering and the public knowledge of brands, and the applicable scope has been further expanded to the whole world, covering diversified global industrial brand fields. This has provided new development directions, operation logistics and rating references for enterprises to implement brand standardization.

The brand standardization of any enterprise is composed of brand releasing, branding and brand reengineering. The first thing to asses is the meaning of brand releasing:

From the establishment of an enterprise, when the policy maker of the enterprise has decided to develop the original operation pattern into a clear brand, the brand releasing will become the most important thing for the enterprise development. Brand releasing is an important ceremony to be prepared by the enterprise after its establishment so as to announce the official birth of the brand to the world, the society, and the related groups both inside and outside the enterprise, release the *Brand Announcement* and make the brand vow to all employees. This ceremony is the necessary baptism to be conducted by the enterprise when deciding to develop its brand. From this day, all production and operation activities of the enterprise will be promoted in the world with an official brand. This process shall not be neglected. The reason that more than 95% enterprises in the world could not become brands finally is that they did not hold brand releasing ceremonies (or brand launching ceremonies), or did not announce that they are brands. Therefore, such enterprises have stayed in the non-brand product stage, and even their employees, clients and suppliers do not think they are serving a brand.

If applicable, an enterprise shall hold official brand press conference, which is an important ceremony to officially release the brand through news media. The development of major brands in the world could not be realized without brand press conferences. Through the press conferences held for the overall brand concepts, sub brands, new products and the updated versions of new products, the brands will become the hot spots of the global brand news reporting, and giant public relationships of brands and medial markets such as new media brand transmission will be established, which are the main supporting strength for the development of the newspaper industry and the new media businesses.

5.1 Brand standardization during branding

The key point of brand standardization occurs in the branding process. Branding process is not only the national strategy and industrial strategy of different countries and enterprises, but it is also the main body of all brand development behaviors for enterprises. The branding process covers the R&D, purchasing, production, quality, equipment, market, marketing network and services of brand products, which is a brand improvement process optimizing and developing every procedure and node constantly, the large-scale process of updating the irregular development method into the mature and stable operation of standardized production and services, a standardized process to make, use and develop standards, and the precondition to further develop the brands into self-adaptable brand biological organizations.

The laboratory status is the main status for enterprises to conduct R&D activities, which includes comprehensive experiments and researches of the product R&D and testing, the production and equipment preparation, the product user experience, and the management flow operation. The laboratory status is the core brand standardization link to identify standard nature, generate standard source, summarize and propose standards and implement standards. The scientific experiments and researches are the key to identify risks and prevent management problems. The larger an enterprise is, the higher the investments, scales and levels of the global R&D center of the enterprise will be, and the larger the research scope of the laboratory status will be. All immature market factors shall be completed under the laboratory status. The formation of such standards will include detailed forms of products at the production stage, product performance design, productivity design, operation mode design, service method design and various brand elements, such as brand images, brand packages, brand highlight design, brand and promotion methods, so as to form a series of documental and manual standard "drawings".

The test production and operation processes are the expanded laboratory status, and are the active efforts made to identify problems and establish standards. After the completion of the standardized drawings, all links such as purchasing, production, quality and operation, are the detailed standard implementation processes. This stage is also an important standard supplementary and adjustment stage. Through the continuous summarization during the market expansion and development, issues will be identified and standards will be developed through combing processes while focusing on various management and market problems, so as to improve the standards, and develop them into a constant brand development power, so as to serve the market through the orderly operation of the brand standardization.

Although the initial productization of the branding has been operated in a mature way, and the productization has been completed, the branding is not yet done. Branding means that a series of important functions shall be realized at any point when it makes contact with the users, and great efforts shall be made in terms of the brand value output method and the identification of the brand value by users. The development focus of branding shall be placed on the brand ecologicalization (brand imaging, details, visualization, vividing and interaction), and the development process from rapid brand, light brand and large brand to group brand clusters. The development of modern international brands has abandoned the original product forms, and production quality as well as other basic elements. The contents and development of branding have the multi-element ecological development structure focusing on users. The virtual modern brand technologies such as the self-learning system of brand users, and the brand user value identification system are replacing marketing to make the brands pay more attention to establishing attracting capacity, leading to fundamental changes to contents and forms of the standardization of enterprise brands.

5.2 Brand standardization of brand reengineering

Any brand would like to be developed forever. However, the changes to the ages of human beings are becoming more and more rapid, and products may be eliminated instantly in case of loss of competitiveness. The aging period of a brand has been significantly reduced. On one hand, enterprises are constantly promoting new products to withstand market competition, and on the other hand, they are doing every effort to develop and maintain the brand user groups. Keeping pace with times has become the common rule for global brand competition. In order to maintain the frontier positions and determine competitiveness, enterprises shall conduct a large-scale brand reengineering at a certain interval (10 years to 30 years), so as to express the development powers with new brand images and the brand leading postures.

If we study the histories of major brands carefully, we could find that the changes to LOGO and the stage promotions of important products, especially their updated versions based on the Internet development, could be seen in the histories of various brands. The development history of the global brands is not only a history recording the historical facts, but also a history of the constant implementation of brand reengineering with dynamic changes and moving evolution. This is the essence of the brand history.

During the large-scale reengineering of each brand, not only could its global LOGO and brand images be fully changed, but its established brand standards could also be subject to large-scale changes, or even branding could be conducted all over again, so as to form a new generation of brand standards.

No matter if brand releasing, branding or brand reengineering, our conclusion is: the development of brand standardization of human beings is a repeated release, development and reengineering process conducted with the brand reengineering as core rules. This is the natural rule for enterprise brand development, and the basic operation theoretical logics contained in the detailed practices of global brand standardization, such as brand standards and brand certification. Handling the rules of brand standardization properly is the important reference for enterprises to effectively implement the brand standardization. Enterprises are using the brand reengineering processes over and over again to fine-tune their development, updates and overall progress, so as to further advance and make the brands last forever.

Exercises

1. Fill in the blanks: _____ are those with thoughts for scaled production, services and commercial mode operations. The development of brands of human beings in fact is a process of brand improvement marked by three standardization thoughts, namely _____, _____ and _____.

2. True or False Question: The laboratory status includes comprehensive experiments and researches of the product R&D and testing, the production and equipment preparation, the product user experience, and the management flow operation.

3. Essay Question: What are the five structures of standardization of human beings?

Chapter 4

Brand Power

The brands power shall be researched as an important subject. The brand power is the change of effects of forces during the development of brands, which could be used to explain the organization effects between forces so as to from high-value brands. Brand power constitutes of A Theory (model of thinking power of brand) and B Theory (brand consumption decision model), which are collectively called the AB Theory. The AB Theory has a dominating position in the principles of the brand science, and is the basis for the application of important principles in brand science.

1 A theory: Thinking power of brand

The thinking power of brand is the important development process of brand power for the establishment of independent brand thoughts. The thinking power of brand includes brand consciousness (height), brand organization power (depth) and brand attraction (width - the collective name of brand attraction powers). The thinking power of brand is the result of the highly consistent and coordinated development of three brand power. The development structure includes the constant vertical development represented by the brand consciousness and brand organization power, and the cross development in the width through the brand attraction. The pattern is the constant and stable A-shaped pattern required for the development of a brand organization, which is named A Theory.

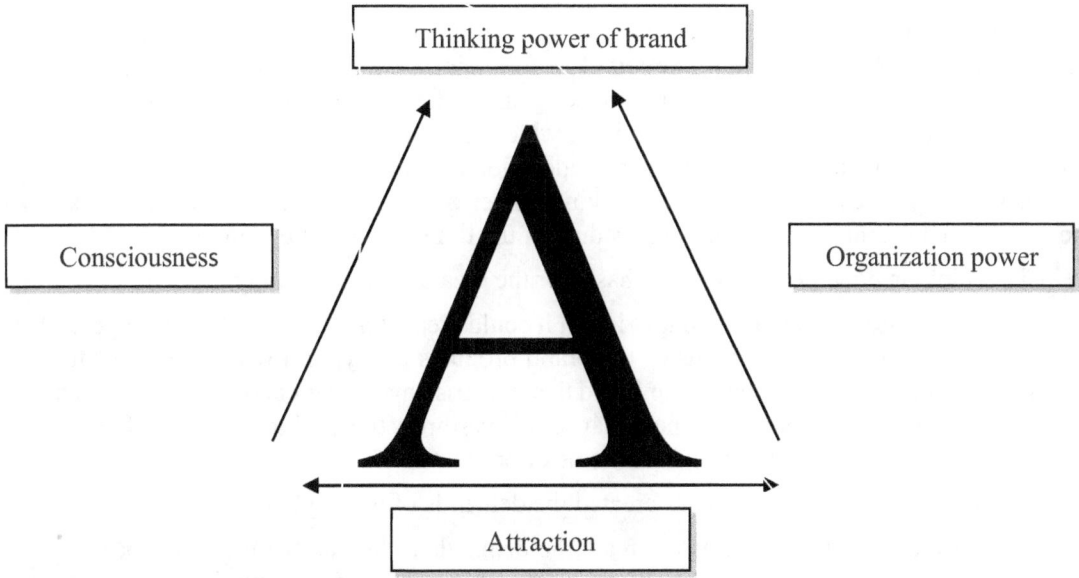

Fig. 4-1 Model of the Thinking Power of Brand

Utilization of forces during the branding process:

Brand consciousness: (1) realize the dreams through prospects; (2) endow with meaning through appeals;

SECTION I GENERAL INTRODUCTION

Brand organization power: (3) take actions through organizing; (4) provide deliverables through the brand organization process;

Brand attraction: (5) obtain trust and affection through the quality and brand experiences; (6) obtain customer base through self-expansion of the brand customer groups.

The difference between the brand power and the management mechanics and physical mechanics is such that the brand power is the important principle guiding the practices of enterprise brands. The thinking power of brand is a height achieved during the process of brand development, and a systematic thinking state achieved by an enterprise through the brand development; this is superior to ordinary thinking activities and creativity. It is the result of the creative brand thoughts and wisdoms that are independently developed through the preparation, development, practices and summarization for a certain period of time.

According to the history of brand development throughout the world, all brands did not have profound influences on human beings at the very beginning, and their unique styles, consciousness and the classic brand images with significant influence on human beings are formed through endless thinking, repeated exploration, practices and researches. Brand thoughts are not only the most precious wisdom of human beings, but the brand realm achieved by human beings through their pursuit for perfections, truths and value contributions. The great and classical brands are generated in this way with huge social influences. These are the gains of the practitioners – great brand achievements and global honor.

Human beings always have pursuits, such as, for future, lives and careers. Brand owners' constant pursuits for brands are the true driving forces for the generation of brand thoughts and the development of brands of human beings. Such precious spirits and virtues could drive the constant development of brands from nothing to something great, and created the brand legends, myths and fashions. It is the brand pursuing spirit that is encouraging human beings to create outstanding brands one after another continuously, and in return abundant brand wealth of human beings are created.

1.1 Propositions of A Theory

(1) The formation of the thinking power of brand is a great creation process with the wisdoms of human beings

The thinking power of brand is the supreme rule for the development of brand mechanics, and the supreme thinking realm of the brand pursuit. The formation of thoughts is a high degree of thought achieved by human beings through constant thinking and summarization during the process of pursuing truths in life, production and operation activities, which is the final summarization result of a series of scientific and philosophic principles that is made after reaching certain thought realm in terms of consciousness, capacities and levels. The thinking power of brand is a higher level of the knowledge economy of human beings – the important product of the thinking power economy.

(2) The thinking power of brand is the basis for the creation of everything

The great significance of brand thought is that it could create all things on earth, change the original ecologies, forms, patterns and methods of the brand products easily, and with a series of thoughts to support the development of new matters in brand that humans have never encountered previously. Thus, brand is equipped with high competitiveness that could overthrow the thinking patterns of human beings, the industrial competition structures and the forms of products.

(3) The thinking power of brand has created the demands of human beings

The purpose of brand thoughts is to create the demands in human beings. It is not for providing resolutions or improvements to certain problems, neither for meeting certain market needs nor satisfying certain consumers. Brand thoughts could create unprecedented new demands of human beings, featuring creativity. If brand thoughts could not complete the creation of brands, such demands could not be generated in terms of the development patterns of human beings. The original creativity of brand thoughts has generated new demands in human beings.

(4) The thinking power of brand is the inevitable result of the highly coordinated development of brand consciousness, brand organization power and brand attraction.

The thinking power of brand is not an original or single huge changing power, but it is the final product of the development and coordination of countries or enterprises in terms of brand consciousness, brand organization power and brand attraction, which is the ultimate collection of thoughts and wisdoms that are being accumulated during the development of brands, and the general brand thought summarization and the general brand designing thought utilization represent the highly coordinated development patterns in terms of heights, depths and widths of brands.

(5) The thinking power of brand is the important milestone of the social and economic development of human beings

The importance of brand thoughts depends on the brands generated by it. To some extent, the purpose of brand thoughts is to make material and creative changes to the development pattern of the productivity of human beings, the product patterns, the business models, and the operation thoughts. Such changes could reorganize the basic understandings and patterns of the business development, and generate powerful driving force for the development of social economic with the branding effects such as group learning, global recognition and general application. Therefore, brand thoughts are milestones for the stages in social and economic development of human beings, and are the firm and new footprints during the development of human beings.

(6) The thinking power of brand is a precious mental pursuit of human beings

The formation and development of brand thoughts are the driving force for human beings to move forward continuously in terms of mental pursuits, which could drive new understandings of brand in human beings and changes of new thinking patterns in human beings. The pursuits could be seen in all processes, links, stages and nodes during the formation of brand thoughts. There are pursuits to scientific discoveries, to technical levels, to knowledge systems, to matter creations, to aesthetic expressions, to truths of lives and to contribution values of human beings, which are the important improvement forces driving the development of human beings, the comprehensive scientific understanding to the development patterns of human beings and the central expression of individual and collective virtues.

(7) The thinking power of brand is the rare core development power for human beings.

The brand thoughts are not formed naturally, incidentally or originally. Brand thoughts are the result of rare and key strategic thoughts, and the thought achievements could be realized through brands. There are only a few ideologists of human beings, and the brand ideologists are even fewer. The thinking power of brand could change the industrial economy, production and living styles, and social and economic development patterns at the national or even international level to some extent, and such change is not a short term change but a long term and sustainable change. Therefore, the development of the thinking power of brand is the highest point of the global competitiveness of a country.

1.2 Brand consciousness

The brand consciousness is a combination of thinking patterns, capacities and levels determining the ideology of brand development. The ideology of human beings is not created naturally, it is developed by contacting matters, identifying the essences of matters, exploring the natural development rules and researching the forms of matters in different living environments. This has denied the assumption that entrepreneurs are born naturally.

Everyone could have dreams, and only a few people could implant dreams into brands. Everyone in the world has fantasies, but most people are living in reality. The brand ideologies are formed initially among a few persons with development capacities – the application and the utilization of power of brand dreams. They have experienced a necessary ideological development process and an action development process, namely, "image – concept – blueprint" and "strategy – action – achievement", so as to make the brand dreams come true firmly.

The brand consciousness is the rational development made by human beings for brands in terms of science and philosophy, which is the reaction of wisdoms when the consciousness level and physical experience utilization level have matched with each other. Possibly, some brand popularities have caught the attentions or is catching the attentions throughout the world and the purchasing tendency of the whole society. However, the brand popularity is not a phenomenon. Behind any brand popularity, there must be a formation logistics, scientific networks, and development rules. Such scientific rules shall be identified, developed and used in the development of new enterprises and brands.

With the global market competition and the comprehensive development of global brands, it's not an accidental phenomenon for a brand to draw attentions throughout the world. It's not a result achieved by an entrepreneur through mere discovery or accidental invention, but a knowledge drawing and application process conducted by handling advanced brand knowledge systems, developing brand scientific researches, and renewing the new brand research achievements constantly. By focusing their thoughts on a brand knowledge system that is subjected to constant dynamic updating, the thoughts of entrepreneurs can then keep in pace with time and drive new thoughts timely, which has important trigging value for the formation of the brand ideologies. In the age of knowledge economy, the foresights and thought level of an entrepreneur depends on the methods, speeds and values of obtaining knowledge.

The formation and improvements of brand ideologies also depend on the true understanding of entrepreneurs to brands. They shall consider brands as the instinct for pursuing missions. Any difficulties encountered in our lives could not stop us from moving forward. When the ideological levels of human beings are improving from developing virtues to conveying social morality and from dedication to the consciousness of sparing no effort to serve the society, the brand consciousness level is also improving. Finally, the precious brand ideologies created great companies, most respected undertakings, ideas that can change the world, and products providing the largest benefits to human beings.

The development of brand consciousness is also subjected to a persisting problem. Brand consciousness may change, and is not a brand power with constant improvement. By contrast, only when the brand ideologies could reach a certain level then can the brand thought be generated. However, the brand thoughts could only stay within certain period of time, depending on the time during which the brand founder (or leader) is holding his or her office. If the brand thinking power could not be constantly improved due to the successors, the brand consciousness may fail. Therefore, the major brands in the world pay great attention on developing the brand successors.

1.3 Brand organization power

The brand organization power is the reflection of the organization capacity of a brand in the whole society. Human is a contradictory body in fact. On one hand, we hope that what we have created could become our achievements, and on the other hand, we hope to participate in a joint undertaking to experience the process and make contributions. We do not like being managed or controlled but we also hope to be led by others and participate in an organization with strict disciplines.

People are shifting between the individual and group relationships. Employees are individuals sometimes, but they are members of groups at the other times. Users are groups, but they may be individuals sometimes. The function of brand organization is to establish the organization group transition process both inside and outside the organization. When the individuals are transferring into groups, huge organization power will be generated.

Therefore, brands are not the products of the development of enterprises, or the liability limited companies in laws. Brands are the organization group power generated when an enterprise has upgraded to brand organization and become ecological brand organization. Brand organization is a special form that may disappear in an instant, which could only be seen when the enterprise has organization power. If the organization power has disappeared, the brand organization will return to the original enterprise form automatically.

The brand organization power is the problem related to brand management and enterprise culture, which will also be subject to a dual synergy problem. The brand organization power is a force represented in the brand organization, but its source greatly depends on the development of the brand culture and enterprise cultural power, which is the order body of the enterprise in the business organization status and the representation of the organization behaviors when the consciousness of all employees of the enterprise has developed to certain level. In term of structure, brand organization power and enterprise cultural power are all within the scope of organization development science. Such determination could facilitate the high-level consistency and the function of the development power of the brand organization. Meanwhile, attention shall be paid to the negative influence of the enterprise cultural resistance on the brand organization and enterprise cultural power, which may reduce the brand organization power and prevent the brand thought power from developing.

Labor function assignment and cultural assignment are the keys for developing brand organization power. In an active and dynamic brand organization, the demands of people for wealth will reduce, and they would like to reflect their labor value to develop certain cultural pattern. This is the instinct for people from individual development to common development. It's vital for the brand organization to respect, acknowledge and reasonably return the labor value of people. It's the ideal development condition for a brand organization to assign everyone and use everyone's talent, which is the base of the fair environment for the coordinated development among the employees in a brand organization. The level of the coordinated development of the labor value assignment and cultural assignment could determine the final development level of the brand organization power.

1.4 Brand attraction

Brand attraction is the comprehensive capacity of a brand to obtain user base, form the foundation of the brand and develop the brand user groups. The brand users shall be obtained through active attraction, which is the mature and stable brand user groups attracted and owned by the brand organization during the self-adaption development process with high quantity, quality, trust and expansion speed.

Different from marketing and sales, what the brands could establish is a special brand attraction method. During the development of brands, the interpersonal network will be used as the basic morphology for the communication and expansion of brands. During this process, Internet and mobile internet have played important roles in the consumption process of the brand users in terms of self learning, self-confirmation, self-purchasing and self-knowledge, as well as the important rules in terms of the application value transition of brand and the self-discovery of the most important brand users to the brand value. The connections with various channels at different levels have made the brand organization into a dynamic system network with brand triggering, brand self-respond and brand communication. The great attraction power of brand is generated in this way.

The brand organization shall improve the deployment of brand contacts to trigger the self-process and value identification of brand users through brand contacts so as to complete the important development of brand attraction. In the modern social network environment, a series of changes will urge enterprises to pay attention to the scientific development of brand attraction during the development of brands.

The generation of brand attraction is a social networking process and an important development process for brand products and services. The brand consciousness could determine the classical level, concrete form and popularity of the products and services of brand, promoting the updating and development of brand to develop its unique charms. The brand organization power could determine the structure of brand organization, labor assignment standard, cultural assignment standard and the standard of brand users to discover the brand values, promoting the brands to attract attentions from all walks of the society in a more active way.

Finally, the developments of the brand consciousness and brand organization power in height and depth could promote the brand attraction to generate powerful attraction, forces and consumer interest guidance among the public and the users, thus the brand users will be attracted to the brand and generate the ever increasing brand effect with ego, self-adapt, self-influence and self transmission.

A highly consistent and coordinated development shall be maintained among the brand consciousness, brand organization power and brand attraction. With the development height of brand consciousness, the depth of penetration of the brand organization in society and the automatic expansion influence of the brand attraction in width, a series of unprecedented brand thoughts, advanced brand activities, and outstanding brand achievements could be made for a brand so as to ensure the historical brand force value in terms of missions and responsibilities, development and progress, and pursuits and honors.

2 B Theory

Terminology

Brand policy-making power: It is the rapid identification method trigging the consumption desires, thus allowing brand consumers to make consumption decisions immediately or in the future.

Understand

- Consumers could only recognize brands but not the business types and enterprises.

- Brands could meet certain consumption desires and eliminate price sensitivity.

- Consumers could make rapid purchasing decisions for brands immediately or latterly.

- Brands are not solely for large enterprises. Any enterprise will be preparing for brands from the first day of establishment.

Trend

The brain consciousness of human beings in the 21st century constitute of brands. Brands will accompany the development of human beings and consume such brands finally.

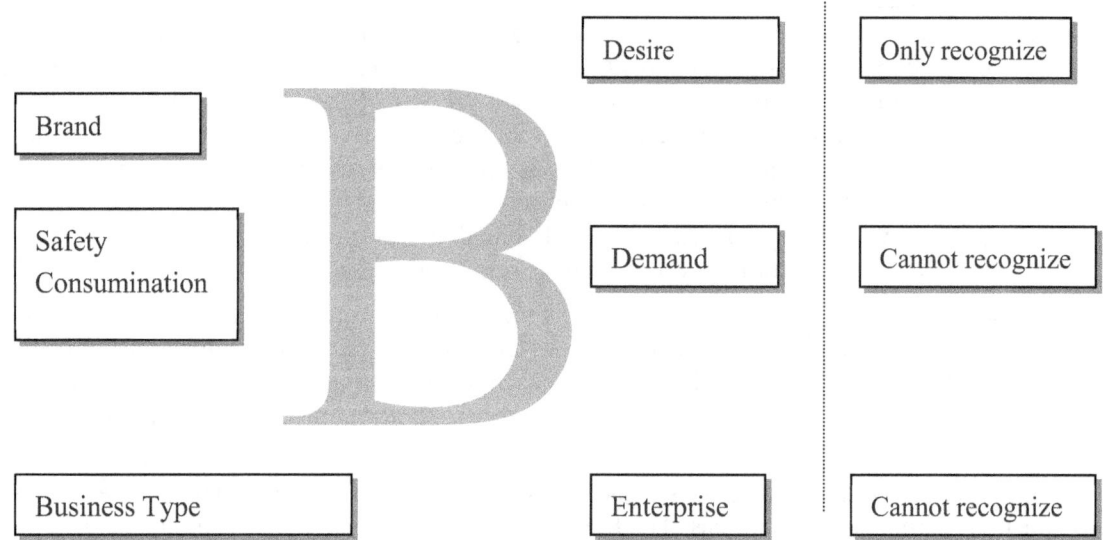

Fig 4-2 B Theory Brand Consumption Policy Making Model

The B Theory (See Fig. 4-2) is also called brand consumption policy-making model which could explain the following to consumers at the market level: (1) Why do you purchase brands? (2) When do you purchase brands? (3) What consumption activity reaction will occur when purchasing brands?

2.1 Key points of B Theory

(1) Brands are the expectations to consumption desires, and the desire for consumers to pay more money. Such purchases shall be completed under the condition of safe consumption.

(2) When desire is higher than demand, brand consumers will pay more. When the desire is lower than brand, the consumer will question about the safety of the brands and may reduce the price.

(3) Consumers could only identify brands and their own desires but not the safe consumption environment and fundamental demands as well as the enterprise names featuring business types.

2.2 Proposition of B Theory

(1) Brands are the safe consumption activities for certain desires.

Brands are stimulations and triggers to desires, and the consumption activities occurred to meet certain desires, which could occur under safe conditions.

(2) People will pay more for brands.

Desire demands are higher than normal demands. When such desires are triggered by the brand operators, the consumers will pay more money for purchases and price sensitivity will be reduced or eliminated.

(3) The desires met by brands are special demands.

Desires represent identities, status, rights, honors, and consumption capacities; as well as leading concepts, outstanding works, high-quality designs, reliable purchasing, stable quality, mature technologies, guaranteed services, fashion elements, cultures and consumption safety.

(4) Brands have consumption levels, and people will do every effort to complete such consumption process.

Brands are equivalent to desires. When consumers are able to consume, they will purchase. When the consumption capacity is insufficient, they will purchase by doing every effort or after the conditions could be met.

(5) People rely on brands and will resist other brands.

Purchasing behaviors are exclusive under most conditions. When the consumers have specific purchasing belief in certain brands, they will have strong dependency on these brands and have strong resistance to other brands.

(6) Consumers will not recognize the business types of the brands nor the enterprises.

There is no relationship among brands, business types (product types and industry types) and enterprises. Consumers can only remember brands, and will not care about the manufacturers of the brands when they are purchasing products from the brand operators (brand owners and brand dealers).

(7) Consumers will rarely purchase new brands and only accept the recommendations from reliable sources.

When the consumers do not have remembered brands in a field, they will find new brands through Internet, brand news or the recommendations from relatives or friends. They will not buy new brands actively unless such brands have been confirmed by news or friends.

(8) Consumers may only make trail purchasing for new brands with strong consumption prevention consciousness.

Even with the recommendations from reliable sources, consumers will make trail purchasing for the brands they have never used before. When the safety consciousness is broken, the consumer will stop consuming the brands.

(9) Violent brand consumption could only be seen in the enterprises with mid-brand capacities. The lower the consumption power is, the higher the consumption requirement will be.

When the desires could not be met, or the brands are homogenized, consumers will reduce their demands for brands. They will make brand comparison in terms of product performance, functions, appearances, types, textures, quality stability, service guarantee, contact attitude, using habits, so as to make selections with difficulties and make purchasing decisions finally. If the brand capacity is weaker, the selection requirements of consumers in terms of prices and utilization conditions will be higher.

3 Brand ternary relation

The ternary relation is an expansion of Theory B, defining the symbiotic relationships among brands, consumption and enterprises.

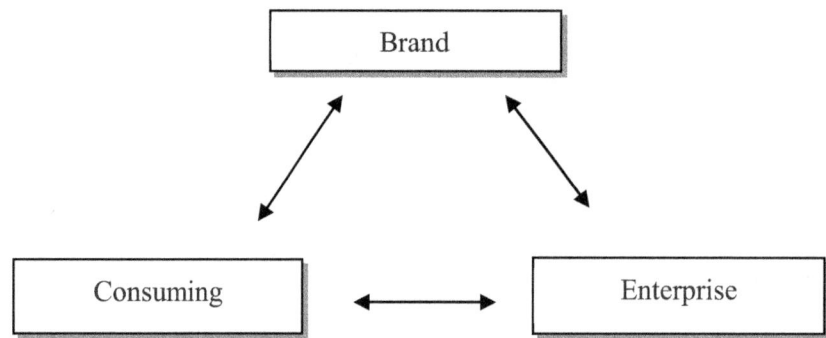

Fig. 4-3 Ternary Relation

3.1 Proposition of brand ternary relation

(1) Enterprises believe that they own brands and belong to certain business types (certain industry and certain good).

Examples: P &G Company has many brands such as Head-Shoulders, VS Sassoon, Crest, Safeguard, OLAY, Whisper, Tide, Gillette, and NanFu; and Hexing of Hong Kong has brands such as Yoshinoya, Diary Queen, and Lion & Globe. They are using different brands to occupy different markets.

(2) When a field has brands, consumers could only recognize brands but not the business types or enterprises.

Examples: Consumers clearly wanted to purchase Pepsi but not Coca-Cola, or beverage or sodas, or the products made by Pepsi Company, the Pepsi is made by local factory. When consumers want to buy shampoo to make their hairs smooth, they may buy Rejoice but not Head-Shoulders.

(3) When a field does not have brands, consumers will only recognize demands but not enterprises.

Examples: Consumers will find the best dentists and the best office furniture manufacturer. They are not recognizing the medical industry or the furniture industry. They will not look for clinics that could provide dentist services or any manufacturers that could provide office furniture.

(4) Consumers will rarely purchase the products of new brands and will only trust the recommendations from reliable sources.

Survey in 14 European countries: 71% of the consumers will not buy products with the brands they have never heard about; Survey in China: 78% of the consumers will doubt the quality and softer-sales services of new companies or new brands, and they will not purchase such products. The reliable sources include: media reporting, friend recommendations. More than 50% of the consumers will search the information of the new brand when they heard about it for the first time. If the brand has not been confirmed by the media, the brand will not be trusted. The other reliable source is through friends' recommendations. The consumers will purchase the products after their friends have used such products or confirmed the product information.

(5) The prices are not the appeals for brand competition.

Example: Even when the monthly income is less than 2,000 Yuan, a young person would like to purchase an iPhone at the price of 4,700 Yuan. BMWs are the dream of many people. BMW and Santana are both automobile brands but not brand competitors. However, an owner of thee Santana may wish to have BMW someday. The people who are able to purchase BMW will not buy Santana. The desire for brands could determine the purchasing behaviors.

(6) The enterprise could accelerate consumption and obtain profits by operating the desires of consumers to brands.

Examples: the brand dealers could import French wines to obtain profit and the furniture dealers may import Italian furniture to meet the high consumption desires in the market. The competitors without clear sources or brands on eBay or Taobao will obtain small profits by reducing prices. The brand operators could only obtain high profit through brand designs, brand influences, brand communications, brand permits or quality goods.

Exercises

1. Fill in the blanks: The thinking power of brand of A theory includes _____, _____ and _____.

2. Fill in the blanks: The ternary relation is an expansion of B Theory, defining the symbiotic relationships among _____, _____ and _____.

3. Essay Question: how many propositions are there in the B Theory and what are their contents?

SECTION I GENERAL INTRODUCTION

Chapter 5

Brand User Groups

Brand user groups are the foundation of brand development. They are formed through the accumulation of brand users after the brand has fully developed, they will be the basic guarantee of the sustainable development and the essence of the constant operation of the brand in the far future.

The brand user groups are realized through three stages, namely, brand communities, foundation of brand, and brand user groups. During the development of a brand, only when the brand has obtained a sufficient quantity, scale and stable stream of regular customers, then can the development of the brand be stabilized, this means that the brand has a good development prospect and a sustainable future.

1 Brand communities

The initial development of any brand is unstable, which is represented by the fact that the brand has insufficient user base before its development, and its users are temporary. Many brands in the world may meet with this problem at the initial stage of development. Given the insufficient users, the enterprises shall focus on obtaining brand users in the early stage so as to survive in the complicated competitive environment. However, since people do not understand and trust the new brands, they will see the new brands with a strong sense of resistance.

Brand risk questionable principle: The instinct for sense of security during brand consumption will form a natural protection for human beings. People will be wary of all unknown matters. Even tiny risk will stop them from moving forward. Such sense of protection is more obvious at the early stage of development of a brand, which could urge the brand to pay attention to this important process.

Most of the people in the world may take a relatively defense position towards new brands. According to statistics, in Europe, about 90% of the consumers would not buy the products of unknown new brands. In China, about 76% of the consumers will have doubts about the after-sales services of a new brand. Before the new risks are eliminated, few users would try new brands within their capacity to withstand risks. It's common for a new brand to encounter user growth difficulties at the very beginning of its development, and this is a very normal natural development condition.

Almost every new enterprise in the world would suffer from insufficient users at the early stage of a brand. All enterprises in the world may encounter this problem from the date of establishment. Nearly 50% of new enterprises may be shut down within 9 months due to significant insufficiency of users at the early stage. Among the enterprises that have survived, only about 40% could maintain the daily to daily normal operations and develop gradually or become surviving enterprises that are sales-oriented.

Among the newly established enterprises, only 10% could develop rapidly into high-growth enterprises thanks to market opportunities, sufficient funds and advantageous products. However, not all high-growth enterprises could become brands and not all low-growth enterprises are unable to develop into brands.

The formation of a brand is not always combined with market development. By contrast, the brands are determined as a special development status, which are the development patterns determined by the founder of an enterprise since its establishment. He or she would select branding as the method to realize his or her dreams or use economic profit method to develop a successful enterprise. Only less than 1% of the emerging enterprises could have firm brand dreams since the day of their establishment.

Whether it is harsh market exploration or stable and rapid development, the original intention of brand development will not change due to good or bad market conditions. The enterprises with clear brand wills only account for less than 1% of the new enterprises, and the enterprises that are able to develop into brands finally only account for 0.01% of all enterprises in the world. No matter large or small brands, they will finally be able to maintain sustainable competitive advantages in the global or local market and obtain the constant brand development features for tens or hundreds of years. Such brands will finally become the splendid marks in the history of brand development of human beings.

Therefore, brand communities are very important to the emerging enterprises which would like to realize the branding development in a smooth way. Brand communities could significantly release the problem of insufficient user reserves of a brand at the early stage, and eliminate the instabilities of the development of the brand at the early stage, which will be the safety transition period of the brand at its early stage. Although brand communities are applicable to other enterprises that would like to develop as soon as possible, not all enterprises would like to spend time and money on completing such change since the brand communities are an enterprise development strategic issue. Enterprises shall understand that the purpose of establishing brand communities is to develop brand user groups that have strong development potential. Brand communities are in the embryo stage to some extent. When the strong foundation of a brand is established, the function of brand communities will disappear.

1.1 Establishment of brand communities

Brand communities are a social organization pattern in essence, which is formed through the scientific development route of "developing brand communicates, releasing brands and developing products", but not the route of "developing communities, following by releasing products and upgrading to brands". The former will forge powerful brands and the latter will develop weak brands, they will have different brand effects and values. The former will obtain powerful brand attraction and stable branding users at the beginning and is able to develop the foundation of brand as soon as possible. The latter, however, may have rapid market expansion and growth during certain periods of time, but its branding process is relatively slow, and may lose the branding development driving force when the foundation of brand is not stable, and will disappear before developing into brands. According to our investigations on some brands, the enterprises that are able to establish brands may experience a very difficult process that requires repeated explorations, this is caused by the brand Parkinson disease due to the non compliance of law 01.

To obtain a more stable brand development foundation, the brand founder shall establish a brand community at first, in order to reserve brand users at the early stage, so as to make active preparation for obtaining the first brand users. At this stage, the brand shall focus on establishing a community that is used to accumulate potential users. Internet and various channels could be used to search and capture potential users. Thus, gathering individuals with an interest or demand and complete the early group transfer of the brand organization.

The community established by the brand initially is not gathered in the name of the self-owned brand. By contrast, a common name may be used, such as skiing club, music fans, and natural coffee forum. In this way, some potential users may find the organizations through search engines or friends. When the first group of users is collected and the community relations with organizations have been established, the groups of potential users will form the "virtual" communities focusing on certain demands. Some brands may use "trial" activities to accumulate users at the early stage. During this process, a relatively stable brand ecological organization may be established through the participation, interaction and responses from the members in the communities, and the first group of users of brands are among them.

According to the golden triangle of brand profit, users of any brands would conduct group transfer in the way of "Users – Clients – Regular clients". The scientific organization process of "regular clients recommending clients" will occur repeatedly. The completion of the process signified that the brand community has fulfilled its value at the early stage, which could ensure that the brand could effectively release the client development difficulties at early stages and develop orderly.

Both large and small brands could obtain stable development foundation at early stages by establishing brand communities. Some large brands, such as Facebook in the United States and the MI in China, have obtained great development opportunities by establishing social network development method for brand communities at the beginning. This has become a special business model. In the internet, mobile internet and every demand preference, the brand communities could be easily developed to certain quantities, for example, Aiyuelan music fans, competitive sports fans, UAV fans or csa community supported agriculture, as well as lighter collection fans. The development of these communities has made great contribution to the development of emerging brands at early stages, and many brands have resolved the development risks at the unstable early stages.

1.2 Operation of brand communities

Brand communities in fact could eliminate the unfamiliarity between a brand and consumers at the early stage. With the shifting function of the communities, the status of users will be shifted from defensive to friendly. The initial trust design and excellent interactions at the time of purchase could be used to change the consumers into the first batch of regular users. With the inter-promotion and inter-influence within the community, the brands would be able to successfully accumulate the first batch of regular users, and obtain the independent development foundation for its ecology.

Through the socialized communities, the fans will be transferred from individuals into early brand user groups. In this way, the users will trust a brand, and the inter-trust within the community will further enlarge the foundation of the trust. The brand could use excellent interactions with users to improve the user attachment, expand community relationship network, and develop friendly brand-user relations. Relatively, such input has low cost and could be used to complete the transition of brand communities to brand foundation with limited funds at the early stage.

The effective organization is the basic assurance for the development of brand communities. To ensure effectiveness and stable growth of brand communities, the organizers may need to input certain efforts, labors and resources to establish a series of community infrastructure, including the software systems required for the community development, third party network systems, offline meeting places, places of meetings for members, accountability rewards provided to the backbone members, activity rewards for the development of the societies, and resources used to encourage the member interactions or promotions. The detailed forms shall be determined according to the actual conditions.

The top stage of the development of any brand is the brand ecological organization and the maintenance of such organization form. The characteristics of brand organizing could be seen at the beginning of establishing communities. In the competition of brands in the world of enterprises, the major value is reflected by the competition in organizing brands, or what effective organization scale could a brand achieve with all resources in the society. Therefore, the brand organization is the super industrial ecological organization with the socialized organization as the core development method. The organization development level, organization capacity construction and socialized organization status are the key points of the organization construction.

For this purpose, initiators and organizers of the brand communities, or individuals or enterprises, shall maintain the normal conditions of the brand community organization from the very beginning, establish the key team or the socialized organization of the brand communities, build corresponding organization rules, develop corresponding organization structures and branches, and build the promotion system, service system, working coordination system and activity systems in the organization. The effective organization development capacity is very important. The organization development science is superior to the ordinary enterprise management methods with common meanings, which is the scientific base for brand culture, enterprise culture, internet chain and flow management, and the socialized organization assurance to obtain extraordinary development capacities, especially in the social networking age with the interconnection of multiple networks. Both local and international brands highly depend on such network organization forms featuring socialization. In addition, brand communities are built on the basic network patterns, the inter-personal network. Therefore, the features of socialization are more obvious, the development capacity of centralized economy will be more powerful, and the development method of the network organizations will be deeper, which could better meet the scientific development rules of socialized networks in the future.

2 Brand Foundation

Brand foundation means the brand user groups are developed with "Tagee" as the main body, which is the basic assurance for early development, market expansion and long-term sustainable operation of a brand and the foundation of long-term brand life. The brand attraction model to be established for the development of brand organizations is based on the stable development of the brand foundation.

Concept of brand foundation: "Tagee" is an online word that is constituent of "Tag" and "ee", which means the persons or experts classified by Tags. Therefore, Tagee is the foundation of all high towers.

The brand foundation is the whole brand user group with solid foundation, expansion capacity and sustainable development based on the development logic of "Tagee", which has emphasized that construction of the brand user foundation is to be noticed by the brand organization from the very beginning. This is consistent to the "Fans Economy".

On the Internet, when the number of the fans of a brand has reached 1000, the self expansion of the brand will occur, and the brand will enter into the process of self-media transmission, self-service respond and self-user expansion gradually. The foundation of the brand users is built in such process and operates based on the law 101, which means that there must be one effective paying user in every 100 potential users, and there must be one active regular user in every 100 paying users who can realize the brand backbone user effect by bringing a lot amount of clients recommended by existing clients. When a brand has 100 brand backbone users, the brand foundation is established, and scaled brand user group self-expansion will occur.

The law 101 is the basic rule for the establishment of brand foundation, which is the key at the early stages of brands. The enterprise shall increase the promotion scale, attract more potential users and transfer them into the clients of the brand in large amount.

2.1 Brand foundation principle

The "Tag" in the brand foundation "Tagee" means the tags in the Internet, which is also called "free classification" or "mass decentralization classification", which is a descriptive word created by the Internet users according to their understandings to matters. This word is widely used in the searching engine and the user visiting catalogs. Traditional catalogs could compare the fixed catalogs with the matters, and the Tags are marked freely for the conveniences of management, searching and inquiry, which could provide excellent flexibility and expandable application spaces for the applications on Internet.

The brands, however, are classified by brand user groups. Each brand will have its fixed brand user groups after developing to certain degree –the typical brand user groups gathered the interests, preferences, styles, and features of brand backbone users, brand regular clients, brand clients and brand users. However, if the brand is established initially, emphasis must be placed on the establishment of the brand foundation as the initial actual foundation for the development of the brand.

Just like the idiom "birds of a feather flock together", the brand foundation is the brand user classification based on interests, cultural styles, hot topics, focuses and using features, which could enable the brand to actually capture special demands of potential consumers and provide the best forms, so as to transfer certain or a series of potential demands in the public into user transformation behaviors based on the operation of brand market.

SECTION I GENERAL INTRODUCTION

The "ee" in the brand foundation "Tagee" means the group of passive people or professionals, which refers to the backbone user groups of the brand in the brand foundation. They will be transferred from passive to proactive after being attracted by the brand attractions to support the long term development of brands, recommend clients, expand the brand influences and transmit the brand concepts with their original passions and voluntary actions. Their group development is the core assurance for brands from birth to expansion and from development to everlasting operation, and the solid base for the stability of the brand foundation.

When the brand has developed to Level A, it will attract the public rapidly, and people will transmit the brand voluntarily and wish everyone could consume the brand for a long time. They will pay higher prices for the brand. Therefore, the enterprises will obtain sufficient high profits and the client transfer cost will be extremely high. The regular clients will use the brand throughout their lives. In such case, the brand foundation will be formed, and the brand will enter into a brand attraction stage with high quality. Even when there are complaints about the brand, the users may protect the brand voluntarily, and a mature and stable self-adapt ecological system will be formed for the brand.

In addition, the golden triangle principle of brand profits could also explain the transfer relations among "users, clients and regular clients". The enterprise shall increase the quantities and intensities of users trying the new brands at the early stages of the development of brands. In such way, the first group of paying clients will be found among the users. When the clients begin to consume repeatedly, they will become regular clients, featuring frequent payments, who will also recommend people whom they know to become the paying clients. After completing the early preparation, the enterprise will enter into the repeated transfer and expansion stage from clients to regular clients. At this moment, the enterprises shall stabilize the brand foundation structure for the brands. The enterprises will enjoy sufficient profits from the constant consumption of the brands. The circle of "Clients – Regular clients" will occur repeatedly, so as to achieve long life of the brand.

2.2 Application of the brand foundation principle

Enterprises shall deploy the brands accurately according to the attributes of the brand users, the key areas to be distributed and the user groups of the brands, so as to complete the vertical system coverage over the chain and flow managements such as the enterprise commanding chain, enterprise culture flows et al. The key markets and accurate brand user groups have formed the foundation required for the power of the enterprise brands.

Examples of foundation in key markets: The *China Times* has abandoned the concept of city news paper and made strategic changes to focus on the CBD area of Beijing to cover the whole country. It has established the position as a "Comprehensive Daily + Business Cycle Newspaper" to become "the first business cycle newspaper in China". The foundation area of the newspaper covers the CBD "golden key business cycle cluster" composed of International Trading Center, Jianguomen, Chaowai, Lufthansa, Wangfujing, Xidan, Financial Street, Sanyuanqiao and Dawangqiao cycles. The target readers are the high-income office employees in the area. The CBD "golden key business cycle cluster" has gathered many famous enterprises and multinational companies both at home and abroad, who have super strong consumption capacities and driving function. With one year's effort, the *China Times* has completed the foundation coverage and become the "pure office life publication and the spirit coffee of the CBD persons".

Example of foundation of brand user groups: In China, for people who are getting married, there is a famous quote "I would like to fell in love with only one person and never be separated". The young couples have attached great importance to figures such as 1314 and 520. When the brands of marriages focus on such links, the brand foundation has formed, or the brand user groups with certain demands have been established, include people who are interested in the quote, in Zhuo Wenjun, in 1314 and 520, in the dreaming blue packages and in the blessing ceremony of Zhuo Wenjun. Each of the above special demand represents a brand user group and all brand user groups could form the user group family. The brand designing and transmission shall only focus on these special users that have been selected carefully. Even each user group has only 10,000 users with special demands, the whole brand user group family will have a foundation established by the users with several special demands. The foundation of brand user groups is a cultural awakening, cultural simulation and cultural response, which could enable those people with certain cultural demands to find their organizations. The people unrelated to the foundation are not the brand users we needed and we do not need to expand the extra market input.

Example of foundation of enterprise cultural flow: The brand foundation of Starbucks is established on the enterprise cultural flows. The coffee culture of Starbucks has been connected to every white-collar worker pursuing quality lifestyle. In the market of China, Starbucks has become a cultural symbol of tasting life. The enterprise cultures could flow in the interpersonal network, and regular clients pursuing better lifestyles will recommend, lead and guide their colleagues and friends into the Starbuck culture. The stores of Starbucks are distributed in business areas with many office buildings, which have become the cultural gathering centers for modern people in the cities, and are expanding in office buildings. You will see that young people in many office buildings are used to having a Starbucks every day. Especially in meetings, about 1/3 attendees have Starbucks on their desks. In fact, what people need is not the coffee but the cultural attribute of Starbucks. Among the colleagues enjoying Starbucks, there is a common cultural resonance, which has isolated them from those who do not drink Starbucks.

3 Brand user groups

The structure of the brand foundation has laid solid base for the long-term stable development of a brand. The key of the true value of the users required in the development of a brand is not the size of the user groups but the inventory and maintenance rate of regular clients.

Regular clients are those who will purchase the products of a brand for more than three times or recommend at least three new users to become paying clients per year. The development prospects and profits of a brand are mainly from the repeated consumptions of the brand, which is unrelated to the market conditions.

The user transfer rate is the proportion of the users that have not transferred within three years to the total amount of the regular clients. The high inventory rate indicates that the brand has powerful user transfer barrier, and the users will not transfer due to other similar competitive products on the market, and will not leave from the brand due to the scale or difficulties of the development of the brand.

Only the inventory and inventory rates of regular clients are the strategic investment values of a brand on the global or domestic market. Even if these brands do not get listed in the stock market, it will still maintain excellent investment benefits. For a brand, this could sufficiently prove that it has good sustainable development capacity to realize the stable and mature development of the brand. Many brands have become hundred-year brands in this way.

The brand user groups, the most valuable sentimental users of the brands, will develop their feelings for the brands through the contacts with the brands for many years, which are the key points for the establishment of such purchase, delivery, introduction, and self-transmission relationships. Such feeling is high-level mutual trust. The users will see the brands as the trustworthy "friend", and the primary substances and spirit conditions for daily lives or personal development.

This could form a brand consumption blood relationship in a family between the son and father, the daughter and mother and the grandchildren and grandparents. For generations in a family, they will see the brand as a spiritual member of the family, for which such activities as repeated consumption, reliance, maintenance and collection will occur. Such features could cause the brand user groups to convey unprecedented values and meanings in the development of the global brands and the development history of all brands of human beings, which could separate the brands from the capital and financial market with investment activities and the ordinary money relationship. In such case, the brand will obtain the features of constant development, to improve the brand to a perfect value presentation and spirit pursuit level, and the true brands will be born in this way.

SECTION I GENERAL INTRODUCTION

3.1 Features of brand user groups

Brand user groups are the high-level stages of the brand users when the brand communities and foundation have developed to a certain level, which have the brand consumption blood relationship and special brand cultural features, including the mental maintenance and inherence of brands, the historical factors of brands, the brand utilization habits, the common brand preferences, the brand philosophy and the brand arts.

When there is no brand consumption blood relationship, the inherence of brands is not perfect or firm, and the firm and sustainable cohesion could not be generated. In such case, the sustainable and reliable brand civilization development patterns could not be established. When the specific cultural attributes could not be formed, the brands could not develop beyond the common products to convey the brand expression attributes with special attractions. Therefore, only when the two conditions are met at the same time, the user groups of a brand could pay active role constantly.

The brand user groups have powerful consistent sense of identity. Through the long-term recognition to one brand, people will feel familiar to each other instantly. For examples, two persons who love Coca-Cola, Starbucks or Tequila will feel familiar to each other when they met in a strange environment. Their passions for the same brands will reduce the distance between each other and eliminate the sense of unfamiliarity immediately. The common preferences and topics could promote the specific effects in the brand user groups.

Despite of different races, nationalities and languages of people in the world, the brand user groups have surpassed all elements such as countries, histories, backgrounds and economic conditions. This is why international brands could be famous in the world, or be heard in every corner of the world. Brand user groups have become the bridges between people based on the passions, interests, habits, experiences, spirits and joys to things.

The powerful consistent sense of identity in the brand user groups has established a stable defense line against similar competitive products. The roles of groups have surpassed prices, appearances, trusts and other features selected by human beings in terms of materials and spirits. Such high-level trust and utilization preference are formed between people and brands for a long time, which is an advanced, powerful and developed socialized organization with the centralized and highly coordinated development of the brands as the development pattern, which is a developing science.

The inherence relations and mutual influences in brand user groups will maintain the foundation for long-term and stable development of a brand, which could cause people to have intensified desire to own and protect the brands. Since people are familiar with the brands they have used for years, stable development patterns, official consciousness, and civilization attributes of the brands are formed. Such brand resonance frequency spectrum generated with these common social attributes could further improve the determining purchasing capacities of people to the brands. The brand safety sense generated through mutual reliance could protect the brand users so as to eliminate all uncertainties in the rapid social development – especially, the purchasing risks of new brands and the sense of insecurity of selection among similar brands will be eliminated.

3.2 Development of brand user groups

The brand user groups are generated based on fixed experience and knowledge system formed during the development of human beings. Given the long term experiences and usage for various brands, everyone could have his or her brand selection and abandon the unstable and unsafe brands. Therefore, this has become an instinct for human beings to develop themselves. Each one may store some fixed brands in the brain. When dealing with certain demand or implementing certain solution, the fixed brands or even the years and codes of the brands will be remembered so as to complete the daily utilization and development through "fixed and mature utilization habits".

This is established on the brand protogenesis theory and brand instinct theory. The Brand protogenesis theory means that people will select brands based on fixed selection patterns, original official consciousness and brand consumption blood relationship. Only the brands that have been fixed for a long time could exist in the form of brand user groups. The protogenesis could be represented through original consciousness. If applicable, users in the user groups of a brand will purchase and use the original parts and services since this is safe consumption, accustomed purchasing and fixed using method in the opinion of people. This could ensure that the brand could be able to develop into a self-adapt, self-operation and self-development brand chain through the original patterns and consumption of original parts.

The brand instinct theory refers to the fixed and historical using habit to a brand in the lives or movements of human beings. The lives of people are limited, and it is impossible for anyone to try all brands in his or her limited life. He or she must save time and prevent risks. Therefore, the brands are selected and used based on recommendations from reliable information sources. Once the utilization of a brand is stabilized, it will be fixed. The transmission of such reliable information is based on the transmission of trust on the reliable facts and experiences.

In addition, people move around in the world. People in periods in their lives will work, do businesses and develop in different places. There are so many intensified and different traffic tools, which are determined by the movement nature of human beings. Although new brands would like to join in the market competition, the instinct of human beings could determine that the brands will become the instinct of human beings to make fixed and necessary selections. Such development forces could enable the brands to establish brand user groups with high level of competiveness and natural development orders in the human world, which has surpassed the brands and developed into the basic brand instinct for brand understanding and purchasing in the future.

The development of brand user groups is the brand organization development patterns emphasized by us, given the resonance and inherence functions of the brand user groups, the brands will have a series special civilized bodies that can be inherited and developed, such as historical origins, spirits, symbols, honors and ceremonies, which will be able to stabilize and fix the brand user groups after their completion through the long-term utilization preference of the brand, including the prints of using the same brands constantly, the familiar brand styles and features, the similar brand utilization knowledge and the same language and names.

The largest rand user groups may have hundreds of millions members, such as Hollywood films, Coca-cola and Disney, or several thousands, tens of thousands or millions members, such as the Longjing Tea and Yunnan Baiyao of China, the French Guerlain make-ups and the RED GINSENG POWDER of Korea.

Exercises

1. Fill in the blanks: Brand foundation means that the brand user groups developed with "Tagee" as the main body, which is the basic assurance for _____, _____, and _____ of a brand and the foundation of the long-term brand life.

2. Multiple-choice Question: Brand communities are a social organization pattern in essence, which is formed through the scientific development route of _____, but not the route of _____. ( )

    A. "developing communities, releasing products and updating to brands",

    "developing brand communicates, releasing brands and developing products"

    B. "developing communities, releasing products and updating to brands",

    "developing communities, releasing products and updating to brands"

3. Discussion: What are the theories underlying the development of the brand user groups? Please describe the related theories.

Section I General Introduction

Chapter 6

Brand Performance

Brand performance is defined as the brand development method that shall be noticed by modern and future enterprises in their development. When an enterprise has developed into a large organization, brand performance will gradually become the core of the operation of the enterprise. With the development of the enterprise, it will come closer to the modern development methods and have higher requirements for brand performance.

Brand performance is composed of five basic performances, namely, the brand perception performance, brand presentation performance, brand value performance, brand essence performance and brand utility performance, as well as the brand performance in the global synergic network. During the development of brands, enterprises shall focus on the related brand performance as the key point, which will be the basic performance status required for updating the enterprise brands to brand organizations.

1 Management of brand performance

The management of brand performance is the collection of all activities related to the brand performance such as general designing, distributed designing, evaluation and optimization. The development of modern brands has been separated from the actual performances such as the quality performance of products, which has become a brand-sensitive ecological organization operation based on the social network organizations. A lot of IT technologies have been included into the daily operation and management of brands. The brands and enterprise users are developed through the direct connection relationships. The services provided to users by enterprises are featured, which means that an enterprise will provide service to any brand user through several departments and suppliers. Although the departments or suppliers have not faced to the users directly, their works will directly or indirectly reflect the brand performance, or the functions of the brands to the end users.

The brand performance shall be subject to general designing. Different from the ordinary product performance tests, capacity analysis, troubleshooting, maintenance and repair, the brand performance are the general operation level of the expanded brand organizations, and the dynamic brand guarantee system with core competitiveness in the organization frames of modern brands.

The brand performance is based on individual brands. By developing the brand thinking level of enterprises, a structured function network chain of brand performance will be established in terms of brand perception performance, value performance and utility performance. With the development of the brand performance, new value chains will be developed and the potential brand value capacities will be explored so as to conduct the brand sense transmission and the brand value transition from inside to outside, optimize the brand performance according to the brand performance heat map, distribute the ecological supplies and resources of the brands and maximize the brand utility.

The management of the brand performance requires an excellent initial trust designing, stable quality and reliable brand safety. During the systematic operation of the brand ecological organization, the system resource occupations shall be analyzed accurately to ensure the best performances and reduce the resource occupations of the brand systems. The brand performance is developing towards the IT network intelligence and into a centralized branding operation system with a more complicated design and simpler operation. Especially at the peaks of brand productions or services, the resource vacancy at lows of brand production and services shall be reduced in order to maintain the best agility productivity and service respond capacity.

2 Brand perception performance

The brand perception performance describes the multi-dimensional perception of brand users to a brand, which is portrayed as a process of exploration, research, perception measurement and data analysis and reporting of the perception levels, degrees, methods and responds of the brand users based on the brand feedback mode. The brand perception performance is not the customer satisfaction measurement or market survey with potentially confusing traditional meanings, but the analysis and confirmation of a brand enterprise of the perception of the brand users regarding the brands and the related products, services, management, business modes that market similar and comparable competitive products during the exploration, research and identification of brand users.

The brand perception performance is totally based on the users of a brand, but not the performances of the products or services provided by the enterprises. Its purpose is to explore how the users on the market look at a brand and its products, what are good, why do the users like the similar products, what are the functions and details of the products, do the users like the products and how much are the users willing to pay for the performances of certain products. In different areas or local markets, how do the users look at a brand, why do they trust or not trust the brand, what has influenced their purchasing decisions, what brands do they want to buy, what factors have led to the resistance thoughts when they are buying a brand, and what are their concerns.

By establishing a series of feedback models for brands, brand organizations could be able to back detect the preferences of the users based on the understanding of the users to the brand, which could make outstanding contributions to the development of brand performance. The feature of brand feedback model is back perception, just like the right hemisphere of a human's brain could control the left body of the human and vice-versa. The brand performance management based on the levels, methods and basis of the understanding of users could significantly improve the development of the ecological organizations of brands.

The brand perception performance has another important role, which is to identify the links that may confuse the brand performance; find out the misunderstanding, acknowledge errors and habit perception deviation of the users towards a brand; correct the expression, experience and flowing processes of the important brand performance such as brand value identification level, brand value transmission level, contact point setting, and the self-learning methods of the brand users, which have significant key values to the brand premium and band effects.

During the development of global brands in the past, much attention was paid to the designing of the highlights of the product performance and brand values from the inside to outside of the enterprise, but not the brand knowledge, understanding and experiences expressed from the brand users. More that 75% of the unsaleable brand products in the world are caused by such condition. 100% of the homogeneous competition of enterprise brands is caused by lack of research on the brand perception performances. In such case, the enterprises could not fully use the competitive advantages in terms of the differences of brand performance and could not establish the determining competitiveness and market protection mechanism with the powerful values in terms of brand performance.

3 Brand presentation performance

The brand presentation performance could determine the brand value performance retroactively. The most important problem of the brand value performance is to present the brand value directly in the best way and from the best angle. No matter if it's a large or a small brand, a brand shall be clear about: what features could it take to the market and deliver to users, and what key brand performance could be given to the public and users. When marketing the brands, the global enterprises can rarely use the excellent brand presentation performance method to present the brands in the good way, making the public and users not be able to see the differences between the brands and other completive products, and neglecting the huge differences in the brand realization processes in terms of raw materials, production, processes and services.

During the actual R&D, production, provision and service processes of the brands, enterprises will use different materials, production processes, technical invention, scientific application or service designs in different links to realize perfect brand pursuits, and such processes could not be directly detected by the brand users in the market as the key links with high costs and they could have influence on the final brand performance. The differences are especially huge between the handicraft brands and industrialized brands. However, if the enterprises could not show the important efforts made during the branding process, the users on the market will never know about the value differences, and there will be no differences between the competitors in terms of market prices. Therefore, it's very important to tell the story to the brand users about the unique brand performance links.

We have noticed that only few enterprises could notice the good expression of the brand presentation performance. They will convey the special attributes and values of the brands to the users who are making choices by displaying the brand details, periphery matters and atmosphere of the brands, such as displaying the materials, crafts, textures or features of each core link, or telling the stories about the R&D or manufacturing of the whole brand, or showcasing the designing ideologies of the designers, aesthetic expressions, the working attitudes of the technicians, and the lifestyles of the service providers.

For example, the applications of the brand scientific technologies and brand philosophical thoughts during the production, the perfect description of the brand products in the brand publicity pamphlets are all the important methods to express the brand values in a living, artistic and stylish way. When the enterprises are developing brands, especially when they want the brand users to feel the brand values through various direct promotion materials, they must use various Medias to make the brand value come in contact with the soul of the users, so as to trigger the recognition, perception level, perception attitude and perception reaction of the brand for the users to value. Only the users could feel that the brand deserves its price at the moment of the trigger, and if the brand value can be correctly presented. Therefore, it's very important to any brand to use the best way to express the brand and present the brand to all potential users. This is the brand recognition level to be achieved by the brand attraction features that could be called as the highest stage in the marketing development level of the brand.

4 Designing and manufacturing of brand value performance

The difference between the brand presentation performance and value performance is that the former could be used to solve the problem of presenting the brand value in the best way and from the best angle, and the latter could be used to solve the problem related to the identification, designing, creation and development level of the brand values.

The value performance of an enterprise could be reflected through value identification and value chain development, which could be transferred through the interconnection of multiple networks. Wall working processes flowing through the enterprise are the attraction, and the core is the brand value designing and brand value development level.

The brand value design shall be started by the brand organization from the brand designing. The value identification system and brand value chain system shall be established based on the brand knowledge development system, which requires the value chain closed loop with seamless connection for working flows and service flows, as well as the value network penetrating multiple networks and facing all users, or the system designing, value chain system and value identification system shall be coordinated to meet the advanced development requirements for the synchronous development.

The general system design of the brand value has determined the performance structures, designing performances and performance evaluations required for the future development of the whole brand organization. The forward-looking view shall be used to reserve the synergy interfaces and the centralized, information-based, interactive, dynamic, distribution-based and interconnected designing method shall be used for the general designing. The key point of the structural designing of the brand performance is to meet the designing requirements of the bottom structure of the management science, meet the dynamic development requirements of the brand in the future, prepare reports and respond to the needs and preferences of the users with sensitive perception and agility detection.

The brand value chain system is the comprehensive development process of updating an enterprise brand into a brand organization through practices. The value chain is the improvement, expansion or detailed extension made by a person to the value chain in terms of value consciousness, R&D activities, working processes, service process, competitive product researches and thinking in other methods, so as to output values to the society or the specific brand users in a better way. All employees, suppliers and services of a brand organization are the creators of the brand value chain, and every link may have new value.

Just like the anti-rub technologies in car paints on the production line of automobiles, or the actual demand highlights identified by the customer service personnel when solving the problems of the clients through telephone by accident, the new materials used by the suppliers to improve the service lives of the product parts, or the suggestions made by the management consultants for the data collection of enterprise brands. The purposes of such works are not only to provide new ideas or advices, ,but also to create new value thinking methods and expression methods for the brands in all directions and links, so as to enable everyone to identify, develop, improve and contribute values in a value creation body with orderly development and to respect everyone, and also to improve such values as product aesthetic feelings, value recommendation points, product performance improvement and market data detection and identifications for the full output of the brand value chain.

The development of tomorrow's brands is based on the orderly creations of such values, the value respect, value recognition, and value expansion. Everyone is a precious value creator in the value chain. The value creation, provision and development shall be consistent with the fair value income increase and value sharing so as to create a stable value ecological development environment in which everyone will create values and benefit from values.

5 Detection mode of brand value performance

The design, creation and provision processes of an enterprise brand on the brand value chain could enable the brand value chain to output brand values in a stable and orderly way. However, this doesn't mean that the brand users in the corresponding networks could effectively sense, experience and identify all values outputted by the enterprise brand.

We must note that the value output of brand towards the users is not a peer-to-peer network. The value development levels of the brand could not reach the level of the peer-to-peer network between the brands and users because: (1) only the brand value output party feels good, there is a brand value chain, but the brand value detection system for the end users has not been established; (2) the brand value chain could not match with the brand value detection system, the value output information is in chaos, the output is insufficient or the output is breaching the commitments, and the output power of brand values has low efficiency and quality; and (3) the brand value detection system based on multiple-network interconnections is not well developed with insufficient designing capacities and low development level.

We shall continue to use the brand feedback mode to establish the value detection system for brand users so as to ensure the stable output of brand values through various network Medias such as the Internet, mobile Internet, and Internet of things. All brand values are valuable only after being detected by users. People will always believe their own discoveries and the brand values from the recommendations of their interpersonal networks could only complete the effective value transfer after the self-investigation, self-learning and self-understanding by them.

Therefore, another general designing thinking link of the brand value performance is reflected through the value detection structural design and the overall development level of the value detection capacities at the users' tend. The multi-network interconnection environment today and tomorrow represents the more-to-one brand organization-to-user relationship, including all persons related to the

SECTION I GENERAL INTRODUCTION

R&D, to delivery and to service of enterprise brands + all brand suppliers and service providers + all operation networks and sales Medias and post-sales service links. The efforts made by all persons shall be concentrated on independent, individualized, sensitive and totally ego-driven network users. At the same time, the information received by everyone per hour may come from all over the world, and everyone could be able to transmit information to the world in the multi-network interconnection method at any second. People are the receivers of the diversified information and the releaser and amplifier of the mood information. The reactions of the users may occur and be transmitted at any instant, which will immediately influence the existence of the whole brand organization.

It's very important to deploy the brand value detection system here, which is the most important action and necessary measure for modern enterprises to develop Internet branding and implement the multi-network interconnection. Only with the value detection system based on various network Medias of the brand users and the extensive deployment of the dynamic contact points throughout the network at full frequency can the system work as the sensitive transmission network with value trigger, user self-response, user self-confirmation and user-self transmission. Only in this way can the brand organization establish developed modern brand value chain and brand value detection system, and establish the highly consistent peer-to-peer network value transmission relationship.

Any value could only be valuable after being detected by users. If the users could not detect such values, they will not become the integral part of the value system. In multi-network interconnection, the brand value detection system is mainly deployed through content marketing, full network marketing and full process perception. The preconditions are the design of the scientific system and the establishment of the brand value detection system. Otherwise, the value network of the brand ecological organization could not realize its value. This is a high value brand development field that can easily be neglected and underestimated by enterprises. Only less than 1% of the enterprises pay attention to this field and effectively develop and use such brand value resources. Standard methods, sensitivity and accuracy are the general performance development requirements for the full-area and full-network deployment of the brand value detection system.

The development level of brand value is the most important frontier position and determining competiveness for the enterprise brand development capacity, development structure and the natural ecological development order of the global enterprise brands in the future, which shall draw great attention from enterprises since the brands in the future must be established on this basis. The development of brand value performance in the multi-network interconnection environment of human beings is formed from the brand value detection at the end users, and this is the future development patterns of the age in which the consumption capacities could determine the productivity.

6 Brand essence performance

The brand essence performance covers the designing and performance compliance of the direct performances cared about by the global enterprises, such as product performance, service performance, industrial designing and package designing. The performance development could be realized by making the quality, productivity design and visual aesthetics reach the actual performance level. Scientists, engineers, designers and aesthetic consultants will make extremely important contributions in the process of brand essence performance. This is the process from product imagination to R&D completion to production, the supply process from delivery to service and the operation process from purchasing to the completion of orders.

Since the brand essence performance is obvious in enterprises, great attention will be paid to the volume of the input made by enterprises into essence performance depends on the working quality requirements, management level requirements and the input-output profit calculation requirements in terms of R&D level, material level, equipment capacities, quality assurance modes, trading safety, delivery convenience, order accuracy and service response. The state-of-art brand essence performance development method and brand skill requirements are included in the extraordinary brand pursuits in terms of brand concept, brand designing ideologies, advancement of R&D, material selection, product manufacturing performance level, process modernization, quality stability, design aesthetics and service levels.

We could see the brand development of the global enterprises, which exists in the forms of brand essence performance fulfillment and brand essence performance pursuits, which could eventually lead to the different branding levels of the enterprises. Despite the fact that the development of Internet or mobile Internet products has changed this development process to some extent, their development principles are basically the same, which are within the two original brand development thoughts, and only the development speeds and patterns required for the updating of products are changed.

In the past, when the brand of a product was developed as a physical matter, special emphasize was placed on the service lives of the products. From the conception to development and then to completion, R&D will require one or two years for a product. After the repeated development processes on the market such as test sales and re-test sales, at least two or three years will be required before a product become ready. However, what the enterprise needs is to comply with the consistence requirements for the R&D and production capacities, the manufacturers and service personnel and the suppliers and services, or meeting the users' basic physical performance requirements and acceptable minimum sense requirements to a product when it has decided to use the brand utilization performance fulfillment model.

Qualification is not excellence. Such enterprise brands will fall into the mid-income trap, which could only freely develop on the market to limit the content based on the homogeny and same price competition at the same level. In many industries such as automobile, mobile phones, home appliances, IT, food, and catering, the low and mid-end brands are gathered, and are competing with each other violently, and there will be specific monopolistic enterprises when the national or regional economic protection policies are applied. Such enterprises do not care about bringing good products to the market, but will focus on the market policy of developing the same products as others. Excellent brands could not be made only with qualification. No matter how sensitive their judgment to the market conditions is, how their technologies are advanced, how large their capitals are or how strong they are, they are class B enterprises. These enterprises may develop at a high speed, which could use the power of capitals, speed advantages and the first-in-first-out method to establish their development patterns based on the general demands of citizens. Only if there is no outstanding enterprise brand in the same field, their brands will be the leading force in the market.

7 Brand utility performance

The brand utility performance includes the brand functions, utilization effects, utilization frequency, utilization results, application scenes, effect improvement, effect solution expansion, and the utility application and evaluation in terms of service development, which is the designing thought from the imagination and R&D stages of a brand and the final expression of the actual applications and consequent values at the user's end. To some brands, it is the source of a sustainable income, or even their fundamental business model and the source of long-term profits.

The brand functions are the basic designing requirements of brands and the functional expression of the actual applications at the user's end. Any product, no matter if it' virtual or physical, will have its basic functional attributes, which may be the solution to a problem, or an experience, or the combination of various new functions. Any product will pay attention to the functional development, but the utility effects of the functions are underestimated by 75% of the enterprises.

We shall pay attention to three utility effects of brands, which are utilization effects, frequencies and results. The utilization effects are the functional performances, performance efficiencies and operation conveniences when the users are using a product to solve a problem, which is the first step to establish a good impression among the users. However, about 75% of brand products may fail in this step. Many products could not establish good impression after opening the packaging or purchasing, and about 25% of the users who have bought such products may announce that they would never use the products again at this moment. This condition is caused by many factors, such as the similar effect with

Section I General Introduction

the same type of products, difference from the users' reference, instable performance, utilization diversion and inconvenient operation. However, users will not directly communicate with the brand suppliers with such feelings, and their decision to abandon the products will be made in an instant.

Utilization frequencies are the utilization weights made by the users to a brand product. If the product is used frequently or occasionally, if it is considered as the major brand among the brands used by the users or the major brand used to solve certain problems, if it is the fungible brand or the brand that may be used occasionally. The researches on the utilization frequencies have determined the determining position of a brand on the global market or a professional market. Although some brands have been established at the early stage, or have sufficient funds or resources to occupy the leading market position, if a new brand has become the major brand for some people in their works and lives, the self-adaptation and self-expansion of the brand will occur, and it may develop into the new leading brand in the market to replace the original leading brands. Such researches on the determining positions of the major brands among users will not focus on the quantity of the existing users, but the selection weights for the utilization of a brand. Good brands will automatically expand through the self-transmission on the interpersonal network. The angel investments and risk investments on the modern capital markets are looking for such potentially quality brands and the expansion of the new brands will be at high speed.

The utilization results are the final judgments made by the brand users regarding a brand. This is the decision made about the end of the service life of a brand. The brand may be damaged or may fail after being used for a while due to instable quality, or the consumers may end the utilization of the brand, or the service life of the brand is expired naturally after a long-term utilization. At this moment, the users will make a comprehensive judgment to the brand product to decide to buy it again, recommend to friends, stop using it or select other brands.

Application scenes are the effects to be obtained by using the brand product in the environments, conditions or fields indicated or implied by the brand organization, and are the brand effects identified by the users in different scenes and fields during the utilization. The brand organizations shall frequently research, collect and analyze such application scenes. The expansion of the application scenes is the value brought by the brand to the users, or the utilization benefits. Such application values are expressed in different occasions (such as airports, hotels, vacations, high-income persons, wedding ceremonies and farms), and in different fields (such as industry, agriculture, catering industry and computer safety field).

The application scenes could match the improvement of utility and the expansion of utility solutions. Based on the researches on the application scenes of brands, new profit-making spaces have been developed in terms of high-end customization, individualized manufacturing, performance updating, product performance R&D in special conditions, and the professional services for solutions in different fields, which could expand the business of the brands, increase the premium capacities of the brand, promote the brand benefits, and increase the attachment of the users, or even improve the dependence of the users on the brand. It will become a business model with stable development due to the repeated or constant consumptions of the users.

The service development is not to provide post-sales services to users, but include the whole service performance in terms of the service methods, service solutions, service respond plans, consulting, delivery and completion that are understood by the users, as well as the initial service response (installation, adjustment and the list of original spare parts), and service updating (increase of maintenance time and service element updating), including the purchasing of original spare parts and consumables, the repeated purchasing plans of regular clients, intelligent service systems, self-recommendations to services by users and service outsourcing. Effective service development is the new profit source of the brand and an important source for the brand to develop the regular client plans to increase constant benefits. The uncomfortable feeling of the users towards services or the interruption of the services may lead to the disappearance of an important user attracted by the brand forever.

The brand utility performance may become an important business model for a brand. Especially, the version updating, performance updating and service updating of the Internet and software brands will lead to the cost reductions of the brand users. The business focus will be on the development of the high-level applicable businesses designed for the paying users after attracting the users free of charge. This means that new potential products or services may be generated based on the special needs of the users to increase the supplies of products and services. The brand utility functions could also be used for product R&D, by making the users participate in the R&D process and buy the products they have designed. Some electric products or computer equipment may use this method to reduce the initial sale prices of the products, such as printers and automobiles, and then improve the brand benefits by supplying consumables, original spare parts or post-sales services.

8 Brand performance in the global synergy network

At first, we must confirm that, with the development of the global brands until today, any brand may become the member of the ecological chain of the global brands and may establish its own brand ecological chain with itself as the center. This is the basic existence form of a brand in the world, which doesn't mean that any brand is the R&D, creation or service process completed by any individual or enterprise independently. It must be the brand ecological chain with the interconnections, interactions and mutual benefits among different persons, enterprises and organization. The differences include the structures of the individuals or organizations participating in the brand ecological chain, their scales, and quantities. You could understand this through the nature's food chain. Even a small brand has such ecological structure.

In this way, a new conclusion has been made that the global brands are existing with the nature of synergy network. Different roles, such as imaginers, implementers, organizers, researchers, service providers, suppliers, operators and users have participated in the process. However, we also have to note that, with the multi-network interconnection development of different network patterns such as the Internet, mobile Internet, Internet of things and vehicle network, the attribute of the brands based on the networking operation has become more obvious, and has become a tendency. When all brands, including the traditional, modern and future brands, have become networking brands, high knowledge capacity, intelligence, sensitivity, flexibility and reliability will be required for its operation, and to realize the seamless connection of the performance requirements related to brand management and brand product or services, so as to participate in the global synergy network consistently.

Today, such synergy effect has become very obvious. Countless OA software, EPR, CRM and other management systems are operating in the internal or public networks of different companies. This is what we can see. However, the flowing methods of the brands in the multi-network interconnection and the process purposes of the users can hardly be identified. People could only be able to identify the known and controllable parts, such as the registered member quantities, data, and connection rates. Most of the unknown fields such as the trigger theories, service flows and advanced Internet brand operation bases have not been deployed. However, people at least know about the existence of the brand synergy, and are using the synergy functions such as brand combination, crowd sourcing, whole-network marketing, information transformation, data interface and opening system to realize the brand synergy. This is the basic condition and requirement for the brand performance development in the future.

The further requirements are based on the brand perception logic in terms of the utilization behaviors of the users such as the feeling behaviors, value identification and utilities. The patterns of the users used to identify and use brands shall be researched to conduct the general brand performance design. The researches on the movements of the users in networks and the policy-making behaviors of the users in different nodes are the top priorities for the brand development in the future. The brand organization shall establish a new networking flexible organization based on the perception and utilization of the brand performance by users. Of course, in terms of the deployment of software and hardware, attentions shall be paid to the performance design, test, analysis and control of the IT systems based on the multi-network interconnection. The 7/24 stable operation is also the important brand performance technical support.

Section I General Introduction

Exercises

1. Fill in the blanks: Brand performance is composed of five basic performances, namely, _____, _____, _____, _____ and _____, as well as _____.

2. Multiple-choice Question: The brand utility performance includes _____ ( )

A. the brand functions, utilization effects, utilization frequency, utilization results

B. application scenes, effect improvement, effect solution expansion

C. the utility application and evaluation in terms of service development

D. A, B and C.

3. Discussion: Please describe the brand performance in the global synergy network.

Chapter 7

Leading Position

Brands are future-oriented. The purpose of brand creation or reengineering is to establish leading position. This is the most important strategic selection made for the brand development directions, and prospects, which could determine the final achievement of a brand. Brands without leading position will become weak brands, or disappear from the market shortly.

When an enterprise has decided to develop into an advantageous brand enterprise through branding, it shall establish the future brand target, the strategic direction of the brand development, the leading positions to be occupied in the market, the method for the consumers to identify the brand clearly, and the way to express the brand strength. If consumers have certain demands, the brand will become their primary choice.

1 Brand development direction

Brand development direction is the important policy determining the future direction of the brand. During the birth or re-engineering of any new brand, the brand direction shall be determined at the beginning or breakthroughs of the brand in the future, the development directions in the future and the way for people to understand the brand.

The brand development directions shall be determined through the resolutions of the board of directors. The CEO or chief brand officer shall have the authority to make suggestions for all decisions related to the brand. Since CEO and CBO could determine the ways of developing the brand, the market actions to be taken, and the brand management technologies to be implemented, when the board of directors has decided to develop the brand, it shall carefully consider about the suggestions made by CEO or CBO. If necessary, CEO or CBO shall submit an official brand strategic leading edge report to the board of director for consideration, which shall contain the strategic targets, major policies, development map, and market budgets.

Under ideal conditions, the board of directors or investors of a company will not participate in the daily operation of the company. CEO or CBO is the core person in brand development direction and will assume the position of chief planner, designer and executor. For any rational board of directors or investors, they only need to know how the enterprise will develop in the future and in what direction, and do not need to know about the details. The detailed decisions shall be subject to the scientific suggestions made by CEO or CBO. Once the resolutions have been passed by the board of directors and the investors, the CEO or CBO shall establish their undertakings according their own thoughts, and any great brand will be created in this process.

1.1 Material reform – deciding the brand development direction

The brand directions are always the big decisions made by the management of an enterprise, which could reflect the collective policy making levels of the board chairperson, directors, CEO and CBO, especially at stages such as new market exploration, market saturation, and industrial transition. Determining the brand direction is almost the only and necessary important decision to be made by the enterprise. The board of directors and investors will pay great attentions to the determination of the future direction of the brands, so as to explore a new way for the enterprise to become a successful brand sharing certain market in 10 years.

Unique, leading and profession brand directions with excellent market prospects may be passed with all votes in this stage and receive the full supports from all members of the board of directors. By contrast, the brand directions without clear features and market prospects will be denied. When the old industrial market is subject to large competition pressure, some brand strategic direction reports with original, wild and adventure entrepreneurship will be supported. The ambitious entrepreneurs and investors would like to create brand enterprises with unique advantages through bold actions, new business giants could be seen in industrial competition. If the industrial market conditions are stable, the board of directors may select strategic directions with safety, and small market and investment risks for development. This is a brand homogeneous competition age without obvious relative competition advantages.

Board of directs wants to determine the strategic directions in the future, investors want new business models and users want professional brands. "What to do and how to do" have become the core problems to be solved in terms of brand direction. Once the direction is determined, the enterprise may be subject to major restructuring, and the market will be subject to major changes. Therefore, the whole policy making process shall be careful and the factors in many aspects shall be considered.

In the board of directors with many conservative and cautious shareholders, the massive reform and bold creative development thoughts can never be supported. The market related personnel may put forward many doubts and opposing opinions since they could not see any direction. The innovators shall be patient and confident to convince the board of directors and investors, or may use small-scaled experiments to obtain proven results to promote the board of directors to make the major decision.

As for the opinions of market observers, since they do not understand the actual condition of the company, they may not be able to make objective, scientific and foresighted suggestions. The CEO or CBO who is responsible for the brand direction reform shall have sufficient confidence to lead the perfect reform of the company in terms of the strategies in all situations. Even one or more enterprises have failed in this aspect, the CEO or CBO who is trying his or her best to conduct the reform shall not lose confidence. Once the time is ripe or he or she has found the board of directors that supports, the great revolution will occur anytime. The CEO or CBO simply needs an opportunity and an appropriate enterprise to fulfill his or her major revolution, and prove his or her capacity. Opportunities are for those who are prepared.

1.2 Scientific analysis of brand development direction

We should note that the factors determining the brand directions are not pure imagination, thoughts or feelings, which are not scientific. The brand directions are determined through industrial data analysis, prospect verification, data obtained from the verified population and consumption data in terms of industrial frontier tendencies, industry operation rules, market competition conditions and the actual enterprise conditions.

CEO and CBO shall start from three aspects to conduct scientific analysis: (1) Industrial tendencies, or how the industry could develop in the future, how to implement reforms to change the industrial competition pattern, what are the client source markets, and if the vertical development shall be conducted against the client source market; (2) exclusive chances, what are the new opportunities in the future, what are the professional markets without powerful brands, if such markets have sufficient capacities that could realize profound development once the brand directions are determined. Too small market capacities or unclear identification of professional markets are the major causes for failure in brand direction policies; (3) what data could be used to support brand directions, population statistics, consumption tendency statistics, market demand changes and the market achievements made by the similar business models could be used as proofing data. The small scaled market exploration or market survey data could be used to support the judgment of market directions.

Next, we shall conduct the detailed research in three aspects to determine the main strategies of the market so as to complete the scientific designing and planning of the brand directions: (1) the shortages existing in the market, including the industrial difficulties, the problems interrupting the industrial development, the concerns of the dealers, and the complaints of clients. Many similar problems could be found in Internet or libraries. After comprehensive analysis, certain industrial laws could be obtained. Market designing of the brand directions shall be started from the largest problems concerned by people; (2) latest competition tendencies of the market and most popular business models in the market; the latest competition tendencies with the common attentions and actions from enterprises in the industry in the market and the most popular business models in the existing economy shall be researched to avoid the existing competitions, and use rational new business models to create new business competition patterns. Markets in the future always belong to the innovators; (3) research the selection habits of brand users, to identify how brand users in the market make selection for a brand, the brand features that they are concern about; in different markets, the selection priorities of the users are different, only the selection patterns and consumption patterns of the users are analyzed, can the powerful brand that can be easily accepted by users be designed.

1.3 Final decision of the brand development directions

After the CEO or CBO has conducted scientific and careful analysis on the brand market to be developed in the future, he or she could be able to propose their thoughts about the brand directions so as to design effective brand direction strategies. Such research data shall be incorporated into the report to submit to the board of directors to verify the accuracy of the brand direction policies.

The frontier report of brand strategies shall contain brand concepts (brand directions, brand cultures, and brand slogans), brand concept application structure, market competition pattern designing (the important strategies, policies and competition advantages to be implemented), general market planning, progress schedule, invest budget and task breakdown.

Among these strategies, brand concept application structure is the brand concept system required by the brand enterprise to enter into the market. The focus shall be placed on the key concepts to support the brands.

The market competition pattern designing includes a series of competition strategies to be used, such as raising strategy, single produce strategy, cultural strategy, client source strategy and news strategy. The focus shall be placed on the difficulties in the current market and identify policy suggestions and highlight the competition advantages of the brand.

The general market planning requires a longer term, such as 5 to 10 years, during which the market targets and priorities should be define in every stage and annually.

The investment budget is very important in the report. If a company has decided to conduct brand reengineering, release new brand or conduct brand market expansion, it will input corresponding starting funds and resources. According to the conditions of different enterprises, such funds may be tens of thousands dollars to tens of millions dollars. The CEO of CBO who is responsible for brand reengineering should discuss with the board of directors or investors to determine the total investment, and should reasonably use such funds to cover various expenditures, so as to maximize the economic benefits with the minimum investments.

In addition to the launching of investment budgets, CEO or CBO shall allocate certain sales income from the long term business operation as the brand management expenditure to ensure constant brand construction and input expenditure for the brand market. For a new brand or the brand released after reengineering, the early brand management expenditure shall not be lower than 5% of the total sales income. This suggestion will generally be passed through by the board of directors.

If the CEO or the CBO has conducted binding development for the brand and the market to unify the brand effect and the market sales effect for management, CEO or CBO may propose higher allocation ratio to the board of directors for the comprehensive operation of the brand and the market. With the increase of the total sales income, the highest ratio may be 30%-15% of the total sales, which means that the ratio at the initial stage shall be increased, and then shall be reduced with the increase of total sales volume. However, with the increase of the base of sales income, the CEO or the CBO will obtain higher personal income, with corresponding responsibilities, efforts and gains. No pains no gains. Therefore, an outstanding CEO or CBO could earn more than one million dollars every year after handling high level brand reengineering technologies.

2 Future of brands

To solve the problem related to the future of an enterprise, the problem of what the future of brands is shall be answered to the board of directors, investors, employees and users.

At the brand economic level, no matter at the global brand framework making level, or in the national, local or industrial cluster economies, or in the emerging brand enterprises with dreams, or in the mature brand enterprise planning brand reengineering, the problem of what the future of the brands is shall be answered to the related enterprises, investors or the whole brand organization.

People are eager to know about the future of the brands, enterprises and organizations they are working for. Any organization or enterprise shall clearly answer this question. In fact, everyone will ask this question, including the members of the brand economic organization, brand investors, backbone members, and employees, who would like to know the answer to this question. They will ask this question repeatedly, and are pondering over it consistently. Then they will use the explanations and understanding from their thinking to estimate the prospect and future of a brand so as to make further decision for investment, staying, growth together, being tired or leaving away.

We always believe that the brands are future-oriented, forward looking, predicable and leading thinking methods and predicating thoughts. The brands shall explain the future of its organization or enterprise. The brands shall make a splendid view in the future. The brands shall ignite the dreams of everyone. The future of brands shall influence all brand users. The brand leaders, brand officers, brand investors and enterprise managers shall understand how to realize the future of the brands step by step, and in order, systematic and scientific way, so as to implement the brand development in real terms.

For users, the assignment of a brand is the new values created by the brand – new environments, new life styles, new feeling experiences, some quality and tastes, some status or good senses. The brand assignment will be measured with monetary leverages, which will become an important link of brand premium. Bands could obtain brand premium capacities by creating new values. This is the bold exploration of the brand for future, which could bring the future to the users and explain what the future of brands is to the users.

In the 21st, 22nd and 23rd century or further future, there will be many brands that are describing the future, and many brands creating the future, so as to bring us new international brands. Many international brands will realize the everlasting development and maintain long-term vigor in the history of human beings.

3 Brand frontier exploration

The frontier exploration is to provide enterprise brand with frontier thoughts, discoveries, experiments, R&D and drive required to obtain leading position which are needed to complete the preparations of information, data and knowledge required for the leading development of a brand – the frontier preparation that can not be neglected.

The frontier exploration includes various thought combinations required to obtain the competitive advantages in the future. Based on the strategic directions that may be encountered in the competition in the future, and various assumptions made by the competitors, various brand performances shall be designed to meet the future development needs of the enterprise brand to maintain the conclusive competitiveness.

Any enterprise shall have a forward looking view to fully understand the challenges and opportunities that it may encounter in the future competition. Such challenges include but are not limited to: (1) brand market protection barriers established from the very beginning to prevent market competition and avoid possible competitions; (2) powerful brand actions implemented to the market to obtain the effective market advantage positions; (3) professional market researches and market conquering measures taken to penetrate the market; (4) joint brand actions used to keep the competitive positions of the brands; (5) the brand market attacks launched suddenly to fight against any potential competitors. The brands shall be able to rapidly respond to such challenges.

Competition is everywhere and business war is more competitive than military war. When an enterprise is determined to conquer the market with its brand, it shall have a frontier position from the very beginning to surpass the common competition patterns and the latest tendencies so as to move forward boldly to identify the latest tendency needs of the world and create wholly new tendencies with the global frontier exploration as its action target.

3.1 Importance of frontier exploration

In the 21st, 22nd and 23rd century or further future, new brands will emerge to challenge the frontier fields and create the new tendencies in the world. Such brand will finally stay in the history of human beings for a long time or even forever.

The frontier exploration is the first action that is used to establish the leading edge of an enterprise. In complicated conditions, tendencies and changes in the future, the brand shall fully understand that it could only become popular through creating tendencies. Only in this way, can the long-term market effects be obtained.

Not everyone could capture the frontier tendencies, and not everyone could create leading position However, for an outstanding CEO or CBO, the creation of leading position is the purpose of brand reengineering and the largest commitment to the board of directors, investors and brand users, as well as the important responsibilities and missions to be taken.

The frontier exploration is the actual preparation made for frontier designing. Through frontier exploration, CEO or CBO could think about the future of the brand in-depth, identify all potential frontier tendencies, conduct a series of experiments over the frontier assumptions, obtain data from analysis of experiments, start the R&D of the brand products, and if applicable, drive more frontier supporting enterprises and partners to implement the frontier design.

Frontier exploration requires the capacity to imagine, follow by the visualization of all imaginations, and finally to fulfill all these imaginations with the board of directors, investors, backbone employees, supporting enterprises and partners. Such future knowledge and images only exist in the minds of CEO or CBO. The transfer of imaginations into actual products, services and matters could be used to test the thinking capacity of the CEO or the CBO.

3.2 Actions of brand frontier exploration

The frontier exploration could be completed through personal thinking, group discussion, scientific experiments, comparison analysis and summary analysis, which requires at least three months.

Such exploration requires the thinking capacity to be fully release. The forward sights, knowledge and analysis capacities of CEO and CBO will have a determining role to play. The frontier exploration includes the following key points:

SECTION I GENERAL INTRODUCTION

Frontier thinking: Creators shall conduct various researches on the industrial data and the market entrance directions to determine the patterns of the brand products, the method to enter into the market, service methods, price elements and the market protection capacities from the competitors, so as to determine the basic outlines of the competition methods of the brand products, such as what they are, what their colors are, which market will be served, what are the value features of the brand, what leads the users to purchase this brand and what are the competitive advantages compared with the competitors.

Frontier discoveries: After completing the frontier thoughts, the creators shall conduct the survey on the products and competing enterprises on the market in certain scale, including market observation, purchasing of samples for researches, package designing and analysis, market survey on the color demands of users, planning, investigation and verification of the identities of important products, the detailed issues concerned by users, and the value discovery of the brand history. The scope of such discovery includes the favorite brands and why the other brands are good. The frontier discoveries also include the thinking and verification of new business models.

Frontier experiments: According to the needs, small scaled detection experiments shall be conducted to confirm, verify or modify the discoveries according to the data from experiments, which may include color sensation experiments, taste implementation, touching experiments, contact point experiments, logistic clash prevention experiments, and pressure withholding experiments. Some experiments shall be conducted during R&D, and the product R&D results shall be corrected according to the results of these experiments.

Frontier R&D: Through the frontier thinking, discovery and experiments, an enterprise will enter into the frontier R&D stage. At this stage, the key point is to transfer simulation images of the products after scientific analysis, thinking and discovery into actual products. The designing drafts shall be completed by describing the designs to the designers, and the final brand products shall be completed through various technicians. However, this process is not easy. Brand products are excellent works that have been developed through much hard work and fine tuning. Generally, several rounds of designs, sample making and experiments done by several designing companies, supporting enterprises and the product R&D laboratory of the enterprise are required. This process may require a lot of funds. Since the brand officer is always a perfectionist, who shall test the products for the market users, all links of the process shall be perfect and excellent. Every link shall be subject to micro adjustment, repeated modification, test making and experiments until the perfect products are produced. During this process, the frontier thinking, discovery and experiment shall be repeated to constantly improve the brand.

Frontier driving: During the R&D process, CEO or CBO shall have powerful driving capacity to motivate the cooperative enterprise in upstream and downstream, the supporting enterprises and various market resources as well as the backbone members and all employees of the enterprise to participate in the implementation of the brand reengineering dream. CEO or CBO shall constantly describe the dreams to the people inside and outside the enterprise, raise the business enthusiasm of all members, and encourage everyone inside and outside the enterprise to make great efforts for the brand reengineering. The brand creation or reengineering process is a forced transmission process targeting at the backbone personnel inside and outside the enterprise, aiming at forming the first group of backbone personnel to spread the brands to more fields and influence more people. The new brand backbone personnel may be strangers, but they may become people who will care about, serve or help the brand based on their confidence on the brand. The formation of the brand organization is a transmission process of continuous expansion, backbone development and brand value transmission, which will become powerful brand belief and win the market shares.

4 Brand frontier designing

To successfully implement brand creation or reengineering, any enterprises shall note that brands could not determine the existing market conditions. Brands are future products, and are the overall marketing designs made by the enterprise for the development of next 5, 10 or even 100 years. The brands have described a series of market views, and future competition patterns that are attractive. Brands are the life stage that may motivate many people to fight for their dreams. Therefore, brands could attract increasing number of brand users to focus on and expand the user base and finally reach the brand market position defined on the brand map.

To realize the leading position, enterprises shall put in many efforts, such as constantly improving the accuracy of indications based on frontier exploration, using predication thoughts, and implement frontier designs, so as to highlight the product performances and service values. In essence, the frontier design is the full scale market design to be conducted for the future development of the enterprise. The frontier designing capacity has determined the brand competitiveness obtained by the enterprise.

The main body of frontier designing is the marketization designs used by enterprises to obtain leading position Such designs include market scale predication, market launching method, market entry strategy, market channel designing, market action designing and market coverage methods, as well as a series of important full scale preparations for competitiveness.

4.1 Pre-designing of brand frontier

The pre-designing of frontier is the accurate predication designing completed based on frontier exploration. The reporting form shall be used to report the complete brand expression methods. The pre-designing of frontier includes product designing, cultural designing, service designing and market designing, which shall be expressed with detailed data. Such designs are the basic preparations for brands to enter into the market. After completing and implementing such initialization designs, brand could enter into the market comprehensively, be verified and improved in the market and become mature.

The product designing is to complete and implement the ideal design drawing of the brand products through the exploration and researches on many brands' perceptions and expression forms such as colors, textures, tastes, qualities, volumes and surfaces. To improve the predication preparation, the test products at each stage shall be subject to small scaled market tests to verify the accuracy of the predication. Since the final products may not be the best forms that could meet market demands, the product designing could be conducted in stages to enter into the market in the form of updating. Potential best designs could be explored through the updating of products such as the generation 1, generation 2 and generation 3 products, so as to achieve the best status for product performance and appearance design.

The purpose of cultural designing is to provide the products with certain cultural connotations, meanings, symbol marks and brand transmission networks. Such cultural attributes may come from the exploration of history of the brand, or from creation of the brand culture, which may be the comprehensive expression of a series of special enterprise civilizations, or the epitome of a new lifestyle. After the cultural designing, the brand will get rid of its basic form and have certain cultural attributes. In such case, the brand could be identified more easily, have higher value and be provided with cultural expression basis for the targeted brand user groups.

Service designing is a series of predictions made for service forms, including the establishment of the intelligent service systems, the designing of the electronic services, initial trust designing, delivery designing, logistic designing, client services, service flows and value-added services. With rational service deployment, the service designing will further improve the brand premium.

Market designing includes a series of deployment of the market capacities required by the market strategies, such as the methods used by the brands to enter into the market, the targeted audiences of the brands, the new channels to be obtained for the brands, the market actions used for the brands, the final purposes of the brands in the market, and the sales volumes to be realized by the brands. Market designing is a series of dynamic actions on the market. Especially, for new brands and brands released after brand reengineering, at the beginning, all efforts shall be concentrated and all resources shall be used to occupy the market shares to achieve the preset target.

4.2 Brand sensor network

Any brand could not be accepted by sufficient brand users at the beginning. When a brand has entered into the market, it shall be subject to a run-in period, during which, the brand sensor network deployed by the brand organization will have an active role to play. The brand sensor network is the detection system to be deployed for any new brand when entering into the market. The period of deploying the brand sensor network shall be within 6 months to 12 months. With the completion of the role of brand sensor network, it will be updated to a higher level – brand interpersonal network.

Deployment of brand sensor network: the brand sensor network is frontier detection and sensing system deployment with the official releasing of the brand and the entry of the brand into the market, which is composed of market analysts and management analysts. The brand organization shall train certain ratio of the members in the dealer network to be market analysts and management analysts. At each dealer service network point, at least one part-time market analyst and one part-time management analyst shall be assigned. Some of their works are to conduct market analysis and management analysis. If possible, they could be updated to MA learning team.

The task of market analysts is to identify the brand demand improvement points in the local market; collect suggestions made by local market and consumers in terms of colors, packages, styles, popular cultures, fashions, prices and meanings; research the localized client sources and market development strategies, market action plans and consumer service packages; and analyze and research the opinions to submit them to the brand committee in reports. The task of the management analysts is to identify various problems and suggestions related to terminal management links such as the problems related to terminal management, personnel management, personnel trainings, logistics, delivery, goods arrangement, and dealer management ,and submit them to the brand committee in reports.

The sensor network composed of market analysts and management analysts assigned to each dealer network point, it is actually a transmission, detection and sensing system for the massive detection of the market, and the early stage of the dynamic brand management knowledge system, which shall be subject to the summarization and analysis to determine the more accurate market predication and product service improvement reports. To strengthen the functions of the sensor network, in the 3rd and 6th months after the brand has entered into the market, the branding committee shall increase the members of the brand dealer committee, the brand-user relationship committee, and the brand quality work committee, which are the sub-committees, by encouraging the dealers, brand users and quality recommendation personnel to participate in such committees. Through the MA learning group summarization and analysis activities among members of the committees, market exploration and collection of management and analysis data shall be further implemented. With the deployment of the sensor network and analysis activities of the committees, the enterprise brand will obtain the improvement reports related to the products, services and management processes from the very beginning, so as to accelerate the marketization maturing of the brand.

5 Brand strength

To achieve the leading position of a brand, brand organization shall pay great attention to the designing of the leading position from the very beginning, so as to convey the strength of the brand from beginning. The process from entering into the market to the market movement includes, in essence, all efforts made to obtain the leading position Only when the brand could occupy a leading position firmly in specific markets, could the brand creation or reengineering be completed successfully.

The leading edge designing based on the brand strength includes brand endorsements, frontier expressions, primary brands, brand image perceptions, market performance, and brand position, which is a mental set process required for the brand to obtain leading position – or how the potential brand dealers and all potential brand users see the brand, and how they perceive this brand. This is a psychological effect in the heart of everyone, and is the basic impression, understanding and profile made by everyone to a brand.

5.1 Brand endorsement

For a new brand, during its initial entry into the market, the market does not know it hence the brand does not specific purchasing rate. At this stage, the brand endorsement shall be the top priority. The purpose of brand endorsement is to use a series of verified brand strength combinations to complete the initial acknowledge of the brand entering into the market. Since more than 90% of the population in the world have purchasing psychological barrier which is caused by the safety concerns in new brands, and consumers may have recognition difference to the same brand before brand reengineering, any new brands or reengineered brands shall be subject to good brand endorsement before entering into the market.

Brand endorsement is through the use of a series of strategic cooperation, brand combination and brand actions to derive an initial verification on the strengths of the brands.

The brands could conduct strategic cooperation with many important organizations, such as the authorized economic organizations, important news media, and well known important technological research organizations, this will help to improve the initial trust and the basic recognition that people have on the brands, and with assistance from the professional forces to eliminate the recognition obstacles for brands so as to help it to enter into the market as soon as possible.

Brand combination is to join enterprise brands or individual brands that have certain influences in the market, this will lead people to trust the brands when they come in contact with the brands for the first time through other established brands. With certain expressed of implied strengthened brand relations, the initial market development of a brand may be completed by taking advantage of the market and brand influences an existing brands have.

Brand actions use certain influential market actions to highlight the great strengths of the brands when they enter into the market, such as the global brand announcement, important brand actions, important brand events, etc.

5.2 Brand frontier expressions

The brand frontier expression is the expression method shown to the market through brand identification system, brand product designing concepts, brand technical strength and brand creativity, so as to lead people to think that the brand products are new products representing frontier technologies, fashions and concepts. The designs with scientific and fashion elements are deemed as the best brand expression capacities.

Expression of brand identification system: brand stories, brand meanings and brand symbols as well as the expression method of LOGO could provide people with certain feelings that are expressed in an instant. The expression methods such as painting albums and brand image articles could further expand the sensations brought by brand to people. The international, scientific, fashion, sunny and young expressions could lead to the enthusiasm people have for the brands. Otherwise, people will have a lagged, old and aged brand sensation.

Expression of brand product design concepts: Design concepts are the perfect explanation to the designing thoughts of the brand products. Through the detailed expressions of product in terms of appearance design, texture experience, tastes and styles, etc. the CBO or designer could express the advanced, fashion and ideal brand designing thoughts, to bring the brand audiences to a higher brand enjoyment level.

The purpose of the expression of brand technical strengths is to provide users with the opportunities to select brands rationally with the help of technical frontier expression, technical leading degrees and technical performances that showcase the excellent skills of the brand in terms of technical levels, historical inheritance, technical environment and details, or by expressing the scientific effect discovered through the frontier scientific and technical R&D.

The purpose of brand creativity expression is mainly to express the excellent creativity of a brand, which is, generally, the expressions of the overthrown creativity such as independent R&D, scientific researches, frontier creation and fashion appearances. New tendencies, new models and new images could help a brand to obtain leading position in certain field. Especially, in the industrial fields with material frontier tendencies, the brands with excellent brand frontier creativity could become outstanding more easily and with a leading position in drawing the attentions from media and markets.

5.3 Primary brands

Primary brands are the important strategic selections made by enterprise brands to obtain leading position, or a series of market preparations and actions assuming that the brands could become the primary brands in some fields.

The brand with the largest market share may not become the primary brand. New brand competitors could emerge constantly, and the brand market disrupter may come at any time. Therefore, being the primary brand is equivalent to being involved in a violent fight. When entering into the market, new brands or reengineered brands may overthrown the rules of the old market, and announce themselves as the new primary brands, they will use powerful market actions to quickly obtain the leading position as the primary brands.

When entering into the market, the new powerful competitors will analyze and research the old brand market combinations so as to make new rules that are different from the old ones. The changes may be made in terms of appearances, tastes, formulas, performances, channels, and the identification methods used by consumers to the brands, so as to make revolutionary designs for the market. The applications of new competition strategies, business models and management technologies could significantly improve the revolution speed of any market.

The new giant may be born at anytime; the new revolutionary creators may be seen on the market at any time. This is the major behavior of global industry competition. Especially, during the material industrial reforms, all enterprises will conduct reforms to some extent, which are differed in terms of degrees and speeds. The possibility for an enterprise to become a primary brand with thorough reform through brand reengineering has been improved significantly. Just like the view of risk investments, the unclear business models with conflicts may obtain great return on investments.

The primary brand is also an important epitome for a brand organization to establish its leading position. From the first day of brand creation or reengineering, the strategic target of primary brand has been determined. Next, a series of massive reforms shall be conducted to define the primary brands in the minds of consumers, and the physiological effect shall be rooted among consumers from the very beginning, so as to use market actions to complete the great changes from imagination to implementation. When the press conferences are held to release such brands, the revolutions with huge influence on the market have started. Sufficient preparation and strategic arrangement are always conducted before the sun rises.

5.4 Brand image designing

Brand image is the active preparation made for leading position of the brand before an enterprise releases the brand, and the general layout of the brand images has been completed. The brand images of today are no longer just simple product designing, it is a comprehensive image provided to the market or consumers through communication media, brand image expression and brand concept highlights.

Firstly, the channels for people to learn about a brand mainly include the Internet and the mobile internet. New brands must use the Internet branding method to show their basic impressions to people. The media attentions, the novelty of the brands and the ways for people to learn about the new brands are very important. To release a new brand, the preparation before entering into the market must be completed through media deployment. The searches, websites and mobile terminals of the Internet and mobile internet shall be used to deploy the comprehensive images of the brands among potential personnel. Of course, the further design of Internet brands shall have in-depth brand knowledge and application capacities.

Secondly, the designing of brand image perception must be conducted from external to internal. At first, people will learn about and know about the brands by accident and generate the initial brand images through Internet, mobile internet and interpersonal network. Next, they will understand the brands through further contact points or self-learning. Such contact processes may be conducted without any physical product, but the purchasing decision may have been decided. The contact with the physical products begins from the outer packages. After using the products for a while, the perception to the brand images could be completed totally. This is a test purchasing process completed by the users of a new brand. Based on such processes, the Internet brand contact points, brand transmission flows, brand knowledge self-adapt learning system and the initial trust shall be designed for the brand, so as to accelerate the purchasing selection and comprehensive trust of the users. This is an important link for an enterprise brand to be upgraded to a brand organization.

Thirdly, the designing of brand highlights includes the important brand concepts to be deployed to news media, potential dealers, potential brand users and Internet population before the brand has entered into the market. Based on such brand highlights, the great attentions will be drawn from news reporters and the target brand user groups. The modern brands are those transmitted through basic interpersonal networks. Digital networks or Internet could not exist without the transmission from people to people. New brands shall accelerate the speed to enter into the sights of the people so as to obtain the initial brand effects from the attention economy, further develop the interpersonal network and obtain the brand foundation required for the further development of brands.

5.5 Brand market performance

New brands or reengineered brands shall express powerful market attacks in the market, or the market movements with high speed and frequency. The brands shall also prepare for a whole scale fight. From the view of media and public, the markets with brands are active. Since the brand images could generate overlapping effects or sudden effects, enterprises shall use such effects to fully showcase their market action strengths.

Market action performance: New brands shall express the active conditions in high speed and high frequency on the market. The action conditions are represented by the market actions by stages and the market plans with high influences, or by the tide rule. Such actions and plans shall maintain certain market frequency. Market actions may have some action codes, which are the methods for the brand organization to enter into the market every three or six months, such as dealer recruitment actions, client relationship actions and market target attack actions. The movements and ranges of such actions shall be large and the influences shall be high. In addition, the media reporting shall keep pace with such actions. The plans are mainly important mid or long-term plans, featuring large scales, high levels and active meanings to social development, so as to transmit positive energy on the society.

The tide rule requires that a new brand shall at least implement the important highlight actions or plans that may draw market attentions every three months minimally, which shall take turns to enter into the market and generate powerful and constant attention effect. Speeds, strengths, power, influences and social advancement are used to determine whether the market action performances could obtain the best brand effect. In the age of rapid competition, the brand with slow market development may be replaced by powerful emerging brands. The market action plans with low level and small coverage without

Section I General Introduction

structural brand strategic designing, can hardly draw attentions, which is negative at the early stage of branding, and may lead to the losing of good chances.

Market performance effect: Expression effects of the market are mainly overlap or sudden effects. Overlap effect means that a new person (potential investors, dealers or users) sees a brand from different media or channels within a short period of time (one week to three months). When one brand is found from more than thee links, the attentions of the person to the brand have been activated. Such person will remember and further learn about the brand, and become official attention payer with consciousness. Sudden effect means that a new attention payer emerge after coming in contact with a brand through reliable recommendation channels or the conscious attentions has suddenly found the powerful strength of the brand, so as to pay attention to the brand automatically.

Any one may become a brand attention payer at any time. The main attention method of an attention payer is to search for brand information and understand the brand through interpersonal network. The attentions are a self learning process for brands. Some attention payers may be transferred into brand users, while the other will become the brand recommenders. The success of a future brand depends on the base of the attention payers. The more the attention payers are, the larger the quantities of the transmission in the interpersonal network will be. In such case, the brand strength will be confirmed repeatedly, and the brand effect will improve.

Exercises

1. Fill in the blanks: Brands are future-oriented. The purpose of brand _____ is to establish leading position This is the most important strategic selection made for the brand _____, _____, and _____, which could determine the final achievement of a brand.

2. Multiple-choice Question: The leading edge designing include: (　)

A. brand endorsement, frontier expression, primary brands, brand image perception, and market performance

B. brand endorsement, frontier expression, primary brands, brand image perception, market performance, and brand position

C. primary brands, brand image perception, market performance, and brand position

D. brand endorsement, frontier expression, primary brands

3. Essay Question: How to become a primary brand?

Chapter 8

Deciding Competitiveness

An enterprise must develop its deciding competitiveness through constant brand reengineering. The essence is to maintain the key conclusive competitive advantages in the global market to realize the key competitiveness for the next brand reengineering period. During brand reengineering, the enterprise shall make active preparations in many aspects and focus on establishing the deciding competitiveness. Although an enterprise may make many choices in terms of brand strategies, and see many brand capacity elements and competitiveness application links, the enterprise shall establish the deciding competitiveness as soon as possible to identify the focuses, eliminate the unnecessary links and actions, concentrate on resources and strengths and realize powerful competitiveness.

The enterprises shall use the brand scientific principles and brand reengineering technologies flexibly to concentrate on the development of the deciding competitiveness. Some enterprises will use diversified market strategies. However, the diversification is not the ideal condition at the early stage of brand creation or reengineering, which will lead to serious chaos at the users' end and reduce the deciding competitiveness. To maintain the clear deciding competitiveness, the enterprise shall highly concentrate on the market, actively find out the market competition key points for brands, products and services, so as to establish the deciding competitiveness of the enterprise as soon as possible.

To obtain deciding competitiveness, any brand shall be clear about what the conclusive factors are, including seven typical competition strengths, namely victory determination, knowledge system, management design, concept route, brand performance advantage, full-scale operation and real-time response. All of these strengths have together formed the brand deciding competitiveness. When the brand has made every effort to use such strengths, they will be rapidly transferred into the competitive strengths of brand organization. Therefore, in this chapter, enterprise brands could be updated to the brand organizations in the ideal state.

1 Victory determination

Victory determination means the consistent predication and determination of the board of directors, investors, CEO and CBO towards brand reengineering. The management of the enterprise shall be clear about why the brand reengineering shall be conducted. They shall have courage to thoroughly implement the reform in order to complete the brand creation or reengineering.

As this is the action that shall be conducted by the enterprise at certain interval, brand reengineering shall focus on the future of the brand frontier to implement the brand reengineering thoroughly with the purpose of completing the material changes of brands and markets.

The long-term predication and firm determination could determine the success of the brand reengineering as well as the final achievement of the reengineering. A brand has its infection from up to down and from inside to outside. Powerful predication and determination could determine the strength of such infection. Therefore, the management of an enterprise would use their thoughts to influence all employees. The result of the expansion of the brand infection is to update the brand enterprise to brand organization so as to generate powerful ultimate influence in the market.

SECTION I GENERAL INTRODUCTION

The brand reengineering will finally express the rapid action power in terms of thoughts, designs, and policy making, as well as the powerful brand forward-moving signals released to the market through the movement of the brand gravity center. As more and more brand members are attracted to participate in, the brand organization will expand without limits, and the enterprise brand will be updated to brand organization, providing guarantee for the material market achievements. Such brands feel safer and more trustable, and will realize long-term development.

2 Brand knowledge system

The core of the brand development is the establishment of the independent and exclusive knowledge system. In reality, few enterprises may concentrate their brand competition efforts on knowledge competition. In fact, the competition of brand knowledge system is the key competitiveness for brand development.

Let's see the process of a brand from birth to growth with the deciding competitiveness: from the brand fantasies, during the process of the brand foundation to form imaginations and complete thoughts, the ecological system has been established for the existence and development of the brand. The founder has to consider how to develop the brand, break the concentrated market links and built market defenses. This brand blueprint contains the initial structure of the brand knowledge system. The following brand practices are the process of the actual development of the brand knowledge system.

During the brand creation, the contributions of all brand participants will be concentrated. The knowledge from different fields will be gathered into the central system of the brand to realize the knowledge establishment in terms of brand R&D, raw material purchasing, production, quality, and services. All brand capacities required for development, the results of brand performance research and experiments, brand flow management methods, brand processing experiences, brand experience data, brand appearance designing thoughts and the actual brand user researches will be gathered as the precious enterprise brand knowledge files and the brand documentation operation orders to complete the initial structure of the brand knowledge system.

During the following brand finalization, and brand scaled development, the stable and mature operation presents itself as a brand requirement. This is the important process for continuous updating, summarization, analysis and finalization of the brand knowledge system. Various dynamic brand issues shall be solved onsite to form professional and systematic knowledge. The brand knowledge system could complete the order arrangement and knowledge division during this process to form the brand knowledge tree.

All efforts made during brand development are generated, developed and finalized in the form of knowledge, which will be subject to important organic application, knowledge reengineering, knowledge expansion or knowledge updating. Such knowledge includes various detailed experiment reports and conclusions during the R&D process, the tests conducted during the purchasing of brand raw materials, the process designing and tests during the brand reengineering, the research and discovery for brand qualities, and the indication about the client-related issues during the brand service process. Any brands, no matter big or small, will realize long-term development by handling the knowledge system in developing capacities. The degrees, depths and width of the knowledge; the advancement of the knowledge tendency exploration; the professional degree of knowledge research; the knowledge development level; and the knowledge application effect could determine the overall knowledge advancement degree of the brand knowledge system in the global market competition.

The competition between two brands is in fact the competition in terms of the knowledge handling degree and knowledge development level of the brands. Those who have knowledge will have the future. The brand development of global enterprises is not a temporary or accidental behavior, but an important knowledge development process involving constant knowledge creation, knowledge inheritance, knowledge development and knowledge application. A brand organization shall organize internal or external trainings, and recruit consultants, experts and analysts to assist the enterprise to develop a better, more advanced, more professional and more powerful dynamic brand knowledge system.

Among the emerging enterprises throughout the world, knowledge has become the deciding competitiveness, especially in emerging fields, since the potential or unknown research fields and application methods will be subject to challenges or changes, and the speed of knowledge development shall be fully accelerated. Only 5% of the emerging enterprises will occupy the competition leading edges with their knowledge of R&D capacities, and 1% of the enterprises will become the leaders in the global market through the high level development of the brand knowledge system. Brand knowledge system can not only provide effective market protection from competition, but it can be used with the help of the competitiveness to occupy market positions.

In traditional enterprises, knowledge is also the deciding competitiveness. Only few enterprises could own the knowledge in a specific field. Even small enterprises could become long-lasting brands given their exclusive knowledge. The competition essence originates from the knowledge discovery, knowledge development and knowledge inheritance of the enterprise. For example, The Jack Daniel has been using charcoal made from sugar maples to screen the whisky to maintain the quality, and this is the exclusive knowledge of the company. There are more than 10000 long-lasting enterprises in Japan, whose development bases are the continuous applications of their own brand knowledge system.

3 Brand management designing

The management designing has determined the final economic scale that can be realized by a brand organization. Many brands have poor performances on the market because the factor determining the brand scale is the management designing capacity, or if the management could support the scale that can be achieved by the brand, but not because the brand doesn't have a good market prospect or sufficient investments or first class talent team.

Management designing is an important designing conducted from the very beginning. To realize scaled economic effect, any brand shall design the market designing preparation at the 100-million-dollar level for the brand designing in terms of management technologies. If the enterprise would like to occupy a larger scale market, the management designing preparation shall be made at the billion or 10-billion-dollar level.

According to our market observation, many enterprises have not paid attention to the comprehensive designing of the management technologies. A new enterprise may be established by several founders, or a brand project may be started with 1 million dollars. However, in most cases, these brands have not been successful in the market and even disappeared short after. The speed from business starting to losing control and failing is very high. Many enterprises on the market survive without good management designing, are limited to the operation scales as small enterprises, and aren't able to develop into high-growth brands.

3.1 Brand management designing capacities

The management designing capacity could be reflected in two aspects, the one is the market volume that can be supported by the management, and the other is the capacities of the management designing talents.

To ensure that new brand or reengineered brand obtains the market volume of hundreds of millions or tens of billions in a few years, the supporting capacity of the management system will have a key role to play. Organization structure designing, HR outline, salary structure designing, management flow designing, production designing and batch service designing are all important management designing links. Since the future management is complicated, the market channels and scales are extensive, and the links for which market actions shall be taken include many aspects such as multi-network interconnection, thus the management designing is the pre-designing of the uncertain changing factors under complicated conditions. The transfer from the uncontrollable condition of the management predication to the controllable condition is the important designing process to be broken through by the management designing.

The second key issue for management designing is the shortage of the management designing talents. No business school in the world could train management designing talents. Therefore, at present, the management designing talents are mainly experienced CEOs or those from management consulting firms. These personnel and services are expensive, which could not be afforded by ordinary enterprises, leading to the small proportion of large enterprises and the inability of most enterprise to develop into large enterprises. This is determined by the shortage of the resources for management designing capacities. We could see that most organizations and personnel are providing management consulting and training services to small enterprises and only few organizations or teachers could provide management technical services to large enterprises.

Finally, the brand scale highly depends on the advanced management technologies and state-of-art management designs. If such determining competitive factors are missed, and no advanced and systematic management technical support could be used, the brand fantasies can hardly come true, leading to the fact that only few enterprises could grow in the market competition and there are only few emerging wealthy stars in most of the countries. The management foundation could determine the brand scale and the final achievement of the brand.

3.2 Greet to the complicated management designing in the future

The management in the future will become more complicated, because the designing of the management technical systems will massively replace manual policy making and works, the scientific intelligent environment will propose higher requirements for enterprise management, and the opportunities for consumers to choose brands will increase significantly. These changes will require the leaders of new brands, and brand managers to pay attention to the application of the management technologies.

If the management is determined as management technology, the changes of the management technological system will lead to the massive discoveries of the scientific management principles, transferring the management from man-made policy-making to scientific policy-making. The technical requirements of management will increase and become stricter. The management technical system will fully replace the old management system. In terms of scientific technology updating, the management technologies could be easily updated to the advanced computer network technical systems, or intelligent systems. The advanced management technologies will be everywhere. Of course, the designing of complicated management technologies is not as easy as informization or software development. The most important thing for the management technological system is to use the leading edge designing capacity of the management technologies to conduct technical deployment. The principles, designing and analysis of the management science are the deciding competitiveness determining the designing of the management technological system.

The scientific intelligent environment will have higher requirements to enterprise management. HMI or various networking conditions have made the scientific intelligence become the material content of the future management environment. Many brands will establish the ecological brand system with self-adaptive development. The demands of brand users will change. We can assert that science, fashion and environment will become the three important competition factors underlying the future brand development. Such factors will require the brand leaders and enterprise managers to have higher level of knowledge. If such knowledge demands could not be met, many enterprises and enterprise managers will be eliminated from the market competition link due to the aging knowledge.

The opportunities for consumers to make choices will increase significantly. Since the global enterprises are constantly creating new brands, the numbers of international brands and professional brands will grow greatly. More and more fields will have professional brands. The large brands previously dominating the market will become pan brands, or non-professional brands. Such future brand competition tendency is occurring at a higher speed. It's estimated, that till 2041, the pan brands will be massively eliminated from the market, and be replaced by the massive and professional brands that are active in all markets throughout the world.

We emphasize that the management is future-oriented, and so are the brands. The future brands supported by the future management will be able to greatly strengthen the brand competition advantages with powerful market forward moving capacities and market occupation capacities. The deciding competitiveness in the future in fact depends on the efforts we made today. Only those brand leaders and managers focusing on the future could become the future presidents of the brand achievements.

4 Brand performance advantages

The brand performance advantages are the performance requirements made for the brand products, services, and cultures. Such performances include the physical attributes, scientific attributes, natural attributes, cultural attributes and management performance ratios. The comparison advantages shall be used to establish the conclusive competitive advantages of the brand products.

For brand purposes, the brand performances are the important issues that may have been neglected in the past. Through the expressions of advantages, the specific demands of the brand users could be identified, such as good brands, good products, good meanings, good materials, good images, high quality, better safety, international and good tastes. However, to determine what or why it's good, the brand organization shall make scientific analysis and effective verification of the performances to be identified for the brands, and provide convincing data, concepts or attribute description.

Despite the fact that some key performances will influence the brand decisions of the consumers, the brand performances shall be carefully explored, analyzed, and identified by the brand organization, so as to find out the brand performances that are more specific and convincing to the target markets. With the improvement of the living standards and the changes of the lifestyles, higher requirements have been made to brand performances despite the requirements only related to the brand performances. A brand organization shall be good at identifying, summarizing and creating new performance demands, such as the comfort degree of the vehicle chairs and the gas saving of automobiles, as well as the clean air required for the wedding photography and housing. The experiment data experienced during the R&D process is the key point for the expression of brand performances.

Some enterprises have explored the key brand performances, and make them into their secret weapons to change the market competition and the consumers' brand selection habits. The brand performances could be identified, felt and confirmed through frontier exploration. Since the brand organization has effectively identified some special demands in terms of brand performance, the brand types, modes and names are changed, leading to the change of the competition method of the brand in the market. From the brand performances, some brand organizations have created a series of classic brand works with independency and specific market demands, realizing the differed competition between the new brands and the existing brands on the market and obtaining unique markets.

Given the protections from invention patents and technical permissions, or the exclusive cultural connotations or manufacturing processes, many brand performances have become unique market competitiveness that can hardly be duplicated or simulated by the market, laying solid foundation for the brand to develop into specific brand or marketing leading brand with deciding competitiveness.

The optimized management performance ratio is the enterprise level capacity for brand performances, which means the input-to-output ratio of management, including scientific performance ratio, knowledge performance ratio, HR performance ratio, quality performance ratio, product performance ratio and service performance ratio.

SECTION I GENERAL INTRODUCTION

5 Concept of brand roadmap

The roadmap is the system capacity development route defined by the brand organization for sustainable development, which has established the competition strategies to be used by the brand organization in the future competition.

The roadmap is the actual route designing required for the long-term development of the brand organization, which will provide the brand organization with extensive sights, obvious brand prospects and the stage targets that could be implemented continuously, so as to express the prospects described in the frontier thoughts in a method that can be realized. The major concept of the roadmap is to establish basic strategic procedures for the sustainable actions, continuous learning and analysis and summarization.

The key point of the roadmap is to deploy the capacities in different stages according to the leading edges. At the certain interval, the roadmap could be corrected according to the actual competition patterns to ensure the close relationship between the roadmap and the market competition demands, market actions and technological updating, so as to keep pace with the time and maintain the leading positions.

According to the roadmap making requirements, a series of future development issues will be proposed and resolved: (1) in the future competition environment, how could a brand organization maintain its deciding competitiveness; (2) in the complicated and ever-changing market competitions, how could a brand organization effectively operate to defend itself from new competitors; (3) to meet the future development needs, what key capacities shall be developed by a brand organization, and how to implement the integration of the management systems in the future.

The new concepts made by a brand organization are always the market strategies used to deal with market competition and maintain deciding competitiveness, which are the major method used to conduct differed competition with competitors based on the analysis of the future competition environment, and could determine the future directions, central thoughts, solutions and a series of activity supporting thoughts for the development of the brand organization.

5.1 Brand roadmap

A roadmap shall span at least 5 to 10 years or even 30 to 100 years. According to the capacity targets encountered in the roadmap, the roadmap could be divided into several development stages, and each stage could be divided into several sub-stages. Such stages and sub-stages could define the capacity construction requirements for the brand organization in terms of development thoughts, capacity frontier, product R&D, frontier preparation, market activities, organization establishment, talent reserves and personnel trainings.

The roadmap will fully use the ever changing sciences, technologies and frontier fashions, as well as hot spots and tendencies to make the combination of deciding competitiveness for the long-term development of the brand organization, so as to reduce the investment risks and significantly improve the possibility of success of the brand organization. The long-term meaning is to define the development strategies of the whole brand organization, so as to concentrate the resources and efforts on the deciding competitiveness of the brand organization.

The roadmap is started from the frontier imagination. Based on the roadmap, the concept system will be further proposed to assist the implementation of the roadmap by stages. The proposal of a group of concepts could help the enterprise employees to understand the capacity requirements, action targets and action methods, so as to improve the effective target identification, task guidance, action commanding, working guidance, process control and corresponding management technologies.

In general, the roadmap has provided four key capacities for the brand organization to realize the leading edge targets, and establish combination of deciding competitiveness: (1) it has clearly indicated the action methods of the brand organization, and conducted task assignments, treatment, development, distribution and progress control for the general strategic targets; (2) it has reduced the risks during the brand development, especially the investment risks during the market fluctuation periods; (3) it has reduced the work load caused by uncertainties of development and optimized human resources; and (4) it has improved the operation efficiency of the brand organization, and prepared various strategic deciding competitiveness for the long-term development of the brands.

5.2 Brand concept system

The concept system is a series of effective competition strategies designed by the brand organization using the frontier thoughts. Such strategies include the imagination of the future, the determination for the current challenges, and the strategies for market divisions, which shall be used as the guiding thoughts for each stage and each period to complete the thought and activity support for the long term development of the brand. Concepts are a series of ideological forms which could be used to guide the central thoughts and action routes of the brand organization actions.

Any concepts that are proposed from the way of thinking based on the basic assumptions for the future market competition, are the advanced thoughts after analyzing and researching the current tasks, emerging competition threats, potential market patterns and the features of the future competition environment.

Concepts typically include task-type thoughts, competition strategic thoughts, and action supporting thoughts. According to the different aging, the concept could last for different periods, which could be determined by the brand organization. The task-type thoughts could propose the clear development tasks, to concentrate the favorable conditions that may be used to obtain the conclusive competition advantages, so as to utilize the commanding of tasks, principles and rules as well as concentrated resources to rapidly make new competition changes for the market and change the old market competition rules.

The competition strategic thoughts are the concepts made for the brand organization to create excellent competition environment, which shall be learned by all employees so as to concentrate resources, thoughts and various capacities to fully use the group competition advantages of the organization to form deciding competitiveness. The action supporting thoughts are a series supporting concepts established for the application of market actions, which have defined the way of thinking, action methods and action rules required for detailed actions, and further improved the action capacities and the all-employee cohesion.

The ideology composed of the concept system shall be systematic, advanced, continued and traceable, which shall be proposed by the brand organization, and implemented through the enterprise cultural reengineering to reflect the thinking patterns and action methods of the employees of the enterprise.

6 Brand full-scale operation capacities

Ocean, land, space, air and network are the deep scope used by human beings to express modern full-scale development capacity. A large brand organization has to operate across regions, networks, cultures, groups and spaces throughout the world, which demand from the enterprise to develop and handle high-level brand full-scale operation capacities.

Market is a battlefield. A brand market action is always a massive global cooperative combat. To maintain high-speed market development in the complicated and ever-changing modern and future global market competitions, large brand organization shall develop the highly sensitive and flexible commanding chain and prepare for attacks, so as to develop the high speed market operation capacities in the world.

Cross-regional capacity means the brand action commanding and coordination capacity and consistency action preparation capacity is spread across regions and market fields; cross-network capacity determines the vertical development capacity in the multi-network interconnection environment including the Internet, mobile internet, logistic network, media network, digital network and satellite network; cross-culture capacity determines the capacities of the brand organization to realize stable development and resolve cultural conflicts in the international diversified cultural environment; cross-group capacity determines diversified user penetration capacities for the target audiences and the radiated groups for the brand development. In modern society, diversified civilizations have generated the great changes of consciousness and ideologies among different groups, and the users of the same brand are divided into different groups with specific preferences; cross-space capacity determines that the brand development environment is not limited to the 2D or 3D spaces. The band purchasing channels, utilization conditions, and application methods have been changed significantly, and the cross-space capacity has proposed higher requirements for the brand products or services.

In the global competition environment with rapid development, the regions, fields, networks, cultures, groups and spaces connected by enterprise brands have been changed significantly, which have brought forward the brand reengineering cycle, promoting the rapid dynamic changes in terms of the technical R&D speeds, technical equipment updating speed, manufacturing capacities, service consciousness, supply chain synergic relationship and the brand user respond method. The contents and forms related to the enterprise brand organization development have become more and more complicated, which requires the enterprise to organically combine various resources to seize the important brand development opportunities in the development environment with high-level commanding and coordination, to launch market challenges by developing the full-scale operation capacities of the brands so as to make, follow and establish tendencies with high speed market operation capacities of the powerful brand.

7 Brand real-time respond capacity

The brand real-time response capacity represents the capacities with real-time feedback, response and reaction that shall be developed and obtained by large brands in the high speed competition in the global market, and shall be used for the early warning, motivation and rapid reaction functions in the brand market.

The real-time feedback capacity is the safety warning line established by a brand for itself, or for a rapid early warning system. Especially in the age of the rapid development of modern network self-medias, any complaints of the users may lead to risks for a brand, which may be magnified through the network media, and become the main focus of the media and the public. The real-time feedback capacity could also be represented by the warning calls to attention to the potential competitors, the latest academic and technical research tendencies in one field, and the new cross-industrial or cross-discipline knowledge and technologies that could change the strategic patterns. The changes of such links will lead to the material changes of the brand product forms, service methods, business models, and competition product strategies. Therefore, the early-warning system of the real-time feedback shall maintain high sensitivity and have the observations, analysis and evaluation functions at the strategic level.

Real-time response capacity is a response system that completes the rapid emergency response reactions after any early warning. Large brand organizations will assign a news spokesperson to rapid screen the market sensitive information, especially the early warning information reported in real time, so as to make written responses, and avoid oral expressions or the explanations by many persons and from many angles. News spokespersons shall pay attention to due diligence and the data that can be verified. The crisis public relations of any brands are not the development core of the enterprise brand organizations. The enterprise brand organizations shall focus on the effective treatment and timely respond to the information provided by users in the ordinary business course, so as to serve every user wholeheartedly and create the best products and service experiences for the brand users.

Another key point of real-time response is to respond to the market competitive products, industrial tendencies and other market information in real time. At first, the brand confidence shall be maintained. Secondly, various improvement opinions and measures from the market shall be accepted reasonably while maintaining own ideas of the enterprises. Most brand aren't perfect at first when they enter the market. There will be various problems. However, the key point of branding is to develop the brand with perfect brand pursuit spirit. If necessary, the zero management or starting all over again are worthwhile. The efforts made to establish perfect brands could be seen throughout the branding process. This is the development based on independence, self-creation, and self-confidence. A brand shall not be controlled by the words of others. The largest concern in the brand real-time response is the shortage of own ideas. Therefore, the designing of the rapid motivation mechanism and the personal using mechanism with real-time influence on leaders are the keys for this.

The real-time reaction capacity means a series of appropriate and rapid reaction (fighting back) actions is taken or launched by a brand organization after the rapid emergency response through real-time response, which shall be handled by the brand organization from strategies to tactics, from management to market and from products and services. It may involve the structure adjustment of the brand organization, its product line adjustment, market action deployment or the release of market measures, which are the global effective motivation and coordination capacities of the enterprises and among their employees.

The essence of rapid reaction includes the reaction actions, as well as the market fighting back actions. These are two market actions with different strengths. The board of directors or the senior meetings shall determine which action shall be used according to the reaction conditions, resource preparation and inventories of the enterprises, the impact speeds and degrees of the competitive products on the market, the damages to the enterprises and the emergency respond cooperative capacities of the supply chain and operation network points. It's necessary for an enterprise to start from the rapid reaction system to abandon the real-time response system and real-time feedback system, so as to establish the real-time reaction capacity of the brand organization, and conduct the resource reserves, organ setting, system designing and periodical rehearsals to some extent, to improve, train and strengthen the comprehensive strategic development level of the enterprise brand. The material changes of national policies and the industries or markets will lead to the market disappearance, product elimination and enterprise closing down immediately.

Exercises:

1. Multiple-choice Question: What are the elements of brand management designing capacity?

A. The market scale supported by the management system

B. The market scale supported by the management system, and the capacities of the management designing talents

C. Organization structure designing, HR outline, salary structure designing,

D. Organization structure designing, HR outline, salary structure designing, management flow designing, production designing, and batch service designing

2. Essay Question: What is brand concept system?

3. Discussion: The brand management designing capacity could be reflected in what aspects?

SECTION I GENERAL INTRODUCTION

Chapter 9

Internet + Brand

Enterprises become multi-network interconnection, and brands are networked comprehensively. In the future, all brands are network brands, and diversified-environment, multi-network connecting branding system, including e-business brand, digital brand, online brand, and mobile brand will be evolved according to the development form. The third decade for internet development in the 21st century is the time for enterprises to comprehensively recreate brands based on internet. Enterprises provide comprehensive networking reconstruction from R&D status, management process and services. Enterprises will completely become network-based branding social enterprises and branding e-business enterprises by virtue of the internet of everything and world-wide-web interconnection. About 5% enterprises will become a highly developed network brand organization.

The network brands develop by structural mode, and are operating under new media environment. The nature is a diversified open system centering at enterprise brand market and businesses, and extending based on department level development. The network brands shall be combined with various multi-network interconnecting solutions effectively to strengthen foundation of brand operation.

1 New media context for network brands

The new media is different from traditional media. The carrier, contents making, mode of transmission, and value embodiment are based on internet and mobile internet. The new media transmits via multimedia and terminals by digital forms such as words, graphics and video.

The new media emerges with internet as carrier. The rapid development of internet and mobile internet stimulates development of content expression form, expands application range of traditional media such as newspapers, video and TV, and publications, as well as attributes of individuality, interaction and self-diffusion, establishes new extensive media transmission form, and thoroughly rewrite media development mode so as to form brand new development power structure and development mode of whole network.

New media appearance is the necessary result of internet development. When more computers, mobiles and digital terminals are connected, the traditional media will lose its weight gradually, and change to social system network between people, people and brand, and people and society with comprehensive and interactive development. The channel of information acquisition, exchange way, opinions proposed and problems discussed by people will change to typical internet application form. New media plays the role of new medium for exchange, interaction and trade between people. The new media is not only a necessary product for networking life, but also the main expression way of information and contents in self-centered social network interconnection.

1.1 Challenges of enterprise brand in new media time

The global new media rises rapidly, and the direct result is to change connection mode between people so that the "interpersonal network", the most basic interconnecting relationship between people, changes for multi-network interconnection form, but the nature will never change. The nature of connected relation of any network is a derivation of interpersonal network. But the changes of remote or direct connection, connection technology or social relation, emerging technology application or human civilization development, or combination change of all meme forms such as interpersonal communication, connection, participation, interaction, strangeness, trust, support, dependence, friendship, kinship, belief, preference, emotion, social relation and investment activities constitute factual basis of multi-network interconnection. Therefore, all networks are set up based on interpersonal relation, and evolve to diversified civilized society of human being.

The trend of global new media changes communication mode between people from all over the world. It makes people freely express themselves by any possible media forms such as website, APP, WeChat, video and photos. It also bridges distance between people, and makes all people in the virtual world under different scenarios. Meanwhile, such social reform urges a series of significant changes in new media technology, new media form and mode of enterprise application new media.

Enterprise brand needs channels which can directly communicate with users. It means the traditional TV or newspaper advertising is cut down. Enterprises do not reduce expenditure on brand marketing, but just cut down expenditure on advertising on traditional media. They transferred the expenditure to multi-network interconnecting media such as internet and mobile internet to more directly express and develop brand attraction by network.

When everyone frequently surfing the internet in the world rebuilds his/her life by networking, he/she will select new preference of reading, discussion and shopping, and, on that basis, rebuilds internet-based new interpersonal cycle. About 75% new friends are strangers from far away. The contact and information transmission mode between people is not limited by face-to-face communication. On the contrary, they will accept all new friends, new brands and new consumption forms with limited threshold of trust.

In a networking environment where all brands are we media, everyone is we media, and any enterprise and any person communicate, interact, mutually know and trust by media mode, any brand owns equal opportunity to develop to a network brand. Any new enterprise has a good chance to become a new brand while any enterprise or person will take brand as a center of interests, trust and interaction so as to build a new development pattern. This is the common media characteristic in the scientific time of new media. It does not matter when new media is outdated or disappears, as long as multi-network interconnection pattern exists, people are living online, and it is always under new media networking status. The attribute of new media is the "gift" sent by internet to all people and enterprises, and also the most basic operating environment for any network brand. The brand can develop if the enterprise knows the law of new media.

1.2 Redefinition of new media

New media refers to all operating strategies and technologies of internet and mobile internet which develop with media property, including any possible contents and media forms such as content marketing, digital publication, media communication solution, display terminal and we media.

Main causes for aforesaid definition are:

(1) The property of networking we media evolved drastically. Everyone is we media, and any enterprise or brand can be we media. All spontaneous contents such as blog, micro-blog, WeChat, micro-journal, column and selfie are revealed to public and open media transmission sources.

(2) Forms of media client increase greatly. Any multi-network interconnecting user clients, such as internet, mobile internet, software, TV, auto GPS navigation, and Internet of Things are inbuilt with setting that allows media transmission, display, review and propagation.

(3) New media is a mixed interactive virtual environment where global enterprises participate in internet operating, users participate in brand development, everyone participates in media contents sharing and transmitting; besides, the new social relation network with direct communication, ordered operation and ecological development has formed between enterprise brands and users, potential consumers and enterprise staffs, person and person, people and brand, and people and society.

(4) In view of aforesaid change, the network-based media property of enterprise brand enhances greatly. However, so far people have not systematically and comprehensively understood the new media.

SECTION I GENERAL INTRODUCTION

The only marketing plan or solutions are partial improvement of certain enterprise new media applications. There is no complete systematic and integrated enterprise-level new media operating theory and practice method. It is extremely unfavorable for transformation development of enterprise towards network. The overall thinking about direction, method and approach is lacked.

(5) The great changes in enterprise operating mode, user attraction mode, market activity mode, product R&D mode, service implementation mode, supply chain mode, service provider mode and social development mode made by new media still go on, so the operating mode, consumption mode, delivery form, management approach and population employment method also transfer synchronically. Such synchronic transfer means enterprises need to make many new changes in concept, cognition, management methods and actions.

(6) The new change of enterprise new media shall pay more attention to management foundation of brand networking operation supported by cutting-edge theories in aspects of cooperation, brand performance, sensitive development, agile manufacture and service intelligence. Moreover, enterprises need to add large amount of new media solution providers, and the service contents and service mode of the service providers will change greatly to acquire cutting-edge status and decisive competition advantages of brands in an ever-changing future.

2 How to change brands by internet?

The largest changes of internet lie in these six elements, "information, time, communication, usage, knowledge and ecology", which are respectively corresponding to "information source, time cluster, communication mode, usage method, knowledge system, and brand ecological organization". The six elements will be shown in network brand process of all enterprises.

Information source: The internet speed development is represented by information source. The internet is the largest information source. In the past, people knew information by newspapers and TV. In the 21st century, the information characteristics of those old media are replaced by internet. People know the latest information from multi-network interconnection, and verify reliable information source and deeply search to know related information of information source at any time according to personal demands. Information source can become the new hotspot almost immediately, and adapt to expanded contents by forms of topics, themes and special subjects to reach any possible content depth, angle and derivative field. The immediacy, flexibility and hotspot cannot be replaced by any other media.

Time cluster: the development of internet efficiency is represented by time cluster. In the 21st century, time is not only the most expensive cost but also the most invalid capacity of human activities. It depends on different choices made by time holder. Once different usage mode is selected for time, the time cluster will change correspondingly so as to evolve to different internet products and services, and transform to different internet use value.

The time cluster refers to time periods of time and people generated under cluster status. People spend most of time every day in movement in the internet time cluster, including online status (computer use time in office and residence), moving status (walking and riding transportation tools), offline status (normal rest time such as eating, sleeping and leisure, and other time not using internet). The time clusters become networking work time cluster, networking study, discussion and knowledge exchange time cluster, and idle time cluster, which are acquired by different internet websites, software, products and services, and led or transferred to specific labor value, new knowledge and ability, user holding valve or entertainment consumption. The effective analysis and management of time clusters of networking users is the most important field to develop competitive advantages during enterprise internet-oriented development process.

Communication mode: The social relation development of internet is represented by communication. The communication mode generates various communication software and tools on internet or mobile internet, and internet communication media such as online intercommunication tools, chat room, forum, blogs, micro-blog, friend circle and social network site. The communication further accelerates media property of brand, and strengthens official reliability certification of brand so as to realize requirements of accurate recognition and consumption safety.

Usage method: The internet application development is represented by usage. The settings of all internet websites, development of internet products, and internet service providing are featured by user demand so as to form diversified internet application environment and usage foundation with professional or individual choice. The network brand operators shall perfect and develop more professional products based on study of user demand, usage characteristics and dynamic usage trend, and thus combine the real products and virtual product services.

Knowledge system: the system development of internet is represented by knowledge. Any enterprise or any person can set up an independent and open knowledge system in multi-network interconnection. The knowledge system comprised of professional viewpoints, opinions, usage method, technology or skills. People interested will spontaneously link individual time cluster and the knowledge system, and meanwhile provide new interconnection support for knowledge transmission and development. The knowledge system may exist by various forms of closed loop and open source, while the development nature of one brand lies in an independent knowledge system established and developed by the brand.

Brand ecological organization: brand ecological organization is shortly known as brand organization. The worldwide brands are operating by ecological chain. About 75% world populations are distributed in different brand ecological chains. Just like the food chain in the nature, they have specific chained labor division. In order to meet management and operation demands on internet, especially when deciding to provide more direct associated interaction service to users, the brand must pay attention to brand organization, include backbone, employees, supplier, service provider and brand use groups to a common brand organization state, and guarantee sustainable development, and self-adaptive operating natural ecology order.

3 Media structure of enterprise brand

The rapid development of internet and mobile internet in the 21st century is featured by many emerging network content distribution center, we media collection center, media interactive expression field and new media solution providers with progress of media technology. The traditional media, such as TV, movie, advertising and games turn towards network to form the boundless world center containing network content making, distribution, response and transmission.

The development of new media field makes internet evolve, in essence, to an enormous super new media industry. Besides, the new media industry keeps comprehensive integration and open development relation with individual and enterprise media. The difference is to build a completely open media center, or to establish a LAN media center with own ecological system.

All new media contents, such as brand news, advertising texts, video, movie, image-text story, internet image, and interactive activity are repeatedly spread, diffused and shared between each media center, and transmit different brand pursuits. Those popular transmission modes and the supporting transmission form easily accepted by people become common product of enterprise brand and new media industry development.

The traditional brands start networking comprehensively, and wish to create new opportunities by virtue of network. Some brands are even willing to change original image, and appear on network by interesting network "cool" brand. The traditional PR companies and advertising companies start trying to develop practices of interactive public relation, and explore enterprise level management solution and marketing activity plan based on network news media.

With development of network news media, many new product forms, brand expression ways and occupations have been created. These processes may develop new concepts, new awareness, new impressions and new behaviors so as to become the new networking interactive bridge between enterprise brands and network users.

SECTION I GENERAL INTRODUCTION

Various easy, professional and serious brand expression style featured by novel creativity can develop on network so that many emerging occupations are generated in links of creation, design, production, story and animation, and many emerging fields such as webpage design, game design, industrial design, news, serial story, four-frame comics and cartoon image keep making new changes. The diversified civilizations of modern society are generated to jointly constitute vivid ecological form in networking status.

3.1 New media movement of enterprise brand

The development of enterprise brand in network shows more centralized and de-platform development characteristics. The centralized development means enterprise reduce or terminate budget released for advertising on traditional media. The overall investment is not reduced, and the enterprise only transfers the cut-down budget to network to establish corresponding network brand department, seek for new network brand outsourcing service provider, and build a series of new frameworks required by network brand-based operation and development.

For large-scale brands, the centralized characteristic is obvious. Enterprises need a systematic and complete network brand development strategies, and shall design by distributed and open mode, and set up efficient operation foundation in network. They shall pay attention to maintaining a more direct relationship between brands and users, and actively apply new media strategies to the whole-network deployment. Some enterprises keep seeking for and purchase network solution providers, merge relevant businesses and develop emerging products. Some internet companies such as Amazon, Microsoft and Google lay emphasis on combination of new network business to keep competitive strength.

The centralized development also means brand operation of enterprises in network has systematic, integral and completed requirements. As various scientific rules in network are discovered, invented and mastered, the centralized brand system operation speed, operation efficiency and mode of brand in network will be improved. The brand application level will change rapidly and dynamically, and will be improved synchronically. The multi-element and multi-level network connection environments such as air, sky, network, ground, mobile and branch make the systematic and coordinative command performance required by network market with efficient command and flexible reaction, and all user groups with potential values. Command does not mean important development opportunity is lost. The de-platform development generally happened on various original e-business transaction platform. Enterprises shall try to build their own brand e-business (B2U), provide reliable and direct products and services to brand, gather users, and develop emerging electronic value added services to make it become new brand economic growth space.

The vast value generated by new media is firstly reflected in American Presidential Election. In the known 2008 American Presidential Election, the candidate Obama set up campaign website, and applied network media publicity strategies to propagandize, attract, link and encourage targeted users to participate in campaign and voting. The social network is used to expand influence and promote small amount campaign donation. Multiple methods are used comprehensively. The campaign is the worldwide social event organically combining new media and old media, organizing highly professional new media application by centralized new media strategy, and finally winning great success.

We can observe centralized uniform development ideas, highly professional operating strategies and fixed movement trail of new media during actual application. This is the movement route left by new media development of enterprises on network ---

How to divide labor strategically? How to group strategically? How to release by steps and combinations? When? What information is produced? Where to release? Etc.

These problems constitute a series of enterprise brand media project clusters, and keep loose and compact two-way interactive relation with network by various networking releasing process. The original characteristic presented by enterprise brand during market expansion is the high-speed movement in the market. By studying the movement paths, developing the movement modes, and paying attention to what people are concern on internet, the information, emotion, attitude, knowledge, thinking, capacity, participation mode, volunteer behavior and purchase behavior will be transferred to effective time cluster which can generate high value based on the effective "brand-user" attraction mechanism set up during network brand development phase.

Therefore, participation encouragement and interactive mode play important roles in application of network brand media operation. Treating contents generated by enterprise brand, contents generated by user and interactive behavior as new media movement path of enterprise brand, the management analyst, brand researcher, market personnel and business cycle can more systematically master scientific rules of brand for internet development, and explore new and effective development way for further brand development. This is the most important development element granted by new media property to enterprise brand, followed by new media technology development, content production or interactive mode problems.

3.2 New media property of enterprise brand - content producer

During multi-network interconnection -oriented development process, enterprises will unconsciously transform into content producer. The brand promotion is transferred to producing quality and splendid contents rather than the former rigid Cost Per Mille advertising. The "content-oriented" competition property of internet is unchanged forever. This is the eternality way of internet brand development.

In order to produce contents, enterprise brands hire large amount of PR and advertising companies to produce massive contents in the forms of news, advertising contents and videos, and ceaselessly strengthen release for powerful transmission. In this way, the strong and weak network brands are generated. The strong brands, relying on their powerful content producing ability and media transmission capacity, release thousands of news to transmit the latest brand information on internet. They transfer brand product release to brand product edition release upgraded once in a while, and ceaselessly make mystery, fresh, novel or interesting points to the market and the entire society. The brand leaders receive various interviews successively to increase opportunities on camera, and attract eyes, and attentions of more media, industries and the public by talking about various brilliant views, opinions and trends. They have already played multiple social roles including the image spokesperson of their brand, starts, directors, producers, chief editors and main authors.

Not only network brands, the emerging companies in any field such as IT, real estate, catering, food, industry, agriculture, movie, TV series, animation and music are happy to do this. If they do not do so, they will soon be emerged by massive information from peers on the network. They must release information at any time to show and refresh the sense of presence on internet. Many leading brands in marketing field and even large sum investment media industry hold shares of newspapers, movie and TV industry and publications to get better transmission effect. It concerns next round of financing and market value of shares. For instance, Alibaba has done in that way.

The weak network brands obviously do not know operating characteristics on network. They care about increasing user quantity and sales volume growth. However, due to the low appearance frequency on network, and even do not show themselves online so that the brands are not recognized by users, user number increases slowly and first trust clients and constant clients are few. The financing and investment is affected, and they may miss the best opportunity for rapid development.

The current network, in essence, exists as we media. The content producers become the most obvious new media property of enterprise brand. The content production contains production of enterprise brand and also user content production. For instance, news agency, experts, in-depth users, we media operator, opinion field and related brand partners all constitute combination of content production strategies. However, the most important contents are that of enterprise brand. The brand contents are deemed as a kind of specific cultural presentation and transmission mode. By incisively and vividly expressing on internet by massive information and multiple forms, the small enterprises can show uncommon market expression on network and become outstanding after mastering new media property characteristics of content producers.

A group of research shows, in any field there are tens of thousands of similar enterprises and experts. However, the brands, good at expressing themselves, showing themselves perfectly by brand mode, and exposing frequently, are easy to stand out among network brands, and have advantages of resources, business mode, investment and income in network market. The public never know 10000 similar manufacturers or experts off the line, but can only see ten and occasionally few famous brands or experts online in the same field. That is the necessary result of redistributing market resources, re-matching advantageous status, and reorganizing market pattern on multi-network interconnection. Even if an enterprise only concerns and develops a very tiny media field on internet, such as healthy vegetable plantation, or pastry making skills, it can acquire its new media success.

3.3 Further reform: change of brand media property

The brand media property appears intensively in the second decade of the 21st century. In this decade, the newspaper industry faces network media crisis, we media centering at every enterprise and every person gains unprecedented development in multiple fields of internet, mobile internet and e-business. The social contact form and communication mode changed unprecedentedly, and brand media property is strengthened comprehensively.

The enterprises approaching internet gradually mastered certain network brand transmission method by exploration and practice in network media trend. Firstly, emerging new internet companies emphasized network media value, and became the network public relation companies with internet as business focus and development foundation. Secondly, leading enterprises deem network as key point of brand content marketing, and they started moving toward network in a large scale. And then, some leading traditional brand making enterprises, advertising companies, started to transform. The transformation way of enterprises in each field and industry in the decade toward network becomes the new enterprise application venture trend, and drive all enterprises and people to accept network thinking methods and operating characteristics.

The brand media property intensively occurs in the period when internet and mobile internet develops rapidly. Global enterprises, population and emerging media companies start concerning and applying internet technology by unprecedented way by such change, and developing media facts of brand transmission based on internet and mobile internet. Enterprises intensively develop brand user relation with users by networking mode in interactions. The orders and services of enterprises turn to the network-centered purchase and service connection structure. The express service and logistics become core delivery carriers connecting online, offline and mobile state, and connecting demand and supply. The new awareness, new life and new environment with virtual environment, social contact and social group relationship, and network social development form as main civilization form reconstruct the daily life and work of people.

Various networking modes extend toward any possible fields such as auto, household appliances and family so as to form connection between information, demand, data and consumption in fields of Internet of Vehicles, intelligent household appliances network, Internet of Things, and health network. The connecting structure continuously expands to each field. By the third decade of the 21st century, all brands will comprehensively and thoroughly complete strategic transformation toward network brands. At that time, all brands will become network brands, and all enterprises, since start up, will strive to develop the emerging competition status of network brand. In the time of change, the only thing unchanged is that the network environment keeps changing, either actively or passively. All enterprises will finish changing finally, either changed or be eliminated.

4 Model of enterprise-level brand media operation system

The operation of enterprise-level brand in multi-network interconnection contains four links, attraction, impetus, brand zone and channel point. The main operating idea is trigger theory. (Fig. 9-1)

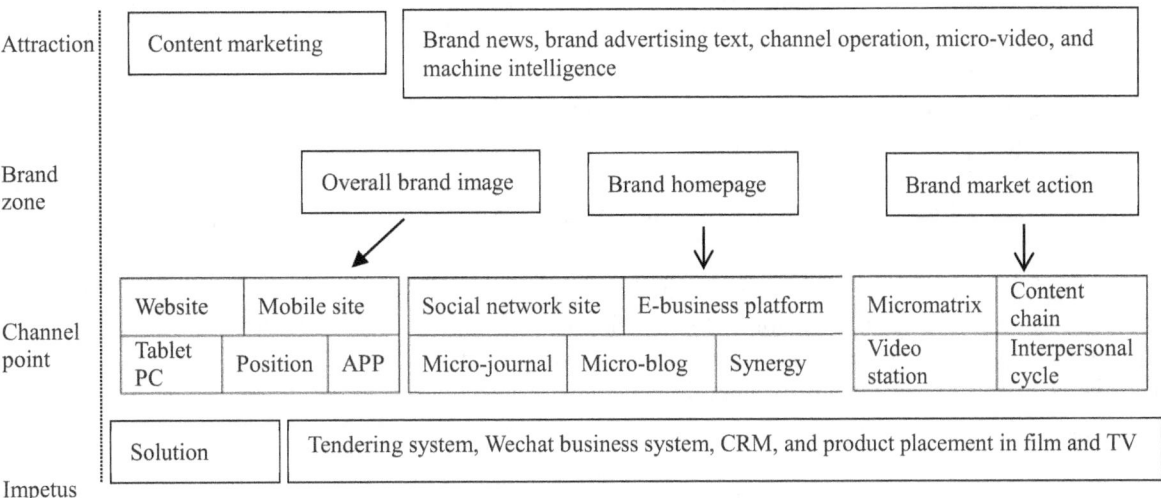

Fig. 9-1 Standard model of enterprise-level brand media operation system

For enterprise brand development on network, the specific development rule is slope development mode; the attraction is from content marketing including brand news, brand advertising text, channel operation, micro-video and machine intelligence. The brands extremely active on internet can develop to a network brand with large influence only by sustainably implementing and rapidly upgrading brand content marketing strategy. The impetus is comprised of various internet solutions, including statistical analysis, tendering system, WeChat business system, payment system, CRM and product placement in film and TV.

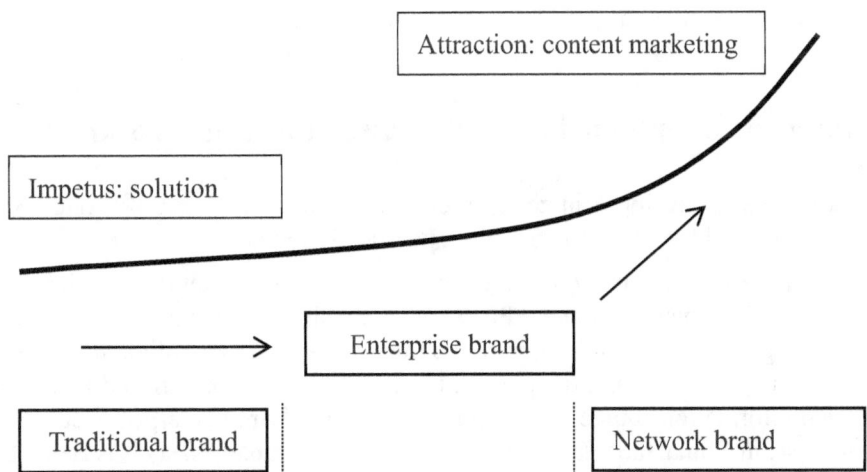

Fig. 9-2 Model of enterprise brand network development

The major development power of the new media is the attraction. If not attractive enough, the brand has no sufficient influence on network. The market field, no matter high-tech or industry and agriculture, adopts traditional brand operation mode. It has not finished network brand transformation from the operation mode. The search engine such as Baidu has pay special attention to the update frequency and capture efficiency of the news contents. (See Fig. 9-2)

4.1 Network brand contents marketing

The network brand development is the necessary result of two-way evolution of enterprise brand and enterprise network, and the final form of all enterprises in the future t at last, all enterprises will be developed to brands, and all brands are network brands.

Content marketing plays the most important role in enterprise network brand process. The large-scale brand enterprise and network brand enterprise pay special attention to the development mode. They transfer more sources and fund from TV and newspaper advertising, greatly cut down expenses on traditional advertising and transmission, and concentrate energy to transmission process of network content marketing.

An article on Forbes column once pointed out within the one year from 2012 to 2013, American enterprises improve emphasis on content marketing about 60%. By 2013, about 93% enterprises have made internet content marketing as one important part of enterprise overall marketing strategy, and 70% enterprises strived to create more content facts on network.

Content marketing is the most important development attraction of network brand. The traditional brand marketing mode depending on network brand has been changed to focus on brand attraction. The development mode attaches more emphasis on brand use group scale attracted directly and indirectly by brands, and direct communication between brand and users. Even if newly established enterprises pay special attention to brand column base construction, one brand can be truly active on network as long as it can attract enough brand users.

Brand news and brand advertising texts play the most active roles on internet. Therefore, they are the main brand promotion and transmission modes selected by global enterprise brands. They unremittingly enlarge production volume of brand contents on network, and evolve to network content producers. Thus, the public relations companies emerged greatly engaging in network content production and release. Enterprises shall attach importance to this aspect. The massive content data and second-based second forwarding speed have become the most pivotal index to evaluate industrial influence of a company on internet. Enterprises engaging in auto, IT, household appliance, film & TV, food, game, animation, education, and medical care have deemed large-scale release of brand news and brand contents as the most important brand promotion mode, and even as the only mode.

4.2 Deployment of enterprise-level brand zone and brand channel point

The brand zone (brand development zone) of enterprise on network mainly contains overall brand image, brand homepage and brand market actions, specifically including:

Overall brand image -Mainly including website, mobile site and tablet PC website for brand image, map location marketing information, brand APP, which are mainly used to display integral brand image. The overall brand image is the official unified brand image center, brand authorized information center and brand network service center, and the portal of unified construction, unified image, unified brand recognition, unified information source and unified networking. Large enterprises can set up the brand portal of general sense. In China, the third party internet service companies, such as Baidu Search Engine and 360 Search Engine, have successively set up open data for enterprise official website such as "Official" authentication mark, real name authentication, and information authenticity verification so that net citizens can rapidly recognize the uniqueness and authenticity of enterprise brand official website. The authentic information is open for consulting. For instances, Steve Jobs loved rounded rectangle. Therefore, the mobile phone icons in the entire world become rounded rectangle. Why everyone must follows the rounded rectangle? You can make a change.

Brand homepage -Mainly including open brand information of enterprise brand homepage, pages, themes and topics in fields of social network website, e-business transaction platform, WeChat micro-journal, micro-blog, talent recruitment, and third party collaborative business platform. These transmission sources are all official homepage of enterprises established officially by enterprise brand, verified by internet service provider or third party, and marked with special authentication and identification marks. The official webpage is numerous and of characteristic of sole official property. Data such as trademark registration certificate shall be provided for authentication on many mainstream brand homepages such as Tencent micro-journal and Sina Weibo to confirm the sole accuracy and authenticity of brands.

The brand home pages are important channels for enterprises to display and spread brand images on internet, mobile internet and various network terminals by multilevel and diversified ways, and are inseparable important constituent of enterprise brands. High importance shall be attached to brand image, brand information accuracy, and authenticity of brand business trader. Besides, the brand images and information are key contact link directly face to face with each internet service provider, network associations and network users. Google and Facebook currently have mainly developed "brand homepage" service. Website of listed companies on some internet service provider may have special page for brand investor relations. The official "brand homepage" of enterprise-level brand is the key for later global network brand development, and also the focus on business competition of global major internet companies. For increasing brand homepage establishment field, enterprises shall arrange special department and personnel to manage, and unify brand image and information. This is an important link for enterprise-level brand development in the future.

Brand market actions -including forms of micro-matrix, content chain, video station and interpersonal circle, mainly interactive access port, interactive mode, information transmission such as brand release, brand image extensive transmission, brand market activities and brand public benefit activities carried out by enterprises for brand development on network, as well as any possible contact point terminal. The contact point and trigger theory are all over every corner of network and the world all the time in every aspect, and exist as multilevel and multiple-spreading and transmission form. The effective management of the major brand transmission information source has been promoted to key brand ability scope of network brands.

Specifically, the micro-matrix is a micro-transmission medium including WeChat, micro-blog and Twitter. Enterprise brand officially spreads and promotes brand market information actively through various mainstream or professional networking channels. Besides, any member of enterprise brand, or member of service provider operating network can release the "official" information or gossips as direct official or semi-official identity. The content chain comprises of brand information transmission, discussion, and friendly support about the brand in direct or related transmission media combination of enterprise brand members, we media comment column, expert column, blog, and community leaders. It comprehensively deployed attributes of self-generation, self-response and self-transmission in parallel.

Video station is the media transmitting videos such as CNTV, Youku, Tudou, LeTV, Ku6, QQ Live, YouTube, Megavideo and AOL. With development of popular films, professional video program producing, micro-film, family video equipment and smart phone, video and graphics or text information, especially "snapshots" become the key way of transmission. Many videos and graphics or text information contain shooting information of brand, such as latest food, new clothing's, interesting brand events on the streets, and even the horrible status during the use of brand. People display all images and information intentionally or unintentionally as "experiencer", "user" or "witness". Other network users are not against the brand information; on the contrary, they are willing to accept and continuously forward the information.

The interpersonal cycle contains interpersonal network of every people, family and kinship relation network, colleagues, peers and friend relation network, online and offline communities, any possible occasional net friends added at any time, and users mutually commenting the same content. The multilayer and accessible interpersonal cycles constitute instant contact and transmission relationship between people and brand, people and internet, people and society, and also the trigger relation directly or indirectly transmitting brand influence.

4.3 Network brand solution market

Massive network solution market is generated between internet and enterprise business development. The market development starts from initial domain name sales and server space lease, develops to mobile management, mobile marketing, payment, bidding, statistical analysis, membership system, preservation and appointment as well as any possible network development forms, and finally evolves and extends to any possible forms such as vehicle-mounted, family, wearable equipment and self-service terminals.

With mature network application of internet citizens, formation of habitual preference and development of self-centered network user characteristics, enterprises evolve from pursuing how to sell products online to focusing on dynamic and efficient operation, agile operation and service intelligence of brand on network. Users initially applied convenient service of internet and purchased commodities by comparing prices, and now pay attention to diversified high-level brand enjoyment such as pursuing individual style, usage reference, fashion, cutting-edge technology, pleasant memory, virtual environment and brand performance. The changes make network brand solution and intelligent terminal increase greatly, the dependency of study on development of emerging technology and network-based brand scientific laws strengthened from all aspects, and network brand solution markets also face hyper competition and drastic changes.

Some emerging network brand solution products emerge endlessly every day, support management and reconstruction of enterprise implementation network from different degrees, and play roles of different degrees in network brand management. From the angle of brand system management, the brand solutions are enhancements of a series of brand ability, and foundation support and functional subsidiary required by network-based operation of brands. They accelerate the process of brands thoroughly and comprehensively to evolve into network brands.

With the development of network brand theory and diversified choice of solution, which is the brand development foundation required by enterprises on network, diversified network brand forms are evolved due to different enterprises, different products and business modes. There is no such thing as same management of two network brands. One enterprise brand is different from another more or less. This is the key strategy to realize different competition on network, and also decided by the instinct of human creativity development. The instinct is to create brand development form on network and insist on its own way. The result is not important. The important thing is enterprises step over toward change, independent creation and brand development along the practical way of network brand. We have been creating and surpassing. The brand ecological development mode with creation and transcending will urge every brand to realize true brand ego on network. This is the development mode we encourage the most. Every brand shall have its own characteristics. With characteristics, brand can realize user group clustering effect, and gain long-term development of ecological organization, and reach a bright future.

5 The third decade of internet in the 21st century

Before arrival of the third decade of the internet in the 21st century, the leading entrepreneurs can see the future clearly in five years. In common sense, enterprises and people need to see the future in 10 years.

The internet competition laws are still the same as that in the first decade, i.e. the forward-looking entrepreneurs and investors continuously lay out infrastructure construction required by LAN user in the future. As a familiar slogan for social development in China, "build roads to get rich", they set up important channels of future ecological system or future network by high pattern. Thoughts and foresights will create the future. Although it seems like a cause with few economic benefits and even in deficiency, in the next decade, their foresight will gain advantages for them. They will own fortune because of their courage and insights. Even, their thoughts will generate new network ecology, while the most important asset they invested is the future. Only they know what the future is and what changes they will make to themselves.

The third decade of internet in the 21st century is the time of enterprise reconstruction, and the time of Internet of Everything and multi-network interconnection. Enterprises will make comprehensive network reconstruction from aspects of research status, management flow and service providing mode, and thoroughly become network-centered brand social enterprise, and brand e-business enterprises. About 5% enterprises will become highly developed brand organization.

At least a third of global enterprises will transform into network enterprises. In the time of highly developed network brand, the brand media development will be the most common application form of major enterprises. Every large-scale enterprise will set up special brand media department to integrate enterprise journal and media for users. The large-scale reconstruction and speed of business splitting will be the largest characteristics in that decade. In order to adapt to development of network brand, enterprises have to make significant changes from organizational structure, competition relation, strategic layout and brand cluster development.

People keep thinking about the latest trend and exploring the latest answers about what media is and what new media is based on, network media practice mode, new media technology development and content marketing value. The in-depth problem that enterprises just started to consider or are about to consider currently is what form the enterprise network brand media will develop to. It is certain that if the first and second decades of the 21st century are years for "declination of advertising, rising of public relations and development of new media", the third decade in the 21st century will be the years for "declination of public relations, rising of management, and development of user reaction mode". The boundary line between new media technology and planning and business management will disappear, and the new media-focused media development will be evolved to scientific research and application with user reaction mode.

The next ten years, next 20 years and 30 years will be the time of reciprocating replacement for N generations by decades. Based on the X generation (population born after the Second World War) and Y generation (population born after 1985), we further propose and emphasize N generation as the time for continuously changes of world population awareness and consumption habits. Every ten years are deemed as one N generation. The new young consumption will grow up, and new brand life consumption mode is cultivated and developed. The old consumers will update life and consumption mode of old brands. The consumers changing every ten years will cause 10% global brands generate replacing change. The leading-edge exploratory study on positional cognition and application of the N generation for brand life style shall be strengthened. It is the key for enterprise brand to keep keen market cutting-edge competitiveness, and develop emerging brand design ideas.

6 Move toward comprehensive reform: change of brand operation attribute

Since the internet is greatly applied by enterprises, the management personnel started developing modern management of enterprises by internet. Therefore, many flows such as R&D, finance, marketing and services are transferred to internet, and IT deployment starts. As the fundamental pillar companies for people to step to multi-network interconnection time, internet enterprises and IT enterprises become the greatest beneficiaries for enterprise brand network development. On the contrary, the cognition on roles of network media, especially new media, of enterprises are delayed for a long time when they realized the truth. The deep understanding of network brands will be truly realized by Internet of Everything and multi-network interconnection in the third decade of the 21st century.

Consistent with the great development and great reform mode of internet companies a decade in the 21st century, in the historically progressing stage, the first golden decade is the time for internet

Section I General Introduction

enterprises and IT solution providers, the second decade is the time for enterprise media development with new media transformation, and the third decade is the time for drastic change, evolution and development of enterprise network brand. Almost all enterprises will be transformed to network brands. The worldwide large-scale brand reconstruction, in return, will rebuild basic industrial business types such as internet, mobile and digital technology, IT industry and media industry.

When all enterprises implement enterprise management based on multi-network interconnection, the multiple internal and external flows of enterprises have made fundamental changes, and integrated together. For many original internal operation frameworks on public internet, large amount of work engagements connects with various internet, mobile internet terminals and data. Until one day, enterprises will thoroughly become the brand ecological organization operating by network ideas completely. Various pure network operation modes based on network gene, network system, data connection, service response, value chain and work flow replaced foundation of daily enterprise management and operation. The large-scale enterprise brand organization reconstruction, brand performance, brand capacity and brand operation foundation development by brand users living online will make all global enterprises finish thorough, overturning, self-adapting, self-response, self-serving and self-organization development process of brands.

Nowadays we can deeply hunch the changes in the future, and deeply feel the overturning power is budding, just like the volcano about to erupt. The magma is boiling and waiting for the new time at any moment. When the brand operation attributive has made fundamental structural change, the highest form brand ecological organization, i.e., brand brain will come into being officially. However, minority entrepreneurs with foresight are doomed to incisively find the development value of such senior brand organization, and the new brand giants are bound to be born. Correspondingly, the traditional internet companies, IT companies, and new media companies will be evolved to traditional enterprises. In the key fields eliminating by trends and facts and facing reconstruction, the brand founders who are creating brand new competitive advantages are poised for reform. All industries in the world will, under status of active and passive change, participate in global network brand reform. The result is rising, continuing or falling.

The nature of network brand development is human's in-depth understanding of brand practice, and the basic ability of human being developed during internet reconstruction process. Enterprises shall deem network as resources like land, air and water. Although it may be invisible basic substances in virtual space, the application level of the virtual substances, production resources and development relation becomes the key to decide whether a network brand can develop. The material basis of such cognition is different from that required by deeming network as a kind of development. In the future, during the process of network brand evolution of global enterprises, brand is the key of operation. It is of material difference than research of certain software, certain internet function service and customer relation establishment via internet. The former is to develop brand network gene reconstruction, business reorganization and brand rebuilding, and the latter is the application to realize business or work solutions.

Exercises

1. Fill in the blanks: The largest changes of internet lie in six elements of "_____, _____, _____, _____, _____, _____", which are respectively corresponding to "_____, _____, _____, _____, _____, _____". The six elements will be shown in network brand process of all enterprises.

2. True or False Question: The brand media property intensively occurs in the period when internet and mobile internet develops rapidly. Global enterprises, population and emerging media companies start concerning and applying internet technology by unprecedented way by such change, and developing media facts of brand transmission based on internet and mobile internet. (   )

3. Essay Question: What are the specific development rules for enterprise brands on internet?

Chapter 1

Brand History

The brand history runs through the history of human civilization and progress from prehistory to the future. The study on brand history is to study an important development process confirming the civilization form of brands. Different from common science of history, brand history is a developing history. It does not only play an important role in the past, but also has important development value for present and future of brands. Moreover, while the prosperous brand work of human is contributing and serving human beings, it is being recorded in the development history of human civilization as precious historical materials.

1　Origin of brand history

The brand history contains (1) development history of the brand, including four stages of brand civilization gene, brand incubation, brand creation and brand development; (2) discovering the brand from history; the origin of many brands or the discovery of brand story shall be sought back from history, and a basic civilization form of a brand shall be laid by protective discovering; (3) development history of every international brand, including origin, reform and transition.

Brand history is an important constituent part of development and transition of human civilization, and a "live" epic from recording trade activities to economic growth and transition of human society, prosperity of the country, and civilization renaissance. The development history of nations, words, languages, clothes, architectures and transportations is deemed as the foundation to study the transition of human civilization. However, as human beings gradually step towards higher civilization stage, the development history of brand has gradually replaced the original fundamental development form of human beings such as nations, words, languages, clothes, architectures and transportations, and became the main line of study on human civilization history.

The trade and market activities in brand civilization form as structure, national brand, brand art and specific fields of agriculture, industry, automobile, aviation, clothes, food, home appliances, urban tourism brand and urban landscape are representatives for social economy and industry transition of specific brand development history in market. The method of expressing human development and transition history by brands will become more prominent in the future. Finally, brand history will replace recording and expressing method of most human civilization history, and become a specific recording method of human history. Therefore, the brand history file is the most important history that records human activities.

Looking back at human history, pictures of historical fragments appear one by one. In the long human history, trade caravans are passing by with camels; ships are sailing on the sea; steam engines are whistling; modern logistic network are interweaving; international network are transmitting rapidly; airbus are flying around the world...

What is brand, and where is it from?

What is the role of brand, and what values does it generated?

Why are human beings obsessed in brands and consumed greatly?

Why does global economy operate around brands?

SECTION II BRAND SUBJECTS

Back in time, you can seek for brand from the progress of human development, start exploring knowledge of brand history, and probe the secrets of the entire world and mankind.

2 Civilization gene of brand

The brand existed as human civilization gene at the earliest. From the development of pictographic images, words and languages, human expressed the earliest civilization by imaginary images, images recording reality, pattern design of decoration aesthetics, and national words and language inventions, which are the main ways that human progress. The images, patterns and national civilizations are fundamental prototype and great gene for human brand development currently, and some brand ideas which generate great influence on later brand development were settled in that period.

It is the brand civilization gene formed from the birth of human being to prehistoric civilization period 4000 years ago that created three main forms of brand civilization for future brand development. The first is brand civilization based on image, which is the origin of brand constituting virtual civilization world such as science fiction, fantasy and dreamlike imaginary literature, film, game, scientific space and virtual community; the second is brand civilization based on reality, which is the origin of brand constituting realistic civilization world of practical literature, film, entity products and actual services such as reality record, actual problem solution and actual development situations; the third is the brand civilization based on artistic expression such as pictographic and abstract image, picture composition, plane and three dimensional image, and decoration, which is the original of brand constituting aesthetic design of mankind.

These great brand civilization genes can be found from places of origin and inhabitations around the world. The archaeologists have ceaselessly reported such latest findings during digging process of important relics of different human prehistoric civilization period. Human have found previous memories left by ancestors to us from historical sites and remains from ten thousand years ago and thousand years ago such as cave rock painting, grave wall painting, cultural relic modeling and decoration in Kazakhstan, Karelia, Spain, France, Siberia, Italy, Britain, Germany, China, Algeria or Sahara in Europe, Asia and Africa.

The ancestors in prehistoric period had laid the most fundamental gene of brand civilization form for the development of human brand. However, it is not the sign for the final generation of brand. Although human civilization usually exists as nation or national group (pan-nation which has not formed normal nation), many human civilizations were disappeared, or dynasties fell, or some civilizations have developed up to now, forming resplendent civilization marks, while these marks are rapidly evolved to expression of brand styles in the time of brands rise. The legends and charm of ancient national civilization of human being are recalled by brand impression. Nevertheless, brand ideas shall lay the foundation for brand incubation and final generation; moreover, conditions of saturated supply of human commodities and fierce competition are necessary. The original brand civilization gene will finally cause vast trend of brands.

2.1 Brand property relationship in early stage

During the period when there were limited commodities, even though the prototype of brand had come into being, they were primitive activities for design of brand prototype for self-recognition, self-use and self-entertainment, recognition of property ownership, and interchange and trade of materials under most circumstances. It is unable to advance to the competitive environment which needs strict laws, property protection, self-recognition emphasis, and seeks for brand development. Therefore, in a long human historic period, brands had only went through brand prototype development to identification property right, and then to property ownership judgment and protection stage with legal sense.

Through the evolution process from rock painting, totem to symbols and labels, finally brands turned up in the basic existing form of "identification"; while the development history from original exchange to commodity transaction and then global trade is the foundation of identifications to evolve to trademark and then to brand recognition. The basic significance is that the identification shows emergence of property relations.

About 7000 years ago, human officially started using various identifications to show ownership of livestock and goods, and subsequently it is used to show goods ownership and work quality of manufacturers. Various special identifications were mostly used on rock painting, bricks and ceramics. The totem belief and ancestor worship were further combined to confirm the origin of ancestors and its affiliations, while "totem" is the symbol for obvious distinction. The totem worship accelerated the evolution of identification.

As trades increase, human started engaging in early branding commodities transaction and distribution by long trade route or trade cycles. Merchandises were emerged, and acquired favorable price difference of commodities from trading of original brand. The major global ancient trade cycles are the Aegean Sea, the Baltic Sea, the North Sea Trade Cycle and the Sahara Trade Cycle, and major ancient trade cycles in China are noon markets and the Silk Road, etc.

Although these trades are rudiments of brands, they not only meet the transmission characteristics of global reach and global premium, but also meet the requirements of brand ability and brand recognition characteristics such as imprints, place of origin, quality grade and quality stability.

While concerning "brands", we need to know the following characteristics of brands:

(1) Global reach: brands must realize global reach, and brand operating network spreads all over the world;

(2) Global premium: brands shall reach enough premium capacity in each market worldwide, and own high profits and high added value.

(3) Imprints owned: brands own recognizable symbols such as marks and badges.

(4) Place of origin: brands have exporting country and original producing area (place of origin), and brands are mainly traded to the world or supplied to global market by export.

(5) Quality grade: Brands owns certain quality grade. The global export is mainly guaranteed by high reliability and high quality grade (excellent quality) so as to allow the consumption of brand to be completed in a completely safe consumer psychological environment.

(6) Quality stability: brands require stability of reliable quality performance. Brand consumers can purchase brand products and services with high stability anywhere, which will not change due to regional difference, climate change and service environment.

Brands meeting aforesaid requirements simultaneously have basic elements featured by global trade output right (property ownership, trade right, market exclusivity, market access right and contracting relationship) no matter in original and proto form or in modern brand form, which are consistent with modern brand economy entity (brand exporting country, industrial brand cluster and group brand cluster) of human beings.

2.2 Process from brand identification to normalized use

During the process of global trade (transaction, market access), the prototype of brands in early stage of human being came into being in brand trading successively, and identification started evolving to identification marks protecting consumers. People used identifications to distinguish place of origin and reputation of manufacturer. The identification protection in this period was not been listed to laws, but people gradually realized identifications are in favor of fair competition among manufacturers. Finally, the recognition property of identification was confirmed.

Therefore, the etymology of brand is formed. The world brand is from "brandr", the Norse word, which means "sear" and "burn" in English. In early stage, people seared different marks on horseback to distinguish their own property. This is the primitive naming method for commodities, and meanwhile the source of modern brand concept. However, it does not mean identification is brand, and trademark is equivalent to brand after human laws on trademark are formulated.

Since ancient times, the human economic activities are dependent on "brands" and supported by logistics and propagation, and various economic variables true brands shall provide, including investment, production, grading, recognition, trade, consumption and cultural elements are generated hereby.

After basic brand trade (transaction) elements are satisfied, brands need certain variables, such as who is the investor? What is the production method? How to rate quality and appearance? How to distinguish valid products from similar products? What are the characteristics of trade (logistics) and transaction? How to successfully meet demands of global consumption? Whether cultural elements are sufficient to improve brand premium?

By investigating aforesaid variable elements of brands, it can be found that the scope of element contents of brands is much larger than what we have imaged before.

Some brand variables are fixed in early stage of human being, forming certain preconditions for transaction. For instance, for the totem of fish-frog pattern painted on pottery in Yangshao Banpo Ancient Cultural Relics in Shaanxi Province, China, the Banpo symbols discovered mostly are engraved in the same part on the same kind of potteries regularly. Some symbols do not only appear on multiple utensils repeatedly, but also are discovered in different relics. In 3000B.C, Mesopotamia measured quality of barley by specific value indexes as the basis of transaction.

The more typical case is the Wensi Crafts Institute brand of Tang Dynasty in the 9th century A.D in China: The royal tea wares made in Tang Dynasty were unearthed from Famen Temple Underground Palace, Fufeng County, Shaanxi Province, China, in 1987. Those tea wares were made in the 9th - 12th year of Xiantong, Tang Dynasty (868-871A.D), with mark of "Made in Wensi Crafts Institute".

The inscription of "Made in Wensi Crafts Institute" is as follows:

"A gold-plated silver salt table made by Wensi Crafts Institute in the 9th year of Xiantong, has a weight of 620g with cover. Assistant to the chief local official: Wu Hongque, Envoy: Neng Shun.

A golden alms bowl made by Wensi Crafts Institute on March 20 of the 14th year of Xiantong upon command, has a weight of 715g; Dozhi: Liu Weizhao; Assistant to the chief local official with purple fish bag: Wang Quanhu; Service official: Qian Yi; Palace Gate Guard General: Hong Que"

The development of those brand prototypes shows brand emerges as a kind of code, and covers elements except identification. Although brands are mainly distinguished by "identification", "identification" is not the true development method of brand. Brand is gradually established during technology promotion, growth, influence of transmission and consumption cognition process based on requirements of order rules. The "trademark" is only a property right delimitation of legal sense as a "graphic or named identification", and has no element and significance of any brand.

2.3 Legal agreements on brand from identification to trademark

The Celtic identification, which is of important representative significance, intensively appeared during the 5th Century B.C to the 1st Century A.D. It is the origin of many important marks in Europe and North America. The identification was rapidly changed during revitalization and declination process of Rome, and monopoly identification appeared in societies and protection guilds. The important dragon pattern in China appeared in the Neolithic Age 4000-6000 years ago, and later was shown incisively and vividly on bronze wares and jade wares. The brand prototype appeared in large amount in Shang and Zhou Dynasties in China for product recognition and protection. Those primitive functions continue up to now.

In China, "signboard", "shop sign" and "emblem" are the specific way in ancient society to express brands. Traces of brands can be seen in documents of wine, sword, ceramics, silk and tea in the early period.

In the 11th century A.D, the earliest official brand image appeared in the Song Dynasty. The Liu's Needle Shop in Jinan, Shandong Province engaged in fine needles particularly designed and made a copper plate for identification printing. The identification is engraved near a square, with white rabbit as mark, and contains words and graphics. The name "Jinan Liu's Fine Needle Shop" is carved horizontally on top. The white rabbit is carved in the middle. The words "the white rabbit is the mark" are carved on both sides. A long excursus is caved on the bottom. Compared with modern brand, the normalized characteristic has been manifested.

The industrial associations in Europe started using official identification from the 12th Century, and some main manufacturers started using identification in the 13th Century. The "Watermark" firstly appeared in Italy. In 1266, Labeling Law of Baker, the earliest trademark law was formulated in Britain and France. Some bakers used identification on breads. In 1353, the trademark ownership appeared, and was deemed as legal evidences when commodities were stolen. In 1365, the blade smiths gained protection. The blade smith in London should register their specialized identification to urban officials. In 1373, bottle manufacturers were asked to engrave their trademarks on leather to allow the bottles and other vessels made by them to be recognizable. In 1452, a widow was allowed to use the trademark of her late husband, and this was the earliest trademark litigation record.

In Europe during the mid-century, the handicraftsmen always smeared identification on their handiwork so that customers can recognize the place of origin and manufacturers. This is the initial trademark. It can provide guarantee to consumers and meanwhile provide legal protection to manufacturers. In early 16th century, the manufacturers of distilled Whiskey put whiskey in barrel smeared with name of manufacturer to prevent from fraud perpetrated by illegal merchants.

In 1618, the apparel manufacturer who used inferior cloths but quality cloth identification was judged as infringement. Since then, the business and trademark started to be closely connected. In 1653, the Royal Delft in the Netherlands, enlightened by ceramics of China, started using identification.

In the Industrial Revolution, Europe and North America started legislating for trademarks. Trademarks became legal properties, and brands became familiar with by consumers. The legislations contain: trademark legislation protection for canvas producers in USA in 1788, USA protected trademark legislation protection from the identification of canvas manufacturers; in 1789, by legislation, the canvas exported overseas should be smeared with commodity label or seals; in 1857, France issued trademark law; in 1862, Britain issued trademark law; in 1872, official newspapers of US Patent and Trademark Office started publishing.

On April 14, 1891, many countries jointly signed Madrid Agreement Concerning the International Registration of Marks in Madrid, Spain to set up joint protection laws for modern marks. By 2003, USA has owned 1,600,000 registered trademarks. Trademarks are used to show independent property nature of products or services.

3 Brand incubation

The increasing and frequent human business activities drive cognition of identification to the trademark on legal sense. However, by owning a trademark, an enterprise may not incubate a brand. Human brand is a combination of brand civilization gene and brand ideas. The brand civilization gene needs sufficient commodities competition in market, while commodities can transform to brand through brand ideas.

A brand can be incubated and born when four special brand development attributes are provided simultaneously. The attributes are respectively (1) brand cultural gene existing and kept in a nation; when the civilization of the nation undertakes historical mission and responsibilities, the brand is the embodiment of civilization revitalization results to a certain degree; (2) the basic original brand ideas, mainly consisting of spirit of the craftsman, scientific spirit, service spirit and civilization confidence; brand ideas play the most direct value of creation to brand incubation; (3) varieties of commodities are increased to the fierce competition degree.

The civilization of any nation or nation group in human history has experienced the great progress of creation, birth, formation and development. However, under most circumstances, the brand cannot be incubated successfully since original brand ideas are not came into being or lost due to the interruption of civilization. Different countries in the world have gone or are going through the course from deficient commodities to abundant commodities. The insufficient commodity competition caused those countries to fail in forming important ideology for spontaneously developed brand. Brand may be potential-level awareness. These countries, which knew that brand is essential but have not make sufficient preparation for brand incubation, will not have any brand emerging yet.

However, brands will not stop developing simply because of certain country or nation failing to incubate brands. On the contrary, as commodity varieties and quantities increase continuously, trade and transaction activities add increasingly, till competition emerges and fierce global competition stage starts, some countries, with international status of brand exporter, occupied upper market of global brand economy, while countries and regions that could not complete brand development will become brand importers. Brands produced continuously from brand exporter, via development of modern market economy, spread all over the world. Even Eskimos in the North Pole or people in poor African countries will not stop the wills to use and purchase brands due to regional limitation or country power.

Brand incubation is the masterwork in human civilization history. The pursuits of knowledge, truth, science, culture, art, commodity, life, family and fortune in the past thousands of years are all gathered in "brand". Finally, the brand comes into being in brand ideas incubation, and grows prosperously and eternally.

3.1 Formation of brand ideas

The nation-oriented cultural form in human history has not formed enough abundant brand sources up to now. The basic cause is the great course of culture inheritance, civilization division and civilization revitalization. Some important ideas influencing human brand development were rooted in civilization of some mainstream nations, laying foundation for human brand incubation and generation. On the contrary, in diversified national culture of human beings, many countries or nations are unable and incapable to incubate and produce brands due to lack of original brand ideas or interrupted original brand ideas.

The formation of brand ideas is an important development mark for a nation or national group to stand among worldwide nations. Brand ideas are from basic ideology proposed by human beings for civilization development. The ideology, by unconscious influence, will exist and get inheritance and development in one nation and generation by generation. Thus, if some nations or national groups disappeared in human history, or failed to exist as the form of country, the civilization has not been interrupted or disappeared, and continue to be pass on generation by generation instead. Conversely, the development by form of country may fail to prepare conditions required by brand generation in overall ideology due to the lack of national confidence spirits. The civilization pattern of those national brands shall be incubated for a long time or a very long human historic period.

For brand, civilization is a great fission process, while brand idea is inherited and carried forward during civilization, this leads to the origin of a civilization to incubate and generate brands. Those important brand ideas mainly contain civilization confidence, spirit of craftsman, scientific spirits, service spirits, contractual relationship, and wealth view, and they are the important structural environment for incubating brand spirits and order. Nations or countries with aforesaid brand ideas own the factual basis to conceive brands.

The formation of brand ideas is a long process for human civilization origin, derivation and development. The nature is the human's overall cognition and understanding of human society generated during development and change process, the specific embodiment of national world outlook, and undertaking of mission, responsibilities and obligations by the nation and descendants for the development of a civilization. It is a civilization trend under potential influence, a conventional order and rules, and an ecological sequence developed naturally.

The modern and later human's ideas of brand cannot develop if the ideas did not inherit and carry forward earlier brand ideas. This is the development of human civilization from the beginning. It is a self-adaptive comprehensive open-source civilization system, and will develop higher-degree civilization when it advanced with the times. It is a self-development process for self-continuousness, self-cultivation, spontaneity and self-improvement of a nation.

The early brand ideas of human beings were generated during 4000 years ago to the 1st Century A.D. The most important civilization time and national civilization origins are centralized in this period. This historical period, when human civilization was generated officially and intensively, lays foundation for basic brand ideas, and constitutes to human society civilization form by conscious structure of orders, rules and networks. Sometimes, historical records are not true because history is written by victors. During that process, many original civilization and original brand ideas which may influence future of human being could be neglected or rarely recorded. However, by the persistence of descendants of these nations or national groups which may have disappeared, human brand finally experienced the long-time incubation process from the Middle Ages to the modern history, and finally came into being.

The four ancient civilization powers, Ancient Babylon, Ancient Egypt, Ancient China and Ancient India had to survive and develop with much difficulty. Except Babylon had vanished thoroughly, Egypt, China and India are formed eventually. However, the civilization period division exists to a certain degree, the original civilization was disrupted numerous times. On the contrary, in modern brand civilization world, the interaction of ancient and modern civilization makes it difficult to incubate and develop cutting-edge civilization facing the future. Therefore, the time of higher civilization stage represented by brands is delayed so as to generate specific medium-civilization progress stage. However, when those ancient civilizations are finally revitalized, they are still possible to become the great civilization influencing human brand civilization development progress.

Not all brand ideas are generated by ancestors of ancient nations. In the stage of highly developed brand civilization, when a nation rises up spontaneously, the self-development process for self-continuousness, self-cultivation, spontaneity and self-improvement will complete brand incubation and generation by powerful national wills. That is because brand is the product of human civilization, great seeking process and pursuit of all nations during civilization revitalization, and final development achievements of national mission, responsibilities and obligations.

3.2 Official incubation of brand

Based on the large amount of historical history of brand origin, we can judge that human brands are intensively incubated in the Celtic civilization originated from Ireland, Scotland and Gaul. Although the Celtic civilization was destroyed by Roman military under the leadership of Caesar in the 1st century A.D, the brand civilization gene and original brand ideas required by human brand incubation were inherited. By the 19th Century, the human brand incubation stage was completed. The great creation process of brand is from the 19th Century to the 20th Century.

It is easy to prove that the Celtic descendants spreading all over USA and Europe (descendants of Ireland, Scotland and Gaul), and offspring and successors of craftsmen in Europe are the main force to finish brand incubation and creation.

This can be proven by the official appearance of the first brand in the world: In 1835, the first brand logo on modern sense appeared on commodity. The Scottish wine makers used the brand of "Old Smuggler" to maintain the quality and reputation for wind brewed by special distillation process.

In the Europe in 19th Century, large-scale nonlocal brands and packaged goods started circulating massively, the industrial revolution created large amount of household goods, such as soap. The centralized factories produced those products massively. Vessels shipped barrels with brand trademarks to other places by batches, the brand at that time has expanded the significance of "trademark". The Ivory soap of P&G (founded by England immigrant William · Procter and Ireland immigrant

James · Gamble) that came to market in 1879 is the outstanding representative in the stage of human brand generation.

Not only representatives of national brand images in USA, such as Uncle Sam, General Patton and Elvis Presley, main originators or reengineering leaders of multiple brands in America and Europe such as Ford Motor, IBM, Microsoft, News Corporation, GE, Hennessy and Jack Daniel are all of Celtic (Ireland, Scotland, Garand and Gaul) origin. They jointly created the earliest brand or the dominant brands in the world as immigrants or their descendants.

Celtic spirit of craftsmen plays an important role in brand incubation process in Europe development history, including processing and transaction of precious metals and jewelries, guidance and services provided to the upper class, ability to create advanced tools and professional ethics for seeking improvement continuously. The Celtics invented wagon with steering mechanism in the 1st Century B.C, and applied in large scale in the 15th Century. It is the prototype of modern auto manufacturing technology, the craftsmen in the Roman period are mainly Celtics, the inventor of improved steam engine is Watt, a Scotland blacksmith. The civilization and blood lineage urged America and Europe to become centralized incubation, generation and manufacture center of modern brands.

From the 19th Century, the large-scale Celtic civilization revitalization started in a large scale, which promoted diversified expression ways of modern brand arts such as literature, design, movie, opera, music and games, and hence created modern civilization centers such as the Hollywood. For large amount of current artistic forms such as TV, the major popular elements in plot design, film making and film music are derived from Celtic civilization, mainly Ireland's and Scotland's civilization. For instance, Georges Melies, a descendant of Celtic magician, created imaginary films, built virtual imaginary world for future science fiction, illusion and fantasy, and drove development of virtual civilization brand.

Over half of the international brands in the world are incubated, multiplied and finally generated from Celtic civilization. So far, the international brands in human history are divided into three brand waves, the important peak periods of centralized incubation and generation. The first international brand wave occurred in the industrial revolution period in the 19th century, the second is around 1921 and the third is after 1975. "Creating dream and perfecting pursuit" is directly related to centralized incubation and generation of international brands, and inheritance of large amount of brand ideas in Celtic civilization.

Through studies on origins of international brand incubation and generation, we found out that the creation of international brands does not occur accidentally. They are intensively incubated and generated by specific human civilization genes and specific ideas in specific human development periods. With human brands being incubated intensively from Celtic civilization, brand effect was developed rapidly all over the world, and affected other civilization entities to conceive brands intensively. International brands may be intensively conceived and generated in one country under three circumstances: firstly, countries, investment, banks and fair competition order are established around new ideas; secondly, links providing products and services to the upper class such as royal family, noblemen and upstarts have not been interrupted due to turbulence; thirdly, in countries and regions with especially strong national spirits, brand is the direct embodiment of national spirits.

3.3 Historical course of human brand development

The first batch of early brands were incubated and generated massively in the 19th century. From the industrial revolution, industrialization produced many household goods by intensive factory production. Factories made more commodities in large scale. The sales managers of factories find that the consumption habit of being only familiar with local products should be changed. In order to win the broader market, products could not only be competing with local products, they must sell to more countries and regions.

People soon found out that in order to convince large number of nondomestic public to trust their products, products should be packaged and transported, and accurately recognized so that the nondomestic public can recognize the advantages of their products. Therefore, the initial "brand-oriented development" occurred. Looking back at the brand creation history of P&G's brand, "Ivory soap", the history in the 19th Century can be restored. At that time, the brand image of P&G has already appeared and continued up to now.

A British beer brewery claimed that their red triangle brand is the first trademark in the world. The Lyle's syrup has used similar claim, and was rewarded as "the Oldest Brand of UK". Its green and gold package has been the same since 1885. Another theory says that brand is from Italy. The stamp or image carved with the same prototype mark appeared in St. Peter's in Vatican City since 1731.

Pears soap, Campbell soap, Coca Cola, juicy fruit gum, and Quaker Oats were the first batch of brands. They have strived to improve the cognition of consumers on the advantages of their "brands". At that time, people started to have in-depth understanding of brands.

Around 1900, James Walter Thompson released advertising of real estate and explained the advertising mode of trademark. Coca Cola also realized canning at that time and started production in different plants. People started recognizing "brands". Enterprises may promote in the early ratio station and TV by slogan, poster, mascot and jingles. By 1940s, manufacturers further realized they were developing mutual brand relation with consumers, and existing by sociology, psychology and anthropology.

Manufacturers soon learned to build their identifying features such as "brand" identity and characteristics, such as youth, happiness or luxury. The "brand-oriented" development started officially, and people started getting used to buying "brands" rather than products. Around the Second World War, emerging brands were created in each country, especially America. The brands focused on the theme of "patriotism", and brand theory developed rapidly. At that time, brands became economic dominators gradually in each country.

The trend was continued till 1980s. Large amount of brand theories, such as brand value and brand assets, emerged. People have already known assets value of brands. In 1988, Philip Morris bought Kraft at a price that is six times of its value. What they truly bought is its brand name.

In the 21st Century, the incomes of consumer rise greatly. Consumers in the 21st Century pay more attention to brand. Brands become the hot spot for economic growth in each country, and the consistent competitive focus of global enterprises. The countries all over the world in the 21st Century have entered comprehensive and in-depth brand process. Enterprises are transitioning toward brand organization, and unbranded commodities are squeezed out from global market rapidly.

4 Development of brand science

Brand science was not a complete subject earlier mainly because brand is a basic subject of human being, it cannot become the important subject in human knowledge field officially without systematic scientific research or before formation of systematic theory.

Basic science subjects of human being:

Medicine: comprised of clinical medicine, pathology, pharmacology and evidence-based medicine

Chemistry: comprised of chemical elements, chemical equation, and chemical reaction

Physics: comprised of physical experiment, Newton's mechanics, theory of relativity and quantum mechanics

Biology: comprised of biosystematics, embryology, cytology, and genomics

Mature basic subjects are generally in the stage of studying essence of things and scientific laws.

Brand science still lacks basic science theories, research spirits and sufficient professional scientific researchers so that the actual application of brand science actually focused on business form earlier. For

Section II Brand Subjects

instance, the theoretical application such as brand public relations, brand communication and brand planning lacks systematic in-depth research on brand principles, brand organization, brand history and brand quality. Therefore, the stage of current brand science development is at the stage of "brand phenomenon and brand awareness".

4.1 Brief formation history of brand science - pre-stage of brand science

Prehistory: formation stage of brand civilization gene

Before the 1st Century: stage of brand idea formation

Before the 11th Century: stage of brand prototype

Before the 18th Century: stage of brand form

Before 1870: stage of brand attitudes

1870-1900: Mainly individual producers owning own brand of consumer goods

1915-1928: Highlight brand publicity in advertising; provide new management method, i.e. brand is managed by functional department

1930-1945: Brand Manager and brand management system appeared (Neil McElroy, 1931)

1950: O&M firstly proposed the concept of brand in 1950; Rosser Reeves (beginning of 1950s) proposed Unique Selling Proposition (USP)

1950-1960: many enterprises, especially consumer product enterprises, started implementing brand management system, and the status and role of brand loyalty, brand management and brand marketing rebuilt in marketing were shown sufficiently. Some scholars started studying brand management theories (Burleigh B. Gardner and Sidney J. levy, 1955)

1960-1980: Brand manager system prevailed globally

After 1960: Manfred Bruhn proposed theory of brand life cycle

1969: Jack Trout proposed brand positioning

1980s- Early 1990s: brand integration appeared, brand assets prevailed (David A. Aaker, 1991)

Since 1990s: Brand strategies and brand management became the important new field of company strategy and management, and many books and operable approaches emerged around how to manage brand, such as:

—— "360 brand" theoretical model proposed by O&M;

——"The global branding" proposed by Sarge;

—— "Brand communication" proposed by Dentsu;

—— "Brand wheel" proposed by Ted Bates;

—— "Total branding" proposed by JWT;

—— "Brand iceberg" theories and ideas proposed by Davidson;

—— The "brand cluster" concept for single enterprise brand system proposed by David A. Aaker firstly introduced the concept of cluster in ecology to the study on brand theory, and pointed out that this is a brand new angle for brand cognition; he further proposed new management method of "brand leadership" in 2000.

——Agnieszka Winkler proposed the new concept of brand ecology, and pointed out brand ecology is a complex, vigorous and ever-changing organic organization.

4.2 From brand manager to brand organization

The important milestone for formation and development of human brand science is the development from "brand manager time" in business activities to "brand organization time". This is an important change of people from pursuing business development target progress to setting up brand ecological organization form with modern social network as operating basis. Brands step forward to a further future by the form of ecological organization.

Main characteristics in brand manager time:

(1) Enterprises allocate a brand manager with highly organization ability to every sub-brand it governs;

(2) Brand managers will take full responsibilities for product development, sales and profits of the brand;

(3) The brand manager shall uniformly coordinate product development department, production department and sales department, and take charge of all aspects of products affected by brand management and the entire process. So far, the operation of business circles makes brand theory generate great business economic and social demands.

Main characteristics in brand organization time:

(1) Brand exists by the form of ecological organization and is of constancy; brand shall face the future rather than the past or present;

(2) The purpose of branding is to provide products and services that are deemed more perfect to human beings and improve on people's lives.

(3) By implementing "brand +management recreation", brands aim to improve efficient and agile operation of the entire brand organization.

(4) Acquire optimal products, optical services and optical management by scientific experiment methods;

(5) The purpose of brand management is to finish efficient and self-adaptive movement of brand organization;

(6) Stable and balanced management order is the guarantee to long-lasting brand organization foundation;

(7) Brand concerns all the staffs, all staffs should participate in brand contribution, and acquire fair return (such as payment, promotion and share options) during contribution process;

(8) Brand management starts from management occupation, pursues professional management, and focuses on next generation agile management and intelligent services;

(9) Brand learning is the assurance for progress of brand organization management; the brand officer must master overall brand design and branding;

(10) A thorough brand recreation must be done at every interval.

5 Digging brand from history

All brands have its origin or source. But not the origin of every brand is from a new name. A major source is to seek once again from history, define brand origin, emphasize historical inheritance of brand and grant new significance to brand.

The Olympic Games is a typical example. Originated from the games in 776B.C, it was held every four years in Olympic, the games aim for peace and respect of Olympic Gods (Zeus and other Gods in Ancient Greek Mythology). The most important event every year among all cities is the great games in Greek. Those games contain Olympic Games, Opicia Games, Nemea Games and Isthmia Games. The four games, led by Olympic Games, were respectively held in four places. In that way, a four period was formed, known as Olympiad.

The ancient Olympic Games started from 776B.C and ended in 394A.D, there were a total of 293 games held in 1170 years. In 394A.D, the Olympic Games were prohibited by Theodosius I, the King of Rome.

On June 23, 1894, Coubertin, the founder of modern Olympics, decided to set up IOC (International Olympic Committee) with 79 representatives from 12 countries. This feat was once satirized by people. However, over a hundred years later, today Olympic Games have become the festivals of the whole world, and have attracted 202 countries and regions to participate in.

Brand origin is of historic characteristics: every brand organization has its origin to restore the story of creation. People always deem brand as a kind of token, similar to totem in early stage. In other words, both totem and brands are physical mark or symbol of human social organization concepts. Their basic forms are combination of name, pattern, color, spirits and significance.

During development of modern brand, brand is also a totem of a brand organization -- token, and meanwhile the perfect interpretation and expression of spirits and connotation. The main brand origins are usually names of historical figures (legend, objects and events) or founders, or the expectations of founders for brands. Naming and historical sources of some typical brands:

For instance, Nike is named after the goddess of victory in Greek mythology, and symbolizes flying in whirlwind.

"Yahoo!" is originated from a savage named Yahoo in the book "Gulliver's Travels". It represents a disgusting guy in appearance and behavior, who cannot be even considered as a person.

Georges L. Vuitton, the son of Louis Vuitton, inherited the family tradition of ingenuity. In 1896, he printed the well-known "LV" trademark, and from then on Louis Vuitton started integrating to ideas and social life of people as symbol of brand.

It is the most delightful thing for human to discover the history of brand origin during branding process. Therefore, many new brands are generated from ancient myths, historical events, historical records, archaeological notes, or many movies and bestsellers such as the Star Wars, Harry Potter and the Lord of the Rings so as to grant meaningful origin to brands.

6 History of international brands

The files of international brand history have become an important historical heritage of human beings, and also an important link for modern brands communication in multimedia and new media. In 2008 when the Federal Government of the United States announced the shabby garage where HP started business in 1939 as National Historic Site, the old and simple wooden "separated garage hailed" as the origin of Silicon Valley is only 30m^2, and attracted over 40000 tourists to seek for venture spirits of the Silicon Valley annually. Some simple tools, including one workbench, one set of vice, one drilling machine, one screw driver, one file, one soldering iron, one hacksaw and some elements bought outside, accomplished HP.

Every brand organization is trying to show its brand history, and express the history in-depth by using the development history either in the past or in the future so as to offer historical expression structure with image, awareness, story and legends to the public. Those brand histories have become inseparable parts of civilization course of human beings. Besides, as human brand varieties and quantities increase, and historical value shows, the history of every international brand is not only the previous memory in human history and national history, but also the story and traces recorded, told and continued by media or passed by people through words of mouth.

The most popular is the variance history of brand LOGO. People know the profound history of certain brand by the change of LOGO. For instance, the mark of BMW is evolved to five stages, respectively in 1917: creation of BMW mark; in 1933: more stable and noble mark; in 1953 (or 1954):

young mark; 1979: mark with more sense of technology; in 2007: modern mark of BMW. LOGO of Apple also has gone through multiple changes in 1976, 1977, 1998, 2001 and 2007.

The variation history of slogan for Coca Cola went through dozens of transitions during 1886-2012. In 1886: Drink Coca-Cola and enjoy it; 1904: fresh, delicious, satisfied – it is Coca-Cola; 1906: the great national temperance beverage; 1907: Coca-cola – bring energy and vitality; 1908: Good till the last drop... 1976: Coke adds life; 1980: Have a Coke and a smile; 1982: Coke is it!... 2007: The Coke side of life; 2011: Coke Real Taste.

The brand organization will express history of brand from origin to development and meanwhile provide brand discovering elements for further branding by multiple forms such as museum, exhibition hall, chronicle, milestone and electronic albums.

6.1 Brand named after founder

Some brands are named after founders, as beginning and origin of a series of international brand history, such as:

Adidas is the name of the founder; Toyota is named after its founder Sakichi Toyoda, who created the company in early 1930s.

Burroughs Wellcome, a large-scale pharmaceutical company is named after the names of the co-founders of Silas Burroughs and Henry Wellcome.

Antoine de la Mothe Cadillac, the French explorer and colonialist founded colony Detroit in 1701. In order to memorize those founders or creators, their names are used to be the name of brewery, motorcycle and event hotdog booths.

Nathan's Famous is the brand of hotdog named after the state founder. It is founded with USD 15 in 1913 in Coney Island. Through over 50 years' operation, it has grown to a chain worth of millions of USD. From 1850, Milwaukee beer is named after the name of its owner.

Walter Disney, a founder of tradition, used his name for the company he founded, and sold products by the name of figures created – Mickey Mouse, Donald Duck and other animals in the zoo. Brands are granted with new origin, not only from figures or places in the real world.

6.2 Personalization of brand history

The brand inheritance cannot be separated. Otherwise, brand will not be integrated. Thus, brand organizations strive to discover and spread stories about brand origin to emphasize the historical significance and initial rising of brands.

Due to a mysterious formula never released, a simple soda becomes the mysterious "Coca Cola"; due to the elegance and hard work of Ms. Chanel, Chanel becomes a synonym for "dignity and independence"; Pierre Cardin, a apprentice in small tailor store due to poverty, set up the inspirational color for "endeavor"; due to the bad temper and arbitrary of Jobs, the youths pursuing personality and fashion automatically become "iFans".

The origin stories are spread by movie, literature, videos, novels and biography, and make personalized charm for brand inheritance. By blurring boundary of stories, combing point between the story and people, spirits and interesting in the real world can be found. People can have more direct understanding of brands only by ingenious combination between brand and people, brand and objects or brand and an organization.

The investment story design about brand origin plays an important role in IPO process of modern enterprises. The investment story tells brand concept, business mode and logic of the Company, and is the potential and highlight for development vividly shown to investors. It greatly influences acceptance degree and share price in capital market.

Section II Brand Subjects

7 Future brands – history of upcoming future brand

Brands not only tell history in the past, but also, more importantly, explain future history, which may become the future. The ambitious brand organizations always express brand future by showing the future simulation view, scene and blueprint, while the composition or description of brand prospects is the imagination science developed by human beings to future brand history.

The ambitious brand founder will strive to depict the future and make the brand cooler, more active and have more expectable prospect so as to attract brand clusters to participate in future brand conception. In that way, the expectant target brand receivers can be formed to jointly create future brand history.

Since international brands always wish to be even better and wish users to pay more bills, the customer groups required by the brand are ideal groups. Brand premium is generated based on ideals. At foundation, the problem to be solved by overall design ideas is what is the idea and wish of people, what is their largest expectation. In specific practices, brand organization will establish "ideal model" – rational future ideas.

For example, fashion brand will depict "what is real woman"; theme parks will conceive "what is the entertainment dreamed by people"; luxury autos will consider "how to reflect identities of people"; consumer electronics will design "what is the future popular fashion".

Brand organization will separate "real life" and "ideal model", and ceaselessly suggest or encourage brand users and public to recognize products by ideal work or life mode, and even simulate future blueprint of brand by digital technology, documentary and advertising pictures and tell brand users group to follow future steps. Some brands have acquired great success, for instance the "Speed of Thought" of Bills Gates and planning of Walt Disney for the Disney Land.

Modern brand will develop towards more popular and advancing future. The popular science fiction, fantasy and fairy tales, animation and games make youth from generation to generation focus on brand experience of virtual reality. Therefore, "virtual reality" becomes the brand future that brand organization shall spare no effort to depict, i.e. for future brand history; everyone has a dream, and is looking forward to the future. The brand combining future with dream and expectation of everyone will have broader future.

Some brand organizations believe brand should be a kind of future expression method, carrying out science fiction by virtual reality, emphasizing brand impression recognition and thus creating considerable brand income and margin income. For instance, Marvel created distinct marks of Captain America, the Mighty Thor, and Agents of SHIELD. "Transformers", "RoboCop" and "Superman", it strengthened transmitting identified brand impression by emphasizing identification repeatedly.

Exercises

1. Fill in the blanks: Brands have characteristics of _____, _____, _____, _____, _____, _____

2. True or False Question: "identification" is not the true development method of brand, and trademark is only to finish a property right delimitation relationship of "graphic or name label" in the legal sense. Beyond that, it has no element and significance of any brand. (   )

3. Discussion: How to understand the origin of brand history

Chapter 2

Brand Principles

Brand principles is a subject studying interaction and scientific laws of brand and global competition, brand economy, brand strategy, consumer and enterprise management mode, specifically cause of brand, brand recognition, consumption mechanism, development characteristics and various regular changes during management process. The subject of brand principles requires seeking and finding various scientific rules of brand behind various phenomena of brand economy, and refining, designing and applying the scientific rules.

1 Brand principles and brand management improvement

Branding is a complex economic phenomenon and management process, and may change under mutual function of global competition, consumer reaction and management method. The researches and explorations of scientific rules of brand science became the basic theories for brand problems. See through the appearance to perceive the essence. The in-depth research of scientific nature behind brand phenomena can provide necessary preconditions for people to get familiar with brands, development brands and prevent brand management errors.

Although many branches of brand science have come into being, and many brand theories are formed, it is the necessary stage of worldwide brand science development to study brand development rules and define basic theoretical structure of brands. The subject of brand principles studies the variation rules and characteristics behind brand phenomenon, and provides systematic theoretical foundation for scientific practices of brands.

The nature of any study on management is a fault-preventing design, i.e. design management process by summarizing complex management phenomena to prevent from any possible fault. It is irresponsible to directly assign management practice tasks to managers or employees. The quality of management is different and management result cannot be assured without management study as foundation and principles as basis. Brand management also faces the essential subject breakthrough problem.

The brand principles and function of brand management practice are of strict cause-and-effect relationship. On the one hand, brand principles are used to guide basic brand management; on the other hand, the subject summarizes scientific rules in brand practice, forms corresponding brand science principles, and combines academic research and scientific practices to deeply push development of brand science. This is the objective requirement for enterprise management improvement, and further for human progress.

1.1 Scientific authority status of brand principles

The subject of brand principles plays unique role in fundamental research of brand science, and exerts core authorized guiding function in development of the entire brand science. As scientific rules, the brand principles are the essences behind brand phenomenon. Any economic phenomenon apart from scientific rules cannot be scientific. The variables of manmade factors will generate any arbitrary changes in brand rising, cultivation, construction and development, leading to failure of brand investment. The individual successful cases cannot replace the knowledge value of scientific rules.

SECTION II BRAND SUBJECTS

During scientific diagnosis, scientific research, scientific design and scientific implementation process for brands, the subject of brand principles plays the leading role. Brand principles are the summary of scientific rules, and can accurately answer multiple causes and crux of various brand problems. The subject can not only meet requirements of large amount of brands cultivated in one country or region, but also play obvious economic effect for creation and recreation of enterprise brands. Through ceaseless findings and research explorations on symptoms, characteristics and new phenomena of various brand problems, brand principles is the ecological subject which can finally diagnose and explain brand phenomena in a scientific way.

The confirmation of brand principles is the most rudimental, basic and important reform in development of human brands. The subject of brand principles is an open research and invention procedure with open sources. It expands by brand tree, ceaselessly summarizes various scientific rules in brand practice process and continuously attracts the latest research findings concerning brand principles all over the world so that all theories and practices with regard to brand, including theoretical research and scientific practice, brand cultivation, brand construction, brand management, brand quality, brand measurement and brand indexes can be changed fundamentally.

It should be reminded that, the entire brand science based on brand principles cannot be studied under a specific national background of one country. The study on brand science must be global and borderless. The brand science is universal, depended on the global market competition that brands participate in. The borderless study without difference is an important factor for brand science to truly acquire progress and generate profound influence worldwide. All theories from brand principles to the entire brand science shall not only adapt to developed countries such as USA and Britain, but also adapt to developing countries such as China, India and South Africa. It is unscientific to study brand phenomenon in one country or one region, and effective progress of brand economy in the country or region will be hindered. The brand problem in any country can be studied by individual cases of certain country, belonging to country branch of brand science.

1.2 Methodology of brand principles

We must set up a most fundamental trunk for development of the entire brand science, while the trunk is brand principles necessarily. Various professional brand subject and professional fields of brand technology such as brand strategy, brand organization, brand quality, brand construction technology and brand communication technology will be developed based on brand principles. The structure of entire brand science is studied on that basis to realize the essential leap of brand science development. The steps of study on brand principles are as follows:

The first step is to set up the brand principle tree, i.e. tree diagram of brand principles. Scientific research on brand science is carried out by tree diagram to ceaselessly generate new research branches, and confirm new brand principles. The brand tree is the foundation for scientific development of brands. When treating various brand principles equally and respecting varieties of brand research findings, any new study can extend branches from brand tree. Any brand science theory can be shown in the brand tree. The study in any field can be branched from the brand tree so as to respect research value and avoid repeated brand study. Various types of brand study activities are centralized intensively to accelerate integrated development speed of brand science.

The second step is to set up the brand terminology, concept of brand theory and model of brand science. The basic terminology structure is established by confirming relevant brand terminology. The terminology shall be explained by scientific explanation and sufficient consideration of the perspective of brand science. The historical explanation in the past may not be new, if the explanation of brand terminology is outdated. Any person can propose new terminology. The terminologies with objection shall be approved and confirmed by academic discussion in batches. Global researchers are encouraged to propose various new concepts of brand theory and scientific model. Theories and models shall meet the basic requirements of scientific rules. The increase of terminology, theory and model can be searched and confirmed by PADS scientific analysis model.

The third step is to scientifically summarize brand practices. The scientific summary and correction during brand practice are important. By extensive application of brand tree proposed in early stage, the practical problems in many brand applications can be collected and analyzed dynamically so as to find new brand scientific laws. The brand tree will surely extend ceaselessly and rapidly based on summary, design and refinery of those new rules. Brand economy entity and enterprise brand practice will have more scientific laws to follow, and acquire more extensive promotion and use. The most important principle that the study on brand principle should follow is to greatly improve brand management level and brand premium ability.

It's necessary to note that cases are not the most important thing in structure of new brand science. Even brand science, in essence, separates from any case collection and case study. The individual cases will not be used as research methods of brand science because they may hinder scientific progress of brand science study. The emerging brand science must strictly focus on the new height of "brand principles – brand science development and brand technology development". It is the correct way to carry out science-based academic studies and practices so as to decode brand phenomenon and scientifically develop brands. With principles of brand science as a research basis, the practical cases of enterprises are carried out independently on the development process of brand science, while various cases are actually derived from brand principles, brand science and brand technology.

2 Brand principle tree

Brand principle tree is the core method to develop basic principle and theoretical structure of brand by form of tree diagram. Currently, the preliminary brand tree contains basic brand principles of B theory, brand construction CBA stage, ternary brand relation, golden triangle of brand profit, brand development mode, and arrow law. The example of brand principle tree is shown in Fig. 1-1.

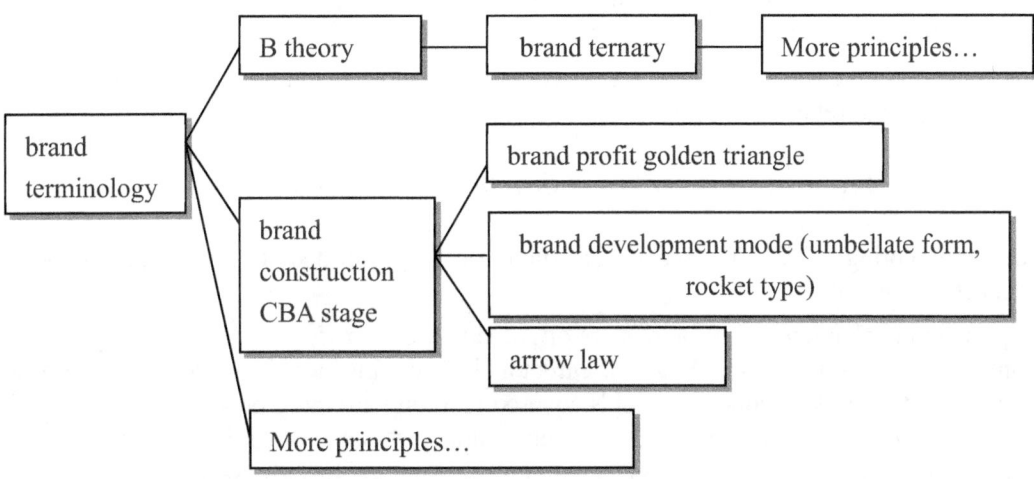

Fig. 1-1 Brand principle tree (Version 1.0)

The brand principle tree is made of open sources, and expandable. Any person can ceaselessly get a new study branch, and add new brand principles, thus upgrading it from version 1.0.

3 Brand ability ranking

The method of brand ability ranking is the ranking system implemented in the enterprise brand development. Brands are divided into Grade C (primary), Grade B (exploring) and Grade A (strategic), and stages of every global brand are defined every year.

SECTION II BRAND SUBJECTS

The ranking for Grade C, B and A brand ability is also applied in the formulation, acceptance and appraisal of brand construction plan. Grade B is subdivided into Grade B-2 (improvement) and B-1 (progress), and Grade A is subdivided into Grade A-2 recommended (or highly used) and A-1 high quality.

Brand ability grading system can be extensively applied to the comprehensive ranking of global brand construction, brand development and brand ability.

3.1 Brand development level ranking –Grade C (primary)

Grade C (primary): Brand awareness stage, primary stage, the most original status of brand

Enterprise brand characteristics: brand ideas are chaotic without brand strategy, and brand management is arbitrary and inconsistent. Enterprises are confused about their brand development. The businesses operated by enterprises are various and complex. Although some brand management methods are formulated, the brands are unordered and without executive power. They never implement brand technology, and rarely set specialized posts and departments for brands. The functional authority of brand is low.

Characteristics of brand investment: the loan and financial ability of brand is weak, and investors are reluctant to invest.

Public recognition of brand: consumers are unable to recognize the brand. People do not know the prospect of the brand, do not trust the brand and do not know how to distinguish this brand from similar competitors. The customer development cost is very high. Enterprises need to spend large amount of money in order to convince people. However, people are still unwilling to buy. The business closing rate is low.

Brand consumption characteristics: customer transfer cost is extremely low. In most circumstances, consumers make choice after comparing similar brands. Although there are some impulsive buyers, they will disappear soon and never come back again.

Brand transmission characteristics: enterprises never carry out brand transmission and promotion, and rarely release brand related news.

3.2 Brand development level ranking - Grade B (development)

Grade B (exploring): this is the brand construction stage, intermediate stage when brand seems mature, but actually is not

Enterprise brand characteristics: brands are oriented to a certain degree. Enterprises participate in market competition by varieties. The Board of Directors believes business is depended on varieties and quantity, covering the market scope. The fields covered by brand are more present. For the varieties of competitors, enterprises believe they must develop similar products and join the competition. The businesses are involved in multiple aspects, but not specialized. Single variety has no powerful competitiveness, and may be accused of abusing advantageous status to monopolize and restrict market development. Enterprises have formulated preliminary brand strategy, formed brand management document system to a certain sense, hired brand counselors and allocated professional personnel such as brand director. The functional powers of brand are higher.

Characteristics of brand investment: investment is a short-term profit-gaining behavior. Generally, it is led by speculating investors. Investors are concerned about business mode, market scale potential and enterprise growth speed. They easily acquire investment and financing. Investors generally exit in next round of investment or at listing. Some investors will carry out long-term strategic investment, but investment is still depended on business mode and profits.

Public recognition of brand: The market has not formed consistent opinions and impression on brand. People that approve enterprises are actively building brands, but they often understand brand in a wrong way. The brand image that enterprises want to form and the brand image usually in people's impression are different. Enterprises believe their brand construction may have problems, and try to improve. Therefore, the brand recognition often become chaotic again.

Brand consumption characteristics: The customer transfer cost is low; if market has other options, customer will be lost soon; for more similar brands, most customers will make comparison and selection. People still are unable to accurately distinguish the brand from other similar brands. They are sensitive to price, and closing rate is mainly depended on low price, discount and sales promotion.

Brand transmission characteristics: Brand public relation and advertising services are subcontracted to specialized PR and advertising companies. Enterprises still need to communicate about market, and try to avoid brand damage. Brand crisis public relation is highly valued.

3.3 Brand development level ranking – Grade A (developed)

Grade **A:** Brand recognition stage, high ability brand strategy stage when enterprises successfully develop to international brand and achieve global reach

Enterprise brand characteristics: Brand strategy is clear, brand recognition system is perfect, and information transmitted to public is appropriate and accurate. Concentrating on development of a single professional brand in each variety, every specific brand is independent, and has a sufficient leading status in one professional market; the brand can stably receive cash flow, and the advantageous status is hardly shaken by competitors. The brand functional authority reaches the highest level. Brand ability is quite mature, brand strategic method is deeply mastered, and can accessed easily access and can make achievements in any professional market. Unblocked in global market, and brand expansion ability and premium ability are strong. They never need discount or sales promotion, and price increase is the main market behavior of the brand.

Characteristics of brand investment: Investment is a long-term behavior, and generally led by strategic investors in one dream, one expectation, one spirit and one pursuit. The trademark (brand) is of asset value, and can acquire loan and investment at any time. Investors are generally unwilling to exit, and hold stock of the brand for a long term even if the company is listed. They share honor with brand, and the investment behavior is deemed as a kind of insight and the highest glory for investment achievements.

Public recognition of brand: In the aspect of certain specific consumption desire, the designated purchase rate of consumers is high. It repels other similar brands, and the public can rapidly and clearly recognize brand, and know why they need this brand. People approve the prospect of the brand, clarify the professional performance of the brand and understand the standpoint of the brand.

Brand consumption characteristics: Brand attracts the public rapidly. People spread the brand voluntarily and wish everyone around can consume that brand for a long time. They are willing to pay a higher price. Enterprises thus acquire enough large-scale profits, and customer transfer cost is extremely high. The regulars are fond of the brand for a lifetime.

Brand transmission characteristics: The brand highly values brand transmission, and lead the public to spread spontaneously. Some international brands with outstanding achievements have never released any advertising. Enterprises rarely have crisis PR, or never need crisis PR. If the brand is accused, consumers will voluntarily maintain the brand in groups. The brand forms a mature and stable self-balancing ecological system.

4 Brand profit golden triangle

The simple diagram for brand profit golden triangle can be seen in Fig. 2-1.

Section II Brand Subjects

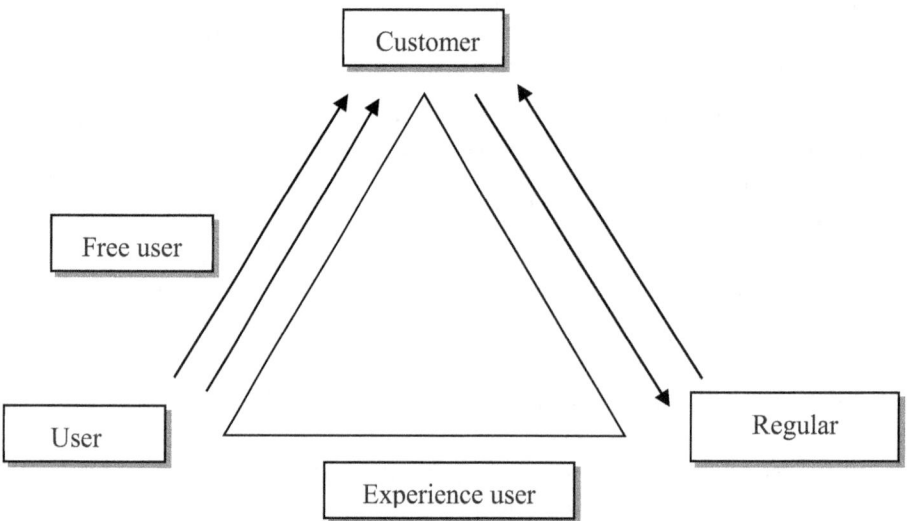

Fig. 2-1 Brand profit golden triangle

Brand profit golden triangle explains the transforming relationship between "users, customers and regulars", i.e. the source and long-term guarantee of brand profits. The long-term source of brand profits is reached by transforming "from users to customers, and then to regulars".

4.1 Main claims of brand profit golden triangle

(1) Primary task of brand is to increase quantity of brand customers (users)

In the beginning, brand has not added customers directly, and customers are generated from users according to certain proportion. In initial period of brand release, the quantity of first time payer is type of a rare resource. It is difficult to create a brand in the early stage and a large amount of interesting users and experienced user foundation are required.

(2) Brand customers (users) are comprised of free users and experienced users

Brand customers (users) contain free users and experienced users: free users refer to users without payment and fans (or people interested in), and paying customers will be generated from free users with certain proportion; experienced users refer to users with experienced activities and large amount of low payment, and customers will be generated from experienced users with certain proportion.

(3) Paying customers will be generated from brand users with certain proportion

The probability of first time paying customers generated from free users is about 1%~3%, and from experienced users is about 3%~5%. It is unnecessary to be concerned about the paying probability or strive to improve payment rate, certain proportion of brand users will be transferred to first time paying users. The early task of brand must be and shall always be to increase users greatly. Brand organization shall make first trust design. The insufficient user base will lead to failure of early brand development.

(4) Certain proportion of first paying customers may be transferred to regulars

The transformation proportion from customers to regulars is about 5%~10%. Brand service focuses on the transforming relation from customers to regulars. It is unscientific to spend large amount on advertising costs for aimlessly attracting target customers. Brand organization shall use more investments in providing the most excellent and ideal services to paying customers so as to accelerate proportion from first paying customers to regulars.

(5) The target of brand organization is not to make customer satisfied, but to realize completely ideal pleasure for customers

Brand organization shall strive for customer relation management of paying customers, and the services provided shall be ideal. The customer services shall be designed by "the most expected and most ideal way required by customers, and making customers regularly find supervises".

(6) The long-term core profit source of brand organization is "customers becoming regulars, and regulars recommending customers"

Only regulars who frequently pay can recommend paying customers to brand organizations, and recommendation is the most reliable source. The brand organization shall strive to transfer the first time paying customers to regulars. The long-term profit source mainly depends on "recommendations to customers by regulars". The regulars are the maximum profit guarantee of brand organization. The long-term development and high brand premium are generated by large amount of spontaneous recommendations of regulars.

4.2 Main applications of brand profit golden triangle

(1) Brand profit golden triangle is suitable for high-speed development of any brand and services

The brand manufacturers of outdoor products may need to set up outdoor organization (outdoor club) in the beginning to cultivate fans for mountain climbing, and then promote brands in suitable time; large amount of potential users may gather due to same interests, and jointly participate in research and manufacture process around the desired product; the company may develop interested experienced users by forms of "1USD experience card" or "10USD registration"; many network products may generate business mode for sustainable profits from large base numbers of free users; the early brand advertising and brand news can be intensively used to collect applicants for experienced activities.

(2) Brand service profit chain will generate high premium of brand

Brand organization shall focus on customer service design making customers more attracted and more pleased; establish user relation committee with the highest level, which is comprised of brand organization and user representative by 50%-50% proportion and strive to develop the most subtle user experience and user pleasant enjoyment; make customer service process of brands a funny and wonderful feeling process, so that customers can find various supervises, motivate energy of mutual influence, and sufficiently make use of psychology of "moving"; design efficient brand service profit chain, dig service potential, make every employee participate in active contribution during service process, and share service premium dividends; develop highly attractive service brand, and drive profit creation of service client by service branding project.

(3) Regulars plan is the key point for profits of brand organization

Brand organization shall strengthen the transforming efficiency from the first batch of first-time loyal customers to regulars; design a series of regular plans, such as VIP club; grow together with customers, and design a series of growth activities, such as reading club and growth club to share individual honors and family happiness, depict and spread stories in growth; design a group customer honor system to allow customers share honors; create the transmission of "happy family" brand value among regulars, and transmit the positive energy of love, caring and dedication to the society. Brand organization shall strive to be a responsible and respectable company.

5 Brand development model

During brand strategy design and brand practice process, brands will finally develop into two typical types - umbrella type and rocket type. See Fig. 6-5.

SECTION II BRAND SUBJECTS

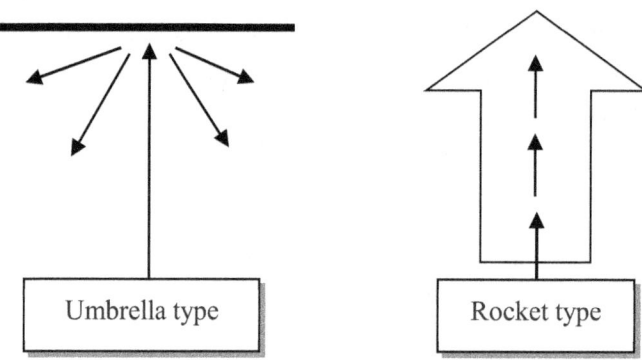

Fig. 6-5 Brand development model

Brand development model shows two typical types during brand development process, respectively umbrella type and rocket type. Brands with Grade C and Grade B ability develop under umbrella type and brands with Grade A ability develop under rocket type.

5.1 Umbrella type brand

For umbrella type brand, when carrying out strategic design or brand develops to certain degree (generally in Grade X and Y brand stage), brand rising channels are restricted, and brand varieties are expanded in a flatted way, deviated from main business and invading other market fields for diversified development. Brands may cover many different market fields such as fashion, transportation, IT, real estate and energy to achieve the purpose of development by sufficient brand market coverage.

Umbrella-type brands mainly develop by variety expansion. Main brands involve in multiple different market fields, and keep profit source of diversified market by unlimited brand extension. The umbrella-type brands may be caused by historical reasons, or maybe from strategic design of brand operators. However, the umbrella-type brands are formed due to limitation of strategic design, less prominent core competitiveness and insufficient market penetration depth. The medium-sized and small enterprises can meet market demands by providing different product varieties (models).

The advantage of umbrella-type brand is that it is easy to access new market relying on original brand influence, competitive advantage and market status, while the disadvantage is that main brand business is indistinct, and market recognition is chaotic. In future global competition, umbrella-type brands there will be less umbrella-type brands, they will finally disappear and get replaced by diversified investment groups and assets management consortiums.

5.2 Rocket type brand

For rocket-type brands, the main business has been designated clearly from the beginning of brand strategic design, and even dominant brands enter global market by single product. The rocket-type brands emphasize on highly consistent brand strategy, highly clear brand recognition, and strict conformance of brand development with high growth strategy, i.e. preparing step by step, breaking out in global market step by step, and maintaining the high speed expansion speed.

Rapid speed is the important characteristic of rocket-type brand. Brand may be the "fast company", and win with rapid market attacking ability. Brand strategy is strictly restricted to the owner, and separated from any non-owner, even from work and business of non-core departments. Instead, the professional outsourcing is adopted.

INTRODUCTION TO BRANDS

The rocket-type brand organization has powerful global market outbreak ability, always strengthened main business field, and forms more powerful strategic access ability and brand market coverage ability by "(1) purchasing other competitors, core technology research companies or business fields; or (2) forming close market alliance with similar competitors to jointly establish larger-scale companies and unify co-brand".

The rocket-type brand aims to rapidly develop into the most powerful brand in certain market, and occupy absolute advantageous competitive status. The rocket-type brand organization aims at single market, and may develop into brand cluster to occupy multiple subdivided professional market by different professional brands or products. Every single, distinct brand market will intensively centralize fields involved, and show high-strength market development ability in both scope and depth.

Rocket-type brand is the mainstream international brand development strategy in global market competition, and also the mainstream brand form for future global emerging brand development and centralized development for recreation of existing mature brands.

6 Arrow theory

The diagram of error theory can be seen in Fig. 6-2.

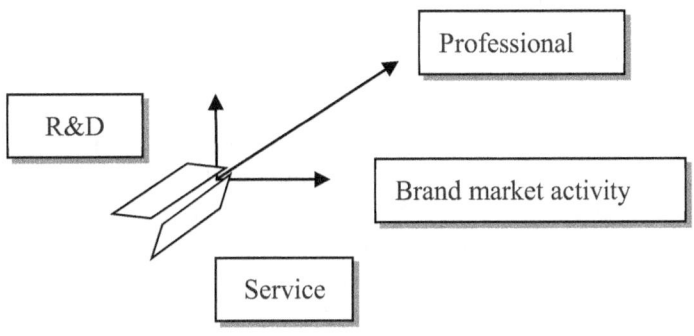

Fig. 6-2 Arrow theory

The arrow theory is a kind of typical mode for brand market access and brand operation, and also usually applied to brand organization development for venture and brand cluster type of emerging small enterprises.

6.1 Principles of arrow theory

Arrow has a history of over 30,000 years. The hominids used arrows in hunting during the upper Paleolithic Stage. Arrow is the most common weapon used in cold weapon time. Although the arrow tip is tiny, it has powerful advantages in remote attacks. Many famous military leaders have died of arrow injury. Modern rockets, submarines, bullets and missiles are created from the people's cognition of "arrow".

Arrow theory is of extensive application prospect in market, and is the simplest strategic market progress model.

Arrow is comprised of the arrow tip (accurate market orientation), arrow pole (R&D) and two end wings at the end (marketing and services). It is the most basic market unit combination, and also a basic typical market access step, specified as follows:

Step 1: mark arrow tip, and select accurate market target. The arrow tip refers to market target, i.e. selecting the most accurate professional market, such as face skin whitening, pimple treating, and eyes fatigue easing. One arrow tip can only solve one professional problem. The more accurate the target is, the stronger the market attack ability will be. It can avoid diversified market targets. The more targets of the same brand (or product), the more market competitors. Small enterprises or brand cluster enterprises can select one easy niche market with certain space, and rapidly occupy one market with professional operation, and maximally gain profits from that market.

Step 2: make arrow pole, research and develop independently and professionally. Arrow pole refers to the process of research and development. R&D shall be carried out independently. Before accessing any accurate market, the products shall be studied carefully and professionally to guarantee the absolute pertinence of products in market and avoid large and all-inclusive situation. In order to meet requirements for entering market rapidly, early R&D of completed products must guarantee not to be carried out simultaneously with marketing and services. Former brands failed mainly because R&D was carried out simultaneously with marketing and services so as to affect market access speed and cause serious dislocation of R&D from market. In particular, for first market access of new brand, R&D must be finished firstly so that the entire venture company can solely focus on marketing, and implement intensive market access. It is infeasible to carry out R&D and marketing of products simultaneously in early stages of market access.

Step 3: Direct wings in the aspect of marketing. After arrow tip and pole are finished, brand organization shall access market most rapidly, and accurately enter market target. Several marketing modes are optimal: intensive access, by intensively releasing advertising and large-scale market actions; direct and repeated marketing: lock the most accurate market customer groups, and carry out intensive and repeated marketing only targeting those market groups; efficient transmission: aiming at accurate target market, rapidly transmit and cover by brand transmission mode and occupy the market for the first time.

Step 4: Stabilize wings in the aspect of customer service. Marketing and services are a group of synchronous actions. After the intensive, high frequency and rapidly accessing marketing is carried out, services shall follow for the first time in order to finish rapid and high frequency consumer response. Marketing and services are synchronous. Rapid service response is the important guarantee to maintain market for the first time, strive for payment from customers and strengthen recommendation ability of customers. The asynchronous marketing and services will rapidly affect next market activities and cause distrust of market.

6.2 Power of brand arrow matrix

The arrow theory is, as a matter of fact, a rapid market access method designed on the basis of professional and rapid brand projects. It strips unnecessary market targets, market activities and excessive department designers and staff.

An arrow brand project is a rapid brand action which can rapidly acquire market profits, and also the optimal rapid investment mode in modern society. One arrow can rapidly finish rapid access and market stability of one professional market.

When brand organization decides to enter more market objects, it must copy the first arrow brand project after it is finished, and rapidly access the second and third professional market successively.

Different from former niche marketing, the arrow theory has strategic ideas, and particularly emphasizes on rapid segmentation of market, i.e. breaks down the original market combination form by establishing arrow-type brand, separate market with competition to new markets of different types and different combinations, and tries to access core profit market of the original market, finish early high-profit return requirements, and occupy core strategic market. On that basis, more brands projects will help the brand occupy one cutting-edge field in one market so as to expand the field.

The arrow theory is applied to combine different arrow-type brand projects. Multiple brand projects will comprise intensive and powerful arrow matrix, which has powerful impact ability to market. Moreover, every arrow-type brand project can operate, and create profits independently. The arrow matrix will finally make brand organization a powerful brand cluster.

INTRODUCTION TO BRANDS

Different brand projects can be named by different professional sub-brands, or independent product models with market impact force. The powerful brand action which applies the arrow theory is also a typical mode for brand recreation.

Exercises

1. Fill in the blanks: Brand profit golden triangle explains the transforming relationship between "_____, _____, _____", i.e. the source and long-term guarantee of brand profits. The long-term source of brand profits is by transforming "_____, _____".

2. True or False Question: the research methods of brand principles are: the first step is to set up brand principle tree; the second step is to set up brand terminology, concept of brand theory and model of brand science; the third step is to scientifically summarize brand practices. (   )

3. Essay Question: How to understand design of umbrella type and arrow type brand strategy?

Section II Brand Subjects

Chapter 3

Brand Pathology

Brand pathology is a new basic subject of brand science we have proposed. Brand principles, brand pathology and brand organizations are collectively known as three key basic subjects of brand science. Although governments and enterprises of all countries in the world deeply know the importance of brand development, the abnormal development of brand is universal among global enterprise brands. Occupations and enterprises such as brand officer, management analyzer, management consultant companies, management consulting companies and management software companies all engage in the work of brand pathology, but people have limited knowledge on brand development since brand pathology has not been officially proposed before. Insufficient understanding of scientific laws and abnormal development status regarding brand development leads to unfavorable development of most brands in the world. Brands with achievements are few, and failures are universal.

1 Proposition of brand pathology

Brand pathology is a professional branch of brand science studying the causes of brand diseases, occurrence mechanism, development rules and pathological state, and a key basic subject required by global development of brand science. The brand diseases and brand diagnosis facts, as well as great development of worldwide brand officer, management officer, management analyzer, and management consultant companies, management consulting companies and management software companies sufficiently show the universal brand development abnormalities. That also means brand pathology must be developed preferentially, and plays an irreplaceable role in the development of global brand science. It is decided by the nature and the tasks of brand pathology.

The human medicine has gradually evolved to modern medicine by the development route of "patient –curer – disease – pharmacology – clinical – discipline - health". Human diseases are usually appreciable. Thus, the professional knowledge of curers and the study of developing medical science, pathology and pharmacology are necessary. People know clearly when their body felt uncomfortable, the diseases will be treated by self-inquiring, inquiring kinships or consulting the doctors. Besides, in the belief of doctors, they clarified the mission and responsibility of "being responsible for life and health of patients" earlier.

However, brand diseases have not been valued during development process, and the "invisible diseases" cannot be shown in specific form, such as pain. Thus, non-professional personnel cannot see through brand diseases clearly and discover them in the early stage. People still fail to realize the hazards brought by brand diseases to enterprises until the occurrence of serious development loopholes, huge brand assets wastes and incontrollable serious management, or even the closure of enterprises. Such "invisible" attributes have greatly increased the abnormal development status and the uncontrollable enterprise management risks. The most direct embodiment is venture failure rate and brand closure speed. The essence is that objective fact of brand pathology decides the economic results and failure facts.

1.1 Proposition of brand pathology

Brand pathology is the important innovative requirements made for global brand science development, and the subject development foundation for comprehensive study integrating brand abnormal status, brand disease naming, common brand disease screening, brand epidemic disease study, brand disease occurrence mechanism and brand diagnosis according to scientific laws of brand development.

The brand pathology is proposed based on four development mechanisms: (1) brand pathology serves for healthy development of enterprise brand; (2) the in-depth development foundation of brand pathology is the scientific practices of enterprise management; (3) the development task of brand pathology is to discover and prevent abnormal problems in brand development; and (4) brand pathology is developed based on highly developed scientific research and analysis.

Brand pathology provides service to brand health of enterprises. "Disease" and "health" are the two corresponding themes for brand development. The development attribute of brands emphasizes that brand diseases of enterprises are generally shown by various symptoms. The pathogenesis and lesion usually do not affect local management problems of enterprises. The lesion complexity, integrity and impact degree are more complex than human diseases, while the treatment using overall diagnosis and reform are relatively complex. Therefore, treatment suggestions are generally offered. The overall development requirement is to solve healthy development problems of enterprise brand, and list "health" as overall development task of brand pathology.

With development of brand science, especially as the role of brand economy in human economic development activities becomes more important, the highly developed brand science should comprise of many specially developed professional branch subjects. The common target and task of the professional brand subjects is to assure healthy development of enterprise brand from different angles, different specialized standpoints and different technical means. The professional property of each brand subject requires that the overall brand science development characteristics should be brand science department. In the future, global enterprise development must be weighted and ranked by the order of "future studies, brand science and management science", while brand science will be attached with more importance than management science, and become the highly consistent "governing" science of enterprises.

The in-depth development of brand pathology is the highly unified development proposition of brands necessarily, and management activities such as study, analysis, diagnosis, reorganization and recreation based on management science. The task of brand pathology is to prevent abnormal development of brands, management errors and uncontrollable management, actually solve site problems of management and improve scientific decision making level.

Brand pathology is developed based on systematic brand science development including scientific observation, analysis, discrimination, summary, refining and solutions. It is the result of comprehensive development that integrated careful study, systematical analysis and scientific summary, and is the systematical science which will systematically diagnose problems of brands, practically solving problems of brands, scientifically adjusting brand development structure and overall designing brand development methods. Powerful brand science study ability, scientific analysis level and brand practice guidance capability are required to set up brand pathology. Therefore, the management scientists, management analyzers and brand officers shall finish the specific study, and benefit all new business founders, brand founders, entrepreneurs, brand officers and each level of management personnel by popularization and professional diagnosis development method.

1.2 Development principles of brand pathology

One important principle in development of brand ideas is the "lancet principle", i.e. brand diagnosis, brand recreation and brand consulting project shall take responsibility for the health of enterprise brand, and treat the diagnosis, operation, reorganization and consulting of enterprise brand like life. The main operator of brand must learn brand science contents for certain time and reach certain standard of brand level; own certain cases of brand project operation and diagnosis, and has overall design experiences. The precise process is the most fundamental for the development of future brand science – responsible attitude and cognition.

SECTION II BRAND SUBJECTS

The "lancet principle" in brand ideas is also the scientific requirement proposed for development of brand pathology. The occurrence of brand diseases is a complex development process of abnormal lesion. The "invisible" attributes of brand diseases caused non-professional brand researchers such as brand founders, business founders, entrepreneurs and management consultants to fail in recognizing abnormal brand development status rapidly and accurately. The brand diseases will in-depth make brand organization generate various lesions, make the reaction mechanism of brand organization generate various mutual changes, and finally show various symptoms, such as shaking the brand organization, brand development without directions and delayed of brand services. The most common symptom is the criticism made by brand users on internet we media to a brand, especially users' complaints, which are the most direct reflection of brand diseases, showing certain link of a brand is ill.

The development principle of brand pathology is an important decision made to officially include brand pathology to a cutting-edge scientific study field, and together with professional methods and specialized technologies to research and develop. The tasks of brand pathology are to use scientific brand development rules such as brand designs, brand principles and brand organizations to classify symptoms and name diseases for various abnormal status during brand development, and confirm pathogenesis, lesion influence and treatment suggestions. Different from pathology development in the sense of medicine which is a study process of "etiology -pathogenesis-lesion", brand pathology is a kind of discipline never before. The subject is proposed to carry out reversal study from classifying and naming epidemic brand disease status which is common or outbursts periodically and spreads. Only when large amount of brand disease symptom characteristics and names of diseases in abnormal brand development are summarized and confirmed, the influence of brand disease occurrence mechanism and lesion on each brand development link in each department can be studies systematically, and scientific treatment suggestions can be proposed. It is the direction and scientific guide on complex and systematic operating treatment, and technical system.

2 Importance of brand pathology

Brand disease is the main factor deeply disturbing the healthy development of global enterprise brands, including insufficient cognition of brand diseases, unobvious presentation of brand diseases and nonscientific brand diagnosis.

People have limited knowledge about brand disease. Only minority of scholars judge abnormal status of enterprise development by the diseases of those enterprises. The suggestions on medical diagnosis, treatment and unhealthy status have not been introduced to brand science and management science, hence, people can neither make accurate judgment for mechanism of brand disease occurrence, nor consider a serious of influence of brand disease in management in each department and each link. Under most circumstances, people fail to find, analyze and systematically solve these management problems from the angle of scientific management. Instead, the endless enterprise management problems are always ascribed to "manmade factor", "individual problem", "individual case treatment" or certain phenomenon, or neglected. The scientific management degree of global enterprises is quite low.

Such cognition directly causes people to understand pathogenesis of brand diseases unclearly. Enterprises are ill, but the specific symptom, disease origin and development cannot be described accurately, and accurate pathogenesis and lesion influence cannot be discovered. Whether the brand diseases are acute, chronic, or relapsed or shown as certain management barrier, corresponding judgment error, distorted information transmission, wrong brand decision will occur. Various management problems occurred frequently everyday deeply depress and restrict enterprise development, but often are neglected.

Due to the lack of necessary study on the names of brand diseases, diagnosis and classification, brand diseases are shown insufficiently and vaguely. Enterprises do not know their disease status, and management consulting companies or management software companies fail to distinguish the name of brand diseases and pathogenesis so as to offer accurate treatment suggestions. It also further restricts scientific and effective development of brand diagnosis and management technology system solution.

The trouble of these brand diseases are more specifically shown in troubles of brand development direction, troubles between brand and products, and troubles of brand organization disease status. People are always helpless for these troubles. Especially under the highly developed complex management environment nowadays, the management problems, contradiction and conflict become more complex and diseases will occur more frequently.

US enterprises need to ease these management problems and eliminate restrictive and problematic influence on enterprise development scale caused by management development problems during growth process by over 800,000 professional management analyzers. Large amount of new theories of market analyzers and management scholars, and management software systems are necessary. Enterprises in other countries are not as lucky as US enterprises, in the aspect of enterprise management. The management problems have actually caused the tough problem that hindered the development of most enterprises.

2.1 Brand pathology as management diagnosis basis

Brand pathology is mainly applied to brand management diagnosis field. It depends on study of human being on "pathology" of brand, while the in-depth and professional study may make diagnosis rise up to "authorized diagnosis".

In enterprises, brand officers, management analyzer, market analyzers and brand management department and management research department generally undertake the task of brand pathology development. They mainly discover and diagnose regular mistakes in management process such as research, development, production, products and services, feedback and study solution mechanism at the first time for frequent and prominent management problems, and strive for management optimization of entire brand management process.

Outside enterprises, generally main research and decision supporting powers for management research and market analysis industrial chain including management scientists, management designers and professional research institutions, management consultant companies, management consulting companies and management software companies undertake brand pathology development task. They mainly solve brand organization structure, brand management way, and lead overall design and management system support of brand recreation by diagnosis, analysis and scientific design.

Scientific brand disease analysis and study mechanism shall be set up for frequent brand problems and various cross management problems in enterprise brand management to name common brand diseases, study disease causes, make scientific management system design for disease conditions and spreading influence, and make effective and rapid solution plans for diagnosis suggestions. These actions are necessary to rapidly improve enterprise brand development level, enterprise management level and market level.

The nature of brand pathology development is to set up scientific basis for diagnosis. By studying common brand diseases and epidemic diseases, and conventional problems and setting up classification system of brand disease conditions, the global brand development speed, enterprise survival rate and high brand growth speed will be accelerated. Brand pathology plays a prominent role in reducing brand investment consumption, brand management cost, and shortening brand development time. We believe that the future scientific development of brand science lies in building key fundamental subjects such as brand principles, brand pathology and brand organizations, and aims to make structural change in overall scientific design of brand development route and brand organization health. It means that all aspects with regard to brand diseases such as management analysis, flow design and management consultant will accelerate cognition level of brand pathology.

Authorized diagnosis is generally the development instinct of brand research and consulting agencies which can rapidly named, analyzed and solved brand pathology, and the key capacity of professional organizations and institutions involving global brand design, management analysis and brand consulting. Generally, the management research institutions and management consulting agencies with high diagnosis ability can rapidly distinguish tiny changes in business management, and confirm cause and solution from the latent management process design flaws. Such special management diagnosis ability and scientific brand management design ability will make some cutting-edge agencies develop to the first-class institutions representing the global management field in the future, and is the embodiment for the world status of academic development degree of brand science and management science.

2.2 Abnormal status of brand development

Various abnormal states will be generated during development of enterprise brand. Currently, since enterprises and management research institutions know brand pathology insufficiently, the abnormal states are difficult to discover. Enterprises' development is bothered by many different links, and shown in various management problems, mainly brand errors and retardation time.

Brand errors refer to the wrong cognition of brand development method, brand management problems, wrong brand information transmission and wrong management diagnosis. The wrong cognitions are mainly the deviations of brand founders, or main brand leaders and main management layer in understanding of scientific cognition. These deviations in understanding bothered scientific development route of enterprise brands, so that brands fail to upgrade to brand organization status or maturely and effectively operate brands. The slow development or uncontrollable management of enterprise brands, or business failures are unavoidably affected by market factors, but under most circumstances they are related with enterprise brand development level and enterprise management level.

The wrong cognition of brand management problems is mainly on management site, generally by business leaders and managers. The frequent basic management problems of enterprises are because, on one hand, business management is not in real-time and dynamically upgraded management operation system, and on the other hand, in case of management problems, people do not know management problems sufficiently in a scientific way, and have no sufficient judgment ability for the roots of these management problems. The bigger the business scale is, the higher the requirements for complex management system will be. The endless management problems will generate cross influence in multiple departments, multiple aspects and multiple directions, thus, restricting the progress of management level. When accumulated problems are developed to certain degree, many management loopholes, redundant management flow will be generated, and all staff of the enterprise will face various management difficulties, work barriers and struggle with management problems.

Brand information is mainly transmitted in brand operation network and brand user terminal. Due to the trouble of brand diseases and cross influence, much information from market terminal and user terminal, and even flow design problems and management problems incurred frequently but are never resolved thoroughly and all these information are wrongly transmitted. Since information transmitters neither distinguish authenticity, effectiveness and importance of the information, nor undertake the first hand responsibility of brand problems. The brand information transmission is distorted, and the direct influence is quite subtle, i.e. customers go away, and never purchase and use the brand. While customers lost faith in this brand, they will spread such dissatisfaction to other users through their interpersonal network. It is difficult to acquire a valid regular, and the cost is high, but it is easy to lose a potential quality customer at any time.

The occurrence of brand diseases and related influences concerned are generally delayed. They cannot be shown momentarily, but usually microscopic and in split moment. They are reflected in management awareness of management personnel, work of enterprise employees, and user service experiences, and generated by management flow design flaws and improper management system design to certain degree. Therefore, the lesion links will last for a long time. Before sufficiently solved, the lesion will last. People do not realize the urgency to resolve until serious management accidents occurred.

The abnormal brand development usually cannot be discovered and solved effectively inside the enterprise. In the case of certain management loopholes or prominent management problems met by brand development or business management, the brand has been seriously ill, and shown symptoms of certain brand diseases. They generally would need to be resolved by high level management research institutions and management consulting agencies. The main solving approach is to adjust organizational structure, redesign management process, and adopt scientific management system solution, or introduce advanced system management method. Unless enterprises have higher level management research personnel or own brand research institutions for long-term strategic cooperation, they cannot find the cause of brand disease and pathogenesis, and cannot efficiently resolve these problems neither.

3 Professional cognition of brand epidemic diseases

The current development of brand pathology shall focus on pathological discovery of common brand diseases and epidemic diseases, starting from universal problems, main troubles and prominent contradiction of global enterprise brands to name and confirm characteristics of intensive symptoms, and apply to enterprise practices and management diagnosis field.

Brand pathology plays an important role in solving universal problems of enterprise brand. The importance mainly lies in the universal, intensive and common abnormal states during development of global enterprise brands. These problems are generated by three reasons. Firstly enterprise brand development lacking systematic and scientific development route and summary of brand scientific development rules, and scientific brand management is seriously insufficient; secondly, the long-standing case management teaching makes enterprises treat management problems as an example or individual case, and development ability of scientific management is seriously insufficient; thirdly, the clinical management ability on management site is insufficient, and enterprises cannot rapidly and effectively treat frequency of various dynamic management problems and scientific diagnosis ability. The management problems of enterprises are frequent and common.

The solution of the first problem lies in scientific system management and design level and the management science is highly valued as a sturdy experimental science. That relies on the development of completed and developed design level and design capacity of overall management technical system. Moreover, large amount of emerging brand management rules, brand principles, brand management rules and laws shall be summarized and refined from practices of enterprise brand development at any time, and risen up to theoretical and academic high from specific enterprise practices so as to promote leap development of enterprise management level based on high level scientific management. The development mechanism of scientific management laboratory is an important factor to effectively develop global enterprise management level. In essence, the management is the same as physics and chemistry. It is necessary to acquire experimental conclusion from scientific experiment.

For solution on the second problem, global associations regarding brand and enterprise management, teaching institutions and enterprises shall jointly improve cognition. Global MBA teaching adopts case teaching and case study. The application practices are easy to understand and treat common and frequent management problems as example or individual case. People always wish to acquire certain experiences or ideas to solve certain management problem from examples; however, they cannot develop natural laws of scientific management from examples, let alone scientific management level. The individual case treatment makes management science follow a trivial and spattered management science development field with too many branches. In that way, the solution ideas and approaches of "individual cases" and "difficulties" in brand management are prominent; on the contrary, the scientific exploration, scientific study and solution of common management problems are weakened.

For solution on the third problem, the scientific management development power level and scientific solution ability development for dynamic solution of management problems on management site shall be emphasized. The development nature of brand science is the progress of the management science. Management problems can only occur on management site, not in CEO's office. If human medicine is able to make great progression because of the scientific cognition of systematic treatment approach in traditional Chinese medicine, and clinical medicine developed by western medicine for which medicine students shall acquire knowledge and grow up to a doctor by clinical observation, meta analysis, disease record, disease case library and evidence-based medicine so as to develop ability to cure diseases of human being. However, leaders and management personnel of enterprise are promoted to certain management post without going through special learning and training, and undertake corresponding management responsibility, while all staff of worldwide management consultant companies or consulting companies, and management software companies have not accepted similar clinical special training, and even practices in enterprises. The work of university professors is to impart knowledge. They do not have abundant experiences in on-site business management, but show up as master of management theory. The universal worldwide extensive management makes management problem finding, solution, and scientific summary and refining level worse.

The professional development of brand pathology, as an important brand science development trend, aims to solve common diseases, and accelerate building brand disease control system. It plays a prominent role in promoting a brand economy (brand exporter, industrial brand cluster or group brand cluster). It is also important for brand development strategy of a country and region, and helps to greatly improve on the development power level of one country, region, industry and a group, and improve the success rate of the brand, effective investment rate of the brand and brand value scientific development method in capital market. A highlighted problem is that brand cluster development contradiction is prominent. One enterprise may be comprised of parent brand and multiple brand projects. Currently, enterprises spent most of their energy and funds in treating structural contradictions, which are key brand disease links.

4 Decision making supporting system for brand health

The development purpose of brand pathology is not limited to treatment of brand disease. The more important development target is to focus on brand health, and help enterprises establish brand health decision making supporting system, check and predict abnormal brand development status, probe and manage problems, and take charge of sustainable healthy status for longer future of brand.

The decision-making supporting system for brand health is a necessary disease-preventing technology development measure for healthy development of global brands, and a kind of dynamic brand knowledge management system. The system shall be developed and designed based on ceaseless development of brand cutting-edge knowledge, brand science, brand healthy knowledge application system, and provide application support to enterprises.

The key development point of decision-making supporting system for brand health is to provide various brand strategy decisions to main enterprise leaders and managers, learn daily brand management knowledge, and provide decision on self-diagnosis, self-repair and spontaneous development for healthy status of brand organization. Different from the expert system, brand management resource or management software in common sense, the supporting system needs development premise of high level system brand science knowledge development ability.

In the era of knowledge-driven economy, the global brand development will necessarily show diversified development patterns. Every brand shall make decisions according to different conditions, different people, different brand ideologies and development levels so as to develop different brands. This is no such thing like identical people or leaves in the world. All brands in the world shall develop independently and explore suitable development way. This is the general premise for highly developed brand science to support healthy development of global enterprise brand. Although presentation forms and brand development results of various global brands are different, the scientific laws, brand system ability matching required by development are consistent or similar.

Brand health decision-making supporting system develops based on scientific development facts orienting at scientific development level of brand system so as to provide the most valuable, most objective and realist application value to specific development practices of enterprise brand directly and indirectly. We wish brand leaders and brand officers could leave office and go to management site to develop and look for the barriers obstructing every employee microscopically from the first day. The influence is no other than lesion cross influence brought about by enterprise brand development and actual brand management.

5 Case of brand pathology: Brand Parkinson

Common brand disease of enterprises: Brand Parkinson

Symptom: The awareness of "customers need brands - we are not brand yet" in each R&D, marketing and service departments is chaotic. The links are shaking, causing slow enterprise actions. Under affection, the clients generate large sense of distrust, and generate the confusion of "should I trust you", causing shaking, low order rate and low renewal rate. The companies are always developing new customers, and few potential customers buy actively.

Pathogenesis: the branding has not been integrated and completed from the beginning; enterprise structure is not developed completely, and enterprises are always stuck in the "0-1" stage of 01 law without distinctive direction and route, disordered subject ideology. Customers fail to rapidly and accurately identify "difference between your product and similar products". Brand Parkinson contains congenital, hereditary and secondary Parkinson. About 70% of new companies will be attacked by diseases rapidly from the fourth month, leading to disordered venture. In serious case, enterprises will rapidly break up and shut down. Even if it survived, business will suffer from development bottleneck. Brand Parkinson of large-scale enterprises will further cause overall management disorder to enterprises, and generate large-scale uncontrollable brand management link, which is the cause that trigger frequent management problems.

Corresponding brand principle: 01 law

01Law is the valuable lifeline for enterprise to develop, and decides the vigorous and sustainable brand vitality.

01Law advocates:

(1) The first thing for the foundation of any enterprise is branding.

(2) If one thing is not done thoroughly, it shall be done again.

(3) Brand failure starts from disordered brand status, and cause of disorder is not to finish from 0-1, and stay between 0-1.

(4) Enterprises grow slowly, and they are ceaselessly developing new customers and always in status of business maintenance, because the process from 0 to 1 has not been completed, and wandered between 0-1.

(5) In order to ignite passion for business again, or open new business, any enterprise must finish 01brand again.

For recreation process, enterprises must recreate the brand again and carry out branding required by opening new business every several years, forming 01-01-01……. That is the brand history formed automatically, and also the branding movement track left by ecological and sustainable development of enterprises. It is the secret for permanent operation of brands.

Exercises

1. Fill in the blanks: Brand pathology is a professional branch of brand science studying brand disease _____, _____, _____ and _____.

2. Essay Question: What are the similarities of abnormalities during global enterprise brand development? What are the patterns of manifestation?

3. Discussion: How to understand common brand diseases of enterprises – Brand Parkinson?

Section II Brand Subjects

Chapter 4

Brand Strategy

Brand strategy is a brand science studying brand strategic design, brand strategic structure, strategic ideas and strategic methods. Compared with former management strategy, brand strategy has a higher design level and strategic requirements. Brand strategy is the highest strategic direction leading all management ideas and market actions of enterprises, and the core program and action guide for strategies and practices of the enterprises.

1 Enterprise brand strategy layers

The enterprise brand strategy layers are studied based on enterprise brand strategy independently, and this is due to wrong cognition, neglected ideology of brand organization and multi-level brand strategy layers in the world. This will lead to a lack of interactive integration among enterprise brand strategy, global competition, human progress and social and economic development. Any enterprise cannot be studied in parts. If an enterprise brand is unable to enter ecological system of global brand economy, the brand is of no strategic significance. Enterprise-level brand strategy layers can be seen in Fig. 4-1.

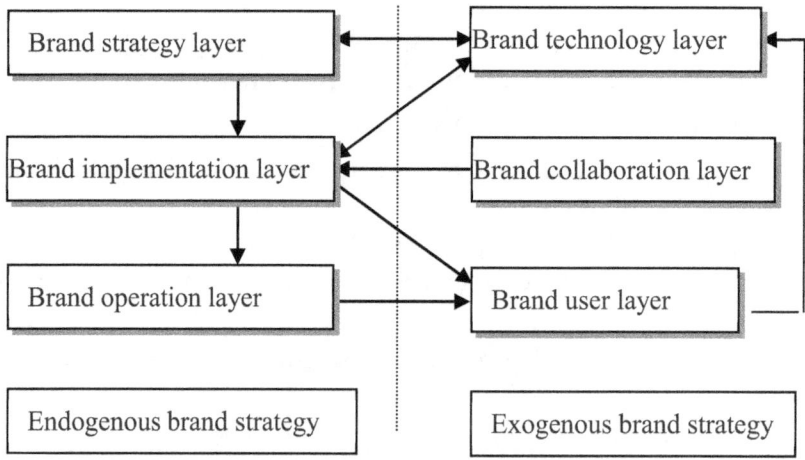

Fig. 4-1 Enterprise-level Brand Strategy Layers

Enterprise-level brand strategy contains six layers, and every layer has close connection with one another. The strategic organization of endogenous brands generally believes that brand strategy is divided into three layers, including brand strategy layer, brand implementation layer and brand operation layer, and all subjects are internal members of enterprise organization. The strategic organization of exogenous brands generally believes that brand strategy is divided to six layers. Brand technology layer, brand collaboration layer and brand user layer are added. All layers are closely combined from inside to outside and from outside to inside.

We examine the movement rules of brand organization by strategic organization of exogenous brands. The first is the strategic layer of brand organization, which takes charge of overall strategic design and strategic command. Enterprise may need a group of brand strategy departments, respectively strategy research department, brand technical committee, quality review committee, etc. Setting up a committee is a typical approach which an organization will take for studying and referencing on the decision-making of higher management. In general, the strategic work of an enterprise is taken charge by a specialized committee. This committee is a cross-enterprise and trans-department decision-making group. If the decisions of enterprises are only made by internal higher management and departments, the strategy is insufficient and incomplete.

Brand technical layer is a special structure of brand organization, and takes charge of specific work of brand technical committee, including some secondary committees such as brand user relation committee as required. The brand technical layer contains of two aspects: the first is the research and analysis team which is comprised of external brand consultant and brand technical experts and takes charge of technical guidance of brand layer; the second is the brand backbone technical team which is comprised of internal brand technology formulation and implementation personnel, including brand officer, brand department, quality system supervisory department as well as management design department and assessment department.

Brand technology is a core strategic technology, and must undergo large amount of global brand knowledge creations and updates, and acquire the most advanced brand strategic ideas and brand technology operators, i.e. enterprises need to make expanded global brand technology knowledge upgrade network to provide knowledge source to technical practices of enterprise brand. If enterprises have no brand technical organization or fail to participate in external academic research activities about brand technology, the brand technologies of enterprises are closed. Earlier, many enterprises particularly emphasize on "layman" and "professional", and intentionally emphasize on industrial characteristics. They always believe brand technologies in other industries are unrelated. Actually, it is a kind of "self-reclusive" ideology of endogenous brand. The knowledge aging speed of the enterprise will be far faster than the norm of the same industry, and the enterprise is easily eliminated by new changes in industry.

The brand technology layer plays the role of "brand order manager" in one brand organization, and takes charge of brand order establishment and maintenance. The brand strategy layer dedicates brand research tasks and brand project tasks, and the brand technology layer takes charge of specific brand strategic design, implementation and advancement. Meanwhile the brand technology layer shall report to the brand strategy layer as well, and provide latest research findings and brand technology implementation project suggestions to brand strategy layer. One important job of brand technology layer is to manage implementation situations of brand project schedule, and make reasonable scientific explanation for brand technical problems. In addition, various feedbacks and researches of brand user layer shall be gathered to brand technology layer immediately.

Brand implementation layer takes charge of specific implementation of brand tasks. The implementation must be carried out according to the requirements of brand strategy layer, under technical guidance of brand technology layer and schedule follow-up. In the past, many companies do not have brand technology layer, and only brand strategy layer dedicates tasks to brand implementation layer. It is unscientific for brand implementation layer to report to brand strategy layer. After all, it is irresponsible to directly assign brand technology experiment, research and supervision to the implementation layer. The brand implementation layer only needs to take charge of job implementation. They are not experts of brand technology, and will generate binary opposition contradiction.

The reasonable order structure of brand sub-organization must be ternary. Brand organization must own independent, advanced and third party brand technology support and own supervisory department to take charge of the management of brand management order and maintenance, while the department must be the brand technology layer. The ternary management relation is the most stable and most basic management order, greatly eases leadership of strategic management level, and effectively assures smooth and orderly operation of the organization. Meanwhile, brand implementation layer shall take charge of the management of brand collaboration layer, i.e. coordination of external supply chain, strategic cooperating network and brand operating network.

The brand operation layer will specifically implement every task, every person's work, daily brand management and work performance. The operating layer covers every grass-root staff inside and outside the company, including temporary employees. All employees are responsible for the brand, and implement and maintain the brand. The brand operation layer shall report to brand implementation layer.

The brand implementation layer and brand operation layer shall, according to different labor divisions, be responsible for brand users. The brand technology layer, by studying trend, opinions and problems of brand users, update the knowledge system timely, and break down more reasonable and more scientific brand tasks. Every department, every organization and every person inside and outside the brand organization will play different levels of roles inside the organization and be responsible for the brand. Only when its entire staff is responsible for the brand, the enterprise is a responsible global enterprise. Based on such responsibility, the brand organization can form powerful, progressive, outstanding and effectively collaborative brand organization.

2 Strategic thinking of brands

The strategic thinking of brands is the strategic thinking way that all brand rules formulators and brand organizations must rely on. Brand strategic thinking decides whether brand rules formulation is scientific, effective and perfect. The main strategic thinking of brands contains eight ways of thinking including thinking of structure, anticipation, order, leadership, science, creation, themed topics or route, and operation.

Strategies are the thinking methods and clear implementation routes or methods applying ideas adopted in order to reach prospect objective, and the overall reflection of strategic ability. Strategies are overall setting of objective, overall layout, structural combination, planning implementation and resource application process. The key points of strategies are to be unprecedented and unique.

Strategies are the strict combination of major strategic objective, guideline and action plan. The strategy formulators master the overall strategy design and implementation guidance.

Strategic objective is an unusual kind of hyper-normal prospect, while the prospect is too ideal and ahead, and it may not be aware and recognized by all people. However, prospect is a kind of dream, and can drive all people toward the objective.

Guideline is the major strategic requirement to realize the strategic objective, and the requirement for strategic stages, directions, tasks and principles. The guideline will be broken down into specific strategic objectives, which are clear and can be recognized by major strategic targets.

Action plan is the specific action program formulated according to strategic stages and strategic tasks. The action plans may involve tactic problems aiming at specific actions (including action target), time, place, personnel and resource configuration and expected action effect.

2.1 Structural thinking

The structural thinking, also known as top-level design, refers to the thinking mode focusing at structure of design framework. For structural thinking, the structural design is made from the highest level of thinking so as to clarify covering domain and emphasis of strategy, and state overall structure in framework documents.

The typical structural framework documents contain *Worldwide Internet Policy Framework, Global Framework of Credible E-Business, WTO Framework, United Nations Framework Convention on Climate Change* and *Corporate Strategy Cooperative Framework Agreement*.

The structural framework documents are of the nature of leadership and outline. It is only necessary to express strategic intention, including subject structure, and mark off the coarsest structure, trivial details are not necessary. The design of framework thinking application strategy plays the role of simple and distinct thinking, and is also the key guiding role in strategy implementation. The strategic tasks are specific decomposition and labor division of strategic framework documents.

2.2 Anticipating thinking

The anticipating thinking is reflected in conception of strategic prospect. The strategic rules are formulated by making anticipation for enterprise management trend and market strategy direction according to serious trends such as future scientific and technical development, market change trend, management reform direction, enterprise organization system and network change.

The anticipating thinking is a kind of prejudgment for unknown challenges, trends, directions, opportunities and crisis. Thus, the anticipating thinking is usually known as "foresight", and sometimes known as acute insight and cutting-edge power of thought.

In fact, the anticipating thinking is from some cutting-edge knowledge flow in the future and sensitive thinking and judgment ability, and can make accurate prejudgment. Since the thinking and knowledge levels of everyone are different, different levels in enterprises, such as grass-root employees, quality supervisors, project engineers and leaders have different understanding. Some people are used to understand and master cutting-edge ideas and future knowledge, particularly analysis in the strategic level; while most people are satisfied with basic job contents and occupational knowledge, hence causing everyone to have different ways of thinking and knowledge structures.

People who are used to think strategically usually capture the knowledge field or cognition direction people noticed or ignored, such as judgment on financial crisis, direction of new technology and crux of management problems. Therefore, they can more distinctly make accurate judgment with trend for comprehensive information. Meanwhile, the formulators of strategic rules are unnecessarily judge by respective thinking. The knowledge source may be provided by think tank comprising of a group of consultants, such as military counselors and advisers in ancient military. The formulators of strategic rules collect diversified decision-making information, and acquire excellent anticipating thinking ability by mastering more professional decision-making reference sources.

Sometimes, the anticipating thinking is a kind of psychological warning. Someone is sensitive to crisis, and can acutely feel the threats of crisis. In order to get rid of unsafe state, they will change strategies in advance, or prevent from unsafe state in strategy design.

2.3 Thinking of order

The thinking of order is reflected as formulating ability of self-adaptive rules, and is an important thinking ability of strategic thinking.

The traffic light is a kind of self-adaptive rules. The traffic order is commanded by alternation of traffic light. The traffic rule formulators will design a series of rules or regulations to guarantee traffic order can be operate more smoothly. The next task is to cultivate drivers to learn and master these traffic rules strictly. Thus, the traffic order can maintain a favorable operating status.

The order organization with the longest history and most profound influence is Celtic Druid order organization. It has once led the order network of over half of Europe. It is the major foundation for stable social order in developed countries in Europe and North America. As the earliest international order organization, some typical orders in Druid order, such as "equality between the sexes", "capacity-oriented" and "immigrant city", as well as formulation and verdict ways of rules for education system, war rules and war verdict generate profound influence on mainstream form in developed countries in Europe and America. The order of many rules of the current United States, international organizations, royalty management, upper class, environmental protection and even some NBA rules are from the earliest Celtic Druid Order to certain degree or partly. Nowadays, many developed countries still have Druid organization, usually named as "Druid Order". The organization takes charge of order formulation and maintenance, while Druid adopts the "ternary thinking" order structure.

The largest order organization in the world is the religious order organization. Some international organizations such as international civil aviation organization takes charge of formulating various general rules in civil aviation field, while except the enterprises, some typical rules of business management are formulated by ISO and securities and exchange commissions.

"Code", "system", "bylaws" and "-oriented" are four typical formulation methods for ancient and modern rules. "Code" is usually for overall formulation, collection and uniform regulations of orders, and is authorized, systematic and integrated; "system" is a kind of self-adaptive rule showing balance and measurement, and is also the most frequently applied rules formulation methods, such as primogeniture, the Qin system, well-field system, constitutional monarchy, accountability system, piecework system, official residence system, recommendatory system and divisional organization; "bylaw" is a kind of rules for basic guideline and operating order released by one country, organization, institution or enterprise, and also known as "articles of associations" and "regulations"; "-oriented" is used for a kind of common order with obvious trend, such as brand-oriented, modern management-oriented, information-oriented, knowledge-oriented, flow-oriented, science-oriented and industry-oriented.

The progress of rules formulation technology is the major reflection of global strategic thinking development. No strategist (strategic leader) can be separated from mastery of rules formulation technology. Thus, the strategic development of the world, or a country, organization or enterprise focuses on developing formulation of self-adaptive rules. All systems which can operate independently will get through a series of self-adaptive rules. The fair competition in future global market and development of future system science will surely further emphasize progress and application of rules formulation technology. The leaders mastering rules formulation technology are the major leading force for future global development and human progress.

2.4 Thinking of leadership

Leaders mainly guide people by ideology, and take charge of management design. The job is essentially different from specific management contents. The thinking of leadership in brand strategy is completely different from the normal leadership. The strategic thinking of leadership mainly is shown in leading-edge leader, commander role and management design ability.

The thinking of leading-edge leaders can be seen in frontier science study, future forward-looking exploration, trend creation, industrial trend leader and ideology leadership style. The world never lacked followers, but it lacks leaders. The leading-edge leader represents the commander of certain market field, and has huge social influence.

The commander role can be seen in the commanding leadership, also known as commanding power. In leadership science, the commanding power is shown in natural commanding capacity, i.e. organization members are consistently led and expected, and spontaneously form unified leadership by establishing actual authority and awareness authority. The overall execution of the organization system is activated, and the entire organization gives play to effective mechanical capacity and vast market impact force.

The management design ability is a kind of specific representation of leadership thinking. Leaders shall take full charge of management structure, management style, project promotion and management results of organizations. The strategic intent of a leader needs to be completed by management system that is sufficiently large, while the overall operating mechanism design and operating efficiency of management decides whether strategic intent can be thoroughly and effectively implemented. Without management design ability, the organization is unable to expand rapidly, or keep enough scale advantages.

The thinking of leadership is the comprehensive reflection of multiple factors, including both mental and will levels, and ideology and specific capacity.

2.5 Scientific thinking

The progress of scientific ideology is the most important component in human progression. The scientific thinking is the comprehensive thinking ability mastering and applying scientific cognition, scientific awareness, scientific deliberation and scientific approach. Scientific ideology is different from scientific thinking. Firstly, they are different in thinking approach, i.e. to know and decide matters by scientific attitudes, promote scientific progress of organization by scientific awareness, and promote mastering of the essence of matter - scientific laws by spirits of scientific study, and investigate study and decide affairs by scientific thinking mode; secondly, the mastering ways of scientific approaches are different. The scientific thinking aims to finish scientific invention and creation by scientific experiments, research, analysis and demonstration, and apply the scientific findings.

The globally leading brands finish scientific-oriented work of brand organization by establishing scientific laboratory and global research and development center. Repeated scientific study and demonstrations for the process of scientific management from product trail-manufacture, research, manufacture, to market research and development, are required to ensure the maximum brand effect.

Science is a scientific-oriented practice process by multi-sample, multi-variety and multi-project experiment research, investigation analysis and contrast based on fact study report and with experiment, actual measurement, data comparison, fact analysis and research findings as subject.

Many brand organizations place particular emphasis on setting Chief Scientists, support and encourage members to actively participate in scientific paper issuance, scientific appraisal between peers, and serve as higher posts of scientific organizations (associations) to accelerate knowledge updating speed. The research, invention and application of advanced scientific technology occupy a great proportion in enterprises.

Many brand organizations strive to develop scientific-oriented management, study and set more reasonable management system by scientific approach, and actively create, invent or introduce advanced technical system to improve comprehensive ability of research, development, production and marketing. The extensive application of scientific technology shall be the main source power for brand organization to get ultra-convention development.

2.6 Creative thinking

Creative thinking is a kind of typical thinking habit for invention and creation. Leaders of brand organization will always have the creative thinking habits such as "How to be unique? The answer must be different from others, must be the most advanced technology and must be the best in the world".

The creation is a quite positive desire. By inventing new things, new technologies, new modes, new concepts, and new behaviors, the expression of creative resultants are finished. Creation is a kind of habitual creative behavior. Such behavior will urge brand organization leaders to make changes, and realize personal and organization's value by continuously creating new method. Such habit will spontaneously resist and boycott various behaviors and methods damaging creativity, such as copycat of business mode, copy of technical results, disrespect of intellectual property right and other ideologies and behaviors damaging creativity.

Creation is a tough thing, and it may require decades or a very long tough period. However, the creative environment in different countries may throttle national creativity and control creative activities. Without intellectual property protection policies, the feasible protective environment for creation, the creation cannot be unified with social contribution. Entrepreneurs have no profit so as to greatly frustrate positivity of creators, and restrain rising of creative economy represented by creativity. That is the predicament of creative generation environment that global emerging creators may suffer from usually.

Education is the major method to cultivate national creativity as well. If education cannot release creative instinct of every citizen, cultivate fan of free creation, create ideas, proposition and self-judgment, or lead independent thinking and independent creation ability from every child to adult, the education is unsuccessful.

The new generation of creators need informal creative environment. Too much administrative interference of policies, too many complex social barriers, and too much restrictive humanized awareness may harm development of creativity. Cultivation of independent leader is the major method to get creative talents. The excessive administrative interference and trivial management process shall be avoided so as not to restrain development of every potential leadership member.

Agile management requirements for future enterprise: acknowledge every employee is a creator; the development of enterprises needs to depend on multiple creators. Small and rapid R&D group, enterprise creation environment with flexible mechanism, and batch cultivation mechanism of independent leaders are the high expression of creative thinking development of entire brand organization.

2.7 Thinking of theme, topic and route

Theme, topic and route are three typical ways to finish thinking expression, and are comprehensive application mode of strategic ideas used in confirming core strategic field, prominent core strategic value, refining strategic ideas, clarifying key competition ability, spreading brand topics, designing strategy implementation route, and designing strategic action steps. The strategic thinking of theme, topic and route can be either used independently or used in a mixed way.

The strategic thinking of theme is a kind of strategic implementation mode designed around certain theme, and typical strategic mode carrying out all brand strategic designs and behaviors around one clear theme, deepening brand market, and forming unique brand civilization form and brand competition pattern with clear main idea and prominent subject. Centering at the theme, brand products, brand derivative products, brand image spokesperson, brand image cartoon, brand image virtual or authentic environment, brand legend, interesting activities of brand, brand television, film and animation can be set. The comprehensive image with clear and independent brand personality can be created by multi-level, multi-angle and diversified shape. And brand fans are gathered to form unique brand user groups.

The strategic thinking of topic is a kind of brand strategy implemented by designing, devising, organizing and leading hot topics. Brands focus on transmitting and making brand topics, gaining attention of news media, topic editors, investors, opinion providers and social public by realizing high presence rate, high exposure rate and high influence of brands via a series of media activities, and attract and form large amount of brand fan groups so as to comprehensively drive speed growth of brands. The strategic thinking of topic has key strategic value during Initial Public Offerings, IPO of an enterprise. Since the topic is well known, the listing of brand organization may be a sensational event.

The strategic thinking of route refers to the strategy implementation way to set key strategic route of brands. The overall concept of brand strategy is directly expressed by perceptional means such as document description, work conception, literal expression, virtual digital technology, scenery model, simulated diagram, imagination diagram and creation implementation, and thus strategic implementation steps, such as Phase I, Phase II and Phase III, for brand prospect are set to clarify key strategic capacity implemented to reach strategic objective.

2.8 Operational thinking

The operational thinking refers to a large-scale thorough action which applies ideas of military war and deems global market as battlefield and brand recreation as comprehensive attack to market.

The modern military operation is the strategy of high technology, the modern war mode linking comprehensive command and multiple-corps rapid combination in the scope of sea, land, air and space, and the asymmetric mode of operation highly orienting future, knowledge, agility, remote services. Wars will depend on the perfect combination of future ideas, command system, new weapons, overall deployment, daily training and logistic guarantee. The traditional ideas of operation have been changed deeply. Modern military ideas always focus on next generation military deployment and weapon R&D. The military organization striving at the most advanced, developed, scientific and knowledge-oriented monetary deployment and weapon development can win the next war, and occupy the advantageous military position in the world.

The market effect of brand organization lies in not only comprehensive application of various operational thinking and modern market operational system, but also the "more positive" and "first-strike" active attack strategy. The influential brand is the brand that actively attack in global market, attacking or breaking up original market structure and building up new market order by launching strategic market or crushable market, while weak brands are mainly enterprises accepting challenges under compulsion or passively, and some are even incapable to accept challenges.

As future operational ideas have been generating a thorough military reform, future market operation will undergo deep reform in terms of operational ideas, operational command, operational target, operational behavior and attacking mode. Tactics and operational means will generate great changes. For any international brand, the war in any market field of the world may be on the verge. Enterprises should either challenge actively or accept challenge passively. No other option is provided.

3 Design of brand strategy

The brand strategy refers to the "brand+" strategy, i.e. each link of enterprise management, market and services, which is closely related with brands. The value of brand strategy is as follows:

(1) The essence of strategy is "unprecedented and unique";

(2) Strategy is a top-level design focusing on long-term vision and future insight;

(3) The strategic entrepreneur always drives progress of business management by strategic ideas;

(4) Strategy is the scientific cutting-edge, forward-looking and decisive anticipation leading cutting edge of ideas;

(5) Strategy aims to realize "distinctiveness", i.e. why is it different from others;

(6) Strategy decides the overall direction in the future, and is the dream target that all employees strive for;

To sum up, brand strategy is the thorough reform of business management ideas of enterprises:

(1) Brand strategy is a kind of foresight of entrepreneurs, usually 10-30 years ahead of common people;

(2) Brand strategy aims to solve brand strategic ideas and policies of enterprises in next 10-30 years;

(3) Brand strategy is the overall programmatic document for future development, and the action program for global development of brands;

(4) Brand strategy tells everyone, including investors, supply chain, employees and the public, what is the future of brands;

(5) Brand strategy is the perfect interpretation of enterprise spirits and actions of high capacity, high quality and high efficiency;

(6) Brand strategy recreates the business backbones and dream of all the staff, and mobilizes the entire brand organization to actively attack brand market so as to advance toward the world.

3.1 Strategic level design: "strategic brain" of trumping brands

Brand strategy is a large-scale consistent action that is mobilized and commanded by brand organization through planning of all human powers, materials and resources. The global brand strategy of enterprises is extensive, and cannot be made by single decision-making force. At any time, it is the uniform research, decision-making and command of strategic brain bank, and the application of brand strategic brain plays the obvious role of strategic command.

Every time when an enterprise decide to release a significant brand to the world, or launch a large-scale attack on global market after brand recreation, the enterprise shall start implementing significant strategic action - trumping brand strategy. The trumping brand strategy is a significant action by pushing out trumping products and occupying leading brand market by absolute advantages.

The trumping brand strategy is designed to finish redistricting of market layout, occupy advantageous position and reorganize business structure of brands. Brand organization usually makes great reform for design research, development, production and marketing where necessary, and mobilizes all members of organization to take actions and attack the market intensively.

The establishment of brand organization's strategic level is emphasized. The research network comprised of external brand strategies, technical and market experts provide advices for strategic

Section II Brand Subjects

decision making of brands so as to assurance established and effective application of "strategic brain". Except finishing preparation of management standard, the management can be upgraded to "trumping brand operation command center" that comprises of IT framework system and mobile system as required. The brand operational system with brand technology and mobile deployment will surely play a powerful role in this action.

The key points of trumping strategic design contain brand operation command center, command chain, instruction system and mobile action terminal. The design can connect each department, each local branch and global outlet of an enterprise, and will realize brand action deployment command at fixed and mobile status such as air, land and ocean where necessary. It can rapidly process various data, manage report of action in each market link, and keep communication between each operational unit of brands.

The integrated trumping brand operational command system comprised of scientific brand strategy design, systematic management analysis, fast connecting knowledge network, reliable and efficient basic information deployment, and rapid mobile management marketing mode will grant modern enterprise brand strategy with the truly sense of "central command operating capacity"; provide functions of dynamic command, real-time management, and accurate attacking ability to attack any market objective on the earth; realize global reach, global coverage of brand by accurate way, and thoroughly improve strategic benefits and efficiency of enterprise brand.

3.2 Process design of brand management

Brand organization shall clarify that brand is an action that all internal and external staff of the enterprise participate in. It needs contribution and implementation of all staff. The old brand management process can be seen in Fig. 4-2.

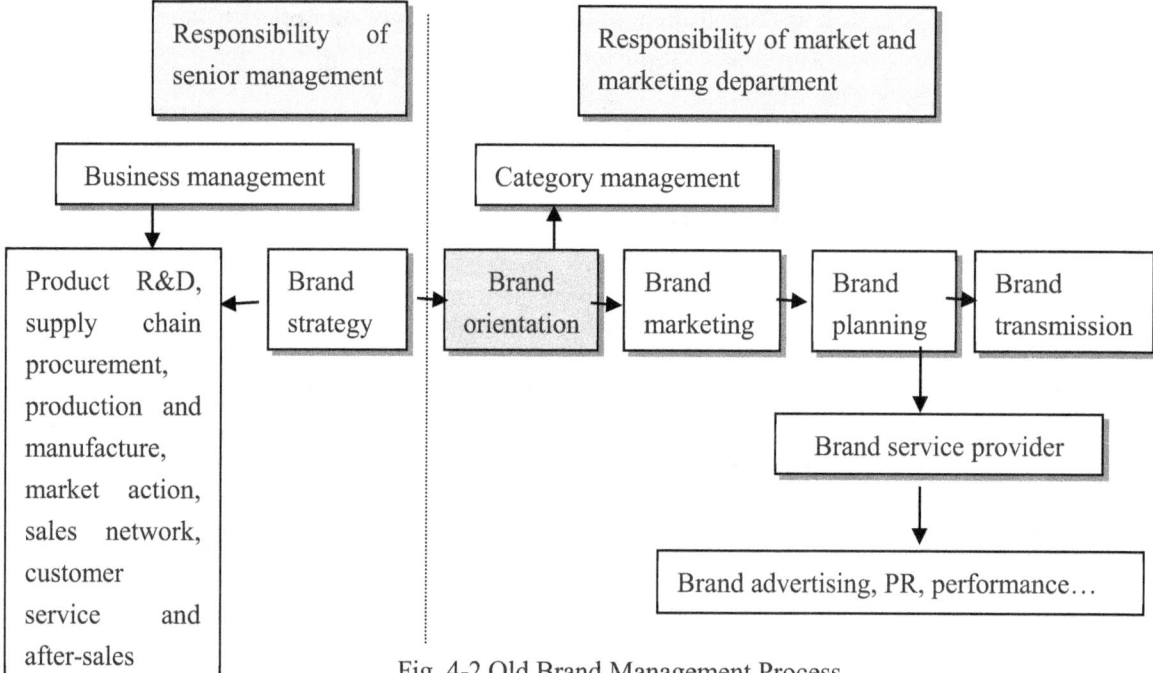

Fig. 4-2 Old Brand Management Process

For overall route of old brand management, the brand is taken charge of by market and marketing department. The brand management is centered at "brand orientation" and transited towards brand management. The marketing department extended contents of brand marketization, including brand marketing, brand planning and brand communication. Enterprises may cooperate with external brand service providers, such as brand advertising, PR, planning and performance companies. Enterprises will formulate brand strategy, which will be managed by separated higher management. They will make certain brand management requirements for product R&D, supply chain procurement, production and manufacture, market action, sales network, customer service and after-sales service.

The drawback of old brand management is that brand is actually managed by the single Marketing Department. The management layer is low, and brand management does not involve all the staff, or other departments. Departments other than market and marketing are unable to enjoy brand premium effect. All staff neither participates in brand contribution nor shares brand market achievements.

CEO takes full charge of brand strategy of new brand management process. The brand management comprises of brand technology, brand capacity and brand recognition, and operation centered at brand work flow. The brand technology department provides brand assistance, suggestions, technical support and report to CEO, and also undertakes charge of brand order management. Jobs involving brand capacity are undertaken by each management department. Each department will carry forward brand recreation strategy, brand strategic framework, brand operation manual, brand learning, brand capacity error correction by means of project system and documentation. The market and marketing department takes charge of brand recognition, including user group learning, brand communication (planning and transmission) and error correction of brand recognition information by means of project system and documentation. The advantage of overall route of new brand management is that all staff participates in brand contribution and enjoys brand effect. They respectively undertake various brand tasks. The overall route of new brand management can be seen in Fig. 4-3.

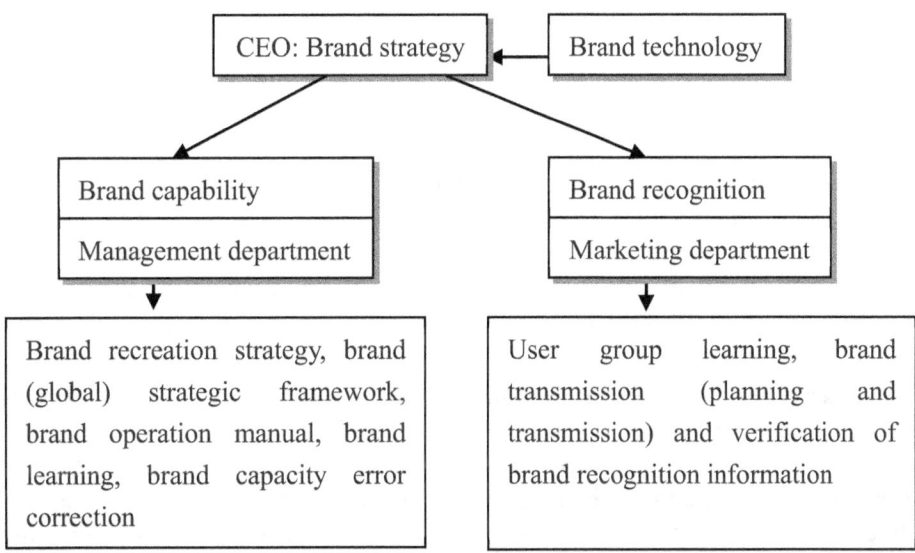

Fig. 4-3 Overall Route of New Brand Management

3.3 Process design of brand premium capacity

Enterprises shall carry out process design with certain sense according to brand premium capacity to make all staff releases brand premium energy in each link while participating in brand contribution.

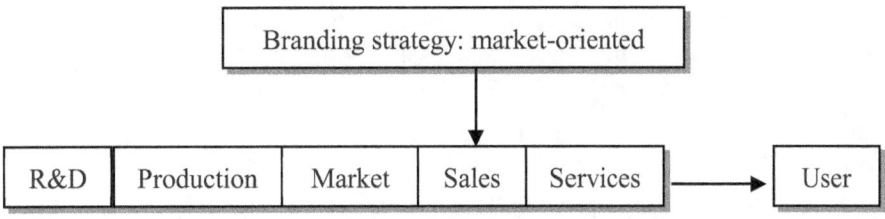

Fig. 4-4 Old Brand Premium Process Design

Section II Brand Subjects

Old brand premium process design (see Fig. 4-6) is a kind of branding design purely centering at market. In that design, the company requires all staff to be responsible for brands, but actually all staff takes no responsibility for the brand. Enterprises always emphasize on being responsible to users. They specifically stated to be responsible to users during many processes such as R&D, production, market, sales and service process. However, the actual case is that all departments are subordinated to the same enterprise. Due to internal relationship, responsibilities are shuffled between departments and persons. No one is responsible for users, and users become guinea pig of immature products; brand premium ability is low; personal competence and contribution are not in direct proportion with payment; personal value cannot be shown; company benefits are decoupled from personal income; enterprises are inactive.

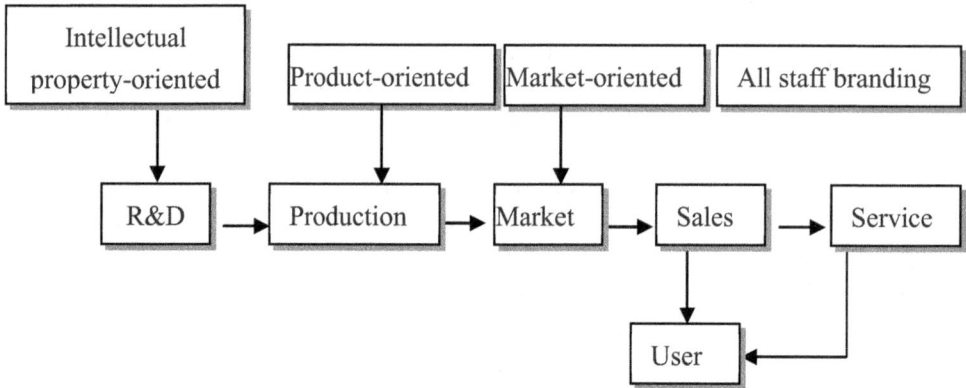

Fig. 4-5 New Brand Premium Capability Process Design

The new branding strategy emphasizes on simulation market. A brand organization is set up by multiple professional companies, and sales and service departments shall both be responsible towards users; department will purchase products and services from the previous department (professional company) according to market purchase relationship step by step; accountability will be held level by level; the nonconforming products shall not enter the next link. The new brand premium capability process design can be seen in Fig. 4-5.

New brand management divides main brand-related jobs to intellectual property-oriented (R&D), product-oriented (production and manufacture), market-oriented (market branding), or more specifically divides to four premium process of laboratory, product-oriented, branding and market-oriented. Such division further emphasizes on the premium performance generated by management, sales and services of each department to brand terminal. Each professional department (company) can acquire brand premium in every process.

New branding strategy focuses on growth of brand premium, emphasizes on direction proportion between personal contribution and capacity, and shows contribution value directly. The company benefits and personal income improve on year-on-year basis, and enterprises are full of vibrancy.

3.4 Selection of brand strategy

Different brand organizations will adopt different brand strategies to develop brands. The typical brand strategies contain ultimate factories strategy, fantasy strategy, environmental strategy, standard strategy, substitute strategy, route strategy and transmission strategy. Different strategies can be either used separately or used in combination.

Ultimate factories strategy: The dominant strategic direction is to make important, popular, influential core products. Typical brands are Ford T, Ferrari, and Apachi.

Fantasy strategy: The dominant strategic direction is to create a hyper-normal dreamy, virtual, fashionable, advanced, amazing and imaginary Sci-Fi or fantasy brands. Typical brands are Hollywood, Industrial Light, Magic, and Disney.

Environmental strategy: The dominant strategic direction is to create a special user environment to increase brand recognition, brand environment experience and brand environmental infection ability. Typical brands are Starbucks, Hong Kong City Brand.

Standard strategy: The dominant strategic direction is to create and develop standard system, and strive for unified R&D, and standard implementation for relevant products. Typical brands are Japanese auto battery, and Sunkist Orange.

Substitute strategy: The dominant strategic direction is to make brand name become common name to solve certain problem globally by representing the application field, performance and functions of brand. Typical brands are Band-Aid and Head & Shoulders.

Route strategy: The dominant strategic direction is perfect design and promotion of market strategic route. Typical brands are Toyota, Marvel Comics and JDB.

Transmission strategy: The dominant development strategy and direction is brand transmission, and the key strategic value of brand transmission in brand value and brand premium capacity process is emphasized. Typical brands are Google, Haier and Galanz.

4 Strategic thinking of brand

The strategic thinking of brand is used to guide basic brand behavior of enterprise. The strategic thinking will govern the overall situations, and guide strategic layout and deployment. It is the key ideological soul and value creation way of enterprise brand strategy.

Each country (region) and enterprise can design some brand strategic thinking where necessary to guide brand practices. For instance, typical brand strategic thinking contains strengthening the country by famous brands, strengthening the enterprise by famous brand, brand economy, brand cluster, brand internationalization, brand professional, brand feeling, making particular brand strong, brand capacity, lean brand, brand security, brand learning, brand naming rate, brand profit chain, and brand user groups, etc.

The strategic thinking of brand is used to distinctly clarify what brand the enterprise should create, what key capacity the brand should develop, what strategic route the enterprise should adopt to implement brand construction, and what brand leading ideas should be used to realize brand achievements.

Actions of entrepreneurs: in the ever-changing global business environment, entrepreneurs spare no effort to develop business foresight, create their world-consciousness by broader vision, and focus on brand strategy for development power and business prospect and set up their own great plan so that they can pay more attention to their brands, carefully create, development and perform significance granted by brand strategic thinking as high speed channel to acquire outstanding achievements.

Exercises

1. Fill in the Blanks: The strategic thinking of brands contains eight ways of thinking including _____, _____, _____, _____, _____, _____, _____, _____.

2. True or False Question: The reasonable order structure of brand sub-organization must be ternary. The ternary management relation is the most stable and most basic management order, greatly eases leadership of strategic management level, and effectively guarantees smooth and ordered operation of the organization. ( )

3. Essay Question: What is the brand strategic thinking? What aspects is it shown in?

SECTION II BRAND SUBJECTS

Chapter 5

Brand Organization

What do brands change? We start to discuss brand organizational structure, organization process, order, actions and culture around brand organization, which is a specific organization form. This is different from the study on enterprises earlier. We believe that brand organization is an expanded internal and external combination form of enterprises. The management characteristics and significance are different with that of enterprises in essence.

Brand organization is a kind of specific organization order environment, and the brand ecological organization exists in an ecological way, including four development stages of "enterprises, brands, brand organization and brand ecological organization". Sometimes brand organizations exist in enterprises, and sometimes it does not. Only when brand organization forms order and favorably gives authorization to organization power, the brand organization can exist; when brand organization loses management order, the organizational characteristics of brand organization will be dissolved immediately. Therefore, brand organization can only emerge under specific situations. It may go too soon or exist for a long time. It is a specific characteristic of fundamental management environment.

1 Structural actions of brand organization

Brand organization is not the enterprise in traditional sense. It is an expanded internal and external combination of an enterprise. A complete brand organization is divided into five categories including brand creator, brand organizer, brand operator, brand collaborator and brand user group. The members of brand organization can be seen in Fig. 5-1.

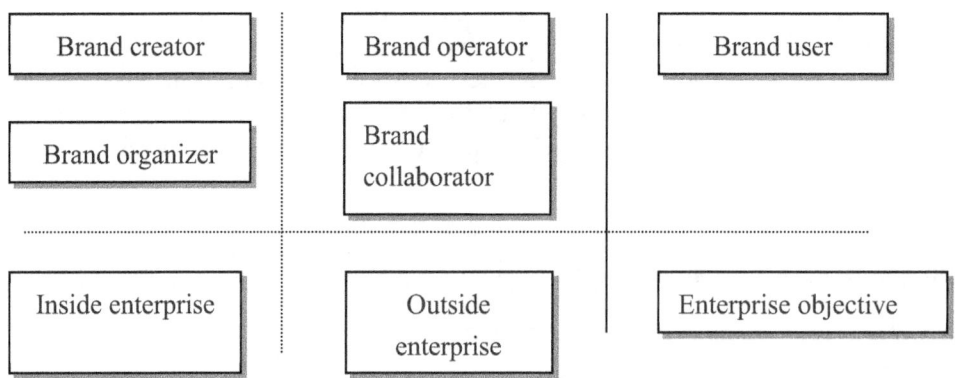

Fig. 5-1 Members of brand organization

The concept most frequently used by enterprises before is the "we and they", which is the most common language used inside and outside the enterprise. People consciously separate internal enterprise members, external members and target group-customers. Such languages are in enterprises internally or externally at any time. Similar expressions are "insider and outsider", "company and customers" and "head office and dealers". People make such distinction intentionally or unwittingly to clarify their role inside or outside the organization, and reject and deny functions and contributions of others in enterprise organization.

As a matter of fact, brand founders, or collaborative factors or unpaid users are members of brand organization. As long as every member deems themselves as an integrated part of brand organization, they can more accurately clarify their role, responsibilities and obligations.

The distinction of various roles intentionally made before is a kind of representation made by informal organization in organizations, and typical consciousness for organizational form separation. It greatly destructs integrated development of brand organization.

A complete brand organization is divided into specific roles, including:

Brand creator (brand founder, leader of brand recreation, brand technical consultant);

Brand organizer (brand investor, brand leader, brand officer, brand organization backbones, brand organization employees);

Brand operating network (brand operating department, direct sales outlets, brand dealers);

Brand collaborator (brand supply chain, brand supplier, brand alliance);

Brand user group (brand backbone user, brand regulars, brand customers, and brand users).

Special note on some brand organization members: brand creators are major persons making vast contribution during final formation process of brand, including initial founder of brand, leaders deciding and leading brand recreation, brand technical consultants greatly influencing brand organization reform, and sometimes brand officers. The specific members are decided by great contribution value for brand creation or recreation.

Brand organization backbones and brand user backbones firmly support development of brand organization with primary passion and sincerity. They may be senior leaders of brand organization, or common employees or common users. Their enthusiasm truly promotes brand development, and spontaneously transmits the brand. Brand organizations shall be good at seeking them, finding them and offering them more involvement, honor and support.

1.1 What on earth do brands change?

The focus of brand strength is brand organizing capacity and brand attractiveness, i.e. brand organization generates strong attractiveness from inside to outside via activities, and finishes efficient conversion from users to customers by attractiveness. The marketing activities of brand are centralized around this focus.

In view of this factor, enterprises shall make reform, and transit towards brand organization via brand recreation. Only a thorough and complete brand organization could finally be the connection between awareness and brand, and could finish branding targets.

Branding is a kind of thinking mode. Enterprises, both internally and externally, generate new brand thinking, and centralize all works, actions and values around brand. Earlier, enterprises may have paid too much attention to internal business management and operating network. However, the new brand organization must concern dynamic management of brand resources and organization activity, and greatly shorten connected relation between brand and person, brand and society.

Since the internet brand thinking is of many-for-one service form, anyone can talk with brands at any time anywhere, conduct purchasing and directly provide feedback through likes and dislikes of a brand, while the direct actions, feelings and reactions of the brand users are transmitting interactively. The contact method, communication method and handling method between brand organization and brand user are all changed. It requires the new generation brand organization behaving like a magnet.

Unfortunately, many enterprises failed to make such wise changes, and only deemed brand as one part of premium or marketing planning. What is worse, they believe brand construction needs a complex and vast investment return process, and take it for granted and think that brand is irrelevant to them.

They deem brand as a kind of dispensable object. Although people pay more to buy brand products, people purchasing other brands never place their brand in a reasonable position and never make deep consideration.

1.2 Fragmentation of brand organization

Even if enterprises plan to upgrade to brand organization, brand organization will not be established efficiently. Since brand fragmentation occurs at any time, the function will disrupt integrity and uniformity of brand organization. As mentioned above, internal members of enterprises are used to distinguish various relations between departments, or internal and external enterprises by "we and they" and reasonably reject or deny other people's function and contribution. Thus, brand organization will have very serious resistance, and hinder the thorough formation of brand organization.

The explanation of organization is: one organization is an entity or collective owning common target and consistent action, and harmonically combining internal and external order, resources and environment. The types of organization segmentation can be seen in Fig. 5-2.

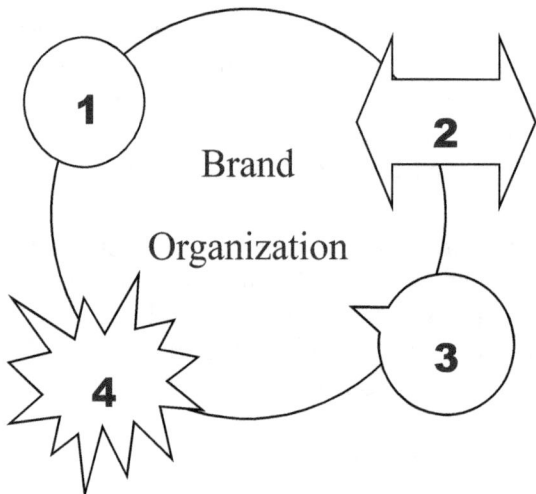

Fig. 5-2 Type of organization fragmentation

However, organization fragmentation exists truly, and plays certain negative role in influence on organizing ability and even destroys organization. There are mainly four types of organization fragmentation, respectively eccentric fragmentation, opposite contradiction, organization dissolution and informal organization fragmentation. From the third month after a new enterprise is found, the organization fragmentation will exist. Many new enterprises lose control in entrepreneurship due to organization fragmentation and then break down. Only 30% or less companies can live through the early survival and development period for nine months in a balanced way. Even companies operating maturely may have four organization fragmentation types simultaneously.

(1) The eccentric fragmentation means the five roles in brand organization are not synchronic. The typical characteristic is to segment the organization to different organizations in the sense of manmade ideology by "you, we, they" and make roles in brand organization in different psychological states. Many internal and external contradictions are generated hereby, and friction between organizations is enlarged artificially. Some departments and personnel in organization exist particularly to handle the contradiction, objection, conciliation and coordination.

(2) The opposite contradiction is the diverged contradiction gap between organizations, especially organization leaders so that organizations form several groups, even conflicting groups. Organizations spend too much time and energy in coordinating opinions of all parties and mediating contradiction. The

opposite contradictions will seriously delay decision-making speed and ability of brand organization. The opposite contradiction between shareholders and partners will emerge after a newly found enterprise operates for three months. Such circumstance may be generated easily for the "newly allocated" leaders. Employees inside the organization often do not know what party they belong to.

(3) The organization segmentation means to segment to the new organization from an organization. Such circumstance is common. After the higher level, middle level and grass-root of a brand organization learned and operated in an organization for some time, they will segment the organization according to former brand organization management mode, product structure and competitive advantages and disadvantages, and create the same or similar enterprises or competitive enterprises with direct market hedging with the former organization by running new enterprise or carrying out investment activities. Sometimes new brand organization will cause serious threats and market impact on original brand organization; sometimes new brand organization will take backbone staff of original brand organization and seriously weaken the organizing ability; sometimes new brand organization will surpass original brand organization leading to end of original brand organization.

(4) The informal organization segmentation will be reflected in composition and structure of the organization. Although a brand organization has official management level and departments, the informal organizations may exist largely, mainly shown as informal "opinion leaders". Since brand organization does not always offer favorable opportunity for performance and expression to every organization member, the "opinion leaders" among organization leaders or employees will generate this opportunity. They express their right to speak and establish their factual "power of leadership" by discussing negative news, inveigling organization members and damaging organization so as to damage organizing ability of original management level and original department. If organization members acknowledge the "organization danger", people will believe the new enterprises or mature brand organizations have certain "dangers", which will trigger collective complaints. Thus, the informal "opinion leaders" will be derived in a large number, and informal organization segmentation will infect and spread rapidly like the plague. That may not be members' faults. Too many faults are always caused by the highest leaders of enterprises. When one person becomes the highest leader of an enterprise, the defects of his/her ideas and behaviors will be enlarged unlimitedly, and fully exposed to everyone. Therefore, the fragmentation will generate rapidly.

Only clearly knowing facts of organization fragmentation, feasibly valuing brand organization science and designing better brand organization pattern by scientific management can effectively prevent a brand organization from organization segmentation in management design and avoid horrible circumstances.

1.3 Motivation of brand organization

The motivation of organization decides the membership composition and characteristics of enterprise culture elements. The motivation of organization is the initial motivation for people to decide to participate in foundation or participate in a brand organization; meanwhile, it is also the overall motivation to clarify existence and development of the entire brand organization. The benign opportunity will promote rapid development of brand organization while non-benign opportunity will generate different degrees of destructive power to brand organization.

First comes the motivation of people. When participating in creation of a brand organization, every shareholder and partner has certain initial motivation, and such motivation may be concealed. There are many kinds of dreams. Some people aim to reconstruct and contribute to society, some people aim to realize their own value, some people aim to acquire short-term economic benefits, some people aim to try new things, and some people aim to operate a business with seemingly stable income and prospect. In initial stage of business foundation, different motivations shall be screened effectively. With consistent or similar motivations, a brand organization can finish hyper-normal rapid development. Different motivations, especially opposite motivations, are like the "torpedo", which may explode within certain time.

Section II Brand Subjects

The motivation of people is reflected in the process of participating in a brand organization. Every day, numerous green hands participate in an enterprise and become a member with various targets. They have different opportunities. Someone aims to get higher payment, someone aims to support a family, someone aims to realize their value, someone aims to get opportunity of learning, and someone finds an easy job to reduce labor time and labor capacity. Motivation is usually covered by beautiful resume. The motivations of job hunters are necessary to screen. Personnel complying with brand organization opportunity can finally stay, and they are the premise for concerted efforts of brand organization.

The second is motivation, i.e. value orientation, of brand organizations. Everyone has different values, and every company has different preferences for brand organization cultures, such as technology, service, elegant environment and personnel with higher education background. Brand organization shall more clearly express value orientation before recruiting personnel and make job hunters clearly know motivation of brand organization. Employment is a kind of two-way selection. Brand organization shall strive to avoid applicants with motivations different from those of the brand organizations. If the personal value is not consistent with enterprise value, they will leave the enterprise soon. Rational and reasonable suggestions benefit both sides and can save time of applicants and encourage them to make more reasonable choices. The motivation of brand organization shows organizational characteristics such as brand features, management style, organizational ideology and key strategy.

1.4 Active reform of brand organization

The active reform of organization is usually pushed by innovator of brand organization. The reform may be made from up to down, from part to whole, or from inside to outside. It is of great significance for realizing organizational reform actions to increase reform sources of enterprises. The active reform of organization aims to promote awareness, attitude, behavior, responsibility and actions of all members to generate more active changes.

The reform environment is the parent that breeds organization reform. Anyone may push organization reform. However, if the overall environment of organization does not allow reform, the vitality of organization will be seriously insufficient, and reform is unable to generate. The organization will be seriously aged. On the contrary, brand organization greatly advocates and supports some tiny reforms. Brand organization owns sufficient vitality, and reform will occur at any time. Benign reforms are generating locally or overall, internally or externally, and the entire brand organization is reforming so as to cope with or innovatively surpass necessary organizational environment required by global market competition.

Brand organization shall deliberately introduce competition mechanism in each management field to encourage new reforms, consciously cultivate ideas of organization reform in reserve leaders and management intern training, and encourage creating value in all possible fields so as to motivate entrepreneurship inside the organization. Encouraging supply chain and brand users to participate in active reform of brand organization will further promote organization vitality, and make people understand more the reform of organization and more actively and enthusiastically urge brand organization to be more ideal.

After the operation matures for a period of time, such as a decade, the higher management level of brand organization shall start carrying out brand recreation to certain degree, and motivate brand vitality by large-scale and thorough brand recreation so as to finish the progress of brand organization towards new goals by thorough organizational reform. The repeated progress of creating and pursuing goals will bring brand organization to a higher level, and make brand organization become a powerful, active and developed vigorous brand life which is more perfect, more ideas and more attractive for new reform powers.

2 Ecological-oriented development of brand organization–group shift

Human beings exist by groups, and connect by interpersonal network. Except special circumstances, people are unable to develop independently without a group. It is emphasized that brand enterprise is a kind of brand organization whereas brand exists by the form of organization. Brand cannot develop separately from organization form, and must highly depend on organization. By applying group effect, the group shift can be implemented to acquire future infinite development space of brand organization.

When referring to the group relationship of brand organization, we divide brand organization groups into three key groups, successively brand backbone, brand staff and brand users.

The group of brand backbone not only contains brand leader, backbone members, but also contains backbone of brand supply chain, service provider and brand users. The backbone group is the frame forming brand organization. The people rich with spirits, power, enthusiasm and endeavor are the dominant pillar for development of brand organization. At any time, the largest loss of an enterprise is to underestimate the support of an enthusiast for brand organization, because you never know who the passionate supporter is. He/she may be the next president or celebrity. Even ordinary people may support you with their ability or resources. The wisest, most significant decision and the most important investment of an enterprise is to win the hearts of all supporters and convert them to the backbone power of brand organization.

The groups of brand staff and users are the groups making contribution to or interested in brand organization. Every one of brand staff and users may be converted to new brand backbone and become the loyal supporter of brand via brand learning and transmission organized by brand backbone group. Although they only serve the brand or preliminarily understand the brand, the brand organization shall spare no effort to strive for them. Enterprises continuously use all means such as publicity, transmission, actions and activities to attract brand staff and users, and convert them to brand backbones so that the great charm of an organization is directly shown as brand attraction effect. Through the group shift process, the brand organization grows rapidly and can reach the long-term objective of sustainable operation.

2.1 Brand group shift effect

Group shift effect means humans always exist by group. When people are on their own, much self-awareness may occur, which can be depressed and pessimistic. When individual state transfers to group state, the self-awareness will reduce, and vitality and positivity will be generated. Individuals need to subordinate to certain group. The formation of brand organization is the process of establishing and organizing group, gathering individuals and finishing shift toward group and forming group awareness. Brand organization helps people finish organizational shift from individuals to group by employee recruitment and employee group actions, and also finish transfer from brand users to groups by setting up customer club and organizing user experience activities.

However, not every ideal organization shift will be smooth and last for a long time. If the organization is not vital enough, employees will lack sense of belonging, or if brand users fail to realize group effect and influence on them, the group division may occur. In that case, employees will leave the group and return to individual state, and may generate new informal organization; user may return to individual state, and turn to other more attractive brand organization.

The group shift and division process of brand organization can be seen in Fig. 5-3.

Section II Brand Subjects

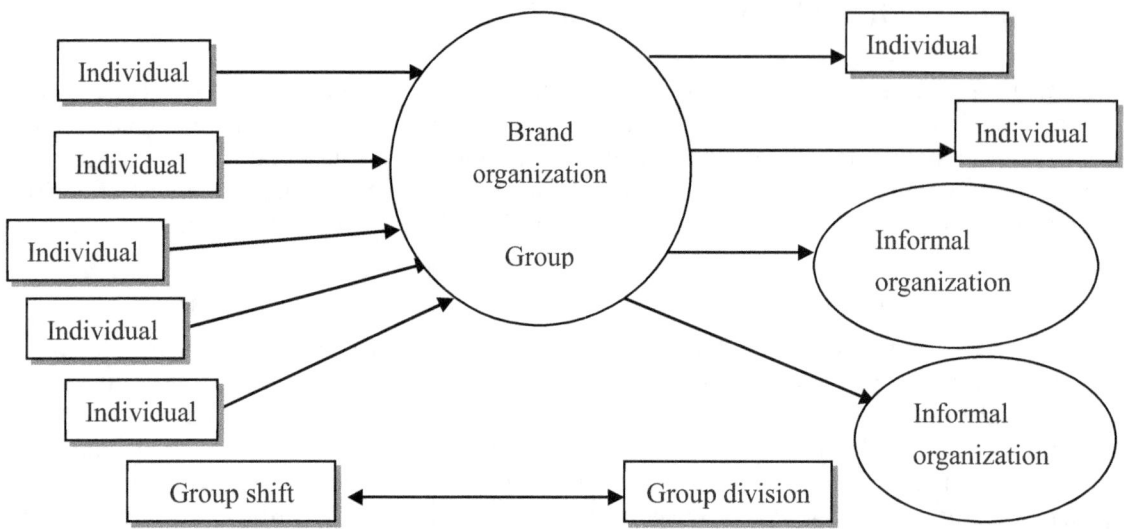

Fig. 5-3 Group shift and division process of brand organization

People often search for and probe groups for "I was a soldier", "I am from rural area", "when I was in college…", "I once watched an inspiring movie", "I am starting a business", "I have used certain brand", "I am the loyal user of certain brand", "I have encountered similar problem" to find consumer groups with same experience, similar circumstance and consuming the same brand. Thus, the seeking process from individual to group is finished. The brand group shift is an important organization process finishing transfer from individual to group.

2.2 Brand group shift process

In view of group shift effect, people always shift between "individual-group-individual", and either transfer from individual to group, or separate from group to become individual. The attitudes, responsibilities, awareness and emotions are deeply changed therewith. Brand organization shall favorably apply group shift effect, and effectively organize groups. The group shift process and characteristics of brand organization can be seen in Table 5-1.

Table 5-1 Brand organization group shift process and characteristics

Group process	Organization shift	Brand organization	Organization division
Type	Individual	Group	Individual
Change of awareness	Self-awareness increases	Self-awareness decreases	Self-awareness increases
Characteristics	Depressed Lonely Tired Pessimistic Anxious Timid Benefit Claiming Passive	Natural Organizing Sunny Happy Confident Brave Responsible Contributing Active	Resisting Worried Depressed Pessimistic Dissolved Escaping Remuneration Slack Rejecting

Everyone wishes to participate in some interest groups, religious organizations and voluntary organizations to seek happiness, mission and value and is willing to pay to get certain group return, such as post, identity, honor and opportunity. Monetary profits and substances are not always expected by people. The spiritual sense of belonging is the major demand for return. Even if enterprises offer profound remuneration, they cannot always attract excellent talents. The more outstanding talents wish to realize personal value. People lacking spirit of contribution and true skills and knowledge are prone to short-term material rewards. Brand organization shall design for scientific remuneration and value return to truly attract the most outstanding talents.

The condition for common personnel to participate in a brand organization is surely due to less economic costs. Under most circumstances, people do not list time spent under costs. However, for brand organization backbones, the condition is less economic cost and relatively high conditions. The conditions shall be represented by technical level, academic value, time contribution and resource network.

To acquire opportunity for learning, exercises and acknowledge growth is the most important selection mode for one person to participate in an organization. In order to acquire more and better talents and supporters, brand must respect everyone. Only by truly respecting everyone can a brand acquire other's respect. The effect is mutual. The organizational design must pay attention to discrimination, such as discrimination of educational background, sex and region. The discrimination of educational background is the most crucial. Over 80% population in the world do not have high educational background, who are the main power for brand development and brand consumption. Enterprises must achieve "everyone is equal for knowledge, and competence is oriented", set threshold by true skills and knowledge, and value capacity and value. The restriction of education degree base line shall not be set. The restriction of education will seriously hinder knowledge creation and production and make knowledge system closed and aged.

When a new member (new employee and new user) selects to participate in a brand organization, he/she will experience a mental involvement process, including expectation, understanding, learning, getting familiar and make a decision to either stay or leave. This process is the perception process of a new member, and the leading program of the process is crucial. Particularly during the transfer process from new user to customer, first trust design becomes an important content for brand design. The process is the process for new member to leave individual state and transit to group state. The attitude, enthusiasm, mental state and psychology will undergo active changes, and the process is non-repeatable or irreversible. For any person or brand organization, the process will occur once, and never again. When one individual becomes enthusiastic for a group, it is an opportunity for brand organization; when the enthusiasm fades away, member will disappear and never go back.

Due to group shift effect, everyone will emphasize group property. Brand organization acquires substantial development by group attraction effect, i.e. common member (user), usually employee relation board, brand user council and user club, cultivate and give play to brand backbone power, and spread among more extensive interpersonal network by group characteristics. In that way, everyone can drive people around him/her and people they know to transfer from individual to brand. Otherwise, brand organization will be too loose, and difficult to generate attraction and carry out valid interpersonal network transmission. There is no group effect in user relation management mode of official customer service program such as Weibo and Micro-journal. Therefore, users still exist as individuals. The organization group effect can be generated only when individuals are organized powerfully.

2.3 Group interaction between brand organization and non-brand organization

People and organization are of compact or loose group interaction relation. Particularly in brand organization and non-brand organization, the interactive relationship between brand user and organization is obvious. The interaction degree of brand users (individuals) in brand organization or non-brand organization are ranked by Grade 1-6 and Grade 6-1 to observe the changes in psychology, emotion and behavior of individuals when the demand for brand organization is satisfied or not. The group interaction degree between brand organization and non-brand organization can be seen in Table 5-2.

Table 5-2 Group interaction degree between brand organization and non-brand organization

		Brand organization	
1	Active interaction	Show status of others, provide help and praise	
2	Active interaction	Show tension release, joke, happiness	
3	Active interaction	Show satisfaction, happiness and comfort	
4	User identification	Provide professional spirits, methods or technology	
5	User identification	Provide suggestions, direction and future	
6	User identification	Provide oriented and accurately recognized information, repeat important information	

		Non-brand organization	
6	Attempting to solve	Seek for status and sense of verification	
5	Attempting to solve	Seek for psychological security, under-assessment and sense of unknown	
4	Attempting to solve	Seek for demand and function substitute	
3	Negative response	Not professional selection; comprehensive integration, confused recognition information	
2	Negative response	Status is nonconforming; give up and reject early; not provide help	
1	Negative response	Show tension and unsafe consumption, and quit as user	

3 Management order of brand ecological organization

The management order is the ecological system of organization, and a balanced mechanism for dynamic and ordered operation after brand organization is upgraded to brand ecological organization. In enterprises without order, management is chaotic, and such chaos creates chaotic of management order. The enterprises will suffer from vague management structure, unclear responsibility, difficult accountability, broke organization, low job efficiency and divided public opinion. The enterprises with order will show balanced and stable organization operation, ordered operation, clear target, distinct responsibilities, smooth flow, high efficiency and concerted effort.

Enterprise is a member of social organization, and thus social order will affect enterprise order. For instance, the social problems and bad morality such as abortion, crime, corruption, non-discipline, and money-orientation will affect brand organization. However, enterprise is also a specific member in social organization. The active, positive and ordered brand organization order can awake conscience, motivate positive energy, develop morality and promote employees and user individuals to make benign awareness, state and behavior in favor of organization development so that brand organization can own vigorous spirits and vitality, operate in order, circulate virtuously and progress rapidly.

Earlier, enterprises are easy to neglect order problems, and apply management contents such as management codes, management system and enterprise culture to sort out and regulate management order, causing disadvantages such as halfway management order design, low management operation efficiency and weak responsibility awareness of employees. In order to give play to efficient, excellent and high quality management order, brand organization must highlight the leading role of management order in enterprise management, and make favorable operating, balanced and stable management order become the core pillar of organization development.

The favorably, orderly and dynamically operating brand management order is the guarantee of all enterprises to keep favorable management level and operation quality. As an independent and specific organization, the management order of brand organization is higher than social order. Some viewpoints treat social problem equal with various enterprise management problems, and shuffle problems occurred in enterprises to the society. The viewpoints are wrong and irresponsible. In that case, an enterprise has not formed organization order. Brand organization can completely create partial social new order by independent management order, and create positive operating environment and favorable operating structure. This is the instinct of brand organization, and can favorably improve social progress. As long as all enterprises dare to undertake responsibilities and actively change order of this enterprise, the social order of human being can make progress more rapidly and significantly.

3.1 Ternary structure of management order

The chaotic human order is mainly decided by binary thinking. The enterprise organization with binary contradiction and binary structure of right or wrong, front or back, all or nothing, active or passive is easy to fall into disorder. Behaviors regarding official leader and non-leader, right and protest, task and implementation, responsibility and shuffle, being a person and doing right thing, right or wrong become contradiction and focus suffered during business management.

The line structure, in which the superior leader takes responsibility of the inferior member, is a very serious binary structure. The binary level of leaders and subordinates increases to generate frequent internal contradiction and problems. The leadership and management layer of the company spends most of its time and energy in handling the complex and snarled contradictions.

People and organization are instinctive to protect themselves. Due to basic emotion and sensible logic, each department and group of enterprise organization have the instinct of self-protection, and various protection instincts are generated due to emotions between people. Various responsibility chains inside an enterprise are easy to be damaged by the protection distinct so as to cause many circumstances such as worse implementation power, improper accountability, insufficient responsibility correction, and unfinished implementation of tasks. The basic level of management order is in chaotic state.

Furthermore, various protection instincts inside the organization will cause disorder of management process flow. Just as enterprises usually use "you and we" to segment or separate each department, or inside and outside the enterprise to different organizations, the enterprise will cause self-closure. Breaking from various external advanced orders, knowledge update, and competitive advantages, enterprises fail to contact with the outside world, and easily accelerate aging of organization.

The optimal way to change business management order is to constitute ternary structure, i.e., command, order and implementation are undertaken by different departments and members. We divide the strategic structure of brand organization into brand strategy layer, brand technology layer and brand implementation layer, which is the scientific ternary structure division of organizational structure.

The brand technology layer takes charge of management order, and the composition form may be the brand assets management companies and brand technology committee. Independent brand assets management companies take charge of brand asset appreciation, and specific implementation of brand implementation supervision, technology formulation, schedule management and brand technical standards by the professional role of brand assets so as to reduce opposite contradiction of brand strategy layer in direct management. The brand technical committee can be comprised of secondary committees such as brand user committee, brand customer relations board, and work efficiency committee, and can form knowledge chain and technical introduction with external brand technology supporting units.

The ternary structure of brand organization plays an important, clear and prominent role in balanced, stable and ordered operation of business management order. In recent years, management modes such as third party authentication, third party outsourcing, third party trusteeship and third party after-sales service are emerging greatly, because the third party professional management has made clear labor division for old-type management, and generates active management effect, economic effect and premium appreciation effect for management responsibility breakdown and value-added brand service premium.

In business management, the third party order entity takes charge of management order formulation, schedule management, management task implementation supervision, technical standard, job efficiency and accountability supervision and is the main structural ecological management mode to effectively improve organization efficiency, improve management level, and improve favorable operation of order. Since only the third party can effectively apply various means and methods for order management to find problems, and promote management progress in a fairer way, each department and each layer of the company, if jointly applied by a third party order entity, will give play to significant management effect. For instance, setting posts to follow up market progress, management task implementation, and supervise management technical standard and accountability will greatly ease direct management pressure of leaders, and accelerate the easing of management contradiction, improving management efficiency, accountability and judgment. It plays the role of justice.

3.2 Justice is the basic guarantee for management order

The fair competition of global enterprises, fair environment in a country and fair order in business management are the soil for normal development of every enterprises participating in global competition. The fair environment is particularly important. For enterprise development, "fairness" is the "law-based" way for organic operation and ordered management of the enterprise.

Fair competition is the primary development principle inside a brand organization. Organization reform shall be carried out based on the principle of fair competition. Employment recruitment, opportunity selection, payment and honor acquisition shall be carried out under framework of company competition. The policies and behaviors not complying with fair competition are not supposed to exist.

Fair accountability is the responsibility environment that brand organization must guarantee internally. The strict accountability mechanism is the premise to implement enterprise responsibilities and arouse awareness of responsibilities of all staff. The vague accountability or false liability judgment will make members of brand organization lose confidence and further lose public support.

Fairness is usually advocated by the brand strategy layer, and implemented by the brand technology layer, i.e. leaders and members of brand technology layer must be fair. Due to ternary structure of organization, the entire brand organization can guarantee overall fairness as long as brand technology layer takes charge of formulation and maintenance of fair competition and fair order. Fairness couldn't be guaranteed previously without order layer. The binary management structure and accountability between leadership layers may vary due to "people". The "people-based" governance may surpass the "law-based" governance, so that the fairness will be meaningless. Without fairness, the organizational characteristics of brand organization will be dissolved immediately.

Fairness is a kind of rational, ideal and ordered "law-based" status. Fairness shall consider the nature of "things". It is the scientific explanation for any management accident, the management environment required by operation of parent enterprise, and a setting process of self-adaptation rules for business management. Regardless of "manmade" factors, fairness guarantees dynamic, ordered and coordinated development inside and outside brand organization by reasonable management order design. Enterprise can effectively participate in global fair competition only when it forms favorable management order for fair competition.

Exercises

1. Fill in the blanks: Brand organization is a specific organization order, including four development stages of "_____-_____-_____-_____".

2. True or False Question: Fair accountability is the responsibility environment that brand organization must guarantee internally. The vague accountability or false liability judgment will make members of brand organization lose confidence and further lose public support. (   )

3. Discuss: What do brands change globally?

Section II Brand Subjects

Chapter 6

Brand Consumption

The limit must appear when human productivity develops into certain stage. In that case, the production oversupplies, and various contradictions about productivity development are generated frequently, including the below average productivity development level, unbalanced productivity structure and excessive production capacity. At that time, humans entered the period of great social and economic structure transformation when productivity was decided by consumptive power. The growth capacity takes the place of productivity and becomes the new topic of the epoch. The consumption growth capacity, including consumptive power, purchasing power, brand ecological order, brand consumer theory, brand consumption authority and brand consumption capital theory, becomes the new global market competition structure and marks the human growth capacity level.

1 Consumers in ecological chain of global brands

The ecological chain of global brands and the nature's food chain are equally important to the ecological development relation between humans and nature. The ecological chain of global brands is comprised of producers, operators and consumers, it operates naturally under brand ecological environment, and develops under the ecological balance; while the nature's food chain contains three roles including the producer, consumer and decomposer as well as the natural ecological order.

No matter if the consumers are in the brand ecological chain or in the natural food chain, the overall properties are consistent, i.e. they do not engage in production, but need to acquire energy, nutrition and substances from producers during growth, development and survival. However, the difference between consumers in the brand ecological chain and in the food chain lies in the transmission modes of the two natural chains.

In brand ecological chain, brand consumption is transmitted among brands occurring as a consequence of producer, operator and consumer handling. Producers take charge of the energy and nutrition production, as well as of the new matter creation and production. The senior form of production is brand. Since global dispersed aggregation and mobility characteristics of population, excluding minority producers who can directly provide brand to consumers, can finish delivery by multiple communication means and delivery mediums, most producers need to deliver brands to consumers through a highly developed global brand operating network or local brand operating network. Producers and operators shall take charge of value improvement and after-sales service for consumers during brand consumption process so as to finish the necessary brand consumption enhancement.

Brand consumers undertake overall demand of brand consumption, they decide to consume according to their own demands, decide about diversified demands of spirits, culture, materials, nutrition and services supplied by brands, and finish the degradation process of natural decomposition during use, for example when certain food is eaten, a certain bag is worn, when equipment loses usage efficiency, and when the sense of priority ends. Such natural decomposition process is the essence of natural circular development for repeated consumptions, and also the core source of brand profits. It is considered to be required by the energy supply, production condition supplementation and the development of brand producers and operators.

2 Consumers in brand ecological chain network cluster

In the natural world, each animal eats diversified foods. Thus, a series of complex food chain networks is formed between food chains. This is the same as the brand ecological chain. However, brand ecological chain network is relatively more complicated.

Limited by movement speed, geological position and natural environment, animals can move in a small spaces. Therefore, animals have few selection rights for producers. They must be restricted by natural conditions, and cannot decide what they would eat today and what nutrition they should acquire tomorrow; they cannot improve spirit requirements, culture requirements and neither the energy supply of producers. The range of their demands only covers the basic survival conditions. The freedom of choice of human beings, however, is much larger. In order to fulfill the requirements for own development, producers need to greatly promote development of various transportations, operation networks, supply channels and purchase delivery ways so as to greatly strive for consumers. In that way, consumers, even in a tiny space, can fulfill the freedom of choice through interaction and communication with technologies and information. Therefore, producers are passively in a global brand ecological chain network cluster, and apply multiple means, methods and opportunities to approach the consumers, attract and communicate with them, and rapidly strive for orders, finish deliveries and improve diversified demands of consumers by brand consumption enhancement. This is the modern brand development that is different from the modern brand development order of basic survival demands of enterprises.

Enterprise brand development shall not only follow development characteristics of brand ecological chain network cluster, but also deeply realize how to acquire effective development in the natural order operating environment of brand ecological chain. Brand ecological order exists in the brand ecological chain. As human productivity upgrades to human growth capacity, consumption decision and consumption mechanism take initiative of human growth capacity, and, in turn, deeply affects development of productivity so as to generate the ecological development order environment in which consumptive power decides productivity and purchasing power decides the consumer market capacity. The problems such as formulation of global brand rules, maintenance of brand consumption ecology, natural balance between brand consumption demand and production relationship, and natural ecological protection during consumption decomposition process are the key points for development of brand ecological order, and also the basic operating orders for the progress and development process of human beings.

Moreover, human development is diversified. People can change roles among brand producers, operators and consumers. One can not only be a producer of certain brand, an operator of another brand, but also a consumer of other brands. This is a special basic characteristic of the development of brand ecological chain network cluster. It is the transformation of people among the three roles that promotes basic demands of human beings for brands to improve ceaselessly and synchronically, as well as updating and upgrading global brands. During synchronous brand development, people can acquire equal brand value by acquiring income, increasing purchasing power, consuming brands and creating production, and make brand growth capacity continuously develop into a higher level.

Comparatively, the food chain is simpler. Except human beings, any creature on the earth has its survival food chain, and plays a role in a certain link of the food chain. The balance of the natural food chain is the foundation for survival and development of natural environment that the human beings need to maintain in order to protect the natural ecological development order. If one link is lost in the food chain, the ecological system will be unbalanced. Similarly, if a brand producer fails to favorably master the development structure of brand ecological chain, then the foundation for brand operation and development will not exist, let alone the brand development of the enterprise. The development valuing the brand ecological system is the most important development instinct and the factual foundation for a future global brand, and an important mark showing the brand growth capacity level.

SECTION II BRAND SUBJECTS

3 Brand growth capacity: consumptive power decides productivity

When human brands develop to a certain degree, the most serious market problem is not the marketing of brand producer - "how to sell products"; but on the contrary, the largest development difficulty encountered by brand producers is how to face the more confused consumers – the difficult brand selection. This is a demand for important ideological change suffered during the marketing development stage and development relation in human market, i.e. a historic transition period from marketing to brand attractiveness. Consequently, the fact of development will be reflected as the extinction of worldwide mercantilism and the comprehensive degradation of enterprise marketing function. Furthermore, the development stage, rules and ways of marketing will face serious changes.

Confusion about brand consumption is presented as an increasingly upgrading contradiction between market consumption demand and producers. It is the development relationship of enterprises in market competition, i.e. enterprises decide what branding development mode can meet the increasing consumption demand, and what professional brand should supply the market. The confusion is not only a significant opportunity, but also a cutting-edge challenge for enterprise brand development. The bottleneck limits the ideologies of the industrial man, social man and brand man. Both brand founders and leaders have great dreams for the brand. Nonetheless, the actual brand development depends on the limit of three basic growth capacities of industrial man, social man and brand man ideas.

The large-scale production and operation problems must be solved if brand production needs to expand its capacity and market. Otherwise, the products of a brand must be restricted to a tiny region and smaller market field. For instance, one can only run a cake shop successfully, but cannot form a cake brand with an operating network owning 50 outlets simultaneously. Without the ideology of social man, brand fails to develop, focusing just on social contribution, social services, social responsibilities and social operation, and brand development can only be in a low and preliminary development level. Without ideology of brand man, brand products have no soul and no life, and fail to reach the condition required by the brand, let alone become an outstanding brand.

The development structure of global market in the 21st Century is that the consumptive power decides productivity. Such development characteristic is different from former producer theories. The transformation of producer theory is an important social, economic and structural turn, from commodity economy to brand economy. Producers put emphasize on sales, raw materials, process, production mode, labor service, good capital, cost and profits, production conditions such as land and real estate, production structure, production development mode, product accounting as well as entity assets appraisal, bank loan and goods capital finance. However, in brand economy, such development and accounting modes will be eliminated successively, and replaced by theory of brand consumer.

In terms of production development mode, due to difficult brand selection caused by consumers' confusion, the key and emerging brands acquire the development authority in order to directly communicate with consumers. For brand consumption selection, producers design and recreate products and services based on feedback model of brands, finished research, development, production and delivery by implementing reverse engineering, and thus changing and optimizing raw materials and production process, while keeping the profitability level and improving the brand performance. Such brand development capacity is on the basis of "making consumers use better and acquire better brand perception and use experiences". The cost accounting mode of input and output will evolve to long-term assets and the maintenance mode will profit. Enterprises will, regardless of costs, carry out raw materials improvement, product R&D, service design and user attraction so as to search for the balance mode for optimal brand profit level and brand value development mode.

4 Ecological order of brand consumption: purchasing power decides market capacity

The market development is limited. The sum of consumptive and purchasing power decides the total market capacity, which is known as shallow-level market and deep market. The purchasing power contains the sum of citizen purchasing power in one country, as well as individual family purchasing power. The family purchasing power contains purchasing power level and expectation. The former refers to total current family purchasing power, and the latter is the brand expectation for purchasing power growth desired by family members and the decision that made them purchase something. The B theory has disclosed that the purchasing power expectation will stimulate a family and its members to acquire better development modes for income growth; while the universal growth of family income represents an overall growth of consumption level in a country.

In the shallow-level market, market capacity undergoes changes of rapid expansion and sharp reduction of growth. In the early stage when a new product enters the market, the market will acquire high speed growth by virtue of capital force under high speed market motion. In that case, enterprises will be in the state of rapid expansion. However, expansion is not unlimited. When market develops to a certain degree, the market growth will slow down. The sharp reduction of growth shows the market has encountered development bottleneck - market saturation. Therefore, enterprises shall make strategic adjustment. They may implement the umbrella-type development strategy to invade other market fields in order to maintain requirements of capital market for market expansion by more production lines. In the event that the enterprise has finished the IPO, the requirements of capital market for enterprise performance will enlarge so that the enterprises are forced to maintain diversified market growth by increasing new products or by investment activities. This is the typical primary market economy with development of producer theory, product life cycle, primary market scale, and ultimate capacity of market purchasing.

Nevertheless, global market will finally develop into a deep market stage led by brand market. The deep market is built around the brand project. Instead of pursuing unlimited market development, every brand pursues limited market capacity of a single brand. A brand usually has clarified combination structure of brand market during the preliminary development, i.e. market development requirements of group brand cluster and single brand. P&G and Apple Inc. have such typical market structure for brand development. Multiple brand markets of P&G only pursue market scale of USD 1 Billion, and develop market by the USD 1 Billion single brand combination. Every brand can keep competitive advantages and operate continuously for a long time. Apple Inc. develops purchasing power of brand product cluster by ceaseless upgrading of main brand, develops markets by engaging in a few main brands, and finishes market growth by upgrading of products.

In general, deep market is a mature brand market development mode, and the final mode for global market, including product market, capital market and market design development power level. The capital demand of deep market is centralized on sustainable profitability level of the brand, and concerns stability and sustainability of main brand business, while the requirement for market growth is low. It is the objective law universally applicable to benign brand market development which develops and deposits the market. The key point of operating mode and market judgment lies in mature, stable and sustainable long-term operating capacity of brand. Thanks to the time-honored brand, the stock holder may get a lifetime benefit, and stocks will be of value for property inheritance. In addition, global deep market naturally eliminates global shallow-level market step by step. Finally, the market requires highly branded products and services which own leading-edge status and decisive competitiveness and stably expand and develop the market and keep the long-term stable operating level rather than products and market which are urgent in rapid market expansion.

Not only global market or capital market, but the consumers' market also develops in this way. In order to get rid of confusion, consumers shall establish a complete set of mature and stable brand system that they require and depend on during their lifetime. These brands will accompany them throughout their life. Thus, consumers will, facing numerous brand products, ceaselessly select, test and screen

SECTION II BRAND SUBJECTS

various products till relatively fixed ultimate brand selection is established in certain category or certain field, and final brands are being used regularly. During development, any brand must keep the lifetime fixed demand, and maintain the permanent development relation by favorable brand operation mode.

Currently, global market is still in development stage toward mature and stable deep market. All countries in the world will universally adopt policy interference to expand domestic demand of consumption. Markets of developed countries mainly adopt multiple policies to encourage highly free market competition, while developing countries usually adopt economic means, including reducing bank deposit interest, reducing tax of certain industrial market, and brand place of origin protection, to stimulate consumption.

It is important to note that the expansion of domestic demand for consumption and simulation of national consumption does not mean that it gets benefits from producers in this country. The difference between brand market and common market is that brand market is not limited by countries, and citizens have the right to pursue better brand enjoyment. The domestic demands that are expanded will mainly focus on brand consumption of exporter, and the consumptive and purchasing capacity will be shown in brand supply. If the producers of the country fail to reach branding requirements, they will be abandoned by consumers in the market. It requires that one country must provide balance between brand productivity and brand consumptive capacity when expanding domestic demand and stimulating consumption, and lay emphasis on improving domestic branding level for policies of domestic demand consumption expansion. Only by accelerating brand development can one country truly improve the development level of consumptive and purchasing capacity so as to enhance the national competitiveness.

5 Theory of brand consumers

We have pointed out that the global market development is transiting from commodity economy to brand economy. Such transition is the unprecedented significant transformation of social and economic structure for human progress and development history in the past 5000 years. It is not only a key fundamental period deciding about the existence of a brand in the next hundreds or thousands of years, but also a long-term future plan for social and economic development and reform of a country.

The theory of brand consumers is comprehensively and rapidly eliminating the theory of producer till it finally and thoroughly eliminates the original production mode of producers. It will develop into a brand ecological organization, integrating "consumption-production" that centers on brand operation, and finally become a stably and maturely operating self-adaptive brand ecological chain in super brand ecological chain network of human beings.

The deep change is also reflected in growth history of human consumers. As the most important link in human brand ecological chain, brand consumers will finish the thorough development in the 21st century. This is consistent with the development process of human basic demands and ecology.

The basic need of human being was mainly survival before the 21st century. Except the freedom of choice which animals do not have, natural human basic demand is the demand for food, residence and traffic. The population in few developed countries and developed regions has the conditions for higher selection, i.e. branding selection.

Human beings were rescued from death when the two world wars ended in the 20th century, and then started eliminating poverty. Previous human development was based on the basic survival conditions. Furthermore, with social development and consumption growth, the growth of human basic demands began to appear and grow gradually, and consumption market was expanded and developed as well. In the past, people firstly wanted enough to eat, then something good to eat, and later something nutritious to eat. Next, they wanted healthy food, cultural enjoyment, good body, long life, and protective system for food safety. People unlimitedly improve and develop those basic demands.

By the 21st century, the basic demands of human beings in aspects of food, clothes, residence and travel have made fundamental changes. The growing part will be satisfied and supplemented ceaselessly by global brands. Brands get development and opportunities herewith. This is the foundation for the future of brands, and the developing distinct of human beings is that ceaselessly increase brand consumptive capacity expand brand market capacity and improve human brand productivity.

Unless one country, region or family are still in poverty and only have the basic demand of survival, the income growth in any region must drive consumption growth, and, in turn, promote formation of brand consumption and develop increasing demand for brand consumption. Thus, brand consumption becomes the new basic demand of human beings. The theory of brand consumption is the basic development mode for human brands based on theory of brand consumption development.

6 Theory of brand consumption development: basic form of brand consumption demand development

From the 21st century, the basic demand of a human being is no longer survival, but becomes the increasingly developing brand consumption demand, brand consumption market, brand producer and brand development power level. Thus, enterprise brands can always be under development, and can be synchronous with brand demand growth of consumers by ceaselessly improving development capacity mode. Otherwise, the brands will be eliminated naturally by the market. As evolution of species and improvement for human beings, enterprise brand developers with ceaseless improvement can acquire development ability, and have the opportunity to improve the development.

The basic forms of brand consumption demand development mainly contain three modes, respectively the development of human basic demand, development of brand preference, and development of brand value. All the three aspects constitute the basic theory for human brand development in the consumption market.

The development of human's basic demands, i.e. brand consumption demands, contains five main forms, including the development of survival conditions (natural environment enjoyment level for food, residence and travel), development of brand basic demands (brand performance development level, service life, quality stability and performance elements), development of special brand demands (personality, identity, honor, nutrition, health, happiness and relaxation), development of brand user group demand (sense of belonging, sense of achievements, sense of identity, sense of value, sense of participation acceptance, emotion, and long-term demand), and development of brand consumption safety (food safety system, purchase channel, reliable e-business, new brand perception mode and primary trust design of brand).

Human brand development is, to a certain degree, the process of brand preference development. The brand producers with development capacity and brand consumers with development demand jointly promote brand development. The brand producers with development capacity promote continuous reform in consumption forms and consumption mode by ceaselessly creating new brand expression form, brand sensory experience, brand product form and brand service methods. Such natural elimination process is the main competitor on the market, combining industrial reform and creative destruction of the combination structure in the old market.

Brand consumers with development demand ceaselessly require international, professional, individual and stylized consumption characteristic so as to promote the generation of emerging brands, and promote original brands to ceaselessly implement brand recreation so as to adapt to new market changes. Various brand preference demands are the main development elements for brand development capacity, and promote diversified development modes of brands. Moreover, original brand markets are impacted ceaselessly, and new brand market capacity is expanded. The professional brand and professional brand market accelerate the decomposing global market, and it is reflected as a flexible change, such as a ceaseless increase or decrease of each market capacity, like the sudden market reduction trend in certain e-business markets during a certain period. When brand producers do not have valid development capacity, the rapid reduction of market trend during the certain period will be obviously felt.

SECTION II BRAND SUBJECTS

Brand value development is a balanced development relation between development of brand productivity and brand consumptive capacity, and established on the basis of brand value development mode on brand consumption side. It is the brand value discovery, perception and creation process of brand performance, and is the enterprise brand organization value chain system based on feedback mode centering on consumer research.

In commodity economy or producer theory, the development of price system is crucial, and shown in financial indexes such as input, output, and cost profits rate, as well as in accounting methods. However, the price system will be weakened in brand economy, because brand will eliminate price consciousness of consumers. Finally, brand value will replace product value and become the basic appraisal element for brand market, brand economy and brand market value of global deep development.

7 Brand consumption right

Brand consumption development is also shown in growth of brand consumption right, including the consumption right development (leading status of brand consumers in market), brand consumption right-oriented development (growth of branding consumption requirement) and brand consumption right organization development.

In the highly developing brand market, the leading right and dominant status of market selection are transferred to consumers from producers, and become the structure of brand development capacity in which consumptive capacity decides productivity. Diversified consumption demands decide brand products, brand services and positive changes in brand market business mode that brand producers should develop, and also propose requirements for a series of active or passive changes in brand product research, development, production conditions, production process and purchase channels.

However, it does not mean that the consumption right of consumers must be authorized, that it has to be universal and publicly-recognized as a decisive purchasing power. On the contrary, brand producers can develop brand right to be in balance with brand consumption right by brand ideology. This is the perfect time for upgrading the producer ideas, from "meeting demands of market" and "meeting requirements of customers" to "actively creating new market demand" and "proposing requirements for consuming users".

Brands are unable to meet extensive market demand, but are only the products provided under specific consumption conditions to specific markets and people with specific consumptive capacity. Brand producers also have the right to require consumers with specific conditions and characteristics as their brand users. Those highly developed brands do not serve the common public so as to develop balanced development mode for producers and consumers with equal two-way rights, and generate the "brand attractiveness" by distance herein. Therefore, the senior brand consumption demand in aspects of identity, status, honor and happiness can be balanced with the increasingly growing income, consumption demand, consumptive capacity, consumption selection right and consumption enjoyment of consumers.

The right-oriented brand consumption mainly shows improving branding consumption requirements of consumers. Those requirements are the essences for development of brand-oriented living standard. Brand is a kind of pursuit and enjoyment of spiritual materialization serving but more important than human life. It has a supply and demand relation with brand value, the equal value market of growing living standard, life style and job and work quality requirements. As people's income increases, many consumption demands will be transferred to specific brand consumption requirements – brands must provide and meet basic cultural requirements of human beings. This is the result of continuous upgrading and evolvement of human's basic demands. The requirements for both basic living requirements for food, clothes and appliances, and for working and living venue environment have been developed, so that brands become standard configuration in many fields.

Brands have consumption grades, for instance the vehicle brand, service brand, shaver brand and central air-conditioning brand used in workplace. Those branding demands have been transferred to the equal requirements of human beings, who serve as and switch roles between producers, operators and consumers, for the development of universal brand demands. People confirm their living standard such as status, identity, and environment based on brand holding quantity, holding mode and brand consumption grade.

The human consumption right organization also improves development of the organization during the process, changing its operation mode from past consumption right maintenance to right-oriented brand consumption, largely in terms of decision making with the consumer participation. Consumer representative shall be added in aspects of rules, standards and policy formulation. The listed company shall add an independent director serving the brand consumer. The customer relation management in enterprises is transferred to interactive relation between producers and consumers with full participation of consumers, and more direct brand user commission and brand consumer representative relationship department emerge herewith. Formal and informal brand consumer right organizations, such as brand consumer association, brand club, brand learning organization and brand community, increase rapidly and become an important link for upgrading from enterprise brand to brand organization. It urges brand consumption right organization to become the most important organization form, mode, status and basic structure of brand organization in enterprise brand ecological organization and in every brand ecological chain.

8 Theory of brand consumption capital

The capitalization of brand consumption is an important development form for global brand consumption. The focus is on the comprehensive capitalization of branding consumption. The specific manifestation is the brand capitalization and brand consumption capital enrichment.

Brand capitalization is the entire assets appreciation and management process of global brands orientating at branding assets investment, financing, capital promotion and brand investor relation management, brand treasure distribution method and brand market value, and brand transaction value.

Consumption promoted by capital is an important and representative mark for global brand development. Global capital fully participates in brand development process by means of investment, transaction and stock holding. Initially used for creation of a brand, the angel investment plays an important role in breeding the new brand; Secondly during the brand growth stage, venture investment promotes growth of brand by supplying funds and resources, makes brand projects enhance the agreement with brand users by using better methods, balances brand market development and brand consumption development favorably, and rapidly accelerates brand user holding quantity during brand market expansion process to prepare the development power for further brand consumption.

Lastly, the market value management of brand in capital market guarantees significant development of brand by favorable stable operation and sustainable market growth. If a brand decides never to list, or delist and privatize operation after listing, it may push the brand to develop by more stable means such as dividends in order to ease a series of growth targets required by capital market for brands so that brands can stably, sustainably and persistently operate in specific market with stable customer source relation. Investors can continuously acquire dividends by holding the brand assets for a long time. The brand equity has favorable capital performance in aspects of purchase and transfer, and is an important value carrier included in financial accounting and financial assets.

Capital promotes consumption. The brand projects preferentially supported by investors will become the main focus of global investment activities in the future. Brand stock holding will also be a key point for capital market development. During that process, brand consumption capital enrichment will be a typical capitalization development form of brand consumption.

Brand consumption capital enrichment mainly contains four development forms, respectively public investment and crowd funding of brand project, brand capitalized consumption, participation of brand consumption capitalization and secondary brand treasury distribution.

Section II Brand Subjects

In public investment and crowd funding of brand project, early consumers participate in brand creation and early development process. The development by public investment and crowd funding is emphasized. In terms of public investment, certain investors participate in brand project development by clear investment participation form, mainly 50, 200 or 500 shareholders are allowed by laws in many countries. Investors only take charge of investment, but don't participate in daily operating activities. In terms of crowd funding, joint operators, partners and consumption driving personnel comprehensively participate in early operation and development of brand project as shareholders. In many countries, those forms have become the legally permitted operating modes. However, the number of shareholders must be within the legal range. Moreover, the multi-level capital market shall be adopted to make shareholder capital input and stock raising legal so as to protect the profits of investors.

The brand capitalized consumption refers to the process of brand consumers that participate in consumption and investment by brand capitalization transfer within the legal range in each country. Generally, the direct sales or rebate modes are emphasized so that the consumers can transfer to promoters for brand asset appreciation. For instance, some internet companies calculate brand development process by periodic stock value through developing core users and content authors. Moreover, some companies and branches implement share option plan by operating network, and allow employees to hold shares so as to meet the brand capital creation and consumption value. The form is flexible and diversified, but must be in legal operating range so as to protect the legal rights of all participators.

Brand consumption capitalization is a structural development relation encouraging brand consumers to be public investors, keep synchronous development of brand, and share long-term development opportunities, development advantages and development level of brand. This is the rational security market process development for stock holders on capital market by holding stocks, from short-term to long-term. It can effectively promote brand development, and allow public brand consumers to share the honor and dividends during brand development process as brand investors and own favorable anti-risk capacity and accident disaster buffer capacity in case of securities market turbulence or brand crisis.

The consumers are willing to hold the brand stocks for a long time because they agree with development ideas, respect the development mission, and are willing to grow and experience hardships with those brands. They keep favorable rational investor relation with brands, and represent firm strengths for development of a brand. The long-time stock holding is the desire and direct embodiment of people loving these brands, the necessary way for capital market to develop from speculation to development capacity with rational, mature and stable development, and also the future of brand development.

Exercises

1. Fill in the banks: The theory of global market ecological chain points out the ecological chain of global brands and is comprised of _____, _____ and _____.

2. True or False Question: The natural decomposition process of brand consumers in use is an essence of natural circular development for repeated consumption, and also the core source of brand profits. (   )

3. Essay Question: What are the main development forms of brand consumption demands?

Chapter 7

Brand Products

The subject of brand products accounts for a large proportion in brand science, and it is the research and application field involving the most disciplines. This is decided by brand products as the development entity. Any brand shall use "product" as the carrier of materials and services delivered to users, while the main incomes of enterprises are from the specific operation of these "products".

The brand product competition is unprecedentedly fierce in the global market, diversified products in target market, and product homogeneity and analogous performance in diversified market competition. It is a difficult challenge for brands to stand out rapidly in the global market. We start from overall situations of brand products and investigate a series of scientific rules during brand product development. As the most valuable and competitive competition subject of brands, it is necessary to get the attention of universities, design and research institutions, and enterprises for the subject of brand products. The subject shall be coordinated comprehensively and developed preferentially.

1 Overall design ideas of brand products

The design of brand products is different from common product design; these include overall design ideas of brand products, design ideas of typical products, and design ideas of brand product development (structural design, breakthrough design, brand performance design, error-prevention design, ecological design, differential design, and product group collaborative design). In addition, new brand product development mechanism, brand product development structure and brand product-oriented development process design shall be followed. Creative R&D, production and delivery development of brand products is the final embodiment showing the ultimate design ideas, development design ideas and perfect brand expression form. It is a brand design idea sublimation process for a brand to ceaselessly improve and develop from the beginning by circular development.

The brand product design ideas need to rely on comprehensive application of design ideas such as craftsman spirits, labor value assignment, enterprise responsibility, brand conception, brand aesthetics, and ecological awareness. It is the perfect expression of comprehensive brand design ideas for brand science and philosophy, technology and art, creation and inspiration, process and quality, perception and experience and value presentation, and reflects incisive driven results.

Brand products are shown by extreme pursuit of brands for creation, typical interpretation and perfect spirits. Different from common product research, development and production, brand products shall not only pay attention to products but also lay emphasis on perfect optimization of brand product-oriented development process. The scope of design is not only limited to aesthetic design or artistic design elements and packaging design, largely including seamless linkage of order, production, delivery and service links, and smooth order flow process so as to perfectly supply brand value to any brand user. The native pursuit essence of human beings is the highest embodiment of human creativity, scientific process of management level, and ultimate materialized product of human development capacity of spirits for materials, labor value for products, cultural connotation for form and natural perception for artistic conception.

The overall design ideas of brand products are for special design based on overall product development, user perception and value discovery. The value display of general brand dream, brand story and brand pursuit for brand products, staged brand product development stages, and extended requirements comprised of future development pattern, future market development interface and production line must be considered. Brand product is not only a brand product-oriented design process finished by product manager. More importantly, the chief product officer, brand officer and brand designer must control the entire brand process to make products meet higher design requirements. It requires that the brand officer must be a perfectionist, and enterprise brand must carefully undertake the liabilities of brand products.

The development of brand products is not just the deal of product manager and product R&D team. On the contrary, brand product is a "brand research entity" that comprised of brand founders, brand consultants, brand designers and product managers. The brand rules of "research is more important than R&D, pursuit is more important than profits and purity is more important than demands" shall be followed. It is a series of overall ideological design on science and philosophy level, ideal expression and cultural value presentation carried out to brands. It is the perfect interpretation for all best things and purest aesthetic pursuits.

Brand product is also known as brand work, which cannot be the product of a single brand. It is the pursuit and presentation of systematic brand ideas, series brand products, integral brand structures, comprehensive brand aesthetics and pure artistic conception, and a kind of "brand product group". It is a systematic system that load brand products and cultural memes to specific brand products and make them perfect. Such classic brand products are usually named by brand works. If enterprises wish to respect and give gratitude to the works of brand officers and brand designers, they will need to hold grant news conference to release the brand works officially to the world, i.e. the brand life process, from brand product breeding, foundation to disclosure, is made public. The main creators of brand works will exist together with these great or outstanding brand works, and be preserved as a basis for verification. As the precious process stage in development history of brand, process and main contributors shall be reckoned to the files of brand history.

2 Design ideas of classic products

Brand products must be developed based on the requirements for creation and design method of classic products, which is the direct embodiment of brand design ideas' mature application. The classic products may be either a single product or a series of products; either entity material or virtual goods. They are not limited to certain specific product form, but are mainly focus on the products.

Products are named by different forms in different market fields. For instance, raw materials in production supporting, industrial products in industry, crops in agriculture, financial services in securities companies, solutions of project companies, training courses of educational institutions, time-based consulting of management consulting companies, game operation method of sports companies, performance works of art companies are all brand products, and can all be developed to classic products.

If material brand products are always presented as finished products, the promotion feeling of artistic conception must be provided. In other words, the sensual pleasure for spirituality and aesthetics shall be shown through design ideas in aspects of brand product model, appearance, texture, color, connotation and packaging to give life to the brand products. The nature of brand product design is to create a deep feeling. Such feeling can flow through the hearts of brand users, and generate collision and resonance with soul of brand users so as to reflect high level spiritual perception and real enjoyment in technology, dignity, nature, flexibility, culture and style provided by brand products.

The brand products can become classic products because of spirits, ideas and life injected by brand creators during branding process. This is the spiritual pursuit that a true brand founder must express during brand product creation process, and the perfectionist spiritual pursuit of brand founders and height of classic product design ideas.

The non-entity brand products will finish perfect brand expression by combining multiple design ideas including words, languages, photography, freeh and sketching, virtual mapping and customer testimony. Words are the most important. It is necessary to extend artistic conception of brands from word reading and comprehension, and show extremely beautiful perceptions and experiences. The graceful, smooth, flowing and fresh words pass through the soul of readers and listeners like splendid melody, and gently touch the souls of brand users, become the "vivid" words, and make people generate mediation and experience and build outline of spirits.

Anytime, anywhere, any true brand founder in the world will create, build and show the wish of perfect and extreme brand expression by ceaseless pursuit of natural spirits and meaning of life to assure that their brands will become classic products, exist with history, shine with life, connect with soul and communicate with hearts. The inherent pursuit of brand founders gives brand the meaning of life under perfect pursuit of brand officers and brand designers, which is the same pure heart pursuing artistic conception, same willing contribution, and same brand language for transmission, expression and interpretation of any brand founders around the world.

3 Design ideas for brand product development

Brand products are developed along the history with sources, development vein and style direction, which is the important guarantee for a brand to extend life by time-honored brands for hundreds and thousands of years. From the time when a brand is started to breed, the brand ideas of brand founders have penetrated the process, and defined the development structure of a series of main brand ideas such as spirits, awareness, expression method and presentation method for next century's development of the brand.

At the initial stage of brand foundation, the early brand founders, brand officers, brand consultants, brand designers and product managers shall make researches, tests and confirmations for overall brand design ideas, development structure and design ideas, and clearly fix brand elements. When a brand becomes mature, the generations of brand owners keep inheriting, continuing and carrying forward the brand civilization, and ceaselessly advance with time so that brand can closely combine time development tide and vein, and perfectly present in optimal expression form and technology. This is different from product design, R&D, life cycle theory of common enterprise products.

Therefore, we hereby disclose some important ideas about brand product development design. As a series of thinking tools, these design ideas are usually for brand design combining multiple ideas. Designers of brand products, compared with product designers and product managers in common enterprises, have superior ideological level, development pattern, inner cultivation and knowledge contents. The design ideas are for structural design, breakthrough design, brand performance design, error-prevention design, ecological design, differential design, and product group collaborative design.

Structural design: Mainly refers to overall development structure of a kind of brand product (comprised of multiple brand products but pushed out by stages, or only developing a classic single product brand), including brand combination structure, components, expression method and main elements of brands, digging point of brand cultural connotation, expression of flexibility and aesthetics of brands, social service ideas and brand design ideas expressed by brand products, as well as expansion of production line, and definition of brand products, development vein and overall direction if brand products are extended. The structural design of brand products is the overall development and final market expression of a brand, and confirms principles, standpoints and requirements of mainline and vein-type design ideas.

Breakthrough design: Mainly refers to the difference that the brand has from others. It may be necessary to reconstruct design ideas for expression method and presentation form of brand products in aspects of reverse engineering, backward thinking and cross-generation design so that the products are completely different from products on existing market. This is a perfect expression of the great creativity of human beings for challenge thinking, subversive thinking and venture thinking, and highly natural confidence for brand products. Creation is a kind of habit, and the nature of creation is to create unprecedented and unique product form. Yet, such thinking naturally rejects simulated, alike and similar design methods, and must be a brave and decisive initiation. The result of brand product is a thorough breakthrough.

Brand performance design: Mainly refers to the optimal performance index and the most perfect performance pursuit of brand according to comprehensive thinking of brand performance. It is the extraordinary refined soul expression for performance pursuit, smooth expression of nature for natural inspiration and spirituality, and reflection of overall design ideas for brand aesthetics in performance expression. Relating brand production to pure beauty, and with spiritual integration, resolution and performance enjoyment of brand users, people can experience the beauty of voice with eyes closed, see the beauty of color and appearance design, and feel the beautiful sense of touch.

Error-prevention design: Refers to perfect expression of outstanding products under various possible circumstances such as crack, damage, scratch, soaking and impact during use by brand users under different environments and conditions and especially severe environment and weathers, and self-adaptive protection of products in case of accidents. The largest difference between outstanding brand products and common enterprise products is the nature of expression. Brand products shall experience tests of severe environment and adverse conditions, and provide outstanding warrant to users during crucial moments. Therefore, the brand users will become the most loyal friends and have the most sincere trust to the brand. However, common enterprise products have poorer performance in these aspects as they wanted to reduce costs, so they will be eliminated by brand users at a rapid rate.

Ecological design: Refers to a series of designs that protect natural environment, guarantee natural resources and keep ecological use status. The ecological design is the social responsibilities undertaken by brands and their brand users based on enterprise responsibilities, the joint endeavor made by brands and users to jointly protect the sustainable ecological development in the world, and also the common pursuit of ecological value, including returning to nature, enjoying sunshine, air and clean natural environment, and natural ecological conditions, such as concepts of green, environmental protection, degradable packaging and ecological nutrition advocated by brands, and actual actions paid to public benefit for saving the nature.

Differential design: Differential design is more direct than the common differential design requirements. It is the direct design for cross-generation, rank difference, use condition and performance aiming at similar products in the market, and can directly change formation, use method and market demand of brand products. The differential design must maintain a further distance away from similar products, the brand must be a more direct professional market than professional brand service, higher brand product performance requirements and service level than similar products in market, distinct and accurate brand recognition method, easy distinction of brand product form, and unique style of brand products.

Product group collaborative design: For development of modern and future brand products, the products are not independent products under most circumstances, and more coordinative cooperation, collaboration and coordinative service are required to complete the comprehensive combination of brand products, while brand products need reserve program interfaces which can be connected in parallel or extension, technical preparation, extension design and extensible solution for further development. Thus, the product design will no longer need to centralize around the products and instead it will be a collaborative design of product group. Multiple parties jointly participate in brand design, while the requirement for consistency, flexibility and intellectual property rights between collaborative parties will be higher. When a product group is finally boiled down to a brand product, any error or collaborative fault may affect the development of overall brand performance, and favorable market performance of brands.

4 Brand product development mechanism

The development mechanism of brand products is mainly shown in the design requirements of brand strategy, the brand operation and management, including the strategic design in the aspects of brand industrial combination, brand product planning, brand main products, brand production line and brand product elements. It is the overall development route, development rules and coordination mechanism of brand that brand development should follow.

Brand industry combination: It is the important core structure of brand development strategy, and decides the development structure of a brand in one or more industrial fields and market fields. No development of brand product will break away from the development trend, development characteristics and development mode of its industry. In order to acquire cutting-edge status, decisive competitiveness and optimal brand performance, brand usually needs to acquire quality resources in industrial field, including company acquisition in capital level, strategic reorganization, strategic product combination between different enterprises, strategic partnership formation, upstream and downstream support during the entire product process, and brand performance optimization of product supply chain.

The industrial organizations in strategic level need to guarantee integrated and stable brand system from certain degree, and prevent attacks from competitors so as to provide comprehensive brand consumption safety guarantee to brand users. Industrial organizations usually participate in negotiation, cooperation and decision making of enterprise brand organization strategic layer, as well as strategic design and strategic coordination made by brand order layer for brand development problems, provide strategic resource supports and suggestions to main strategic investors, brand consultants, and strategic partners, and make strategic resource reserve and preparation for future development of enterprise brand so as to protect the strategic development status and absolute competitive advantages of brands in industrial development field in the long run. External or internal talents, including brand consultants, brand officers and product managers may be deemed as important strategic resources and play key competitive role in the strategic-level industrial combination. Enterprise brand organization shall maintain high competitiveness of brand capacity.

Brand product planning: Product planning is a series of specific long-term, medium-term and short-term development tasks and development schedule of products, including outline guiding specific combination relation of development route and brand products and requirements by market development process, development stage planning, R&D upgrading and updating planning, reflection of brand value competitive advantages, brand product price range strategy, product strategic organization planning, and market action plan during brand product development process.

Brand product planning is a kind of development strategic design which can effectively prevent competition, the main structural line for development of brand products, the visual design drawing of production organization relation, the staged competition implementation process for brand products to develop, research orderly and enter into the market, and specific strategic guidance and operation requirements guide for brand product-oriented development process. The brand product planning is featured by global, long-term and strategic pre-design performance, and may be responded and corrected in time according to important changes of market situations during actual development process.

Main products of brand: Refers to the major operating fields and model of a brand, and the overall product development route preferentially designed in brand product design. All brands should have its main market direction, advanced and unique brand combination solution so as to realize highly product-oriented, brand-oriented and system-oriented development, and make breakthrough development intensively in main product market, and acquire long-term development.

Brand production line: Brand production line is the main strategic product line and the depth of products designed for development of brand organization, and the summarized product combination relation which are refined and verified during long-term brand development. The brand production line highlights key advantages, develop characteristics of intensive economy, and provide professional services to professional market users in limited field covered by production line. The brand production line is deemed as a kind of comparative advantage for comprehensive competition. It should provide reasonable ecological layout and organic reasonable industry depth, and give play to the coordination ability of valid market development and market protection.

Section II Brand Subjects

Brand product elements: Refers to main element constitution and product element combination relationship among products of enterprise brands. Product elements are valid element combination through scientific design, experimental analysis and practical verification. The elements shall have comparative advantages in key element market, and some could be independent element brands. Elements contain highly knowledgeable, professional and modular core element development abilities such as scientific research findings, technical innovation, product characteristics, professional function, application and practical ability, and system solution ability.

5 Development structures of brand products

The development of brand product is mainly shown in the design method of brand products, i.e. what kind of design development idea is adopted to define development structures of brand products, and allow a brand or a group of products in future group brand cluster to develop along a fixed, mature and stable way. This is a key structural development way for a brand to develop into a time-honored brand.

From the setting of brand development structure, brands will continue and inherit along a fixed development structure. Unless significant structural recombination of brand development during future development process changes the gene of the development structure, the core problem that brand development structure shall solve is the way to keep the brand surviving and operating permanently by development order.

Many time-honored brands in the world can solve the problem mainly because they have established a set of structural development model, i.e. stably expand market by fixed brand development mechanism, development characteristics and brand organization management progress. The typical structures are P&G, Microsoft or Cummins. The development structure of the brand products is relatively fixed, which guarantee continuity of brand organization development.

We divide development structure of brand products into five categories, including systemized products, functional products, industrial ecological products, morphological products, cross-generation products, and N-generation products. Brand organization can freely select one or multiple development ways for strategic combination of brand development structure.

Systemized products: Refers to the development structure formulating main brand products, extending production line and marginal supplementary products for brands from the beginning. The main brand products can be deemed as central development system of brands, and the trunk for brand product development. By developing main products, the brands can own powerful market status and sufficient market share, and become the main role supporting the entire brand development structure. On that basis, several auxiliary production lines are extended to support the main line. As required, some supplementary products shall be developed during brand product research and development process for new market test, or to cover small market field nearby. IT enterprises and film & TV industry mainly launch new products and finish product upgrade by upgrading and sustainably developing main products so as to facilitate key market status of main brand products.

Functional products: Refers to the development structure that mainly develops key products aiming at specific use function, specific environmental atmosphere and specific people. Functional products are commonly specialized professional products. One brand usually only solves one specific user problem, or creates a specific purchase and user environment or application scenarios, or opens its products only to people in a specific field. The development structure of functional products is to divide and decompose market effectively, and target at main market objective by developing multiple key products in different single professional specific field, environment and people. Functional product is the most common form in global market, which may be a brand cluster containing multiple brands, or multiple branding products of the same brand, and may have market structure clearly forming brand.

Industrial ecological products: Refers to the development structure of brand products carrying out ecological combination in one industry or field. The brand concentrates on expanding the user market field of one industry, carries out ecological market layout by ceaselessly developing new products, and carries out overall product design by market combination relation, application connection relation, consumption demand sequence and cross and interactive ecological development between brand products. Usually, an industrial user acquires relevant solution in a fixed industrial market field, or a user with certain specific consumption demand finishes related consumption during industrialization process of brand consumption.

Morphological products: Mainly refers to product-oriented development way using conceptual application for intensive brand development. Brand products are deemed as form of classic products, best-sold or marketable products, and physical products, virtual products or brand projects are deemed as development structure. Through popular, topical and themed market operation, a product or a series of products can become fixed regular consumables in one period or one field frequently used and sold goods. Some popular products with physical concept, such as consumer electronic products, or TV program, performance art, themed park and software, or continuously marketable products with invariable tastes and techniques, always use this method.

Cross-generation products: Refers to the development method adopted by brands with cutting-edge development ideas and advanced research and development capacity. Generally, enterprises shall create the popular consumption trend by researching and developing next generation products in advance, and ceaselessly push out products overturning basic knowledge of people by highly developed professional knowledge system. These products exist as a kind of global development trend of technology, culture and education, and acquire market achievements by conforming to the trend. The advancement, super-reality, tendency and professional performance of the brand products are usually the key development targets of brand products, or the characteristics of next generation products which may impact the market and overturn old production combination relation, product formation and product use habits in the market. Perhaps the products may split a certain market field and acquire its own independent professional market, and own certain number of regulars. For instance, the automobile modification brands have such characteristics. For research of robot, only early pioneering research is invested in, and products cannot be finalized until perfect status is achieved.

N-generation products: N-generation is the definition that we have for emerging consumers that have grown every ten years as an age of change. The N-generation products carry out cutting-edge research and probe brand product field and ceaselessly usher in demand change of the latest generation with ceaselessly change age of growing population as main market development method. There are two major classic N-generations in the world. One is the emerging N-generation market, in which the market of emerging young generation brand products is the latest adults; the other is substitutive N-generation market, in which the market of emerging aged generation brand products is the new aged population. The generation for growing change demand of emerging population is every ten years. Due to different backgrounds, growing up environments, cultures of time and thinking methods, the demands for brand products may generate different styles, and thus show obvious characteristics of age change. With ceaseless change of brand demands required by the N-generation population, the application market for evolving habitual emerging brand products is formed.

6 Advantages of brand product-oriented development process

The idea for brand product development is the overall development idea for systematized brand products with strategic significance, ideology and structural advantage. Except specific order for development organization, the product development shall be deemed as an integral branding process for strategic management and harmonious development.

The advantage of brand product-oriented development process is firstly established on specific order structure of development organization. The core members of a brand product development group contain brand consultant, brand officer, brand designer, person in charge of R&D, product manager, technical engineer as well as management analyst and market analyst with certain management and market design level. The external brand consultants and internal brand officer and brand designers of

Section II Brand Subjects

brand organization take charge of overall brand product research ideas, branding requirements and brand product research project management; person in charge of R&D takes charge of promotion of technical structure and specific product-oriented R&D process of overall projects; the product manager takes charge of comprehensive branding of brand products; technical engineer takes charge of technical deployment in the aspects of production, quality and delivery, and supportable research and design of technical conditions. These roles correspond to the complete closed brand product-oriented design, experiment, tests and scale production process covering overall branding design, R&D design, product-oriented development, scale process flow and market-oriented development respectively. The roles shall finish the entire process of brand product-oriented development by constituting different project stages and project groups.

The advantages of brand product-oriented development process are shown in nine key development fields of three categories including the entire process (product planning, product devising, product-oriented design, and product-oriented management), brand cutting-edge design direction (cutting-edge study, order flow design, flexible application, perception and experience, and agile manufacturing) and re-productization. The re-productization process is the product-oriented development which can stretch, extend, combine, support and collaborate in the future. In other words, one product may become the connecting point or combination configuration structure of other enterprise brand products, or be used for second and third development in other enterprises, or extend to new product series and production lines.

During brand product-oriented development process, product planning is the overall systematic planning for key strategic markets such as future development direction of brand products, product existence form, competition field, and market development method, and is the overall development guideline and staged implementation requirements of the brand for a long time. Product devising contains the strategic-level brand planning design that includes concept, development route map, product form, product expression form, product selling points, cutting-edge status, decisive competitive advantages and product layout management.

The brand product-oriented design is for technical conditions, technical preparation, technical equipment and technical requirements, including specific market research, technology research, product element combination, product module development, product supporting capacity, production conditions, product quality requirements, product experience design and product service design during the entire process, as well as complete product-oriented system elements such as R&D, experiment, test, raw materials, equipment, personnel, job, delivery, marketing and after-sales services. The process of brand product-oriented design is the entire process to propose requirements for product-oriented management, establish corresponding management mechanism work flow and specific management process to meet various requirements, carry out overall technical design, experiment and test of management process, and prepare brand management documents and included in brand management file.

Brand product-oriented design can be ended after brand product-oriented management completed its deployment and the design requirements are satisfied, and shall be transferred to test and error correction report collection stage according to system optimization requirements. This is the requirements for mission and responsibility of brand consultants and brand officers for entire brand product development process during the entire brand product-oriented development process. All brand products must complete the final perfect interpretation of brand products in strict branding order. It is an extremely irresponsible and serious brand accident of enterprises, if they only let brand managers, brand designers, person in charge of R&D or product mangers to carry out entire design and research of brand product. This accident is a serious loophole which may damage future development of a brand. All brand officers are perfectionists, and must take the highest responsibility for brand products passing through them and flowing into market. Therefore, the higher level brand consultants outside the brand organization have the same specific consulting value in brand product development.

The direction of brand cutting-edge design contains potential cutting-edge ideas of brand products such as cutting-edge study, order flow design, flexible application, perception experience and agile manufacturing, and shall be carefully considered during the process of design, R&D, technical preparation and management practices. The cutting-edge research may be undertaken by brand research department of enterprises. Order flow design, centering at brand product delivery, brings production side, delivery side and service side to a complete and closed-loop system management process for work flow management. The flexible application is the flexible and variable product design idea for dynamic development of brand products aiming at market research status which may vary at any time, and it is a guaranteed system with stable quality. The perception experience is a series of design for perception level and experience results made from the perception status of brand users. The agile manufacturing is a flexible combination design structure for brand product meme-type capacity, a flexible production structure and a delivery way carried out according to the minority development trend of market.

Exercises

1. Multiple-choice Question: The design ideas of brand product development contain: _____.
( )

   A. Structural design, breakthrough design;

   B. Brand performance design, error-prevention design

   C. Ecological design, differential design, product group collaborative design;

   D. A B C

2. True or False Question: The development mechanism of brand products contains strategic design in aspects of brand industrial combination, brand product planning, brand main products, brand production line and brand product elements. ( )

3. Discussion: Discuss advantages of brand product-oriented development

SECTION II BRAND SUBJECTS

Chapter 8

Brand Service

The subject of brand service is an emerging cutting-edge discipline in modern times. It is not only an important part for national strategy of service economy, but also a key strategic guarantee capacity for sustainable development capacity of an enterprise. In the time when modern service industry grows rapidly, the contents, forms and methods of service have undergone in-depth changes, while such changes accelerate transformation of brand service industry from ideology, technology, behaviors to systemic, intelligent and complex service science.

1 After-sales service ideas

The after-sales service ideas do not only refer to after-sales service of brand, but also specifically refer to the strategic ideas for long-term service that a brand should establish, including extension of producer's responsibility, rethinking of service objective, service-oriented ideas, leading edge detection, service profit chain, service upgrading and service marketing. It is the source of main competitive thoughts for brand to set up service value chain and carry out systematic design of brand service flow.

Brand after-sales service appears as a kind of service idea. Such idea is based on service profit chain development structure of "after-sales service reselling". It is the key development capacity to guarantee that an enterprise can develop into a brand organization and sustainably acquire brand profit source during service process, and the strategic development ideas and long-term service value planning for constant survival of brand. In terms of capital market, sustainable and constant high level brand profits kept by any brands are from repeated consumption process of regulars under after-sales service ideas. Without that process, enterprises cannot generate sustainable profit level, let alone brand construction.

People always believe after-sales service is unnecessary for restaurants, and they believe after-sales service is only applicable for household appliances, automobile, large IT system, medical equipment, facilities or issues related to industrial machinery design. However, this is not true. When a customer enters a restaurant, he/she enjoys after-sales service when eating delicious food and accepting services of service personnel. Customers will immediately decide whether to consume in this restaurant again, or decide to invite important friends to enjoy the food and service here again, and this will expand the growth level of repeated consumption.

Corporate planner in charge of restaurant development, designers in charge of environmental design, restaurant manager in charge of management as well as chefs and service personnel in charge of different service processes all participate in the process of "after-sales service reselling". Therefore, the after-sales service is reflected as after-sales service design and immediate service process on site. Thus, the after-sales status becomes the key competitiveness of long-term profits for the enterprise.

Both presales preparation and on-purchase service are the endeavors made by any brand for the reselling after products are sold. After-sales service is deemed as important sustainable development idea of brand strategy and repeated consumption value generating continuous sales and become a series of specific operating targets. The holding quantity of regulars who repeatedly consume one brand becomes one important link for the entire brand value chain, is an important strategic resource reserve and decisive competitiveness, core economic income source generating sustainable brand profits, long-term strategy for after-sales service idea to generate direct economic development effect, and the basic ecological development order that allow brand to develop into organizational operation.

1.1 Brand service idea

Brand service idea is an important extension and branch out field from branding idea. It emphasizes on basic ideology, in-depth service and smooth service during the entire servicing process provided by the brand, and has important service value to be discovered and improve on the actual profit level and long-term development prospect of brands.

Brand service is deemed as service idea for the development process of a brand organization. Sometimes service idea accounts for relatively important proportion in strategic ideas of brand development in some emerging enterprises, and gradually exists as common cognition, consciousness level, height of strategic thinking and future career development pattern of entrepreneurs.

Services firstly exist as extended responsibility of enterprise producers, and are provided to brand users by the form of combination of product and user development relation, or products. In the future, global enterprises will focus on developing into modern brand organizations that are service-oriented. Service providers will gradually replace manufacturers and become the main brand development form in global social and economic development. The service range, property, model, capacity and service performance will be developed and extended unlimitedly.

Therefore, when a brand decides to develop, it needs to consider the value of service in brand development, particularly development model for brand user. These enterprise responsibilities are reflected and developed by brand service idea. When an enterprise has brand service idea, brand organization will rethink service target during development process, and develop to advanced service level and service abilities such as cutting-edge exploration, service chain profits, service upgrading and service marketing. The development here is deemed as characteristic results with development capacity which can generate new services, new products, new profits and new values by labor value enabling. The final development capacity level of a brand depends on emerging development capacity generated during development process so as to develop different brands, different markets and different results. It is the transformation of emission and responsibilities implemented to brands in market by instinct of enterprise responsibility development.

The cutting-edge exploration of brand is the overall in-depth study on overall brand service demands of brand organization to research on brand users, find market problems and develop brands. It is the market cutting-edge sensor network established based on favorable after-sales service ideas, and collects market surveillance, research, discovery report and analysis and research data during contact with brand users by product details and subtle links of services.

Since brand is the comprehensive reflection of management level based on perception reaction. Brand performance and brand contacting process in any subtle link may change perception of brands. Brand organization shall strengthen this aspect, give play to information sensor network of brand during entire process, entire range and entire user link by applying after-sales service idea, and develop brand product R&D and service design by the most direct analysis data from front line of market. This is a complete closed link of information flow with important feedbacks and opinions. The cutting-edge exploration is the true foundation for development capacity serving the market with due diligence and acquiring favorable market development.

1.2 Brand profit sources: brand service profit chain and service upgrading, service marketing

Service is the main source of brand profits, mainly including three aspects. The first is designing of brand service profit chain; the second is brand service upgrading service; and the third is market expansion during service marketing process.

The brand service profit chain greatly enlarges creation of profits value by service through valid design of value link in service process. We use 3SCR service profit chain structure to distinguish profit value link during service process, including service defect (S1), service recognition (S2), service responsibility (S3), customer's feeling (C) and regular customer plan (R). We believe the improvement of service profits starts from study on service defects, mainly the system service design and troubles hooting by PADS. The dominant recognition of service price shall paid attention to service recognition. Since service is a kind of virtual product, brand users cannot know the specific difference between one brand service and another in advance. In many countries and regions, since brand users fail to make valid recognition for service value, it is difficult to show as valid price difference. In addition, the main focuses of service competition are service intelligence, service contrast experiment and service transmission.

Service upgrading occurs more frequently for modern automobile, IT and internet products. The service requirements of brand users are graded by service level and service price. Usually a brand only provides conventional products. The additional value added service or service options, such as 24*7 specialized service, or different service components and service combination, all these mean that brand service is upgraded as a kind of typical product sales structure, and included as important operating income.

After-sales service is important income source of many brands, including income from original accessories and original consumables, and income from product refitting and product maintenance. For instance, automobile and printer mainly improve additional service profits of products through after-sales service and consumables. Maintenance of mechanical equipment, extension of warranty period and technical upgrading of main parts are all deemed as newly increased profits of service product.

Service marketing provides new profit sources from repeated purchase, increased consumption and customer instruction through service reselling process. Theoretically, many brand users depend on and continuously increase consumption of certain brands with their growth and development. For instance, one person, from child to youth and then to middle age, will ceaselessly enhance income growth capacity, consumption capacity and purchase decision making power. During favorable product and service process, a brand user will bring sustainable and long-term profits return to brands when he/she have dependency consumption habit and purchase decision habit, and becomes a most valuable backbone brand users for large consumption. The holding quantity of regulars is a key point for a brand to maintain lasting and joint development relation with users, and for service profit development and service profit growth. Service marketing is directly related to sustainable service investment and service level of brand organization.

2 Value chain of brand service

The value chain of brand service is the level line of brand life value that is generated when brand service demand chain, brand service supplement chain and brand service profit chain developed jointly, coordinated with each other and reach highly coincident level value. The separate service value chain that is solely established by enterprise does not exist, and is an incomplete and serious service defect.

The value chain of brand service shall firstly be established based on service demand chain. Various clear demands or hidden demands of brand users for services may be depicted by service research and market exploration. These demands are key points for the overall design of brand service system and service project development every once in a while. However, the systematic design and development of brand service needs certain time period and service capacity preparation, so brand organization will provide a series of supplement links and services for temporary brand service resources to meet the instant and dynamic demands during the service tendered to brand users. These real-time dynamic service connection chains will be deemed as a complete brand service supplement chain.

Brand service supplement chain can carry out dynamic adjustment for brand service, service measurement and service experiment, and collect service data according to real-time change of brand service demand chain. According to interaction of brand service demand chain and brand service supplement chain, brand organization can carry out dynamic service shrinking flexibly and thus observe and summarize new service development direction and stable service quality supply in service system.

The brand profit chain that are enhanced and developed based on these links will have more factual interactive service profit link and service profit level.

The development of brand service value chain is the process of strategic-level service value appraisal, service investment and service management. It means that not every service link will generate profits. Some profit links can be deemed as service investment required by brand organization for long-term development, and will not be listed in profit sources in a stage so that brand can pay more attention to development of future long-term profit level. The service value chain of brand is an important part in the entire brand value discovery system and brand value chain design, and shall be investigated and appraised bilaterally from overall design requirements of brand performance so as to confirm the optimal brand service value chain.

The development nature of brand service value chain is the closed-loop connected relationship between brand organization and brand value, and the value proposition and interaction system for mutual dependence and collaborative development among brand organization, brand users, and suppliers and service providers of brand organization. Brands finish brand value creation, supply, delivery, after-sales service and service relation maintenance by dynamic interaction of brand service demand chain, brand service supplement chain and brand service profit chain so as to establish, acquire and develop brand service value chain with high performance, high quality and high level.

3 Social and ecologic value of brand service

Brand service value is firstly shown in economic value, and gradually transits to brand social value. Service economy is an important part of economic strategies in one country, and the economic field with the highest weight and proportion in GDP and involving most population during modern economic development. For brand exporters that mainly develop service economy, the proportion of service industry to GDP is at least 60%, and the proportion will be over 80% in highly developed countries. The occupied populations engaging in service industry and consumption demands for service are the most important contents in statistical analysis of domestic economy.

The economic value of services for enterprises is also obvious. As mentioned above, brand after-sales service ideas are the most important brand service process and brand profit sources of a brand organization, and also the life line created by a brand to keep its business long lasting and develop into a time-honored brand.

The development progress of human from 20th Century to 21st Century is an important historical transition process for human beings as they transfer from producers to service providers. In the 21st century, the number of producers reduces greatly, while the dominant market role represented by service provider acquires unprecedented development therewith. The enterprises directly or indirectly providing services to market solve employment problem for over half of the global labor population, and make daily life and work process of world population in highly developed service-oriented social network.

With economic growth in one country, the service demand and service consumption of people will increase greatly, and meanwhile, the requirements for service level will increase. During development process of brand organization, the service value must be transferred from economic value to social value. Finally, the highly service-oriented economic organization with social service as main development structure will be established so as to build operating structure required by orders of brand organization when a brand is deemed as a brand ecological organization.

The nature of service socialization is to make service public. It is the necessary result for development of services' social functions. When a brand provides services to its users, these services are provided to citizens in the public social environment. The service flow process, terminal reached by service, and supply, delivery and comprehensive service process are all in public environment. This is also the ecological organization development relation which helps brand organization to achieve bidirectional balanced development between social value and economic value, and the foundation for healthy and stable operation of brand organization with ecological and sustainable development.

SECTION II BRAND SUBJECTS

No brand can exist by breaking away from the society. When a brand organization develops to certain degree, and after it completed its enterprise responsibilities, they will turn to enterprise social responsibilities that brands should undertake so as to thoroughly reach the ultimate development significance of public social services. During human development process in any time, any country or enterprise shall take bidirectional balance of social economy as the most basic development order, and pay equal attention to social value and economic value. When economic conditions are developed to certain degree, main development way of future brand is to drive economic value by social value, and finally human society will surely develop into the contribution-type social development structure acquiring economic profits by social contribution. Brand organization serves the society and acquires economic return given by the society. People in the organization contribute to the brand organization, acquire economic return given by brand organization and create the economic form of development capacity with benign circulation of social contribution.

4 Business model of brand service

Service is a scale economy. "People" serve as development subject of service industry during the service process, and service is the occupation and industrial field consuming the most population. Brand service can be deemed as a kind of independent business model, and mainly contain three typical service development forms including service business model industrialization, product process business model and service-orientation and product service model.

Service business model industrialization refers to the development where a brand takes service as its business model and makes it large-scale and industrialized. The express courier delivery industry is a well-known modern service business with intensive labor population. The express courier delivery can be designed as a business model. The industrial combination between express courier delivery and e-commerce retail business is the most important entity of service industrialization. The service business model is also shown as brand service provider model (BSP model). In other words, some brands develop to brand service providers in specialized field. They mainly develop systematic service solution, service infrastructure, service outsourcing and service trade, and provide specialized services to other enterprises or customers. During the time when modern science develops rapidly, BSP will develop to major representative business type and the key investment target with long-term strategic development advantages in global service business model market in the future.

In order to meet requirements for future enterprise development and transfer of profit point section in market competition, and cope with complex products, technology and service under complex management environment, the service orientation of business model during product process becomes key development field of global enterprises. Such transition process of brand organization is the key transformation of service structure from developing productivity to developing consumption capacity.

In modern global competition, many enterprises have transformed from producers to service providers, and developed to emerging brand service providers with modern service awareness and service level. They strive to improve and get rid of impression recognition as producers by people. They play the new market role of "brand service provider", and spare no effort to extend its market ability to service market field and transfer key original business income to service profits. Typical enterprises such as automobile and software have transferred key point of market development to after-sales service market, and developed them into the new generation brand service providers through generating service profits.

Many enterprise brands between brand producers and brand service providers mainly develop services by the product service system (PSS). In order to adapt to the ceaseless change of market, enhance service viscosity for brand users and probe future development of service market, these enterprises develop by combining products and services so as to mainly develop product service system. The current PSS mainly aims to solve customer consultation, customer service response, and provide remote service support and on-site service support. This method is the complementary competition combination of brand products in product market to shift to service market. Surely, this is the transiting development period of modern service industry lasting for a long time in global market. In the future, these enterprises will finally transmit to the stage of brand service provider with strengthened brand and brand service value.

Although global brand business model is experiencing the three typical service development forms of service business model industrialization, product process business model, and service orientation and product service model currently, the value cognition of service as business model and business investment has been common and mature. With improvement of human beings' understanding of brand service and development of human social network, brand service providers will finally replace brand producers and become future service subject competition form and common global brand service status. The global brand service provider will share development results of brand services with the entire human being, and strive to help people live better in ecological environment of global brand service.

5 Design of brand service flow system

The flow management is the new requirement proposed by management recreation for modern enterprise management model. Under the increasingly developed multi-network interconnection environment, service, as a kind of real-time and dynamically transmitted process flow, flows through each link of brand organization, including brand service performance management, service output side, service transmission network, service distribution system and service user side. This is the management model of tomorrow which is featured by service flow deployment, service flow process, and efficiency ratio of service output and input.

Due to the cross-network operating characteristic of future management, the chain management and the flow management will become the new basic management models, and order flow, service flow and enterprise culture flow are the three most important management models. They replaced the former product management forms, use advanced order flow and service flow during product flow process management to organize product process respectively, and improve service connotation of service flow and enhance brand value transmission ability by enterprise culture flow.

The future development attribute of service flow management has higher requirements for design capacity of service system, and pays attention to requirements of real-time dynamic cross-network transmission. It does not only differentiate emerging service management model from former service management methods, but also generates essential distinction with popular service management software in modern sense or IT service solutions. The systematic development of service flow will be the leading-edge direction and latest trend of future service development method, and the organization form of scientific service development capacity based on high flexibility, cross-network and integrated development. All service links are organized effectively and give play to power brand service flow organization effect of brand organization by open, distributed and direct-contact development results.

The systematic design process of service is the necessary development process for human beings to service science; the highly organized and scientific process for enterprises to advance with times and establish leading-edge status and decisive competitiveness; the system upgrading based on social network service of service flow, network branding and public service nature; and the ecological organization process of service which is finally improved to highly self-adaptive ecological self-transmission represented by "service flow".

A complete systematic design structure of service flow contains brand order layer, brand management layer, brand operation layer, brand collaboration layer and brand service layer, which are respectively corresponding to brand strategic decision making, brand order management, brand management department, brand field operation and brand collaborative network, and the service layer providing comprehensive service to all brand users. The structure is consistent with organizational structure of brand organization, and attaches importance to flexible, network and ecological development requirements of brand organization. It is the permanent structural operation order and forward-looking deployment made for service science to usher in development in the future age of service intelligent network.

The systematic design of service flow is, with overall brand design principles as main design ideas, the complete system design process cooperated and implemented by brand officers, management scientists, management analysts and market analysts. As required by scientific development of brand organization, certain number of service science working teams shall be deployed. Enterprises which are unable to deploy service science working teams can deploy large amount of MA groups for service system design, maintenance and operation. A typical professional division characteristic of management recreation is that, future management system is designed scientifically by overall management technology system led by management scientist. Brand officers, management analysts and market analysts take charge of operation and maintenance of the management system, leaders and managers in enterprises are specific users of the system. It is irresponsible to rely on external consulting companies or internal management personnel to take charge of service system design. It may cause large amount of consumption of service flow.

The future service flow of brand shall develop conforming to basic development order of ecological service system. For instance, studies on basic natural ecological system development characteristics of food production, water flow, climate improvement, disease suppression, human body nutrition circulation, and crop fertilization process are all the ecological science research fields that brand service flow system can refer to for future development. Besides, the ecological system of brand service flow is an important branch of ecological system that is highly integrated, and coordinated, in parallel or collaboratively operated with urban ecology and industrial ecology. The ecological brand service flow is an important approach for human being to ceaselessly improve understanding of natural ecology and make it act on ecological development of human beings, society and economy.

Furthermore, the brand service shall develop a culture according to the understanding of nature, and apply the culture to services. It is a development model that ceaselessly recognizes and improves pursuit of philosophical, artistic and esthetical property required and emerged during various services. This is a development process with synchronous and coordinated progress for ceaseless self-improvement, and ceaseless self-development of service demand and service providing, and also the necessary results of scientific and philosophical bidirectional development for a brand organization to be a brand ecological organization.

6 Brand service learning

Human's cognition for service is a process of ceaseless self-progress and self improvement, and the in-depth understanding based on basic cognition of service spirits, service ambition and service state formation. It becomes the self-development process of everyone's basic ideology. When an enterprise brand decides to develop into a brand organization, it must improve brand service level comprehensively, and upgrade brand service by learning. The brand service learning is a necessary experience and crucial service development process. When a country wishes to become a strong service power, it shall establish in-depth and developed modern service industry, comprehensively improve service ability, proportion and value of brand economy, and carry out nationwide service learning. Brand service learning here is a structural strategic resource reserve for development model of national service economy.

Service learning is a kind of important learning method, and a state maintained when providing services. There are many differences between learning and education. Human beings are parts of rapid dynamic learning network. Learning comprises of instant learning at anytime anywhere and knowledge dynamic update of system topology. Everyone in the world is in a self-centered learning cycle everyday for knowledge supplementation and adjustment. The task of education is to systematically impart and master existing knowledge. The differences become obvious during modern science development and social progress. Learning and education will surely be divided into two different strategic development fields in the future.

The brand service learning of enterprises is the preparation of service ability that helps to develop service level with high quality, high performance and highly matching self-adaption capacity. When an enterprise brand tries to grow into a brand organization, it shall select competent service talents by brand talent screening technology and allocate them to each service link. Service learning contains five levels of contents that include brand service learning for brand officer, leaders, backbones and all the staff, and brand collaborative network. The five aspects can be combined according to intensive learning courses and learning hours.

Not everyone can engage in service management. In a brand organization, main members engaging in brand service shall be selected by brand talent screening technology. The talent measurement technology is mainly used to seek for specialized personnel with service spirits, active service awareness and service status. Voluntary and active persons who can sustainably remain passionate towards others are required to provide services. Only when accurate service personnel play important and due diligence role in links of leadership, management layer and key service operating link, the service ability and the service value of a brand can be completely, systematically and organically combined and give full play to service capacity.

In terms of national development, in order to develop modern service industry, nationwide service learning must be carried out to transform its population to high quality service personnel. Not all citizens of a country can have service capacity. Service capacity depends on the most basic service accomplishment of citizens. The proportion of population with basic service accomplishment in one country depends on population accepting specialized service learning among strategic resource reserve of national economy. The universal service awareness and service ability of citizen are mainly cultivated through national basic service accomplishment carried out to newly grown population. The elementary school, middle school and universities are important stages for service learning. The service learning here is carried out by national universal education. By carrying out service accomplishment education, popularizing brand service science, and developing social voluntary service spirits in schools, the future economic form of a country can realize nationwide brand service-oriented development.

If a country fails to learn services in the universal meaning, the population who can effectively engage in service industry in the country will be rare, the service economy of the country will face structural fault, service talents required by enterprises will be seriously insufficient and enterprises will face the crisis of service talents exhaustion. People with brand service development capacity have important advantages of strategic resources for service development in venture economy and service economy in countries and regions.

7 Brand service intelligence

The intelligent development of brand service is the leading-edge field of service science that modern brand service has encountered and is developing rapidly. The service intelligence of brands shall be established at the beginning based on deep understanding of service. It does not change the expression way of technology, and the key development orientation is the comprehensive intelligent design of service process.

Currently, the development of intelligence is only in the initial stage for future intelligence of human beings. Service intelligence can only simulate form or part of self-service, or be applied to experiment, test and study of service in a small range, such as self-service devices deployed in large amount. The response service of intelligent service robot and personated service reception of intelligent robot are still in immature laboratory state for subjects of brand quality and brand experience.

Brand service intelligence shall still develop with the principle of systematic thinking and overall design. The orientation is management and technology development based on brand service order with self-operation, self-adaption and self-ecology of brand service flow. In order to meet requirements of future brand service intelligence development, the service network system capacity, local service and multi-network interconnecting environment development shall be noticed.

SECTION II BRAND SUBJECTS

At present, the service process management of global enterprises still has large amount of service design defects, and the service flow does not flow smoothly. Those service defect, and unsmooth and unstable brand service flow process hinders ecological and further intelligent development of brands to certain degree.

The preferential development link of current brand service intelligence is mainly shown in customer service system of enterprise brand. Few enterprises develop brand user supporting system. Under the network branding and e-business branding (B2U) development environment, more brands will further integrate e-services with original entity products and services so as to create a new form of future brand intelligent services.

The ultimate development of brand service intelligence is oriented on the rapidly developed brand brain science and the developed service intelligent network so as to deeply change the existing cognition method and acquisition method of people for services.

Exercises

1. Fill in the Blanks: The value chain of brand service is the brand life value level line generated when _____, _____ and _____ develop jointly, coordinate with each other and reach highly coincident level value.

2. True or False Question: If a country fails to learn services in the universal meaning, the service economy of the country will face structural fault, service talents required by enterprises will be insufficient seriously and enterprises will face the crisis of service talents exhaustion.   ( )

3. Essay Question: What are brand after-sales service ideas?

Chapter 9

Brand Quality

Brand quality, also known as science of quality, is a branch subject of brand science that is obviously different from the ordinary quality science. The essential difference is that the ordinary quality science focuses on quality assurance, quality process control and quality conformance, which is deemed as a kind of inspection means. It is implemented through quality control, constraint theory and quality activities; is based on overall quality control and factual constraint theory meeting quality requirements; is shown as dependence on common consumption demand; and finally become the warranty for minimum quality conformance. For brand quality, it aims to pursue better state, optimal experience and stable quality, and is deemed as the most basic enterprise responsibility. It is implemented through brand quality system, quality design and quality process; is based on development theory ceaselessly pursuing overall quality level; is presented as the highest target and factual foundation for comprehensive pursuit of quality; shown in perfect expression of brand self-pursuit; and finally become the provable brand quality science and philosophical practice results.

1 Brand quality science and brand quality philosophy

Brand quality develops both as a kind of brand quality science and brand quality philosophy. It has dual development requirements for science and philosophy and final expression form with high standard, high level and high requirements. The brand organization reaches the purpose of self perfect pursuit for brand products and services by developing brand quality science. It is a spontaneous, initiative and transcending rationality-sensibility bidirectional quality level cognition pursued by brands from internal to external.

The development of brand science is based on overall requirements for brand quality system design, and improvement of scientific laws of brand quality is accomplished through ceaseless summary. Quality problems are discovered through scientific experiments, brand products and services, and steadily improves reliability, stability and guarantee requirements of brand quality by overall staged progress. As a quality pursuit in aspects of cognition, understanding and attitude, the brand quality science develops system quality value of all brand organization members to the maximum.

The brand quality philosophy aims to improve expression level and presented value of brand quality aesthetics through ideology, awareness level, spiritual pursuit and quality experience standpoint of brand quality and by ceaselessly feeling the nature and understanding the natural ecological system. As an important part of brand thinking, Brand A Theory, brand quality philology appears as source of idea, thinking, cognition, will and awareness and spiritual pursuit, and provides cultural interpretation ability for cultural connotation, artistic presentation, philosophical quality of artistic conception and aesthetics to brand quality development.

Brand quality science is equally important as brand quality philosophy, and provides important supporting leading-edge development power for structural brand development capacity to brand quality development. It is the ultimate quality pursuit of brand products and services to ceaselessly improve the overall quality level, show the best brand quality demand, develop favorable quality expression and presentation form, and encourage and mobilize all members of brand enterprise organization to make endeavors with good attitudes and actions. Therefore, the development of brand quality science is obviously different from the ordinary quality science in the aspects of ideology, cognition, strategy and management.

SECTION II BRAND SUBJECTS

The development of brand quality science is the optimal expression form of brand development mission and enterprise responsibility, and the basic quality state during quality development of enterprise brand organization. Finally it enable brand quality to reach perfect reflection through output, transmission and use of brand products and brand services to brand users, and thus drives self-response, self-induction and self-transmission of brand users and make brand quality an important carrier of brand for automatic expansion, transmission and marketing. It is the brand attraction during brand development, and gives full play to dual value of brand science and brand philosophy.

2 Brand quality standard theory

Brand quality standard theory refers to the basic functions, central role and main competitive state of brand quality in the entire development history of brand and the expression process of brand products and services.

The development of all enterprises is always to pursue the fulfillment of enterprise responsibilities first, while the key point of enterprise responsibilities is to control quality of products and services, develop market by quality, win market by quality, facilitate market status by quality and establish the essential development route for quality pursuit of enterprises and countries from "strong enterprises based on quality" and "strong countries based on quality".

No enterprise can develop without performing basic enterprise responsibilities of "controlling product, service and quality". Enterprises shall extend social responsibilities based on preferentially performing enterprise responsibilities. The order shall not be reversed, i.e. laying more emphasis on social responsibilities than enterprise responsibilities. Only when an enterprise strives to develop to a responsible global enterprise, its brand can be respected by the whole world.

Quality plays the role of main market competitor in development process of any enterprise brand. It is not only the firm resolution of an enterprise brand in market, but also the highest pursuit for development of enterprise brand. More importantly, it is the basic brand cognition and endeavor of all members of enterprises.

Brand quality cannot be assured by promise or guarantee, or recognized by detection, or improved by PDCA quality link. However, it is completed by structural design as overall structure of a brand, and it completes staged brand quality advancement by overall design, quality pursuit and overall improvement; it is the global progress of brand quality reliability, stability, advancement and development quality system; it is the fundamental development idea and structure to guarantee long-term future development of a brand, ability to guarantee overall prospective pre-design and cutting-edge position and systematically solve any possible quality problems in future brand development, and the key factual basis for decisive competitiveness development ability.

The brand quality standard theory also requires that brand quality should not only value quality of entity products, virtual products or product experience process, as well as ultimate quality which users can feel, but also strive for perfect quality requirements during any process such as management and service process. Brand quality is the development foundation based on comprehensive brand quality rating, the basic precondition for a brand to create all realization results of optimal brand quality, the self-upgrading process by ceaselessly eliminating oneself, developing oneself and improving oneself, the development requirements for upgrading self development pattern and the highest quality, and a kind of quality awareness level and quality status that all members of brand organization can achieve. Thus, it is the key development idea of leading brands to acquire outstanding brand achievements in enterprise brand development history and market performance of brand products.

3 Stereoscopic expression form of brand quality

The perfect expression of brand quality is mainly realized by stereoscopic structure of brand tensile theory from the aspects of perceptibility, technology and art. In order to show it in three-dimensional, drawing art must apply 3D perspective relation so as to establish 3D visual image. The expression of brand quality, similarly, shall not be presented separately through certain angle or certain side. Otherwise, the product quality will not be expressed stereoscopically, and fail to form the comprehensive perceptional impression and the integrated judgment to brand users. The common product quality science is always concern about certain aspect or several important links. The quality shown in this way is two-dimensional, and incompletes.

Quality perceptibility: Brand quality establishes a kind of perception and creates a kind of feeling. It is a series of spiritual pursuit and perfect expression which will comprehensively realize perception. In order to surpass oneself and the reality, and perfectly present overall brand design ideas and design concepts, brand quality shall keep studying materials, procedures and manufacture process, and also pay attention to expression form of artistic and aesthetic design ideas.

The scientific experiment, scientific analysis, scientific research and technical innovation with regard to brand products become every important. Brand should spare no efforts to carry out scientific research on these fields. Therefore, the scientific laboratory and global R&D Center take charge of long-term fundamental research with the highest weight, largest proportion and the most profound influence. The perception of brand quality will be evolved into multiple research projects and quality perception data, for instance study on figure, glossiness and color of fur, or experimental test for tastes and flavors. The optimal presentation quality of brand shall be created and designed through thorough and meticulous scientific findings, materials contrast, fundamental disciplinary study, technological standard and perception impression.

Quality technology: Key point of quality technology is to deem quality as a comprehensive embodiment of pursuit, requirement for quality stability to be reached, and requirements for quality management process and quality rating requirements. These technical links have expanded people's basic understanding of quality.

(1) The requirements for quality stability promotes brand products to strive for perfection, and keep stable operation, favorable use status of products delivered to brand users. The quality stability of industrial products is complex, and the development of quality stability concerns high quality requirements for manufacturing technology level. The research and development will attach importance to advancement and developed degree of technology, expression model of optimal product performance and outstanding quality technology development level.

(2) Quality technology shall be based on quality level development of the entire management process. This is the requirement for quality in the aspect of management, and cover quality guarantee capacity, operation maintenance level and fast response mechanism in multiple cross-management technical fields and cross-management systems in terms of R&D, process technology, production equipment, production process, storage & transportation process, delivery process and after-sales services.

(3) The requirements for quality rating of each link contain quality level rating, high level quality requirements combination, collaboration and application of physical materials, work quality and virtual products including supply chain purchase quality, service quality, supporting service quality and content quality. The requirements for brand quality involve multiple aspects. Quality grading is the clear requirements for quality of various aspects in the entire quality system, and the system screening and selecting quality grade of each link. It can keep consistent interactive development level of quality. As long as all links that are related to quality achieved the high level of quality grading, the entire brand can show high overall quality development standard.

Quality art: This is the requirement for quality aesthetics based on philosophy and artistic expression form. The internal and external brand designers of brand organization mainly take charge of art reproduction process of brand products. Brand products improve in aspects of scientific standard, cultural connotation, and infinite development space of art design through quality art expression forms such as product form, originality and creativity, concept design, industrial design and package design, and quality develops the cultural property as artistic work.

SECTION II BRAND SUBJECTS

The requirements of brand organization for art are mainly shown in finished products of brand, which are the branding products stereoscopically and visually pushed out to the public. Through artistic processing such as color application, appearance design and brand perceptional impression enhancement, the products are finally expressed as quality pursuit property in specific links including exquisite raw materials, fine workmanship, and artistic expression, and are easy to be discovered, recognized and memorized by users. They are the approval of brand users for brand cultural value, and the motive for brand purchase with high cost performance and enjoyment of use.

4 Brand quality failure theory

The expression of brand quality is obviously far higher than the common requirements for product quality, and must finish stereoscopic presentation of complete brand quality from three dimensions. The optimal perfect form of brand can be displayed by comprehensive stereoscopic form such as inside, outside, vision, smell, performance, quality, shape and packaging from any angle or side. This is a kind of integrated, comprehensive, and in-depth function of brand quality tensile theory so that brand can show perfect and complete quality aesthetic perception and fixed brand quality impression based on original virtual or physical form.

When any consumer first met a new brand product that he/she has never heard of, he/she may know nothing about the use form, performance characteristics and application time of the product due to the lack of "experience-based" perfection. At that time, consumers are very vigilant to the brand, and have the "tentative error test psychology" for any service state in any link and during brand delivery process, and any problem after purchase. This is based on self safety protection any unknown matter with potential risks. For instance, people will not approach the edge of high buildings without protective measures. Once approached, the mental and physical safety warning will start automatically. The fear hinders the body from moving forward.

Human being may keep high potential risk appraisal process during the contact with brands that are unknown or never been used before. They will list such products as key matters (or services) for monitoring and risk control, and feel assured after safety requirements are fulfilled. The vigilant psychology of self-protection will enlarge any minor defect instantly during the usage of product, if "risk" is being detected at the beginning, and people are being stopped from continuing under the protection consciousness. The product will have no chance to explain. People will immediately receive warning from the heart, and stop using the product and directly give up further understanding of the product. Few people will take the risk to use any other products of the brand.

The inherent prevention mechanism of human being urges brand to notice complete expression of quality. No detail or failure can be occurred. Therefore, the highly branded quality must start from stereoscopic and complete brand quality development impression indicated by brand tensile theory to complete the attempted use, first time trust and cognition of quality stability and quality advancement of brand users to brand products so that "brand selection and usage experience" rises up to specialized, safe and fixed consumption behavior by usage experience. This is the new experience generation, experience transfer and experience fixation process of a new brand user for a brand.

People finish complete quality perception and quality approval of a brand by the safety recognition experiences, and experience results after use. If any product failed in any minor link during the result process; all endeavors made by the product and the brand will be ruthlessly abandoned by consumers. They may deny the brand in the whole life.

5 Brand quality development theory

The early development foundation of global quality theory is mainly the restraint theory. It pays attention to development idea of "quality control" management process, gives determinate objects under control by applying conditions of quality system, restraint device and people restraint quality, and finishes quality guaranteed by quality activities such as operating technology and supervision in each link and PDCA quality improvement.

The quality control idea focusing on constraint theory occurs because of the nonconforming, substandard and unsatisfied factors in all stages and links of the entire quality chain due to quality design defect, quality instability of production process, and non-integration of quality elements to guarantee production and provide and deliver qualified products to consumers.

However, the brand quality development had apparently exceeded the range of conformity assurance. The purpose of brand quality is to produce excellent products, and supply branding products through perfect processing to the market. The "qualified" products are obviously the lowest level quality requirements in market rather than the dominant development route developed by brand products.

Therefore, brand quality idea is based on the development theory, and emphasizes on development level of brand quality. It is a scientific and philosophical expression with "brand quality pursuit" as an overall development target of one brand. In order to create the dreamy, ideal and rational perfect brand, the brand founders, management scientists, brand designers and brand analysts will spend days and nights to create a perfect brand work.

In brand quality science, quality depends on neither inspection nor guarantee. Brand quality is the perfect quality pursuit results finished by staged overall upgrading and development of quality. The possible brand product defect and usage experience under various environment including mal-conditions are all proposed and attributed to brand design link. The brand perception performance, brand presentation performance, brand essential performance, brand efficiency performance, as well as brand performance in global collaborative network are deemed as complete brand quality pursuit links so as to comprehensively complete the optimal performance design of brand quality.

In Qin Dynasty 2200 years ago, the standardization time of human beings is initiated for the first time. The weapons such as crossbow, Pi, halberd, dagger-axe and bronze sword, and even war horses were realized according to large-scale standard production and digital standard requirements. Those weapons were not produced through common production control, but represented deep weapon study and high design level development. The body of war horses shall follow accurate and uniform laws. The brand quality development laws shall be "large amount of studies and experiments – seeking for the best performance – fixing and becoming the standard – reproduction (scanning)". Any classic product that is constantly sold the best worldwide must experience similar brand performance design process so as to develop outstanding brand quality and show excellent brand performance. This is the "outstanding" performance of worldwide brand products during brand quality development process. No matter in the Eastern Hemisphere or in the Western Hemisphere, brand products have similar brand quality pursuit ideas.

On the contrary, it is popular in enterprises with common quality management to use restraint theory to supervise actual quality process, identify defects and fine for faulty quality problems mainly because of fast product upgrading and low requirements for product quality. In order to push out new products which meet superficial competitive demands from the market, enterprises will deem "users" as "experimental subject" and check quality performance of products by users in the market. Therefore, all users purchasing the product become the experiment subjects. Large amount of design defects and unstable quality bother enterprise development for long, but enterprises are not aware.

The launch of new products means quality defects are accumulated and enlarged to serious quality accident, causing ceaseless product recall and "quality scandals" in the world. The essential cause is the non-branding awareness in the aspect of quality management ideas. When enterprises do not truly have basic cognition of brand quality, product quality will occur frequently as a kind of complicated and confusing management problems, repeated feedbacks of market difficulties and complaints of consumers, which are the natural barriers for enterprises to stride forward toward brands. There is major difference between brand quality science and gap of brand development capacity and flattering itself as "brand" due to its popularity to becoming the true brand.

SECTION II BRAND SUBJECTS

6 Brand quality system design

Brand quality development is the brand quality pursuit model with excellent quality design as main development model. The key points are system design and laboratory status. It aims to finish overall upgrading of brand quality system design level and development degree by nature of the entire brand quality stages, and improve level of overall brand quality development capacity by integrated system.

The systematic design of brand quality is the overall design arrangement and system design practices made to meet various performances of brand, and the important brand quality presentation link in overall brand design. The systematic design requires that brand must pay attention to the ideal development status and various quality advantages of brand quality while developing brand quality. It is the advantage cluster, performance embodiment and perfect expression based on brand development instinct.

In order to create the optimal quality status of brand products, brand organization shall carry out comparative study on the highest brand quality level in the entire market. However, this is not the main purpose. The research range of brand quality shall cover the most cutting-edge, most advanced and most developed brand quality ideas and quality pursuit aspects in all possible fields. Moreover, it seeks for the optimal cognition of brand quality and achieves the optimal status of brand quality based on ceaselessly summarizing and refining natural scientific development laws and human philosophy development ideas.

It should be noticed particularly that brand quality is the self-creation and quality realization for the pursuit of perfect brand quality. It is neither restricted to the study on similar brand quality status in the market, nor the quality development based on reference of quality of peers. The idea source of brand quality may be study on animals and plants, or understanding of natural ecology, or more possibly a comprehensive understanding of the latest hot development trend and competition form or quality development level of worldwide popular products. These ideas finally integrate to the independent thinking that a brand requires for development, i.e. the final development results of brand thinking ability in brand mechanics.

This will also mean that on certain degree, brand organization may change brand product form, brand quality expression form and brand performance reflection and cognition model in the existing market. As a kind of advanced creative result of thinking ability, the brand quality result created by any excellent brand product may overturn the market, and also make brand new understanding of brand quality in similar market in the same industry. It is the latest height that one brand may reach in global and industrial competition field for product quality. Such creation starts from, develops based on and achieves the brand. It is the ultimate embodiment of completely independent brand quality idea in global market, and also the optimal performance of brands in market by cutting-edge status and conclusive competitiveness advantage.

We always emphasize that all brand officers are perfectionists. The brand officers striving for rigidity, perfection and free ideas, and keeping fair, just and independent thinking are the actual people in charge of decision making and performing the inspect, check and control brand products on behalf of any possible potential consumers. The brand product design that any brand officer believes that it is not perfect enough and unsatisfied will not flow to market, or appears the sales and delivery links. The brand officers must seriously and prudently treat the emission and responsibility of brand profession, and the final control and signing right for brand products. This is the huge sense of mission, sense of responsibility and power endowment responsible for market, brand and themselves. Therefore, the product design defects or defects during manufacture process are actually eliminated by brand officers. It neither depends on the control of quality personnel, nor relies on the information fed back by consumers in quality complaint.

In all brand product links that are completed upon agreement and signature of chief brand officers, the optimal status and perfect expression of brand products shall be sought ceaselessly by the standard ideas, zero management and meta-analysis of brand products. These brand products will be studied repeatedly, analyzed scientifically, and tested accordingly in strict brand laboratory. On essence, the systematic design of brand quality is always in scientific experiment and study under brand laboratory state. Only with the approval of chief brand officer by signature, the preliminary research of brand products can end. Next, the experiment state can be thoroughly finished and brand products can officially enter market by further experiments on production management process and service process of brand quality.

In order to reach the target of brand quality pursuit, brand organization will apply completed model of systematic recognition, performance experiment and stochastic approximation to finish optimal reflection of brand quality. System identification is the repeated experiments and distinctions of all problem links of brand products. Performance experiment is the comparative study made by specific practices of various brand performances so as to find the optimal brand perception level, optimal quality method and optimal quality expression form to finish the perfect construction of brand quality. The stochastic approximation includes the random optimal quality expression links of brand performance to study and actual measurement during actual scientific study and scientific experiment process, and summaries scientific laws of stochastic approximation under brand laboratory state and applies these scientific research results by acquiring optimal performance in stochastic approximation. It is an important way for valid development of brand quality.

7 Brand quality process

Brand quality process is a key means for brand quality development, and the staged overall quality level upgrading process after brand quality design is ended. The brand quality process contains three typical brand quality process development structure and development methods including value engineering, overall optimization and MA solution.

Value engineering: Value engineering is the value creation and development of brand quality cognition cultivation and brand performance system implemented by all members of brand organization before and after the brand products are launched. In order to capture important brand quality elements, optimal performance and optimal expression way in brand design link, value engineering has both high management level and competitive advantages for development of brand value chain.

Brand is finally shown as value discovery model in the market. It has equal value realization and value expression pattern as that of brand organization. The former refers to the self-finding of brand users for brand value, and the latter refers to new value creation of all brand members in each link of brand quality realization process.

When a brand completed the whole brand quality design, the brand value engineering is implemented systematically on brand organization user side and development side to verify brand quality level and develop brand values and correct errors during the entire brand management process. It is a systematic engineering to guarantee brand to further reach self-adaptive and self-operating brand ecological organization development level.

In order to create conditions for development, promote and accelerate brand organization creating brand product quality with high quality guarantee level and high stability, brand organizations shall apply comprehensive optimization and MA solution to upgrade systematic level of brand quality.

For overall upgrading, brand quality development cannot focus on random improvement, perfection at any time and subsequent change. PDCA quality link that is mainly concerned on quality improvement model is prohibited during this process. Due to the restriction of local optimization, PDCA may suffer from management problem accumulation, redundancy, and management flow stability damage. This is the reason for ceaseless management problems, complex management flow and lower management efficiency discovered during business management once in a while.

The brand quality management must have systematic, integral, global and overall upgrading of brand quality by system correction, system cognition and system analysis, and finish scientific design, scientific development and stable brand ecological order development level of complete quality system of brand organization through complete brand quality system upgrading. It is finished by trans-department MA groups distributed in brand organization and MA solution model.

MA solution covers problem collection, meta-analysis, scientific design and science popularization by PADS model of MA management and analysis group aiming at specific brand quality problems and quality instability during brand quality system upgrading process so as to guarantee scientific development level of the entire system during brand management process.

Exercises

1. Fill in the blanks: brand quality science pursues _____, _____ and _____, which is deemed as the most basic enterprise responsibility and shown in perfect expression of brand self-pursuit.

2. Multiple- Choice Question: The development of brand quality science is obviously different from the ordinary quality science in aspects of _____. ( )

   A. Self-response, self-induction and self-transmission

   B. Ideology, cognition, strategy and management

   C. Cultural connotation, artistic presentation, philosophical quality of artistic conception and aesthetics

   D. The highest weight, largest proportion and most profound influence

3. Essay Question: What is brand quality? What is the role of brand quality in enterprises?

Chapter 10

Brand Experience

Brand experience is an emerging subject during modern brand development process. With rapid development of global brand products and services, the scientific, cultural and aesthetic demands of brands increase greatly. In the beginning of the 21st century, brand experience is deemed as an important field, thus specialized professions such as brand product manager and brand chief experience officer are generated. The subject of brand experience emerges herewith and becomes a rapidly developing branch subject in the field of brand science.

Brand experience is the imagination and experience process of the experience study, not the purpose. The final purpose of all brand experiences is brand perception, i.e. the cognition results of deep and long-term mental feeling and experience during brand use when brand is deposited, perceived and memorized by the user. If brand feeling cannot be realized, brand experience can be only known as a marketing stunt and a variation of a sales promotion.

1 Emerging of brand experience

The emerging trend in brand experience science is a wave of worldwide manager such as Steve Jobs, the founder of Apple Inc., who enhanced the product experience design in the globally popular electronic products such as the iPhone, iPad, iPod and iMac in the beginning of the 21st Century. Product experience is deemed as an important product development field during the development of modern enterprises, and introduced rapidly and valued greatly. However, global enterprises, especially technology enterprises, have added product managers and positions regarding product experience and successively set facilities such as brand experience pavilion. In terms of development of global products and brand experience facilities, brand experience is currently only deemed as a global wave and fails to form an ideal brand experience branch subject with developed systems, except the minority brands which have effectively improved experience level of products and favorably applied a directly interactive brand user relation development form.

As a matter of fact, Jobs noticed the development of brand experience earlier than the others. From the beginning when Apple Inc. was founded, Jobs started applying design idea of brand experience to develop the production line, which is a thinking power of brand based on systematic brand perception philosophy. The brand experience idea has been completely applied when Apple Lisa was launched in 1983 and iMac in 1997. For brand experience science, the number of excellent product managers is not the decisive competitiveness of a brand. The key point of brand experience development lies in systematic brand perception philosophy, brand experience benefits and thinking ability development structure of brand user relation. In other words, it depends on roles of brand entrepreneurs and brand officers with a high level of brand cutting-edge status development ability.

That is because brand experience is not the change in a local or a certain detailed product form or experience degree, but a development result applying the high level of brand thinking ability, a comprehensive presentation of complete and perfect brand experience ideas based on global leading-edge development level, and the original creativity, ambition and courage to deeply change brand product and service form and deeply drive the reform of original industrial combination relation. There are but a few entrepreneurs with great brand experience ideas. As restricted by various development causes, entrepreneurs who can create miracle of brand experience and transfer to brand experience achievements are quite rare. However, it will not hinder us to establish a series of brand experience ideas, summarize the scientific development laws, and establish a theoretical foundation for more entrepreneurs and brand officers with outstanding brand experience ideas in the future.

SECTION II BRAND SUBJECTS

2 Philosophy of brand perception

Brand is a leading-edge science based on the development of human's perception level. The development focuses on scientific invention, scientific creation, scientific realization, philosophical thinking, philosophical expression and philosophical transmission for perception. Minority with development capacity favorably applies scientific and philosophical value of brand perception development level during brand development process so as to give the full play to brand experience globally and create a series of economic miracles and changes in overturning of market experience ideas.

The development of human brand economy in the 21st century mainly shows that consumptive capacity decides productivity. However, the leading role is the development capacity of brand idea, while brand users are always passive percipients and only accept specific brand products and services created by brand organizations. Although some academic opinions believe that in the 21st century the consumers are not the passive receivers of information, and emphasize the development of participating marketing and interactive marketing. This is actually a strategy of brand from a market's perspective deemed as marketing. From the main competitive role in global market, the change made by brand users in brand participation is limited. Users can only change the microscopic link of brand products or promote brand organization to develop brand form in a rational way. The main development role is still dominated by brand organizations.

Only when brand organizations release out brand products, users have the opportunity to use these brand products, and the products have the opportunity for a dynamic experience and upgrading. If one enterprise has no strategic, dominant, independent and decisive brand ideas, the brand organization will not exist. Therefore, users fail to independently decide on the development direction of brands by subjective consciousness and self-judgment capacity. Enterprises going with the flow and extremely expecting to meet all demands of customers are the temporary substitutions in market, and will fail in the end.

The development of brand perception level comes from the great creativity of brand organization leaders, which is the thorough release and application of brand perception philosophy deduced from leading ideas and an absolute competitiveness and development power in market. It contains brand perception creativity, brand reality perception transformation ability and the scientific application of perception and learning process, and it is the decisive competitive advantages mastering progress psychology and also developed in the market; while the development of such user perception level is shown as a brand experience effect –it is the brand experience plantation in the global market.

2.1 Development of brand perception level

What the brand wants to create is perception. This is the human history development process in which the human beings ceaselessly evolve and improve during consciousness improvement. The growth of common economic income promotes the growth of physical and cultural consumption level. A large amount of new brand perceptions are continuously invented and created, and new brand perception is more complex and difficult to create, since human beings ceaselessly know and understand perceptions, and habitual perception experiences increase. Therefore, the creativity of brand economy becomes more challengeable with the growing development of human brand perception users. Moreover, when the perception of human beings develops to certain degree, the new brand emerging speed will slow down, and gradually will the small new brands emerge when brand perception saturation is reached by the end of the 21st century.

Firstly, perception is a two-way development process for both science and philosophy, based on perceptive organs and on the feeling psychology of human beings. The human organs participating in this feeling are the eyes, ears, tongue, hands, feet and human nerve network, which respectively takes charge of different feeling judgments such as vision, hearing, taste and touch so as to generate experience aesthetics which are beautiful to see, good to hear, taste good and feel comfortable. The comprehensive feeling level of everyone's sense organs is formed with the growth of feeling experiences of sense organs and development of feeling psychology, such as the sense organ reaction for comfort and judgment ability for beauty and ugliness.

The changes in feeling psychology are mainly from the feeling judgment made by sense organs, such as the mentality and brain for experiences, including the development of more complex and high level feeling judgment ability such as language perception, aesthetic identification, artistic apprehension, natural inspiration and dreamy fantasy. It is the comprehensive growth of feeling, perception, knowledge creation, identification level and cognitive ability formed by comprehensive growth of environment, knowledge growth and independent thinking of one person.

The comprehensively and synchronically growing perception level of human beings as well as different perceptive level growth of every person decide the creativity level and brand cognition and ceaseless evolving progress for perception level acceptance degree of brand users. The typical cases are the changes to mainstream fashion styles in different times and the staged perceptive changes to daily materials and tools such as food, communication tools and transportation tools, which are recorded by the concept of "change of time".

The nature of brand development value is to invent, create and develop perceptions, such as inventing a flavor, creating a style and developing a new tool. The brand perception creation shall be realized by rational scientific creation process or perceptual philosophical creation process. The former is deemed as new invention, or findings and development following the new scientific laws, which grant popularity and value of human science application to brands; the latter grants new significance, value and expression form to a brand by creation of ideology, development of concept and expression mode of art aesthetics.

Both rational scientific or perceptual philosophical developments can develop brands. For instance, the optimal temperature 4°C of Coca Cola (flat area) for the former, and cutting art of Sashimi in Japan for the latter can both develop perception level from scientific or philosophical angles. However, in terms of science, perception can develop normally and on a large scale, while in terms of philosophy, perception can develop individually with varieties. Only when the two aspects of development try to keep in bidirectional and balanced way the balanced rational scientific or perceptual philosophical perception level, enterprises can develop popular brands and brand products and services which not only meet large-scale development demand of market, but also have philosophical thought value with certain perception level.

2.2 Brand progress psychology

Brand founders only create new brand feelings, but the market will not necessarily accept such brand feeling. The transition of full brand perception process and landmark development process of brand perception level can be finished when the innovation of brand perception and brand user experience reach synchronic development status. Otherwise, the brand perception creation may wait for a long verification period by human beings, and can finish a thorough transition after long historical changes for years, dozens of years and even hundreds of years.

The historical period division is generated mainly because perception creation is advancing, is surreal and even ahead of human thought development and aesthetic experience cognition level during a certain period, or because the perception market scale cannot be expanded effectively, as it is restricted by multiple development achievements. Therefore, no matter how good the perception is, it is unknown to people. Along reality-perception transformation process is required to create common perception and acceptance of brand users by perceptions of brand founders, while this process is the change process in humans for cognition learning, i.e. the development process of brand progress psychology.

For instance in 1983, the failure of Apple Lisa launched by Steve Jobs lies in the generation division between brand perception creation level and brand user perception and acceptance level. The iPhone mobile series, by reality-perception transformation in 3 years and with three generations of products of iPhone1, iPhone2 and iPhone3 after firstly launched in 2007, and continuous accumulation of brand user since 1976, finally ushered in the worldwide craziness and sales wave when the fourth generation iPhone4 launched in 2010.

Wong Lo Kat Herbal Tea, founded in 1828, was still an unknown local small brand till 2000. After 178 years, the herbal tea got combined with hotpot market, "heat syndrome + heat syndrome prevention".

Section II Brand Subjects

Due to the market operation, the brand finally becomes a well-known brand after large-scale market application for ten years.

During brand experience development, brand organization needs to experience a transition process of "reality-perception transformation". This process is not only the rational brand cultivation process when brand founders, brand officers, all members of brand organization and brand investors all keep quiet, but also a conception learning process required by the first batch of early brand users in global market when they touch a new brand product for the first time. No good brand can miss out on this historical development stage.

People need time to accept a kind of perception. As the ideas may get delayed for at least a decade, the classic accuracy of a new thinking can be verified on time through large amount of application in an expanded range after people tested and experienced valid application. Market also needs time. The worldwide brand users need time to experience, digest and verify the latest perception of advancing brand products. Therefore, they may spend a very long time in updating their original perception level, adjusting the cognition state, forming new perception habits and transmitting and spreading the new perceptions.

It is difficult to change the habit one has formed. The nature of brand perception is to create new perception. It means brand users must give up or adjust some perceptive structures formed already, accept new perception and form new habits. This is a necessary process for human progress, and also the perceptual learning of everyone in the world for reality-perception transformation. Brand users must combine new perception with various perceptions in reality. No matter such perception is virtual, realistic, visual, impressive, has taste or uses' habits, it shall be transformed to the habitual perception that can be accepted in real life, and included in a fixed thinking of brand perceptive structure.

Fortunately, human beings are ceaselessly developing individuals and groups, while some people always love to accept new challenges, new things and try new experiences. Especially in the time of rapid development and fast change, people have the progressive idea to accept new things so that new brand develops brand perception process faster. New brand perception can effectively release the development potential in a short development stage of 2-3 years. Brand investors are willing to pay for the transition process of brand perception level, and even invest in such perception. The universal brand progress development psychology is hereby established. The favorable environments, in which the capital market pursues new business modes and investors, are willing to provide capital support for new brand perception study by jointly promoting the common development of brand perception level.

3 Brand experience benefits

The brand progress psychology is the accelerator for development of brand perception level in common sense. Both the active attitudes of brand founders pursuing new brand perception invention and powerful supports of capital market on brand perception development urge the brand experience effect to become an important development trend and universal hot wave in the global market. Thus, brand experience effect develops into social and economic benefits of brand experience, and acquires unprecedented development in the 21st century thereby.

We should notice the important development mode of brand culture selection development theory, brand memetics and brand evolution and application in modern and future social economy. The reason why brand experience becomes a highlight in development of global brand economy is that brand organization favorably applies the process of human beings from preference transfer to emotion transference, so as to develop brand scientific developing capacity structure for mental pursuit.

The overall human development is the history of ceaseless evolution and development in different categories of civilization, and also has a history of ceaselessly inventing and creating world multi-culture. Thus, the human culture spectrum is formed. Brands supply abundant cultural characteristics, creativities and significance of life for human beings in modern life by ceaselessly giving new cultural connotation. Most of the global population may be unable to freely select the civilization attribute with national characteristics. However, everyone is free to know, understand and accept diversified civilization forms and multi-culture modes. Free selection of culture lays a basic factual foundation for brand diversified development.

Since brand culture has the same multi-culture attribute as that of the culture type of human beings, brand can expand the global market and be accepted by development mode of brand memetics. The attribute of brand culture selection is the cultural preference transmission of overall memetic factors from one group to another. For instance, leading-edge technology, consumer electronics, European architecture, American country music, or classical Chinese literatures, all have fixed cultural preference groups. Brand culture can be designed on that basis or new brand cultural characteristics can be created beyond existing cultural styles. Such culture preference transfer is featured by universality and collective trend in certain range. Brand is established based on development of culture selection and overall preference development of brand memetics, and owns brand user groups within specific category of culture.

When a new brand emerges as a cultural characteristic, the group preference transformation will appear among global brand users via market operation, i.e. the development process of "brand characteristic culture learning – accepted by individual brand users – perceptive experience development – brand use group expansion". In the beginning, only a minority and even individual brand users are willing to accept and try the new changes brought about by brand. They acquire new perceptive experience during learning and use, and make changes to their habits, judgment methods and cultural attribute preferences. The experiences are transferred to deep perception and fixed by the form of "experience".

When the scope of "culture selection –preference –feeling -experience" is expanded continuously in the global market, the perceptive experience achieves development in a common sense, and a brand thoroughly finishes transformation of brand experience benefits between market and user groups so as to become a stably developing brand. When the brand experience of a user develops to a certain degree, the experience will be further transformed to transference. Due to high dependence on the special experience value given by the brand, the brand user will generate deep development relation with brand emotionally. At that time, the relationship between brand and users becomes especially important, and becomes the foundation for permanent development. Therefore, the final result of brand experience benefit is the spontaneous development process from "brand culture selection preference" to "brand emotion". Brand can further develop the pursuit for brand spirits so as to reach the high-level dependent consumptive demands in the aspect of deep cultural spirits of brand users.

4 Brand experience facilities

We have disclosed main sources of brand profits in the "golden triangle of brand profits" on the subject of brand principle. In the starting development period of a brand, the most important process is to expand the trial range, and enlarge the scale of trial brand users so as to transfer them to paying users and regulars. Some brands may have not carried out the systematic brand construction yet, but have realized the importance of acquiring paying users by brand experiences. Some brands enhance the spiritual resonance between brand designers and brand users in a small range, and only maintain and keep a small amount of brand users as a minority brand to acquire stable development foundation within a limited brand cognition range. Regardless of brand experience, the brand experience in the 21st Century has become a common brand subject of brand science.

When a brand decides to build brand experience facilities, the basic target is consistent, i.e. to expand first experience, experience feeling level and trial the first trust design of brand users. The brand experience facilities developed by brand organization contain typical forms such as brand experience pavilion, brand virtual scene, online brand experience technology and brand experience activity development.

Brand pavilion are a pavilion building and shop type experience facilities in the 21st century, built by brands to make users more directly be in touch with brand use process, the sensual pleasure, brand consumption environment and brand development prospect, known as brand image shop and brand flagship shop. Brand pavilions are usually built in cities with dense population and convenient traffic, or in the countryside or farms with characteristic brand experience environment. Generally, brand experience officers or brand experience receptionists will be defined. The first time experience of users can be promoted by independent participation, oriented invitation, and brand experience activities. Generally, the brand experience process management shall be the main focus. Some brand pavilions adopt open strategy, and welcome any brand users to freely participate in the experience process. They do not focus on sales, but pay attention to direct experience and interactive process with any potential brand users. Some brand pavilions integrate consumption environment and free experience process, and provide loose and free consumption experience. For instance, McDonald's and Starbucks actually integrate free consumption and free experience.

Brand virtual scenes contain online brand experience pavilions developed by computer technology, reality enhancement developed by virtual reality technology, and simulation experience scenes built by forms of themed parks. Brand virtual scenes mainly aim to create a dreamy natural environment and wonders for brand users, or to realize the sensual pleasures by virtual, simulation technology and entity environment that brand users cannot experience in real life. They can arouse the memories of brand users by using the product under certain circumstances and the scenery environment of these technologies, and trigger the demands of brand users.

Online brand technology experience mainly develops direct online interactive brand experience. By modes of intelligent service Q&A, brand user guide, interaction system, third party use of testimony, discussion among brand users, photo taking of realistic application scene, video report, user feeling rendering, competition, lottery drawing, and interactive participation, the interaction process of brand experience is established on the PC side, mobile side, multimedia side and various terminals so as to enhance the universal application benefit of brand user group.

Brand experience activities contain experience games, brand night galas, vocational tours, factory visits, industry-oriented tourisms, TV program live recordings, free application samples, interactive recommendation of brand users, brand tour experience meetings, group gathering experience centered around family, comparative tests of brand use effect, brand lectures and learning activities, and technical seminars. The activities integrate online application and offline activities, and encourage brand users to extensively participate in brand interactive experience by sending large-scale invitations so as to acquire the brand experience effect. Brand experience activities are generally attributed to marketing department of brand organization, and combined with market development, marketing activities and sales, marketing public relation, and customer relation management.

6 Brand product experience

The great concern on brand product experience in the 21st Century is mainly due to the worldwide wave for pursuit of brand product experience drive by the miracle of iPhone sales created by Steve Jobs. Major global IT and internet companies successively add the position of product manager and start paying attention to brand experience officer cultivation.

However, brand product experience is only a universal demand shown in the market side. Actually, most entrepreneurs, brand officers, product managers or experienced officers failed to systematically develop brand experience in terms of structure of brand experience science and as a standpoint of brand perception philosophy. Brand product experience is only a kind of brand product framework developed according to the demands of product-oriented and marketing brand product design and brand user interactive relations.

In specific brand product experience process, brand experience contains brand experience design (BXD), brand participated marketing (BPM), brand experience management (BXM) and interactive perception enhancement (IPE). Most enterprises have only developed to BXD and BPM stages. They still have a certain gap from BXM and IPE.

Brand experience design (BXD) mainly appears in user feeling and use during the entire process of brand product, and is the specific design of experience system based on concept, structure, branch and details. Currently, BXD is applied greatly in specific product fields such as consumer electronics, software, Website, mobile APP and in home appliances. Certain BXD environmental and process design is made in service industry. BXD mainly adopts the product manager system and experience officer system, and pays attention to outstanding performance, detailed expression, perception presentation and emotional reflection during brand product and service process.

Brand participated marketing (BPM) is a kind of interactive development mode encouraging users to participate in brand experience design, service and application process. Some brand products have extensively invited users to participate in the entire design process in the beginning of research, and listened to product ideas and suggestions based on user experience so as to improve the products. The R&D, launch and self-propagation and self-dissipation marketing process is realized during development of interactive brand design and brand user communication by establishing brand communities.

Brand experience management (BXM) is a management mode with ceaseless upgrading, optimization and dynamic development based on brand experience process. The key development point is to apply scientific research and philosophical thinking to inventions and research of new brand experiences according to ergonomics, feeling tests, scientific experiment findings, comparative studies and especially analysis and study on hand/eye coordination of users when using products. BXM ceaselessly develops more scientific brand experience mode by research on changes and preferences of different brand user regions and cultural selection styles, and uses certain artistic creations and aesthetic expressions to improve the cognition, acknowledgement and interaction between brands and users' mind so as to develop high level brand ideas and brand perception philosophy.

Interactive perception enhancement (IPE) uses the effect enhancement method to scientifically develop brand interactive perception level by studies on touch point deployment, value finding way, brand value expression method and brand consumption education method during direct or indirect interaction between brands and users, and uses technology, cultural creativity and brand design strategy to comprehensively enhance key perception effect of perception distribution, ability, effect, presentation method and expression approach so as to comprehensively improve brand performance. IPE is a strategic foresight for long-term development, and the key application field of highly developed practical brands of the future brand organization.

7 Brand user relationship

The ultimate purpose of brand development and brand experience is to develop and keep favorable brand user relationship. It is the development demand of brand competitive ecology, the social and economic development value for brand users to participate in brand, and the ultimate form for development combining development category of rational brand organization leadership science and theory of brand social network structure.

In order to keep favorable brand competitive ecology of brands in global market, brand organizations must reserve and maintain a certain number of brand user groups, and maintain a certain number of backbone brand users - holding the volume of regulars. However, a new brand has no such characteristic. Thus, the brand use relation shall be deemed as a brand progress process in common development.

Brand users' participation in brand development is that, in a deeper sense, brand users participate in social experience development value of brands. It is a historical change process that brand experience economy promotes economic growth of emerging brands. In the fierce modern global competitive environment, users of enterprise products transfer rapidly. Users of one brand product may turn to the other in next second or when making a purchase selection. The brand organization is deemed as brand ecological organization because the development nature is of social and economic characteristics. Brand experience economy promotes the transformation of such social and economic values, i.e. enterprises must consider endeavors made for social development and economic contribution in their future development. This is the basic attitude that brands shall bear enterprise liabilities and social liabilities in global brand economy.

Under social network environment, a brand will own a branding interpersonal relationship network connecting multiple relations. The interactive, multidimensional, multi-element, interpersonal, inter-group and cross-domain brand relation circle, which exists in the form of social network, has thoroughly changed the ecological environment for the competition, which was required by the future brand development. The development process has a special social organization network status for brand penetration and diffusion, brand interpersonal group partner and brand user interactive relation development, and exists as a direct, distributed and concurrent brand user ecological form. This also brings a new challenge for ecological existence form and ecological development form of brand organization.

The infinite magnifying social and economic value of brand and naturally developing social network relation among brand users make global brand society form a new structural form. The brand networking, branding e-business and multi-network connection mode all deeply change the social form of brand in the emerging transformation. This provides new opportunity for brand organization to discover and value the directly interactive brand ecological development form. In the future, any global brand must be an existing and developing brand ecological organization based on such construction theory of brand society.

Brand users urgently try to keep the optimal direct, interactive and integrated development relation with brands. The brand users' participation in brand development process is represented by time stage. Some brand products need to establish participating interaction with brand users in the beginning, take product upgrading and brand reengineering as timeline of brand development, or enhance brand experience interaction by use of interests and the collection of brand fans. When those brand users experience brand development progress together with brand organization, and witnessed the brand history of a brand's growth, from dream to realization, from small brand to well-known brand, and from unknown to world famous, the brand organization development will make outstanding achievements due to deeper interactive development relation with brand users.

It should surely be noticed that brand experience development must contain rational brand organization leadership, powerful brand dream charisma, and legends during brand development process, great creative power of brand, leading service spirits and contribution of brand to social value, which are all spiritual strengths and ultimate value expressions required by great brands. The best brand experience is the future achievement development based on independent opinions of brand leaders, and brand experience is finally a kind of vast economic value transferred from enterprise responsibilities to society dedication. Otherwise, brand experience will become a kind of economic approach, and the brand will be unable to create vast achievement due to the great sense of responsibility to serve the citizens and the society. The relation between brand and users will finally develop into a deeply interactive, inseparable and long-term friendship.

Exercises

1. Multiple-choice Question: in specific brand product experience process, brand experiences contains_____. (   )

A. Brand experience design (BXD), Brand participated marketing (BPM);

B. Brand participated marketing (BPM);

C. Brand experience management (BXM);

D. A B C

2. True or False Question: Perception is a leading-edge science based on the development of human beings for perception level, and a two-way development process for both science and philosophy based on perceptive organs and feeling psychology of human beings.   (   )

3. Discussion: How to understand the benefits brought to enterprise by brand experiences?

Chapter 11

Brand Planning

Brand planning faces a crisis of development, mainly because of the non-scientific factors of brand planning during the global brand development process. Due to lack of necessary cognition for brand science, in the early development stage of global brand economy, brand planning has once more played the major role in the early brand generation process characterized with "omnipotence, panacea". However, with the emergence of brand science, the original mystery of brand planning is fading away, and it getting replaced by the correct role, function and effect of rational brand planning in brand development. This is the key problem to be discussed in brand planning.

It is important to notice that brand planning is comprised of brand planning and brand scheme, and prone to brand philosophy and art. It is necessary to pay attention to the application of brand science and keep a rational development status in brand governance, brand strategy, brand management, brand market and product development. The excessive cognition and opinions on brand planning may be of more importance to brand planning than brand governance, brand strategy or brand management. Such cognition is unscientific, and will not effectively create a brand, but it will lose the normal development capacity of brand.

1 Rational brand planning development

The early brand planning seemingly played the role of "omnipotence, panacea" due to insufficient competition in commodity economy. People believed that a brand can finish the creation and good marketing sales with an unconventional "opinion" and with a large amount of advertising on TV and in newspapers. During the next decades, people found out that the smart "opinions" were not effective. Therefore, they realized the "conceptual packaging" as well as large-scale advertising and they also figured out that media reports may greatly promote the development of brand. Therefore, CI and VI became popular worldwide. By then, enterprise brand development had upgraded to complete brand planning stage, and brand advertising, brand transmission, brand public relation, brand marketing companies and star spokesmen agency correspondingly appeared for the purpose of sales and marketing promotion so that brand planning became the main role in brand market.

Subsequently, people found out about the large number of management problems during brand management process. Therefore, brand management companies, brand consulting companies, brand design companies, and brand software solution companies emerged greatly, and brand gradually developed to a supporting form to serve the purpose of complex brand strategic management mode and brand design services.

Finally, in the beginning of the 21st Century, brand had followed the two-way interaction development in terms of brand science and brand philosophy. It is the creation and development process of brand science that improves brand value by brand philosophy, cultural connotation and artistic performance based on brand science ideas and objective development laws and with brand science development as the main line. At that time, brand had been developed to a comprehensive and systematic science centered on complex structural governance, scientific management, ecological order, interactive form and value development. It is the brand governance and brand strategic structure development stage for long-term development of enterprises which need overall design. Except actually solving existing brand problems, a brand should be able to cope with potential and unknown challenges for a longer time in the future.

SECTION II BRAND SUBJECTS

The development crisis of brand planning started emerging at that time. The value, weight and content of planning for brand development had made essential changes, and global enterprises gradually realized the defect of brand planning in strategic value during the long-term development, mainly shown in:

(1) Brand planning is the overall brand governance idea aiming to create long-term stable development strategy, and can only solve problems of short-term market expansion and growth. It is the historical development and natural transition process of brand to transfer from sales to marketing, and from marketing to core value of scientific management in human social and economic development.

(2) The brand development in the 21st century mainly depends on the process of making the brand scientific. Brand planning follows artistic ideas, just as the military, which are deemed as both a scientific development and an art application; however, with the development of science, the proportion of art decreases greatly. Today, people no longer take the brand art or military command art as the most important core of development, and advanced and developed scientific technology has become the main basis to judge the development of things. People are concerned more about the development direction of the latest leading-edge technology, while the art of military command is, for instance, the content of a historical documentary. Similarly, brand cannot develop by separating from basic scientific laws of brands and by purely developing philosophical reflection or artistic expression mode.

(3) Brand development has no shortcut or certain occasional lucky opportunity, but needs progressive and systematic development and self-adaptive expansion through practical, diligent and stabile approaches. The key point of planning is to organize favorable resources and external powers and rapidly reach the development expectation. After human beings started developing brand with their endeavors, hard work and determination, planning has been given up by progressive entrepreneurs as an opportunity theory of abnormal development.

As advertising is replaced by public relation, public relation is replaced by brand transmission, and brand transmission is replaced by brand user relationship during the development process of human brand, planning also had experienced ideas, conceptual packaging, CI, VI, and productivity resource combination and finally integrated with overall brand design. It becomes a method, content, a job or an occupation of the main development line of global brand science so as to become an important branch and supplementation of brand science. The structure of modern brand development capacity will not be changed due to planning, and no brand will last forever due to planning.

Such rational brand planning cognition makes rational changes in tasks, function and value of brand planning. The rational cognition and development mark the brand planning and acquire a more accurate position and role, and play active roles and have actual values in future development process of human brands.

2 Brand planning as operational research

The subject of modern rational brand planning belongs in the development category of operational research serving the brand governance and brand strategy, and the main tasks are to provide the decision making reference for brand governance structure and brand strategic development route, provide opinions to technical decision supporting system, apply external and internal think tank, manage resource combination relationship, undertake thinking and approach the assemble of specific research activities, and undertake optimization and implementation of specific planning projects and schemes. The planner takes charge of operation participation, resource management, strategy and tactics formation, specific planning projects and originality implementation, and of optimal scheme for specific links. The brand documents are comprised of three standard texts including the brand proposal, proposal on key points of brand strategy and brand plan.

In general, the disciplinary division is the reference to the decision making of brand governance, the overall coordination of brand strategy, planning and organization of brand development resources and intelligent imagination activities, and specific implementation of planning and scheme projects.

According to different project forms, planning is dominant in specific marketing activities while scheme is dominant in specific optimization projects.

The fact that enterprise brand should upgrade to brand organization status is decided by the brand governance mission required by long-term development. In other words, in order to solve the fundamental development problem required by a brand to keep long-term development target and longer survival from brand organization order, brand development structure and brand operating form, enterprises need at least a brand consulting institution, also known as the overall brand consultant, to provide long-term and lifetime brand guidance to brands with along-term perennial contract, and accompany the brand in growth and development. If a brand expects to be a time-honored brand, the long-range knowledge interaction in brand ideas and foresight level is especially necessary. In the aspect of brand governance, brand planning plays the role of reference indecision making.

The development strategy, generally for 5-10 years, or 30 years, of an enterprise brand mainly solves medium and long-term strategic development problems. It aims to confirm the main conceptual form, development roadmap, brand strategic planning, planning operation structure and planning management in the next strategic development stage. In terms of brand strategy, brands need to provide clear reference points and suggestions on route selection for brand strategy development, provide support to technical systems such as brand strategy construction expert system, brand cranial nerve network, intelligence gathering system, database analysis system and customer relation system by assisting and providing decision-making support to design and operation of brand strategy so as to, in a scientific way, make better suggestions on decision making, decision data analysis and brand strategy development resource coordination for a long-time development of brand organization in the future.

Brand planning exists in forms of decision preference and decision support in terms of brand governance and brand strategy, and values the scientific development mode of brand. The management of brand planning, based on imaginary science, carries out association and approach practice with creativity, originality and solution ideas for the imaginary science, develops the networking of ideas of conceptual network, develops the exploration network and resource allocation network, supports the system networking capacity, makes a brand effectively apply the imaginary science, organizes effective resources systematically, and finishes systematic and scientific development process for strategic support of brand development. The philosophical thinking of brand, cultural connotation exploration, artistic expression and presentation form will provide resources and capacity for brand value creation inform of decision-making, strategy and scientific development support so that the brand can realize a perfect reflection of duel-value of science and philosophy in terms of strategy.

For modern brand development, the proportion of science takes a dominant position in the development mode. The high-level philosophical ideas give awareness to development, and also thinking and artistic conception to a brand. The two aspects are indispensable and supplementing to each other. The development nature of all operational researches is based on scientific design, scientific statistical analysis, scientific matching and organization resources. Thus, under such circumstance, brand planning can neither serve brand strategy separately, nor undertake strategic capacity preparation for long-term development of brand strategy.

During brand development, few global enterprises have acquired brand achievements up to now, because enterprises neglect the long-term brand governance order and development structure construction, and lack firm enterprise development prospect and long-term emission and enterprise responsibility establishment during their development. Brand planning can be deemed as a short-term development measure required by a brand for economic benefits in the beginning of development, shortage period, and depression period and for other short-term benefits so that the long-term brand development is misjudged as a behavior seeking for urgent market expansion activity and income increase. Thus, the function of brand planning is amplified infinitely, and it has become a good development way as "omnipotence, panacea "during ascertain period. It is actually driven by short-term market profits, and is the scientific decision not established on scientific data research and analysis of brand development foundation, and scientific planning development.

SECTION II BRAND SUBJECTS

As an important approach that seeks solutions, the operation of brand planning also contains market layout design, research on strategies of valid customer service development, as well as overall research on strategic distribution, task assignment and personnel transfer. Moreover, brand planning devises production steps and product package, supports system decision making analysis with fundamental research and data digging, and particularly provides important constructive and smart opinions for design of industrial engineering and logistic system.

Sometimes, brand organization needs to carry out independent planning for certain projects, including industrial development planning, quality planning, production process planning, brand image planning, product packaging planning, marketing activity planning and service planning. It is deemed as a suggestion on systematic operation and strategic system thinking, or as an implementation of originalities, and it is implemented after getting approval from brand organization.

3 Strategies and tactics of brand planning

It is scientific to take operational research as the development foundation of brand planning. This is the rational progress to scientifically recognize development relationship between brand planning and brand governance, brand strategy, brand management, brand market and brand operation, and effectively apply strategies and tactics, the two core functions, of brand planning. *The Brand Proposal* is the main text to propose plan and suggestions, and to propose the review plan and implementation program.

Strategy is a thinking method that can solve problems, but isn't systematic nor scientific. It may be branched, scattered, crossed, multi-directional or interdisciplinary. It needs to be based on an idea set, and it needs to form suggestions on decision making of brand strategies, and further develop into main strategy set for implementation of brand strategy. By then, the strategic function of brand planning can be applied completely.

Strategy is proposed in form of suggestion and listed as policies or as a themed thinking orientation required by implementation after resolution is passed, playing the role in the thinking level. Strategy is formed from thinking. It is the most basic idea creation process of a human being, and the key development point of imaginary science that is different from empirical science. An effective strategy may be devised by one person or a group of people who have good ideas. It is the intelligent result developed during intelligent thinking process, and the thinking, refining, gathering and integrating process of new ideas, new methods and new actions ceaselessly generated by human thought.

The other important function of brand planning is to give play to tactics required by market development, including actions adopted to perform strategies and tactic application required by active occupation in key markets. The technology and art of planning is developed by specific preparation, deployment, commanding, coordination, organization and driving function.

Tactics are mainly applied to the strategic development mode of brand market. Whenever a brand organization carries out a full-speed market expansion, the high market movement status similar to military action will appear. At that time, the brand command chain and brand tactic application will be in full swing. The strategies, methods and behavior modes used in military actions will be gathered with tactics as the main market operation mode. Brand organizations use such mode to finish a series of rapid market operations.

Once the market access mode of brand is transferred from stable development to the "war state" of an active attack, the brand organization needs to include all links of brand market war in clear, effective and rapidly driving brand command chain with simple structure with the help of highly developed, systematic, consistent and flexible brand command system; the more resources to be organized and more links participating in competition required by the market, the stronger the brand access power, and the longer the war preparation time required by brand organization, and the fiercer the competition. The tactic application will be rapidly raised to the highest state and rapidly-driving interactive operation will be required.

3.1 Application of brand strategy

The medium and long-term development strategy of a brand should combine a series of strategic key points as development theory, main concept set and implementation guide in each link that is under different development structure. Strategies aim to solve problems. The problems may experience development difficulty, business bottleneck, or a strategic decision, or a market approach or an independently developed project.

Brand strategy is an important function of brand planning, and is mainly shown as suggestions on brand strategic services and planning activities for strategies required by market development. Strategies are a series of thinking activities refined, summarized and extended for strategy and market development, and are knowledge creation results of intelligent thinking and imaginary science.

Strategies are a series of solutions, opinions, skills and methods established by a brand organization to solve various forward-looking development problems. They support corrected strategy decision making process and operation efficiency, and are implemented in the implementation layer and operation layer within specific management work while being guided by policies and thinking.

In order to seek for ideas and solution approaches, brand strategies are firstly devised by valid imagination. The strategy consultants with independent thinking, experienced experts, and managers good at coping with complex emergency problems propose preliminary structural ideas based on analysis of strategic intention, concept orientation, facts, resources and background materials so as to make them become purports and key strategic points adopted during conceptual actions and operation implementation.

Strategies shall be proposed by people who have high level of expressing ideas frequently. This is decided by professional labor planning division. Different people can form the main special group combination that provides strategies effectively due to their different levels of knowledge and ability development, such as the thinking ability development level, standards of judgment, range of professional knowledge, rich experiences, and important past experience.

The valid proposition of planning depends on two keys. In terms of application value, the environments and thinking modes of different people are divergent. A person who is good at thinking always has his own idea networking system, i.e. frequently communicates with people with a similar key thinking and resolution ability. The ideas are a knowledge gathering and refining process formed over a longer time period. In another sense, planning level depends on the ability of resource organization. People with different resource conditions have development ability, and are able to effectively organize reasonable resources and coordinate and configure resources to a certain degree. Sometimes, the strategies can be finished with a group thinking process such as field investigation, conditions understanding or brainstorming of strategy proposers.

The strategies finally proposed and adopted after review will be provided to the implementation link as the main policy and strategic key points, and certain principles and thinking process will be followed during development process. These strategies contain product R&D planning, report strategies attracting media's attention, psychological pricing strategy, disputing user communication strategy, transaction strategy and campus recruitment strategy. The valid strategic system construction process provides support in methods for development of implementation of enterprise strategies, effectively saves manpower, time and money and other cost loss, and has a certain application value for development of uncertain future, unforeseeable emergencies, and uncontrollable matters, and for coping with complex unknown problems.

However, strategy is also a specific transition stage of scientific development of a brand organization. When a brand organization has established favorable dynamic brand management system, the application of strategies will be reduced inevitably, and be replaced by systematic operation instruction manual comprised of system management method, dynamic problem collection and analysis, brand scientific principles and brand planning. The systematic management will comprehensively restrain the emerging of uncertainties and prevent the development of faults.

SECTION II BRAND SUBJECTS

3.2 Strategic and tactic application of brand market operation

Market is the major strategic practice field of enterprises which moves rapidly and varies dynamically in the real time. All strategic preparation and management levels of brand shall be comprehensively reviewed in market. Therefore, strategies and tactics are deemed as important parts of overall brand design, and are applied specifically by systematic design. Planning takes charge of specific market research, market analysis, market operation suggestions and implementation in this link, as well as of proposing the product selling points.

A series of strategic supports are necessary for market development. Strategies must be devised firstly from market research, including market structure research, consumer purchase motive analysis, research on expected pricing range, research on market characteristics of competitors, research on production competition combination, market development mode research, market partner research, and sales proposition research, which may differentiate market implementation. Moreover, the key strategies for development based on current market status, including basic market differentiation strategy, consumer strategy, pricing strategy, competition defense strategy, market development strategy, market cooperation strategy and sales proposition strategies shall be confirmed on the basis of aforementioned researches.

In order to improve market development, brands need to establish a corresponding market operation plan for brand attraction, brand value finding ability and marketing activities. Brand market strategies and brand marketing activities accomplish an important task of brand planning. Based on overall brand market layout and development structure of brand strategic market, brand planning can carry out flexible and driving market combination as required. Business level is the key field in which the brand development planning is good at, and can provide intermediate energy transformation between brand market strategy and market implementation.

When a brand organization decides to launch a large-scale market action for market development, brand organization will actively attack the market with great power during a certain period. At that time, brand organization will enter the market operational command state, and all market links will become operating units, naturally combined as brand command chain, and act rapidly in market while operating under the tactical mode. Some military terminologies will be introduced to market operations, including organization and actions in aspects of military strategies and military tactics.

Military strategies contain the advantageous opportunity formed by weather, landform, time and other favorable conditions; while tactics contain tactic formation and tactic actions such as front attacking, outflanking, ambush, strike, fire support and maneuver. Organizational rapid market attack and maneuver process will be implemented in tactics. At that time, brand organization can flexibly apply such military strategies and specific tactic implementation in command and coordination of large-scale cluster operation and local or regional operation.

Some brand organizations maintain the stationary market command system, and establish command chain which can rapidly be deployed at any time and flexibly implement market operation. The preparation is for an immediate operation. In the fierce global brand market competition of the 21st century, the conventional fighting capacity and combat capacity have become important brand strategy reserve capacities so as to adopt the necessary measures and actions at any time in order to cope with market changes. A typical market access method in global market competition is the use of military-like means and the establishment and implementation of global military-like flexible operation preparation state, while the impact of rapid expansion operation in brand market, with similar codes such as "Hurricane Act" and "Blue Shield", has become universal in the modern business war and market competition. Many brand organizations know well that, when the business scale becomes larger, they must adopt the military-like actions to strive for market competition status and key market share. It changes the significance of brand planning, and becomes an important thinking mode and supporting power of market operational strategy, design and market tactics implementation.

4 Brand scheme

Brand scheme is the main approach to optimize the project details. Different from decision-making suggestions, implementation focus and thinking activities of creativity in aspects of management, strategy and tactics provided by planning, scheme is a thinking behavior for systematic conception, meticulous optimization and creativity refining of process, link and plots of a specific project. The difference between planning and scheme lies in different functions and values. The former proposes conceptive approach, action and behavior mode of solution, while the latter optimizes and expresses specific links and details.

Scheme is mainly applied to improvement links of product development, product reform and production process, management site scheme, market acceptance investigation and research, and media content creation and optimization promoting links such as TV program, animation, micro-video and publications. Brand enterprises use special brand plan for refining and creation.

In order to promote brand quality during product development, the scheme shall collect product sales index (such as listing time), operating indexes (such as investment budget and personnel input), analyze problems in each quality link required by brand products, such as product performance requirements (durability, comfort), and quality requirements (appearance, degree of finish). Scheme collects information according to the satisfaction degree of brand users and achieved sales requirements; it designs according to necessary requirements for products; it judges, diagnoses and analyzes details required by finishing product development requirements based on reverse engineering of objective market demand analysis; and it keeps improving till brand products completely meet the optimal product performance state in user expectation and comply with standard production.

Production improvement is the improvement of main product optimization links according to further market investigation, analysis and research, in accordance with the latest satisfaction requirements and expectation of brand users. In the improvement link of production flow, study and analysis are carried out in order to find out the details of project that need to be improved during production and to gradually improve productive efficiency, production rhythm and production quality of each link. For more accurate market research, brand market scheme is subject to specific market investigation and research; it measures the market by schemes, such as taste scheme, hand feeling scheme and foretaste activity scheme; it verifies products, actual market acceptance degree, specific requirements for optimal satisfaction degree of brand users, and perception level required by brand product premium with scheme implementation; it makes specific and actual research, measurement, diagnosis and analysis in order to give play to optimal market performance of products; and it strives to improve the integrating degree between brand product supply and brand user demands.

Scheme plays an important role in promoting the creation level and market acceptance degree of media contents such as movie, TV series, TV programs, animation, micro-video and publications. Scheme needs to start from market research and market analysis so as to find out the most popular, most characteristic, most easily transmitting factors with the greatest branding perception demand, and particularly optimize links making the works keep being vigorous and with persistent vitality.

All links, big or small, to scheme are of the equal importance, including the overall conception, uniform image, character modeling, connotation and personality, props, change of important plot, background information, significance elaboration, as well as an important philosophy which should appear and be expressed repeatedly. Scheme also considers extended links required by promotion such as poster and sales promotion, media report, and brand derivative products so as to comprehensively build a clear and vivid figure, express high quality contents, deepen the impression and memory of people and arouse an in-depth reaching to every reader and audience by means of simple and highly unified themes. The form of continuous creation makes audiences ceaselessly strengthen the impression and records, urge people to read and to watch continuously with great interest, and strengthen the brand transmission effect ceaselessly.

SECTION II BRAND SUBJECTS

5 Document forms of brand planning

Brand planning is usually submitted in three fixed document formats, respectively including brand proposal, proposal on key points of brand strategy, brand plan. The formats and functions are different, and the documents shall be effectively distinguished and used.

Brand proposal is the consequential report proposed by integrating various research findings and thinking results after research and analysis. This is a relatively fixed literary form defined by program. The present contents are overview, conclusion and abstract, current status, main problems, market analysis (market investigation results), brand decision-making suggestions, main strategies in each link, implementation schedule and budget, as well as consequent documents or project lists.

The same as brand governance, brand strategic decision-making suggestion, brand operational research category, brand strategy and brand tactics undertaken by brand planning, brand proposal is a conclusive document of suggestions, and proposed to the strategy level or to superior leaders. When the contents are independent, themed and integral, the brand planning will be proposed by a special brand proposal; when the contents are simple and timely, the planning will be proposed by simple documents (or simple table) such as suggestion on main brand strategies.

The brand proposal, with important research and decision making value, is generally devised, researched and proposed by third party planners or planning institutions. The marketing planning of marketing department is proposed by planners of the department or external planning service providers. Sometimes, when brand proposal has complete program characteristics or if an amount is too large, it bidding or competition may be proposed by the market planning service institutions by means of outsourcing, and brand organization will select the bid winner and implement the proposal. However, it is important to note that contents involving brand long-term governance, long-term development strategy, management level and overall market development are very important contents which will profoundly affect the future development of brand. They should be supported and finished by high level brand consulting institutions. Brand planning institutions generally have no service ability for long-term strategy and overall brand design.

The common suggestive documents involving strategies, proposal and tactics can be submitted by simple suggestions on brand strategy, i.e. simplified brand proposal. Some brand strategies may be just one page of brief words rather than a systematic and complete project proposal, and they will not use the format of complex brand proposal. However, it should be noted that brand planning contents, or significance and degree of adoption, should be recorded and kept, and that they are of equal important development value during the brand development history and serves as an important reference together with traceable documents during the development process of a brand.

History will provide information and past experience to many influential brands in the future, some key ideas and concepts may derive from the historical thinking during ascertain stage, or the problems will be subtly discovered and effective solution approaches will be proposed in the early stage of some brand problems. However, since those ideas will give up or neglected, the brands will cause inevitable economic loss by misjudging decisions temporarily. The traceability of brand record documents can avoid some losses, or provide open internal references to future decision making, extended overall brand design and brand planning.

The difference between brand plan and brand proposal is that brand scheme is deemed as a tool for planning, and the contents of brand plan are generally comprised of documents, including the enterprise management table, scheme tools and scheme steps made with separate design according to different projects and demands of schemes, or comprised of standard plan documents used in certain series of schemes.

The key points of brand plan contain plan structure and content design, and plan implementation. In plan design, the person in charge of scheme project, management analyzer and market analyzer cooperate to regulate the process, tools, requirements, and results required by one scheme project, and then prepare a blank plan. In accordance with the schedule, labor division, steps and key plan points, the plan implementation personnel will carry out the specific plan contents pursuant to the regulated form and finally submit the plan.

Exercises

1. Fill in the Blanks: The documents of brand planning are comprised of three standard texts including brand proposal, proposal on key points of brand strategy, brand plan. The formats and functions are different, and the documents shall be effectively distinguished and used.

2. Multiple-choice Question: The scheme shall collect product_____, and analyze problems in each quality link required by brand products, such as_____. ( )

   A. Sales index, operating index, and quality

   B. Product performance and quality

   C. Operating index, product performance, and quality

   D. Sales index, operating index, product performance, and quality

3. Essay Question: What is the composition of brand planning development?

Section II Brand Subjects

Chapter 12

Brand News

From the birth of news till the 21st century, the specialized reports on business, technologies, life and consumption or climates have become the key fields in the global news report. The development of journalism in the 21st century is not so much established on public news level as it is based on specialized news report except the significant news regarding politics, society and military. Global or national big media is not necessarily the only main power for the development of the journalism. On the contrary, the journalism attaching the most importance to specialized news service or local news has become the emerging media-oriented way to get rid of the transmission relation between the old media and the new media report. Particularly when brands are more closely related to national economy and human life, the specialized news report will turn to the specific development route centering on brand news.

The key point of brand news is to apply the professional brand impression management to brands, and improve brand reputation through media-oriented application of brand news so as to acquire various brand effects and become an important link in brand assets value. Employees, talents, investors, competitors and third party analyzers will visually judge the value of a brand and make corresponding decisions based on brand reputation created by brand news. In that sense, brand value is not only the price of enterprise brand by financial accounting, but more importantly it is the universal brand value recognition made by people. Governments, industrial organizations, investment institutions, analysis institutions and grading institutions often make judgment based on the number of reports in media, contents of report and report level, as well as forms of brand news report on digital media. For instance, one of the application conditions for green card for outstanding talents immigration is that the applicants submit various reports and materials from key media.

1 Value of brand news

The development of business news has started since the Middle Age. Except the official media, such as the court notice released by the Ancient Chinese Imperial Court or government information announcement released officially by European countries in early stage, and various "commercial information" distributed by correspondents who collected and sold business opportunities, penmen, and merchants by handwriting or oral transmission, the troubadours also took charge of extensive publication, morale encouragement and public relation transmission. However, restricted by large-scale printing and publication form of media in the early stage, the news was rarely released to the public regularly; while the "business news" can be only deemed as a small-range transmission of information about internal business opportunities.

Since the ancient times, the communication forms of parliaments, chambers of commerce, beacon towers, local stations and correspondents as information interaction centers and transmission channels all played important roles in human development. The value of news and significance of correspondence have not been confirmed by modern transmission form and developed into modern news media pattern until the successive emerging of official newspapers such as the London Gazette, as well as the telegram network, TV network and internet.

Except reports on relevant enterprises, business news also attaches importance to information in aspects of important business policies, economic environment, market trend, investment and finance. Up to now, almost all large-scale comprehensive media have had specialized channels or categories for business (or financial) news, while industrial news was the main news media mainly concerning business development in a certain market field.

The current business news has developed to the medium pattern centering on brand news and highly focusing on brand economy. With emergence of new media, the public relation and we-media transmission further replace many factors and transmission patterns in news media, and the boundaries between social media and news media have been blurred. In such time, all news media shall be considered as competition in online and mobile news which can be read at any time anywhere. The robot news is further overturning original news generation form, and everything seems changing deeply.

The news value and communication mode shall be noticed. News value decides the mission, subject and theme of a media report, while communication mode decides the pattern for contents transmission. No matter at handwriting stage, printing stage or internet new media stage, different media forms may be generated due to development of news value or communication mode. Modern technology deeply changes communication mode of media so that news, no matter news unit or we-media, pay more attention to "social public" contents.

Certainly, there is a certain circumstance when few large brand news agencies monopolize all news media and social media. Such circumstance is caused because news media always take passive news follow-up as the standpoint of value when judging value of news, i.e. they only report the existing and well-known brands, figures and events that people are familiar with. In that way, media enters a vicious cycle of "pan-social identity", and in people's opinion, media cannot survive if they fail to report the hot topics people that want to know. The excessive focus makes the mission, pursuit and value characteristics of media loss their vitality.

Media always neglects the public. Regarding the problem whether the media provides the contents people want to know, a noticeable fact is that, while the nationwide subscription volume to newspapers in USA has dropped, the subscription volume to community newspapers is rising. It shows that people actually pay more attention to news relevant and close to them. Brand news thus acquires unprecedented development opportunity, and becomes an important opportunity for layered and decentralized development mode of news media. The variety and professional performance of branding media in the future will deeply establish media interactive relationship between society and the public, and between brands and users.

Many media have realized that the small enterprises and common citizens are of disadvantageous status in media reports, while many enterprises have found out that brand should more directly interact with users. Therefore, "making news closer to people" is not only an important trend for brand news to judge the news mission, value characteristics and development opportunities, but also the future development opportunity for media, brand and the public. The brand We Media rises because every enterprise brand has found out that news media fails to meet their further demands. They wish to develop media aiming at their own brand users in a more professional way. Many smaller brands wish to segment market and media by media-oriented contents and directly acquire opportunities to access brand users.

If the development history of global media industry is following the path of "rise of advertising – development of news" to "declination of advertising- rise of public relations", and then to "emerging of new media –time of brand transmission", then finally, it will evolve into the stage of professional report of brand news, i.e. the brand news boundary between news media and brands disappears. No matter big or small, brands will realize the externalization of internal news report, and gradually occupy main contents of business news, technology news, life and consumption news or climate news by independent brand news.

Such direct, true and practical news report pattern of branding contents will make the new brand founders and future presidents realize that they not only urgently need brand news with similar experiences, but also need brand consumption news related to their daily requirements. When the world is not comprised of minority brands, there will be more development opportunities for new brands, and new content demands and news of brand daily consumption will be concentrated on the position the nearest to people as the geological position information of mobile communication tools. The new generation brand media attribute generated by such brand news value will further improve news pattern of the existing world in the future.

SECTION II BRAND SUBJECTS

Particularly when business news, technology news and climate news gradually changed to the report pattern, when the presentation mode and news value cognition changed the approach to brand news, and particularly when brand news directly accelerated the segmentation speed of old media in the self-centered internet media time, the public no longer loved the repeated "flash" news which was only used to find out the social trend information, but truly needed the news with a more direct relation with them. For instance, they care about the latest contents regarding home environment, individual beauty, food, cooking and eye care, and they need the business venture news with their similar background experiences. The news is represented by brands. Brand users subscribe to brand news in order to have the updated information at any time and acquire knowledge about new products. When news appears by brand consumption pattern centering on themes and topics, the application mode of brand mode has been generated.

2 Social status of brand news

Brand news is on the rise rapidly in the global news development. In terms of human social and economic development, brand news plays an important role as the leading power for progress of human society; in terms of development value of journalism, brand news is replacing social news, business news, technology news and ecological news; in terms of brand user-oriented services, brand development and news reports pay more attention to social service, and brand's participating in social public service is becoming a common sense.

From the level of human social and economic development, we will notice that the major creative product of human civilization, technology and economic development is the brand. Highly branding characteristics are the main development patterns for outstanding outcomes representing the economic development level of a country, the direction of industrial economy or main information known from the social public. People are familiar that the news about certain brands lead the cultural development, technological progress and fashion trend of the world, or that certain outstanding entrepreneurs and brands have developed new brand outcomes, and created new cutting-edge inventions and popular trends. People can usually judge the development degree, economic level and living standard of a country in the world by the number of world brands, international brands and whether the country is a brand exporter or international brand transaction center.

The market competition among global brands is infinitely enlarged to a comprehensive competition level in aspects of culture, technology, fashion and trend. The exploration and establishment of brand history and brand cultural connotation contributes new scientific and civilization pattern to human society. Besides, the enterprise and social responsibilities undertaken by these brands promote the development of socialized value and exploration and creation of economic value including the historical value, civilization pattern, scientific research, technical invention, family health, social network, energy development, public welfare and charity and natural ecology.

The socialized enterprise developed by brands, socialized spirits of enterprise responsibilities, and development of entrepreneur consciousness make brand bear more liabilities for social progress. Moreover, the scientific research and charities such as donations and subsidies made by enterprises play an important supporting role in aspects of poverty elimination, disease treatment, digital gap, regional balance, social problem easing, natural disaster prevention, endangered biological conservation, natural science research and cultural relic protection. The favorable social development pattern of brands is not only an important social contribution, but also a supporting power for sustainable ecological development of human beings.

Take global warming as an example. Green food, energy-saving brand, environmental products, low-carbon life and green companies have all become important links in global sustainable ecological development modes. More global brands join in ecological brands through compulsory or natural certification, approval and association such as green and organic food certification, labels of origin, energy conservation label, environment evaluation, forest certification, farmland emission, air detection, urban green space and water quality treatment. They are willing to protect the earth's natural environment through product or ecological development awareness, and spare no efforts to participate in globalization process of global warming prevention. The brand news in this aspect has become an important part of global climate news.

The services provided by brands to users have stridden toward social public services. Global brands have tried to contribute to comprehensive development of urban infrastructure construction, social network development form, social population and brand sharing economy, and cooperative relation between community and brand. The major development mode of global brands in the future is to, based on socialized form in aspects of society, population, region and life, more directly provide various services to people by global network or local service system. As the socialized degree of brand is higher, the multi-network interconnection application degree will be higher, the development relation between brand and population will be closer, and the development brand development will have more sustainable vitality.

It is the in-depth ecological development relation between brands and civilization, technology and economy that makes the brand news report break away from its product form, and gradually evolve into principal part in news about human progress, social progress, population development and community development, as well as business news, technology news and ecological news. Brands deeply participate in this process and are the leading role in these news reports. Brand news will be separated from common news reports, and become an important link in future global news reporting more professional and deeper development way.

3 Enterprise value of brand news

In terms of enterprise brand development, brand news is the most basic and practical strategy for development of a brand, and the most important brand capital power during brand impression establishment, brand reputation development, and brand asset value establishment process. In terms of brand users, brand news is a brand knowledge-self learning system created to discover brands, promote professional choice and maintain brand emotion.

When any brand wants to approach the public, it shall establish a favorable media public foundation from the public level, and develop it as the public brand. It needs to finish three transformations: investor relationship transfers from internal minority investor to attracting potential investors among the public; enterprises and employees transfer from self-introduction to social cognition of brand; enterprises transfer from building favorable brand image to operating brand reputation capital.

The active endeavor made during this process will make brands acquire support of potential investors and wide recognition of the public. This is the development process of "brand impression– brand reputation – brand emotion – brand credibility". During that process, the social public will finish the recognition, observation, understanding, touch and interaction of a brand from the public media.

The key point of brand impression management is to establish a favorable perceptive impression for brand in the public media, and cultivate the sub-consciousness of public users for brand cognition. Enterprises shall maintain a favorable image of brand in public media, and give certain brand reputation foundation to brands; they will develop emotion between brands and users, and make users acquire unique habitual consumption with brand cognition. Through various endeavors, enterprises mainly develop enterprise responsibilities and social responsibilities so that the brand can acquire favorable public reputation and brand credibility construction.

As an important approach to realize the aforesaid task, brand news will play a great role. This is the most intelligent brand investment. Brand reputation is valuable. It is the assignment capacity and value that generates the brand effect, and plays an important part which can be calculated to assets value during the development process of brand. Although people cannot obviously realize such economic transformation value in the beginning when the brand is founded, but the brand will soon find the credibility of partners and new brand users will obviously be increased, there will be more cooperation opportunities, and the space of cooperation return gets expanded. The number of brand news will be accumulated and gradually transformed to premium of brand products and services.

Enterprises adopting high influential brand strategy are easy to acquire support from various market and resources from the beginning of brand development, and they can acquire brand effect of brand influence after function and value assignment from recruitment, talent acquisition, order realization, new market expansion, active investor support, analyst awareness and industrial media viewpoints so as to obviously improve the competitive advantages.

The brand reputation, formed by accumulation of brand news, is not only the important premise for investment, but also the important foundation of estimation. When investors decide to invest in a brand project, the investment interests and credibility will obviously be changed, and the valuation of enterprises will be improved. When a brand is listed, it concerns the value foundation of company stocks. Besides, during the merger and acquisition process of brand project, brand reputation will become an important brand appreciation in asset value.

4 Development structure of brand news

Different from common news, the news about brand is a pattern generated jointly by the brand party, media, and brand related party, and a special communication pattern jointly generated with cross spreading and interactive ecological chain influence in multi-net interconnected media medium. It is also a fundamental ability to review brand from enterprise brand upgrading to brand organization status. Moreover, the purpose of brand news development is to set up and maintain the brand image, develop brand reputation, and acquire brand effect, brand premium ability and brand assets value increment speed due to increasingly improving brand influence.

First of all, the content of brand news surely comes from the brand side, i.e. released, opened and spread by enterprise brands. If a brand never releases news, the outside world will rarely know the brand in an active way. Particularly in the environment of networking social media, if a brand never releases any news, it will be a totally unknown brand on internet. People will neither find outany information about the brand by searching and inquiry, nor will they acquire and evaluate the brand from the public level. Being unknown is apparently dangerous for the development of a brand. About 90% people are vigilant and suspicious about a brand they never heard of before.

News about enterprise brands is always released by news media or We Media. The news released by news media is usually information toward the public, industrial users and potential public investors, and the news will be selected by news media after judging the news value. We Media contains various network journals, WeChat Official Account, Weibo and internal enterprise journals run by enterprises. A typical change is that internal news communications of enterprises successively changes to public media in the time of we-media, such as customer relation media established by brand to maintain brand user relation, themed customer source media established for customer resource development, enterprise culture media established to display enterprise development process, so as to form media characteristics of open enterprise internal information, public brand dynamic development, and direct brand user relation.

Large-scale enterprises usually establish a specialized brand news center, and listed companies usually set specialized financial relationship department and brand media editing department, and small enterprises set news assistant, media personnel, PR consultant, and network media editing department to strengthen transmission effect of brands as media. Internet enhances the opportunity of brands 'self-introduction. Therefore, the social network and brand media characteristics allow brand to accept brand news and brand content marketing as an important strategy for brand development.

The news side contains public news source, industrial brand media, professional brand media and brand customer source media. The public news source is generally the media with news transmission capacity and is capable to extensively put forth and spread brand news report through multiple media such as Internet and Mobile Internet. The news side is comprised of major media forma certain country and of local main media. They supply news contents to search engines in the form of news source. The industrial brand media and professional brand media mainly focus on industries and professional fields of the brand. For instance, the industrial media of wines are food media and wine media. The professional brand media may be academic journals for breeding technology, or life magazine promoting the wine-tasting lifestyle. The brand customer source media are media mainly deployed mainly to strengthen the transmission effect in order to acquire the customer source market, such as the tourist source country and key customers source market media corresponding to one tourist attraction.

Brand related party contains all parties which may directly or indirectly generate a connection with brands such as human resources, finance, purchase, investor, peers, users and public welfare. For instance, brand news is released to human resource media to improve the brand impression of employers; latest brand news is released to investor media to attract the attention of potential investors; the brand preference of brand users is cultivated in media with centralized users, or experts of the industry that make third party opinions on the media to the brand, or investors that express the prospect and value of a brand.

5 Professional report of brand news

Brand news is striding towards professional reports of brand news. Journalists engaging in brand news, or brand news editors and correspondents of enterprises, shall learn the necessary professional knowledge of brand discipline and carry out practices of analyzing brand report. They need more brand consultants, management analysts and market analysts that proficient in brand science in order to finish the professional report of brand news through cooperation.

Without enough scientific brand laws, and without the latest terminology and professional knowledge of brand science, or professional analysis resources of brand category, it is not difficult to imagine the awkward situation: just one journalist engaging in brand report, or brand news writer in an enterprise that can finish an excellent brand news report, but fails to make an accurate judgment on brand development, and even fails to describe the brand by terminologies of the brand.

Brand news needs not only to judge the development situations of a brand from angles of overall global society and economy, overall market, and competition level of the industry, but also to analyze brands from comprehensive angles of scientific laws, terminology, rules of brand science as well as brand technology and brand culture, or to acquire professional contents required by enterprise brands from internal practices. It is the process of publicity transformation for the brand internal news publicity. In order to write good brand news reports, one must be deeply invested in specific brand practices, or may need to master the necessary professional knowledge. For instance, the journalist can write high quality professional news about gene science brand as long as he/she deeply and effectively masters the knowledge of human genome.

The professional report of brand news is different from publicity and PR-like reports. Enterprises may get used to report brand news through publicity mode or PR mode. However, since more professional contents are added to brand news, the objects of universal publicity and PR change greatly.

During brand media development process of human history, troubadours, publicists and PR personnel have successfully played important roles, and various fragmented ages occurred. Humans have experienced important transitions of two brand media processes, the publicity mode and PR mode in the 20th century. By the beginning of the 21st Century, PR and brand transmission industry became stronger, and the status of news producers became weak, due to public consumption being established on a public level from the beginning.

However, as comprehensive branding deepens and branding speed accelerates, the professional characteristics of brands will have spilt the public media to many decentralized and local independent media. The underlying structure of social group consists of socialized and decentralized citizen mode. The layers of brand customer sources and brand users are obvious so as to speed up the professional reform of brand media. Brand users and brands directly generate the interactive dynamic knowledge system relation so that producers of brand news feel energized again, and the development trend of public relation declination and brand news rising might occur. The brand media attribute in the future will take brand news as the main form. Particularly while focusing on internet contents, it is actually the

Section II Brand Subjects

perfect moment to deliver a professional report of brand news and professional brand content marketing, making and distribution.

6 Press conference of brand news

The press conference of brand news is a typical form during staged the development of modern brands. Brand is an important work finished by a brand founder or a chief brand officer, a chief brand consultant or a chief brand designer when comprehensively controlling the brand operation, or while conducting the overall design of brand products. Every brand needs to officially release or carry out a thorough brand recreation every once in a while (5 years or 20 years) so as to adjust ceaselessly and usher in new challenges. At present, thousands of official press conferences are held on a daily basis all over the world as significant ceremonies for the birth of a brand life, while their number will increase dozens of times in next few years.

It is not impossible to release 10,000 brands simultaneously none day around the world. On the contrary, development is necessary in the next 15 years since the emergence of the fast development of global brand market. As global enterprises accelerate the deeply understanding brands, the brand separation speed will increase several times. The past enterprise group will turn to group brand cluster, industrial cluster will upgrade to brand industrial cluster, and emerging small enterprises will start comprehensively developing branding. Brand products ceaselessly enter market with staged upgrading by holding brand news press conferences. There will be more service brands, and a large-scale brand cluster development time will experience a marvelous reform power in the 2030s. A great example is that more enterprises attach importance to overall brand upgrading and product brand release. One enterprise may convene multiple press conferences for brand news in one year to release products that display the great progress of brands.

The press conference of brand news is not only the important ceremony of a brand's life, but also a centralized news report process that publishes the latest development stage of brand to the media, public, industry and associated parties. The release of brand news is comprised of three stages including warming-up of press conference, live report of press conference and follow-up report after news conference. As required, more professional report modes should be added, such as report of brand founder and brand image, exploration of brand venture story, interview of brand leaders, report on viewpoints of popular figures, planning of brand conceptual news hot points, planning of brand concept series news, and themed report of hot market trends.

The press conference of brand is usually combined with brand recreation. It combines strategic preparation of enterprise, market layout, market expansion, invention, technical revolution, partnership construction, investor relation management, market value management or brand image upgrading, and brand impression recreation of enterprises to make them become important milestone development stages during development process. As proven by facts, brand news conference has an obvious driving effect in aspects of investor concern, market attraction, brand user development and brand assets appreciation.

Exercises

1. Fill the Blanks: Brands experience the development process of "_____ _____ _____ _____" to acquire support of potential investors and wide recognition of the public.

2. True or False Question: The release of brand news is comprised of three stages including warming-up of press conference, live report of press conference and follow-up report after news conference.( )

3. Essay Question: What is brand news? What are its functions?

Chapter 1

Brand Technical System

Brand technical system is the first advanced management technology among the global management technology family, which can bring direct economic effect to industries and enterprises. Neither limited by the national background, nor by the industry scope or the enterprise scale, the brand technical system is now developing itself from the enterprise practice to the industry practice on a larger scale in China. It can be widely applied in the brand technology practice of various industrial organizations and enterprises in the world.

1 The overall framework of global management technology family

Global management technology family is the general term for the development of management technology research project, which represents a leap from the global management thinking theorization to management technology application, having profound influence on the development of management knowledgeization, management systematization, and management professionalization. A large number of new complex uncertain factors in enterprise management will emerge in the 21st century, the 22th century, the 23th century and in the distant future, but the development of scientific technology will account for a large proportion of management in the future, and focus on the development of world management technology, not only as a technological revolution, but also as an important frontier exploration. The previous global enterprise application of fragmented management thinking will be transformed to the systematic advanced management technology, which is conducive to the business community by effectively improving the management ability, training specialized talents of management technology and cultivating responsible enterprises serving in the global market.

It is inevitable that the future management will consist of three levels of management technology structure— industry, enterprise, and department. Any type of industry will eventually form a number of enterprises with decisive competitiveness occupying the leading position in the fast-growing market. Enterprise-level management technology serves as an enterprise-level senior management center based on the enterprise level, playing a decisive role in competitiveness of some enterprises and operating across multiple departments or independent branches. In the operation of basic management, department-level management is the center of all enterprise operations, and the integration of management technology is composed of various department-level management thoughts, scientific principle support and system technology in the enterprise.

The global management technical system includes four technical system links, namely framework, order, action and technology implementation. The framework determines the frontier exploration, conception and prospect, the order contains necessary structure level and operating mode design, the action is made of concepts and main actions required by market operations, and technology implementation consists of technical rules, document records and rectification reports. The technical system, with the above four links complementing and connecting each other, will ultimately enable each management technology to become an adaptive management ecosystem.

Framework system is there to build the macro-long-term outlook of the competitive environment, industry transformation, operation mode, market design and market exploration, etc. including all industrial changes and technological innovation, around the following questions:, what type of market power is needed and which supporting scientific theory can be applied to make the frontier exploration and conception for the next 10 to 30 years, which determines not only the deep thinking of the trend of national economy and in-depth industry reform, but also the decision-making reference of the frontier position of the enterprise brand. As a higher stage of knowledge economy, future thinking economy requires enterprises to exploit knowledge advantage, decision-making advantage, and technological advantage in the future. All these explorations, ideas and prospects provide references for guiding a variety of industrial transformations and enterprise strategy developments, and are the prerequisite premise for scientific decision.

Order system is the required operation basis to achieve the scientific operation. Order and chaos are relative, which means if there is no healthy and orderly operation order, the management confusion of different degrees will occur during the operation. In essence, any enterprise should be an orderly body that can operate independently, which is the most fundamental structure for the operation to ensure that enterprises complete the sustainable development, maintain competitive advantages, become a centenary brand and make the foundation everlasting. Since order is the most stable structure for civil society and corporate governance, the construction of an order body is the vital part in the development of company's organization structure and the management system operation. It is also the core market competition structure design to get rid of market risk volatility.

Action system is the measure taken by enterprises to operate in the market. In the hyper-competitive global market, enterprise management transforms from static management and experience management into dynamic management. Management changes will bring positive action according to the predictive changes and the uncertain competitions of hearkened it will be continued under the dynamic fine-tuning in order to better adapt to external competition changes. The enterprise dynamic management integration system is established around the leading edge with market action as the core, enabling enterprises to maintain decisive competitiveness with more agile management mechanism to participate in global high-speed market competition.

Technology implementation system transforms the management system into new scientific and technological productivity while paying attention to scientific thought and technical practice. It combines the advanced frontier management thought with practical management technology to complete the combination of vitality and reality needed by future management. In the future, all human beings will mainly live in virtual reality, that is, half of the imaginary space and half of the real environment, while enterprise virtual reality corresponds to employees, internal and external partners and customer relationship. Technology implementation carries out framework system, order system and action system ultimately for solid practical technology application, and eventually completes the management technology implementation. Technical implementation includes four types of technology applications, which are technical rules, document records, rectification reports and group reports.

Global enterprises are facing the critical transition from information-based to knowledge-based, from management structure to management system, from the traditional modern management to management of tomorrow. The establishment of world management technology will fundamentally change the structure of the national economy, the mode of industrial competition, the mode of enterprise management and the development of management career. The contribution of management technology research development and practice will gradually emerge in a decade, and this large-scale management technology reform will have an active impact on the world economy.

1.1 Taking a broad view on future management

Any forward-looking business leader and manager should take a broad view on future management in order to make an active preparation for the management of future. The original point for management progress should be a leapfrog study for a target time node, every 30 years, in order to determine the appropriate decisive competitiveness required by enterprise development strategy. The focus of the research is to transform ideas, concepts, individual management technology practice paths, and enterprises holding on the management of tomorrow for all market changes that may occur in the future. With all efforts of tomorrow's management, enterprises will simultaneously complete the enterprise strategy trend, product form, service performance and specialized talents of management technology through the full implementation of brand reengineering.

Since management progress in the era of industrial manufacturing is relatively slow, enterprises can continue to use the theory and experience formed a few years ago to guide the production. However, changes in the era of knowledge economy are so rapid that the type of enterprise competition is full of uncertainty. Future management becomes the primary task of the future leaders and managers who participate in the competition, and the research of future management becomes the top priority on which any enterprise must rely to become the leading one.

Changes are occurring at all times, and the research of future management should focus on occupying a frontier position, starting with the strategic conditions which are most likely to produce decisive competitiveness. Even the smallest management node is likely to become the key for competitiveness while reflecting the overall enterprise strategy. Therefore, management technical system will be carefully designed for the future development of the enterprise.

Although the road ahead is challenging and uncertain, and while many aspects of the future are obscure, the determination of the enterprise to move forward must be firm. Brand reengineering, in essence, is a management technical system that helps enterprises succeed in the future. It encourages global enterprises to focus on longer-term future development from now on and make preparations for future management, and it will continue to adjust the staff's understanding of the future based on the leading edge, concept, plan, design, operation and rectification, timely adjusting the pace to move forward, because negative treatment of the future equals self-defeating.

1.2 The accelerated global management change

Today's management has undergone profound changes and modern management is the perfect fusion of science and management while the role that art plays in the management is minimal. Management is a future-oriented science whose intent is not to resolve the remaining or happening problems. The more important significance of management is to establish a management order with more smooth operation and develop the adaptive management rules, focusing on the longer-term future to perform scientific design, subversive creation and professional implementation. According to the prediction on the future development of management and the forefront competition in the market, the company's management layer will gain an edge in order to adapt to the management progress during a long period in the future.

In the modern management and future management, future science technology are changing today and shaping the future management mode and content, such as artificial intelligence, ergonomics, awareness uploading, new material invention, space exploration, unmanned system, industrial extraction, service intelligence, agile manufacturing, computer system, interstellar Internet, Internet of Things, trusted ecommerce, digital network, sensor network, etc.

Today, everyone in the business world should be clearly aware that we are in the era of social change and its speed will be faster and faster. New business models, new modes of competition, new product forms, and new service states will constantly be refreshed by the progressive enterprises. Enterprises throughout the world are in a hurry to carry out reforms of knowledgeization, normalization and digitization. If an enterprise wants to remain competitive in the future, it must deploy management reform ahead of time. Enterprises will soon pay an irretrievable price for not correcting the conservative management thought and management behavior mode formed over a long period as soon as possible.

Future management is the progress on management thought. The application of management technology is the reform of enterprises considering management as a solid advanced technology application, which will pay more attention to scientific thought including scientific principle of management technology, and its change in disciplines and technology. The technology application system should be established with the operation of the orderly body and the level of management department as the backbone by PADS in order to make more enterprises participate in and pursue practical applications of future management thought, development direction and specific technology. As the leading dynamic management knowledge network, it will not only develop the particular economic form of ideological economy, but also provide effective technical guidance for long-term development of future leaders and technical personnel of management.

SECTION III BRAND TECHNOLOGY

1.3 The proportion of advanced science and technology in management

There have been too many non-scientific factors in management, mainly reflected in economic performance and ideology. The proportion of science and technology in management is relatively small, and must be changed through global efforts.

"Economy" usually covers up the truth of "management". The reports of various media around the world are focused on "banking", "finance", "economy", "new trend of industry", "move of popular entrepreneurs", "business activity" and "business opportunity". They hide the important value and role of management action as the backbone of economy, which throws a curse on the future competitiveness of enterprises and makes waves of new entrepreneurs, potential presidents, who will ignore the effective application of enterprise management, resulting in high rate of the venture failure, ups and downs of industrial economy, high risks of project investment all over the world.

The number of economic losses caused by "economy over management" every year is astonishing, followed by enormous waste of earth resources, productivity, employment opportunity, labor value, etc. Repetitive economic waste, economic redundant action and the instability of basic economic activities seriously restricts the progress of mankind, restricts the human to develop economy in a faster, better, more professional and more advanced way and makes all components engage in economic activities and not achieve the best economic ratio and economic effect.

Usually, the difference between management and art cannot be distinguished effectively, and the application of management is mainly on the level of "way of thinking", "ideology", "experience management" and "static management". There is only a very small proportion in the books, concerning management and business published in the world each year, which analyzes management and market from a scientific point of view. The progress of management is very slow and the proportion of application of research results of scientific and technical management is small when compared with medical science, physics, chemistry and other sciences emphasizing on experiments, tests, principles and technology research.

Therefore, present management research circle and business community have not been prepared for the future management at all. There are very few ideas on how to develop in the future mentioned in the management papers and publications around the world, e.g. practical guidance on "how to do" in management theory. Drawback caused by undeveloped scientific management during the training of either leaders or managers of various departments in enterprises still remains in the stage of "management thought + experience learning".

Surveys have shown that in most cases, business leaders and managers do not regard management as advanced science and technology. The lack of consensus will make it difficult for the management application to be in an effective state while applying science and technology.

1.4 Frontier exploration: What is management?

The development history of global management is a multidimensional combination of multidimensional space. If we review the history of management since the birth of mankind, we can find that these multidimensional points together will be enough to bring astonishing changes to the development of management.

These multidimensional points include: the civilizations of order and education founded by a margin, who first led the troops to land on the island of Ireland; the secrets of standardization and Shang Yang Reform that took place in China in the second century BC; the civilization development shaped during China's Han and Tang periods; the factory formation process during the European industrial revolution; the development of network structure such as railway network, cable network after the Civil War; American medical reform process in 19th and 20th century; the research results on scientific management of Taylor, his followers and following researchers in early 20th century; the sustainable influence on industry quality, site management, lean production and other management reforms made by Dai Ming in Japan from 1950s to 1970s; scientific and technological reforms presented by Microsoft, IBM, and Apple from 1980 to the early 21th century; the frontier development of future army from 1990 to modern America; the tide of science fiction culture, fantasy culture and creative design initiated by the United States, Britain and South Korea from the 20th century to the beginning of the 21st century.

The abovementioned formation of the thoughts, management application and cultural tide change had a comprehensive influence on the formation of modern management, thus forming the double value components of science and philosophy, which are bound to be developed by future management. Integrating the above advantages in management or in civilizations is sufficient to form a powerful force so as to create a profound change in management.

Global management technology group is a brand new management technology frontier system combining the formation of the ideas above, opening up a new field of study - the global management technology. Compared with the ISO, IEC and other standards in the world, the standardization activities now attach importance to "standard" and "continuous improvement", focusing on the future development of open resource dynamic management technology knowledge system.

The global management technology group focuses on the "order" and "stability", whose R&D and application of various management technology projects are composed of "scientific principles, mechanics, disciplines and technical systems" and other relevant links, developing emerging management technology from the perspective of science, system, and practical technology. It is just the beginning of the major frontier exploration for the development of world-wide management technology. We would like to welcome and mobilize more researchers and businessmen around the world to take action, develop advanced management technology and bring practice to more enterprises, so as to help global industries and enterprises develop management technology practice, promote management progress, and create better products and services, thus making humans live a better life.

2 The overview of brand technical system

The brand Technical system is the most important reengineering technology centered on the brand in the whole management. The brand technology has firstly established the leading position of the brand management in the future enterprise development. Centered on the brand, it develops the other management technology and then forms the systematic "management integration" for the future enterprises.

Currently, non-scientific brands are the prevalent prominent problem of global brand theory that global brand researchers and business circles usually regard as "concept" of the main theory on brand management, marketing and communication, while, due to a lack of systematic science management thinking and the support of practical management operating guidance link for "concept", the concept is a vague brand operation horizon and practical value should have deeper research space.

Brand technical system is a complete and systematic management technology focusing on solving massive scientific problems of cultivating international brands so that the development of brand is no longer an independent implementation of every enterprise. During the short period time of two to three years, the branding of enterprises can be completed massively by the promotion of state, by combination of industry and other forms.

Brand technical system highlights important factors of brand competition in the brand performance such as brand capability construction, brand experimental status, brand leading edge, brand decisive competitiveness, brand classification, brand rating, etc., refreshing the previous people's theoretic cognition of brand. At present, brand reengineering has shifted from theoretical research to large-scale brand practice, and more and more Chinese enterprise brands are applying brand reengineering theory to obtain even more demonstrable economic effects.

The theoretical part of brand technical system is the practical basis of guiding brand reengineering, and provides scientific, objective and practicable management ideas for brand technical system from the academic and technical layer. In particular, it is divided into brand scientific principle, brand discipline, brand practical technology and brand culture.

Brand scientific principle: it consists of brand economy, brand reengineering principle, brand force: Theory, brand science principle, brand philosophy principle, frontier position, decisive competitiveness, professional spirit and so on, each of which can be applied alone.

Brand discipline: it is made of three future extendable subjects, namely brand history, brand strategy and brand organizations.

Brand practical technology: it is composed of brand performance technology, brand construction technology, brand management technology, brand recognition technology, brand marketing technology, brand communication technology and brand collaboration technology. Every technology can be carried out with meta-analysis and scientific design by PADS so as to create the abundant, practical and operable brand technology.

Brand culture: it is composed of brand philosophy, brand artistic conception, brand aesthetics, brand culture consumption, brand culture connotation, brand image promotion, brand art performance, brand international integration, etc.

3 Global framework of brand technical system

In general, global framework, including global brand reengineering declaration and global industry declaration, global frame document, multilateral strategic cooperation framework and so on, is a programmatic document needed by the global implementation of brand technical system to define the technology implementation framework of brand reengineering and the overall program of industry branding long-term development. In addition, framework document is the overall programmatic guiding document of business cooperation worldwide, including global declaration, programmatic document, cooperating framework of brands belonging to enterprises.

Focusing on the overall development of brand technical system, global framework forms a specific system by supporting and separating each other among various framework documents and constitutes an organic entity of brand technical system in global active development by influencing each other among them. Between top and bottom, diversified and multilateral develop relationship has created a developed, advanced, complete and mature development system of global industry and enterprise branding.

Belonging to strategic application of brand technical system, global framework is different from the previous management methods in the independent development of different enterprises. Brand reengineering and technical systems of the entire global management technology group change the situation of separated industries and enterprises in every country, during the self-development and repeated exploration and investment by the comprehensive use of global power and the dynamic knowledge sharing system completed by country, industry and enterprise to keep the global synchronization update of knowledge management. When some industries and enterprises take initiative actions to connect to a new knowledge system, the ability of exploring frontier will be greatly strengthened and knowledge will converge into a new advanced knowledge productivity, thus greatly speeding up the industrial upgrading, the operation efficiency and the success rate of continuing business, furthermore, fully optimizing the brand performance of the participating companies and providing a strong impetus for the relevant brands in every country to successfully upgrade to international brands.

In the high-speed market competition, enterprise decision is a race against time, an important process to get frontier ideas and advanced management technology. In order to successfully achieve brand success, enterprises need to participate in global competition in a more open and inclusive attitude and complete the deployment of new competitive strategy through mutual knowledge creation, technology sharing and market cooperation. Due to great growth of the collaborative enterprise in future competition, multiple cooperation among enterprises will become particularly important. The previous innovation mode of enterprise market relying on the concept of market trends is playing a smaller role in enterprise management change.

3.1 The pause of new business cycle and the delay of knowledge cycle

In market observation, we find that some popular market trends, popular practice concepts, and development experiences will become the target to be generally imitated by the business community in a period of time, but because of the empty trend concept, the practical level of enterprises cannot keep pace with change. The enterprise community is in the stage of discussing concept, trying ideas and exploring practicing by itself, whose action and technology practice are behind the concept schedule, and even most enterprises are still in place after exploring and trying without any practical influences from new market trends or new concepts, the moving mode of which has been a general new economy cycle break. There are few enterprises getting benefits from the concept of emerging economy. Because this way is a drawback and keeps wasting economic resources, enterprises must find new changes and unite to create a new form of knowledge economy to gain more frontier, more practical and more valuable management technology application.

In fact, the global framework is an integrated knowledge system application on the basis of the development of knowledge globalization. Through the "Knowledge System Integration" freely participated by nations, industries, and enterprises, the necessary knowledge of frontier detection, market design, product development, service design and management technology implementation is jointly developed, thus speeding up the collection of knowledge, meta-analysis, scientific design and scientific popularization speed, and better supporting industrial upgrading, business decision, enterprise specific implementation.

The enterprise's knowledge level also has the characteristic of classification that usually only entrepreneurs and research departments maintain (visionary ability), the middle maintain action capability and mobility, and the operating layer implements specific affairs. However, because individual leaders and researchers are able to identify and recognize vision, the lower layer in the enterprise lacks more vision and the internal knowledge updates are often synchronous, enterprises cannot prepare a sufficient talent pool and knowledge for strategic development of next generation. Establishment of global framework in the enterprise is to make the efforts to maintain enterprise knowledge synchronous. Only when the whole staff understands the future direction of enterprise, the huge loss of enterprise caused by knowledge delay cycle will be slowed down.

In general, the delay cycle of thought is 50 years, the delay cycle of thinking way is 15 years and the delay cycle of concept is 3-5 years. However, the delay cycle is the delay cycle of new economy frontier of industry and enterprise imitation, and also the knowledge delay cycle from top to bottom.

4 Brand order layer

The essence of company governance is to establish the orderly operating enterprise management, and the order management is the basic requirement of any enterprise and the establishment of enterprise order is the first priority of any enterprise organization. The order is composed of a series of rules of self-adaptive operation to constitute the smooth operation of system.

Owing to exclusive dominant position of brand in future global industry and enterprises, the establishment of brand order body is an important organization structure and its establishment should be focused on the implementation of brand reengineering for any enterprise. More and more combinations of management department units will occur in future management such as research development department, production department, Internet department, business department and so on, which will change with the development of enterprise. Although there are new departments conforming to new development occurring, the integration of management is necessary to achieve the general trend and its operation objectives the brand order body.

SECTION III BRAND TECHNOLOGY

Three development trends determine the core strategic advantage of brand order body in the enterprise:(1)The new form of economic development determines the outstanding important effect of brand in the enterprise, so future enterprises must put the brand in the highest position of enterprises and all the management operates in the way of branding.(2)Before products and services step into market, emerging enterprises, brands or economic organizations should step into market by means of completing branding to enhance brand premium, avoid the competition of product price and keep the competitive advantage and profit advantage of enterprise for long-term development.(3)Enterprise brand assets management will be the most important asset of future enterprises to complete market-oriented economic activities of brand such as assets appreciation, financing, investment, IPO, etc. by asset operation of brand management.

4.1 The establishment of brand order layer

The establishment of brand order layer is defined by the scientific development structure needed by the future enterprise organization, as well required by the enterprise ideology in the enterprise culture. The brand order layer set up in ternary order governance structure is not only a kind of important change in the development history of modern enterprise organization structure, but also the necessary strategic decision to meet the long-term development of enterprises, and even a general consensus mastered by the whole enterprise.

Brand order layer is the enterprise management order structure of the overall operation of brand, the unified name of branding committee, whose responsibility is to report strategic layer to enterprise, guide the brand document specification of the executive layer and the operating layer, and find different kinds of brand organization in terms of brand users. The brand implementation layer and the operation layer carries out the corresponding management of the suppliers, the service providers and the dealers, and is responsible for the brand users.

In the implementation of enterprises' brand reengineering, the first step is to establish a brand order layer as the core of the company governance order, and establish the highest layer of branding committee in the enterprises which is the key to implement brand technical system and is responsible for detailed implementation of planning, advancing and reporting at the company level. In the formation rules of branding committee, the main work and division of labor in brand organization structure and brand technology layer will be clear and responsibilities and tasks of brand technology will be defined.

4.2 The value of brand order layer

The establishment of brand order layer is an enterprise-class organizational structure designed by ternary order structure opposite to the previous organizational structure of enterprise binary opposition structure. As early as in the early civilizations of Europe, the ternary nation and social order structure existed for a long time and reached its peak. With the establishment of the United States achieving separation of three powers and after the World War I, the continent also restored the social structure of the ternary order. However, today the world's major developed countries operate in ternary order body to complete the governance of the nation and society, the unprecedented economic prosperity and the unprecedented degree of civilization, and at the same time social operation is generally stable.

In the enterprise operation, the enterprise order mainly refers to the systematization, stability, openness and expansibility of the management order, and should maintain the best management performance ratio. The enterprise order is the basic composition to decide whether an enterprise organization can go on with orderly management, smooth operation, and high-speed expansion.

There are usually many drawbacks such as contradictions between the superior and the subordinate, uncontrolled management, management leaks, customer complaints and so on, the main reason of which is that enterprises build enterprise organization on basis of binary opposite structure and the essence of binary opposite structure is binary, This kind of structure is extreme and rigid concerning the relationship between leaders and employees, and that between employees and work. Because of it, there will be a variety of new work conflicts, process obstacles and opposing thinking between the various links. Over time, a variety of complex management drawbacks will be formed, and sometimes enterprises will sort out problems with the help of external management consulting firms, but the crux of management often cannot be completely eliminated.

Any enterprise should be a stable order body and the branding committee is the necessary order layer of smooth operation of enterprises. Reporting to the board of directors, the order layer leads the formulation of brand rules, branding guidance, enterprise culture and other things, and deals with media relations, customer relations, dealer relations and quality of work. It should be responsible for enterprise brand mainly by the appreciation of brand assets management, brand promotion and brand performance construction to build up new decisive competitiveness of brand market centered around brand users, and to achieve the perfect changes from outside to inside, from inside to outside, from nonexistence to existence and trans form weak brand to powerful brand. Besides, it should make a positive contribution in order to attain market resources, strive for brand users, and obtain brand premium.

Because of the existence of brand order, the board of directors, administrative department, production department, R&D department and other departments in the enterprise can be freed from the complicated market affairs without facing market and customers, just focusing on developing professional spirit, delivering their own performance, going into battle with a light pack and changing the previous situation that any department is responsible for the brand, but any department of the brand cannot afford full responsibility for the brand chaos. In business process, there will be a high degree of concentration, clearness and efficiency of brand identification and communication, reducing of sales pressure and decreasing of the complaints. Correspondingly, R&D of enterprise has been strengthened, brand service has a higher premium capability, the brand enters the market faster, brand has it easier to mature in the market and the misunderstanding of "Brand is the accumulation of long-term market" has been changed. After the establishment of brand order body, brand reengineering will complete enterprise branding process at an unprecedented pace.

4.3 The operation of brand order layer

First of all, the brand order layer branding committee is the core role, on the basis of which the brand organizational structure is divided into: the brand strategy layer (board of directors, senior managers), brand order layer (brand technology department, management technology departments), brand executive layer (middle managers in the administration, production, quality, logistics, sales and other departments), brand operating layer (roots operation staff). The members in branding committee are: principals in brand strategy layer, brand order layer and brand executive layer.

The principle of branding committee: branding committee works mainly in the form of brand official meetings, which will be divided into two types - the whole committee meetings and the weekly meetings. The whole committee meetings are: participated by all the members of committee once or twice a month, in case of major brand cases held once a week. Weekly meeting is: the brand technology layer holds a regular meeting regarding brand on Monday afternoon to conclude brand technology progress and new issues, deploy new jobs and report the decision of every regular meeting to the whole committee.

The composition of the branding committee: the branding committee composed of the progress office, the brand center and other management technology departments can be divided into several secondary working committees, such as brand dealers work committee, brand quality work committee, customer relations committee and so on, and select representatives of dealers and customers to join them according to the need, in order to jointly promote the brand progressing.

The formation of the branding committee: every department proposes the person who can enter the branding committee, decide the final list after discussing the resolution and the time of setting up the branding committee, and announce the list of committee in the form of company documents.

4.4 Responsibilities of branding committee

(1) To discuss and decide the overall promotion of brand work in the form of brand official meeting.

(2) To propose and decide to formulate the overall planning program, prospect brochure and brand management principle of company brand technology.

(3) To formulate and decide brand documents of company and recording management forms of brand, and to confirm a regular investigating responsibility of brand records.

(4) To propose and deliberate every brand design, final design draft(sample), BVI image and other brand identification system.

(5) To propose and deliberate the overall brand planning, and financial budget and final accounts planned to invest into brand management stage.

(6) To manage regular brand technology of brand executive layer and operation layer and supervising the implementation.

(7) To organize the studies and work objectives of brand backbone team and all the personnel.

To organize brand exchanging and technology updating work.

4.5 The responsibilities of every management layer

(1) The responsibilities of brand strategic layer: to regularly participate in brand learning, to understand brand ideas of the strategic layer, liquor and wedding market brand trend; to make major company decisions regarding brand work; to audit brand investment and financial management; to supervise brand technology implementation.

(2) The responsibilities of brand technology layer: to propose the work recommendations and work reports to the branding committee; to be responsible for specific brand promotion work and manage the progress of brand project tasks; to edit brand plans, brand brochures and brand technology documents; to guide the brand normative work of brand executive layer and operating layer; to organize studies of brand backbone and all the personnel; to organize collaborative work of external brand services, brand dealers, brand customer representatives relevant market experts and consultants; to update the brand technology exchanges and technology.

(3) The brand executive layer: to propose recommendations for the brand technical work and to participate in the formulation and discussion of brand technology-related documents; to implement the division of work on the relevant brand project tasks; to carry out brand technology document requirements, the execution of brand documents and supervise recording documents; to explore brand backbone talent; to participate in the backbone learning of the brand or brand learning for the whole personnel.

(4) The brand operating layer: to do their own work in accordance with the requirements of brand technology documents and brand recording documents; to propose recommendations for brand technology work; to participate in brand backbone learning or brand learning for the whole personnel.

5 The sequence of brand technical system documents

Brand documents are divided into four layers, generally consisting of brand framework documents, brand order documents, brand action documents and brand technology documents.

Brand framework documents include: brand global declaration, brand five-year plan, brand prospect brochure, brand strategic cooperation framework, etc. It is the strategic guiding document for enterprises to meet the strategic development of the brand and plan the future competition of the brand.

Brand order documents include: the rules of the branding committee formation, the rules of brand project progress management, the rules of brand office meeting, the rules of brand communication, the rules of brand official training and so on, which are the order documents needed to establish the brand operating order.

Brand action documents include: brand strategy execution, brand marketing plan and so on, which are the executive documents to accelerate the required brand market movement. After brand reengineering enters the market, we must speed up market execution to maintain a dynamic and efficient high-speed market movement, to complete market access and market coverage as powerful brands. Besides, brand action documents include the corresponding requirements of brand technology, brand records and brand rectification reports.

Brand technology documents include: Branding Mission Document (BM), Brand Rule Document (BR), Brand Operation Document (BO), Brand History Document (BH), Brand Communication Document (BC), Brand Correction Report (ECR), and Management Site Report (MSR), which are the document sequence required to complete brand daily implementation of technology.

The weight of the brand documents is classified into five categories: confidential documents (9), important documents (5), briefing documents (3), general documents (2), and temporary documents (1). The corresponding archiving time limits are a permanent preservation of confidential documents, and important documents should be kept for more than 15 years, briefing documents should be kept for more than 8 years, general documents and temporary documents should be kept for at least 5 years. The least maintaining date of any document should not be less than 5years. Among them, the briefing document is included as the company corresponding document in brand briefings.

6 Access and deployment of brand technical system

Brand technical system applies a principle of technology access and deployment and it is the application mode for a nation, industrial economic organizations or enterprises to obtain the brand technical system. The access of brand technical system is mainly a process of brand learning. The brand technical system deployment needs to take a brand recycling period of time (2-3 years) to complete the branding mentoring. The frontier detection, marketing design, product development, service design, and management technology implementation of brand should be completed together with the brand reengineering so as to finish the process of branding from management theory to the full operation of the advanced brand technology. It can also help the enterprise to cultivate the necessary brand leaders, brand officials and talents of brand technology for all aspects to indeed produce economic effects for enterprises. Therefore, the principle of technology access and deployment will bring more substantial benefits for the enterprise.

A typical deployment process of enterprise-class brand technical system is:

BR1 - Establishment of the introduction plan

BR2 - Formation of the branding committee

BR3-Training of the brand technology introduction

BR4- Rule of brand postgraduates (training program of brand leaders and brand officers)

BR5- Brand audit

BR6 - Brand strategy decision

BR7 -Document formulation of brand framework

BR8- Document formulation of brand order

BR9- Research and development of brand products

BR10 - Design of brand service

BR11 - Planning of brand execution

BR12 - Document formulation of brand execution

BR13- Document formulation of brand technology

SECTION III BRAND TECHNOLOGY

BR14 - Brand press conference

BR15 - MA report

BR16 - Brand rectification report

BR17 - Brand technology update

BR 18 - Ending reports of brand reengineering

7 Members of the brand technical system

Brand reengineering is to meet the needs of the global open-source management technical system during the global competition of enterprise brands. Members of brand reengineering consist of government department's staff, industrial economic organizations and enterprises, brand researchers and management analysts. It is an enterprise organization with active participation in the world, and a dynamic knowledge network of personal sharing.

Brand reengineering advocates the combination of principles of brand scientific management and brand technical practices and it offers double values of advanced brand management ideas and practical brand technology for enterprises. Moreover, it makes an organic combination of enterprise's work and market development among the most advanced exploration, products development and service design so as to establish the brand leading position and decisive competitiveness.

Brand technical system's practice on comprehensive open-source exists dynamically based on PADS scientific analysis. Common departments in enterprises such as management analysis group, industrial product research and development department together complete the works of industry and enterprises' frontier trend exploration, product development and service design, even the process of problem collections(P), meta-analysis (A), scientific design (D) and scientific popularization (S) of brands and other businesses. Therefore, it can help enterprises gain valuable new knowledge, new management and new technologies, to make decisions fast and to help the market design. By applying the dynamic management knowledge, brand technical system is a vital leading-power of innovation active in the area of global knowledge economy. It is also a learning network type for future enterprises' management and leader cultivation.

Exercises

1. Multiple-choice Question: There are more non-scientific factors in management, mainly in the aspect(s) of_____ , the proportion of science and technology in management is relatively small, so it must be through global efforts to change the consensus.

A. Economic indication, ideology

B. Ideology

C. Science and technology of management

D. Economic indication

2. Essay Question: What is the brand technical system?

3. Discussion: Please make a brief introduction about the responsibilities of branding committee.

Chapter 2

Brand Technology Preparation

Few people have noticed that brand construction or brand reengineering is a very complicated and magnificent system management technology project that has failure rate greater than 90%, and it would be doomed to be a failure from the very beginning. People just think they are lucky dogs or believe that they themselves are the brands. It is believed that so long as they have superb products, good quality or services, excellent marketing or brand image and in addition with the long time accumulation and test, their brands will become the excellent and famous ones in the market. However, we do not think this belief is right nor do we think that it is wrong. What exists is reasonable.

What we want to remind companies that have decided to do well in brand construction or brand reengineering is the importance of preparations for brand technologies. Every company's brand should make good preparations for brand technologies before starting while carrying out the rigorous and scientific brand construction or brand reengineering technologies with complete system, which is crucial to determine whether brand construction or brand reengineering is effectively and smoothly carried out, and it is an important guarantee for realizing the system branding successfully. Any large organization, corporation and project requiring the professional brand construction or brand reengineering should get down to the preparations for brand technologies prior to carrying out the brand project.

1 Brand strategic resources reserving mechanism

When any company determines to develop a brand, it shall go through a brand process with complete system, conforming to the scientific laws and requirements on brand technologies; however, the company may not have the conditions sufficient for brand construction or brand reengineering from the very beginning. A brand needs to complete the brand technology implementation process during the branding system with a dynamic system. With the development of brand science professionalization and increasing requirements of world competition on branding systematic technology capacity, what a company should do well is the brand strategic resources reserve so as to effectively and smoothly complete the branding based on the brand technology requirements in the proper time whenever acquiring the brand construction conditions or brand reengineering conditions.

In essence, the brand technology preparation is a brand strategic resource reserve mechanism. It is not only the comprehensive preparations on the brand technology construction ability and resources by a company for the purpose of developing a brand in the future, but also the brand technology preparation systematic engineering made by a state for comprehensively carrying out branding among the domestic companies.

The brand strategic resources reserve at the corporate level is a long term strategic reserve made for keeping the brand's leading position and decisive competitiveness and independent competition ability and self-owned strategic reserve resource allocation ability necessary for brand development. The brand strategic resources consist of brand technology resource reserve, brand talent resource reserve, brand capital reserve, brand cooperation resource reserve and brand emergency strategic resource reserve.

The brand technology resource reserve is a long term reserve made by a brand on independent technology competition ability and consists of brand consultancy power, professional knowledge on brand technology, brand knowledge updating and technology capacity reserve on brand product, services and competition; brand talent resources reserve consists of brand leader reserve plan, brand talent training plan, brand backbone team construction, brand professional talent reserve team and personnel brand study system; brand capital reserve refers to the capital reserve used for carrying out brand construction, brand reengineering and brand marketing as well as brand investor relationship maintenance.

Brand cooperative resources reserve includes the strategic cooperative resource reserve covering the brand study, brand product research and development, brand supply chain, brand production, brand industrial portfolio, brand market development and brand service provider, etc. The brand emergency strategic resource reserve is for coping with emergencies at any time such as changes in market competition, unexpected disaster, unexpected accident and important policy changes, etc. and could ensure that immediate strategic adjustment can be made immediately, and provide the brand emergency guiding system necessary for rush market movement and the resources reserve such as public relations, materials, talents and substitutes necessary for the brand emergency reaction network, brand market emergency operation training and brand emergency.

A state's band strategic resources reserve shall mainly focus on branding professional technology education besides the reserve on brand materials, policies, finance, etc. Therefore, it is necessary to give certain time of education on the brands' common knowledge in the high school, college and vocational education and select the prospective brand leaders to provide the professional brand technology training and service study, particularly, combining with the entrepreneurship education.

The competition among companies in the future shall mainly be represented in the deep competition of the brands; whereas the brand development in a country requires a large number of brand founders, brand leaders, brand officers, brand designers and management analysts, market analysts, etc. It is obvious that it is far from enough for these brand technology professionals to study by themselves and it is also unprofessional.

Education in a country should assume the relevant liabilities and be committed to providing the talents with certain basic brand knowledge, brand awareness and brand technology ability in the market sector. It is also required to train many brand officers with certain brand competency and future leaders with the brand leadership competence so that they could make the active contributions to the development of the country's social economy with their ambitious enterprising and entrepreneur spirit for pursuit of beautiful things. They will be the hope for a country's future brands.

2 Rules on brand technology preparation

Whenever a company decide to carry out brand construction or brand reengineering, the company should give prudent consideration as this means that the company would make a series of significant changes in development strategy, organization structure, form of operation, human resources demands, product and service status, management method and supply chain, value chain relations, brand culture, corporate culture, etc. and such changes must be fundamental, complete and systematic.

Brand construction and brand reengineering are very complicated system projects, as they do not only require long construction (reengineering) period, but also might be a failure, which applies to law 91. Whenever a new brand is created, it begins to engage in natural elimination competition applicable to law 91. This is the market's natural elimination process for the brands, i.e. survival of the fittest. In other words, 90% of brand construction and brand reengineering would be a failure at last and 90% of the brand projects cannot obtain investments at earlier stage. As for the remaining 10% brands, 90% brands among the remaining 10% brands needs long term brand technology remedy method to maintain its brand status and similarly, 90% brand may not acquire the next round of investment.

The new brand, after three rounds of natural elimination of 91, could be developed into a steady and mature B-class brand with complete system and a brand shall go through another two rounds of 91elimination before developing into A grade and then might become a famous industrial brand with great influence. A maturely operated brand would be in the process of branding reengineering in the form of brand reengineering; however, if the brand reengineering is not conducted with a prudent and rigorous attitude, the brand reengineering would be a failure or become inefficient. In many cases, the reason why a long surviving large brand could maintain good anti-risk capability for brand reengineering despite of a failure during the brand reengineering is that the overdrawn unique resource strength, brand market accumulation, brand reputation capital, etc. formed for a long time have relieved the impact formed by brand reengineering; nevertheless, it is easy for the companies to ignore the failure of brand reengineering and the implicit dangers.

The rules on brand technology preparation is to decide the preparations for brand technologies based on the specific brand features, brand status, brand consultancy contract, branding project requirements and technological level of brand technology consultancy agency, and make it the preconditions for the preparation procedure of brand technologies and brand technological practice.

Brand features: every brand status is different and there is no completely identical brand status in the world. Therefore, every brand shall complete its independent branding based on the actual conditions, brand cultural connotation, strategic orientation and market field. Brand status: the environment where every brand is, place of origin, source, technical conditions, current resources and brand leaders' thoughts and ideas are quite different, and a company shall decide how to make the branding after going through the study of original conditions and development.

Brand technology preparations are decided by the content of brand consultancy contract. Every brand needs a brand consultancy agency with whom a long term development consultancy and guiding relationship shall be maintained and the professional support provided by the supported brand service provider. The effectiveness of brand construction or brand reengineering will be affected by the technological level of brand consultancy agency. Therefore, generally speaking, the brand technology preparation and brand technology practice shall be specifically carried out by the brand owner under the guidance of external brand consultants. The brand owner shall select or bid the relevant brand service supports provided by external brand service providers based on brand project requirements and then voluntarily allow brand certification by third party after completing the branding based on demands.

As the world brand ecological chain covers 75% of the world population, a company's expenditure on brand has become the greatest expenses consumed by the global companies and brand industry chain has become the industrial clustering brand service organization process covering most brand service providers. Branding needs to solve the future development issues of the companies or the dream of hundred year's brand requires the efforts of several generations and it is impossible to complete the branding only depending upon the brand's own strength and brand awareness. The companies, for the purpose of meeting the long term and future foremost challenges and implementation of a hundred-year brand dream, would complete the brand technology preparation by systematic guidance, diversified cooperation and common coordination while carrying out the brand technologies. The branding technological process of the companies requires the advanced brand technologies for support.

3 Requirements on brand technology preparation

The first thing that any company has to do from the very beginning is branding. In America, success in creating a brand requires 100 million dollars and the complete brand construction or brand reengineering would take two to three years. The reengineering costs of a large brand would be much higher than such investment. During the process of actual investment, branding is a staged brand. As branding is above all and the center of guiding strategy, product, service, management and various related relationship, a company's expenditure in brand maintenance and promotion every year would be much higher than investment in brand product research and development, and design. The small enterprises would not worry about the excessive expenses required for brand construction, as they could make the staged investment based on the development process of rapid brand, light brand and big brand of branding.

However, a brand's long term strategic investment value is consistent for all brands, no matter it is big or small. What a brand solves is the strategic orientations and governance structure issues concerning a company's long term development. Therefore, it is quite necessary for a company to attach great importance to the brand and take the prudent attitude in decision making from the very beginning. The brand technology preparation is applicable to all the companies that want to develop into professional and international brands. Studying the common knowledge on brand is necessary for every potential president who is preparing for startup and the future corporate management talents.

Brand technology preparation refers to all the preparations from planning to brand development for a company to officially carrying out the brand construction or prior to the brand reengineering. To maintain a high quality from the beginning to the end of brand construction and brand reengineering, companies need to accomplish the preparation conditions as required for brand technology preparations. The whole process is referred to as brand technology preparation stage.

Purpose of brand technology preparation: make the advanced plan for carrying out the brand construction and brand reengineering with high quality, conduct professional knowledge reserve, allocate the resources, and coordinate the organization and the staff of a company shall make preparation for the official brand construction and brand reengineering. In addition, brand technology preparation is also the center of brand construction or brand reengineering. As any error or hidden trouble in brand technology would result in the brand strategy failure or market loss or lead to the brand construction or brand reengineering to be a failure. In that case, what a company loss is not only time, money, talents, but also the development prospects and competition strength. Therefore, it is necessary to earnestly do well in the brand technology preparation.

Basis of brand technology preparation: the brand technology preparation is based on the latest brand study achievements, comply with the general brand design principle, lancet principle and the principle of natural ecological development, and carry out the systematic brand construction and brand reengineering based on the brand technology rule and brand reengineering principle, and in combination with the scientific law of the brand. The companies also need to keep the brand in the dynamically updated world branding knowledge system in technology preparation and technology implementation process so as to timely update and supplement the brand rules, technology requirements and dynamic supplement to knowledge.

4 Brand technology preparation stage

A brand may not succeed from the very beginning and there is long way to go from expectation to create a brand to growing up into a real brand. It is not only a dream, but also a kind of pursuit and even more as a representation of brand spirit, brand mentality, degree of consciousness and value of a brand organization from top to bottom and from inside to outside. To achieve the dream of creating a brand or reengineering a brand, a brand also needs to go through a long time of brand technology preparation stage.

No matter brand construction or brand reengineering, the brand technology preparation specifically consists of four stages which are brand dream, brand conception, brand general design and brand technology preparation. This is the full process of preparation from creating a brand dream to dream, conception and imagination before completing the implementation of brand technologies to the time of officially creating the brand.

Any brand begins from a dream and every brand shall face the future. The brand dream will firstly have appeared in the dream of brand creator, brand leader or chief brand officer and it is at the self-consciousness creation stage for longing and enchantment. People would intensify their dream constantly by dream reinforcement and then make it practical through virtual and fiction. Such imagination has driven people to put their dreams into practice and transformed their dreams into the practical creations; however, being limited by funds, resources and professional knowledge on branding, the brand dream would just remain in the brain of dream architect for a long time and only the dream architect himself or a few people with close relationship with him may know of such a brand dream. Maybe everyone in the world has a brand dream; however, only a few people could put it into practice.

To further put the brand dream into practice, the brand dream stage shall be transferred to the brand conception which might take several months, years or even decades. This is also the stage of strategic resources reserve for brand technologies. Please note that brand dream must be your own and it is the fruit of independent thinking on the basis of environment adjustment, resources changes and knowledge supplement. There is no identical brand in the world and every brand should become itself. In other words, the brand dreamer expects that any brand consultant, brand technology or brand talent, entrepreneur team, the subordinated or the external conditions could give support, coordination, collaboration and replenishment for the brand he has created. The brand dreamer must complete the brand creation and development following his original thinking, brand development orientation and manner of brand value expression and the efficient brand support would enable the brand dream to be reinforced, accelerated, expanded or improved; nevertheless, the brand development mission and subject form would never change and only in this way, a created brand could survive after going through the long time test and eternally keep its charm and attraction.

During the brand conception stage, the brand dreamer would constantly set up the structure for a brand, add different brand elements and competing forces, refine and build it to a definite brand concept. During such process, different talents and material resources such as brand consultant, potential investors, professionals, technicians, family, friends, peers, subordinates, clients, etc. would be added to jointly promote the brand concept to be more vivid, strategic, effective and scientific. The brand concept would go through a stage from one person's dream to a group's conception. Furthermore, with professional brand creation, planning or conception group and external brand consultant and some other professional forces, brand conception may be completed by the form of grouping organization and grouping decision. Therefore, brand concept includes multiple-dimensional thinking, concept and experiment such as brand's organization order, brand's governance structure, brand's ultimate status and brand's development status.

When the conditions for brand construction or brand reengineering are satisfied, the brand technology preparation stage shall be transferred to the brand general design stage which shall be completed with the support of external brand consultants, technological experts in different fields and company's brand officer and brand service provider. It is a stage promoting brand concept into brand drawing, i.e., the brand construction plan or brand reengineering plan, completing the brand concept concretization, brand visualization recognition and brand roadmap and also consists of the preparation for design such as brand's overall program, brand's commercial model design, brand product design, brand service design, brand document serial design, etc. It is also a process to complete the general branding structural design by applying multiple brand technologies-- brand classification technology, brand construction technology, brand recognition technology, brand management technology, brand marketing technology, brand communication technology, brand collaboration technology, etc. so as to finish the brand general design by taking the brand construction plan or brand reengineering plan as a design task.

Brand general design stage is the systematization organization for brand technology preparation and requires setting up a professional brand order layer-- branding committee so as to effectively push forward the brand general design program in the form of branding committee meeting and duty division of brand technology with the purpose of completing the brand construction plan with high quality.

The fourth stage is the brand technology preparation stage. It is a process of preparing various technological conditions, technological resources and technological documents while working out the brand construction plan during the brand technology preparation stage and also a stage that the whole brand organization makes the full mobilization and does well in preparation for technological implementation. However, during the stage, what the brand technology preparation goes through is a particular and dynamically developed status, i.e. the brand technology preparation status. So long as the brand's main affiliated persons, all the brands' participants and resources get into such state, the brand technology preparation will be sufficient and make the full and sufficient preparation for successfully carrying out the brand construction or brand reengineering.

5 Brand technology preparation status

No matter a company is carrying out brand construction for brand creation, brand updating or conducts the fundamental thorough brand reengineering for the next round of development, and no matter brand construction or brand reengineering is required for updating the big brand or small brand and the brand industrial clustering, group brand clustering or product brand, it is required to go through the same brand technology preparation stage. The brand development shall be a great event during the history of a company's development or brand project development, which requires prudent treatment

SECTION III BRAND TECHNOLOGY

and requires all the leaders and personnel of the company or brand project department to get into a positive, stressed and rapidly proceeded status in brand idea, brand spirit, brand awareness and brand development level. Therefore, it requires the full involvement of all the personnel and it is the kind of awareness, honor, action and motive of active involvement from spirit to action for brand creation, vision of brand prospect, participation in preparation before brand launching and involvement of the history of brand development.

Only when all the staff have got into such status, could we say that a brand has effectively reached the brand technology preparation stage and efficiently mobilized all the brand potential, ability, passion and resources. All the staff has acquired a deeper understanding. A brand dream belongs to the whole company whereas a brand belongs to every employee. A successful brand has converted its enthusiasm, professional spirit and value from every brand employee to every brand user by virtue of such deep charm and appeal.

Brand dream is a kind of future vision and creative thinking, brand concept is the thinking blueprint whereas the brand general design is the blueprint drawing. During the formulation of brand construction plan, what is involved is product status change carried out among the staff, management process adjustment, management method updating, production technology change, new technology and new material introduction and use, new supplier selection, new distribution recruitment, new market development, measurement on the new users' brand experience, etc.

Like all buildings' blueprints, the buildings cannot make any material change once the construction started and will exist for several decades and several hundreds of years once being completed. Therefore, it is very crucial to make sufficient technology preparation before working out the building's blueprint and construction and then get into the prudent and scientific technology preparation stage. This is the occupational spirit, career mission and professional dedication for duty performance.

Brand construction or brand reengineering has the same historical features as it is not only the operational orbit set up for future development of the whole brand, but also the operation on the whole brand management process. It is not only the refinement and expression of the brand's overall technological implementation and brand cultural connotation, but also the consistent direction and target of all the staff. Once the brand construction or brand reengineering has been officially implemented, all the links and detailed achievements such as technological links, management process, service forms, product status, etc. might not have any change in the coming several decades and it requires the technological preparation for IT brand technology system such as upgrading into the intelligence and network, etc. in the following step.

Therefore, all the participants, no matter it is the brand strategic management, brand management, brand executives, brand operating teams and brand supply chain and brand operating network, so long as they are involved in such important branding system project, should make every effort to get into the scientific and prudent brand technology preparation status and make the comprehensive preparations for brand technologies of each link subject to the duty division of brand technologies so as to prepare well for the upcoming brand construction or brand reengineering. Whenever the decree of general mobilization for brand construction or brand reengineering is given out, the brand technology preparation shall be started orderly, effectively and rapidly till all the preparations for brand technologies have been completed. While officially starting the brand construction or brand reengineering (opening ceremony), the brand development shall be promoted into a new historical stage and the brand ceremony will be very critical in such a process.

6   Content of brand technology preparations

The specific brand technology preparation content of brand construction or brand reengineering technologies includes six aspects: brand study preparation, brand organization preparation, brand system preparation, brand condition screening, brand construction plan (brand reengineering plan) preparation and brand technology basis preparation.

Brand study is an important process for a brand to solve brand development idea, strategic intention, brand direction, brand professional knowledge popularization and staff's brand awareness. It consists of different layers of brand study content. To be specific, it is an organization of study process such as brand idea study, brand ability training, brand awareness error correction, etc. Different from the education, training or examination, brand study is systematic, professional and instant brand knowledge guidance and replenishment and the training on brand capacity combination and brand skills.

The modern enterprises would face the rather complicated competition environment during their development and various new technologies and new knowledge would have changes at any time and massive unknown management issues might appear; whereas brand study is the instant strategic support, scientific law and knowledge supplement and ability replacement under the status of updating dynamic knowledge so as to make strategic preparations for coping with complicated completion environment and market challenges and to explore for knowledge elimination at any time based on the leading knowledge. Therefore, it is obvious that education institutions such as colleges and universities cannot meet such study demands which need to be highly operational and dynamically updated, and the company's brand study requires a new brand study system.

In addition to set up the higher level of branding committee, brand organization is also an organization status with high tension, high capacity and high order. To be specific, it needs to put in efforts for brand updating and brand ecological organization status based on the requirements of brand organization science. Brand organization is a fleeting organized process and only exists when a brand reaches the organization status from top to bottom and from inside to outside. Only in this way, could a brand be in a world brand ecological chain effectively.

Brand system preparation is the systematic technology preparation by considering brand technology systems, brand performance, brand's leading position and brand's decisive competitiveness and requires making the integrated planning and arrangement on the scope of brand technology implementation, brand technology participating departments and links, funds for brand technology implementation, brand talent, brand ability construction, etc. by applying the brand's systematic tools and brand talent screening technologies. It is the concretization, projection and documentation of brand organization preparation.

Brand condition screening is the comprehensive investigation and study made before brand technology implementation and the screening for brand issues and brand obstacles that might exist. It is also the basic data statistics and statements made on brands' future expectation, branding suggestions at each level and brand's potential advantages, disadvantages, existing conditions, potential resources, competitions, etc. so as to get the preliminary understanding and report before officially carrying out brand construction or brand reengineering technologies, make preparations for brand diagnosis report before officially starting brand technologies and provide first-hand condition analysis report, study report, reference content and original files.

The plan on brand construction or brand reengineering shall be worked out based on the requirements of brand construction technology on brand construction plan. Only after completing the brand construction plan compilation and official release after review and confirming the implementation of relevant technology preparation, could the brand technologies be officially started and carried out based on the standard brand construction process. Brand reengineering shall be carried out by integrating the brand construction plan and standard steps on the basis of DID brand reengineering principle.

The preparation for brand technology basis is not only based on the brand construction plan, but also dependent upon the technological requirements and technological key points of brand theories such as brand scientific principle, brand specialty and brand rules to carry out the brand technologies. In particular, the basis of brand scientific law is most important. The source of brand technology basis is mainly from professional brand consultants and brand technology study force.

Any peer review, external views, personal opinions, etc. cannot be the direct scientific basis for brand technology and could be only used after being reviewed by professional institutions and professionals such as brand consultant, management scientist, management analyst, market analyst, etc. to prevent the professionalism of brand technology and scientific system practice from being intervened by non-professional opinions. If the brand leaders do not have insight and independent judgment, different opinions would result in the overall orientation or partial important links of a brand having changes at any time. As a result, a series of implementation of brand technologies would take change and lead to a failure of brand construction.

7 Quality rating on the brand technology preparation

The implementation of brand technologies, as a whole, is a process of science to make governance on brand order and design of brand system. To ensure successful completion of brand construction or brand reengineering, and to ensure that brand technology will effectively obtain the ultimate achievements, the quality rating shall be made on each link during the brand technology preparations.

The quality rating on the brand technology preparation consists of the level rating on the brand construction plan (A-1, A-2, B-1, B-2, C-1, C-2), level rating on the cooperative resources of brand technologies and brand service providers and the rating on work quality during the process of brand technology preparation. Accurate use of the brand quality rating system in the preparations for brand technologies could guarantee the quality, efficiency and science of brand construction or brand reengineering and reduce the potential threat of non-scientific factors on the implementation of brand technologies to the minimum extent and prevent the brand technology measures from any mistakes.

The preparation for brand technology rating is done simultaneously with the quality rating of the brand technologies. For instance, the rating on the quality of brand study would guarantee the perspective, scientific, professionalism and practicality of the brand study content to the greatest extent, so that the brand study content and mastery of different learners could meet long term, current and future study objectives and study task allocation and result could be effectively accomplished.

The quality rating on brand technology preparation is also closely related with brand construction (brand reengineering) cycle, budget and project process. Although the period of brand construction would take 2 to 3 years, based on the competition speed nowadays, market competition would have changes at every moment and the company would face external or internal unknown challenges during the period of brand construction; therefore, budget and process management of brand technology implementation should be within the controllable extent. Lastly, the quality rating of brand technology preparation shall be completed in a summarized report which shall be an important reference after the official implementation of brand technology.

As a whole, brand technology preparation is also a systematic brand technology deployment. By making various preparations such as dream, organization updating, task allocation, resources portfolio, etc., it would reduce any threats and hidden troubles brought by the potential risks during brand construction so that the whole process from brand technology preparation to the specific implementation of brand technology could reach the optimum state and achieve the highest quality.

Exercises

1. Fill in the blanks: No matter the brand construction or brand reengineering is carried out; the brand technology preparation specifically consists of four stages which are   .

2. Multiple-choice Question: The specific brand technology preparation content of brand construction or brand reengineering technologies includes_____ ( )

A. Brand study preparation, brand organization preparation, brand system preparation.

B. Brand system preparation, brand condition screening, brand construction plan (brand reengineering plan) preparation and brand technology basis preparation.

C. Brand study preparation, brand organization preparation, brand construction plan (brand reengineering plan) preparation and brand technology basis preparation.

D. Brand study preparation, brand organization preparation, brand system preparation, brand condition screening, brand construction plan (brand reengineering plan) preparation and brand technology basis preparation.

3. Essay Question: What is the brand strategic resource reserve mechanism? What reserves does it include?

Chapter 3

Brand Construction Technology

Brand construction brings an overall improvement in brand premium, enterprise management and service.

Brand construction technology is a profile portfolio array that completes brand construction at a quick speed and takes into account the *Brand Construction Project* of high quality and six-step methods of brand construction as the core. It aims to divide missions of brand construction into several sections, and accelerate the brand construction process. Certain principles and technological methods, especially scientific brand construction design, are necessary for brand construction to clarify its constructing process, make it organized in an orderly manner with high efficiency, and at the same time, substantially solve the low quality, low efficiency, and overlapping problems while shortening brand construction period.

Brand Construction Project, to some extent, is as crucial as *Construction Design Plan* and *Business Plan*, and it strictly reflects the design meaning and specific working process. Otherwise, a *Brand Construction Project* that is casually made and without scientific support will contribute nothing to execution of brand construction and won't lead to great losses in human resources, material resources, and financial resources. The end result is that enterprises might construct a brand with low efficiency and quality, or even miss out on the best time to construct a new brand or reconstruct a brand.

1 Brand Construction Technology Study

Anyhow, we should always bear in mind that *Brand Construction Project* is the core and main structural file to ensure that the effect of brand construction is favorable in the whole implementation of brand technology.

Brand construction should meet the requirements of three management upgrades: upgrading from extensive model to professional model, conception to system, and information-based to knowledge-based.

Brand constructing should solve three problems of transformation upgrade: industrial transformation upgrade, traditional enterprises transformation upgrade, and small-sized enterprises transformation upgrade.

The purpose of study: to learn how to utilize six scientific steps to complete brand construction, and understand more about the steps, procedure, methods, and tools of brand constructing; to understand the establishing techniques and three principles (prevention first, mission classification, and elaborate management) of *Brand Construction Project*; to achieve the three abilities in brand constructing which are "three decisions, three usages, and three work arrangements."

2 Brand Construction Project Overview

Overview:

Brand Construction Project is a template that can be applied worldwide, which provides enterprises' executives with an advisory document as well as a schedule plan and mission classified document, which can be divided into several levels according to established quality: Level C (the disordered level), Level B (the groping level), and Level A (the advanced level, which can be further divided into Level A-2, the adoptable level, and Level A-1, the high quality level). Level C and Level B, due to its relatively lower quality, are not recommended to enterprises.

Purpose:

Brand Construction Project is an open source program, which aims at making an overall plan in brand construction, giving initial advice, and sharing each working assignment on the basis of overall steps of brand construction so as to help enterprises obtain practical achievements in brand construction.

Significance:

Brand itself is so personalized that different enterprises will have their own personalized brand. Open source ensures enterprises to have an overall unified structure of brand construction, while their brand capability and brand characteristic can be displayed independently. In addition, by quality evaluation and brand index comparison, open source can also make a comparison between brand construction methods and advanced experience as a way to make them draw on others' strengths to offset their own weaknesses.

2.1 What is brand construction project?

Brand Construction Project is an advisory document applied to enterprises executives, which helps design a scientific construction plan for a ready-to-release brand, clearly analyzes every upcoming work, and conducts mission classification of brand constructing.

In the past, most enterprises failed in brand construction, one important reason of which is that they didn't have a systematic, scientific or logical *Brand Construction Project*.

As an open source program, a standard template and its application rules of *Brand Construction Project* has been offered to global enterprises without any charges.

The complete version of *Brand Construction Project* can be divided into three levels according to the establishment quality: Level C (the disordered level), Level B (the groping level), Level A-2 (the adoptable level), and Level A-1 (the high-quality level).

2.2 Why we establish the brand construction project

Brand Construction Project is a guideline to make a scientific plan for an upcoming brand construction.

It is an advisory file submitted to enterprises' executives

Brand construction is always considered as a crucial decision. Therefore, *Brand Construction Project* has to play its role in helping enterprises perform it. Its application, however, whether to become a formal plan or a back-up plan, lies in the hands of enterprises' strategic decision makers.

It is a guideline for enterprises to construct a high-quality brand

Brand Construction Project is a blueprint for enterprises to conduct brand construction. It also provides enterprises with scientific basis for their future management and development, which serves as a tool to help enterprises bring out their full potential and achieve important upgrade. Top executives and investors expect to have a strategic, high-quality, and adoptable brand construction plan. Enterprises with global vision, innovative thinking and internationalized trend would be better equipped with an ambitious *Brand Construction Project* that is full of challenges.

It is a controllable file that controls the prospective time, budget, and outcome of brand construction.

Brand Construction Project is an adoptable practical project, it contains various upgrade plans from senior-level management, middle-level management, and grass root-level management to supply chain, which requires specific time schedule, steps, mission list, and high-quality improvement. As a highly controllable project, *Brand Construction Project* has the characteristics which can be quickly put into practice and effect, and reach a rapid response.

2.3 Why *Brand Construction Project* is highly valued by enterprises' top executives

Top executives and investors of enterprises have to shoulder the risks when conducting brand construction. Implementing an improper brand construction project may be like running an electric motor that will never stop once it starts. After a so called vigorous brand construction, enterprises may lose market opportunities and waste lots of time that will finally lead to great financial losses due to bad strategy decision.

All enterprises need a high-quality *Brand Construction Project*

Brand construction is an important event and a profound transformation in enterprise strategy development. Before formally conducting brand construction, far-sighted enterprises will spend plenty of time to deploy many human resources in order to design every detail in brand construction project.

The larger the enterprises are, the more complicated their brand construction will be. *Brand Construction Project* provides strategic reference for enterprises, in which it allocates missions to executive level and operating level workers. In the next 2-3 years period, *Brand Construction Project* will bring out its key function in instructing enterprises to construct brand.

Brand construction may fail to reach its ideal outcome

In most cases, brand construction cannot meet its initial goal, which is caused by knowledge discrepancies. The promoters of *Brand Construction Project* are usually the managers in relatively lower level, or other brand PR (planning or consulting) companies, which aren't part of the enterprises' top management level. Thus, these people have insufficient understanding towards the enterprises' long-term brand strategy, which directly leads to an ineffective *Brand Construction Project* without strategic vision.

The *Brand Construction Project* that doesn't comply to scientific brand rules, once it's put into practice, will turn out to be nothing but an empty slogan in the end.

Brand Construction Project is a classification profile for brand management

The frequent mistake that people tend to do is to regard *Brand Construction Project* as the only document that enterprises can rely on when conducting brand construction. Therefore, *Brand Construction Project* has been crammed with lots of unnecessary or wrong information, or it has been produced to be a PR file on brand position and brand publicity that only reflects market function.

Brand Construction Project is not only a business plan, for it calls for a higher quality. It is a mission classification file that contains detailed instructions and all the profiles that are necessary in brand construction, clarifying the time schedule, execution, operation method, and expected outcome. In addition, a single brand construction project cannot fully replace the systematic, completed, standardized brand management document.

2.4 *Brand Construction Project* is related to four layers of users

Brand Construction Project is not presented by chance, but by brand technicians, and its application will not be suitable for advisers themselves nor for the brand technology layer, but for people in the four layers objectively.

(1) Brand Strategic Layer: senior leaders of enterprises (decision makers of enterprise strategy) are the ones who have the rights to decide whether to adopt a *Brand Construction Project* or not in its entirety. They also have to promote the project inside the enterprise, figure out the budget accordingly, and expect a final outcome.

(2) Brand Executive Layer: all the middle-level managers in enterprises have to conduct *Brand Construction Project* in their respective management department, as well as raise their brand capability.

(3) Brand Operating Layer: the whole staff in enterprises should shoulder their respective responsibility according to the *Brand Construction Project*, and improve their work performance.

(4) Brand Collaborative Layer: this layer aims at providing enterprises with purchasing supply chain, brand operating net, brand service agency resources outside the enterprises. They will have a deep understanding of what *Brand Construction Project* requires from them, and make improvement.

2.5 How to ensure the high-quality implementation of brand construction

Brand construction technology has triple assurance modes to ensure its quality, which are three logical protections to avoid the casualty, deficiency, inefficiency, low quality and performance of brand management system documents. The triple assurance modes are:

Quality rating for all brand management system documents

In the study of brand principle, there are three stages in brand construction: Level C (the disordered level), Level B (the groping level), and Level A (the advanced level). All brand management profiles must be compiled with prescriptive framework, method, and comply with the compiling structure, process, approaches, and tools of the brochures.

In addition, all the finished documents and brochures must be rated according to three levels: Level C (the disordered level), Level B (the groping level), and Level A (the advanced level, which can be further divided into Level A-2, the adoptable level, and Level A-1, the high quality level). The application version that the enterprises must reach are either A-2 or Level A-1. Level C and Level B, due to its relatively lower quality, are not recommended to enterprises.

Using audit and analysis-based document establishment method

Brand Audit Report existing in document establishment is of great importance, for it submits audit and analysis documents to enterprises aiming to point out the existing issues and give improved suggestions. In general, management document cannot perform that operation.

Before the implementation of brand construction, enterprises have to first check whether there exist deficiencies in management, after which they can further establish management brochure and document. The PADS technological analyzing model and brand comparison analyzing technology are based on enterprises' dynamic management and optimized management.

Establishing brand with a fully standardized pattern

The establishment of brand management handbook is not only a compiling job based on existing working procedures, institution requirements, recorded charts. Management brochure must conduct scientific establishment with standardized pattern, for instance, Reform of Lord Shang and Taylor's Scientific Management Mode. The standard is accompanied with the conception of "optimization to adoption", which aims to make sure that every step of brand development delivers its best performance.

3 The Formal Establishment of *Brand Construction Project*

Brand construction project is a task file and a compiling file established on the purpose of enterprise's implementation of high-quality brand construction process according to specific requirements of form and content, aiming at making guidance and implementation for top executives, investors and for the whole staff in the enterprise and leading the task schedule, quality and requirement of the overall brand construction process.

The establishment of *Brand Construction Project* consists of standard structure, establishment requirements, establishment process and establishment skills, for which the brand technology layer should be responsible for.

Brand construction project is subject to brand expectation in the next five or ten years with an explanation of the expected outcome "what it wants to be, what it hopes to be and what is the best to be if so".

After the establishment, brand construction project and every document system should be rated and formally adopted up to Level A.

3.1 The list of *Brand Construction Project* documents (eight division methods)

The list of *Brand Construction Project* documents is divided into eight key links of the sequence of document establishment with the eight division method, except for the introduction page and brand strategy page.

The list of preludes:

(1) The cover page;

(2) The introduction page: key summary information;

(3) The content page: content information;

(4) The brand strategy page: brand declaration, brand program and strategic objectives.

Eight lists of documents:

(1) *Brand Construction Progress*: The progress administration office manages it and has a clear schedule and accountability.

(2) *Brand Audit Scheme*: Relevant arrangement of brand audit.

(3) *Brand Management System*: To propose a preliminary management upgrading plan and arrange the standardization of management.

(4) *Brand Identification System*: To propose the preliminary identification ideas and plans.

(5) *Brand Marketing System*: Documents about market design and sales design.

(6) *Brand Communication System*: Brand communication requirements and documents.

(7) *Brand Reporting System*: The time and requirements of rectification report and completion report.

(8) *Brand Construction Budget Project* (equivalent budget).

3.2 The standard structure of prelude list of *Brand Construction Project*

The cover page

A clear and distinct project cover is pleasing and makes people urge to open it. The cover page should be expressed in a concise form, placing words like the company's logo, company's name, brand construction project words as well as the " the first draft" and "version for advice", and if necessary, adding a document number and bar code and noting "trade secrets", "attention to confidentiality" and other similar signs.

The key information page

Pages starting from the title page are the welcome page, the address page, the overview page and the right information page according to the specific standard defined by the enterprise. The welcome page can include the enterprise spirit, enterprise belief, or acknowledgment such as "Dedicated to people who pursue great dreams", which will give readers a strong conviction and will also show ambitions of enterprise brand. The acknowledgment page, in general, is addressed by the chairman and CEO, expressing requirements and aspirations of proposed brand construction; the overview page delivers the main outline and key information of task content of the brand construction; the right information page announces the list and contact information of the Chief Brand Officer and the Brand Technical Committee, and at the same time, a department and two liaisons are necessary to remind all the people to contact the one that is responsible for a certain topic and make an official explanation, if there are questions or doubts.

The content page

The content page lists brand construction tasks, and notes the page number as well as the emergency and announcements.

The brand strategy page

The brand strategy page includes the brand global declaration, brand programmatic documents, brand strategy objectives, brand construction policy and other key information. If the brand declaration and other relevant documents are unfinished before brand construction, it should be included in the brand mission documents and marked in the brand strategy page. As the brand construction is a prospective per-design document for the company's brand expectation for the next five to ten years, and the document is primarily for internal use, the document does not include information such as company profiles and existing organizational structure.

SECTION III BRAND TECHNOLOGY

3.3 The standard structure of eight division methods lists on *Brand Construction Project*

(1) *Brand Construction Progress*

Progress files are grouped according to the exact completion time of the brand task item. Brand construction progress includes *Brand Construction Schedule,* promoting time and requirements, and checking points and accountability. The schedule can be made by using tools such as the Gantt chart. The progress document is typically managed, reviewed and reported by the progress administration office of the Brand Technical Committee and the progress managers at each management level, reporting to the Brand Technical Committee supervised by the corporate strategy group.

(2) *Brand Audit Scheme*

Brand audit scheme clarifies personnel, time, audit research schedule, and audit report form. The PADS scientific analysis model and brand comparative analysis are used to having a scientific audit of the existing brand situation. Brand audit should be done under the guidance of technical advisers in an external brand for the third-party audit, helping to find brand management processes and other major problems and designing a scientific brand management standardization system. Brand audit should be carried out for the brand strategy layer, brand technology layer, brand executive layer, brand operation layer, brand collaboration layer and brand user layer, completing an intensive investigation with a certain number of people. The focus of the investigation is to investigate the management process and brand awareness, and to further present audit opinions and submit *Brand Audit Report* after the completion of audit.

(3) *Brand Management System*

Brand management system proposes a preliminary management upgrading plan to arrange matters and time of management standardization, and the brand management manual requirements and completion time. The weak foundation of management has always been the main drawback of global enterprises. All aspects of enterprise management are researched and standardized rigorously, completely and thoroughly through the standardization of brand management. This is a key point to comprehensively upgrade the quality of brand research, manufacturing, management, marketing and service. Brand management targets all staff. It is of great significance for the implementation of brand management standardization to enhance the management level of the brand organization. Brand management standardization is guided by the brand technical committee to carry out a thorough action to enhance management level in all the departments and all the staff. The result of brand management standardization is the completion of various brand management brochure file systems (including a number of specific management operation brochures, such as R & D management brochures, production operation brochures, dealer's operation brochures, marketing operation brochures, etc.).

(4) *Brand Identification System*

Brand Identification System proposes preliminary brand identification opinions and plans. The *Brand Identification Manual* should be finally submitted. Brand identification design is an independent operation of the brand identification system, which includes brand naming identification, brand LOGO identification, brand feeling identification, brand environment identification, brand first trust design, brand safety design and other accurate identification information presented to public and users. Brand identification program is different from the previous CI system(Corporate Identity), because the new brand identification system extends the meaning of the brand image, puts forward the design requirements of the brand idea and the brand image identification, and emphasizes design requirements such as feeling design, trust for the first time and brand safety and other psychological feelings.

(5) *Brand Marketing System*

Brand Marketing System is the document to propose market design and sales design to complete the system design with marketing brochures and operating brochures. Brand organizations should pay special attention to the brand's market design, market action and sales management in order to lead market-oriented brand marketing. Brand marketing system should also focus on modern marketing methods, such as the Internet, mobile Internet, Internet of Things, ecommerce, new media, social network, supply chain and other new trends and new changes to marketing. This system should express the design results with brochures (such as market design brochures, brand marketing brochures in Asian market, and service marketing operation brochures).

(6) *Brand Communication System*

Brand Communication System consists of the brand interpretation system and brand communication system and other components, and completes the design with the brochure documents. Brand interpretation system, containing brand origin, brand story, important events, important figures and other important information, is the main content source of official interpretation of the brand. All brand communication work is based on brand interpretation of dragnet-style coverage, carrying out strong brand communication with application of new media, Internet and interpersonal communication principles. Brand communication document is a brochure document, and a number of brand communication tools are widely used in communication technology such as wave chart, business plans and others.

(7) *Brand Reporting System*

Brand Reporting System includes rectification reports, management site reports, brand construction stage reports and acceptance reports, which are used in various work situations, awareness and behavior rectifications in the brand construction process. They are also used during meta-analysis of questions related to the site management. Through the phased implementation of brand construction and brand construction acceptance, the reporting system will be committed to an efficient completion of brand construction work.

(8) *Brand Construction Budget Project* (equivalent budget)

Brand Construction Budget Project is an equivalent budget plan, putting forward all kinds of investments in deliberation, validation, and final settlement of brand construction. Brand construction itself is seen as an important investment activity, as important as the investment significance of major shareholders, because the brand construction investment will not only generate significant premium capacity for the brand, but also lay an important factual investment base for a new round of important strategic investment shareholder recruitment, IPO and others. The equivalent budget is a two-stage budget, that represents the Brand Technical Committee and the brand construction executive units come up with a budget respectively from their own needs, having a comprehensive comparison with two budgets as the scientific basis for budget deliberation, preview and decision, since the budget of one party alone is often prone to bias.

4 The Requirements of *Brand Construction Project* Establishment

Brand Construction Project has certain requirements for the establishment technology, which ultimately can give a great guide and detailed implementation to enterprise's brand construction by means of *Brand Construction Project*.

4.1 Four elements of Brand Construction Project(4W)

High-quality *Brand Construction Project* should meet the following four elements:

When——When to do?

Brand Construction Project clarifies the promoting schedule and the ending time of every brand task.

What——What to do?

Brand Construction Project clarifies various task items of brand construction forming an establishment document of tasks.

Who——Who should do it?

Brand Construction Project clarifies who or which department should do every task item.

What quality ——What quality is achieved?

Brand Construction Project clarifies the quality requirements of every task item and the whole process of brand construction.

4.2 Three decisions of the project

High-quality *Brand Construction Project* contains decisive information in three areas.

(1) Decide: the definition of brand

Define the recognition system, brand expectation, user differentiation, user group characteristics, education method, and trust design for the first time of brand.

(2) Decide: the nature of brand

Define the practical methods of brand strategic route, brand performance index, brand capability key point, brand standardization and brand communication strategies.

(3) Decide: the organization of brand

Define the organizational structure of brand, the scope of management progress, the process of brand construction, the management operation and review process of brand, the mode of brand audit report, the scale of brand market, the allocation of personnel and rule, management of brand supply chain and operation supply.

4.3 Three guidance of the project

High-quality *Brand Construction Project* reflects the following three characteristics of guidance:

(1) Action guidance of brand construction steps

Define the overall action goals, task items establishment, task division, time and checking points of six brand construction steps.

(2) Operation guidance of brand construction action

Define the action plan and establishment guide of brand identification brochure, brand management brochure and brand audit report.

(3) Capability guide for brand construction action

Define the main action plan and construction capability key points of brand capability project, brand implementation project, brand promotion project, and brand report project.

4.4 Three items

High-quality *Brand Construction Project* contains three items:

(1) Study item

To collect brand issues, assemble analysis data, study brand construction standard and brand strategic route by using brand capability element table, PADS scientific analysis model, brand contrast technology and brand tools.

(2) Discussion item

To discuss and decide the key points of brand capability construction and the brand identification method according to different management levels. Besides, to discuss the covering links of brand data capability, and to discuss and establish task items, implementing key points and checking methods.

(3) Rule item

Every management layer separately takes action, practices operation, plans the overall task schedule, implements the results of tasks and achieves the whole project of brand construction according to established task items.

4.5 Three rules

High-quality *Brand Construction Project* contains three rules:

Rule One: prevention first

The primary task is to prevent the upcoming large number of brand decision errors and brand management errors by strategic vision and scientific management, because the management awareness and management base of brand-importing countries(developing countries) not only have a large number of errors and shortcomings, but also are management problem-prone areas.

Without strategy and scientific law, brand construction is inefficient and cannot foresee future results, which will result in the failure of brand construction investment. Brand construction project by itself is inefficient, and also causes serious decision errors, which can be reflected as a waste of time and can produce economic losses for the enterprise.

Rule Two: establishment of tasks

Brand Construction Project formulates the promoting schedule and task items for upcoming brand construction. These task items should be divided and four Ws should be put forward: Who to do? How to do? When is it done? How is the quality assessed?

The implementation of *Brand Construction Project* is not one person's responsibility, but an integral job done by the whole staff from top to bottom in the enterprise, which should overview the job and define the whole process of job.

Brand Construction Project is also a decision document for suggestions given to senior managers containing resources and budgets to use, the requirements of implementation and necessary implementation conditions.

Rule Three: lean brand

Brand Construction Project must meet the principle of lean management to implement brand construction. The method of "subtraction and addition", namely the enterprise should do "subtraction" first and "addition" should follow shortly. Enterprise should concentrate on developing the core products and business, highlight the core business and the core competitive advantages and cut marginal business and unnecessary links to analyze what not to do, what should be cut and abolished, and then focus on the development of brand core competitiveness.

5 The Establishment Process of *Brand Construction Project*

Brand construction project is as important as architectural design. Once brand construction starts, it will be the brand blueprint of an enterprise at least in the following five to ten years and it will bring great brand effect. Therefore, the enterprise should be cautious about the project itself.

The establishment process of brand project consists of eight processes:

(1) The project approval project: to make a project approval on brand establishment project, to set up brand technique committee, and to confirm the person in charge of starting the design process of brand establishment project.

(2) The project design stage: to try to find out the primary situation, to put forward constitutive contents of *Brand Construction Project* and to draft brand strategy documents.

(3) The preliminary design: the establishment process of draft may be corrected several times or appraised and elected among several projects to establish the primary *Brand Construction Project*.

(4) The validation stage: after completing the primary draft, it is submitted to Brand Technical Committee to deliberate and correct according to deliberated suggestion. It is accepted after convening several deliberation meetings.

(5) The construction and starting stage: according to the passed *Brand Construction Project*, brand construction starting conference is held and announces all the personnel to step into the concrete

implementation stage of brand construction tasks.

(6) The implementation stage: in the stage of concrete implementation and execution, every concrete task item should be put into practice according to brand construction project.

(7) The schedule management stage: the schedule is made of a unified management, such as following up the schedule and solving every schedule problem in time.

(8) The checking and accepting report stage: this stage contains phased acceptance and results acceptance. The actual schedule and results of brand construction project should be reported in various ways.

5.1 The Characteristics of Brand Construction Project

Brand construction project has the following characteristics:

(1)Creation

Brand Construction Project is a scientific and cautious design job, as well as a planned and purposeful creative behavior. The creative job is based on various thinking and creative capability including scientific basis, imagination, brand artistic conception, science frontier technology, prospect anticipation, etc. The creative process cannot be compared with repeated and modeled producing actions.

The creation of brand construction project is the balance between people(brand builders, brand organizers), staff (brand contributors, brand makers), and users (brand users, brand objects).

On the one hand, brand construction project should face different enterprise management environments, intricate management issues and all the personnel with various suggestions in the enterprise. On the other hand, brand construction project releases intelligence of the brand fully and solves all the contradictions, conflicts and problems in the group. On the third hand, people have high-quality requirements of brand and executives in enterprise will put brand imaginary mode into effect in the future on the basis of concrete decision suggestion, enforceable measures, creation awareness and change capability given by presenters of brand construction project.

Therefore, it is required that presenters of brand construction have imagination, creation and aesthetic capability on brand and an intelligent and open-minded approach, changing the psychology of overcoming difficulties and the decision and the willpower of challenging authority.

(2) Comprehensiveness

Brand is a comprehensive subject including sociology, psychology, management, group learning, economics, aesthetics, science, technology, law and more other elements. Different groups should be known such as strategic leaders, administrators, departments of enterprise, staffs of enterprise, brand users, high-income classes and general citizens. Work contents in every aspect should be planned as a whole, such as research& development, design, suppliers, production, after-sales. The overall construct of brand development that could never be completed due to limited project is necessary to put into the project and attain to the purpose for realization by learning to answer various elements, meeting different needs and putting all kinds of elements into practice.

(3) Frontier

Brand construction project should have sufficient frontier, forward-looking and other anticipating capability to show a variety of management changes, the future shape of product and the future user structure which will occur in the future as much as possible, which describes a grand blueprint of future development for the global development of enterprises. Besides, brand construction project should have internationalized characteristics defining competitive factors in the world market, internationalized management and developing capability of international market.

(4) Dualism

Brand construction project reflects the dual role of designers and operators. The proposer of brand construction project is not only the designer and the guide for technology implementation, but also the guarantor for the implementation of the effect. Therefore, the proposer of brand construction project should master and use the process of analysis and research, conception and design, analysis and selection, and make good use of imaginative thinking, frame thinking, ternary thinking, brand design language and other knowledge & ability to perform the necessary learning and practice on the ability of design and implementation and to participate in the process of design, implementation, practice and independent leadership of several enterprise brand items as a brand graduate.

(5) Sociability

Brand services society, but brand is not a general sense of goods. No matter which brand it is, from the date of appearance, it has a wide range of sociability and becomes part of a human's life. Whether people like it or not, we should try to live with it, because the brand has an objective and real impact on humans, because it is inevitable and permanent for decades or even hundreds of years.

(6) Procedure

A lot of labors, materials and financial resources should be invested in brand construction and a quite rigorous project procedure is necessary.

The most important objective of brand construction project is to realize the effect of implementation and the basic premise of ensuring that brand design is scientific, reasonable and feasible, and also whether the initial design stage of project or the validation value of project should be done systematic and with the overall research and thinking.

The proposers of brand construction project need to think and imagine boldly and deeply, listen to different opinions of users, managers, brand technology consultants, experts and consumers, select the better project on the basis of extensive argument, make constant adjustment, development, refinement and improvement, which is quite a logical stage in line with the cause and effect. In this stage, there is no shortcut, but the need for completing the reproduction of brand blueprint by following the project constantly, scientifically and realistically.

5.2 The process of proposing and validating brand project

The process of proposing and validating the brand-building plan includes three steps: preliminary design, validating design and project completion, which are further divided into first draft, second draft, first validation and second validation.(See Table 10-1)

Table 10-1 The process of proposing and validating brand project

Preliminary Design		Validating Design		Project Completion
First Draft	Second Draft	First Validation	Second Validation	Project Validation
Research Analysis	Project Adjustment	Project Optimization	Project Correction	Project Announcement
Conception Proposal	Further Refinement			
Project Proposal				

SECTION III BRAND TECHNOLOGY

5.3 The comparison of multiple projects

Brand Construction Project can be compared with multiple projects, the necessity of which mainly reflects in:

Multiple projects are required by the purpose of project design. The project design is not purpose, but a process whose ultimate goal is to achieve an ideal and satisfying implementation project to verify which project is the most reasonable and to find an effective way to analyze and compare multiple projects.

The basic principles of multiple projects:

To put forward as many great choosing projects as possible; to learn to survey problems from multiple angles and multiple orientations; any project should be established on the basis of meeting the needs of brand construction, otherwise no matter how many projects - it won't make any difference; to deny those unrealistic, unscientific and impossible projects and methods in case of waste of time or energy.

The basic conditions of project optimization:

To analyze which construction project conforms to the development goal and conception of the brand organization by comparing; to analyze which project has scientific management characteristic; to compare which project is more feasible after correction and adjustment; to comprehensively think about the implementation of project.

6 Six Scientific Steps of Brand Construction (Six Steps)

The purpose of brand construction: the capability of brand management attains to the A stage of brand construction, in which the brand management is ordered, cycled, balanced, stable, auto-operating, auto-adaptive in order to form a brand ecological balance system for enterprises and bring enough brand profits to enterprise constantly.

Besides, in the implementation of brand construction, the needs for IT management and knowledge management are apparent. Pay attention to: anytime and anywhere, the system of brand management can be seamlessly upgraded to the world-leading IT structure and mobile management technology, and is committed to the comprehensive integration and auto-adaptive management needs of management modernization, management information and management knowledge of enterprise brand.

The brand construction can be completed quickly by six steps. They are:

B1 The stage of brand strategy

B1-1 The middle and senior managers learn brand awareness and decide to create or re-engineer brand.

B1-2 To establish enterprise brand committee.

B1-3 To apply brand talent screening technology, and select brand technology backbone and brand backbone.

B1-4 To choose the route of brand strategy (using *Brand Capability Element Table*);

B2 The stage of brand organization;

B2-1 The establishment of *Brand (Global) Strategy Frame Document*;

B2-2 The establishment of *Brand Construction Project*;

B2-3 The overall audit of brand;

B2-4 The reengineering and restructuring of brand (start restructuring organization structure, restructuring management, etc.);

B3 The stage of brand standardization;

B3-1 Brand standardization in every link (using PADS);

B3-2 The establishment of *Brand Management System*;

B3-3 The establishment of *Brand Identification System*;

B3-4 The establishment of *Brand Marketing System*;

B3-5 The establishment of *Brand Communication System*;

B3-6 The establishment of *Brand Collaboration System*;

B4 The stage of brand study;

B4-1 The first level study: brand backbone study;

B4-2 The second level study: full personnel brand study;

B4-3 The third level study: brand group study;

B5 The stage of brand communication;

B5-1 The announcement of *Brand(Global) Strategy Frame*;

B5-2 The organization of brand declaration;

B5-3 The action of brand communication;

B6 The stage of brand ecology;

B6-1 The management of brand audit report;

B6-2 The management of brand construction phased reports and acceptance reports;

* B6-3 Brand strategic commanding system (depending on needs);

* B6-4 Brand knowledge management system (depending on needs).

6.1 General Problems of Six Steps in Brand Construction

Brand construction in the past was mainly from different sources of theory and method so that the enterprise became an integrated body with various theories, views and methods. Then enterprise had different experiences and starting points of brand idea, and in addition, brand document was not standardized and quoted terminologies were inconsistent, which led to an obstruction of the overall understanding and communication of enterprise leaders, brand officers and brand project specialists with enterprise brand strategy, brand strategy got seriously detached from enterprise management, and the implementation difficulty of brand construction got increased.

The new six steps in brand construction focus on the top-level design of strategic level to support enterprises to establish an unified brand strategy frame; to distribute key strategic capability in the systematic methods; to deploy enterprise organizational structure, brand implementation unit, the management process and the framework structural brand strategy ability centered around the market; to establish an unified, consistent, professional brand strategy system and to meet the enterprise's new standard for rapid brand command, fast brand operations, rapid, responsive, and dynamic brand management.

The six steps in brand construction also make basic preparation for brand IT structure of enterprises and mobile management of brand. It is suitable for a timely upgrade of enterprises to deploy information technology and efficient brand management strategy. Command chain, collaboration chain and management network connect the command department of brand strategy, the associated department of brands, global brand business network and global brand groups to form the new IT order link with sky, land, sea location and online, offline, mobile and ecommerce.

6.2 B1 The introduction of brand strategy stage

When an enterprise decides to implement brand technology by six steps in brand construction, it should set up a special brand committee with the CEO leading the next brand audit analysis, brand strategy reengineering, brand study, brand communication, brand correction and other jobs of brand strategy structure comprehensively.

Brand talent screening technology should be paid special attention to.

Brand talent screening technology is a very important step in enterprise management specialization. Every link in the enterprise including brand command, brand management and brand marketing needs to strictly choose the talent with special potential to assume the main leadership and implementation. Brand strategy needs different kinds of brand talent, because the enterprise never carried out scientific screening for brand managers in the past, so employment error became the part of enterprise brand construction that failed the most.

The new six steps in brand construction require appropriate specific talents that should be selected to be take charge of brand work and the talents with different characteristics should be employed to realize the shortcut to efficient brand management. These specific talents include:

Brand leaders of enterprise must choose those systematic and thoughtful leaders who are keen on reforming and that will focus on science, law, organization and management. They will play a decisive and crucial role in shaping the brand strategy system due to their aggressive reforming. In most cases, the enterprise brand construction failed because there were no competent leaders.

Brand officer must be the fairest person and perfectionist whose IQ is much higher than that of ordinary people. They cannot tolerate any product defect, strongly defend the brand, cherish every progress of brand, and cannot put up with corruption in procurement, product defects and after-sales problems. They are very sensitive about any criticism from brand users and will try to reduce the recurrence of errors.

R&D supervisor and product manager must be perfectionists. These R&D supervisors working in the world-leading international brand will be mainly engaged in brand product research that is generally regarded as a kind of trend. The frontier challenging ability of R&D supervisors leads in the world for at least a decade. The world trend is created by them, because they try to make samples that become perfect artworks and give them a perfect definition.

Purchasing supervisor and quality supervisor must be the fairest persons who do everything that the public demands rather than to be selfish so as to avoid the corruption of the purchasing source and the outflow of substandard products out of the factory. The supervisor in customer service must be a person who gets very upset if a user problem cannot be solved in a day, which can ensure that the user's problem gets completely resolved. All the key personnel of service terminal must be selected from the people who possess volunteer spirit and their spirit will ensure the user's best satisfaction.

Subsequently, according to the Brand Capability Element Table, enterprises can quickly determine the brand key capability of focusing on development quickly to define necessary capability elements on specializing and strengthening their own enterprises. The identification of brand strategy route indicates the correct direction of brand strategy and the strategy guidance route of mobilizing the full personnel in the enterprise.

6.3 B2 The introduction of brand organization stage

Companies should draw up *Brand (Global) Strategic Framework Document* with a long-term strategic significance. Brand global strategic framework is the overall principle for enterprise's brand strategy. It is also the central guiding ideology for enterprise's brand development for the next few years or even hundreds of years. Enterprises can then make a brand-building schedule as the guideline for real brand strategy implementation.

All staff, from top to the bottom, from inside to the outside, but not the leaders on top or a single department of the enterprise, should be involved in brand development. Within the brand global strategy framework, an adjustment should be made on the enterprise's organization structure, work division and other units when the enterprise determines to develop the core competitiveness of the brand. All staff should dream, be confident, and be powerful. A deeper revolution is better for the brand strategy.

Both brand audit technology and comparative analysis technology should be applied in the B2-B3 brand standardization stages.

When brand reengineering has been decided, brand strategy reorganization can be done at the same time. It can be divided into four parts, which are brand restructuring, organization restructuring, management restructuring, and elite brand restructuring.

Brand reengineering: The main tasks of the brand reengineering are to fully arrange the brand's key capabilities in all units of brand-building, to redesign the brand identification system, to set the brand targets and to optimize the brand's capability elements.

Organization reengineering: The main task of the organizational reengineering is to optimize the organization structure to make it suitable for rapid development of the brand strategy capability framework nowadays. Incorrect organization structure is the major obstructive factor for the brand development. A key point of organization reengineering is to make a scientific division among research and development, production, marketing and servicing and to establish the internal market procurement relationship. The internal market simulating can help create products to satisfy our customers. In the past, problems such as product design flaws, instability of product's quality and poor after-sales service were the lack of marketing-oriented mechanism in the internal enterprise.

Management reengineering: Management reengineering is mainly for the comprehensive optimization of management processes. Errors occurred in management processes are the roots of various problems of brand development. Besides, those wrong and outdated management processes cause a big harm to brand development. Management reengineering should be conducted under the guidance of management scientists and management analysts. Gross errors of management processes often occur. But these errors cannot easily be found by us and management consulting firms. They can only be found by more advanced scientific inventions.

Elite brand strategy reengineering: Elite brand reengineering is also an important part. When an enterprise decides to start a global or a local brand war, the highest level of elite brand strategy should be performed. Elite brand strategy requires enterprises to make a boldly reform of the brand. Product lines, producing and marketing of the enterprise should be focused on a major "first product" to make the market map become disintegrated. Certainly, it requires the enterprise to be more focused on brand strategy. On the basic of management promotion, elite brand strategy can develop a more advanced IT structure and a mobile solution so as to achieve a high-efficiency command of the "brand marketing operational command capability".

6.4 B3 The stage of brand standardization

There are three major processes of brand standardization:

(1) The first process is laboratory standardization, which means the standardization of product research & development processes.

(2) The second process is management standardization, which means the standardization of enterprise management and supply chains.

(3) The third one is market standardization, which means the standardization of markets, sales, communications, service processes and networks of brand dealers.

Enterprises should complete relevant document preparation on management and operation pursuant to brand management standardization technology, PADS scientific analysis model and brand comparison and analysis technology.

The main function of brand audit technology is to capture and to analyze dynamic management issues rapidly and to re-engineer processes. As for PADS scientific analysis model, P means problem investigation, a means meta-analysis, D means management design, and S means scientific popularization. We can achieve rapid management analysis, management promotion, management process reengineering, and management method invention by PADS scientific analysis model. We can form a complete brand management audit report through the scientific analysis of the enterprise's leadership, management, operation, supply channels, customer groups and users so as to provide scientific basis for new brand strategy framework formulation.

Brand comparison analysis technology is used to further enhance a brand's key capabilities. If necessary, enterprises can use it to make a comparison and analysis among the global outstanding brands, similar international brands on management elements and marketing elements. After that the enterprise can establish its brand bench-marking goal, in order to determine more accurately the brand strategy framework and achieve stricter management for globally leading brand development. Enterprises using brand comparison and analysis technology to set the brand bench-marking goal should focus on the aspects of brand support abilities, brand quality, brand management and brand identification ability to establish brand improvement project objectives.

6.5 B4 The stage of brand study

Brand study is a very important stage for us all.

In brand strategic capability construction, brand study is the most cost-effective and the most important way for its key capability construction. Developed countries and countries with strong national beliefs usually have a strong brand study ability and a better brand quality foundation. While in developing countries' enterprises, brand study is the most overlooked step with worse brand quality foundation.

(1) Brand study in developed countries

Service study in the United States, Hong Kong and other countries and regions has been going on for more than 30 years. This service study has spread throughout primary and secondary schools, universities and communities. Children had been cultivated with the spirit of service and the sense of social contribution when they were young. When they grow up and enter into the enterprise, volunteer spirit and social service consciousness will be deeply rooted in their awareness and make them become rational and systematical at work.

"Disruptive Innovation" in the United States, "Lean Production" in Japan, manufacturing workers' social status in Germany, romantic culture in France, creative culture in South Korea and specific culture in Italy, all of these have a profound impact on international brand construction. The Government of Hong Kong Special Administrative Region has always reminded the public that "cheap equals to no good goods" which has led to a fine consumer awareness. The cultivation of enterprise' brand quality has already begun when they were young. And the cultivation can also lay a foundation for their international brand construction.

(2) Brand study in developing countries

As for enterprises in developing countries, when promoting brand technology, they should focus more on brand study. All employees should be included in this deep study. Owing to their close relationship with brand with which they have been dealing with, all of them should be passionate about brand, know what they are doing, be professional about it, and be willing to make all efforts for the rise of brand. Obviously, independent development, products, quality and services of an enterprise are from staff's sincere efforts.

In developing countries, brand construction and reengineering have become a kind of brand organization. We need to promote brand talent screening technology and the brand development from the maternal to the trunk through brand study. We should take efforts to cultivate brand key staff who are the real brand lovers and send them to the important positions of brand construction to make services wholeheartedly. Constant learning will walk you throughout the whole life of the enterprise. Every new employee must begin his or her work with brand study, and brand study will never end.

(3) Three levels of brand study

Brand study is the most cost-saving brand construction method for enterprises designed through brand technology. In the meanwhile, it is also the biggest one to be overlooked by enterprises. In that case, we have three effective study processes which can promote enterprise's brand capability rapidly.

Brand backbone study process: brand talents are the "brain", "center", and "backbone" of a brand. We select the most appropriate brand talents through brand talent screening technology and sent them to the most appropriate work positions. Leaders in many important departments such as brand leaders, brand officers, purchasing supervisors, quality supervisors, customer service supervisors and after-sales supervisors need to be selected in a special and serious way. Not everyone can do it. Unsuitable employees in these areas may lead to a lot of problems such as purchasing corruption, defects of products and service incidents. Therefore, those who work for brand management and brand marketing communication such as brand leaders, brand officers, purchasing supervisors, quality supervisors, customer service supervisors and after-sales supervisors should focus more on brand study especially.

All Members-study process: this is a very important process. Brand study is not a process for senior leadership or a department, but all the employees should be included. We rebuild their faith, enthusiasm, responsibility, spirit and morality to the brand so as to perform better during the international brand construction. Their enthusiasm for the brand will affect people all over the world. That is to say, employees themselves can be the best examples for brand external communication.

Brand users' study process: this process is unique for brand users, brand customers and the public. It aims to cultivate brand impulses, brand identification abilities, brand consumption habits, similar brand rejection abilities and brand reputation spread abilities for them. The success of an international brand relies on a group of regular consumers to help gather more users in the public. However, companies often ignore those customers who are the real brand lovers and cost lots of money to advertise goods and focus on those users who do not like it. This can be an unforgivable mistake.

6.6 B5 The Stage of Brand Communicating

(1) The announcement of *Brand (Global) Strategic Framework*

When enterprises have finished the brand strategy framework, the brand construction project, the brand strategy rearrangement and the first brand study, they need to choose a "big" day to hold a press conference or ceremony so as to declare *Brand (Global) Strategic Framework* and *Brand World Announcement* to the public.

Brand strategy framework can be divided into three different versions: internal version, consensus version and public version. Public version is designed for the public to identify new brands and to avoid disclosure of trade secrets; internal version is designed for suppliers and partners to reach a consensus on brand prospects and responsibilities and rights; and internal version is designed to be a guidance document for the whole staff in enterprises, coordinated with brand strategy manual.

Key staff, all the employees, suppliers and dealers must declare their responsibility to the brand, but small enterprises can simplify some steps within the scope of the brand strategy framework.

Brand itself is a kind of belief, an honor, and even a kind of responsibility. If staff have no passion and longing for the brand, brand construction itself will be a failure.

(2) Brand-intensive promotion actions

After the announcement of brand strategy framework, there will be a series of brand-intensive promotion actions of large scales to let the public know how to recognize the brand clearly. Brand identification itself is a kind of psychological set rooted in people's deep hearts to make them clearly know how to choose the best solution when dealing with a professional question, and it can help them to make an equal comparison between a consumer's desires and the enterprise brand as soon as possible.

Even small enterprise should focus on the promotion of brand, although small in scale. More than 50% of people choose to learn about new brands on the Internet. If no news about the brand can be found in the search engine, they will have extreme doubts about the brand. In that case the business opportunity goes away.

Large enterprises usually outsource the work of branding promotion to a professional brand promotion company or a public relations company. But it should be noted that – once the brand identity information has been wrong for us, it will influence users' impressions on the brand. In new communicating plan, the work of brand recognizing communication should be treated strictly to make sure that every piece of brand information which is communicated to the outside is consistent with its capability elements, the brand interpretation system, and the correct brand identification information defined by brand identification system.

(3) Long-term brand communication strategy

There have been many successful international brands such as Google, Starbucks, Louis Vuitton,

Parker, Zippo, and China's Glanz that have shown that their success is achieved without advertisement or with less focus on advertisement.

Those high-level products attract customers through public praise. But some brands attract customers through advertising with a massive investment to make the brand be famous so as to form a large regular consumers group.

Brand communication has no limits. There are less TV viewers and newspaper readers nowadays. More young consumers use the Internet to obtain information, thus brand subsequently transforms into Internet brand. In the future, all enterprises will live on the Internet, and all brands will be completely become Internet brands, too. Therefore, enterprises should pay more attention to Internet brand construction.

(4) Micro-communication strategy for "Micro-brand"

In the era of social networks and micro-mobile applications such as Facebook, Google +, Twitter, Photo bucket, micro-blogs, videos and pictures can also have certain brand communication effects. Enterprises need to pay attention to the construction and maintenance of micro-brands, even the scientific laws of micro-communication.

Micro-brands are mainly based on the so called "brand home" on social networking and micro-tools. They aim at attracting regular brand user groups which can make a certain value of online timely consumption.

"Topic" is the main communicating method of micro-communication, thus enterprises should focus on topic effects of design, fashion, transshipment and transfer. Besides, some creative "micro-activities" also has a certain micro-communication effects.

However, in general, micro-brand and micro-communication are a subsidiary and extensive communicating method of the brand strategy. There will be more harm than good, if the strategic capability construction, common brand identification, brand strategic rearrangement, brand management and brand marketing are ignored. Moreover, mobile phone is not the only carrier for mobile management and mobile marketing information of the brand capability promotion. Mobile management information is usually based on specialized mobile terminals, and has been separated from daily entertainments and call functions.

6.7 B6 Brand ecological stage

(1) Brand correction -- Brand ecological stage

The correction is a continuous process emphasizing on rectifying during the implementation of the brand strategy, which includes rectification of the brand strategy thought, brand identify information, processes of brand management and marketing, and work behavior of personnel who are in charge of implementing brand strategy. Regular rectification reports and reports on emergency must be reported to brand technology committee of the enterprise in time.

Regularly using the PADS scientific model and comparative analysis method, companies can analyze the brand rectification report so as to figure out the source and reason of the problems. The measure taken in the rectification report is not a repeated recycle of a continuous improvement process. Except from the timely repair of the urgent and critical error information, enterprises should avoid change in the management process at any time, which will lead to greater error of management process or major management accidents -- every management procedure must be connected seamlessly, otherwise a minor change may cause deviation of related work procedure.

(2) Avoid management improvement at any time

The PDCA (Plan, Do, Check, Adapt) cycle applied in former quality management is not perfect. Modern management requires that the enterprise management itself should be a systematized and self-adaptive order. Besides, more and more management links will achieve automatic deployment with the help of electrical system, information-based system, software and other systems. What 'seven more important is that man and machine can be separated, that is, the function of man in specific work can be sharply reduced and replaced by automatic system. The continuous improvement of PDCA is in fact to patch at any time, to change management process and to modify the program, and it is the significant factor causing management process error and BUG(vulnerability) produced by auto-adaptable system.

PADS scientific model of brand strategy does not advocate change at any time in the management process. In the initial implementation period of brand technology, when there are quite many rectification reports and once concentrated on rectification of brand management system, it must be carried out after every certain period of time to ensure each management process can be steadily jointed. As the brand running becomes more mature, the number of rectification report will be less and less, and so will be the concentrated rectification.

(3) Brand ecosystem

In 2-3 years within the brand building period, brand building will be completed and brand association will become the most stable brand ecosystem, which smoothly functions and is flawless and will grow into a mature brand management method. It will also make sure that the enterprise will be a qualified brand management system upgrade to integrated information system and achieve core competitiveness of outstanding international brand in an automatic, rapid and accurate way. An ideal brand ecosystem is known for its stability, which cycles in order, remains in the balanced and stable stage, and rotates automatically. Brand balanced ecosystem -- scientific brand being, can bring significant profits continuously to enterprises.

6.8 Benefits of implementing the six steps in brand construction

(1) Implement top design of brand strategy

Through the framework design of brand strategy and brand capability structure, to enhance the competitiveness of an enterprise brand, set up a long-term strategic objective and build a first-class international brand.

(2) Develop competitiveness of competency-based brand

The global market and professional market competition directly reflect the enterprise comprehensive management level and brand market management level. To develop brand technology as the core, to build the first-class brand as the pioneer, and to effectively enhance enterprise management level in an all-round way.

(3) Introduce the world's advanced brand management methods

With strategic view and advanced management philosophy, the company will above all concentrate on brand through scientific six brand construction steps, management tools and methods so as to comb management process and optimize the management efficiency.

(4) Implement lean-brand strategy

By removing unnecessary links, reducing needless expenditure, cutting redundant departments, all the staff will become brand-competence-centered and the core competitiveness of brand strategy will be highlighted.

(5) Promote the efficiency of the whole staff

Through the implementation of brand strategy, to revitalize the morale; through the entire personnel learning brand knowledge, to establish faith, spirit, responsibility for the brand and to maximize the quality of work at the lowest cost.

(6) Increase brand equity rapidly

An enterprise's brand strategy is the most valuable investment of this enterprise. Advanced brand technology will help brand equity increase steadily, improve brand investment and brand financial capability, realize the goal of being an international brand and make global brand profit.

SECTION III BRAND TECHNOLOGY

Exercises

1. Multiple-choice Question: Functions of establishing *Brand Construction Project:*
   - It is a proposal submitted to the senior personnel of the enterprise
   - It is a guidelines to guide the construction of enterprise brand with high quality
   - It is a controlled document command the time, budget and effectiveness of controlled brand construction.
   - The above are correct.

2. True or False Question: Brand construction should satisfy three management upgrade issues: from extensive management to professional management, from management structure to management system, from information management to knowledge management. (   )

3. Discussion: There are several scientific processes of brand construction. What are they?

Chapter 4

Brand Classification Technology

Brand classification technology is a kind of classification for brands. It helps distinguish characteristics and brand ability elements through conducting overall classification towards different types of brands.

In the past, when there is no brand classification, people or enterprises think brands are confusing, which makes them unable to rapidly figure out the context of brand ability and accelerate brand construction, because all the brands look similar. As a result, people cannot distinguish LG, Intel, Samsung, Shell, Toyota, and other brands, leading to brand becoming a relatively confusing topic.

As the first time in this field, according to the key abilities necessary for brand development, we divide brands into the following types: professional brand, trusted brand, premium brand, tide brand, leading brand and international brand. After classification, brands are marked with brand key ability factors and ability elements, because of which different brands are easily distinguished, and brand organizations are able to quickly choose certain brand ability elements as their strategic guideline for brand construction, so as to speed up brand construction.

1 Brand classification technology

With respect to brand cultivation and enterprise brand construction of brand economic entities, brand classification technology has thoroughly solved the key problem of "how to carry out brand construction", thus equip brand construction with clear strategic guideline and development direction of structural brand ability.

As a scientific and professional classification of global brands, brand classification technology divides the overall brand ability into the following six key brand abilities.

Professional Brand -- Whether the brand has occupied a professional market field?

Trusted Brand -- Whether the brand is able to make people trust it and buy it?

Premium Brand -- Whether the brand has high profit and whether people are willing to pay more to buy it?

Tide Brand -- Whether people buy the brand for the purpose of following a certain fashion or cultural factor?

Leading Brand -- Whether the brand plays a leading role in a market?

International Brand -- Whether the brand is international enough to develop throughout the world?

* Classification technology is used for professional division of global brands.

* Enterprises can focus on developing one kind of or multiple kinds of key brand ability combination.

Brand classification technology's essential significance is to let investors and employees know what their brands on earth are. Investors know which kind of brand ability will be emphasized by the brand invested, while employees know the specific category of their brands, thus allowing all kinds of investment and strength of all the employees to concentrate on a few brand abilities, so as to avoid unclear selection of brand abilities and rapidly complete brand construction with lesser time, input and hard work of staff than before.

SECTION III BRAND TECHNOLOGY

There is no need for enterprises to develop brand abilities that are unsuitable for them, or follow the brand ability structure of "large and all-inclusive". With brand classification technology, enterprises can focus on developing key brand abilities and choose the quickest brand strategic route. Thanks to substantial reduction of efforts on unnecessary brand construction method, period of brand cultivation has been fundamentally changed, with brand investment and construction period being significantly shortened to 2-3 years. Brand construction no long entails long-term hard work. Brand cultivation has entered a "brand batch production age" characterized by large-scale, large-batch, highly efficient and rapid brand development.

Structure of brand classification technology

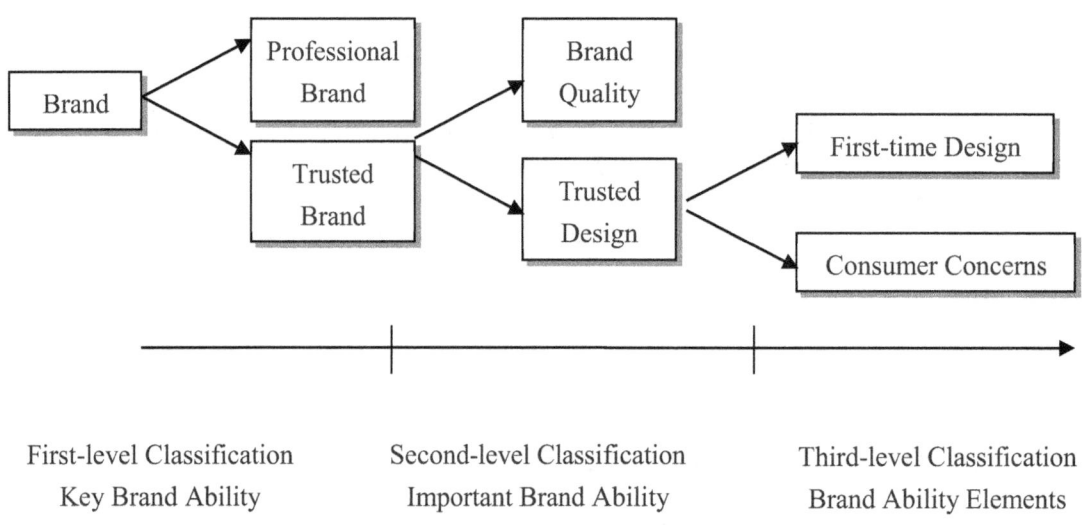

Fig. 9-1 Structure of Brand Classification Technology

The structure of brand classification technology is based on the tree diagram, consisting of three levels of classification: the first-level classification is key brand ability; the second-level classification is important brand ability; the third-level classification is brand ability elements.

Brand classification technology aims to solve the problems of brand diversity, brand ability comparison and formulation of brand strategic route. That is to say, pay attention to brand diversity and divide brand abilities into several groups based on the tree diagram according to different characteristics, thus visually displaying various possibilities of brand construction; conducting brand ability comparison can help enterprises to rapidly improve specific brand abilities and optimize key brand abilities, which allows enterprises to focus on the key work of brand management and then significantly improve their brand management level and user satisfaction degree; during the process of formulating brand strategic route, brand classification technology can help enterprises quickly choose their brand strategic routes and their own list of brand ability elements that needed to be focused on according to the list, so as to greatly improve the brand cultivation success rate and brand construction speed.

1.2 Brand ability element list

Brand Ability Element List consists of 6 key brand abilities, 60 important brand abilities and 240 brand ability elements.

With the birth of Brand Ability Element List, the concept of brand which was vague in global brand theory has a clear classification from now on, and brand construction has come into a new stage of clear brand ability construction. The list is an important milestone in brand history. It marks that enterprises only need to select a small number of appropriate brand ability elements to quickly determine their brand strategic routes and then complete brand construction in a period of 2-3 years, thus realizing the full speed improvement from professional brands to international brands.

Pursuant to arrangement and decomposition of brand ability elements, enterprises have no need to expense too much energy in aimless brand construction. The three-level structure of brand ability elements not only reflect the inner structure of brand ability, but also eliminate relevant influences of brand ability, allowing enterprises to concentrate their attention and investment on improving a small number of brand abilities.

The application value of brand ability elements remains to be confirmed in the whole world. Some international media and research institutions have applied brand classification technology and brand ability elements in selection of brand awards and comparison research on brands. What's more, the brand ability element list can contribute to the establishment of brand index and improvement of brand ability performance in the same industry or relevant categories.

1.3 Invention significance of brand classification technology

The invention of brand classification technology mainly depends on the following five factors:

(1) Being similar with the periodic table of chemical element. Invention of periodic table of chemical element means a lot to the improvement of chemical industry. It allows scientists to decompose elements, invent new compounds and discover new elements based on combination of chemical elements.

(2) Carrying out benchmarking management. Improve management level by establishing explicit management samples and standard as the benchmark and studying the scientific law, nature and methods of management. Benchmark research on comparison of individual brand abilities can be conducted based on the brand ability element list.

(3) Selecting brand strategic routes. By employing brand classification technology, brand organizations can quickly select the ability elements fit for themselves in the brand ability element list to formulate their own strategic routes and rapidly conduct brand construction, thus thoroughly overcome the common problem of "how to carry out brand construction".

(4) Rapidly conducting brand diagnosis. By comparing the brand ability element list, rapidly conducting brand diagnosis according to the brand strategic routes selected by enterprises. With more specific and explicit brand ability elements, diagnose specific brand problems, so as to contribute to improvement of brand ability.

(5) Establishing the basis for brand rating, evaluation and index. Brand classification technology is the main basis for establishing brand rating, evaluation project or brand index. Through the selection of brand specialty categories or brand ability elements, brand classification technology can help conduct brand ability performance rating of brands all over the world, especially the peer review or comparison review with respect to the same brand ability element, which contributes to the brand ability improvement of a same industry or relevant enterprises in the global range.

2 Professional brand

Definition: A brand focusing on one thing and eliminating unnecessary links.

Objective: The first step for any brand is to be professional, because only professional brands can be accurately identified by people.

Tasks:

(1) Centralize advantages to realize accurate identification;

(2) Eliminate unnecessary activities to create a lean brand;
(3) Segregate users to occupy the professional market;
(4) Quickly acquire investing and financial ability.

2.1 Characteristics of professional brand

Establishing professional brands is the key strategic route for enterprises especially for small and medium-sized enterprises to win in competition. Professional brands can enter the market and segregate users rapidly. By representing specific needs of users, professional brands can occupy the commanding height of market, thus acquiring higher profits and help enterprises realize fastest and maximum development.

For consumers and enterprises, professional brand means: right purchasing choice, optimal choice, preclusive purchasing, no purchasing risk, higher expense, enjoyment of professional service, professional solutions, repeat recommendation to friends, repeat purchasing, investment focus, rapid growth of enterprise and strong market defense ability.

2.2 Examples of professional brand

Nike: Representative of professional sports goods in the world.

DuPont: Always committed to building professional brand, known for plenty of chemical inventions – new materials and technologies.

Dolby: Dolby laboratory is always committed to developing sound technology.

Band-Aid: Synonym for skin wound hemostasis.

Vienna: the City of Music – Vienna New Year's Concert.

2.3 Ability Element List for Professional Brand

1. Brand strategy	2. Brand cluster	3. Brand definition	4. User division	5. Ingredient brand
Market selection	Brand portfolio	Brand position	Usage division	Ingredient definition
Strategic framework	Brand professionalization	Key strategy	Group division	Ingredient enchantment
Strategic resources	Brand investment	Positioning communication	User locking	Collaborative purchasing
Strategic management	Brand asset	Brand substitution	User group	Ingredient charm

6. Brand recognition	7. Professional market	8. Professional competition	9. Tide concept	10. Brand state
Professional recognition	Professional status	Core competence	Fashion elements	Brand diagnosis
Exclusive identity	Professional sources	Competitive ability	Fashion trend	Brand evaluation
Professional features	solutions	Industrial competition	Hot topic	Brand report
Recognition system	Professional application	Competition defense	Conceptual trend	Consumption data

2.4 Cases of professional brand

As sports brands, adidas, BILLABONG and Quiksilver have implemented different professional brand strategy.

Adidas is a German sports goods manufacturer that focused on producing footwear products. Mainly through sponsoring sports events, adidas has established its professional role as the best sports goods equipment provider for professional athletes, thus attracting sports enthusiasts to follow.

BILLABONG is an Australian surfing leisure brand. At first, it was a water sports brand for surfers, and gradually combines with Australian surfing life style and establishes its brand style as today. It focuses on board sports and its design best represents the street style in various water sports brands, which makes it popular in teenagers in recent years.

Quiksilver is defined as a fashion clothing company. As an international surfing brand, Quiksilver pays great attention to interpreting the beach culture which has been a new favorite of fashion.

2.5 Development of ingredient brand

Ingredient brand is a key method for brand development in the category of professional brand. In addition to market supply of ingredient products, license fee is the main technical income of ingredient brand. Ingredient brand refers to brands providing essential ingredients including materials, elements and components for products of some brands. Famous ingredient brands include Dolby NR, Gore-tex waterproof nylon and Teflon non-stick coating, etc. Ingredient brand is aiming at making consumers form adequate recognition and preference, so that they will not buy any product without its ingredients.

Typical examples: DuPont Teflon, used in insulating materials, anti-sticking coating, etc., has become an irreplaceable professional brand product; the automotive technical department is the largest and the most profitable department in BOSCH Auto.

3 Trusted brand

Definition: Acquire long-term and stable income with trusted design, unfailing performance, reliable quality and quality stability.

SECTION III BRAND TECHNOLOGY

Objective: The foundation of any brand is trust, because only when a brand is trustworthy then people buy it without hesitation.

Tasks:

(1) Make people rest assured to buy and remove their doubts;

(2) Have a long-term and stable source of income;

(3) Become a first-class brand and more reliable than other brands in the same industry;

(4) Make old users spontaneously recommend the brand to new users.

3.1 Characteristics of trusted brand

The first key factor for any successful brand is trust. If a brand is trustworthy, the consumer decision-making process will be significantly shortened. Known and trusted brands can improve sales results at the greatest extent.

For consumers and enterprises, trusted brand means: trusted product source, stable and excellent quality, extremely low purchasing risk, fast recognition and purchasing, reliable brand, repeat riskless purchasing, recommendable brand, enterprise quickly obtaining operation returns and basis of enterprise competitive advantages.

3.2 Examples of trusted brand

Made in Germany: Always committed to trusted brand construction; started to adopt the brand marking of "German Engineering" in 1960s, emphasized on the outstanding quality of Made in Germany.

American Cotton Mark: Cotton products containing over 50% American cotton can use the American Cotton Mark.

Intel: Committed to producing chips that are most reliable in performance.

Singapore: Providing the best environment for business.

3.3 Ability element list for trusted brand

1. Brand quality	2. Important information	3. Trusted design	4. First-time trust	5. Reliable support
Faith in quality	Product source	Reliable communication	Purchasing attempt	Management style
Synonym for quality	Brand mission	First-time trust design	Application risk	Brand ability support
Quality behavior	Brand commitment	Trusted contact point	Damage the trust	Brand strength
Quality stability	Brand background	Remove doubts	Continuous trust	Brand performance

6.Brand safety	7.Brand dependency	8.Informing user	9.User evaluation	10.Information correction
Quality guarantee	Dependency elements	Enterprise movement	Third-party evaluation	Information asymmetry
After-sales guarantee	Market area	Product development	Comparison evaluation	Purchase correction
Secure purchase	Reduce identity cost	Information disclosure	User interaction	Trusted information correction
Safe consumption	Market defense	Implicit information	Expertise evaluation	Brand communication correction

3.4 Studies on trusted brand ability: service brand

Service brand is a key field of trusted brand. By providing professional service, service brand can realize explicit service identity and brand service premium. Typical service brands include Blue Wrench, Golden Wrench, First-time Service and Cheverolet Complete Care.

4 Premium brand

Definition: Premium brand is brand that has successfully lowered people sensitivity towards price, and people are willing to pay more to purchase its products.

Objective: Handsome profits can be generated from brand premium ability; strong premium ability is equivalent to high profits.

Tasks:

(1) Develop premium ability and significantly increase the band profit;

(2) Sell at a higher price than other brands in the same industry;

(3) Eliminate people's price sensitivity;

(4) Obtain the brand asset.

4.1 Characteristics of premium brand

Premium brand sells products at a higher price than other brands in the same industry and obtains higher profit. It helps enterprises to obtain a good return on brand investment including brand designing, product investment, management investment and service investment, and makes enterprises change essentially in various aspects including market scale, customer quality and customer consumption capacity.

For consumers and enterprises, premium brand means: enterprise management upgrading, enterprise product upgrading, enterprise service upgrading, better brand trust, more exquisite design, better quality, better enjoyment, first choice for distinguished group, symbol for quality and status, a must-have for consumers when they are ready, high ROI for enterprises and strong revenue ability.

Note: after-sales service can be developed into an independent premium brand, such as IBM. What's more, printer original consumables, automotive original components and medical equipment after-sales service are all designed as service premium brand.

4.2 Examples of premium brand

South Korea: The South Korean Government prohibits South Korean brands from discounting or selling at low price and requires these brands to pursue high quality and high premium. The slogan of South Korean brands is: Hanyang people who are active in the Presidential Council on Nation Branding strive for their best to earn a high international reputation for South Korea and improve the national value.

Made in America: Made in America -- High premium ability

LV: Committed to high brand premium

Korean Ginseng: Its export price is 10 times of Chinese ginseng.

4.3 Ability Element List for Premium Brand

1.Brand profit	2. Customer classification	3. Brand awareness	4. Brand system	5.Brand shape
Profit design	Specific customer	Brand faith	Brand history	Science brand
Key profit	Customer requirements research	Awareness design	Brand story	Manufacturing brand
Profit chain	Customer development	Specific element	Brand communication	Element brand
Profit optimization	User reference	Awareness manufacturing	Self-adaptive brand	Service brand

6.Brand impression	7.Brand quality	8.Brand investment	9.Brand information	10.Service profit chain
Brand intuition	Brand feeling	Promotion investment	Background information	Service
Brand characteristic	quality leadership	Management investment	Performance information	Whole staff after-sales service

Brand price	Users feeling	R&D investment	Technology information	Salary structure
Newest and hottest	Quality stability	Service investment	Comparison among the industry	Regular customer plan

5 Tide brand

Definition: Trigger and lead the trend, or attract interest group with certain culture, environment and element.

Objective: The trendsetting ability of tide brands will lead people to rush to buy their products; it is able to fully make use of emotional consuming and human desires.

Tasks:

(1) Create a fashion trend;

(2) Employ the trend to realize large-scale impulse purchasing;

(3) Have a fixed consumer group with specific elements;

(4) People hope to satisfy their desires through consumption.

5.1 Characteristics of tide brand

Tide brand can stimulate people's purchasing desires and lead the fashion trend, so as to trigger impulsive buying and chasing purchase. Tide brand is the preferred choice for people pursuing trend, fashion and specific cultural pleasure. It divides users according to their preferences and only serves the wants and needs of certain users who met the requirements, Tide brand can help enterprises to find their own user group and realize repeat selling via direct marketing.

For consumers and enterprises, tide brand means: fashion trend, preferred choice for coolest and the most fashionable group, specific follower group, fashion elements, fast-selling goods, meeting specific demands, must-have for certain consumption, the simplest way to get return on investment, low market development cost, direct marketing effects, returns on multiple repeat selling.

5.2 Examples of tide brand

Apple Inc.: Create a fashion trend.

Starbucks: Create a kind of coffee culture.

Uniquely Singapore: Tourism fashion.

Italian Furniture: We are the symbol of design philosophy.

5.3 Ability element list for tide brand

1.Brand desire	2.Concept brand	3.Cool brand	4. Tide brand	5.Popular brand
Desire decomposition	Concept compose	Cool positioning	Tide positioning	Popular element

SECTION III BRAND TECHNOLOGY

Desire positioning	Concept product	Cool element	Tide sensory	Popular movement
Desire background	Industrial design	Cool shape	Fashion trend	Popular trend
Desire catch	Package design	Cool topic	Tide warm up	Popular market

6. Topic brand	7. Theme brand	8. Fast brand	9. Integrated brand	10. Dream brand
Hot topic	Theme structure	Fast company	Brand strategy	Future brand
Topic trigger	Theme element	Fast consumption	Product integration	Shocking brand
Topic guidance	Theme diffusion	Fast feeling	Market entry	Brand imagination
Topic diffusion	Theme guidance	Fast popular	Intensive promotion	Brand attraction

6 Leading brand

Definition: Take the leading position with respect to a kind of market demand; have enough strength and influence; set up defensive barriers.

Objective: Its strategy design ability based on trends and attacking ability will determine the brand competition pattern in the market.

Significance:

(1) Determine the industrial direction and affect the competition pattern;

(2) Take the leading position with respect to market share;

(3) Have market authority influence and speaking right;

(4) Set up automatic defensive barriers to protect its market share.

6.1 Characteristics of leading brand

As the center stage of media public opinion, the focus topic of people from all circles and the fashion leader followed by the market, leading brand means the focus of all the attention. It represents the future of the whole industry, takes the largest part in market share and the most authoritative market position and has the most powerful voice. Representing the outstanding leader image of enterprises, leading brand drives the overall market revenue with its leader's charisma, and centralize the best resources in the market.

For consumers and enterprises, leading brand means: preferred choice, must-have, necessity, essential elements, assured purchase, exclusive purchase, repeat purchase, repeat communication of consumers, self-adaptive sales, the most desired return on investment, market resource maximization, market profit maximization, market scale maximization, future market space maximization and the strongest defensive ability in local market.

6.2 Examples of leading brand

Land Rover: Pure British blood
HP 6L: Birth of classic products
Microsoft: The world's IT leader
Google: Committed to making the world's best search engine
Sunkist: Authentic American Sunkist orange
AK47: Birth of a world's classic legend

6.3 Ability element list for leading brand

1. Brand status	2. Lead brand	3. Power brand	4. Strength embodiment	5. Public consciousness
Leader status	Lead trend	Powerful design	Capital strength	Public recognition
Market share	Front exploration	Show of strength	Development strength	Public communication
Market strategy	Lead opinion	Brand ability	Scale strength	good selling process
Brand ally	Heroic figure	Brand potential	User strength	Public relations

6. Strong brand	7. consumption attitude	8. Brand experience	9. Lead element	10. Brand market
Brand strength	Brand purchase by name	User experience design	Brand quality	Brand substitution
Market attack	user preference	Brand feeling	Brand performance	Brand coverage
Brand association	Consumption	User attention	Leadership	Block and

Section III Brand Technology

	consciousness			compete
Milestone	Consumption ability	Experience correction	Leader effect	Brand defending

7 International brand

Definition: Meet the international standards; realize global outreach; enter the brand development phase of biological balance.

Objective: International brand is the synonym for first-class quality and high reliability. Its products are appropriate for the market in any country.

Tasks:

(1) Global reach ability;

(2) Global premium ability;

(3) The whole brand chain is a self-adaptive ecological balanced system.

(4) Strong ability and strategic competition advantages.

7.1 Characteristics of international brand

International brand has comprehensively entered markets throughout the world. By integrating international popular elements, it has become the best choice for international users and can help enterprises to obtain revenue in various places and forms. International brand makes it easier for enterprises to obtain revenue from high-income countries and make use of international trade gap. It grants enterprises with higher revenue guarantee and strong market occupation ability.

For consumers and enterprises, international brand means: the most trusted one, the best choice, preferred choice when they can afford, the most trusted high quality, cutting-edge design, the best R&D ability, the most exquisite manufacturing technique, the best material, the best talents, optimal operation method, symbol for lifestyle, international enjoyment, faster market speed, wisest investment choice, largest market scale, strongest revenue ability, markets in high-income countries, markets in developed countries and the strongest defensive ability in overall market.

7.2 Examples of international brand

IBM: During the time when Thomas ·J· Watson changed CTR to IBM, he has showed his brand aspiration and dream

Coca Cola: Brought to all parts of the world by the US army

FedEX: The global dream of second-day delivery

Hong Kong: The Asia's World City

Ireland: Celtic Tiger; European headquarters economic cluster

7.3 Ability element list for international brand

1. Global brand	2. International brand	3. Brand Internationalization	4. International market	5. Brand Influence
Brand reach	Brand positioning	Brand strategy	Market entry	Brand reputation measure
Global reputation	Brand ability	Brand design	Market coverage	Brand concept
Recognition	Brand feeling	Brand image	Market access	Brand culture
Brand pattern	Brand information	Brand identity	Market response	Brand fans

6. Brand credibility	7. Quality trust	8. Mature brand	9. Brand property	10. Brand expansion
Public credit	Lead level	Brand maturity	Brand trust	Brand strategy
Specific credit	Brand enjoyment	Brand stability	Brand valuation	Brand investment
Brand effect	Brand trust	Representative brand	Brand finance	Brand extension
Crisis public relations	Brand pursue	Brand management	Brand economy	Brand equity

8 Application of brand classification technology

Band classification technology divides the brands into six brand types which also known as six key brand abilities, which are professional brand, trusted brand, premium brand, tide brand and international brand. Each key brand's ability contains 10 important brand abilities and a brand ability element list which is composed of 40 brand ability elements.

An enterprise only needs to rapidly figure out which type of brand it wants to build, determine their choice of brand strategy development route, select several ability elements from the Brand Ability Element List to focus on, and then the selection of brand strategic route is completed.

By employing brand classification technology, "brand" is no longer a confusing and vague concept, and has turned into an accurate, scientific and effective ability elements combination. The completion of brand strategic route designing only needs enterprises to select several brand ability elements and rapidly combine them, which is so simple and effective.

Section III Brand Technology

8.1 How to develop brand ability elements?

Application of brand classification technology mainly manifests in enterprises' brand construction and improvement of brand management ability. Any enterprise needs to answer the following question:

(1) In your opinion, which key brand ability should your enterprise develop?

(2) Which brand ability elements can you find in your enterprise brand?

Enterprises application of brand classification technology and Brand Ability Element List is mainly completed via four steps: strategy selection, advantage analysis, problem diagnosis and implementation.

Step one: Strategy selection. Figure out the brand business separation of the enterprise and select a development strategic route from the Brand Ability Element List.

Step two: Advantage analysis. According to selected brand ability elements, analyze all the existing advantages by employing PADS scientific analysis model.

Step three: Problem diagnosis. With the assistance of brand technical experts, find the existing problems through problem diagnosis and then improve the strategic route and advantages.

Step four: Implementation. Take the finally selected brand ability elements as the focus of brand improvement or rebuilding, and improve on such elements.

8.2 Examples: Used for formulating brand strategic route

The A brand should strengthen the professional brand in brand classification, which is the strategic foundation of its development.

The current strategy of B brand should be focusing on developing professional brand in brand classification and develop into leading brand.

The C brand should focus on developing premium brand in the classification and complete the concept design and industrial design in concept brand, as well as thematic structure and elements in theme brand. Strategic route of the brands in C country: Focus on developing trusted brand. Brand quality is the key work of this brand. Without high quality, the brand will lose its root. Even though it can develop in quantity, brand premium cannot be realized. As a result, the brand can "go out", but will not develop into a well known international brand.

The strategic route of M Brand: Focus on developing user preference, market attack, brand quality, experience correction, brand substitution, category coverage and other brand elements; give play to leading brand effect in terminal brand market; take service-learning and whole-staff after-sales service as the driving force of brand marketing network.

8.3 Examples: Used for brand diagnosis

Brand Diagnostic Report

Brand: LINING

Brand status:

1) Massive decrease in brand profits, decline of the market position.

2) Previously apply the ZIBA methodology, make mistakes during execution and product definition comes before brand positioning. Divide the users into athlete, sports participant and sports enthusiast. Subdivide the product line into professional sport, urban light sport and sports life.

3) Still insist on the tide brand line, focus on young consumers. Late in its brand strategy execution, shifted focus to sports life series, and suffered a crushing defeat.

Symptoms:

1) Wrong method for brand classification. ZIBA method implements a pan-brand classification route, which forms a similar products competition with Adidas and ANTA, leading to the loss of competitiveness.

2) Give up the core part -- Professional brand area, severely weakened in professional ability. In professional sports area mainly relies on a relation-based market; show a weak international competitiveness when it comes to normal circumstance and public level; unable to internationalize the brand without the special national conditions of China.

Diagnostic opinion:

1) Brands R&D approach must be changed. Sports goods brands must follow the brand tribalism route. In other words, brands must develop products and enter the market with some sports lines or interest lines. For sports lines, such as tennis line and cycling line, we can develop a series of peripheral products focusing on professional sports events. For interest lines, such as skiing lines and glider line, a product line about interest is feasible. Sports line is professional, and interest line is tide user.

2) Brand product line development. Focus on project management and sports lines, accompanied by interest lines. Every project development must ensure that the product meets the highest quality standard of international, aiming at international competition. Stabilize a professional market of sports lines, or an interests market of interests lines, then develop the second professional market or interests market, and so on.

3) Brand development route: Firstly, develop the key abilities of professional brand. Secondly, develop the key abilities of international brand. Thirdly, develop the key abilities of tide brand. Premium brand can be highlighted. And do not rush to be the leading brand currently.

Exercises

1. Fill in the Blanks: As a scientific and professional classification of global brands, brand classification technology divides the overall brand ability into the following six key brand abilities: _____, _____, _____, _____, _____ and _____.

2. Essay Question: Which factors constitute the basis of brand classification by employing brand classification technology?

3. Discussion: Why brand classification technology can solve a large quantity of brand cultivation problems?

SECTION III BRAND TECHNOLOGY

Chapter 5

Brand Recognition Technology

Brand recognition technology consists of three aspects, namely brand idea recognition (brand ideology), corporate identity and brand impression recognition design. By focusing on these three aspects, we can build a unique brand image that the public, costumers and investors will see.

Brand recognition methods based on new media, social network and interpersonal communication network of the modern society are quite different from the corporate identity in the past. It is no longer limited to the reified image recognition, but the display of brand impression in multi-dimensional structure and multiple perspectives, which needs to establish a kind of ideology, psychological sense, memory elements and impression recognition.

1 Brand idea (brand ideology)

Brand ideology refers to the forming of unique brand idea, brand concept and features of brand recognition. This kind of ideology can be understood as a kind of comprehensible imagination and a kind of methods and specific memory for observing and judging matters.

Ideology refers to various sensory thoughts that people generated on things and conceptual understanding of ideas, views, concepts and values, etc. Strong brands usually can form independent brand ideology, while weak brands generally cannot form distinctive recognition features of ideology expressions.

For instance, Vidal Sassoon (VS) is always committed to lead the fashion trend of hairdressing. Using a pair of scissors with limitless inspirations, it has not only created numerous classic and remarkable hair styles, but also raised fashion booms round after round on the fashion stage. VS deduces inspirations from all fields, from nostalgic rock music to modern T-stage fashion show, from classic architecture to the universe waiting to be explored. Each hair style created by VS displays its creative spirit, building a new age of hair style trend advocating the pursuit of fashion and personality.

People always associate VS with hairdressing fashion trend, thereby forming a social ideology about hairdressing. As a result, people remember this brand in a stable structure, and every time they mention VS, they always can recall this association. Brand organizations build exclusive user understanding and cognition through all kinds of specific and unspecific elements, feelings, environments and symbols.

1.1 Unique brand proposition: brand ideology construction

Brand ideology construction must firstly form a unique proposition which is fully independent, including unique thinking structure, unique management style, unique awareness transfers and unique culture type. This kind of unique proposition develops from unique to exclusive, which is the prerequisite for the forming and the further mature development of brand ideas.

Unique brand proposition may not always be consistent with unique selling proposition (selling point), but the former is far above the latter. Brand proposition is a kind of culture and value transfer and also the unfailing historical mission along with the development of brand organizations, while selling proposition may vary to an extent with times and locations to adapt to the specific markets at different times and locations.

In the idea construction process of brand ideology, unique proposition as a group of brand ideas is the "superstructure" of brand organizations, and it can deeply influence the way of thinking, value orientation, using habit and exclusive choice of the public and users with a series of ideas, views and concepts.

What we need to think about is: what has been changed by brands on earth and which lifestyles have been changed by brands? For example, Nescafe has brought high-quality and tasty coffee and coffee culture to the worldwide markets; Amazon has changed the way people purchase books; Facebook has changed the interpersonal communication patterns on internet; the invention of Diners cards has changed people's payment method.

1.2 Brand sense portraying: Portray brand image

Brand organizations try to make a deep sensory impression on people in various aspects such as product quality, appearance, packing, performance, taste and advertisements, and hope that while hearing of or talking about their brands, the brand users and the public can promptly recall the memory of the brand images, which allows the specific senses to pop up in people's mind immediately.

UPS Express is committed to international courier that covers the whole world. Its coat of arms logo with the well-marked "UPS" stresses the speediness, safety and stability of UPS; the advertisements and brand news launched by UPS try their best to give a specific description on the safe arrival and advanced scientific and technological capacity during the global delivery process of important, influential and special things, all of which combining with the exploration of special ways of delivery help to form a completed classic brand impression.

For instance, UPS has carried out a series of advertisements and brand news that are built around the delivery of The Terra-Cotta Warriors to form a group of brand images, which was made on a series of themes including *From Qin Dynasty to America – A Magic Journey of The Terra-Cotta Warriors*, *UPS New Logistics Ensure The Terra – Cotta Warriors A Safe Journey*, *UPS Meteorologist Ensure On-time Delivery with The Latest Technology*, and *No Afraid of Challenge – UPS Successfully Delivery The Terra-Cotta Warriors*.

IBM builds brand sensory images through real stories and people of small and medium-sized enterprises solutions, so as to let people associate the brand images with the work site environment of enterprises' daily IT application. Through the TV advertisement "Want to check whether your computer is excellent? Please find the logo of Intel", Intel explicitly emphasizes the specific brand image that "Excellent computers must have the logo of Intel".

When these images have taken roots in people's memories, people will have a relatively clear and complete brand images in mind while talking about or seeing these brand names.

1.3 Brand users division: divided by trends

It is impossible for a brand organization to make the whole population in the world to become its users, so it can only selectively distinguish a portion of market of users. For this reason, brand organizations have formed a series of different trends in terms of colors, patterns, styles and beliefs, namely, black, blue, red, white, purple and other typical colors, or American style, European style, Chinese style, Korean style, Japanese style and other different cultural styles, so as to segregate users. In order to further segregate the users, special cultural styles which are more classical such as Italian design, British fantasy style and American Hollywood style may be adopted.

These cultural elements formed in terms of colors, patterns, styles and beliefs help international brands to be ever successful in the global market. Sometimes, in order to enter the market in a foreign country, international brands may add the local cultural elements to their publicity. According to the specific cultural custom, they make the corresponding TV advertisements. In this way, these brands are deeply rooted in local markets.

There are also some brand organizations creating their own brand styles to form their special recognition elements which may be the environments, packing or users' usage experience, thus forming their unique trends in a certain sense. These brand organizations intensively promote these trends, so as to make users adapt to and get familiar with such typical unique trends.

Obviously, differentiating trends aims to segregate brand users. The series of *Harry Potter*, with the global total sales of over 500 million books and total box office returns of USD 7.8 billion, is the highest-grossing film series in the world's film history, and has revitalized the Celtic cultural style and also brought back a strong upsurge of cultural root-seeking. Not everybody likes *Harry Potter*, but the effects cultural trends have on user segregation are strong enough to make global brand organizations to consider creating their own brand trends. It is a kind of achievement that a brand is able to satisfy a kind of cultural type, find a fashion trend and create a fashionable style.

1.4 Brand image expression

Marlboro represents the typical rough cowboys in the Western United States; State Express 555 shows the typical British gentlemen style; LV always shows the lifestyle of graceful upper-class women in its advertisements; Haier has influenced a generation of Chinese young people and their deep understanding of Haier brand by producing the cartoon – *Haier Brothers*; Singapore tourism has enriched people's impression on Singapore with the fashionable Merlion statue.

By concretizing brand images, many brands have always been committed to give specific expressions to their images and try best to create a kind of recognition memory which can impress people deeply, integrating brands with specific lifestyle, spirit and style, so as to improve the recognition rate and create recognition images which are totally different from that of other competitive brand products of the same kind.

Concretized image memory design of brands makes people habitually associate brands with their images, which can reduce the recognition costs incurred by brand users, therefore help brands bypass the "price" issue and create better brand images with higher prices. This kind of design aims to comprehensively realize the brand premium.

The most typical example of brand image expression will be Disney. It has created Mickey Mouse, Donald Duck and other virtual images as well as theme parks, and such virtual images in turn have become Disney's best image representatives, showing Disney's new type of cultural delights, while the Disney theme parks which are similar to magical and dreamlike kingdoms further emphasis more distinctive image expressions such as dream, creativity, fantasy, smile and naivety.

In addition, countries and regions may build typical images by constructing landmark buildings or employing typical image design, such as concretizing abstract images through urban landscape, characteristic architectural styles and city dreams.

For instance, Dubai has directly attracted the global attention through building the world's first seven-star hotel (Burj Al Arab Hotel), the world's highest skyscraper (Burj Khalifa Tower), the world's largest shopping center and the world's largest indoor ski slope, which has made it into a synonym for luxury, and then rapidly developed into a global economic and financial center. Besides numerous huge construction projects, Dubai spreads its strong influence with its active real estate market and competition and conference holding. Another example is Xi'an City in China. By shooting the documentary *Xi'an in 2020*, Xi'an has presented the future blueprint of the city and inspired people's longing, confidence and passion for the city's future.

1.5 Heavy brands and light brands

Nowadays, brands develop in a watershed with two kinds of development types, namely heavy brands and light brands. Heavy brands refer to brands that are developed with heavy investment in advertising such as TV advertising, outdoor advertising, magazine advertising and TV program sponsoring; light brands refer to brands that are developed through communication methods such as internet communication, mobile communication and interpersonal communication, therefore people usually cannot see any advertisements posting by light brands.

Heavy brands attach importance to visual presentation of brands and brand products, which lead people to form recognition memory with repeated appearance of LOGO and product images, while light brands emphasis on the natural communication of brands, which lead people to memorize the brand image with the ever-present process of using, discussing and communicating.

In the modern development of brands, we believe that the trend of light brands will become more obvious. Brands are spreading imperceptibly everywhere via people's causal media communication and interpersonal communication. Unlike heavy brands which aim to shape images, light brands emphasis on communication characteristic, laying particular stress on people's discussion of brands and self-communication.

Light brands have another characteristic -- young-oriented. That is to say, aiming at developing into fashionable and young brands, light brands pay attention to combining brands with the fashion medias used by young people, and conduct communication with young people's communication habits and trends, so as to develop their brand user group among the young generation.

1.6 Brand planning proposal (market activity project)

Marketing planning proposal is a type of writing which is used for brand market activity planning. It reflects the originality, resource combination and market arrangement via planning, so as to achieve certain market action goals.

Planning is the arrangement of creative thinking, originality, plans and resources. The thoughts in planning depend on the creative consideration at the ideology level; the nature of planning is different from the rest; the planning ability and scale depend on the resource assignment. To be precise, planning mainly depends on the application of strategic resources. Based on different levels of resources application ability that are supporting the planning, some important factors include the possible scales and locations of activities, level of participating people, news media which can be employed, cooperating organizations and investment amount may vary, thus planning proposals differ in thousands of ways in the forms of levels, grades and effects.

The essence of planning is achieving success with original ideas. Only the novel, creative and distinctive ideas can produce the best planning effects. The function of planning is to gain maximum effect with minimum input. We are not saying that there is no input or little input, but this kind of input shall correspond to the effect, so it takes great efforts to realize the most appropriate ratio of input to return.

Centering on brand planning activities, planning proposal is the overall practicable text scheme of planning activities. A planning proposal is completed through detailed arrangements and allocations for each link such as inviting people according to the planning content, site service, activity process, media support, light and stereo, site ambience, personnel arrangement and budget for expenditure, and then submitted to relevant departments of the brand organization for review and discussion.

Generally speaking, a brand planning proposal is also an execution guidance which a brand organization can follow in accordance to execute all the links specified therein so as to fully complete all kinds of tasks and achieve all the effects required in the brand planning proposal.

In the history of modern brand technology development, it is impractical to only rely on brand planning to complete the overall construction and development of a brand. More often it plays a role of assisting, serving, subdividing or extending in the whole task. Brand planning proposals are generally managed by the brand marketing department or communication department, and exist as a type of writing used for carrying out daily brand marketing communication. According to demands, a brand planning proposal may include: activity planning, evening party planning, advertising planning, website planning, project planning, public relations planning, communication planning and other specific works.

SECTION III BRAND TECHNOLOGY

1.7 Brand project proposal (special project management)

Different from brand planning proposal, brand project proposal is mainly used to design the execution details of a specific brand task or discuss about an improvement plan.

Proposal originated from Japan. Generally speaking, the first page of a project proposal is about a concept or improvement for a problem, that is to say, propose a specific and distinct concept or problem and then complete the study and development of such concept or problem via the overall process of formulating the project proposal.

When an enterprise decides to make a picture album, contents of a syndicate column, a TV ads script or a brand website design, it can employ project proposal to complete the setting of each role, pilot, expression form and the compound model of key elements, and then form standard elements and process. Comparing with planning proposal which is just "semi-completed" and cannot present standard elements and process in details, project proposal has stricter making requirements and execution guidance, thus the specific designing, making and shooting works shall be conducted in strict accordance with the project proposal.

Project proposal can also be used to improve the existing problems, following the process of proposing a problem, conducting strategic analysis and improvement analysis and then proposing an improvement strategy.

The purpose of project proposal is to conduct specific and detailed study, improvement or design and production of a creative design or an improvement project. Project proposal in Japan has formed various patterns, various mature application methods and various project tools, which can be used as reference for everyone. Project proposal can be used in combination with planning proposal. However, in our opinion, planning proposal cannot replace project proposal, because project proposal as an important type of writing used in enterprise marketing and communication has greater application values and effects and is more precise, scientific and regulated than planning proposal.

2 Corporate identity recognition

The use of corporate identity recognition system is pretty prevalent today. Enterprises in the world all attach great attention to corporate identity recognition system design. There are a large number of design companies, designers and books in this field. It has become a relatively wide and professional design service area, and we do not need to talk about it any further here.

The only caveat is to pay attention to the design of brand name. Some enterprises like to name the brand after the enterprise, thus it easily caused confusion between enterprise name and brand name. Certainly the two names can be the same or different, which is decided by the enterprise's strategy. However, according to actual observation, most international enterprises hold more than one brand, so they have to design every brand individually in order to let different brand focus on different specific market.

Brand name should be as unique as possible. When you are about to name a brand, Google it at first, the less search results come out, the better. Because the brand name itself can become a search keyword. When it is becoming a hot search, every search result under this word will point to the brand. On the contrary, if there are too many namesakes, it will cause brand ambiguity, which can adversely affect brand recognition. Today brand recognition may spread just via oral or written communication, without image, costume design and other factors. It must be ensured that when users look for new brands on the Internet, your brand will be there at the first time round, and search engines will show the complete information about your brand.

3 Brand impression recognition

Unlike the previous corporate identity, today and future's brand recognition is impression recognition dominated, which is accelerated by internet, mobile internet, new media and interpersonal network. Brand recognition has entered an age of multi-dimensional network-wide communication. And it is gradually out of the existing forms of vision recognition, such as LOGO, television advertisement, mail, costume, car body, environment and picture albums.

In many cases, brand recognition has simply evolved into written or oral communication characterized by telling names and descriptions, in which content communication plays a very important role. So we need to figure out how people find, get to know and remember a brand, only in this way can we design a modern, brand-impression-based brand recognition system.

The process of designing and building a brand impression system is a kind of research or exploration that is completely based on brand communication and memory characteristic. We have to do experiments, tests and amendments, in order to build a high quality brand impression recognition system which has unique differentiation and can be distinguished from all others.

3.1 Brand recognition principles: Self-promotion

Brand organizations should pay attention to visual or objective information presentation method such as searching online and referring to friends, thus systemically construct a new overall impression system for brands.

Brands have an obvious characteristic of self-promotion. Seeing, hearing, considering and consciousness are four typical brand impression identification ways. The self-discovery, self-seeking, self-recognition, self-recommendation and self-judgment of brands have constituted a kind of highly self-organized behaviors, rather than passive brand promotion as before. Brand organizations should pay attention to the rapid development of this trend, so as to form a new generation of customer self-perception system and then speed up the process of brand impression recognition, as shown in Fig12-1.

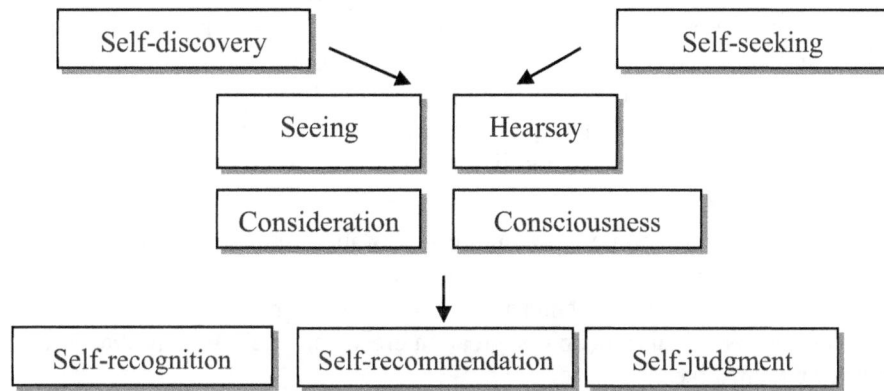

Fig. 12-1 Brand Recognition Principles: Self-promotion

People know about new brands mainly through reading online news which are mainly text news and rarely image-text news. If people intensively see a brand while reading news, they will have a deep impression of this brand. A story referred in an online article may contain an introduction of a brand, while people may consciously search and understand the brand via search engines or online links. "Seeing" may also be realized in daily life unwittingly, for example when people are shopping, at the office or at a friend's home.

"Hearsay" happens between known or unknown friends and even strangers. Modern internet and mobile social tools allow people to know others at any time, and people gathered via each social tool may talk about a brand. These talks may cause some potential brand customers to be interested in such brand, thus triggering new customers' identification towards such brand. In addition, the circumstance of "hearsay" more often happens via discussions, references or introductions among schoolmates, colleagues and friends, through which a new customer's identification of a brand has been completed.

"Consideration" means that when a new brand customer has a problem, he acquires information about some brands by referring to the people around or social tools or searching online by himself. Since

Section III Brand Technology

this information may involve several competitive brands, brand customers may further recognize and select the brand that they wanted most after enquiry or self-seeking, which is a screening process conducted by customers themselves.

"Consciousness" happens in every choice that people made. Most people have their own brand preference, which has already existed before purchasing behavior happens. They haven't bought it simply because they are not ready for it. Once they are, the purchasing behavior will happen immediately. So brand organizations should focus on developing a capability that the brand can be the chosen one when any potential user is ready.

50% of new users, when coming across a new brand which they have never heard of, will spontaneously get to know the brand by visiting brand website, reading brand news and free comments online and watching online video via search engine, so as to further confirm their recognition judgment on such brand. Through this kind of self-help learning, users will have deeper memory on the brand and make their own judgment. After the first try of buying, they may reconfirm their buying decisions or abandon the brand directly.

3.2 Brand market recognition

New users firstly prejudge a brand from three aspects, namely "the largest", "the most professional" and "interested". That is to say, people often choose the world's largest brand in the field, the most professional brand in the market or the brand they are interested in and can gain happiness by joining or possessing from.

In order to speed up this kind of memorized recognition, brand organizations often add certain descriptions in their brand news and introduction to give certain labels to their brands. These labels usually appear in the first line of brand news as a kind of brand recognition explanation, for example, "the world's largest indoor and outdoor ocean park – Ocean Kingdom" and "one of the world's largest ferry companies – Stena from Sweden", or "the international leading integrated circuit OEM company – Dolphin" and "Tuoren is a world-leading medical instrument company". Especially for market fields and emerging companies whom are not familiar to people in daily life, to accelerate the recognition process is very important.

Brand recognition may also come from "interests". Brand organizations design these interest points through some market activities, such as publishing professional technical articles, the latest research results, the latest investment news of enterprises, the latest highlights of products, cases of helping customers succeed, so as to raise people's great interests on their brands and allow new users to recognize brands by themselves.

Brand market recognition builds a kind of brand image which can show market position, specialization degree, technical abilities, research and development level as well as brand influence mainly in a multidimensional way. Even a new company can form the preconceived market impression recognition through effective brand image designing.

3.3 Brand triggering recognition

In many cases, people obtain brand information via the triggering recognition model designed deliberately by brand organizations. With various media such as news, pictures, colors, experience, attempts and fun, brand organizations trigger people's recognition and understanding of brands and then complete the building process of brand impression.

TV ads and posters can be considered as a kind of explicit triggering. Via presenting a specific group of pictures to users, TV ads and posters can cause people to have a strong sense of recognition as if they are the people inside the pictures, or make them desire for the brand, thus helping this brand to form an impression identity in people's mind.

In addition, product experience activity is also a triggering method. However, triggering recognition should pay attention to study and measurement on triggering effects, because only when triggering happens exactly when, where, and how people are most in need then it can be an effective one.

Triggering happens wherever possible. Triggering design aims to effectively attract people's attention, interests and recognition, following which people are likely to confirm the problem solving ability of the brands.

Triggering itself is a kind of psychological effect, and the triggering process is completed via psychological suggestion, emphasis, self-adaption program setting and brand knowledge recognition system of users, etc.

3.4 Brand sense recognition

Brand sense recognition generally appears while users are observing, experiencing or using products, and perfectly shows brands' sense effect in various forms including texture, touch sensation, color, grade and style.

Close your eyes gently, feel the appearance of brand with your fingers and put your heart into the feeling that brand gives you, and then you will understand the deep influence of sense on brand, and through the whole process brand itself is generating feelings.

Japanese researchers found the early forms of sense marketing in 1970s. They sensitively realized that there will be significantly more liberal arts undergraduates engaging in marketing than science undergraduates. However, this finding did not develop into a theory.

Brand is the creator of feeling. Brand sense recognition is multidimensional through the involvement of taste, color, style, texture, emotion, impulsion, culture, interest, spirit and enterprise responsibility, etc., from appearance to connotation, from aesthetics to soul, thus forming the secret of originality of international brands.

In our opinion, an international brand by itself is a creator of feeling or trend, such as a kind of taste, desire or function, so that the whole world can exactly recognize this brand.

3.5 Brand style recognition

Each brand has its own distinctive style. This style can show strong and specific style design in various aspects, such as LOGO, color, pattern, brand news, brand website and brand brochures.

Brand styles have their own characteristics. For brand users, they represent specific manners. When seeing or finding a brand, users may find one of the following classic brand images:

Bright and clear; romantic and gentle; simple and healthy; natural and peaceful; positive, energetic and sporty; luxury and noble; noble, august and leader-like; fresh, pure, beautiful and artistic; classic, practical and tough; scientific, fashionable and futuristic; mysterious, dreamlike and charming, etc.

To go further, we can take out a piece of paper and write down some phrases to make these image types clearer and simpler and to consider which phrases are more representative, such as advanced, gorgeous, beautiful, rational, august, elegant, delicate, romantic, scientific, concise, quality, glorious, modern, oil painting, calm, alive, graceful, powerful, hopeful, cheerful, fresh, joyful, healthy, pure, etc.

Individualized description will make brand style clearer. By selecting suitable phases and conducting brand impression recognition test within a certain scope, brand organizations can create their own optimal brand styles.

3.6 Brand value recognition

Brand value recognition is mainly expressed via price, grade and value.

Price recognition itself refers to price difference among the same kind of brand products and non-brand products. C level brands always hope to lower product prices and aim for excellent quality and reasonable price; B level brands always compare themselves with competitive brands and hope to keep moderate prices in homogeneous competition; A level brands care little about prices, they will eliminate price sensitive and create brand premium.

In fact, people prefer to pay more to buy the best brand and this is a kind of instinctual free choice of people. However, many enterprises fail to create successful brands because they wrongly judge this psychology of people, by always thinking that most customers in the market are at the level of mass consumption and cannot afford products which are too expensive. Z level brands adopt the best materials, best technicians, best packages and best designs without hesitation to perfectly show their products. Prices of these brands are always prohibitively high for common people, making good use of the common understanding of consumption value that "the best thing must be the most expensive". By providing whole-hearted services for a small group of selected users, these brands successfully create their brand legends.

Especially for Z level brands, people always associate international brands with taste of life, thus forming a monopoly brand market expectation for high-and-middle-end users. As an ideal objective for designing, taste helps to build a specific market with material and spiritual satisfaction by forming humanity space, grade of living and lifestyle, providing a series of brand expectations for people pursuing ideal life.

In addition, some brands form their brand images by promoting specific brand values, and thus changing people's understanding of brand consuming patterns. For example, pump brands fixed prices according to usage and maintenance term, and thus expanded the financial purchasing method of pumps, largely changing the old value judging way based on one-time payment and forming a special promotion method of values. As a result, the consumption pattern of pump brand market has been changed.

3.7 Specific culture element recognition

A brand culture must develop from its special and independent recognition elements with deep historic root. We take *Harry Porter* created by J.K. Rowling as an example. *Harry Porter* may not have its original cultural elements, but it has been developed based on special and independent cultural elements existing in the Celtic culture. These elements include a series of essentially popular elements, such as magician, old castle, elf, druids mentor, highly intelligent life entity, centaur, the god and goddess, fairyland, legend, pure love, color level, natural scenery, natural spirituality, music epic and spectacular adventure, which constitute a special cultural element combination.

This combination of popular cultural elements has bred a series of epics and fantasy and sci-fi culture forms, including The Lord of the Rings, The Chronicles of Narnia, Harry Porter, Avatar, Star Wars, The Avengers, Tristan and Isolde, Braveheart, Merlin, World of Warcraft, Dungeons and Dragons, etc.

Creation of modern brand culture also highly relies on the combination, creation and development of specific culture recognition elements. Disney can be an example that develop into an outstanding popular brand by employing specific culture forms. Generation of new brand culture must begin with studying, designing and developing the combination of specific culture recognition elements, so brand organizations should consider in the first place on which specific culture elements of brand recognition they can design and develop.

3.8 Brand consumption security recognition

Brand consumption security is the comprehensive embodiment of including purchasing channels security, reasonable premium security, product performance security, using security, re-recommend security, emotional security, etc. It makes users repurchase trustingly and enjoyably, without any concern. In theory B, we emphasize that purchase and repurchase can happen only on the premise of security. Any insecurity in any time will immediately break purchase process and push users away. Brands in Z-level are paying great attention to the designing of security attributes.

In order to reassure consumers and make them purchase for life time, brand organizations have established a large number of experience stores, exclusive stores, regular chains, franchised stores, or released official websites and hotlines. Through a series of measures, they try to streamline their marketing networks as far as possible, so that they can protect the authenticity from fakes and bogus. Meeting the consumer demand with a small but safe number of selected, intuitive, reliable sales outlets, this trend will still be distinctive for a long time in the future.

Brand organizations would try everything to improve the quality and service, in order to convince brand users that the brand is worth it. They emphasize the concept of quality, design the brand with great verve, and deliver products in a spirit of meticulousness. Brand's global R&D center spares no effort to show the superb technology elements. They try to embody the brand premium in all-dimensional. In the perspective of consumers, this premium is reasonable, worth the price, or even beyond it. "Must, shall, looks like, can be worth the money" is a kind of consumer psychology that brand users are pretty sure of.

"The performance is superior for sure", "the usage is absolutely safe", a series of positive psychology establishes a high recognition in brand users. On the contrary, users are always psychologically resistant to those products in B-level, C-level or off-brand, wondering if it lives up to the advertisements, and worrying about the quality. Rare consumers will raise complaints or ask for exchange when they confront the exaggerated advertisements and quality issues; mostly they choose to live in silence. However, silence does not mean that there is no protest. Actually, in their silence most users have abandoned the brand and decided to never buy it again.

Re-recommend security appears in the process that brand users spontaneously introduce or recommend brands to other people. This is not only the main form of brand operation, but also the key point of brand marketing. Especially for high-end luxury brand and professional bands which have narrow market and are not familiar to people, such as printing machinery brands and optoelectronics brands, they have a limited quantity of users with a centralized distribution, therefore word of mouth re-recommendation becomes the most typical and major brand communication and marketing method. Only when people use and highly accepted a brand, they will spontaneously recommend the brand to others. Recommenders know that their recommendations are secure, while the recommendation itself is a kind of active and spontaneous behavior, which represents the identity, status, reputation and reliable influence ability. For this reason, recommenders are often cautious in making recommendation, and only when they are sure of the security of recommendation then they will recommend or even intensively recommend the brands to others. On the contrary, if the brand products recommended have poor quality and malfunctions sometimes, it will be quite embarrassing for the recommenders, and the credibility and influence of the recommenders may be lowered.

Emotional security is reflected during the whole process of buying, using and recommending by brand users. People's ideal psychological expectations are happiness, health, gratefulness, trust and respect, etc. they do not want to have bad mood and negative emotional reactions such as anger, sadness, lose, depression, complain, suspension and guilt after recommending at any link of brand contacting.

3.9 Brand contact point recognition

Brand users can perceive brands at different contact points at any time. Any brand organization can analyze and develop brand contact point strategy with respect to the whole process of brand establishing, discovery, understanding, observing, experiencing, using, purchasing, customer service response and after-sales service. Whether the automatic service acquiring under smart service model, or contact point in site recognition, purchase determining, product service and service delivery process, they are equally important.

In the past, people over-emphasized on shopping environment and service attitude. Actually, in most cases shopping environment is not a big problem, while service attitude is. Service attitude sometimes is under control, but under many circumstances it may be out of control. Especially when a brand organization's operation network is overlarge, service attitude of shopping guides in the business outlets may be out of control when directly in contact with brand users. Service attitude in the after-sales service process may also be easily out of control. This is mainly because sales personnel at outlets think that they are not members of the brand organizations. On the other hand, they are neglected by brand organizations in the past and are treated as unofficial personnel, temporary staff or sales support personnel. So they have not received specialized brand training and do not even know the characteristics of brands, therefore their service for customers often receives complaints, to which brand organizations should pay great attention.

In addition to recognition contact, another important link is contact with people or "thing". This kind of contact is mainly reflected as the physical contact feeling such as people's feeling at the first sight of products, people's impression of products after unpacking and people's touch sensation when they are holding the products for the first time. For this reason, brand organizations should pay attention to specific recognition design at such links in the product research and development process.

All the links which may directly contact users should be integrated into the contact point management scale of level A, level B and level C brands according to the degree of importance, and brand organizations should conduct study and test on the optimal contact method, so as to realize the optimal contact presentation method and pay attention to providing good brand experience at contact points.

3.10 Brand first-time trust design

For a brand which is new-found or in its early stage, when public and pro users have not been familiar with it yet, a good first-time trust design is very critical. For an existing brand which is going to launch new products or new services, it is also necessary to do the first-time trust design.

90% of the public do not have faith in brands which they never heard of. Their trust is highly dependent on reliable recommendation sources

In theory B, we point out that users will tend to be suspicious of the brand which they are not familiar with. They will see this brand with a hypothetical and skeptical attitude, regardless of identifying, knowing, buying, or using process. Once they feel any uncomfortable, psychologically, emotionally or practically, they will immediately deny it. If poor service occurs in their first purchase, or quality defects are found during use, their mere interest and expectation will be gone, and they will decide to never use it for lifetime. In addition, this is always a many-to-one relationship.

Therefore, based on the brand contact point design, every part which may have first-time contact, such as consultation, enquiry, viewing, delivery and service, needs the first-time trust design. From sense, behavior to mind, it will help users to build first-time trust all-dimensionally.

Besides first trust design, trust design is a long-term experience process. Brands always face the first trust design challenge whenever they are about to release new products or new services. In practice, many brands often relax the management of research, quality and service after a long period of development, causing new products and services to be brought to market hastily without being tested. If such a product is sold to direct users, especially regular customers, they will immediately realize how bad it is and abandon this brand forever.

Situations like that are pretty common, so we always see that many people are changing brands frequently. Even if they have trusted a brand for a long time, they may lose their trust because of a little accident and turn to other brands. Brand organizations can use directional tracking or PADS science analysis model to analyze the average time length of users, the amount of recommendations from new users, and most of all, the reasons for clients' dissatisfactions, then find out why people turned to competing brands. In this way, we can extract some vital information about first trust design.

3.11 Brand after-sales service recognition

After-sales service is not as simple as people think. It is more than changing, repairing and promising. Brand after-sales service is a vital part of improving premium, and the core of service value chain and service profit chain.

Many industries all over the world are turning to after-sales service market. Automobile, inkjet printer, large medical equipment, machine tool engine, software, information technology, these industries are all making profits by after-sales service, in some fields, after-sales service even accounts for 70% -90% of profits. Many professional-grade after-service brands and companies are growing rapidly into the major player in the market.

According to GDP (gross domestic product) statistics, in global markets more and more countries have turned their economy forms into service-oriented economy. Service industry accounts for a great share of national and personal incomes.

After-sales service can be understood as a source of repeated business. For example, if a restaurant offers excellent environment and services, customers will be more willing to come back. From this perspective, we can say that after-sales service is the key of keeping sales repeating and gaining profit from it.

In specific design of after-sales service, there are four classical development models to produce premium.

The first is free after-sales service. Through effective science design and durability experiment, brand organizations define these products as disposable products, which spare the maintenance process. These products usually have a "use-by" date. While designing a free after-sales service product, brand organization will make its lifespan far longer than the "use-by" date that they promise or regulate.

The second is distinctive after-sales service. Price decides the after-sales service content and priority level, and users can choose what they want.

The third is building an independent after-sales service brand, strictly distinguished from other competitors.

The forth is defining after-sales service as a main business. In this model organizations purely achieve brand profits and continue earnings through after-sales service.

4 Brand recognition system

A typical brand recognition system generally includes three aspects:

Brand idea recognition

Includes brand strategy recognition, brand advocate recognition, brand user cluster recognition, brand visual expression recognition, brand theory recognition, brand concept recognition, brand jargon recognition, etc.

Brand image recognition

Includes brand naming recognition, brand LOGO recognition, brand standard color recognition, brand environment recognition, brand package recognition, brand products recognition.

Brand impression recognition

Includes brand impression recognition, brand trigger recognition, brand sensory recognition, brand style recognition, brand value recognition, brand consumption safety recognition, brand first trust recognition, brand after-sales service recognition, brand behavior recognition, etc.

Unlike the single, old-model brand image recognition, new brand recognition system is more all rounded and suited for modern and future brand overall recognition design. It becomes brand-idea-recognition-led, accompanied by corporate recognition, and strengthens the recognition vision and pattern of corporate identity.

Section III Brand Technology

At the same time, we believe that the previous CI/Corporate Identity (including MI / Mind Identity, BI / Behavior Identity, VI / Vision Identity) is no longer suitable for today's brand recognition models. If we still lead the entire brand recognition design, it will inevitably cause a huge loss. The main problem of it is that design companies of corporate identity may ignore the great value of brand idea and brand impression in brand design, thereby ignoring a series of design factors in transmission, communication, feeling, and perception process of modern brand communication which is based on content marketing

Brand recognition system also needs the support of brand communication technology, including brand interpretation system, brand communication system, etc.

4.1 Process of brand recognition system design

Brand recognition system design is an integrated process of pre-designing, fully investigating, discussing and examining. It emphasizes predictive design, namely that brand recognition design should be based on the enterprise's strategic thinking for the next five, ten or even one hundred years. It shall not be done according to the current market pattern. To get the design task done effectively and proactively, we need the trilateral cooperation among the external branding technology organization, brand recognition designing company and the internal brand technology committee.

Brand recognition system design is an integrated process that can completely show brand strategic vision, reveal brand management techniques, unify thoughts and actions and reflect design thought. It is a big event in enterprise development. In brand restructuring, the general process includes:

1) Hold the brand recognition system launch meeting

2) Set up particular joint working group in charge of the design task

3) Comprehensive investigation

Conduct comprehensive investigation through group discussion, group survey, interview and field investigation, using PADS science analysis model. The comprehensive investigation content includes: Expectations from different levels of strategy, technology, management, operation, cooperation and user. What do they want most? How employees view the enterprise? What's the future of the brand? Which is the most critical brand recognition idea? What markets does the brand plan to expand? What aspects will the brand recognition system be applied to?

4) Research and analysis of information

Search all kinds of information, enter the stage of enterprise real-time dynamic research and analysis, including conditions that the enterprise should have and already have, enterprise personnel state observation, enterprise reality observation and comparison analysis of brands in the industry.

5) Propose the first version design scheme (the first draft, the first impression)

Decompose each factor in brand recognition system. Collect various schemes through different ways such as calling the whole society, full taking part of the enterprise, etc. Then pick out a relatively comprehensive collection of schemes after comparing all of it. Discuss it one by one, and decide on the initial version design.

6) Propose the second version design scheme (the second draft, the second amendment)

Amend, enrich and improve the design schemes that have been selected in the first version. Conduct a number of simulations on each application. Use image or comparative data to demonstrate the second version scheme. Hold a multipart meeting of recognition design illustration for discussion and selection, thus decide on the second version design.

7) Propose the third version design scheme (the third draft, the third formation)

Further amend, enrich and improve the design schemes that have been selected in the second version. Convert the abstract description into intuitive works. Stimulate all the finished products, sample drafts and examples. Compare every colors, shapes, sensory responses and see if they can create new possibilities. Invite representatives from all fields to experience it and propose suggestions. Keep these records for determining the final scheme.

8) Examine and release the final version design scheme (the final approval)

Finally, complete the final version design scheme with all its details in place, and get it approved. Make corresponding files and materials that brand recognition will require for.

9) Hold a grand brand press conference

Choose a big moment for holding a grand brand press conference. Publish the completely new brand recognition and brand statement to the world. Together hold the corresponding oath-taking ceremony.

10) Enter brand learning stage

Brand learning is divided into three stages: learning for brand backbone, learning for all brand staff, and learning for brand user. This is for completing the application of brand recognition system.

Exercises

1. Multiple-choice Question: Even though brand recognition has an obvious characteristic of self-promotion, which are the four typical brand impression recognition ways. Which have constituted a kind of highly self-organized behaviors, rather than passive brand promotion as before.

A. Seeing, hearing, considering; self-discovery, self-seeking, self-recognition, self-recommendation, and self-judgment

B. Hearing, considering, consciousness; self-discovery, self-seeking, self-recognition, self-recommendation, and self-judgment

C. Seeing, hearing, considering, consciousness; self-discovery, self-seeking, self-recognition, self-recommendation, and self-judgment

D. Seeing, hearing, considering, consciousness; self-recognition, self-recommendation, and self-judgment

2. True or False Question: (   )

Brand consumption security is the comprehensive embodiment of including purchasing channels security, reasonable premium security, product performance security, using security, re-recommend security, emotional security, etc. It makes users repurchase trustingly and enjoyably, without any concern.

3. Essay Question: How to achieve first-time trust design?

SECTION III BRAND TECHNOLOGY

Chapter 6

Brand Management Technology

Management standard technology emphasizes on the way to enforce standardized management, which was previously focused on normative jobs such as global techniques, methods, product models. However, brand standardization is a factual standard that is stricter than any former ones.

"Brand + management standardization" constitutes the brand standardization. Compared with the former standardization, it pays more attention to the developed management standard of the enterprise, advanced products, leading technology and scientific management, whose objective is to manufacture the best, the ideal and the most advanced products and establish a factual standard that would also be the world's leading standard. Therefore, in terms of brand management technology, brand standardization is worthy of more creative thinking and exploration.

1 Brand management technology

The goal of brand management technology is to create leading and perfect products by finding the most advanced method of management, and to provide a better life for people and promote progression of mankind by the best products and service.

Specifically, the implementation of brand management technology includes:

(1) To create the best product: to design product by experimenting, reserve the outstanding design and apply it as the constant form of products.

(2) To establish the best management method: to work out the management method by experimenting, to reserve the best management method, to establish systematic files of brand management standardization and implement *"Program of Brand-building"*.

(3) To carry out brand audit and rectification: to implement management optimization and process reengineering and realize overall improvement of management by scientifically analyzing management links and process and by making audit reports.

1.1 Constitution of brand management system

Brand management technology is a document system. As for brand management system, it consists of five parts, namely establishing management rules, conducting management experiments, formulating management brochures and SOPs (Standard Operation Procedure), managing brand recording documents and finishing brand reports.

(1) Aiming at establishing the self-adaptive rules of scientific system, formulating management rules helps to establish a series of new management methods and turn them into management system. Management rules may be general rules of enterprises in the world and also be established by enterprises themselves, such as airspace classification criteria of ATS (Air Traffic Service) of ICAO(International Civil Aviation Organization), tracking technology criteria of future airliners, *"Manual of Style"* and *"Social Media Instruction"* released by Associated Press.

(2) Carrying out management experiment indicates that both R&D (Research and Development) of products and acquisition of management technology should follow the principle of scientific experiments by labs and experimental approaches, especially the management technology of enterprises should also follow the principle to obtain the best management technology. By establishing management rules and management experiments, establishment of systemic management methods shall be encouraged, which includes 6sigma, TQM (Total Quality Management), pharmaceutical administration on OTC (over the Counter), CMM (Capability Maturity Model), etc.

(3) Management brochure and SOP should be drafted. Management brochure serves as a document of management in detail, including specific management experiments, practical methods, constitution of management system, managing tools, management practice, management process, management steps, notices, etc. Document system arranged in the form of a brochure is of substantial significance to define management contents and avoid managing documents becoming dispersed, fragmentary and unsystematic. On the premise of scientific process analysis, SOP decomposes operation content in detail. Therefore, both execution layer and operation layer should strictly adhere to introduction requirements when carrying out management and operation. The contents in management brochure and SOP should meet the requirement of introduction and application of new technology in the future, and the need of future AM (agile manufacturing), promoting the transformation management and manual work into IT management technology and automatic production if conditions permit.

(4) Brand record document composes of record charts which include statements of facts and analysis record, respecting scientific and factuality when recorded. Record documents should be tracked, inquired and managed. Besides, other features should be paid attention to, such as electrification and remote management. It is necessary for enterprises to value design of brand record documents, because the results of management are mainly achieved by effective guidance and scientific design of management record charts.

(5) Completing brand reports is the major way to implement brand management technology including brand rectification reports, MA reports, brand construction phase and acceptance report. As for brand rectification report, it emphasizes on brand awareness and management process, and it's used to rectify errors made during the process of management instead of the behavior of man. After analyzing and auditing emerged problems occurred in management and optimized process, MA report is completed by designing analysis project of site management. Enterprises should encourage cultivation of management analysts and management postgraduates. Together with external organization of management technology, enterprises should also encourage management analysis group in the departments or trans-departments to carry out multilevel and multi-range site management analysis projects, so as to improve management technology of every procedure.

1.2 Advancement of management technology

The advancement of technology is mainly presented in 3 stages, which are: "formulation of management rules", "management of scientific experiments" and "management standard and system".

Reflecting on the history of humans, it can be found that in different historical periods there were corresponding representative figures, which were of great significance to improve management technology. Their management ideas and methods had profound impact on modern civilization, and posed to establish important departments of management technology in both modern and future enterprises' management.

The formulation of management rules must refer to representatives such as Amergin, the Duke of Zhou, Shang Yang, Li Si, and Gaius Julius Caesar Augustus. Druid Order created by Amergin poses profound effect on the Celtic civilization and modern western society in the formulation of order of social administration, of engagement and of adjudication. The Duke of Zhou formulated management rules such as primogeniture, square-fields system, which are the origin of oriental management of rule-making. Shang Yang and other legalists, mainly known as Li Si, established a series of management rules including the military exploit rank institution, law of Qin dynasty, system of prefecture and counties, etc. The Roman Empire, represented by Caesar Augustus, made a pact of reformation for promotion, county and Roman law.

In terms of management of scientific experiments, Shang Yang, Taylor and his followers must be mentioned. The weapon standardization manufacturing philosophy of Shang Yang and Lv Buwei is a solid foundation for Chinese unity and uprising. A great deal of modern archaeology discoveries has unearthed the world's leading scientific standardization. Taylor and his followers Bath, Gunter, Gilbreth and his wife, Emerson Ford and Fordism, the Hawthorne experiments, all of them defined typical scientific management era of management method with the experimental method.

Section III Brand Technology

In terms of management standard and system, First Emperor of Qin Dynasty, Dai Ming, Ono Chi, Tsien Hsueshen must be mentioned. The first emperor of the Qin Dynasty and Li Si formulated the policy of "unifying words, the width of roads and weights and measures", which poses profound influence on the official beginning and the origin of human standardization. Dai Ming and Ono Chi and other Japanese industrial management representatives made an outstanding contribution on the establishment of quality management and production management system. Tsien Hsueshen and other scientists made great contribution on the academic ideas and practical theory of systematics and management science.

2 PADS management audit analysis

In *The Theory of Brand*, we have introduced PADS scientific analysis model and now let's use it for some practical dynamic management applications.

Let's study the application of the PADS from an example:

The M company needs to design a set of service management systems, and on this issue the PADS scientific analysis model is adopted to make audit analysis. They invite a management analysis expert group of a third-party management consulting company to research and audit the company. The group designs a survey questionnaire which has such questions as – what are the current positions and job descriptions? What positions in some departments influence your work? What complaints, if any, have you received? What aspects of your work do you think customers will pay more attention to? How is your ideal state of work? In similar enterprises, what brand do you think does better in some fields?

After the panel's one-to-one research, or face-to-face survey among the members of the company, we will find that there are a number of errors mutually hindering the process in the company management process, such as improper set of the command chain, inconsistent work interface, cumbersome interdepartmental work cohesion, purchasing management affecting the production quality and supplier's after-sales service underperforming and other management difficulties and problems. And at the same time we will also find out some effective process recommendations.

By troubleshooting the P stage of PADS, we can classify and analyze all kinds of problems in the management process in order to design a more fluent management system. In fact, no matter how good the work is, many problems such as complaints and responsibilities that are difficult to determine will be displayed. Because the enterprise could have a lot of process breakpoints across the years, which could hinder the employee's work, resulting in many management problems. The PADS management analysis model is an effective brand management tool to improve the enterprise management foundation and redesign more ideal management process, which can be widely used in many fields.

We now use PADS to analyze and survey the cases.

2.1 Problem audit on the D company's current service system

(1) Brand issues

The Group has no clear concept of service culture, and the contents of the core concepts of service in enterprise culture are not enough. In the process of enterprise service, there is no announcement to highlight the advantages of service, so customers can not identify service features and advantages of the D brand compared with the same kind of brand; customers can not clearly feel any difference between the D brand and other service related competitive enterprises, not forming its own service difference and strategic advantage.

(2) Function issues

There are no sound service organization structures, no service department at the group layer, no medium and long-term planning for after-sales service, no service research, no effective support and supervision regulation in service timeliness, accessories validity and technical adaptability in the group. All business departments do things in their own ways with no uniform basic service requirements and discordance between supervising and subordinate divisions, resulting in waste of resources and uneven service levels.

(3) System issues

The enterprise does not have a complete service system and lacks of a complete uniform standards and system documents. There are a lot of shortcomings in controlling links of service management. Although developed large business departments have initially formed the service system, the rules and regulations are not perfect and service testing method is not proper. In recent years, most of the newly formed business departments haven't had a complete service system, and some of them have just arranged service rules and documents, still being in the trial run. As a whole, the service system is not standardized, not standard and not systematic. The group does not have a unified guiding programmatic document, and has not established a proper working-hour calculation, charging standards, service processes, SOP.

(4) Research and development issues

In recent years, the enterprise has picked up pace with the new products from the research and development department and is remodeling them quickly. Trial products are put into production too much while mature products are produced less, which results in unstable product operation, in too many models of products' components and in poor universality of components. Over-quick modification makes many components supporting incomplete, especially after the period of Three Guarantees (for repair replacement or compensation of faulty products), many components are difficult to buy or cannot be bought, affecting the normal use of products, which is reported by business department, agents and consumers and is a pressing problem to be resolved. In addition, the main reason for the complaints is caused by a large number of products lacking security protection equipment. When such situations occur due to overweight, overload, overuse, overtime in frequent use and no regular maintenance, there is no warning reminder and no automatic protection design. When products fail, the responsibility is too difficult to be defined. Whether it's the users' problem or the product design and quality problems, which leads to many troubles and is short of bargaining weights when the enterprise is negotiating compensations.

(5) Quality issues

Some products have poor stability, and more serious quality problems in the manufacturing process, components and cooperation components, there is mutual disjoint and no effective link with the after-sales service. The quality of the components and cooperation components, to a certain extent, affected the market reputation of D brand.

(6) The timeliness issues

Service timeliness is not efficient and the process to send staff is much more cumbersome. After the customer has made maintenance applications and waited for maintenance code, staff could be sent, thus customers are waiting too long. No co-movement exists between business departments. The enterprise doesn't design scientific divisions and the division of labor process with after-services radius, and the matching of service is not high. In addition, lacking of service equipment, the company doesn't widely use GPS to command service vehicles to first arrive at the nearest situation to know the problems and audit breakdown and dispatch appropriate service staff to take maintenance measures to respond to the system. The construction of "A machine, a file, a map" has not yet been established, and the past maintenance records, drawings calls, and fault prediction of products are not accurate, which seriously affects the quality of service and service efficiency.

2.2 B-class Brand Problem Audit

Customer relationship problems

There are phenomena such as inconsistent answers and less detailed records for too many departments and interfaces of the enterprises accepting appointment, consultation, repair, complaints, etc., and phenomena like people appointed for accepting, replying orally and personally handling questions during stages of design, on-site construction and after-sales.

(2) In the 400 hot-line, there are wrong names of the brand on display and some customers with the right names. Currently, 400 after-sales service hot-line of enterprises cannot service around the clock,

for example, generally after 5 pm only one person is responsible for answering; the telephone operator's expertise is limited, for example, they cannot accurately understand the problem customers put forward and cannot accurately transfer it to the corresponding business department; the phone response is not answered and is not enough due to busy lines; customer service system works in an outdated way and is still operated in the form of manual reports, which is not helpful to improve the quality and efficiency of after-sales service.

(3) The confidentiality of customer files should be protected. Customers indicate that they have answered sales calls in the name of the Y brand but found that they are not Y brand staff.

(4) The enterprise has no functional departments on customers 'PR (public relationship) (consumer relations). It should strengthen advertisement of public relations and public relations activities among customer groups as well as customer relationship maintenance and word-of-mouth marketing.

(5) Customer satisfaction research should follow the KANO model in order to research and improve methods of consumer satisfaction. The problems of customer satisfaction research: the survey methods used now are applicable to the average level of enterprise satisfaction, but not applied to individual customers; although a few time points are set in the research process, but the content is not integrated organically; the departments and their responsibilities of customer satisfaction survey are not clear; some departments don't agree with the current results from satisfaction research; customers are not satisfied with satisfaction survey and its results.

Analysis of cause

(1) There are too many departments in the enterprise, and too many links serving customers and affecting customer satisfaction. Therefore, there is no service framework design that takes the lead in the customer service.

(2) The customer files' call procedures need to be improved. The files of customer whose construction has been finished should be transferred to the after-sales service department of the enterprise Tobe on unified file management and then placed into the after-sales stage in order to further develop and utilize customers' data.

(3) Customer relationship model should be "several to one" and "one to several" structure and be adjusted according to the structure. Pre-sales and sales stage: several to one—several departments are responsible for one consumer; post-sales stage: one to several—one department is responsible for several consumers, and then the second round of customer transformation begins.

(4) Research about customer satisfaction should be strengthened.

Impact Analysis

(1) The contact between customers and the enterprise is cumbersome. Too many people trying to solve one thing will reduce the efficiency and lead to information distortion. The brand relation of Y brand enterprise is not developed, but the private relations between the designer or the foreman and the guest room are.

(2) The overall customer relationship maintenance needs to be focused on, word-of-mouth marketing is not efficient, and customer re-conversion rate is low.

(3) The link of customer dissatisfaction is not connected with the assessment of the enterprise, which cannot be continuously optimized and improved.

Correction opinions

(1) The enterprise should comb and clarify the customer acceptance regulation as well as unify statements, data collection, analysis, management, and filing.

(2) The enterprise should improve the 400 hot-line and its standardization of service response. In the call center, the enterprise should set up the position of consultants such as designers, engineers and project stewards to professionally answer customers' professional questions. Tracking posts should be also added in the call center, and do tracking investigation on problems raised by customers for the first time, and be responsible for the first question.

(3) The enterprise should add customers' public relations departments and positions.

(4) The enterprise should improve methods and means of customer satisfaction research.

2.3 Analysis of public management issues

Analysis and recommendations on major accidents about public traffic safety:

(1) Prompt legislate: *The law of public transport safety* should be established as soon as possible, starting from the source with comprehensive judgments, to realize long-term stability. The scope of legal supervision includes design, production, installation, and maintenance of all major public transport infrastructure, as well as bid inviting, procurement, inspection and dispatch of operation units. Departments concerned will increase greater punishment of penalty, and will conduct a thorough investigation on major traffic accidents happening in the future, initiate a prosecution, and strictly ensure accountability.

(2) To manage strictly: departments concerned should conduct a comprehensive investigation on all public transport infrastructure and equipment whether it is new construction, under construction, or operating, comb all upstream and downstream enterprises in the supply chain, and establish central database on national public transport safety. Departments concerned should establish a file for all involved manufacturers and operating units. Drawings and products designed and produced by various batches and batch numbers should be included in the statistical analysis. All links that have hidden dangers should be included in real-time dynamic data management and set the alert level. All ordinary maintenance staff and artificial dispatchers should accept strict security education and induction training.

(3) Increase transparency of public transport facilities information: departments concerned should timely establish the bill and rule of "National Public Security Emergency Information Transparency", reform transparent information disclosure regulation, conduct a rigorous training for spokesmen and spokeswomen in the core posts of all the areas in public service so as to unify press releasing statements, ways and contents. We should mainly state facts, but not jump to conclusions, and not use "may", "probably" and other inaccurate words to determine the cause of accidents. Everything shall depend on the due diligence report.

(4) Other aspects: departments concerned should strengthen research and budget on the emergency management of public emergencies, and civil aviation, transportation, railways, subways and other links should have a regular evacuation, rescue, logistics and other training and exercises. We should urge all kinds of enterprises to accelerate the pace of modern management, and enhance research and development, acceptance check and daily monitoring technology of the signal system, electrical system, fault audit system, automatic forewarning system, automatic protection system and technologies. In addition, the audit authorities should have a specific audit focused on bidding, procurement, maintenance and other aspects of all kinds of major facilities and equipment affecting public life and safety, and resolutely put an end to all types of bidding corruption.

3 Design of PADS system management method

The best method of management progress is to achieve the best research achievements in scientific experiments. The frequent bursting problems of modern enterprise management and long-term existence problems always appear in the management design while the management design in nature is from the management of scientific experimental methods. This is the D in PADS which plays an important role in the link of scientific design.

For example, in the salary structure, although popular performance system replaces piecework system, it doesn't mean the end of piecework system. We find that the piecework method is still a scientific salary calculation method after many piecework experiments. However, it changes a little with the progress of the times.

These experimental research findings - approved workload, piecework payment and other tasks could be calculated by the method of piece measurement and multiple programs could also be calculated by task program piece, for instance, telephone volume, web page making volume, document handling volume, and customer transaction volume. According to the degrees of completion, they can be divided into Grade A, Grade B, and Grade C, depending on the work results measurement. In this way, work efficiency and work quality will be substantially increased and its relevant position will be included in the same service payment calculation system. Business accounting of workload and work quality can be decomposed into daily or weekly accounting way, which will also greatly enhance work enthusiasm and work speed.

We hope and expect global management research colleagues as well as global enterprises to focus on scientific experiments to achieve management research results and apply the management result. The progress of future global management must highly rely on the overall development of management subject, the progress of management technology, the discovery of management experiment and the new establishment of full development management system.

The establishment of management system is an important strategy that modern enterprises must take to cope with competition. Due to the rapid changes in the competitive environment of enterprises, many management concepts and methods will soon become obsolete. Therefore, the establishment of new management system method requires being higher and faster more than ever before. The establishment of overall methods in management system is the strongest driving force for modern management and future management progress.

4 Brand tools: practical methods of management technology

The establishment and application of brand tools occupies a very large proportion in management technology. The establishment of brand tools depends on global management researchers and enterprise managers to work together to create new management technology.

We design some typical management tools, such as PADS scientific analysis model, brand analysis technology, command chain technology, tree diagram, wave diagram, which could be used in daily brand management and management progress.

4.1 Brand comparing analysis technology

Brand comparing analysis technology is a method for benchmark analysis of the same problem which originates in the early study of the author. At that time, people learned all kinds of management theories by themselves and they used to find out the different descriptions of the same theory to compare and study. For example, according to organizational structure, they would buy all the books about organizational structure on the market and read all the possible different explanation points about organizational structure and comprehensively absorb various explanation points. Then they would write again according to their understanding about organizational structure. They would get their opinions by learning widely from strong points of others. This is an effective learning method for forming independent views and avoiding insisting on school statements.

In the study of brand management, we also make this aspect exceed to brand comparing analysis technology. We require that the same question should be divided into different research points. At the same time, we should compare with different countries, different management methods of different enterprises to find the best way applicable to the enterprise. Enterprises can also be based on the *Brand Energetic Element Table* to choose different elements of the brand to make a comprehensive comparison. Comparison shouldn't be only for the country or the industry, but should be for a wide comparison and study, and also understand the methods of the same management problem in United States, Germany, France, Britain, Japan, South Korea and other different countries and different enterprises. According to the concerned problems of comparison, we should compare the methods taken by different industries and comprehensively take in the advantages and disadvantages, so as to create the best management method of our own.

A typical case of brand comparing analysis: why Korean ginseng export price is ten times of Chinese ginseng? (See Table 11-2)

Comparing items can be divided into brand origin, brand quality, brand price, brand strategy, brand management and brand extension for the analysis by comparing.

Table 11-2 Comparison table of ginseng brand of China and South Korea

Comparative item	Comparative comment	South Korea	China
Origin of brand	Chinese and South Korean ginseng is of the same root.	—	—
Quality of brand	Overall similar	—	
Price of brand	Difference of ten times	The export volume of South Korean ginseng is 1/20 of that of Jilin ginseng. The price of 1kg Korean red ginseng is $120-200.	The output of Jilin ginseng occupies 70% of ginseng in the world. The price of 1kg Chinese red ginseng is $12-20.
Brand strategy	Difference of strategy	In 1899, South Korean government founded KGC (Korean Ginseng Commune) and was especially in charge of Korean ginseng's manufacturing and export. "Korean Ginseng Corp" is a Korean ginseng made by KGC. The management of every step from planting to field management and processing of "Korean Ginseng Corp" ginseng is very strict, for example, sifting and managing land has been done one year before planting ginseng seedlings. From planting to product molding, there are at least five times. After more than five times pesticide residue examination has to ensure ginseng with low pesticide and high quality. In addition, most of the farmer's plant Korean ginseng according to orders, so KGC supervise and give technical guide to farmers from soil preparation constantly, planting, and management for harvest.	There are about 5,000 ginseng enterprises, but none are famous. Chinese ginseng planting is still in disorganized management that farmers separately operate and manage. The farmers plant, harvest and process ginseng without any management and guidance like the cultivation of other crops, so the scale of planting changes is like a roller coaster ride in price fluctuation. Since 1990s, the planting area of ginseng has blind expansion, so supply exceeds demand constantly, together with disorganized market management and malignant price competition, which lowers the price of ginseng drastically. There is a big difference of quality of ginseng from the same piece of land. There is pesticide residue and heavy metal content that seriously damages Chinese's reputation in the international market.
Brand management	Grading standard	—	—
Brand extension	Industry in depth	—	—

4.2 Command chain technology

During American Civil War (1861-1865), President Lincoln (Abraham Lincoln, February 12, 1809- April 15, 1865) commanded the war by telegram in the basement of the White House. In 19th century, the rise of the US stood on the rapid development of telegram net. Military, government affairs, journalism and commerce are established on the basis of rapid telegram, for example, the fastest command information is concentrated on one piece of telegram paper.

Based on the understanding of telegram form, the author believes that the high-speed management operation of modern enterprise should be based on the construction of the core command chain with quick decision command information as the backbone network. Regardless of adopting virtual or realistic branches or operation network, numerous information and documents of electronic company step in for management and resolve the command chain, which will effectively enhance the speed of enterprise operation.

In the design of organization structure, some organizations themselves are designed as command structures with rapid reaction, for example as the US police organization sets up bureaus, offices, departments, groups or smaller action units, appointing a commanding policeman at each level and assigning other departments as supporting units and coordinating units to coordinate the backbone command system to realize high-speed maneuvering reaction ability in command network.

4.3 Tree diagram

Tree diagram is shown in Figure 11-1.

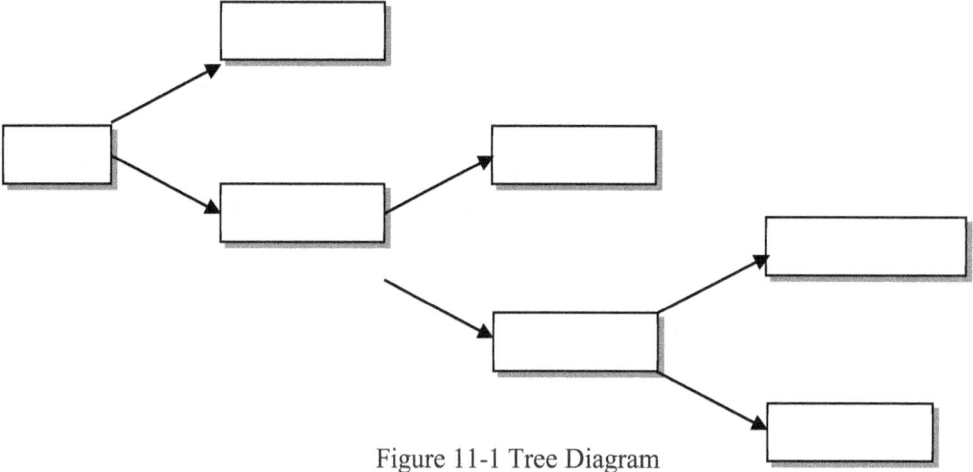

Figure 11-1 Tree Diagram

The tree diagram is a management tool characterized by tree branches to be used in a variety of fields, such as training or development of subject, design of information structure, launch of management strategy frame, decomposition of management task item, screening clues study of management questions, constructional deployment of knowledge system, diversified explanation of management theory, division of management content and so on. Marking and resolving in a tree diagram is convenient to understand and think clearly.

4.4 Wave diagram

The principle of wave diagram (see Figure 11-2) originates from the authors' paper from the early years, in which the motion law of a competition is explained. Normally, there is just one peak of wave in one market activity, one management activity, one competition or hot spots in media, then declining rapidly after a climax. Soon after, people will transform into the period of interest disappearing from expectation and experience.

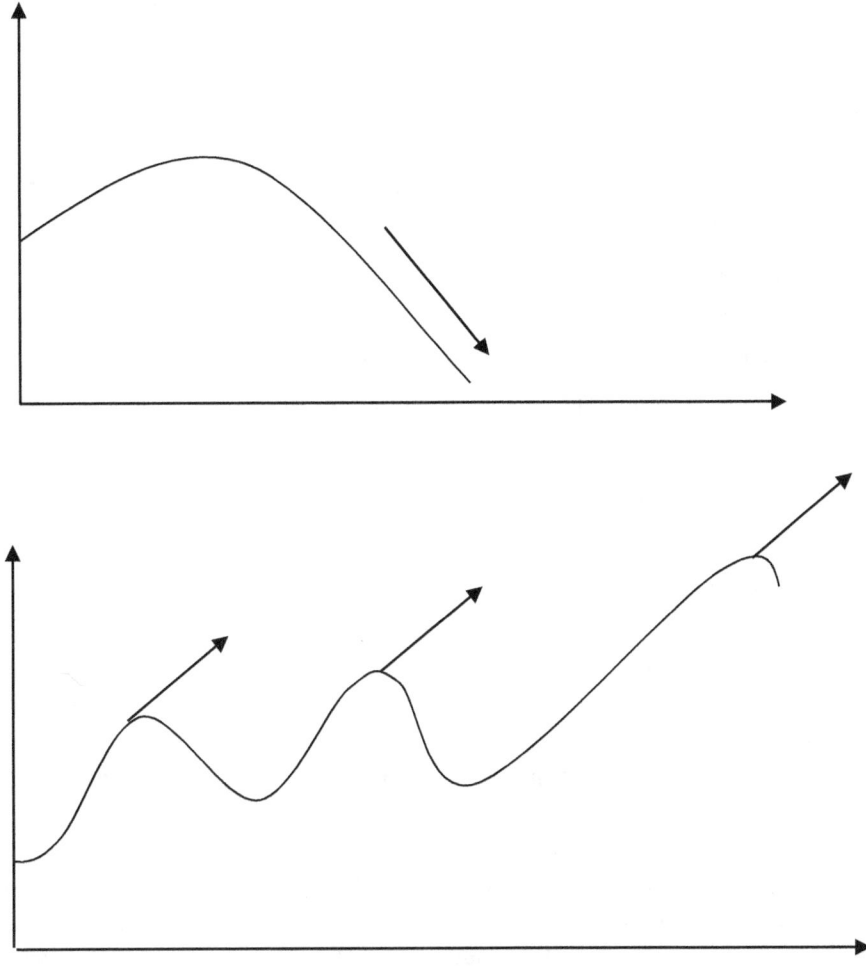

Figure11-2 Wave Diagram

By means of the design of wave diagram operation, consciously designing several pull-up channels for the whole process of activity arouses people's dying interest again, and eventually several rounds of pull-up will continue elevating people's attention to the highest point, which results in the biggest enthusiasm and attention. The design structure of wave diagram can also be for the plan of literature or films and television programs, as well as an important design method of brand communication.

5 Brand document technology

Brand documents are usually expression methods on some typical documents in brand management design, most of which are often used in industrial enterprises and major enterprises. Besides, we also should pay attention to that with the help of scientific experiment of management and scientific analysis process, optimizing these brand documents can lead to the best management level. Here are some typical brand document technologies we list.

5.1 Typical structure of brand management system

(1) The standard structure of brand management system is divided into:

Strategy layer (task requirements);

Brand technology layer (task requirements);

Execution layer (task requirements);

Operation layer (task requirements);

Coordination layer (task requirements of supply chain, business chain and brand services)

(2) The compilation process of brand management system.

(3) The compilation methods of brand management system.

(4) Brand standardization is divided into:

Important characteristics of brand standardization (optimization standardization);

The standardization of brand labs (research and development of products);

The standardization of brand management (the department of management);

The standardization of brand service (the department of service);

The standardization of brand marketing (the department of marketing);

The standardization of brand IT (the department of information);

The standardization of brand coordination (supply chain, business chain and brand services)

(5) The rating of brand management system.

(6) *"Brand Rectification Report"* (The competitiveness of brand).

5.2 The compilation of brand document system

The compilation of brand document system is time-consuming and energy-consuming, and an important job that should be strictly and reasonably boosted on the basis of task items of PADS management analysis model, the requirements of brand standardization and brand construction plan.

The reason why the job is time-consuming and energy-consuming is that many companies and management consulting firms think little of the great role of this job and believe that is has lack of reason and thoroughness in the executing process.

Brand technology committee manages the compilation of brand document system from top to bottom and from inside to outside. Corresponding brand technology groups established in every management department and brand technology professionals are in charge of this job and it takes about six months to one year to do a complete and thorough compilation of brand document system.

Different from the compilation of ISO standard document system, the compilation process of brand document system is more scientific and rigorous. The key point of brand document system is to clear and ease the false management process, to raise brand awareness of staff, to put the brand learning into effect and to pay attention to gain management methods and operation process standard in a scientific manner.

5.3 Operation guide

Operation guide is the document to officially guide management function process (such as operational procedure and detailed working items) including operation process, operation requirements, measuring methods, essentials of quality control, recording period, etc. Operation guide indicates the methods and order of operation in detail, and what methods to implement for quality inspection. The staff engaged in specific jobs must complete the work in accordance with the contents of the operation guide strictly.

In order to ensure the completeness, efficiency, quickness and standardization, and to complete procedure documents established in the operational level, operation guide presents operation and work instructions of operation according to a series of relevant specific operation activities (such as product, service, plug-in, debug, assembly and training).

If enterprises want to realize management standardization, the system of operation guide should be designed, planned and operated. Enterprises not only design operation guide scientifically by means of repeated scientific experiment to find the best working methods, managing MA report activities to improve operation procedure and practically calculating time to formulate the best working beat manually, but also pay attention to train operators and examine proficiency of them. After working on new positions, all the new job-transfer staff must learn from the beginning and become regular staff after a certain internship (three months or six months). Without internship and position examination, they should not be regular staff.

5.4 Management site report (MA report)

Management site report (MA report) plays a role of management audit and analysis in the process of brand management standardization and regards the release of the site management report as a key work of brand reengineering.

At first, the report is an after-sale service management of all the consumers, which means that trans-department management analysis group reverse engineers the source of problems and moving process of problems, including investigating the product quality problems occurring from the after-sale service side, complaint records and users' opinion surveys in reverse.

The second key of the report is to reverse engineer the source of problems and moving process of problems based on the PADS science model. Then the defective design of management process and wrong links of management process can be determined.

The third key of the report is to research and analyze concrete management site project set up relying on existing management problems and advanced management methods of other enterprises, and to put forward the new research and analysis about the ability of partial management work or management system, new methods of management, etc.

Management analysis group is a small group spontaneously composed of several employees similar to QC group (Quality Control group), but the actual content work of which expands to the entire management site including service terminal, encouraging the establishment of trans-department management analysis group and encouraging management learning and management research activities throughout the work of the management analysis group.

The leaders of management analysis group should be trained in a certain training of management analysis methods to ensure to scientifically apply various management techniques in order to manage and analyze management site reports released by management analysis groups regularly. The quantity of management analysis project led by the leaders of management analysis group is an important ability of management. As an important reference to the position promotion, a good leader's ability of solving management problems shows the important level of leadership.

6 Brand management level on basis of process reengineering

When brand associations decide on implementing brand reengineering, the foothold is the process reengineering. Brand associations can achieve success of brand reengineering from the fundamental significance by thorough process reengineering. The reengineering must be thorough, decisive and fundamental.

In 1990s, more than 70% of large enterprises in the world implemented a large-scale process of reengineering movement. Actually, the change of brand reengineering is obviously more thorough than that of pure business process reengineering, because brand process reengineering doesn't mean changing management methods of a department or an association, or optimizing and improving original management process, but it has a profound meaning—self-denial and reform fission of brand associations.

Compared with the last process reengineering, reengineering is neither the change of brand associations by advanced science, advanced technology, and IT information technology, nor the strong pursuit and improvement of cost, quality, service, speed and other process elements. First of all, brand reengineering is a deep understanding of new brand trend and an initiative to think about the strategy, concept and structure of brand more thoroughly and deeply. Old management ideas and old management methods have taken forever and many old ways have changed, the enterprise should re-engineer brand associations in competitive trend of new global brands to realize the next development objective beyond the normal.

SECTION III BRAND TECHNOLOGY

The classical management ideas (such as specialized division, piecework system, rank, standardization) advance with the times and present enduring charm in new brand reengineering. The development of some important management concepts and management techniques will change the meaning and essence of reengineering order to make brand exert stronger nuclear power.

6.1 The core of process reengineering is brand value chain reengineering

Is the core of brand process reengineering consumer satisfaction? NO!

The core of brand process reengineering is to arouse the users' expectations and it is a reengineering action centered on brand value chain reengineering. It is not only a reengineering centered on business, but a reengineering on brand managing of the whole association, the total staffs, and the full process.

The core of new brand process reengineering is the importance of "value" in the overall brand process. Value can be shown by core value proposition, enterprise responsibility, work value and service value. The composition of the value chain identifies value contribution and value output of every department, every process, every task and everyone in brand associations. However, the output of value is the realization of brand profits and the profit chain of deciding brand premium ability.

Only when the enterprise staff are aware of their value contribution and the mode of making profits, brand associations can really release brand premium performance, and enthusiasm of brand full participation. Only when every one in every department can clearly identify the value and the profit made in the process of brand reengineering, the enterprise can transform into a strong brand of mighty associations centered on value and profit, which is the deep meaning of brand process reengineering.

The proposition of brand core value shows the main links of brand value. As a specific key point of brand core value of brand associations in the strategic level, enterprise will increase the investment and clear requirements of strategic links established by itself. Every enterprise has different brand cores, which depends on enterprise preference, research and development, manufacturing or service. For example, "IBM is service". Although IBM works on manufacturing of IT equipment, it proposes advanced reliable technology service in the world, and Cummins regards leading engine power technology as brand value core.

The enterprise responsibility is more considered than enterprise social responsibility, so we put forward highlighting the practice and significance of enterprise responsibility. Enterprise responsibility is confirmed to perform in the world. Most brand associations devote to developing into a responsible world enterprise and express high awareness of brand responsibility in every aspect, such as investor responsibility, employer responsibility, social responsibility, product responsibility, service responsibility and so on. Enterprise responsibility is bidirectional, namely staff should also be responsible for work, salary and value of enterprise. The overall implementation of brand associations is the direct presentation of brand value and responsibility is the basic management style and brand spirit genes.

Work is valued throughout the whole process of entire brand management and operation including procurement, research and development, quality, equipment and other management links. The value of work is the expression of putting enterprise responsibility into effect and being responsible for responsibility awareness, professional spirit and value contribution from the hearts of staff who participate in management or operation. Enterprises arouse the active work concept of every staff to promote every staff to realize the reflection of value, the creation of value and the contribution of value. The main reason why the quit rate of enterprise backbone talents is high is when one person is employed by an enterprise association a soon after he finds out that personal value cannot be realized. After observing, we can find that when a new staff steps into a new association, he will try his best to show himself to realize the process of personal value being admitted, but unluckily, most of enterprises don't set up the process to expressing value admitting value in the management process.

Service value has become the focus of brand organization in the world, because many industries (such as automobile, engineering machinery, machinery manufacturing, IT.) have found the value of service profit chain and they realize that after-sales service makes the most profits for enterprise, so they lower the price in the first purchasing, but put original after-sales service components or after-sales service of original factories into the key points of brands. 3SCR, a new generation of service profit chain we designed includes service shortcomings (S), service identification (S), service responsibility (S), customer experience (C), and re-consumer plan (R) to constitute the service process reengineering structure centered on the service value as the core.

The market acceptance value and premium ability of brand is produced by brand value chain. The study centered on value found that they are shown on finished products—expression mode and service methods of products. "Value" can help staff in brand associations release enthusiasm, creativity and initiative.

6.2 The essence of brand process reengineering is innovative brand reengineering

As a brand organization operates for years, process management might become outdated, cumbersome and improper, which results in efficiency decline with process congested, bloated and stagnated. In order to put an end to the current dilemma, once in a while the company will invite the management consulting company from developed countries or domestic advanced areas to audit their management, reanalyze their management process, implement management upgrading, and finally complete the process reengineering.

But what we are trying to say here is to re-engineer the process by innovative means, among which the innovative destruction is one of them. It is not only a challenge facing the brand organization, but also a profound change for internal and external organizations.

Through the investigations towards a number of enterprises, we found that in most cases, enterprises and management consultants over-weigh and make improvement based on the existing management process, which in fact is not rational and scientific. The management process itself may be wrong, or not advanced, therefore the improvement conducted on the original basis will only lead to more faults and finally cause the failure of reconstruction. In fact, many process errors are caused by improper setting of process itself or by setting process without perspective thinking, lacking capability of avoiding new management problems.

Therefore, propose the concept of innovative reengineering, we stress that enterprises need to break the limitation of the original process, and give new energy to the reengineering of management process with an independent, more superior, more comprehensive and more advanced ideas. Management process can be flexible, which means we can deploy every single process step by step and the present the brand new process design approach, straighten out various process interface, and ensure processes have a seamless connection as well as an efficient and orderly operation.

A large engineering machinery company may wish to solve problems that occur in after-sales service process. Given that the construction site generally operates 24 hours a day, research shows that the most daunting difficulties reflected by customers are the shutdown problems caused by machinery maintenance. Therefore, how to reduce the maintenance time on site has become the priority in designing management system. The new solution to improve after-sales services can be achieved by three stages of maintenance, which also means to encourage enterprises to develop more system components. First, when engineering machinery problems occurs in the construction site, customer service personnel should arrive to the site as soon as possible, make a quick analysis of the problems, and fast call in remote electronic drawings to tackle the problems. Second, when components do need to be further repaired, customer service personnel should replace the components rapidly to ensure the machinery gets back to its normal pace. Third, set up a maintenance center inside the company to provide professional repairing and maintenance service. Three stages of maintenance will effectively shorten the repairing time, and avoid huge losses caused by machinery downtime.

There are 4,000 construction sites operating simultaneously every day in one decoration company, and in which an important position has been set up—decoration manager. As a service brand, the duties of decoration manager are to record and supervise all the renovation process on behalf of customer in case that customer cannot always reach the site on time. But in fact, decoration manager could not work for the benefit of customers, which not only caused distrust, but also many conflicts. It has been proved that the decoration manager is set improperly. The management position is arranged on the branch and has been in the same level with department of procurement, construction, quality, etc., which caused that the decoration manager cannot effectively fulfill their supervisory duties. By reengineering the process, we can transfer the decoration management department to the headquarters, so that decoration manager can fulfill their supervisory duties as headquarters staff. Responsibility and judgment department should be in place to assist decoration manager in judging issues concerning responsibility. Only when decoration manager performs in a relatively higher level can we then accurately carry out supervision functions.

A software management service company for the bank reflects that the company's marketing software often has vulnerability, poor user experience, which in fact is also caused by improper process. Due to the software company's R&D department and sales department belong to the same enterprise, the two parties have a bond to maintain each other, leading to software with poor performance flow into the market. The solution is to implement the internal market mechanism for enterprises, dividing enterprises into two independent companies—R&D company and sales company. The sales company can purchase the products made by R&D Company, and then sell them to customers. Sales company has the rights to set the market purchase price according to the quality and performance of the software. In addition, they can also conduct accountability and compensation approach according to quality problems from market feedback. The establishment of internal market mechanism improves the comprehensive brand capability of software research and development. Only when the software R&D Company outputs products with more professional and superior techniques and services can products be sold at a higher price, at the same time, enjoy high competitiveness in the market.

The above cases of brand process reengineering show that the essence of process reengineering is an innovative recreation. That is, re-establishing the management process in innovative and bold way, which is of great significance to the successful accomplishment of brand reengineering and for the best application of management process for brand association.

6.3 Brand process reengineering should focus on future agile management

Modern process reengineering is still the professional division that any type of reengineering must go through, but only creative characteristics have emerged in some links of the management process like the film production process in Hollywood which constitutes many groups of creators with different work division working on the process production. The other characteristics more important, and that is the process reengineering should focus on the standardization of future agile management, in which agile production is the main requirement of future management process reengineering.

In the future, E-commerce is going to be the main method to placing orders for production in the world. E-commerce must run in the frame of global trusted E-commerce, the precondition of which is that the enterprise that intends to be in trusted environment must have enough capacity of manufacturing, which can be complicated by factory inspection report. Enterprises can produce nothing without necessary equipment and producing environment, even if foundries still need these production requirements to do large-scale batch manufacturing, which constitute the prerequisite for Internet users to judge whether a company is credible or not.

The main fields of future E-Commerce are Data E-Commerce, Route E-Commerce, Subject E-Commerce, Group E-Commerce, and synchronized system integration, which show the competitive advantages and order generation methods of E-Commerce companies. No forms of E-Commerce can run without the process of starting from the customer placing the orders, collecting the data to batch production, in which synchronized system integration should be paid more attention to. This is the closest connection of production relations between networking and manufacturing departments. The order requirements of the customers are systematically synchronized with company's manufacturing equipment and produced according to customer's order and multiple-customized production.

Brand associations should meet customers' need with faster reaction speed. The objective requirements for the future trend of process reengineering are market flattening, sector flattening, scientific research and development, synchronization of production, mobile market and prompt and effective reaction within the whole brand organization. Agile management is going to be the most used

INTRODUCTION TO BRANDS

management trend for next-generation brand associations and all enterprises, and then the great revolution, from the trend to action, will be achieved.

Exercises

1. Fill in the blanks: The system of brand management composes of six links. They are_____,_____,_____ and_____,_____,_____.

2. Multiple-choice Question: The measures of brand management techniques includes: _____ ( )

A. (1) Create the best products; (2) Invent the best methods of management

B. (1) Create the best products; (2) Invent the best methods of management, (3) Implement brand audit and rectification

C. (1) Invent the best methods of management, (2) Implement brand audit and rectification

D. (1) Create the best products, (2) Implement brand audit and rectification

3. Discussion: What is MA Report?

Section III Brand Technology

Chapter 7

Brand Marketing Technology

Modern marketing has been out of old traditional marketing method and evolved into a multiple marketing era in which marketing happens always and everywhere, characterized by complementation between marketing and communication. Marketing technology has two links, namely marketing and communication. Marketing link mainly focuses on marketing concept, market design, market actions, service marketing and sales management, while communication places emphasis on marketing methods featuring communication such as systematic marketing, content marketing, penetration marketing, brand news professional reports and new media communication.

The original meaning of the word "marketing" refers to market actions and sales, which contains three parts: market design, market actions and market management. However, most companies neglect market design and replace market actions with market activities, and their sales management is likely to remain in the early stage, i.e. relying on sales force management.

1 Marketing concept

Many radical changes have taken place in modern marketing concept. Many marketing methods which are neglected in the past have been explored and developed into new marketing concepts. For example, academic marketing is a marketing link neglected in the past, while technology research and development and medical institutions pay more attention to carrying out academic marketing and use technical articles, scientist inventions and academic research results as the typical manners to show their strength; in addition to attending domestic or international academic conferences, they also sponsor academic seminars in industrial sectors, companies, institutions and hospital departments, which has become a main marketing method. In the era of knowledge economy, knowledge researches, inventions and development will account for a growing proportion in marketing.

Modern marketing environment mainly shows three features, namely systemic sales, direct response and automatic sales. As a result, companies with no salesman will emerge in large numbers in the near future. With the brand identification process becomes more and more systemic, intelligent and automatic, a large number of brand marketing principles will evolve into automatic sales process by employing information technology, thereby creating many new marketing professions and professional skills, as a result marketing concept will continue to have essential changes.

We divide the evolution of the overall marketing concept into four stages, namely promotion stage, hard sell stage, marketing stage and brand attraction stage. Comparing with the old stage division method, our division adds the brand attraction stage, which is a new stage in marketing. What's more, we particularly emphasize that brand attraction is the essence of brand marketing and is also a brand new marketing stage and the last field which is worth studying and exploring.

1.1 Improvement upon traditional marketing stage

Promotion stage:

Promotion methods mainly include printing and distributing publicity brochures and business cards, publicizing business promotion information everywhere and visiting from door to door, which attach great importance to obtaining attention in short term to generate profits.

Hard sell stage:

Hard sell goes further than promotion, and it is carried out through intensive advertising and market promotion activities, employing a large number of people to implement huge-crowd strategy and attracting customers with various stunts, gifts and returns promise. It pays attention to the transaction rate of salesmen.

During the hard sell stage, merchants have very low requirement on the quality of customers, and what they only care is completing a transaction, so they may sometimes employ aggressive salesmen. Hard sell may lead to excessive promotion, which main consequences are unmatched items, shoddy products or products do not fulfilled its claims, etc. Therefore, customers who have bought the products think that they have been fooled or have experienced poor services, and dissuade other people from buying such products.

Marketing stage:

Turn to marketing-oriented, aiming at attracting public attention.

Marketing focuses on marketing activities research and divides an enterprise's marketing department into two parts, namely marketing department and sales department. It places market as the priority, makes thoughtful arrangement for market planning, market development, personnel recruitment and resources allocation, and attaches importance to market data analysis reports such as rejection rate, transaction rate and customer satisfaction, etc.

Marketing also attaches great importance in cooperation with professional companies in the field of market survey, public relations, planning and communication, outsourcing to a certain extent, analyzing competitors and taking further actions at any time.

Generally speaking, enterprises that lay emphasis on marketing have established brand awareness and realized the specific effects of brand positioning, brand planning and brand effect have in the market. However, they often think that brand is the issue solely owned by the marketing department, which often lead to the circumstances of "valuing marketing over products and sales over services", so that maintaining of customer becomes a new challenge for marketing.

1.2 Brand marketing stage (brand attraction)

Brand marketing continues to take market as priority and takes attracting certain brand customer group as the marketing objective.

Some enterprises begin to really realize the charm of brand. They adhere to the dream of developing a brand in one field and are committed to do brand-related works well: paying attention to product quality, attracting more customers of a certain category, being known by people through word of mouth, trying their best to create a certain work and life style that are full of happiness, enjoyment and fun, and never analyze or rarely follow competitors.

Brand attraction leads marketing back to its original state: relying on word of mouth promotion, which means using the characteristics and charm of brand itself to naturally attract a steady flow of repeat customers, and then continually scaling up and speeding up such spread through word of mouth. By taking this strategy, companies can get a growing market share and set up new outlets to provide services for newly increased regular customers, thus build up successful brands.

1.3 Comparison between marketing and brand marketing

Process of marketing is as follows:

Develop market development plans – develop advertising plans – prepare directories and promotional materials – make market cooperation and visiting plans – develop specific market plans for different regions (links) – set up sales follow-up plans.

Process of Brand marketing (attraction) is as follows:

Focus on products and services – create a work/life style – massively increase the number of customers – make additional investment on regular customers.

SECTION III BRAND TECHNOLOGY

1.4 Seven main marketing methods:

Main marketing methods all take market as the priority, including:

(1) Personal sales method

Massively increase the number of salesmen and launch various promotion activities.

(2) Direct selling method

Sell directly via TV, internet and other ways.

(3) Advertising-driven method

Make a heavy investment on advertising and find customers who will pay the bill from the public.

(4) Chain operation method

Set up chain stores or recruit franchisees to output category lines and supply chains, without quality requirements on franchising.

(5) Distribution-driven method

Develop channels and carry out channel distribution and terminal sales direction.

(6) Third-party terminal method

Directly develop sales terminals and set up terminal outlets.

(7) Investment agency method

Develop business agents and conduct agent management.

1.5 Seven main brand marketing methods

(1) Direct marketing method

Only provide services for members and repeat customers, aiming at increasing the quantity of repeat purchase continuously.

(2) Factor marketing method

Do not produce any finished products; only focus on research and development of specific technology and product components.

(3) Brand chain method

Maintain strict quality requirements on brand operation and brands export and supporting supply chains.

(4) Word-of-mouth operation method

Never conduct advertising; focus on experience of brand customers and batch communication among specific groups.

(5) Brand advertising method

Conduct brand image advertising on specific media instead of public media.

(6) Brand activity method

Carry out special brand activities to promote communication, learning and knowledge sharing among customers to bring them happiness and fun.

(7) Co-branding method

Carry out mutual brand promotion, mutual brand construction and win-win brand cooperation on the basis of co-branding.

1.6 Automatic sales design

Automatic sales design mainly refers to designing a series of automatic sales methods through studying sales principles, user actions, user analysis data, etc. and finishing the whole sales process through sales degree setting and technical processing. Generally speaking, automatic sales design are made by management scientists and management analysts based on sales principles and customer analysis.

The following are two typical automatic sales designs, through which we can show that all sales processes can be studied and designed to be automatic sales method so as to improve sales results substantially.

(1) Automatic sales design for online advertising

By employing precision marketing methods such as conducting keyword advertising on search engines and contextual advertising, brand organizations direct the users attracted to specially-designed sales webpage.

In addition to directly completing sales, another purpose of the sales webpage which is more important, is to attract all the interested potential users to leave their e-mail addresses, so that enterprises can send specially designed sales letters to specific customers by setting auto reply emails. Such sales letters are generally used for giving away free materials and technical articles, etc.

Generally speaking, a successful transaction usually needs no less than 7 times of promotion. Most salesmen give up after contacting new customers only for 2-3 times, while seven sales letters will be sent to customers automatically according to time setting to let customers experience the process from unfamiliar to familiar. Using automatic reply emails is quite common in some countries, where people effectively apply this kind of automatic sales design strategy to let sales website automatically complete the overall process including attracting customers, contacting customers, completing transactions and electronic delivery.

(2) Automatic guidance sales design

In the early stage of internet operation, I have operated a self-service website construction project, which means users can create personal websites or company websites on the website system through registration. Obviously, self-service website construction is convenient. What we will focus on is not the contents of operation, but how to design the self-guidance program.

After observation, I found that over 47% of the new users would see a lot of website construction tools at the same time when they enter the system after registration. This circumstance often made new users feel at a loss, so that many of them logged out at this moment. Therefore, the number of users was quite less than that of registrants. Even though many users had completed registration, they would not become users.

For this reason, I ask our technicians to redesign the guiding program. Newly registered users, after entering the website system, can go through the website construction process according to the following steps: first, create a website name; second, upload the LOGO; third, design the website's background; fourth, set up columns of the website; fifth, publish the first article; sixth, check the construction result. After completing this process, new users can directly see their websites, making them more interested in using their websites and unwilling to give up the fruits of their labor. Guiding program for new users only appears at their initial registrations, and users will not see it when they enter the system for the second time.

2 Brand market design

As the first step of marketing, market design plays an important role in modern marketing, but it is likely to be neglected by people. Market design is quite important from the beginning of establishment of a new enterprise or brand. According to the market size that you have planned, it provides the market-focused structural strategic design from the aspects of organizational structure, market characteristics and market management, following which you can conduct a series of market actions including market launch, access, development and coverage. The main function of sales in market design is collecting and following-up orders.

The first key point of market design is that modern marketing is a kind of systemic marketing, namely integrated marketing. The success of marketing does not only depend on the hard work of one salesman, but also the visible or invisible efforts made by all the staff for marketing. Salesmen should be aware of it and be grateful for all the efforts made by all other departments and their staff. Only in this way can systemic marketing function well. In the past, we found a phenomenon that most startup enterprises over-valued their salesmen, even aligned employee compensation just with their sales performance instead of the entire organization's effort. This resulted in other departments being unwilling to cooperate with the sales department, and this non-cooperation often evolved into an internal conflict. There are countless cases that businesses failed in this way.

The second key point of market design is market-oriented structural design, that is to say functional division and working process containing workflow, order flow and product flow. It also includes business model design, project group design, product line operation design and other design contents.

Reasonable market design contributes to the implementation of market strategies and defines future market size from the very beginning. It helps startup enterprises to develop into high growth enterprises and helps mature brand organizations complete market structural optimization through brand reorganization.

Brand systemic sales

Systemic marketing refers to considering the sales of an enterprise as a comprehensive system consisting of market subsystem, communication subsystem, sales subsystem and other subsystems, carrying out integrated marketing targeted at directional sales projects and completing the whole process from concentrated development of customer intentions to sales leads follow-up to order fulfillment. See Fig. 13-1 for brief structure of systemic marketing.

Difference between modern marketing and traditional marketing: modern marketing organizes business development and executing personnel to conduct many-to-one sales by means of internet, CRM software and video transmission, etc., while traditional marketing generally adopts one-to-many sales model.

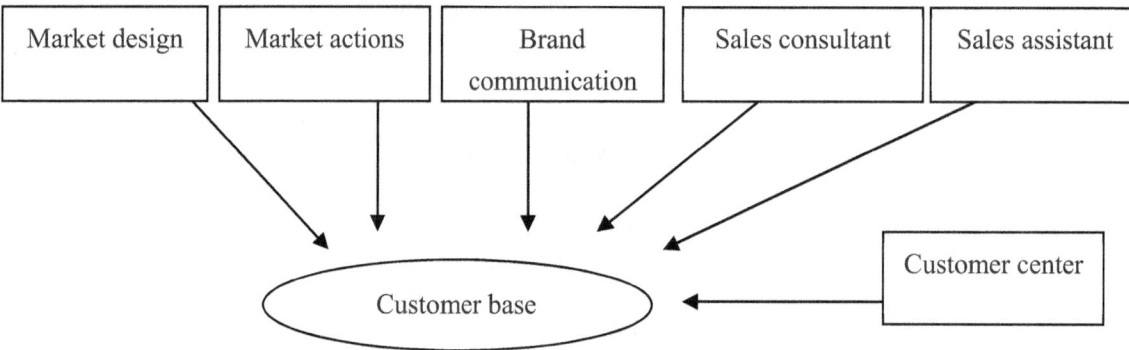

Fig. 13-1 Systemic Marketing Structure

The five parts, namely market design, market action, brand communication, sales consultant and sales assistant, constitute a clear division of responsibilities. They make joint efforts to complete concentrated development of customer base.

The whole brand organization, which consists of research and development department, product department, manufacture department, brand department, sales department, after-sales service department, customer center, administrative department, financial department and human resources department, aims to serve sales business. It is an expanded network of systemic marketing direction, supporting, coordinating and operating.

2.2 Brand market-based structural design

See Fig. 13-2 for the typical market-based structural design

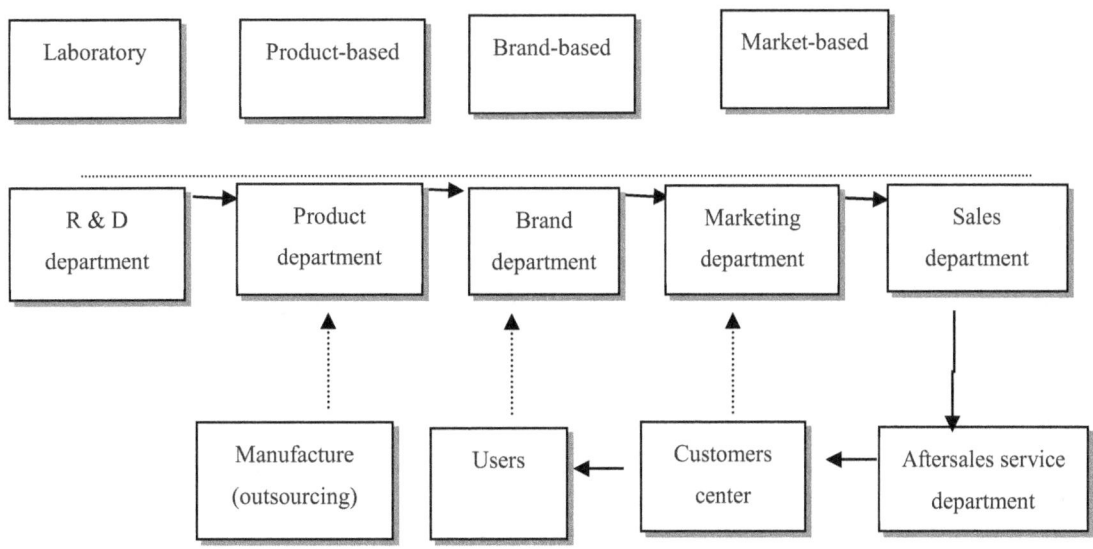

Fig. 13-2 Typical Market-based Structural Design

A typical market-based structural design contains four processes, namely laboratory state, product-based process, brand-based process and market-based process. One product is in the laboratory state when it is under research and development, and then it needs to go through the product-based process, brand-based process and market-based process successively before entering the market, which is a strict logic relationship. Different kinds of enterprises design their own market-based structure according to their own circumstances and define the organizational connection relationship between related links.

In the organization, each part has its own function and responsibility. The research and development department function as the laboratory; the product department is responsible for implementation of the product-based process and quality control; the manufacturing department (or manufacture outsourcing) is in charge of batch production; the brand department is responsible for brand-based process and brand management standard; the marketing department, sales department, after-sales service department and customer center jointly carry out the market-based process. Feedback from customer center should be sent to the marketing department, while user research and analysis is under the management of brand department.

Here it involves generation and operation process of three specific flows – work flow, order flow and product flow. Next, we will have a further discussion about them.

2.3 Work flow, order flow and product flow of brand

(1) Work flow design (See Fig. 13-3 for the typical work flow design)

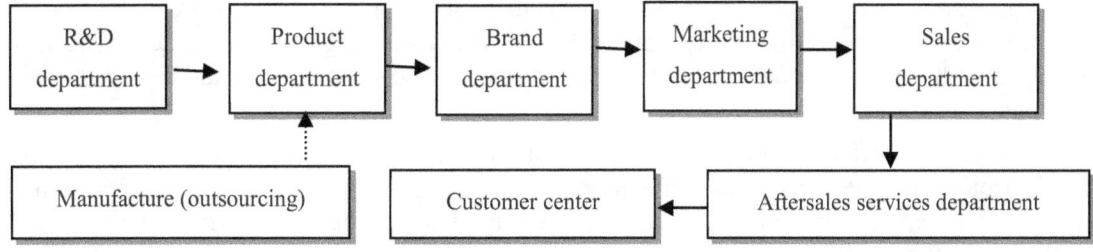

Fig. 13-3 Typical Work Flow design

SECTION III BRAND TECHNOLOGY

In work flow design, each functional department has its own working contents which are mainly as follows:

R&D department: focus on technological research and development and provide technical design according to technical strategy and product demand.

Product department: responsible for technical product-based research, product type design, quality control and technical guidance in product services.

Manufacturing department (manufacture outsourcing): responsible for batch product production and supply.

Brand department: responsible for product brand-based design as well as brand technical management, communication, making-up, transmission and other aspects.

Marketing department: responsible for market-based designs and market actions, activities, analysis and management of products.

Sales department: it is divided into multiple business divisions to conduct intensive marketing for different market segments and complete order conversion.

After-sales service department: responsible for the professional services process of following up the orders fulfilled.

Customer center: responsible for incoming calls and outgoing calls for customer consultation and troubleshooting, following up of customer problem and customer relationship management.

(2) Order flow design (See Fig. 13-4 for the typical order flow design)

Conduct partition and settlement of work flow by orders and do research on the generation method of orders.

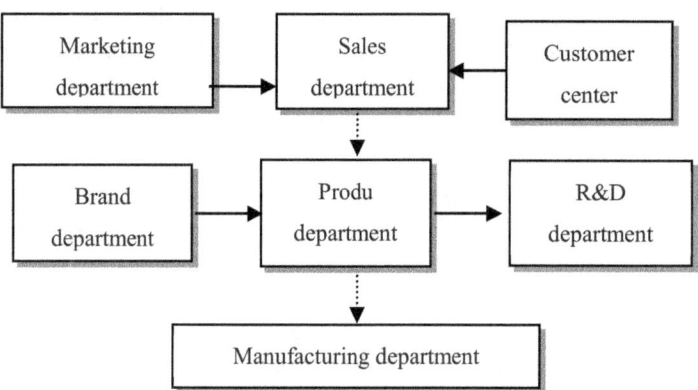

Fig. 13-4 Typical Order Flow Design

The marketing department completes batch production for market orders through market action and market development (cooperation). Customer center may have access to a great number of recommended customers, for which the sales department is responsible to follow up. The brand department is responsible for directing brand management for products. Shaped products should be supplied by the product department or produced by the manufacturing department according to the product department's arrangement; research and development of new products should be undertaken by the product center.

Order methods of different enterprises may vary slightly. Order flow design will effectively speed up the flow from order batch generation, intention development, order production, order research and development to order delivery and further develop requirements on key management links, so as to improve the order flow result.

(3) Product flow design (See Fig. 13-5 for the typical product flow design)

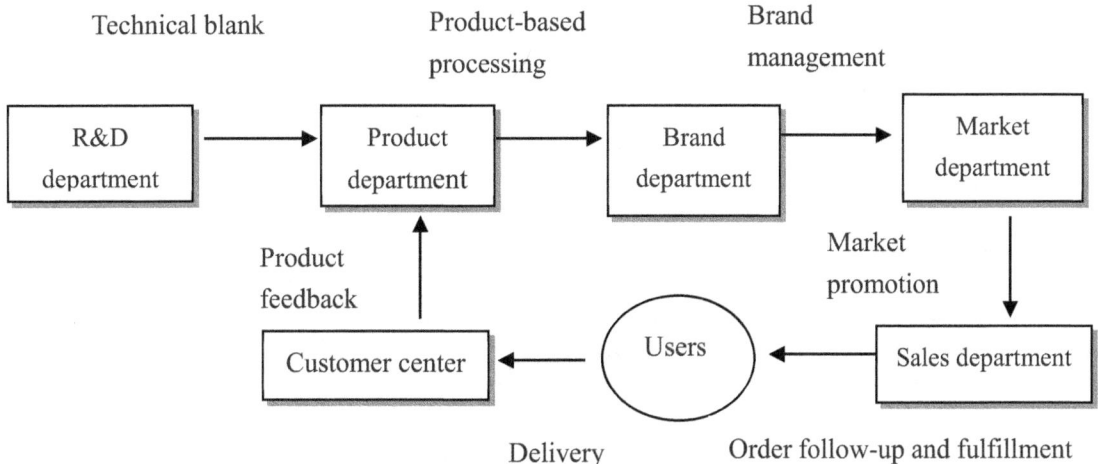

Fig. 13-5 Typical Product Flow Design

We take a typical product flow design as an example and define the typical task of each phase that products go through. The R&D department provides technical blanks (semifinished products); product department is responsible for product-based processing (finished products); the brand department is responsible for band management (to establish brands); the marketing department is responsible for market promotion (market-based products); the sales department takes charge of order follow-up (product order fulfillment) and delivery to users; customer center conduct customer follow-up services (product service response) and send product feedback to the product department (product maturity).

2.4 Brand business model design

Business model deign is suitable for staged product market structure. It divides the future development of an enterprise into three stages (the first stage, the second stage and the third stage) and designs according to each specific stage, so as to ensure the enterprise has a smooth development of key markets in each stage.

A typical SNS has different sources of income in its two stages (See Fig. 13-6 and 13-7):

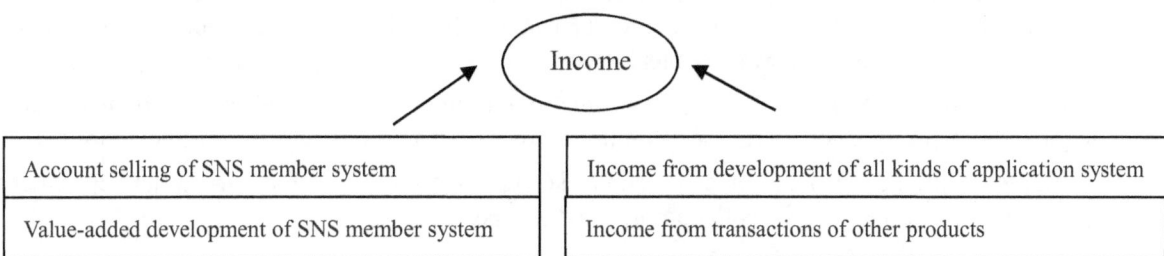

Fig. 13-6 Business Model Example in the First Stage

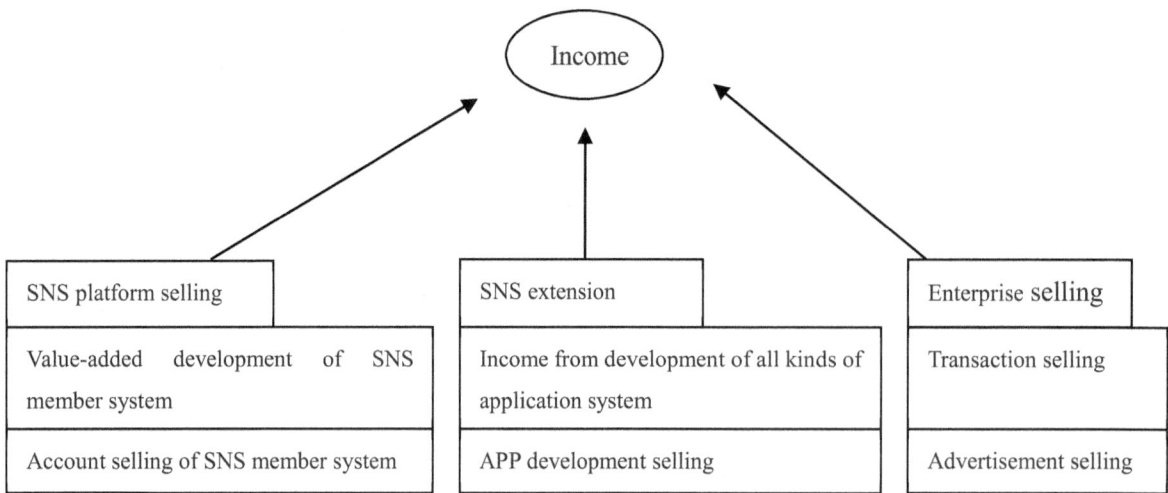

Fig. 13-7 Business Model Example in the Second Stage

Business model design helps enterprises to determine the important level of income sources in each stage. In the first stage, enterprises should focus on sales income of specific and single (which is preferred) type of business, and then expand their income sources in the second or third stage, so as to avoid some problems such as dispersed market capacity caused by engaging in too many businesses while lacking of capacity.

2.5 Brand project group design

According to the actual need, enterprises may set up project groups to ensure adequate market strength and specialization. That is to say, enterprises may classify the work tasks based on certain standards, for example classification based on user groups (old age and middle age, male and female or medical institutions, disease control institutions and health care institutions) or based on market action (Plan M, Plan C, Plan Y), and then set up different project groups for specific work tasks to complete the projects. Under some circumstances, expanded business division can be employed to conduct management.

Project groups have two types, namely long-term project groups and temporary project groups. Long-term project groups are widely existed in all links including R&D department, product department, brand department, marketing department, sales department, after-sales service department and customer center, mainly responsible for designated long-term tasks. Each group under the charge of one project supervisor and is under the management of the department director or project group manager. Each group is built up mainly based on five key members.

Temporary project groups are set up upon designation for temporary tasks, such as striving to make technological breakthrough, conducting one-to-one customer services or market offensive actions.

According to the actual need, enterprise may set up long-term or temporary trans-department project groups in a flexible way, so as to complete work tasks rapidly.

2.6 Operation design for brand product line

In order to serve markets more precisely, companies may launch professional brands or product lines to carry out segmenting management on markets. For this reason, companies can adopt several set of business work flow in actual business operation to match the joint development of strategic main businesses and subsidiary businesses and ensure the reasonable application of resources. See Fig. 13-8 for design for brand business division (product line operation center).

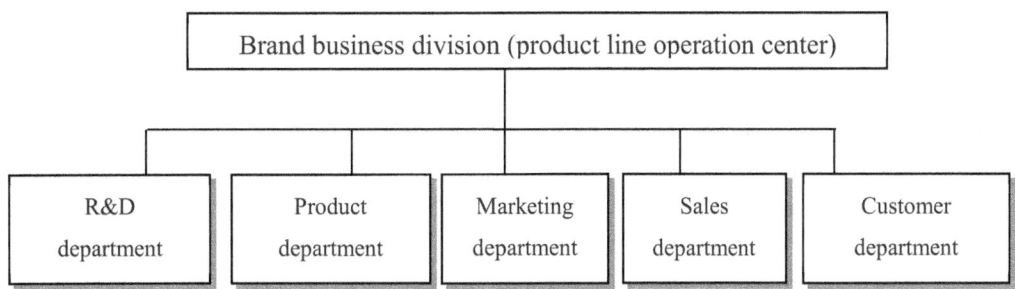

Fig. 13-8 Design for Brand Business Division (Product Line Operation Center)

Aiming to meet the strategic market development, the normal organization structure and product workflow of enterprises may set up one or more independent brand business division or product line operation center in the normal work flow to take charge of all kinds of product line technical services which may be provided and conduct operation management independently. Each brand business division (product line operation center) is responsible for full access to a certain key professional market and the professional service assurance for it.

3 Brand market action design

The first thing of market action design is designing for market size programmatically in order to meet market action objectives. And on that basis, the next step is decomposing market action into reasonable parts, of which there are three critical three parts: method design, standardization and execution.

Market action is essentially a dynamic market operation. Specifically, it is a mobilization of all the staff. All departments, organizations, co-manufacturers and brand service providers may be involved in. Just like commanding a campaign, only by taking the offensive strategy aggressively can the enterprise maintain a continuously strong brand in the marketplace.

Of market action there are two main involving departments: Standardized Management and Brand Communication. The former is mainly responsible for studying, researching and standardizing the methods of market action. Besides, the latter, brand communication department, can heighten the atmosphere, strengthen the market power, boost morale and win customers by widely advertising. We will talk about this part later in Chapter Brand Communication Technology.

3.1 Market size design

Market size design is a kind of prediction for market's future development. When starting out, a new enterprise has to forecast future market prospect, in order to envision how large the enterprise scale is going to be. This is the key point which investors, stockholders and new employees care about mostly while considering whether to participate in.

Everyone wishes to join an entrepreneurial enterprise that is likely to gain a superior market scale. However, enterprises like this have been very rare. Even if there is one, most investors and job seekers are not able to distinguish the potentiality in its early time.

Investors can be divided into two types. One type of investor concerns about how large a brand's market scale can be. They firmly believe that superior market scale can be formed only by supercorp. Angels and early investors of Microsoft, Apple, Google and Facebook are acutely aware of these super projects, so they wrote down their investment myths.

While on the contrary, the other type is lack of the vision. They cannot catch those talented entrepreneurs' dreams and even think that they are unrealistic jokes. Although envying investment myths, they still prudently set their sights on those WYSIWYG investment projects. Listing or delisting, selling out profitable projects and earning dividends are their main investment methods.

Market scale is determined by entrepreneur. But to realize it, the enterprise must have powerful execution. Personally, I believe that a super brand needs at least 100 Billion dollars of market scale. The new generation of entrepreneurs shall analysis the marketplace's capacity of scale at first to build a supercorp.

3.2 Market scale model selection

We divide market into two types: general trend (major trend) and market gap (blank market). Talented entrepreneurs usually choose the market with mega scale and great trend, while common entrepreneurs choose the market gap. The former's scale is at least 100 billion dollars, while the latter is at most 10 billion. Actually, an entrepreneur's (a brand, an enterprise) achievement is already determined by his market scale model selection at the very beginning.

If an entrepreneur aspires to be a tycoon and build a super brand, he will never be tempted by a market scale under 100 billion dollars per year. For example, markets of e-book and SEO (Search Engine Optimization) is quite hot today, but their scale is only billions of dollars. Those market is too small to be called potential. The whole scale of the market limits the enterprises in it from growing big. Great entrepreneurial firms will never be born here.

Many entrepreneurs and investors seem to be far-sighted, in fact they keep doing blank-filling on market scale selection all the time. Market does exist in this kind of blanks, such as online group buying, coin collections and housekeeping services. Entrepreneurs in those fields failed to see the global trend of the market, even worse, in such a narrow segment of the market they still believe that there must be market gaps somewhere and they can fill them. Or they pile into the markets which are already competitive like e-book or stock software with some new inventions, hoping to extend those fields, in the end they will find themselves confined in a narrow market space.

Talented entrepreneurs are always the rule-makers of the game. They could see the future trend, then change the rules, point out a direction and lead the market, finally accomplish great enterprises.

3.3 Market action decomposition

Whether it is choosing a mega scale market with great trend, or a gap market with few blanks, it is certain that entrepreneurs and investors both have great faith in their project initially. So they have to make a prediction about the prospect of brand. Such as a market value of 100 billion dollars, a market value of 10 billion dollars, an annual income of 100 million dollars, or an annual income of 10 million dollars.

Step one: Make a plan of decomposing the market action. Firstly, you should determine duration to reach the targeted market scale (ten, eight, five, or three years). Then break the market action into several stages (the launch time of the first, second and third generations, or market scale stage one, stage two and stage three).

Step two: According to the stage-wise design. Determine the financing target for every stage, major action mode, product's form and user volume.

Step three: Focusing on the target market scale which has been set in step one, plan and distribute all the tasks and targets. Make a powerful action scheme and enter the stage of execution.

There are two kinds of brand which are more attractive to investors. One is fresh, unprecedented, interesting and influential. A brand with these characters is more likely to become a super brand. The other is feasible, with certain capability of R&D and mature commercial pattern. This kind of brand is a good choice for listing or funding.

In consideration that today a brand's development is mainly dominated by its investors and this pattern is quite matured, the combination of entrepreneurs and investors has become the most primary of a super brand. When a brand launches its market actions, investors have already been involved in. They are the chief factor behind the rapid rise of the brand.

3.4 Market action method design

New creative enterprises and reengineered enterprises usually emphasize on developing and designing its own strategy of market launch, market entry and market management. Table 13-1 is the 4M Market Launch System of Dealers Localization (4M System).

Table 13-1 4M Market Launch System of Dealers Localization (4M System)

M1	M2	M3	M4
Market Access	Market launch	Market Development	Market Coverage
System key capability deployment	Market launch schedule management	Market development schedule management	Dealer motivation management
Headquarter market invest management	Market launch problem meta-analysis	Market development problem meta-analysis	Brand standardization Service profit chain
Market launch design	Market launch resources analysis	Market developer management	Regulars project
Market research	Market launch staff plan	Intention customer data management	Brand communication plan
Initiate plan	Market targets break down plan	Localization market invest management	Whole staff after-sales service
Group buying analysis	Market launch work plan		Whole staff learn and improve plan
Distribution analysis	Market launch release plan	Localization brand recognition	
Retail analysis	Market launch expenses budget	Localization sales management	Whole staff incentive promotion plan
Customer groups analysis	Market launch release list		Backbones project
Entry barriers	Market launch warm up management	Localization field-management	Customer resource competition analysis
Entry advantages	Training management	Market distribution management	Total market coverage plan
High quality resources investigation	Product management		
Localization market synergy	Model store management	Channel construction management	
Market entry route design	Experience store management	Branch management	
	Material management	Terminal automation management	
	Channel invitation		
	Intention of signing management	Promotion management Service management	
	Market launch release field-management	Market supervision management	
	Channel invitation	Dispute management	
	Market launch summary		

In this example, we design a 4M market launch system of dealer localization. This system can be used in the specific market actions and market management links for dealers aiming at channel development. It is composed of a series of specialized terms, action method guidance, management tables and supervision. It breaks a market launch process down into four parts: market entry, market launch, market development and market coverage.

3.5 Standardization of market action

Standardization means strict requirements for brand managers and dealers. It is too important to be ignored. However, standardization is much more than unified and standardized image, which is only the early and primary stage.

Standardization of market action is stricter than common standardization management. The establishing process is to research and test every procedure in practice, and find the best method, movement, language and exhibition.

PADS Analysis Model, Brand Comparison Analysis and Experimental Science Management are all efficient tools for establishing standardization.

Just as "4M Market Launch System of Dealer Localization", there are generally two ways of market standardization design. One comes from research institutions. They invent a series of solutions for common situations in market. Such as Automobile 4S shop management, TQC management and OTC management. These solutions are universally applicable and have great value in promoting global industrial development.

The other comes from enterprises. Sometimes enterprises would do the market standardization design by themselves to suit their own needs. It must be done under the direction of management scientists and analysts. In some situations, information technology is useful, too; it helps to build market action knowledge management system, market action command system, market management system, etc.

Designing the market action standardization scientifically and effectively contributes to rapid replication of market models such as market development and market launch, and also brings in good operation effectiveness.

3.6 Market action implementation

After market standardization, decomposition and action, enterprise should take a further step to implement the above processes by conducting specific projects, and practice the project management method to define every project's schedule, effect, reporting system, responsible departments and responsible individuals

Market action execution is a strict management process. Standardization can enhance the effect of market action significantly. Marketing department of an enterprise should build a specialized institutions or organizations, which is responsible for training, guiding and supervising of market construction, focusing on training market action specialists. Only specialists that have been trained professionally can enhance the efficiency of market action.

On brand dealer level, strict market action standardization training is necessary for everyone. It is important to make sure that the market launch process of sample market and key market is operated by market action specialists, and all of the market action specialists are under vertical management of headquarter. Only in this way it can ensure that the market action functions efficiently.

Especially in the early stages of an enterprise, labor division of salesmen and market action specialists must be clear-cut strictly. Salesmen shall not serve as market action specialists at the same time. Specialization and efficiently functioning mean everything to an enterprise that is entering the market, especially in its first year and second year. Only efficient and specialized market action can maximize the enterprise's rate of expansion.

Brand communication plays an important role in market actions, including publicity, promotions, pulling, and large-scale orders development. Its targets are the public, professional markets, and users. Brand communication is implemented by brand communication department, accompanied with departments of sales, after-sale service, customer service, etc.

4 Sales management

Even though modern marketing tries not to talk about sales and believes that sales methods have been outdated, in fact sales still hold a dominant position in most counties. Up to now, it is still a subject that we cannot bypass. The fulfillment of market design and action also depends on sales, especially for most startup enterprises in the early stage; sales take a great proportion in most cases. Operation of some enterprises engaging in insurance, household articles and real estate still depends mainly on large numbers of salesmen.

We do not need to ignore the important role sales plays in the overall marketing. What we need to do is use better sales design, sales training and sales management to carry out business development and expansion of brands.

In the market, some enterprises have entered the stage of robot selling and smart selling based on their own operational characteristics, while most enterprises still try to use more effective sales methods to grow their brand organizations.

4.1 Light sales

Light sales means that some enterprises deliberately separate sales from research, development and production, so as to concentrate their attention on research, development or production. Not every enterprise needs sales. Some enterprises such as R&D enterprises, market development enterprises and allied enterprises, may remove the sales link from the very beginning. These enterprises generally focus on the research and development of core technology and products or construction of key brands in terms of strategy design, or operate by way of joint market development, strategic alliance cooperative operation and others, which can help them fully concentrate on research and development, services and other high-tech links. In addition, some enterprises remove the sales link from their operation by adopting third-party sales so that they can focus on research, development and production, by which they can reduce investment on sales.

For instance, management trainers in the past often not only needed to teach lessons, but also conduct selling. Since their energy is limited, they could not concentrate their attention on course research and teaching. What's more, selling may not be their specialty. After the emergence of some third-party sales platforms or institutions, trainers are encouraged to focus on course research and teaching, while sales works are removed from their duties and handed to third parties.

This circumstance also exists in R&D enterprises and productive enterprises. For instance, R&D enterprises which focus on product research and development operate by way of OEM, technical license, technical sales or technical transfer and totally get rid of the sales link; real estate enterprises make rational division of function by setting up different kinds of specialized companies for building construction, real estate selling, property management and other functions, and conduct effective market combination.

The rational division of R&D, production and sales appeared as early as the 18th or 19th century. For example, *The Wealth of Nations* has discussed the problems of shoemakers to explain the importance of separation of sales from production: A shoemaker can make over 300 pairs of shoes in a year, while his family may wear out no more than six pairs of shoes in a year, so there must be at least 50 such families buying shoes from him otherwise the shoes that he made in a year cannot be sold out. As social division of labor continues to accelerate, light sales will develop into an important trend. In our opinion, only when the enterprises adopting the method of light sales have realized a great development will the social division of labor, technology maturity and market specialization level have a great improvement, and then release unprecedented creativity.

4.2 Robot selling

Robot selling refers to automatic selling without salesmen and this is realized through reasonable self-adaption and automated management. With respect to robot selling, all sales works are completed by automated purchasing equipment, automatic warehouse and automatic services, without people participating in the sales process directly. Typical robot selling examples are automatic vending machine, automatic e-commerce ordering terminal and other technical achievements.

Along with the development of modern systematics and management science, robot selling's links and forms will have a rapid development in the future. For instance, enterprises operating via internet and mobile internet are most likely to remove or reduce investment on the sales department through online selling of rechargeable cards, third-party e-payment and other methods, and focus on market development and cooperation instead.

Robot selling is an important trend. A growing number of enterprises will complete reasonable business model design and reduce or remove the proportion of sales in business process. In addition, application of various new technologies and maturity of industries will further accelerate the development of robot selling trend.

Robot selling is the optimal stage of sales development, in which there is no sales department or salesman. Whenever brand attraction reaches a certain level, the effect of sales will decrease accordingly, and then the self-adapted automatic sales environment will be formed. We emphasis that brand is a form of organization. Thus, brand organization itself has a strong systematization tendency to integrate the works of enterprises' internal personnel with the brand attraction for external users. Triggering identification, problem solving and delivery after completion all can be designed in accordance with the self-adapted sales flow.

Customer center is most likely to become an important link in automatic sales. It can turn customers' consultations into sales opportunities and then help realize repeat sales. It can also establish a customer conversion mechanism with high reliability by employing sales psychology, systematics and other science.

4.3 Smart selling

As an important method pursued by modern enterprises, smart selling refers to carrying out sales by employing scientific and intelligent methods. Smart selling can give a reasonable design of the whole process from order processing, human-machine interaction, smart response, agile manufacturing to batching delivery, during which human do not participate in sales and customer service. The whole process from order processing to order fulfillment is intelligent and automated.

We will usher in an era of great development of smart selling technology. Smart selling can identify users' explicit and implicit demands automatically and match them with selling methods actively and automatically. Thus, responding to their demands efficiently and safely.

Smart selling has different layers including intelligent analysis layer, information transfer layer and interactive processing layer. The intelligent layer is mainly responsible for generating consumer types, states, behaviors and other data, identify user characteristics, study consuming demands and match selling results. Smart selling may further integrate users into the process of opportunity management, as well as obtaining and responding to sales orders through self-adapting promotion, sales lead generation, customers tracking and sales information linking. The transfer layer is responsible for transferring all kinds of information paths and assigning directions. The interactive layer is responsible for managing the interactive interface and providing interactive experience of user to user, user to enterprise and enterprise to enterprise.

4.4 Sales design

Sale-based enterprises mainly rely on personal selling, sales design is the first step of sales management, while sales force grouping is the key content of sales design. Generally speaking, whether the sales teams of small enterprises or the sale calling centers each consisting of hundreds of people or thousands of people of large enterprises, all should conduct sales force grouping and division of works appropriately. See Fig. 13-9 for work flow of a typical sales group.

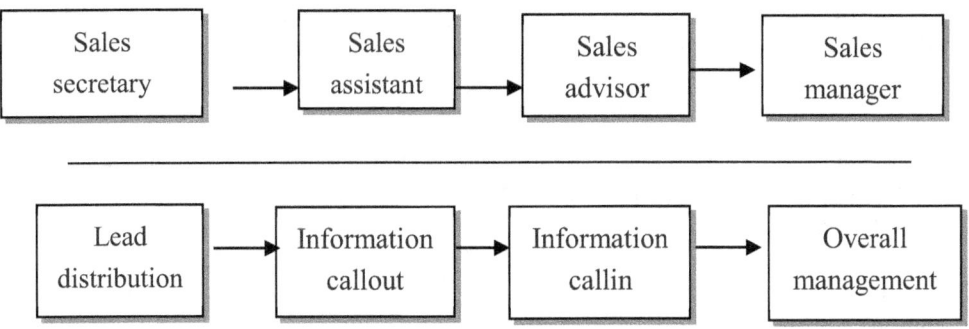

Fig. 13-9 Work Flow of A Typical Sales Group

The recommended size for a typical sales group is 10 to 15 persons, consisting of project managers (sales managers), sales advisors, sales assistants and sales secretaries (sales clerks). Project managers are project management personnel responsible for the sales business in a certain field; sales advisors are senior sales personnel who have strong capability of understanding and responding and can directly negotiate with customers; sales assistants are primary sales personnel responsible for sales leads, outgoing calls, faxing and mailing; sales secretaries (sales clerks) are responsible for phone answering, name collecting, distribution, data statistics, analysis, sales recording, etc.

This structure is mainly based on the ability to reasonably distribute sales works to fulfill orders. Sales assistants are only responsible for calling out, faxing or receiving or sending mails, and do not take responsibility for whether orders are concluded or not. This structure has the following advantages: effectively match personnel with duties so as to reduce personnel assigning problems caused by a lack of sales experience; effectively reduce costs and improve sales output; provide a promotion channel for sales personnel and further define sales levels, providing sales personnel with a promotion incentive mechanism.

Remuneration design is also an integral part of sales design. It includes two aspects: One is the remuneration design for sales personnel. In order to carry out appropriate incentive mechanism, it is more reasonable to tie to sales pieces; measure by figure not proportion whenever possible; emphasis the task fulfillment rate and the reward scheme for excess portion; focus on encourage outperformance and take it as the incentive objective. The other is that the result must be tied to efforts of other departments and individuals, and this part should be assessed and settled reasonably, so that the entire staff will contribute to sales. If staff from other departments especially those connected with the business feels that their salaries are not linked to sales, a serious crisis will emerge. Specifically, contradictions and conflicts (for example, different departments are not willing to cooperate with each other) arise frequently. Soon the enterprise will find itself stuck in troubles internally and externally.

4.5 Sales training

Sales training is the core of sales management. A learning-oriented enterprise understands the importance of training to sales. By providing sales training every week (every two weeks), enterprises can improve employees' sales passion, sales knowledge and sales skills and help employees share excellent experience. For most new employees, the primary goal for joining an enterprise is to have adequate learning opportunities, let alone sales personnel. For the sales personnel, an appropriate learning incentive scheme is more needed which can raise their confidence and passion.

Generally speaking, the main reason for poor sales results for an enterprise is due to its lacking on sales training. As a result, their sales personnel cannot give more professional and clear explanations on products and answer various puzzling questions raised by customers; they cannot have persistent sales passion; they cannot get to know new knowledge, new trends and new concepts about sales, let alone apply them to sales business flexibly.

Sale itself is a sales knowledge network with knowledge updated rapidly and dynamically. Update of optimal sales skills training, optimal verbal tricks, optimal negotiation skills, optimal sales services examples, latest selling points of products and application cases is completed mainly through systemic training. Without adequate sales training, there would not be outstanding sales results.

Enterprises should attach importance on Chief Training Officer, Sales Trainers and other positions, strengthen the external and internal professional sales research and keep training contents updated. One possible drawback of sales training is over-closed, which makes enterprises only know the sales knowledge about the industries they are engaged in and do not connect with external knowledge. The sales knowledge management of such enterprises will fall into an accelerated aging stage and soon be eliminated in competition.

Sale is a knowledge domain which always needs to be widely connected with social hot topics, best-selling elements and new industry trends, otherwise sales personnel will not be able to have topics to further communicate with customers. Whether it is sales courses or sales training contents, they should be designed from the perspectives of common use, common knowledge and all-round persons, keep absorbing the latest and most advanced experience and skills in various industries and fields. Open and inclusive attitude and rich knowledge are the foundations of excellent sales results.

4.6 Sales techniques

Sales techniques include sales skills, sales psychology, sales verbal tricks, sales tools, sales management methods and other techniques involved in the whole process of sales, which are the main driving force for sales management performance and work performance of sales personnel.

Sales skills include knowledge structure and basic abilities which sales personnel should possess, namely deep understanding on brands, mastery of products and product application cases, product usage techniques and sales abilities such as dressing, response and negotiating. Sales psychology refers to the method of designing sales techniques by studying all kinds of psychological experience and response of customers. Grasping customer psychology will effectively improve the success rate of sales.

Sales verbal tricks refer to the standardized process of unifying standard expression language to customers, questions, answering and response language. Sales tools refer to a series of tools combinations providing explanations, recommendations and management by using presentation tools, videos and forms, which greatly contribute to the substantial improvement of sales results.

Sales management methods refer to the management techniques at the sales management level, for example employing sales progress control, honor incentive management, monthly launch meeting, morning conference and other various methods to conduct effective management on sales works and sales personnel.

Modern sales are increasingly using all kinds of IT technologies to develop customer tracking system, sales opportunity management system, sales knowledge management system and other internet-based and mobile sales technologies, so as to improve sales management efficiency.

Exercises

1. Fill in the blanks: Modern marketing environment mainly shows a full service marketing concept of namely systemic sales, direct response, and automatic sales. The evolution of it can be divided into four stages:

_____, _____, _____, and _____.

2. True or False Question: Process of brand attraction is: Focus on products and services – create a work/life style – massively increase the number of customers – make additional investment on regular customers.

3. Discussion: How do you understand brand systemic sales?

Chapter 8

Brand Communication Technology

With the rise of modern journalism and public relations, marketing has begun to attach great importance to the value of media communication. Within the coming of times when all the media such as online news, community forum, social networking, wemedia, video, and mobile media. Have carried out the communication marketing, the content marketing-based brand communication has become the top priority.

When a brand organization decides to mainly develop a brand communication, an independent brand communication center could be established and shall be responsible for all the affairs relating to brand promotion, brand communication, brand market impetus, brand activity scheming, brand public relations, etc., so as to expand the communication effects of the brand.

1 Brand communication

Modern brand communication is a form of communication based on brand news, brand articles and brand video throughout the network and at the full range and based on the news, publicity, public relations(PR), and sales copywriting.

A lot of brands worldwide such as Google, Microsoft, Coca-Cola, Starbucks, LV, Benz, BMW, Haier, and Granz are the winners in brand communication. Every global corporations and PR companies would spend several millions each year on communication writing training and spend billions US dollars on content marketing releasing such as brand news communication.

World Intellectual Property Organization (WIPO) reported: the world brands would spend up to 500 billion USD each year in brand promotion which exceeded the investment of global corporations in R&D or design and account for one fourth of the intangible asset investment.

CMI North America reported: more than 94% of the large corporations would often publish news release and more than 72% of the large and super large companies would recognize the rewards from news release.

PR Newswire 2013-2014 reported: 85.3% of the enterprises would preferentially choose "news release" as the most common instrument for company communication and 64% of the companies believe that the news release would bring the highest returns on brand or sales promotion. 93.1% of enterprise brand PR directors use news release most often and 73.3% of the enterprise brand PR directors recognize its rate of return. Please refer to Table 14-1 for brand communication guiding the living consumption.

Table 14-1 Brand communication guiding the living consumption

№	News Type	Form of Operation	Form of Revenue
1	Movie news information	Sales of tickets	Box office income
2	Concert news information	Sales of tickets	Ticket income
3	New cell phone news information	Sales of cell phone	Income from types of cell phones

SECTION III BRAND TECHNOLOGY

4	News information on specialty demonstration	Sales of dishes	Income from restaurants
5	News information on seven star hotels	Sales of guest rooms	Income from room reservation
6	News information on English training institution	Sales of courses	Income from tuition

Brand communication has affected our living consumption and people would establish the guidance and make the choice for their way of life, work and purchase based on the information from such soft news.

1.1 Principle of brand communication process

Please refer to Fig. 14-1 for the simplified view of principle of brand communication process

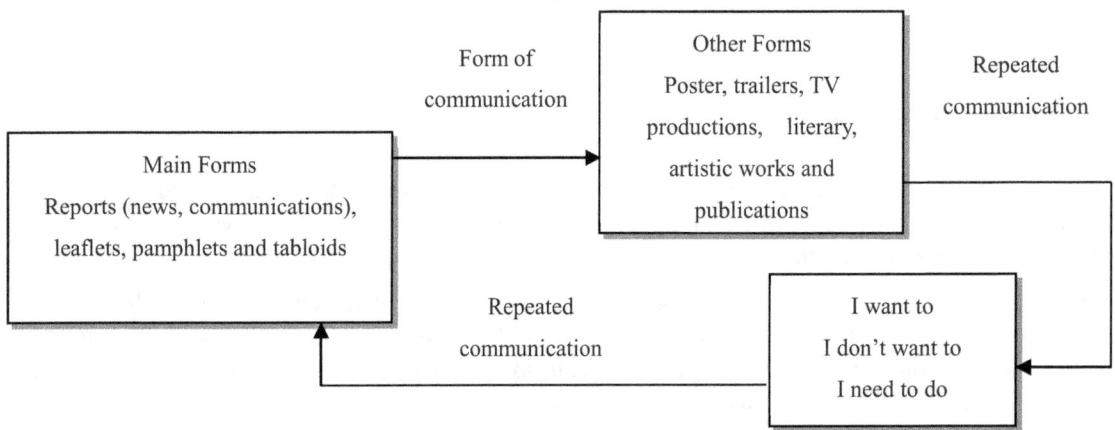

Fig. 14-1 Principle of brand communication process

Brand communication is a kind of diffused communication based on news value and communication value. It is mainly in the form of brand news report (news, communications), leaflets, pamphlets and tabloids or in any other forms such as poster, trailer, TV productions, literary, artistic work, and publication. By repeating communication continuously, it managed to build up the selective ideology of "I want to, I don't want to and I need to do" in potential consumers.

News value refers to the subjective opinion that is sufficient to lead the relevant public or a particular group of people so as to guarantee the media's extensive attention and reports. The media in different countries would have judgment on news value. The media in US generally believe that small enterprises are most newsworthy and would have important social and economic impact on the American economy; whereas the media in China thinks that the large corporations are newsworthy and would usually ignore the news of small companies. Different judgment on news value would determine the number of reports on certain type of news and involvement of the media would write in a country and would also determine the mainstream directions of the national ideology.

When the country and social media gave insufficient reports on the affairs of companies, in particular the small companies, the company should increase their awareness on brand communication and advertisement investment, which is not only a difficult, but also an opportunity, as it means that the branded companies would have more chances to stand out from its competitors by the virtue of brand communication.

1.2 Principle of three levels of brand communication

Please refer to Fig.14-2 for principle of three levels of brand communication.

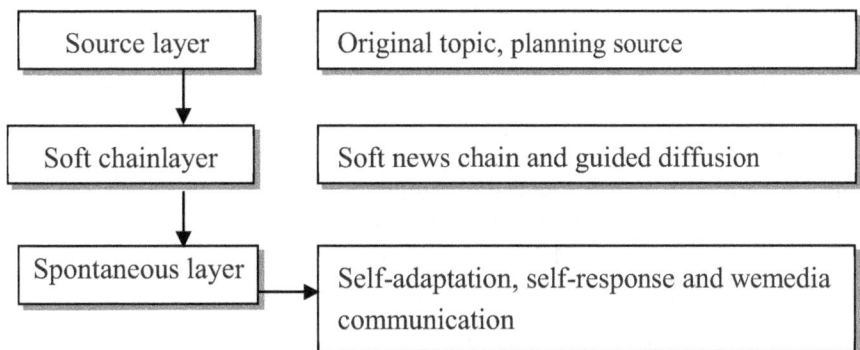

Fig. 14-2 Principle of three levels of brand communication

Principle of three levels of brand communication is a structural design that we have made for the form of brand communication. The modern brand communication is a self-communication process of self-adaptation and self-response. The brand communications could be classified into the source layer, soft chain layer and spontaneous layer.

The source layer is mainly the original topics sent by the brand organizations or the planning sources formed by brand planning; soft chain layer is the second communication of the soft news, content and so on via the important communication channels such as media or opinion leaders via communication layout, so as to guide to diffuse the communication effect; the third is the spontaneous layer and it is the spontaneous communication process to be reviewed, interpreted and explicated by the media reporters, opinion leaders, readers and netizens. The media communication effect shall be mainly reinforced by the second and third layers and then achieve the final communication effectiveness.

1.3 Principle of brand systematic communication

Systematic communication refers to the systematic communication structure classified for the media in which the professional team or professionals shall be liable for different media. Please refer to Fig.14-3 for principle of the brand systematic communication.

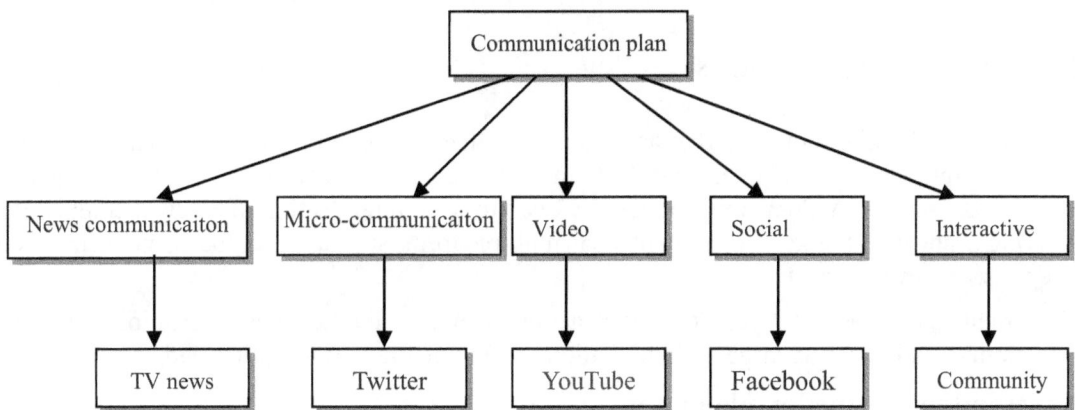

Fig. 14-3 Principle of the brand systematic communication.

Modern communication is a systematic communication. The typical systematic communication is a set of complete marketing strategy deployed by Obama campaign during the early stages, including propaganda, fundraising and communication with voters which has built up the three-dimensional network image for Obama.

1.5 million volunteers from different places who supported Obama have set up 770 offices and access to nearly 400,000 votes each day on average. By a whole set of systematic operation and via the new media such as the traditional television media corresponding to Paid Media, plane media and e-mail marketing corresponding to New Media, online video, Blog, SNS, it has achieved the whole network communication.

For instance, the video production team for online propaganda had been responsible for making a production carrying more than 20 five-minute videos, which aroused great response. There are designated people to be solely responsible for Obama propaganda column on special video website YouTube and specified people to be solely responsible for leading dozens of volunteers to produce the propaganda videos on Obama for making publicity across America.

All the volunteers shall participate in communication and the campaign has set up several leading teams and every member in the leading team have a clear division of duty, such as team coordinator, data coordinator, volunteer coordinator, voter registration and contact coordinator, and family party coordinator.

1.4 Main forms of brand communication

The main forms of brand communication include news communication, word-of-mouth communication, warming-up communication, thematic communication, topic communication, etc.

Brand news communication: such as Facebook, Google, Twitter, would mainly communicate the latest news on its brand and emphasize the real-time trend.

Word-of-month communication: such as LV and Starbucks would mainly communicate the sense of brand value, the sense of brand ownership and sense of use.

Warming-up communication: such as Olympics, Hollywood movies, and Daming Palace, would mainly communicate the brand expectation such as future and prospect.

Thematic communication such as XP, game communication (Red Alert), crazy bird, blue tooth, and Android, would communicate on a specific topic, the usage methods, forms of application, and fun of communication.

Topic communication: hot topics (transformation and upgrading, weight loss, Silk Road economic belt, self-driving trip and road book) would obtain the content of self-communication mainly in the form of topics.

2 Brand market actions

The purpose of taking brand market actions is to realize the brand influence or sales lead by the strong brand communication. It is best that the brand communication department would be responsible for brand market actions. A Company would carry out strong communication of a new market concept, a self-driving event and a market scheming plan via multiple forms such as news focus, media interactive, action reports, and event reports.

The brand market actions include market action planning, market communication plan, brand concept communication, brand large scale invitation communication, brand sales lead, etc.

2.1 Brand market action planning

The brand market action planning mainly consists of two aspects: one is the overall market action and the other is the brand activity.

The overall market action is generally a large scale action organized by the brand such as "quality month", "customer service month", "customer experience day", and "thematic activity". In this way, it could greatly improve the brand awareness by brand action, and demonstrate the comprehensive or professional management and service levels so that the media and brand users could further understand the brand value and show the brand strength by involvement and participation. The overall market action is generally a work in the following aspects of the technology upgrading, service plan, customer service pushed by each department of the company or in a whole process. The brand communication department shall be liable for the all-around drive and communication.

The form of brand market action could be classified into large, medium and small, such as customer club, test-driving activity, brand party, charity dinner, and public benefit activity, which could be organized by the brand itself, or jointly held with the others or by naming sponsorship, which is mainly to increase the brand influence, popularity, reputation, customer interaction, etc.

The organization and publicity of the brand market action should be generally integrated so as to play the important role of brand communication. The brand market activity shall focus on the novelty of action or event originality which should have the sense of news and point of dissemination.

During the process of communication, special attention should be given to the flexible application of such functions as interview, compilation, and editing, so that the action or activity is reportable and could be reported with strong effect. The enterprise members and consumers should be given more opportunities to express their ideas, suggestions and thoughts during the action process so as to make the brand stories lively and vivid.

2.2 Brand communication plan

The brand communication plan is generally prepared by the enterprise every year, it is used to notify all the personnel and distributors of the whole-year communication plan arrangement, including the brand marketing strategy, market activity, media placement plan, brand communication cooperation, etc.

Brand marketing strategy shall clarify the brand concept, brand idea and brand demand focus. A company would carry out a consistent brand marketing strategy for a long time or may launch different brand focus in different years and quarters. At the same time, the company would publish the related history, interpretation, strategy requirement and demand focus and way of expression of the brand concept.

The company would plan the year-round market activity which shall be presented by the projects so as to promote the starting time, pushing process, executive department and principal of each market activity and some activities might be carried out continuously. The company shall avoid having too many activities and the activities are too scattered. Every year, there should be one to three core activities and five to eight key activities. More focused the activity is, the greater influence it has, and greater effect it produced.

The media placement plan has released the year-around advertising time, and the list and quantity of advertising regions of brand advertisement, brand marketing film, brand news and brand activity and it has also stated the advertising focus, demand subjects and contents.

The other brand communication events also include design style and production requirements, placement time of the brand marketing materials such as TV advertisements, picture posters, and DM sheet.

The brand organization shall regularly publish the brand communication plan which is good for continuity of brand communication. For all the employees and brand distributors of a company, it would greatly increase their confidence of the brand prospect so that the brand is in sufficiently active status. Therefore, the brand is very active in the market and the brand operation is in good condition.

2.3 Brand concept communication

As for brand concept communication, generally, only the strategic leading brand organization has the ability to create new concepts and develop into a trend. The brand concept communication generally consists of three forms, which are economic phenomena, typical model and application concept.

A few brand organizations could combine the self-development with the social and economic development and achieve greater success via creating the important popular concepts. For instance, Buffett advocates "all-out donation", Goldman Sachs proposes "BRIC countries" and one of Intel founders Gordon Moore presents "Moore's law", Apple founder Steve Jobs proposes "users' experience", Alex Rampell puts forward "O2O", Chinese leaders bring forward the "Silk Road Economic Belt". By the extensive communication of popular concepts, it has established the position of these brand organizations or leaders in economy and society.

A few brand organizations could create the brand new popular economic culture or management model, so that these models could become the world or regional target for copying. For instance, "Toyota model" created by TaiichiOhno, GE model created by former GE CEO Jack Welch, "Haier model" created by Haier's CEO Zhang Ruimin and "Qujiang model" created by DuanXiannian. The creation of these models has enabled the brand organizations to obtain the extensive study and copy effect.

Most of the brand organizations are devoted to creating the application concepts. For instance, P&G Head & Shoulders created the concept of "anti - dandruff", Geely created the concept of "safe shaving", Crest created the concept of "moth-proofing", Safeguard created the concept of "bacterial reduction", JDB created the concept of "anti-inflammation", Band-Aid create the concept of "simple protection of the wounds".

Creation of new concepts, models or market use concepts would play the great promotional role in marketing, which would not only arouse the extensive attention of the media, but also lead to deep thoughts and imitation from the other organizations in the same industry. Some concepts would further intensify the brand recognition role in brand users.

2.4 Large scale brand invitation communication

The purpose of brand invitation communication is to attract a large amount of users by carrying out the large scale market action. The game manufacturers could attract the potential users by releasing a large amount of test accounts, the software manufacturers may gather the potential consumers by carrying out the large scale actions such as "blue storm" and the property developers may acquire the cooperation resources and excellent customers by holding the large scale property finance conferences.

At the early stage of a brand birth, the large scale market action marketing would be an important method to effectively solve the insufficiency of market development competence. *Brand Nuclear Force* has emphasized the value and implementation method of large scale invitation brands.

At the early stage after a company is founded, it could complete the market entry and coverage by a large scale of market actions and strong communication. Firstly, the company shall make the accurate market division, divide into different market action programs, make the comprehensive package and enter into the market quickly. Market action plan program, such as "plan on trial use by millions of users", "card application plan by millions of users", and "car club green revolution plan" shall independently design the market action plan, conduct the planning, organization, implementation, completion statement and then form different project teams based on the plan for strong implementation and communication.

Secondly, it is necessary to adopt the model of faster sales for coordinating with the product sales. The products must be approved and could be rapidly distributed to the users so as to realize the faster distribution and usage needs and satisfy the large scale market shopping demands.

The development target at the first stage during the early period of a company could be the professional grading of the users so as to find out the most central target groups. By carrying out the large scale market action, it is to accelerate to realize the users (customer) scale, obtain the sales revenue circulation or become the hot target of venture capital.

2.5 Conceptual communication mainly by advance sales

The real estate developers, concerts and movies would generally focus on the conceptual communication with the purpose of "advance sales" and make the warming up on the brands to be sold by the working sketches, planning drawing, 3D or 4D marketing film, trailers or highlights, etc., so as to achieve the purpose of advance sales.

Nevertheless, some concepts such as "next generation network, interplanetary transport network, New York 2030 planning, US grid 2030 planning, US future soldiers plan" have adopted the form of advance demonstration concept. By proposing a super forward concept, it could arouse people to give consideration, research and discussion in the future. The conceptual communication mainly by advance sales could refer to communication cases.

The conceptual communication mainly by advance sales could arouse the great attention of the investors and improve the investment value. At the same time, it could increase the users 'expected value of the brands, and bring the sufficient benefits for improving the brand premium and obtain the brand scale effect and could enhance the brand capital turnover rate. Therefore, the companies could flexibly apply such strategy.

2.6 Brand sales leads

As for the simple Fig. for principle on large scale sales production, please refer to Fig.14-4.

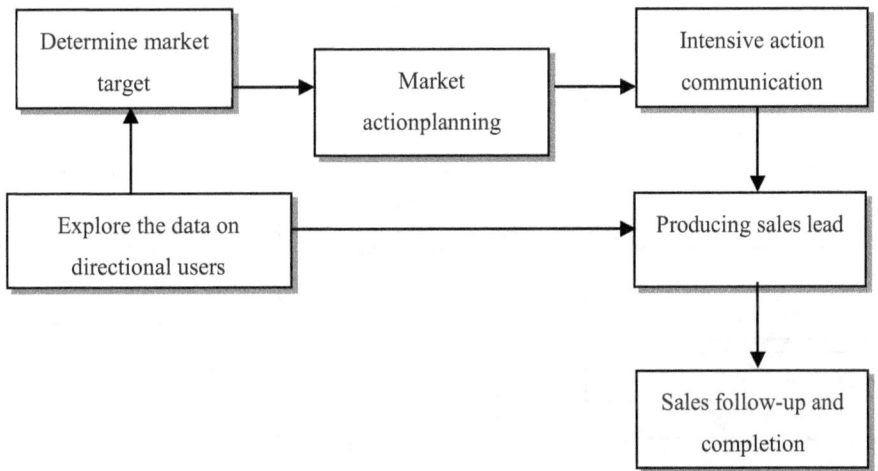

Fig. 14-4 Principle on Large Scale Sales Production

An important purpose of brand communication lies in finding out a large number of sales leads. By the close cooperation between a company's market department and brand department, it is required to determine the clear market target, work out the strategic market developing plan and design the market promotion documents such as the meaningful videos, texts and pictures and prints. Through a large scale intensive communication, it is necessary to intensively carry out the market actions and stimulate the large sales leads produced by the market and the sales department shall follow up and pursue the sales.

Sales leads refer to the intentions that might lead to purchase orders. The sales lead, no matter generated online or offline, are the most precious assets for a company. There are many forms of generation sources of the sales leads. The form of generating the online sales leads could refer to Fig. 14-5.

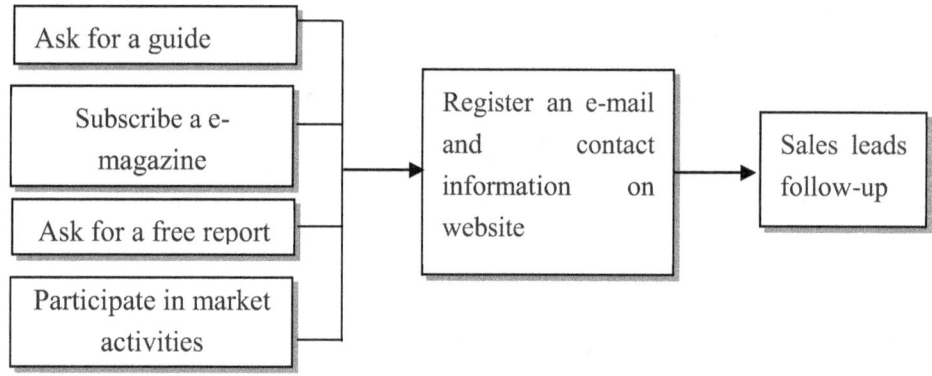

Fig. 14-5 Form of Generating Online Sales Leads

Online sales leads could obtain the users' personal information when the online users were asking for a guide, subscribing the e-magazine, soliciting for a free report and participating in a market action, registering their e-mail address and contact information on the website and the sales could follow up with the sales leads.

Offline sales leads might come from the telephone inquiry made by the users, participation of questionnaire survey activity or seminar or real-life experience event, or purchasing of the catalogue list with the information on the target users. The sales department may follow on the sales leads based on the personal traceable information. The form of generating the offline sales leads could refer to Fig.14-6.

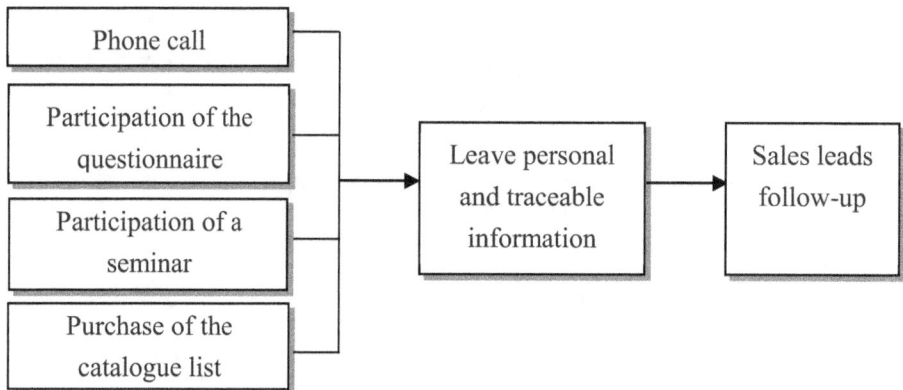

Fig. 14-6 Form of Generating the Offline Sales Leads

3 Professional report on the brand news

The value of brand news lies in creating a brand or production of a hot concept.

Brand news is always the main content in brand communication. Most of the famous companies would place the communication of brand news in the top priority and then appoint a professional press spokesman, news officer, news secretary and brand news center and other appointments. At the same time, brand organization also pays special attention to the important role of press conference.

Brand news report presents more and more professional development mode, breaking off from the original scope of commercial or business news and stepping forward to the professional brand news reports. Some news media have already actively carried out the reform of professional report of brand news and allocated professional news reporters and editors who shall only focus on the brand market of a particular industry or the content of brand management and brand marketing.

Correspondingly, the brand organizations are also actively developing the news center or communication department and training the in-house professional news reporters, brand news communicators and news writing enthusiasts.

Furthermore, in recent years, media crisis PR has been promoted to an important link. Large corporations, in particular, the listed companies would generally employ professional crisis PR personnel, set up crisis PR leading organization or outsource to a professional PR company to be responsible for brand crisis treatment. They have shown their focus on real-time monitoring on the public opinions on the brand.

3.1 Brand news organization in a company

The brand news organization in a typical large corporation consists of four links: the first is the professionally outsourced brand PR companies that are responsible for the publicity of the brand; the second is the news center in a corporation (or PR department, marketing department) which are mainly liable for preparation, compilation and printing of the brand news, press release management and internal magazine of the company; the third is the news management for senior executives. Generally, there is a professional news secretary who is responsible for direct contact with the news medias and is also responsible for scheduling the interviews of the company's leaders during different events and the question-and-answer management in news; the fourth is the internal correspondent network in a company which is generally built in different departments in a company and employs full-time or part-time news enthusiasts to be liable for internal news drafting.

Powerful enterprise news would generally place special importance in the construction of internal communication network so as to build into a professional organization like a "news agency" to be responsible for internal and external news materials collection and news report for the brand organization. The company's news center shall be liable for news drafts organization, drafts assignment, drafts collection, approval and examination and external circulation.

A powerful brand organization shall, for the purpose of enhancing the communication effect, set up the fixed news resources which would cover the strategic layer, brand technological layer, management layer, operation layer, collaboration layer, users' layer and the internal and external expert team. In particular, in the market action and market activity, there should be necessarily the draft collection, compilation and writing teams so as to obtain the latest and most comprehensive news materials.

To strengthen the news transmissibility, truthfulness and objectiveness, a brand organization should provide regular professional training on draft collection, compilation and writing for the teams who are mainly responsible for brand news, and also design the outline for brand news compilation and use regularly and build up the incentive mechanism. We believed that the best brand news materials must come from the internal brand organization, the touching stories that happened among the workers at the front line, the cases arising from the brand after-sale services, the new concepts and ideas of a department leader, and the detailed technologies that could be publicized during the brand study which are all the best news to report.

3.2 Brand interpretation system

Brand interpretation system is a system to make the interpretation, construction and identification of every aspects and it is composed for brand concepts, brand ideology, brand corporate culture, brand history, brand stories, brand management cases, brand marketing cases, brand figures, etc. A company needs to build up a set of standard resource library so as to use such materials extensively in the media report, communication, advertising making and marketing material making.

The construction of brand interpretation system shall lay the solid content material processing foundation for brand communication and all the reports and communication materials shall build upon the core foundation of brand interpretation system. After multiple studies in the past, it has been found that the communication of many brands is feeble and futile without deep and profound content mining. Besides, there are no photos, documentaries, the first hand speeches and interviews on the important historical materials. This would lead to insufficient important historical materials during the brand communication.

A corporation might set up historical memorial museums such as the company's archive or brand museum based on the needs of brand development history and enterprise history for the new employees, news media and clients to pay a visit. However, we have found that a lot of content in the substantive exhibition halls have not been properly demonstrated in the modern company's website and only a few brand enterprises have paid the attention to the consistency of internal and external brand interpretation, including construction of an online electronic hall that coincident with the history of the company.

Brand interpretation system shall also be used by professional service providers such as brand planning company, brand promotion company, brand advertising company and brand consultant companies fondest processing of the brand's materials. It has unified the main aspects in brand publicity, the marketing specifications, the way of marketing, the interpretation statement, the report highlights, the communication styles, etc.

3.3 Brand knowledge system

The brand knowledge system is a modern knowledge library consisting of a whole set of knowledge tree, knowledge points, knowledge materials, etc. set up for brand identification and brand communication. The knowledge system should be dynamic and constantly record different knowledge such as the latest R&D and product application. It should be able to upgrade; access and apply the collection and communication mode.

What is more important for brand knowledge system is that it consists of knowledge such as brand history, the market field which the brand is in, product usage method, and product application cases. A wine company would collect all the knowledge in relation to the place of origin of the wine, grape plantation, wine drinking, wine health, etc.; whereas a software company might collect all the knowledge related to software usage method, application cases, application field, technical problems and solutions, R&D features, etc. The brand knowledge in these systems is extremely effective in communicating brand.

Using knowledgeable communication that serves the market with professional knowledge and provides the guidance and help to the users with professional knowledge has positive significance for building up core user groups of a brand. In particular, many brands would use their unique knowledge system which is rich in content to complete the education for their brand users. This enables the users to use the knowledge gained from the brand to identify the competitors in the market. This has played an important role in building up the brand competition strength and defense against the competitors. The future marketing would place importance on who could teach their users, enable the users to be more professional and intelligent to and progress with the company.

It is best for the brand knowledge to be creative. Some leading world brand would constantly release the latest and unprecedented products. These corporations would extensively publicize the knowledge on the products and teach people on how to use these latest products so as to maintain its unique market leading position.

3.4 Training on brand news writing

The brand news writing requires certain professional training so as to come out with quality brand news within a short period of time.

Writing requires the integration of heart, brain and hand. "Heart" is for the sensitivity towards everything, "brain" is for the processing of knowledge materials and coming up with thoughts and "hand" is responsible for completing the work. Only the highly unity and harmony of heart, brain and hand could reach the master state in writing.

As a beginner, the most important issue is how to begin the writing. This is mainly due to the insufficient material accumulation. As a matter of fact, 65%~80% of the content in the article of a reporter is from the interview and 20% is supplemented by observations and research of background materials during the interview.

Therefore, I have designed a speedy training method for basic writing using "interview, compile and write". This requires the writers to complete the writing training of "selecting for writing-compiling-writing" from the very beginning. Selecting for writing would enable the writers to master the skill of collecting materials and compiling would enable the writers to improve their word structuring ability and finally begin the writing training so as to rapidly and greatly improve their writing skills.

As a matter of fact, the training of selecting for writing, compiling and writing could effectively resolve five issues encountered during writing: selecting for writing-has solved the issue with lacking of materials and topics and having no idea on how to start writing; compiling- has solved the issue of having no idea on materials organization and solved the issue of language being not vivid and concise; writing- has solved the issue of inability to compose a writing quickly and easily.

The specific training includes the interviewing and writing stages: people (interviewing and discussion techniques) matters (recording and investigation techniques); compiling: compiling tasks (subject editing, topic editing and independent editing techniques), compiling practice (article organization, writing and excerpt techniques); writing: special writing (news release writing and sales copy techniques) and style writing (review writing and special column techniques).

3.5 30Brand news templates

The writing method of brand news mostly has certain style or pattern. We have listed 30 common brand news templates. Based on this list, we could find reports of media on brand news which are similar with the named style of the templates and speed up the writing of brand news.

(1) Strategic news; (2)Trend news; (3)Background news; (4)Interview news; (5)Viewpoint news; (6)Problem news; (7)Event news; (8)Celebrates news; (9)Hot news; (10)Topic news; (11) Communication news; (12) Technique news; (13) Research news; (14) Digital news; (15) Special topic news; (16) Professional news; (17)Cluster news; (18) Story news; (19) Insider story news; (20)Analysis news; (21)Merchant invitation news; (22)Creative news; (23)R&D news; (24)Fashion news; (25)Fixed news; (26)Reminder news; (27)Joint news; (28) Relation news; (29)Customer news; (30)Responsibility news.

3.6 42 Brand news standards

The rapid writing of brand news also originates from the organization of professional materials and content combination and realizes the brand news standardization to certain extent by professional collection, professional responsibility division and complete records. Using these materials could rapidly make the brand news and satisfy the features of batch writing and massive distribution.

We have listed 47 news standards and the companies should pay special attention to collectsuch materials so as to make the standards or material package for massive professional report of brand news.

Background

(1) Founder's background; (2) Founder's important strategic ideas; (3) Key leaders; (4) Brands' vital origin and background; (5) Company's key development background; (6) Brand's concept interpretation system; (7) Company's history.

Products

(1) Product history and honor; (2) New product records; (3) R&D process; (4) Manufacturing process; (5) Product performance; (6) Product charisma; (7) First access; (8) Product usage; (9) Product application; (10) Product's relevant network.

Services

Service investment; (2) Customer service; (3) Service process; (4) After-sale service.

Enterprise and brand management

Organization development and strategy; (2) Key management method; (3) Scientific and advanced leading concept; (4) Company (brand) profile; (5) Enterprise's responsibility and Corporate social responsibility.

Brand users

User's point of contact; (2) User's experience; (3) User group; (4) Users' key evaluation; (5) Story of typical users.

Brand market

(1) Users' preference; (2) Brand presentation; (3) Brand interpretation; (4) Market policy; (5) Consumers' studies and applications; (6) Market analysis; (7) Key market and trends; (8) Key data, viewpoints and evaluations; (9) Promotions.

Pictures (marketing materials)

(1) CI system; (2) Symbolic environment and important scenes; (3) Important process pictures; (4) Key product demonstration pictures; (5) Key product figure pictures; (6) Key marketing event pictures; (7) Pictures on brand image communication.

3.7 Modern public relations

The technical means and realization form of modern internet PR include the creation of a series of communication information around a product, service, enterprise or person by message, Weibo, Wechat, etc. These PR forms will continue to exist and will continuously increase the media and communication forms.

The purpose of public relations(PR)is to avoid the users from accepting contradictory or confused information, more accurately identify the brands and more rapidly to make the selection. In case where there is crisis impacting the organization, the company could instill the concept to prevent from being doubted and to share with the media about the development issues with the brand.

The socialized media marketing and digital marketing are on the rise. By the internet instruments and technologies, such as search engine, socialized bookmark, relation with the new media, interactive communication of social media, and the interactive PR, could enable the company and organization to establish the communication without solely reliance upon the mainstream news and magazines for information communication and could communicate with the public, customers and potential customers directly.

PR practitioners might always depend upon media, such as TV, radio station, magazine and new media to promote their ideas with customized information for specific group of customers. In the first year for any news media release, the PR practitioners and the public would have difficulty in catching up with the new technologies but should make every effort to keep in pace.

4 Brand We Media

Modern brand communication is experiencing the times of We Media and the brand organization shall enhance the study and application on "We Media".

Brand We Media is mainly organized by the brand organization and oriented by the brand organization by certain modern brand communication form such as information production, editing and processing, content sharing and communication and achieve the communication purpose by multiple forms such as single-direction dissemination, multiple transmission and interactive communication. It is a form of communication with least investment and higher profits.

The forms of We Media are diversified and the advantages of constructing We Media are to communicate their brand information without confining to the known public media, enhance the attraction to brand users, release promotion activities and improve the interactive relationship between the brand employees and brand users.

A company should have an eye upon their own We Media which might include the TV programs, video interview programs, special syndicate column, customer relation E-papers, user email list, Weibo, e-magazine, etc. and gather the brand users by collecting the information on effectively subscribed users.

4.1 Special subject editing and topic editing

Firstly, we need to be clear on the forms of editing content. We shall divide the editing function into special subject editing and topic editing. These are the basic features to be equipped by all communication forms.

Special subject editing is to systematically collect and edit the manuscripts on a certain subject.

Special subject is the content editing featured by designated field and scope and only collects all the materials closely related to the content.

The special subject could be categorized into:

Professional special subjects, such as new three boards, medical reform, provision for the aged, Nobel Prize, internet finance, XP skills, health methods and Hetian jade appreciation.

Event subject, such as home violence, quality issue, environment deterioration, financial event and medical accident.

Subject project such as blue design series, colored decoration style, beauty of nature, fantasy movies, thematic garden, and fun of pets.

Topic editing means to systematically collect and edit the manuscripts about a hot topic.

Compared with the subject editing, the topic editing is featured by timeliness, rapidness and communication and it is a key editing trend after the rising of Weibo, WeChat.

Source of topics:

(1) Search engine billboard, hot topics in Weibo and hot topic library of every media.

(2) The discussions on hot movies, popular fashions and popular viewpoints.

(3) Focus of discussion: the long term focus of the brand users and readers.

Topic examples:

Who shall become next Google, tyrant king, questions to Sima Nan, salary showing off, how to celebrate Valentine's Day, parent-child, emission standards for vehicles, love stories, don't cry baby, house price and parents say to me before leaving home.

Difference between the subject and topic:

The topics is mainly on the long term issues, periodic hot issues, hot events, certain phenomena, hot topic figures, controversial discussion and hot discussions and it is the highlight concerned by micro-communication and news media.

4.2 Tasks of editing team

Editing could be one person's independent work, or the divided work by a team, or the divided layout work.

Editing could be subdivided into manuscript organization editing, manuscript dispatch editing, manuscript revision editing, front page editing, layout editing, visual editing, reading and editing, editing and translating, etc.

Basic tasks of editing team:

Determine the editing content: determine the next month's (next) editing focus, draft direction and the editing team shall make sure the highlights for editing and highlighted topics by the form of team discussion so as to dispatch the manuscripts to the reports and writers.

Determine the editing quality: the purpose of editing is to examine the manuscripts so as to make sure that the depth, importance, representative opinions, etc. of the manuscripts conform to the quality requirements for publishing.

Manuscript revision: the editors could make the revision, greatly deletion and excerpts and compilation of the manuscripts at any time before layout.

Completion of editing works: every completed works, whatever in electronics or paper form, should be presented to the readers with elegant appearance and superior content.

The editing tasks might include:

Editing a group of series of leaflets (highlight a group of sales proposition);

Editing a group of activity records (follow-up records on whole process of market activity planning);

Editing a group of special content (interview scripts, data compilation and documentation organization);

Editing a booklet (users' guide, purchase guidance for potent customers and manual of brand user groups);

Editing a small magazine (e-magazine on customer relations, e-magazine on brands, technical study briefing);

Editing a report (investigation report, investigation and study report, study report and analysis report).

4.3 Brands We Media: brand users' own media

We are at the times of being discarded by the media and the big newspapers and websites are only concerned about the celebrities and big companies. They are away from the ordinary people. In most cases, it is impossible for them to communicate a story of a common people, nor possible to report the development of a small company. What we are inspired by the US community newspaper is that it would be a better choice to maintain the users (customers) of a brand organization.

A community newspaper could solve: why we have nothing to write and why the articles we have written lacks of attraction?

Obviously, the community newspaper has answered the question. Whatever a website, a company and an organization has a lot to be reported with a lot of small stories happening. However, we would always ignore the news and stories around us. Even through a salesman who has many customers would have different stories with you every day. The relevance, proximity and pertinence of such content must be very attractive for certain people and could produce the cohesion among them. The question you should think is why your website, company and organization lacking of attraction to the targeted public.

A local website, no matter being loved by the local people or not, is a channel for the local people in the other places to know the information of their hometown. A company engaged in sales of paper cutting crafts would have a lot of customers who want to know the historical stories of paper cutting, the information on paper cutters and collection of paper cutting crafts. A website engaged in sales of Swiss Army knife might attract a lot of Swiss Army knife lovers who might need the relevantinformation and stories. A brand printer company would have a lot of printer users who want to know the troubleshooting, applications and skills and a 4S store would have many stories between people and cars. Every service story would touch and even change more people who plan to buy a car…

The reports on great news and celebrities might attract people easily; however, too many people have made the similar reports. Sensationalism and preachment could drive the development of entertainment news; however, it is not the real reflection of social panorama. In a blundering society, what people need is the more real and true information and stories. Despite of small figures and events, they have particular readers. Therefore, such reports could not only survive but also exist in an increasingly better way.

Brand We Media with unique competitive strength

Brand We Media should learn from the community magazine and the content will change greatly. The brand We Media should not just report the big events and only focus upon the "brand" and "localization". It may report whom the brand might help and the brand user growth with the help of a warm-hearted man and a new special featured experience store will open soon. These contents will not appear in the other newspapers and websites, they are truly the exclusive unique content and closest to everyone's life, authentic and full of fun.

The contents of brand We Media is mainly for reporting the brand news and localized brand users and it is closely related with the common benefits of the brand users. It is the content that is most concerned by the localized brand users and has the strong sense of belonging so that they could identify themselves as a member of the brand's We Media and integrate into such atmosphere. The brand benefits, brand features, brand history, brand honor, brand figures, brand life, brand activity and strong sense of integration and participation will attract a great number of loyal readers.

4.4 Pamphlet: consumption education for brand users

Besides the fixed independent editing tasks, the brand organization could regularly compile pamphlets to educate the brand users.

Examples of some typical booklets are as follows:

Manual series of International Breast Milk Association;

Advantages of breast feeding, suggestions to the vocational women, how to add supplementary food to the infants;

ISO guidance series;

Teach you how to use ISO9000, ISO selection and user guidance, ISO's suggestions to medium and small enterprises;

American medical disease and treatment guidance series;

Guidance on diabetes mellitus, guidance on seasonal diseases, guidance on cardiovascular and cerebrovascular diseases and guidance on cerebrovascular disease;

Flexible and applicable guiding pamphlet;

Guidance on home decoration, environmental protection guidance on building materials, healthy cat food and spring women's clothing.

Exercises

1. Fill in the Blanks: the main forms of brand communication include_____, _____, _____, _____, _____, etc.

2. Multiple-choice Question: modern brand communication is a form of communication throughout the network and at a full range based on_____ and is a form of communication integrating.

   A. Brand news, brand news video, marketing, public relations, sales copy

   B. Brand news, brand articles, brand video marketing, public relations, sales copy

   C. Brand articles, brand video news, marketing, public relations, sales copy

   D. Brand news, brand articles, brand video news, marketing, public relations, sales copy

3. Essay Questions: what is brand knowledge system and what is it used for?

SECTION III BRAND TECHNOLOGY

Chapter 9

Brand Collaboration Technology

The future companies shall focus upon the collaboration which shall be the main feature of production and operation. Collaboration shall be presented in the most concise form. Different enterprises and people shall form into a collaborative enterprise or network to realize the cross-enterprise, cross-department and cross-market diversified cooperation in the form of collaboration.

In view of the diversified collaboration organization in work and business, there will be a large number of virtual collaborative companies (departments) to be liable for handing more and more affairs on work flow, business flow and collaboration relationship between the cross-enterprises and cross-departments. The collaborative companies (departments) shall study the consumption demands in the manner of collaboration, share the data and study the products so as to guarantee high quality of products and services to the users consistently. The collaboration between the companies and users, and e-commerce shall enjoy further and rapid development.

1   Brand collaboration companies

Collaborative companies are an important form of brand organization at present and in the future, all collaborative tasks of brand organizations shall be completed by working collaboration and business collaboration. Collaboration is the fruit of socialized professional work division, the main trend of modern information and technology and also the main form of future enterprise organization.

The socialized professional work division is accelerating and increasing number of enterprises are divided into professional brands before entering the professional market, and there are decreasing number of big and comprehensive enterprises. In this way, more companies arising could be more flexible and smart to be engaged in professional research and development, professional production and professional market services. The companies have to adopt the collaboration form to maintain their core competitiveness and integrate the research and development achievements and business strengths of different professional brands for maintaining their competitive strength.

To satisfy more consumption demands, the companies shall be united in developing new products and launching new professional brand by sharing the user data and analyzing the market demands. As this is a win-win choice, such cooperation based on data, market and business will be increasing and the collaboration management will be put as an important agenda.

The development of modern information and technology and the rapid development of new technologies such as next generation of internet, future internet of things, future sensor network and future network of knowledge, etc. have resulted in the business network among enterprises to become the main development form. The cooperation shall be closer and the data network enables the collaboration among the enterprise to achieve full and comprehensive seamless connection, collaboration production and collaboration goods supply.

Collaborative companies, as a virtual company form, shall play an important strategic role. The collaborative companies may or may not have offices, and do not have the traditional organizational structure. Only the cross-enterprise and cross-department collaborative chains could closely combine the departments of the collaborative companies and there are not even any employees managing it. All the collaboration shall be completed during the self-adaptive connection and combination in information network.

1.1 Features of brand collaboration companies

Different from the previous virtual companies, the collaborative companies emphasize the cooperativity between the companies and departments. To increase the collaboration effect, it is necessary for the companies to set up professionality department in the collaborative company. The professional study department will capture all the possible collaboration trends and study all the possibilities for future collaboration among the companies, make the advanced planning, design the network organization structure of collaborative enterprises, collaborative command chain, collaborative work flow and collaborative product form, etc. and work out a collaborative corporate form that is more rationale, more ideal and perfect.

Collaborative company, as a design of work, business and market combination from the strategic level, means that two or more companies shall be organically combined and it is required that the management shall be highly consistent, data shall be synchronously integrated, business shall be synchronously operated and service needs to have uniform cooperation. The after-sale services shall be strictly seamless and the reporting systems shall reach the collaborative parties. Therefore, the collaborative companies are not the business network cooperation or information networking from the traditional sense and in essence, they are the highly developed strategic organization form.

The development of collaborative companies requires the linking, interactive, sharing and cooperation of research network, information network, knowledge network, logistics network and user network and during the process of collaboration, there might be new combined enterprises and new brands.

The strategic factors of collaborative companies include research, cooperation, experiment, connection, contract, consistence and continuity. Research is the beginning for the collaborative enterprise organization to study the collaboration possibility, establish the collaborative company with the possibly cooperated companies, experiment and test the collaboration effect in the form of experiment, and form the closely cooperated and integrative strategic collaboration companies by the contracting relationship, and then maintain the good collaboration relationship via such contracting relationship, consistently provide services for the users (or market users) and substantially produce the collaborative effect.

The collaborative companies could be built in multiple forms, including strategic collaboration and business collaboration, etc. In addition, in supply chain, operation network, brand service provider, e-commerce, IT and mobile management, the companies basically exist in the form of work and management collaboration. If the brand organization is deemed as the collaborative company, it shall provide the new concept for the development of an organization from the strategic level.

1.2 Establishment of brand collaboration companies

To establish a collaborative company, the parties participating in the establishment of the collaborative company shall set up a collaborative committee or office to be responsible for the joint affairs and coordination of all the collaborative companies. The collaborative committee (office) shall include the senior representatives and officers appointed by the participating companies. It might require the collaborative technological experts, industrial study experts, management consultants and management analysis, etc. to participate in the collaboration. The main form of establishment of the collaborative companies includes:

Technology and data integration collaboration. The highly automatic and informational, information clustering technology and network connection technology for company use with higher level of knowledge program shall connect the information on production, processing, storage and goods supply information of difference enterprises. This is to achieve the purpose of adaptive and automatic supporting production facilities. The companies with lower degree of automation shall realize the united production; matching and goods supply by technological interface and data sharing, and be committed to the logistics determination and zero storage, etc. so as to reduce the costs such as storage.

Production plan collaboration. Based on the order source, it organizes different collaborative companies to make the production and matching support, and organizes the matching of different production resources. This is to achieve the connection and response of production information among different companies and complete the production processes such as local, the other places, assembly and parts, etc.

Agile manufacturing synchronized collaboration. Based on the dynamic order, it realizes the synchronization of order and production. Through the organic combination of dynamic production units during the agile manufacturing, it could reasonably allocate the product resources and batches, and rapidly complete the combination of the production requirements in different orders.

Brand market collaboration. It would complete the collaborative combination from the market level, set up collaborative enterprise system and manage the comprehensive collaboration of the operation process such as sales, order, delivery and quality control of different collaborative companies via development of cooperative resources of different markets.

The special attention shall be given to the harmonious factors of dynamic collaboration during the collaboration process. The collaboration consistency should be realized by the collaborative experiment and test and the emergency measures shall also be in put to prevent the occurrences of collaboration interruption caused by uncontrollable factors such as fire, man-made accidents or shortage of raw materials, etc. So long as it meets the orderly and highly effective collaboration operation, it could guarantee satisfaction in production and operation continuity.

1.3 Progress made by brand collaboration companies

The collaborative companies shall, on the basis of in-depth study and cooperation, carry out the in-depth market study, management progress, market collaboration and customer services, etc. This is to establish a more perfect collaborative company with a more open and tolerating attitude. Such progress might include:

(1) Sharing of data. Sharing the store sales income and the relevant data may impel the collaborative parties to make efforts and achieve success together. For instance, increasing the accuracy of sales forecast shall reduce the costs of the suppliers and buyers.

(2) Transparent operation. Transparency shall bring great commercial benefits. Many companies may not know it during the collaboration. If all the collaborative parties could conduct the forecasting, sales, goods replenishment, warehousing and promotion in a more transparent manner, it would become more popular among the collaborative companies than ever before. There would be more opportunities emerging. For instance, it could be seen that the collaborative companies of the whole profit structures would be more willing to offer higher brand premium.

(3) Creation demands. The ideal "consumption society" is to constantly create more diversified and new profit demands. As for the features of cooperative development market, the key cooperation point of both parties is to satisfy the specific professional market and mutually obtain the high profits in every independent professional market.

(4) In view that the consumers cannot find and complete their own demands by themselves, one foundation considered by both parties is to define the collaborative company as the "production department" of end product companies. Both parties shall take measures to create more ideal production department and develop more appealing new products to satisfy pickier consumer groups.

(5) Both parties shall mainly focus upon their ongoing cooperation and jointly solve the problems on substantial link such as reduction of the goods shortage, improvement of the forecast accuracy, reduction of inventories, price optimization, effective promotion and after-sale services, etc. which should be the attitude for cooperation. The end product manufacturers shall set the core objective as whether the collaborative parties could better cope with the market development.

(6) The forecast accuracy among collaboration is crucial. All the parties hope to increase the sales, realize the profits and satisfy the customers. Their main concerns to sell out their products at the end of

the day, which requires the accurate inventory forecast. However, at present, it is usually a complicate game guessing.

(7) The brand collaborative parties actually occupy the initiative power and discourse and the consumers at present are very familiar with the purchase rate of designated brands; whereas the brand itself has the weight for negotiation. The influential of the brand depend much on the respective brand efforts of the parties involved and the consumers would not have much choice in end market. The advantaged brand collaborative companies may occupy the majority of market share.

2 Psychological contract for brand collaboration

Psychological contract for brand collaboration is the natural balance that cannot be broken. The perfect balance relationship between a company's brand and each link is to reach the stable, persistent, and balanced natural balance with higher quality. With the orderly operation among the parties, the company's brand shall demonstrate the "native, natural, constant, orderly, balanced, vivid, cheerful and happy" life status and full of vitality.

Any company shall be devoted to approach the balance of psychological contract of the brand during Grade B and C brand construction with the expectation of reaching stage Ain brand construction (strategic level, high-level stage)- the ecological stage of the brand. However, in most cases, the company may loss balance in certain aspect. The cases on balance loss would happen in most of the companies; therefore, only a few companies have realized their dream of international brand.

2.1 Main form of psychological contract for brand collaboration

Psychological contract is the key factor to balance a company internally and externally, and is also the basic condition for collaboration. The main contract consists of:

Brand leadership contract: the tacit agreement among the brand leaders has guaranteed the greatest achievement for a company's material brand transformation and reached the rapid and consistent powerful move in brand restructuring, organization restructuring and management restructuring. Unstable psychological contract would result in many difficulties for implementation of brand strategy from the very beginning. The interference, obstruction and disagreement of different leaders at different level would disrupt the brand strategy and delay the timing for market battle and result in the brand construction to be long and indefinite.

Contract on key talents for a brand:

The loss of key talents for a company's brand is an important demonstration of unstable psychological contract. The psychological contract between the company and key brand talents mainly demonstrates the standard on talent treatment. In different cases, the companies would have different views in talent management. Some companies focus upon the talents' education; whereas some companies would attach great importance to the ability; therefore, the talents are only the specific resources and they will be different in different companies.

Psychological contract for brand employees:

The fair competition environment of the company, an employee's ability is directly proportional to the contribution; the company's respect to the talents, the company's coordinative supports for talents, the environment created by the company, respect the knowledge creation and whether the company encourages the adventurous spirit.

Psychological contract for brand supply chain and operation network

The company's requirements for the quality, R&D and form of delivery of the supply chain shall be converted into the psychological contract between all the suppliers and the enterprises. The company knows how to provide the raw materials and supporting parts with what quality, workmanship and materials for a company's brand. The brand operation network also knows how to interpret the brand, what brand features to recommend and what services to provide to the customers during the process of operation. Any minor purchase corruption would result in the imbalanced psychological contract between the brand and supply chain.

Psychological contract of the brand users:

There is also certain tacit understanding between the brands and users. In particular, the regular customers (the fixed consumers for a brand) have the best knowledge of differences between the brand and the other brands. They rely on certain features interpreted by a brand and do their best to recommend such features to new users. They love the brand from the bottom of their heart and know clearly how to reject other similar brands and communicate such recognition form to new users.

3 Brand strategic collaboration

The strategic synergy consists of multiple forms. The typical synergy is to establish the collaborative alliance company, strategic alliance collaboration and strategic cooperation collaboration which are jointly established by multiple companies for the target of common competition market.

The case for typical strategic alliance collaboration is the alliance of industrial organization in Japan. The difference from the loose alliance, Japanese industrial alliance is featured by unified operation, unified management, unified production and unified collaboration. On the strategic level of industrial alliance, the industrial alliance has together established the operation committee for unified negotiation. All the companies participating in the alliance shall be organized in "super virtual enterprises" with large scale. The companies in the alliance shall only be engaged in production or operation that is based on different work division and only center upon their own center business; in other words, it is "a factory" in the alliance; whereas the other supporting business shall be finished by the collaborative factories. For instance, the industrial alliance of iron and steel companies in Japan is rather special.

The strategic technological alliance is an important form of strategic collaboration among the global companies. Some companies are united to research and develop the technology standard and formed into the close technological study and license alliance so as to jointly obtain the abundant royalties from the world market. In particular, the Japanese companies would always emphasize the consistent cooperation on technologic research and development and they are very sensitive to the technology license. The typical technological study and license alliance is Japanese Automotive Battery Technological Research and Development Alliance, which has attracted the elites of different automotive manufacturers and automotive battery research institutes in Japan so as to jointly make breakthrough in automotive battery technologies. 6C alliance was the patent protection alliance firstly established by six technological developers including Hitachi, Panasonic, Toshiba, JVC, Mitsubishi Electric and Time Warner and was famous for charging DVD patent royalties worldwide.

Visa card, Master card, American Express and China UnionPay,etc. are devoted to link up the middleman of technologies and develop into the solution institution of close technology collaboration by provision of global technological connection services for the financial institutions, government, companies, merchants and card holders. Visa card could be accepted in more than 29 million merchants worldwide and could withdraw cash in 1.8 million ATM. There are 1.85 billion Visa cards circulated worldwide. At the time of American Express opening, there were over 17000 merchants who signed up, and 150000 card users from US Hotel Alliance and 4500 member hotels joined too. The connection technology alliance shall become a main collaborative corporate form.

The loose technology standard alliance and technological support institution are represented by Automotive Industry Action Group (AIAG) which was jointly founded by three largest car manufacturers in US (Chrysler, Ford and GM) and is committed to development and organization of car standard technologies. Besides, the global or regional technological alliance or technological support companies such as W3 alliance, broadband alliance, WAPI industrial alliance, etc. and ISO, IEC, ICAO, ICANN, Standard & Poor's, Institute for Scientific Information Science Citation Index (SI) and Chemical Abstracts are also an important organization form of strategic alliance.

3.1 Strategic cooperation collaboration

Strategic cooperation collaboration consists of multiple forms such as strategic cooperation units and strategic market cooperation, etc.

Out of the purpose of exerting the core competition strength, some companies are spontaneous for organizing the collaborative companies and every company shall be devoted to R&D and production of core technologies and jointly providing the products and services with higher quality for the users.

Such strategic cooperation collaboration is generally centered upon R&D technology of core parts. For instance, the automotive manufactures would form into the close strategic cooperation alliance with the world leading engine manufacturers, gear manufacturers, axle general assembly manufacturers and car body manufacturers, etc., which would stride over the supply chain integration from the general sense and form into a strong brand matrix. The first class chip manufacturers, computer operation system OEM brand owners and internal memory manufacturers, etc. would be united to form the similar strong brand matrix.

As all the collaborative companies would focus on R&D and production in their respective field and any product would be developed into a first class product integration for several strategic key technologies and brand competitive strength, as a result, it has greatly improved its market core competitive capacity and every brand users would be formed spontaneously and influenced interactively so as to greatly enhance its brand competition status.

The collaboration of strategic market cooperation is mainly represented on the alliance of different brands in the same target market and exists in the form of brand market cooperation, brand bundle sales and brand united promotion, etc. The importance of brand collaboration lies in the cooperation in market operation, reduction of marketing costs and implementation of bilateral penetration marketing.

The strategic collaboration in whatever form should be established upon the consistent management of collaborative companies. So long as the collaborative parties keep providing highly reliable market services and highly dynamic collaborative synchronization, they could exert the greatest effect in management and market operation.

Only the more closely consistent collaboration could produce more farsighted strategic value. For instance, the collaboration between the retailers and suppliers, both parties are combined into a large scale virtual collaborative company with the target of jointly occupying and sharing the market share and establishing the strategic complementarity. The future retailers would surely make every effort to occupy the advantaged market and attempt to obtain greater profits from the specialized or specific commodities, instead of continuously expanding the product structure of groceries. The retailers and the suppliers could be collaborative, such as jointly developing the hair caring product department with the value of billions. For example, both parties may conduct study and investigation and jointly change the catering consumption structure against the population aging and more diversified population.

3.2 Composition form of strategic collaboration

The strategic collaboration could be formed in different possible forms and the main forms include industrial value chain collaboration, core competitiveness collaboration, product core value collaboration, united competition collaboration and diversified collaboration, etc.

The industrial value chain collaboration is based on the composition structure of an industry. A company or investment institution may play a role of industrial organizer and preferentially choose the combination of different link of industrial chain via investment and collaboration. For instance, in iron and steel industry, it might include the whole industrial chain such as miner selection, iron making, iron steel, steel processing, ferroalloy smelting and sea transportation, etc. The industrial organizers would make investment in the advantaged combination of the whole industrial chain.

The core competition collaboration is based on the core competitiveness of up-steaming industry, combining brand assets with the strongest in the combined industry and comprehensively forms the brand cluster in the world market. For instance, Hollywood, Wall Street, Broadway, Dubai, etc. have concentrated the most competitive production, supply and sales resources in the world so as to form the world-class strong brands industrial cluster and exert the scale effect of brand collaboration.

The product core value collaboration is to meet the products' highly competitive core competence and organize the most excellent brands in the industry to develop into the new generation brand products with larger scale, highlighted core advantaged products and strong combined competition competence. This is to reach the overall advantaged competition for the market and bring diversified brand premium.

United competition collaboration. To meet the technologic advancement and occupy the market, many companies with competitive strength shall be united and develop into the united competition alliance mainly by research and development, production or sales, and make the scale market occupation by integrating the strengths.

Diversified collaboration. To expand the product line and satisfy the demands of professional markets, the company and different types of companies shall extensively combine into a multi-dimensional, multi-directional and multi-market diversified collaborative company for carrying out the diversified cooperation forms such as mutually implementing the product customization, cooperative research and development and joint provision, etc. and conducting the market coverage interactively.

4 Brand business collaboration

Brand business collaboration is a further and specific collaboration. The collaboration is mainly conducted with the business as the base and the number of OEM manufacturers liable for R&D in the future shall be increasing. They would conduct the business collaboration mainly by cross-enterprise, cross-business and cross-services.

The company might focus more on research and development and expand the business by the form of cooperation or outsourcing, rather than engaged in business. However, it does not mean that R&D companies would not care for the after-sale technological support and services. On the contrary, the company should attach more importance to the comprehensive collaboration of business technologies and service technologies in the business field. Comprehensive production and sales companies shall entrust R&D companies to provide technologies and requires fast and timely collaboration with R&D companies on information such as the technological issues, technological services, maintenance guarantee and maintenance and repairing, etc. after sale.

The business collaboration would appear in the design, research and development of crossing business. Two or multiple parties shall jointly provide the diversified services for the market and the business collaboration between brands would become more complicated. Proper treatment of business collaboration of different links is the in-deep development topic arising from the collaborative enterprise alliance.

Many venture companies at earlier stage should care about the formation of brand business collaboration from the very beginning so as to obtain the competitive strength and market position from the brand business collaboration and cooperation. As a result, the enterprises at the early age could avoid the direct fierce competition in market in the form of finished product brand and be protected from establishment to maturity.

5 Brand supply chain collaboration

Many companies inevitably have a large amount of supply chains. The production of large products such as automobiles, airplanes and rockets, etc. would depend upon the worldwide collaborative companies to provide the superb general assembly and parts; whereas the large retailers shall be liable for strict and comprehensive management of the suppliers so as to promote the rapid and accurate goods supply and satisfy the retail distribution demands.

To seek the demands for rapid and effective supply chain development, many companies have put the supply chain collaboration in the key position and established closer collaborative production and supply relationship via the collaboration from the organization level, production and demands data and information, and logistics and storage data, etc.

A company shall, while selecting the suppliers, fully consider multiple factors such as R&D level, production quality, production promptness rate and delivery accuracy rate, etc. and requires the suppliers to be fully aware of the development of collaboration management ability, preferentially choose to join in the supply chain network and be included in the unified management.

Supply chain collaboration requires establishing more stable and closer collaboration relationship among the companies and conducting strict and consistent information management for resources, production and supply process so as to exert highly effective collaboration effect.

The companies might need to establish the unified supply chain collaboration system, integrate the management information of the supply chain companies, realize the real-time and dynamic information interactive and set up the collaboration management rules and optimize the business process.

6 Brand management network collaboration

The collaboration of brand management network comprised of direct retail terminals such as franchised stores, direct distribution stores, franchised outlet, 4S stores, etc. and the big stores and retail websites, etc. is playing the increasing role.

The treatment of dynamic data and information such as the management standardization of retail terminals, dispute settlement, retail business information, merchandising of retail terminal market, etc. shall be operated in the form of diversified collaboration.

The collaboration of brand management network shall be further implemented in market demands forecast, production forecast, goods delivery, storage, etc. The companies might need to further study and deploy the raw material purchase, production schedule, establishment of central storage, regional distribution center, etc., and also need to reduce the intermediate cost of the commodity circulation, save trading costs and improve the terminal information application rate of the brand operation.

Future O2O (i.e. Online-to-Offline) refers to the combination of offline business opportunities with the internet so that the internet shall become the front office of the offline transactions. This concept originated from US] times and attached more importance to the combination of offline and online sales and focus upon the operation effects of localized brands. The brand shall go through the route of "worldwide strong brand – world leading brand- localized leading brand" and develop into the localized brand rooted in every country and region from the deepening of worldwide brand. The establishment and cultivation of localized brand is rather crucial for the development of brand organization.

Many companies are actively developing the localized O2O business collaboration model so as to set up the new brand management network collaboration relationship via localized market starting, market action, market activities, etc.

Due to the transportation convenience such as car popularity and development of commercial buildings, the range of activities that people engaged in the future would be enlarged or narrowed. Enlargement means that people would go to farther and larger comprehensive stores for shopping; however, people would also just purchase in their small town or community. E-commerce distribution has changed the operation status to certain extent, and therefore, it becomes more important to make the effective strategic operation office layout and strategic operation structure design.

7 Brand service provider collaboration

To realize the greatest strategic value and largest brand effect of the branding development, brand organization should set up the extensive collaboration relationship with many global, national or localized brand service providers, which include the professional brand technology study institution, management consultancy company, brand advertisement design company, brand advertisement releasing company, public relations company, brand planning company, brand exhibition company, brand communication company, brand performance company, etc.

With the repaid development of worldwide brands and release of periodic important achievements of brand theories, there are more brand service providers in type and quantity. More professional brand service providers start to derive and more brand study organizations have come into being.

Large listed companies have extensively used the outsourcing services to outsource their brand advertisement design, brand public relations, brand communication, etc. or market investigation, human resources management, etc. to the third party brand service providers. They may select the best brand service providers worldwide. Small companies might depend upon the local service providers; however, there might be poor quality in brand design or brand service, etc. which would affect the brand premium ability.

The collaboration between the brand organizations and brand service providers is inevitable and exists objectively. With the repaid development of new concepts, new technologies and new media, the traditional brand communications mainly by TV is transformed to the online, offline and vivid brand communication form such as network and mobile network. The companies will need to study the popular trends, create the creative brand communication form, and select the newer and professional new general brand service providers.

Comparatively, there are fewer brand technology research institutions. The brand organizations should pay attention to such cooperative opportunity. The new brand theory and brand research achievements might bring the fundamental transformation for brand development. A brand technology committee consisting of the external brand technology experts, internal brand leaders and brand backbones has played the crucial transformation role in brand development and is the important transformation leading power for carrying out the initial brand construction or brand restructuring.

8 Brand user collaboration

We have emphasized the concept of brand organization, and reminded enterprises to pay attention that a company itself might be a brand organization. In the modern brand development and communication, the brand users are the important driving force in brand organization development. Such driving force is mainly represented in brand participation, brand interactive, brand user backbone, brand communications, etc.

The brand organizations are accelerating to form its own independent brand user organization by the establishment of brand user committee, brand club, brand activities, etc. and encourage the brand members to participate in the brand organization development and action by various organization forms and organization activities. Some brand organizations have taken the forms of setting up member card, point card, regular customer plan, website registered member, etc. from the very beginning and focused on the brand user registration and membership management so as to firmly lock the brand users in the brand organization.

Many brand organizations are aware that the relationship between the modern brand organization and the brand user is close and interactive. Therefore, they would make full use of such relationship structure. The brand shall set up the official interactive source of the brand organization via establishment of online brand community, Apps and Facebook brand home page on mobile terminal, G+ brand home page, official website on Twitter, Sina blog, etc. In the future, the interactive comment, reproduction, game, tool use and connection among the brand users would be more frequent and the interaction among the brand users shall be an important ability of brand active development.

Some brand organizations begin to attach importance to the cultivation of brand user backbones and actively train the brand users who are interested in it via establishment of brand school, online school, mobile classes, etc. to understand the brand in-depth, study the relevant brand knowledge and serve as the leading role in brand action and activity, and make them to be the vibrant image representative or action spokesman in the brand organization. These common volunteers shall grow up with the brand organizations due to assumption of the roles in the brand organizations. In this way, it has not only reserved the future potential leaders for the future brand development, but also made great contributions to the overall vitality of the brand organization and the attraction of new brand users.

The brand organizations should give special attention to the communication value and re-communication value of the brand organization. Many brands such as Starbucks have well applied the word-of-month communication effect since opening its first store. Google is another company claiming that they would never attract users by advertisements. On one hand, they give attention to the users' environment and users' experience and on the other hand, they highly focus on communication strategy and constantly exert the brand news and brand value communication effect. As a result, they have rapidly developed into world popular leading brands in the new generation.

9 Future e-commerce collaboration

The company shall also take care of the future e-commerce development which is inevitably the highly collaborated e-commerce. It mainly depends on the role of three aspects.

The first is the collaborative integration network of e-commerce, i.e. obtaining the e-commerce order from e-commerce retail terminal and company's official e-commerce website; whereas these orders would be highly collaborative with the company's agile manufacturing system and the synchronous system integration has been formed thereby.

The second is that the company should attach importance to the change of e-commerce contact points. The future e-commerce contact points would not be limited to the online, offline, mobile e-commerce, e-commerce terminal, digital terminal, neural network, consciousness analysis, search preference, retailer database, etc., which would cause the new changes to the demands, production and supply of e-commerce.

The third is the formation of global framework of reliable e-commerce. With the development of reliable technology, the reliability among the global e-commerce in the future shall be greatly increased, and the small brand enterprises may evolve into new and reliable brand organization by reliable, recognizable, digital certification, etc. via the reliable quality, service, etc. For the brand organizations that depended upon the reliable organization of big brands before, they would undoubtedly meet many new opponents.

There would be surely many emerging changes during the development of e-commerce in the future and corporate e-commerce shall center on the company and take the externally extended e-commercial technological transformation on the basis of department level, supply chain and the users. The companies shall be the main bodies of e-commerce and the external e-commerce technology shall be the e-commerce solution provider. The comprehensive development of corporate e-commerce shall bring positive change to the development of e-commerce and enable the application of e-commerce to step forward to a new trend of times.

10 Brand IT and mobile management collaboration

To meet the rapid development of brand organization and demands of scale expansion, and with the great emerging of IT and brand management collaboration of mobile deployment, the brand collaboration shall satisfy multiple applications of brand organization of the worldwide collaboration office, management issue settlement, market action guidance, market management, etc.

For instance, Walmart's logistics management information system, ticket processing system of US Ford car, and IT technology used by Nestle for managing the finance, capital and quality of over 400 subsidiaries worldwide. Shun Feng Express has applied the transparent management of mobile terminal to manage the flowing time and location of express parcels.

SECTION III BRAND TECHNOLOGY

IT and mobile management collaboration system constructed in multiple forms such as computer, network, satellite, mobile terminal, etc. are accelerating its transformation to modern enterprise management. The significance of flow reengineering has been transferred from the traditional management flow into thorough and new technology introduction and application.

In additional to the internal IT and management network, more brand organization networks are connected with the users and formed the multidirectional transmission relationship of the whole network so that the home electric appliance, office equipment, personal application, etc. could be connected with the intelligent network. Many traditional companies are evolving into network companies. All the things could be handled online through the flexible, rapid and highly operational high-speed network.

11 Future of collaborative technologies

The future collaboration shall be developed in the more rapid and advanced manner. Whatever the brands, products, users and companies are, they shall be operated in the form of collaboration. The collaborative network includes multiple forms such as collaborative corporate network, work collaborative network, service collaborative network, supply chain collaborative network, operating network collaborative network, etc. and exist by surmounting any possible network such as net generation network, planet network, mobile network, next generation internet of things, satellite network, digital network, sensor network, awareness network, interpersonal network, etc.

The intelligent cities, intelligent lifestyles, intelligent products and services are accelerating into the experience and popularity stage and the corporate management should be more systematic, self-adaptive, automatic, unmanned and knowledgeable. The intelligent experience and intelligent services of the brand shall become an important trend.

Human beings are moving away from the function-based brand status. These brands are far from satisfying the people's demands for the future and the brands might enter into the consciousness status with more advanced thinking. People will not be satisfied with imagination, conception and fantasy. The virtual reality would become the new product status. The brands with advanced thinking would be more popular among the Y generation (the generation after 80s, 90s and thereafter); whereas the magical brands with science and technology, supreme thinking and future would become the main brand trend in the future. As a result, it has changed the status and form of industrial design, architectural design and product concept.

The brand collaboration will come into being in the unprecedented manner and the collaborative companies will focus upon the future of global companies. Brands shall highly depend upon the collaboration to set up more foresighted brand future. The brand reengineering disintegration based on the development of collaboration technology development will let the company's brands become more thriving and step forward to a more distant future.

Exercises

1.Multiple-choice Question: the progress of brand collaborative companies include ( )

A. Sharing data, transparent operation, creating demands and consumptive power production

B. Sharing data, transparent operation, creating demands, optimizing the operation structure, accurate operation and collaborative position

C. Optimizing the operation structure, accurate operation and collaborative position

D. AC

2. Essay Question: How to establish the brand collaborative corporate committee, in what aspects can the collaboration mainly represent?

3. Discussion: Simply describe the psychological contract of brand collaboration.and its main forms.

Chapter 1

World Brand Pattern

The reason why a brand could achieve the global reach, world market, world premium and world identity is that, in essence, a brand carries the peaceful co-existence, national integration and mutual harmony of the human civilization formed during the long term diversified development and it is the basic demand of the human beings to conduct communications and exchanges and the common requirement for the people in mutual agreement and consistent development. Besides, it is also the joint efforts of every nation worldwide for unity and friendship, mutual respect and development demands and the common representation of the human beings in simultaneous sublimation of material culture and spiritual culture. Therefore, it is the target, the hope, the purpose, the action, the development and also the factual basis, the future and the worldwide effort.

Therefore, the role exerted by the brand is a progressive and developing process for the human beings to constantly improve their vision of thought, constantly develop the civilization, constantly create the material level, and constantly and continuously develop and create and change based on the people's original demands. This is great. During such a great process, the brand has been developed and spans across the state and society, connects the people and the world and stimulates the human beings to step forward into the future.

1 Brand is the highest end of material cultural and spiritual cultural sublimation

The study on the development of material culture has been laid aside and limited to a small scope of academic field. For instance, in archaeology, anthropology, architectural aesthetics, art forms, it determines the historical cause, thread of civilization and regional and ethnical diversified cultural history, and various expression methods formed during the development of human civilization by studying the human beings' creative processing project, historical development, civilized status, form of expression, expressed connotations and preservation and protection of the materials. The spiritual culture originally takes the human beings, states or ethics as the development force unit, and exerts the directional role on and gives guidance, awareness and behavior to humans and encourages the people to use it as a certain spiritual object, state of consciousness, value, thinking and spiritual attitude; therefore, it is an important form to make the social governance from the social ethical structure.

The common ground of the material culture and spiritual culture is to take the material production and spiritual development of the "human beings" as the development force structure of human beings during the process in order to create things and promote the social development force, and it is the essence to distinguish "human beings" from animals.

The material culture is a kind of cultural status created, processed and made by the "human beings" designed around materials with the help of labor value enablement and the materials whose original status has not been labeled as the labor value enablement by the human beings and shall not be in the scope of material culture, just like stone and stone art, iron and car. The spiritual culture is the spiritual awareness and ideological level refined and summarized by the "human beings" in the pursuit of limited life value, seeking for the truth of life and ideal pursuit. It is the spiritual force guiding the human beings to change themselves, change the society and the future and the spiritual force basis by using the spiritual culture to develop the material culture, so that the human beings could make the constant improvement of spiritual status and enhancement of material culture, and it is also the general representation of orderly

Section IV Brand Culture

balanced and steadily improved human progress for the development target and development relationship.

Before the 20th century, the material was rather deprivable and the population mobility was limited by the long transportation and the spirit was only represented in the a few subjective consciousness. Only until the latter half of the whole 20th century, the human beings, after the World War II, ended up with the peaceful light and people began to rebuild their lives from the war disaster and the long-lost peaceful development started. Only from that time, the human beings started recovery and the development level of productivity had been greatly enhanced than ever before. The material creation had been greatly accelerated and the material culture went back to the world citizens from the common sense, whereas the importance of the spiritual culture has converted to the social public in common sense. This is an important direction and factual basis for the material culture to step forward to the public, the spiritual culture to face to the public and serve the world citizens with brand as the particular medium.

From such stage, the existence status and form of expression of material culture and spiritual culture had caused the human beings to take the unprecedented changes and the brands have rapidly become the most important social and economic carrier and ultimate development achievement in the worldwide. The whole world's acceptance and enjoyment of the brands is to enjoy the ultimate pursuit of the human beings for the material culture and spiritual culture and enjoy the "popular" cultural achievement, which signifies that the human beings' pursuit and development of material and spiritual culture have reached the highest state. The development target is all the human beings, all the citizens and all the related parties. This is the universal value of the brand from the common sense.

1.1 From hierarchy to the common people- the evolution of culture

In the 20th and 21st centuries, the carrier to complete the constant and continuous sublimation of the material and spiritual culture is – brand. Brand is not only an important produce necessary for the human society to intensively develop the materials, endow the materials and the culture, materialize the substantive materials and meet the people's material demands during the constant growth and development, but also the process of the material and cultural creators to constantly enhance the ultimate pursuit of human beings for spirit. During the development process of promoting the material culture with the good spiritual culture, it assumes the more vivid, direct and obvious representation of the culture of human beings and it is a general development process for refinement, summary and enhancement.

During the historical formation era, the material culture in the past was only an exploration, communication and enjoyment within a small scope. Besides only a few noble men, elites and artists who were entitled to enjoy culture, only the archaeologists, architects, collectors and scholars and cultural researchers understood culture. It was not only being laid aside, but also a forbidden area. Besides, the people in the world were divided into different classes based on it, such as the upper class in Great Britain, noble life in France, social celebrities in Hong Kong, capital class in the US and scholars, farmers, artisans and merchants in China. During its long history, the culture was only the privilege enjoyed by a small group of people and it was unrelated with the common people.

The thought and movement of progress and reform is the long history of struggle in human's thought and culture and it is the victory belonging to the common people, which is mainly represented in the development of spiritual culture. In history, the leading requirement in spirit was the thinking limitations implemented towards the common people in the form of political decree, laws, education, religion and hierarchy etc. so that the citizens were limited to the fixed national or regional area, complied with the fixed thinking and form of culture expression such as the ecclesiastical feudal theology in ancient Europe and the Confucianism worship in Ancient China. Only after the middle age, with the cultural renaissance, industrial humanism ideology, pursuit of freedom spirit and scientific development and ideological emancipation in the 20th century, culture began to be enjoyed by the common people and the spirit was finally born for freedom.

The birth of a large number of brands was not only the inevitable product for the social commodities to develop into a certain stage, but also the main labor form for the public to develop the material culture and create the spiritual culture. It was also the human development process to represent the labor value and share the labor achievements. It was not only related to the civilianizing movement of the US brand after World War II, but also related to the fact that most of the brand creators and producers and operators were common people. Thus, the brand, for the common people, was the inevitable direction of cultural development, with the principle that all men are created equal. The brand creators have delivered their brand development achievements to the common people and used for the common people. The brands' "public cultural features" enabled the brands to ultimately become the final representation form for the human beings to develop the material culture and spiritual culture and thoroughly connect with the creativity, value pursuit, spiritual demands, use demands, daily demands and life style in the "dream of most people". The brand reached every corner of the world and the process of brands stepping into tens of thousands of families was also the process to excellently develop the value pursuit of material and spiritual culture shared by the human beings.

1.2 Changes of human culture- brand has become the cultural pursuit with the common value

The brands' social value had been comprehensively developed from the 20th century and the overall representation of the brand's social value is the comprehensive expression of the value pursuit when the human beings have reached the certain higher level in material and spiritual culture.

The main brand creators and responsible world corporations have the consistent development target: change the world and live a better life. The brand creators, company leaders, politicians, scientists, artists and brand designers and producers have constantly repeated such an important universal value dream of the brands. They expect to create and bring more and better products and services by creating, producing and developing the brands so as to make people live a better life.

The reason why the pursuit of universal value in the brand field could become the universal value mainly lies in the four development structures: (1) the development of mass culture demanded mainly by the common people; (2) pursuit of universal cultural state for people to live a better life; (3) the social value contribution consciousness for the people to demonstrate more advanced science, more refined technologies, more perfect brand, better products and better services; (4) the development force thought of friendship, peaceful coexistence, mutual progress and shared development achievements among the people.

During the great historical cultural change from the cultural rank in the small scope to the mass, the new government leaders, new companies and entities, and new brand creators were mostly from the common people and common families. Their development targets and service targets are the common people. Such development structure has driven the worldwide brands to face the worldwide common people in the broad sense and enabled the science and technology and art development to target the "socialization" as the key development direction. As a result, brands have become an important universal value pursuit and the constantly upgraded common demands, common development basis and common pursuit of the material and spiritual culture enjoyed by the people worldwide. Such pursuit belongs to the great progress of the whole society and it is the value contribution of human beings in the pursuit of peaceful co-existence and shared development. Besides, it is also the unprecedented change of important value and signifies the pursuit result of an important value for the human being's development force.

1.3 Cultural popularity during the great change period- brand's social value

When the people's pursuit of brand has been comprehensively developed, people would attach more importance to the expression and enjoyment from their spirit, which enabled the pursuit state of the material and spiritual culture to exert the bilateral value and become the coordinated development achievement; whereas the pursuit of spiritual realm would gradually weaken the people's seeking for short-term benefits, and consequently, the concession of the utilitarianism. Such role is the specific and unique development value of the brands during the material and spiritual cultural development and enables the people to get rid of the original sense of survival and turn to development of the spiritual pursuit mainly in the form of the life, ecology and sustainable development. As a result, the human civilization at a higher level shall be developed via the more peaceful and friendly spiritual world with common development and pursuit of higher realm.

Such development changes of the world material and spiritual culture have made the mercantilism, interest group and utilitarianism etc. to show the sign of extinction gradually; whereas the new creative concept, scientific concept, cultural concept, service concept and social concept developed by human beings based on the brands have been rapidly developed and become the social and economic development basis for the human beings to develop the social culture, create and enjoy life during the great change period; as a result, the cultural universality has been developed and the daily life of every person in the world has been fully branded. People begin to use and enjoy the achievements created by the latest material and spiritual culture.

The human beings are still in the great change period of social transformation and such great changes are mainly represented in the three transformation features: (1) the development form of social production force has transformed to the form of the production force decided by the consumption power; (2) transformation of social and economic development form featured by new science, new culture, new business type and new socialized demands; (3) transformation of material and spiritual culture taking advancement, science, fashion, trend, happiness and natural ecology as the value demands.

With the development of modern culture during the transformation and the great change period and constant growth of the people's life, culture has appeared in different layers of demands, which has enabled the coexistence and mutual and cross development of elite culture and mass culture. As a result, the diversified civilizations with multiple layers have been formed and the culture has been protected, developed and sustained. The cultural development has stepped forward from the original cultural limitations to the more indulgent and loose cultural development environment. In the development pattern of seeking common ground while putting aside differences, it has gradually enabled the social and economic value and orientation to be consistent and laid the basic development trend and development road for the comprehensive development of material and spiritual culture in the future.

2 Perfect combination of science and philosophy

The development of modern brand is an output of constant development and integrated combination of science and philosophy, as brand is epoch-making for the perfect combination of people's science and philosophy. The history of human science development is the dynastic history. Human beings first developed science rather than philosophy. No matter in Europe or China, they have gone through the long dynastic development process. Science's role in the people's development and the development of science began to get rid of the restrictions of religion and ethics till the 19th and 20th centuries, grew out of nature and society and rapidly played an important role in the people's life and development.

Despite of development of science and technology with rapid change, it has not fully exerted its scientific value. Even though in the modern society, the development of science and technology has not been completely mature, but quite the opposite occurred, because there are many structural and significant science vacancies in many important fields and the people's application of science is still rather low. The scientific law has not become the effective habit during the people's daily work, life and behaviors and it is still rather common not to respect science, comply with the scientific law in the daily life. We can only say that at present, the development form of science has been basically formed; however, the scientific development force, development structure and development form still need improvement.

Compared with the science that was developed at earliest and had the longest dynastic time, what lasted the longest development circle was philosophy. Philosophy had rapidly developed exceeding science in the history and once occupied the leading development thought in the history of many countries and regions. The reason is that it is easy to use and understand. Facing the complicated and difficult natural science and social science, the general philosophical interpretation could confuse the boundaries of all the things and blur all the related concepts, rules and behaviors. Compared with science, it is much easier and simpler in national governance and easier to be understood and used and easier to communicate and interpret.

Comparatively, science is much more complicated as it requires much more scientific thinking and concept, study and invention, exploration and findings and experimental proof. What's more, the scientific application requires a long time to make promotion and popularization. Therefore, during the long human development, philosophy had superseded science and played a leading role in the social governance of a state and also played the role of basic thinking power during the vicissitudes of dynasties and thought application etc. By studying the development history of science and philosophy since the existence of human beings, there were only a few scientists before the 20th century; whereas philologists were in vast majority and enjoyed the higher social status, and even in the 21st century, the philologists are still holding an important ideological status in the development of many countries.

Nevertheless, brand has perfectly combined the new scientific and philosophical thoughts in the unprecedented form and developed the double value of science and philosophy with brand as the main body. The newly developed science and philosophy freed the people's production force and welcomed the golden times for the great development of science and technology in the 20th century. The role of science to people, to human beings and to the future has been rapidly demonstrated and science has become an important field for the development of human beings. More and more products, services, management, production form, deliverables and its whole development process have taken the scientific invention and R&D and investment in technological system as the main development force. In particular, the general and systematic design of company's management technologies has become the newly emerged power for the scientific development and the new materials and new technologies shall be developed intensively with brand as the parent carrier. The people are to face, access to, feel and develop science and create the leading science with unlimited future imagination.

The philosophy at this time has evolved into the practical philosophies with the development of brand and developed the more practical, intuitive and efficient philosophizing understanding such as management thought, strategic thought, product through, aesthetic design though, design concept and consumption idea etc. The deepening process of practical philosophy is quite different from the previous expression form of philosophy, as it is much closer to people and takes people as the individual or group and regards the material and spirit as the specific culture carrier. It is also the philosophy with constant development and evolution. The ancient philosophy has not become extinct because of this; on the contrary, the great philosophical thinking that topical for a long time has survived in the specific form of brand history and has been added to the modern culture elements and developed the premium performance standard configuration of the new brand culture, brand thinking or brand product.

From the sense of more farsighted development, the role of brand construction mainly lies in the development of creative thinking space, creative scientific realization form and creative artistic expression manner, so as to develop the all-round scientific creation, multiple-layered cultural demands, diversified product forms and multi-dimensional philosophy understanding and diverse international integration.

People have completed the creation and formation of brand and its product thinking by imagining science, empirical science and cultural expression and also promoted the double value expression of science and philosophy by putting their dream into practice. This is the "hand-in-hand synchronization" of science and philosophy and has laid the important foundation for the human beings to develop more advanced civilization. In addition, it has also promoted the economy to invest in the construction of brand projects and provided the basic preconditions for developing more, more advanced science and more practical philosophy.

3 Brand is the inevitable process of cognition, identity and recognition

The brand development is a great process of worldwide and diversified civilization to make the universal cognition, identity and recognition, the universal understanding and development process of the countries and races all over the world to make the comprehensive integration and seek common ground while maintaining difference and also the civilized status jointly developed by the human beings during the process of developing the regional uninformed times to the times of global information explosion.

In essence, the brand's process of "cognition-identity-recognition" is the brand's development of "functionality - culture- realm".

During the history of brand development, the reason why the brand had been developed lied in its unique functional demands. In the worldwide transactions, the commodities from different places had acquired the trading attributes due to their different uses. Such basic functions included identity, status, honor, appreciation, treatment, military etc. With the development of transportation, from the carriage to car, from the sailing boat to cargo ship, from airship to plane, the worldwide transportation network had become increasingly prosperous and the increasingly developed transportation tools had greatly shortened the transportation time and the people's common demands for the daily used commodities had been constantly expanded. At last, due to the intensive emergence of brands, people would select the reliable brands to reduce the time for repeated choices and this was the beginning for the people to have the universal knowledge on brands.

From the transactional activities at the earlier period, the precious commodities, such as precious metal, luxurious silk and refined china were the most important subjects for transaction and afterwards, the high value commodities matching status and social positions such as clothes, cosmetics and household articles required by the people would mainly develop the cultural attributes. With the increase of commodities, people particularly attach importance to the place of origin, materials, workmanship, technologies and enjoyment. As a result, cultural attribute had been preferentially developed and cognition had been enhanced to the universal identity on brand.

The role of a country's cultural attribute in trading activities is rather obvious and has always played an important role, which is particularly true in the US development in the 19th and 20th centuries. America, the immigrant country composed of diversified culture, has rapidly developed into a new world cultural center by virtue of their unlimited natural creativity and freely developed culture, gradually created a great amount of the brand culture with most distinction and popularity, and driven most countries in Europe and Asia, that attach great importance to cultural development, to grow into the great development of brand culture from the common sense. The national image has been gradually integrated with the brand culture. The advancement, development and classics of cultural attributes represented by the culture and the development attributes of a country's culture have been elevated into the common culture identity which would be developed with the process of countries worldwide growing into the developed ones and made the cultural memetic transfer in the civilization circle of human beings.

At last, a country's brand premium ability is highly identical with the premium ability brought by the brand culture. The people's form from national identity to the brand identity has become the friendly and common viewpoints among different nations and as such the universal consensus is the very important social understanding and the friendly common development environment of cultural popularity during the interactive among the nations.

From the 19th century to the beginning of the 20th century, people would frequently use "all nations" to represent the universal culture integration of all countries and they would be very surprised while meeting foreigners from different countries, of different skin and speaking different language. Thus, people attempted to make the distinction and recognition from the conditions, features and characteristic culture of different countries and step forward to a gradual recognition from the understanding and cognition. Nevertheless, with the rapid shortening of world from transportation to the information distance, people began to use "globalism", "globalization" and "global village" to express our common earth and the former cultural barrier has been rapidly eliminated. It has become very common for people to see the foreigners and foreign brands, which has laid the common foundation for the brand's global development.

Globalism is a typical brand development thought. In earlier days, people began to take land as the main development from, from the Celts, Rome in earlier Europe, to "the sun never set" Great Britain or "the concept of world" and "unity" in China's original civilization. All these were the concept of "globalism" formed during the process of human development and just represented through the territory awareness in politics, military and culture.

What has truly exerted the role of "globalism" in the world brand field was the brands' globalized thought formed in the 20th century. US missile thinking taking world market as the "globalism" had promoted the formation of international corporations and Fortune Global 500 and the "international concepts" among European countries have driven lots of development of international brands, whereas the "exogenous brands" in Japan and Korea have caused the brands in these two countries to have the globalized attributes from the very beginning. These development thoughts have driven many companies in these countries to take "globalized companies" as the development mission from the date of its establishment, or take "the international corporation" "international brands" as the core development target, which has laid the factual basis for development for further globalized recognition of the brands.

Recognition is the test of use result completed on the brand exporting country, brand's original place, brand creators and specific brand products and services during the process of long term use of brands. The different brand development thinking and brand products in different countries have been confirmed during the long term use, long term self-communication and long term reliable authentication among the public and a lot of brands survived and formed the recognition on such products and specific brand products in these countries on the basis of cultural identity and cultural distinction. Such recognition is not only the sensible impression, but also the rational choice and the reliable recommended sources. As a result, a global and reliable brand ecological system has been formed and connected based on the reliable facts and with mutual trust.

The brand is rated and the brands from different countries would have the reliable national brand grades and every brand has the specific reliable grade. Such grade is the rapid brand screening system set up by every person and a screening system with brand rating identification and self-safety protection developed from the brand consumption environment and brand application process in the society with the common self-perception of human beings. People would constantly add the newly emerged brands and testified brands into their own reliable brand list, which not only includes the distinction of recognition on brand exporting country, but also consists of the reliable recognition on specific brands. In addition, everyone has also set up a simple grading system to make distinction on the brand recognition as a rapid brand reliability determination and identification and defense system. This is the security instinct of everyone to make the rapid screening and reliability on different brands used in their limited life. Whenever the consumption ability grows in a country, people begin to pursue the enjoyment of brands and such feature has become an important demand in spirit and culture developed after reliability development.

4 People's enjoyment and brand's sustainable development

With the constant growth of people's revenue in every country, people's consumption level has been constantly improved and correspondingly, people's requirement on branding consumption in daily life has also increased. Such growth has mainly represented in the cultural demands with motivational growth. When people are seeking for the best products, services and experience in each consumption or expenditure field, people begin to attach importance to life and brand has been commonly understood as the upper requirement in spiritual and cultural aspects. The brand requirements and brand supply are relatively balanced and such balance has the subtle mentality resonance between the brand producers and demanders.

Every detail on brand creator's thinking, brand designer's understanding and brand value creation chain could be transferred to the brand users via brands. For pursuit of better life, the brand users would improve their cultural connotations in aesthetics, fashion, trend, personality, taste, leisure and nutrition etc. and attach importance to the pursuit of brand value such as identity, status, honor, reputation, ecology and health; whereas such common spiritual upgrading of the supplier and demander has been commonly represented in the pursuit of brand's artistic conception and this is the ideal brand value choice. Even though the consumers have not been improved into the corresponding cultural status, they know well to use what brands to express the social class they are in and their life style in the social class and friends circle.

Therefore, brands have been elevated into a pure enjoyment of the human beings, which includes "my" and "his" social culture expression. "My" is the brand choice of the brand users that expressed their cultural connotation and individual culture demands whereas "his" is the brand choice of the brand users with the purpose of enabling the others to know and understand his social status, social class and life. With the people's constant improvement of their spiritual world, "I" will express more and more whereas "he", as the group demonstration, would gradually reduce after enhancement of a certain period of brand needs and would more and more demonstrate in self-brand enjoyment needs just like "I should do like this".

Brand plays the leading role in the increasingly growing consumption demands of the human beings. During the process of developing the world market or expanding the domestic consumption market, the brand plays the main role in social and economic development that has been constantly replaced and it is also the important strategic reserve resource for a country's economy. A country's future and significant development capacity depends upon the country's brand's quantity. Whenever a country has the increasing growing demands for the brands, it shows that the country's economic demands are increasing constantly and the people are stepping into the consumption enjoyment times urgently requiring the branding from satisfying the basic living conditions.

The whole 21st century is still a period of time that the newly emerged brands could at least enjoy the development; however, after 21st century, with the growth of people's economic income and gradual finalization of worldwide brand competition, the brands in every field such as people's life and consumption etc. have been basically formed and maturely and steadily developed and there is fewer and fewer room for the new brand development. The main reason lies in that the brands enjoyed by the people are sufficient and the brands survived in each specific market sector have become the fixed reliance of the human beings.

If we say the focus of the global brands in the 20th century was to develop the corporate responsibility, and concentrate on the products and services, the highlights of the brands in the 21st century shall be the companies' social responsibility and focus on the socialized responsibilities such as the global environment and green ecology, elimination of poverty and fighting against the epidemic diseases etc. Nevertheless, any country, in case of developing its own brand economy, shall not escape from the development stage from "corporate responsibility" to "corporate social responsibility"; and the complication of the competition structure in the world market requires that corporations in the 21st shall assume the double liabilities for "corporate responsibility" and "corporate social responsibility". The impetus of the brand socialization is also the common cognition that should be supported by the consumers and this is the future of the brands' sustainable development as well as the sustainably developed order of nature ecology of the human beings.

5 Method of the market position classification for world brands

From any brand's development pattern and market representation, we shall apply the methods on brand market position classification to divide the brands into world brands, international brands, national brands, domestic brands, local brands and niche brands. Such classification method is there to divide a brand's future development direction from the date of creation and the actually realized market structure.

Firstly, whenever determining to create a brand, the brand creators must have the market target for the future development of their own brands which might be a global or a small region. Its development pattern, in addition to the good development manner, has finally decided what market position the brand has worldwide. The new Fortune Global 500 would appear constantly and everyone could be the founder of the next Fortune Global 500 and might be the creator of a world famous brand, or would become a legend of a hundred-year's brand.

As for the brands' development pattern, there is no big or small brand and everyone, every country might create the new world brand or international brand at any time. As long as you want it, it might become true. In particular, in the times of public startup worldwide, nothing is impossible; however, provided that the startup must follow the scientific laws of brand development and comply with the brand rules and focus on establishing, being rooted and developing the powerful brand concept from the very beginning.

The future market competition worldwide will be the high level of knowledge competition and the founders without studying the systematic branding would be difficult to have a bright brand start. Furthermore, the world has generally noticed such an important trend, i.e., in the future, the company's president would be CBO (chief Brand Officer), rather than CEO (Chief Executive Officer), or someone combining both; however, the brand would give priority to the operations, which is decided by the highly developed brand in the whole 21st century – the internationalized, professional and occupational development of the overall development of human beings.

The competition of global brands is the fierce global brand competition tournament and brands will be challenged constantly in the world market ranking on its survival and development. As for as the overall progress of the brand is concerned, any brand would belong to one of the six brand market positions, i.e. world brand, international brand, national brand, domestic brand, local brand and niche brand.

Among these, the brands mainly developed shall be the international ones and only a small part of international brands have the chance to become the world brands. The conditions on determination of the world brands are that the brands must be active in the world markets across at least three continents (such as North America, Europe and Asia) and hold the leading market position in the professional market; besides, the brands must be marked in at least three languages in the main part of the brands, such as main demonstration area of brand LOGO, package and instruction etc. (including brand name, product name and place of origin etc.), and the language shall be determined by the number of population using such language worldwide.

The number of the international brands is an important representation on whether a country is a brand exporting country. An international brand must be marked in at least two languages in the main part of the brands, such as main demonstration area of brand LOGO, package and instruction etc. in the professional market of at least three countries, including the native language and an international language or the language of a country where the company has its presence.

The national brand is a country's representative and symbolic brand. It is the brand mainly developed by the country for its economic development or with the cultural features and also an important development form to improve the country's overall brand premium ability. However, these brands must become the highly branding ones with the higher brand premium ability; otherwise, the bad reputation or the cheap image of these brands in the international market would pull down the whole country's brand premium ability and make all the brands of the country be in the awkward development position. From the worldwide consumers, the first is to make the country identification of the brands. The brand premium of a country shall be determined by the country's overall brand premium ability and the brand development level and the premium ability of different countries would be in different premium level, which would decide how much the people would increase or to what trust extent the people would have to judge the brands from the country. It is the potential exporting currency value of

Section IV Brand Culture

the national brands as well as the most important economic competition strength of the country in the future worldwide economy competition.

The domestic brands, local brands and niche brands hold their market positions featured by the demand markets in the national market, localized market or certain field and it is also the main brand development form mostly by newly emerged corporation and the maturely operated corporations and the main source of economic revenue of more than 90% corporations and population.

Brands also have the cultural heritage brand attributes to a certain extent which is mainly decided by the role of brands in the development of human history. When some representative brands with special cultural attributes are developed, the brand will be listed in the very important material or non-material cultural heritage no matter whether these brands exist or become extinct thereafter. The protection or the protective discovery of these brands is an important process of culture continuity during the process of brand development. The files of some brand creators at an earlier age and the original place of the brand creation have been successively listed in the national cultural relics and cultural heritage of each country.

Under the precondition of the world peace and development in the 20th century and seeking for sustainable and ecological development in the 21st century, brand will play a more and more important role in the human development. It has not only become the most important economic power in the leading society, the most common need in the people's daily life, but also the important economic pillar in the economic development and development engine of science and technology, culture and education. Besides, it also marks the human beings as the more advanced civilization and the cultural heritage of the human beings.

Exercise:

1. Fill in the blanks: In essence, the brand's process of "cognition- identity-recognition" is the brand's development of "_____ _____ _____ _____".

2. True or False Question: The brand requirements and brand supply are relatively balanced and such balance equals to have the subtle mentality resonance between the brand producers and demanders. ( )

3. Essay question: What has become the cultural pursuit with the universal value in the process of human cultural transition? What development structure it includes?

Chapter 2

Brand and Enterprise Culture

The relationship between brand and enterprise culture has plagued the business community in the world. The focus of our study is to analyze commonalities between the brand and enterprise culture in order to explain how they develop to different departments engaging in the two sectors for consistent and coordinated development of the two.

1 Property of brand and enterprise culture in the organization

To make judgement on brand and enterprise culture, we must pay attention to their consistency and differences in functions and explain their development course and influence. It seems easier for people to understand brand culture, and it may lead to a better understanding of brand and enterprise culture from the perspective of brand culture and enterprise culture if both fall into the category of culture and coexist in enterprises as important cultural factors.

However, misunderstanding occurs when the relationship between brand and enterprise culture is examined only from the perspective of brand culture and enterprise culture, because brand culture and enterprise culture, in a strict sense, are beyond the scope of culture and are a special cultural competence that is different from and higher than social culture. From the overall viewpoint, brand culture and enterprise culture remain a discipline of organizational development, and serve for the brand and for brand users and development. Therefore, brand is essentially more general than enterprise culture, and serves as an important tool to guide overall development.

Any enterprise culture cannot be separated from the brand itself, especially in future socio-economic formations that feature highly developed branding. Brand, in the regard of enterprise development, is highly exclusive, strategic and comprehensive, and enterprise culture and brand culture should be put on the equal foot and assume different tasks for development. This is the most objective explanation of brand and enterprise culture, and the issue of "difference" and "consistency" should be reviewed from the aspect of brand.

Brand is the soul of an enterprise as well as the overall development strategy, which needs not to be specially noted. When the brand competency of an enterprise is stronger, the brand would have a more powerful leading role in all work, tasks and market of the enterprise. On the contrary, if an enterprise is faced with serious brand competency constraint, the brand would be easily viewed at two different levels of market and organization, leading to independent development and inconsistency of brand culture and enterprise culture as a result of their different extrinsic and intrinsic attributes. In addition, brand culture and enterprise culture would be easily regarded as two different development areas and undertake different development missions and tasks. Nonetheless, when a brand of an enterprise has developed to a certain degree and enterprise culture has progressed into organizational culture, the need of organizational development and organizational ecology for brand development would naturally combine brand culture and enterprise culture together, which is inevitable in the history of brand development of an enterprise. All cultures will be eventually unified and it will be possible to produce brand civilization at a higher level.

1.1 How brand and enterprise culture evolve in overall development

In order to explain the important role of brand and enterprise culture in the development course of an enterprise and the future development trend of global brands, we have established a new organizational culture theory to clarify the development relationship between the brand, brand culture and enterprise culture as well as how brand or enterprise culture evolve.

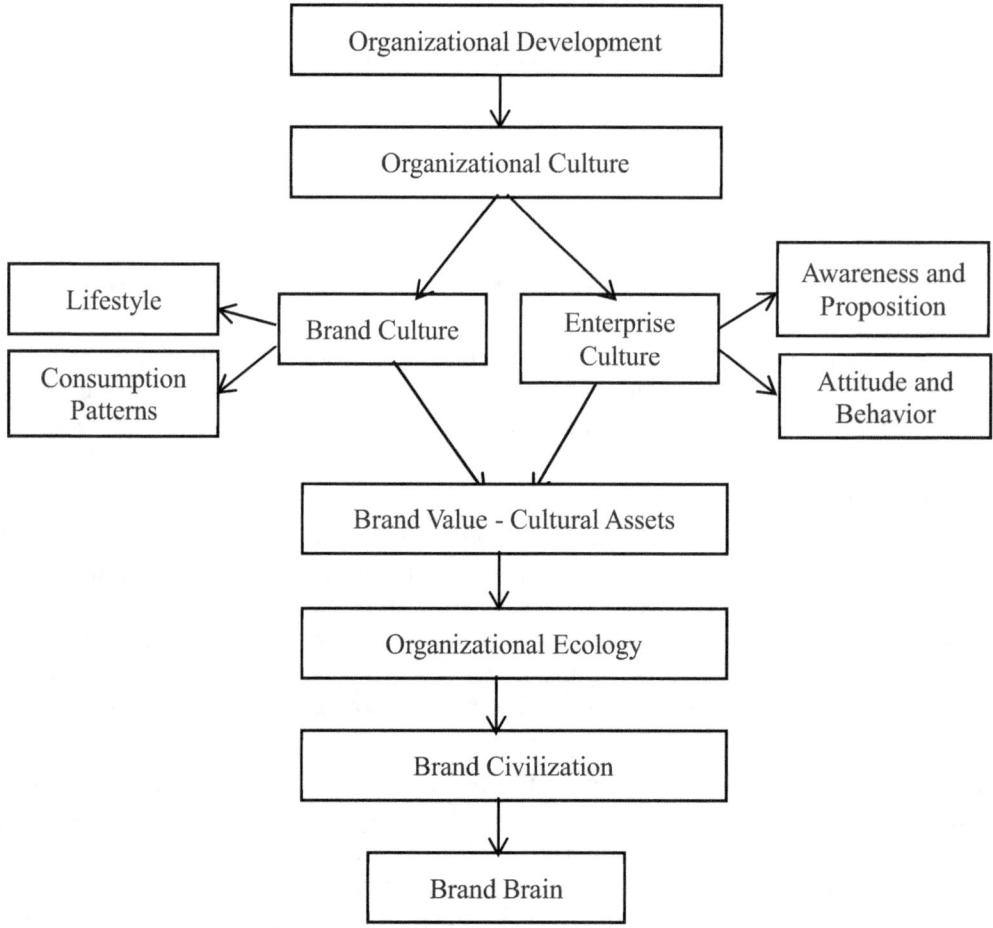

Fig. 2-1 Theory of Organizational Culture

Brand culture and enterprise culture fall into the category of organizational development, and brand organization is a higher stage of enterprise brand, an ecological and organizational stage of brand as well as a short development stage of an organization. To achieve the goal of upgrading an enterprise to a brand organization, organizational development becomes an important development mode representing the development level, structure and ecological order of a brand.

Rational brand organization regards the organizational culture of a brand as the task of organization development, and its development goal is the requirement of organizational ecology on the process of brand organization. The essence of organization is the process of individuals forming groups, and brands users and enterprise employees as individuals share the same task of organization evolution.

The task of organizational culture is to organize and combine leaders, investors, supply chains, employees and brand users within or outside the enterprise for highly coordinated, consistent and organizational development. Organizational culture is highly consistent here, and brand development mission, values, enterprise responsibility and enterprise social responsibility are designed and managed from the level of organizational culture, and brand culture or enterprise will not be artificially separated into different ideology, values or behaviors. Especially in the era of social network, the boundary between society and brand, business organization, socialization, service and network has become quite blurred, and exclusive and antagonistic relationship between "we" and "they" can no longer be used to deal with all social relations relevant to business organizations. Instead, all people should be defined as "us".

From the very beginning, organizational culture is the unified development idea in an enterprise brand or culture, which is determined by the needs of development of brand organization and is the long-term strategy and the highest requirement of decision-making. Future brand economy, national brand wealth as well as the nation, society, enterprises and consumers will follow a highly branded development pattern. Brand as a symbol of development capacity of a business organization is essentially higher than enterprise culture that should serve for the brand, which provides important basis and prerequisite to properly handle the contradictions between brand and enterprise culture development.

1.2 Development goals of brand culture and enterprise culture

Brand culture and enterprise culture assume different tasks in the brand organization, outside-in and inside-out respectively, thus creating a two-way development route and making the two cultures parallel and coordinated.

Brand culture is a specific cultural element for systematic interpretation, cultural explanation and cultural development of a brand. Its key point is to study, analyze and develop and decode cultural causes of lifestyle and consumption patterns of brand users, define the main official interpretation and explanation of a brand, design and manage culture and values based on needs of brand users, and in this way develop a pattern of consumption culture unique to the brand. And it works in an outside-in approach. In the meanwhile, brand culture provides enterprise employees their needed brand value identity, including but not limited to logo, spirit, brand story, cultural heritage, style, sense of brand honor, brand perception, cultural theme and cultural presentation, which constitute causes, origins and soul of enterprise culture as well as the main part of branding requirements and brand value.

Enterprise culture refers to the organization process of specifically dealing with the organizing capacity of an enterprise, developing awareness of employees, fostering enterprise attainment, eliminating enterprises culture resistance and striving to stimulate positive attitude and value-producing behaviors of employees. It develops the actual ideological level and main awareness of behaviors of enterprises, contributing to positive attitude and actions of enterprises in market operation and in individual employees. It provides action capability and guarantee to achieve brand development missions and goals.

Enterprise culture, developed from the inside out, is delivered through the value chain. Due to more social and networked development of modern brands, in brands that are operated in social network, value of labor and direct contact with the public of each employee are increased, and even business executives and key employees not only directly contact with brand users in work flow and service flow, but also own their we-media and communication and exchange ways to associate or interact with anyone and anything. Thus, everyone's behaviors are meant to deliver the image of a brand to the public. Future development of enterprise culture is no longer limited to the enterprise, but requires efforts made by the all people concerned. Enterprise culture should be operated on the basis of branding, and be incorporated into the brand development capacity and it structure for corresponding cultural development, management and supervision as well as transformation of enterprises to brand culture and quality culture exporting.

1.3 Cultural assets of brand and ultimate goal of ecological development of organization

From economic point of view such as investment and finance, roles and cultural effects of both brand culture and enterprise culture are eventually included in cultural assets of an enterprise and considered as an important part of brand value. They demonstrate the development prospect, competence and capital stock and can be calculated as investment value and the market value in company listing, merging and selling.

The goal of organizational development is organizational ecology, which is a discipline that puts brand culture and enterprise culture on equal foot for development and a concrete outcome of enterprises to create brand value and develop cultural assets. In the ecological development structure of the brand organization, a brand has increased its adaptive capacity to guarantee orderly and favorable operation and has acquired the capacity for sustainable ecological development. Being open, united, coordinated, integrated and inclusive, the capacity for sustainable ecological development is formed after brand culture and enterprise culture that are highly developed, and makes value development of brand employees and users ecologically sustainable through outside-in and inside-out organizational process. The orderly ecological development of an organization ensures the long-lasting vitality of the brand and the organic balance of operation.

An enterprise, after branding, organization, socialization and networked development, in the end has the opportunity to progress into the stage of brand civilization, in which the brand entirely becomes a certain form of civilization. Brand civilization is not only a stage of brand development, but also a highly unified form of civilization with brand culture and enterprise culture having progressed to a certain advanced level. It emerges after the enterprise has produced fixed, specific, obvious, independent and inheritable forms of culture, and civilization itself enjoys strong future development value, cultural heritage value and competitiveness.

Ultimately, the enterprise brand may move forward to the highest stage of brand brain, which means that brand culture and enterprise culture will be eventually transformed to adaptive and automatically upgraded brand brain in social networks, and brand employees and users will fully merge together and initiate the stage of memory, wisdom, knowledge, thought, creation and higher civilization. The brand neural network and brain intelligence will push forward the brand to an unprecedented level of intellectual development.

2 Scientific expression of brand culture

The cultural expression of the brand is embodied as important functional value in three aspects. Due to the three value factors, brand culture is different from enterprise culture and is dominant in all cultures, and it enjoys social and economic value and is the most important investment and sustainable benefit in brand value assets.

(1) Ecological development value of brand culture: the primary task of brand culture is to make a structural design of brand value from the cultural level, make a comprehensive brand interpretation and official explanation, as well as to design, promote and supervise branding elements, behaviors and styles at the cultural level. This is the functional mission and responsibility assumed by brand culture as the enterprise is moving towards a highly unified brand, and constitutes the foundation for sustainable development of the brand. Brand culture also serves for brand value appreciation and all brand users. Its cultural role cannot be replaced by social culture or enterprise culture.

(2) Brand culture is essentially higher than all cultural forms of enterprises: brand culture is the highest cultural rule of brand awareness, spirit, branding process and employees' attitude and behaviors, and works as the core that carries the enterprise brand to progress into brand ecological organization and then into brand civilization, to establish brand loyalty among brand users, and to ensure employees' creation and users' two-way value expression and realization in brand value chain.

(3) Monetary value of brand culture from the perspective of asset attributes: brand culture is an important process to promote artistic conception of brand products, enrich cultural background of brand, create sensory properties of the brand, arouse sense of honor of brand employees and enhance brand premium. As the monetary and financial valuable asset that plays an important role for transaction in assets in the capital market, it is a way of financial pricing that can be evaluated, calculated and sold.

These characteristics make the expression of brand culture, in the scientific and philosophic sense, focus on effective utilization of brand science and technology and perfect expression of philosophy and aesthetics. The most important part of a brand lies in culture that gives a conception of the whole brand and its products and service, and makes the brand perfectly express the brand ideas of valuable cultural sympathy and spiritual pursuit based on the physical form of its original product or service

2.1 Theory of brand expression

As for specific understanding and interpretation, we use the theory of brand impression, which means that people's cognition and basic expression of a brand are based on at least three types of contacts or at least three dimensions, i.e. the influence of theory of brand stretching or extension. Logo, name, artistic expression of products, visual image, brand story, service experience and other dimensions directly stimulate people's three-dimensional impression and perception of the brand, that are intuitive and lasting and can arouse sympathy of customers and meet consumers' expectation, desire of possession and spiritual needs, for synchronous interaction between brand creators and customers in spiritual pursuit regardless of time and space.

Theory of brand impression is a specific brand image form established brand culture in a deep level as well as the real pursuit of the development of brand culture. A typical example is the VI system designed and produced by the professional brand design company that is hired by the enterprise. VI system is designed not only to make manuals with materialized quality and visual decomposition, but also ensure consistent brand image on the facets of all entities. Potential consumers through brand homepage, content, employees' clothes and mental attitude, commercials and other comprehensive sensory impression, can only be recognized as potential brand users and pursue the brand. Such kind of pursuit exactly expresses the science, culture, aesthetics, spirit and ideas of the brand and is manifested as clear cultural characteristic.

Text, language, commercials and publicity materials of a brand should be based on the expression of its artistic conception. Only in this way can users perceive the important elements of artistic conception and the brand becomes "alive". When a brand fails to deliver brand builder's pursuit of artistic conception, the brand would be "dead" and be misunderstood as a trademark, business name, product portfolio and business form (a familiar trademark, some famous name, physical products or publicity materials), rather than to be presumed as a true brand, unable to reach the brand's scientific and philosophical requirements.

Brand culture will vitalize the brand, and highly developed brand culture will infiltrate the soul of the brand into its products and service, so that the brand shows signs of life in vivid detail, arouses sympathy of everyone, and is delivered outward through commercials, business cards, websites, pictures, statements, internal documents, service policies, instructions and other physical forms as representatives of permanent and competitive cultural value in spirit, science, art and identity, thus constituting the premium capacity, exclusive competitiveness and market space of the brand. Works of disappeared civilization and artistic expression that are discovered by archaeologists in ancient sites and historical relics and design works of brand masters are preserved as important cultural heritage of human beings, and possess a collectible value and memory value of a good brand that reflects the characteristics of the brand culture.

2.2 Principle of formation of varied brand cultures

The brand culture has the obvious characteristic of centralization. Cultures in the world have their own centers, and different cultural centers constitute different civilization or cultural pedigree, which is an indispensable part of the development course of world cultures and the source of today's diverse cultures. Exploration, inheritance and development of cultures mark the premise of human self-awareness, development of civilization and cultural exploration.

SECTION IV BRAND CULTURE

Any civilization that exists in the world features various cultural centers and pedigrees, being historical, traditional, modern, fashionable, future or international. The combination of these civilizations and different cultures and subcultures marks the origin and cause of diverse cultures, provides cultural inspirations for brands and works as the "pilgrimage center" for cultural tracing and" future center" for develop mentalism. For example, American country music culture, Silicon Valley culture, Hollywood culture, space exploration culture, French customs culture, British culture, Irish harp culture, Celtic fantasy legend culture, sinology or Chinese knot culture, may inspire new brand and brand culture.

In general, the brand culture is the inheritance and development of mankind's diverse civilization. Cultural centers of different civilization cultivate brand civilization, and stimulate cultural beliefs, style and pursuit of each individual brand. In the process of interaction, collision, connection, opening up and integration of different cultures, diverse human civilization, international cultures and brand civilization are fostered through tracing the existing civilization, developing new civilization or new cultural characteristics from combining and interpreting a culture or creating a new popular culture.

Brand culture has its cultural origins for inheritance and creation, and this is the reason why brand culture can more easily win global recognition and international exchanges than enterprise culture. As a result of global awareness of countercultural aggression, cultures in the world can coexist and respect, protect and influence each other, and then each brand culture can be widely accepted around the world and capture followers and fans. In this way, international brands can enter all global markets, and meet someone who respects and loves their brand culture in every corner of the world. Such overlapping and coexisting diverse cultures are incorporated into cultural spectrums of human being, laying a theoretical and factual foundation for brand development.

2.3 Centralized structure of brand culture

The feature of centralization of brand culture is manifested by specific extraction and coordinated development of various cultural centers of the brand, which means that, each brand has its own CBS (centralized branding system) in the world to assume tasks of cultural tracing, integration, extraction, development, implementation, commanding and coordination, and has its outside-in delivery methods. This is an important profess for a brand to create and develop its independent cultural pedigree, and the focus of brand interpretation including brand mission and story.

Brand culture will appear out of nowhere, and brand founders and creators will decide whether to inherit a culture or subculture or absorb different culture and develop their own culture on the basis of various cultures. Each brand culture must be independent and in the meanwhile add new cultural elements and develop its own systematic cultural pedigree on the basis of subcultures. In this way, the brand can exist with typical cultural characteristics that can distinguish it from its competitors or other brand cultures.

Successfully building a brand culture is a lonely and arduous task, and many enterprises have failed, and only a few brands can finally systematically explore and create their own brand culture. In the following stage, the brand organization should focus on its brand culture and attract more people who recognize the brand (backbones and employees) to develop, inherit, protect, communicate and deliver the brand, which is similar to the relationship between queen ant and her ant colony for ergates and reproduction.

However, this is limited to the development of one brand and its employees and users. If a brand aspires to create more new independent brands and a brand group in which each brand is targeted at a specific market segment, the theory of brand order system for brand development is needed. The Celtic once occupied most of Europe and managed hundreds of different countries at the same time, and the orderly operation was exactly the outcome of order system. Founder of the world's first and most successful group brand cluster model P&G with the Celtic background utilized skills to manage several brands at the same time, and finally developed a divisional organization and brand manager structure to manage the great brand family featuring various products and complicated technology. In 2015, sales revenue of 26 brands from the family exceeded 1 billion US dollars.

The centralization of the brand and its centralized brand operation mode will create a centralized systematic structure for the brand. Each brand and group brand cluster have a brand center to assume the task of systematic development for central branding and to be embodied as mature, clear and stable brand order. Issues of brand development and diversity that are generally encountered by global enterprises are a major challenge bothering stable scale development of global brands. Having its own laws and development structure, the centralized brand development mode is a management scope and idea that cannot be hedged by enterprise founders and leaders who are ambitious to enhance their brands and group brand clusters. Enterprise brand is in urgent need of centralization to develop the brand in an orderly, reasonable and clear way.

Brand culture is delivered from the brand center to users and then from users to the center again in a direct way that gets rid of employees. In a highly developed and branded organization, interaction between enterprise leaders and brand users is direct. Development of modern networking technology further supports the direct brand delivery, sympathy and response. Today's enterprises expect to develop social and networked interaction with brand users in a more direct way of networking development, which comes back to the essence of brand establishment: brand, since its establishment, has the purpose to serve for its users and their interests and consumption, to contribute to better lifestyle, happier experience and perfect service, and to deliver spirit, ideas and culture.

3 Consistency and cultural conflicts between brand culture and enterprise culture

Brand culture and corporate culture share the same ideological and cultural heritage such as brand mission, value and spirit, and such consistency is reflected in that brand culture is the source and cause to create enterprise culture. And brand culture itself comes from inheritance, combination and development of one or some typical cultures and has its origin and source.

On the other hand, enterprise culture usually lacks origin and trace ability, and cannot be separated from culture of a brand for independent spirit and values. The ideological inconsistencies will lead to serious cultural conflicts. The brand is the product that is closely related to dream, while conflicts in enterprise culture mainly occur when dream and reality contradict with each other. A highly branded enterprise is bound to be an outcome of coordination between brand culture and enterprise culture. Or there are frequent disagreements between brand culture and enterprise culture, which leads to conflicts and contradictions and seriously hinders employees in their awareness, mentality and behaviors.

Collectivism in some countries is regarded as the main culture, but in fact it is not. Creation of brand culture is relatively easy with effective combination and organic creation of various civilization or cultural factors and expression of mission, consciousness, storytelling, artistic conception and aesthetics. However, enterprise culture is imposed to the enterprises by complicated social and cultural factors. Enterprise culture is constrained by the society and its cultures as various social trends of thought, phenomena, contradictions, religious, politics and cultures initiate dramatic and complex changes in ideology of people. Therefore, to create enterprise culture, it should be considered more important than social culture.

Only when negative factors of defects, contradictions and worries imposed by social culture on enterprise culture are eliminated can the enterprise culture be positive and stimulate employees in their awareness, attitudes and behaviors, so as to accomplish the mission of enterprise culture. It should be noted that in the context of liberalism and the trend of individualism in the age of social network, collectivism can hardly exist. And in some countries and societies that emphasize freedom and individualism, it has become a trend to respect, develop, organize, coordinate and serve individuals. This is a form of organization featuring interaction between individuals and the cultural bond for connection and coordination. Structure and content of organizations have generated tremendous changes in "collectivism" in social patterns, and given rise to a new ecological organizational order based on social and culture forms with representatives of organizational socialization and coordination, which lays an important foundation for development of modern enterprise culture.

Enterprise culture is responsible for the ideology, values, work attitudes and behaviors in the modern enterprises. By transforming brand culture into general cultural state of orderly, positive and coordinated employees who bear two-way responsibility, it is reflected through awareness, attainment and attitude of employees. It also initiates active understanding and action and responsible attitude in groups. Especially in each point of direct contact between employees and investors, suppliers, service providers and brand users, such kind of rational enterprise cultural state is created to contribute to integrity of enterprise culture, playa role of showing and complementing brand culture, and encourage brand users to perceive, understand, discover and recognize brand image and service. In this way, enterprise culture can only meet their functional requirements of the enterprise.

3.1 Service subject of enterprise culture

Brand culture serves for brand users in a direct way, and deals with their awareness, perception and response, while enterprise culture is to stimulate employees to better serve brand users. Regardless of differences in the principal role and value in the enterprise between brand culture and enterprises culture, the two share the same service object and outcomes.

We have established a structure for the development of brand culture and enterprise culture development structure, in order to more clearly identify cultural effects of the two cultural factors and results on brand users.

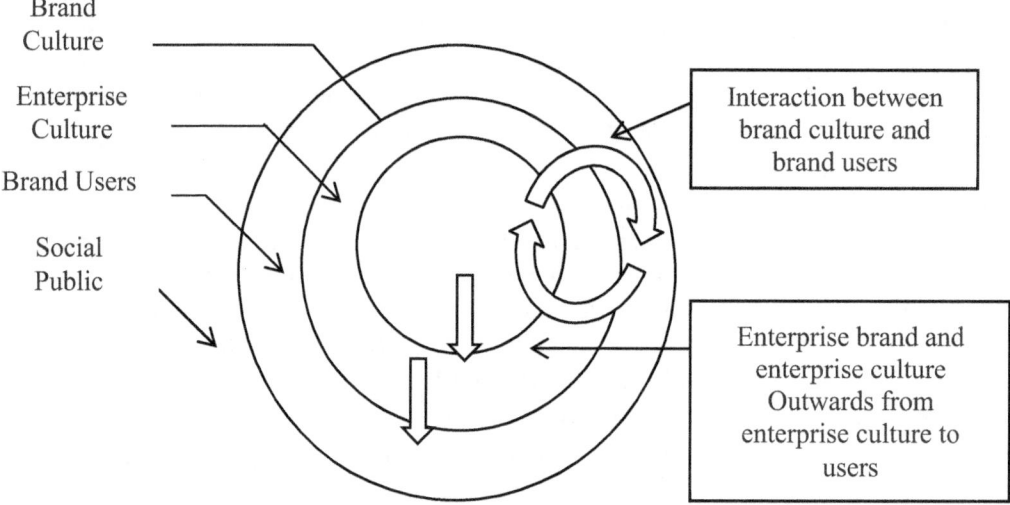

Fig.2-2: Delivery of brand culture and enteprise culture

We divide the delivery of culture into four parts, including brand culture, enterprise culture, brand users and social public. To begin with, brand culture breeds enterprise culture. Especially in the recruitment of new human resources, outstanding talents are attracted by the strength and development prospects of the brand. Then some talents join the brand and contribute to brand expression. Such contribution, being good, pure, real, professional, in many cases have nothing to do with money or material conditions. Instead, it is a spiritual pursuit, value embodiment, life philosophy, noble virtue, volunteering action from the bottom heart, as well as the basic form of human social civilization for mutual respect of people. The enterprise culture, as a transformation mode of spiritual expression factor, atmosphere, attitude and behaviors, works to respect cultures of individuals, recognize the value of labor, encourage initiation, praise good behaviors and contribute to ceremonial cohesion.

From the perspective of enterprise culture, the basic form of civilization created by brand culture is delivered to enterprise culture that is then transformed to enterprise culture power through specific implementation of brand value and actions, and finally enterprise culture is delivered to brand users to perceive, feel and experience. In the end, brand users deliver the enterprise culture to social public, encouraging more new brand users to join the users' group of the brand. Cultural conflicts happening during the process need to be considered.

And from the perspective of brand culture, as the brand is for brand users, interaction between brand culture and brand users is direct. For example, the latest development goals and service policies of the brand that are stated by brand leaders in press interviews will be directly delivered to brand users and social public through social media, and problems encountered by users in product application, after getting published by users through we media on the Internet, may be immediately identified by the brand monitoring system and reported to managers.

3.2 Recreation of enterprise culture and cultural conflicts

The origin of a brand culture and the core value of a culture are enduring in general, and will not be forgotten with the passage of time and the development of history. Since the primitive times, when people kept records and accounts by tying knots, people have been attaching importance to recording, preserving, protecting and inheriting various cultural creations, figures and events, collecting them in museums, historical materials and archives as an important part of human civilization, and repeatedly advertising to draw people's attention. In such a unique way, culture is preserved and developed. Change of brand culture depends on whether its way of expression meets the latest needs of aesthetics, and it is a matter of deciding how to present the brand and develop market of the brand.

But the biggest difference between enterprise culture and brand culture is that enterprise culture may suffer aging at any moment. As a result of social trends of thought, culture, concepts, phenomena, trends and issues, enterprise culture undergoes dramatic changes in a fixed time frame. To be specific, there was a fraction in social culture between different generations (30 years), and now with the net generation, social culture witnesses sudden changes in every ten years.

During different stages of development of an enterprise, fraction and breakthrough in social culture would impact people's ideas and ideology, and the way of working and life of each member of the leadership and employee would change, and ideas and value judgments would evolve with social and cultural changes. Social changes are the main reasons for changes in people's ideology, and cultural resistance in an enterprise would at the same time influence social culture. This requires re-creation of enterprise culture every once in a while to rejuvenate the enterprises before aging of the enterprise culture.

Cultural conflicts in enterprise vary, including conflicts between brand culture and enterprise culture and between different organizations and loss of enterprise culture in delivery. There are at least two very prominent problems in this process:

First, whether there is a true brand culture. If the brand culture in the enterprise is not strong, thorough and far-reaching enough, the enterprise culture will be more high-profile than brand culture, and the brand organization will be downgraded as general business, brand products as general products, and brand gravity as normal marketing development. As a result, the enterprises will suffer brand parkinsonism again, and brand development capacity will be replaced by general needs for enterprise development such as enterprise spirit and values.

Second, in delivery of enterprise culture, problems of decreased enterprises awareness and behavior will occur. As transmission of electricity, sound waves, wireless signals and trains cause a lot of loss, systems of reception, amplification, sending and supply should be set at regular distances for smooth operation. It is the same for enterprises. Enterprise culture is delivered from too many enterprise hierarchies (leaders, executives and employees) to users and the public, so the question is how to deal

SECTION IV BRAND CULTURE

to losses of culture in the process? How to eliminate culture resistance rising from non-official organizations in the enterprises, pressure of employees and negative social phenomena?

Therefore, it is necessary to further study, experiment and establish the theory of enterprise culture. New theories of enterprise culture cover areas of enterprise culture power, re-creation of enterprise culture, enterprise business theory, enterprise order, enterprise attainments can enterprise cultural memes, contributing to the active role played by enterprise culture in its development, delivery and value system. Any enterprise has a culture, and whether it is a proactive one or a depressed and passive one depends on cultural complexity that generally leads to failures of creation of enterprise culture.

Exercises

1. Fill in the blanks: The centralized branding system (CBS) assumes seven tasks of _____, _____, _____, _____, _____, _____, _____ of culture, and always has its own outside-in transmission path.

2. Multiple-choice Question: Brand culture is a specific cultural element for _____, and its key point is to _____ lifestyle and consumption patterns of brand users, and define the main official interpretation and explanation of a brand. ( )

   A. systematic interpretation, cultural interpretation, cultural development study, analyze and develop and decode cultural causes of

   B. systematic interpretation, cultural development study, analyze and develop and decode cultural causes of

   C. systematic interpretation, cultural explanation, cultural development study, analyze and develop

   D. systematic interpretation, cultural explanation, cultural development decodes cultural causes of

3. Briefly describe consistency between brand culture and enterprise culture and their cultural conflicts.

Chapter 3

Brand Artistic Conception

The human mode is always stricken by the natural and beautiful things to immerse in an enjoyment of feeling and sense, which is the origin of birth and development of brand. In this Chapter, the topic about intelligence of brand will be discussed, namely the deep thinking of brand in philosophy and aesthetics.

Brand artistic conception shows three focuses: a kind of pursuit of the aesthetic things in the nature; the philosophical reflection of the truth of life; the understanding of the balanced thinking in the ternary order.

1 Human will eventually develop into brander

Human is divided into general man, economic man, industrial man, social man and brander, which is the existing main form of human. Essentially all the humans will step into the stage of brander. The countries are made of brand-exporting countries and brand-importing countries, a small part of which are brand builders and the rest are the members of brand organizers or brand consumers.

General man is the human characterized by material exchange and the original economic transactions of cars, real estate, precious metals (such as gold, silver, jewelry, etc.) and gems, which depends on the prevalence of mercantilism in some countries, and it shows that general man relies on economic man and parts of them are still characterized as general man.

Economic man is the man who takes monetary and wealth further as a measure or a criterion of things. If the proportion of economic man in one country is too great or occupies the economic dominance too much, the country will become a deep brand-importing country and the rise of quantity and quality of international brands in this country will encounter a huge impact.

Industrial man refers to the man who has the characteristics of the social division of labor. The countries which went through the industrial revolution in Europe or understood the professional division deeply have completed the collective progress of industrial man a hundred years before. On the contrary, the countries that did not experience the industrial revolution struggle to complete a smooth transition for a very long time. Professional division is embedded in the national general thinking and also reflects on the division ways of social labor, meaning that the core competitiveness of enterprises specialization releases a large number of peripheral business and employment space to achieve the specialization of social division of labor so that the small enterprises that occupy the most of all the enterprises in the country get great vitality, which is an important premise of a country changing into a brand-exporting country.

The progress of general man, economic man to industrial man exists in any country and any person in the world, and specialized division society where major nationals reach the stage of industrial man will be based on it.

1.1 Future society measured by social contribution

Social man is the population with civil society attributes. When the citizens have a great proportion in social participation, social strength and social contribution, civil society will be based on them. Civil society is a responsible society, where the population and enterprises actively perform their civil obligations, the citizens in the country generally have a sense of respect, responsibility and the whole society will progress into the stage of civil society. Covering the whole country, the civil society network of social man is highly permeable to all social affairs and is a platform for people to communicate, trust, respect, understand and contribute each other. The social man in the society has the characteristics of love and dedication, generally the rise of the quantity and quality of international brands will be an unprecedented increase, the country will become the major brand-exporting country in the world and nationals will enjoy great brand premium bonus from brand exporting countries.

Most global countries are in a form of a republic. The republic means the state is owned by all the citizens and the social man characterized by the civil society is the leading population and the goal of global efforts. We believe that the future society must be based on the social contribution of population, meaning that the social contribution becomes the measurement of all criteria. All kinds of public or private services from education, job promotion, bank loans, policy support, medical care, and even the state and public institutions are based on social contribution, credit, service as the standard. A good credit society is the primary stage of the civil society characterized by contribution.

The discussion on the relationship between the general man, the economic man, the industrial man, the social man and the brand-importing country, brand-exporting country is viewed from the perspective of the ternary relationship among the state, the citizen and the society. The dominant population of a country is the general man, economic man, industrial man or social man, which determines the international brand prosperity of one country, and also deeply depicts the main economic incoming mode, economic structure, main creativity and consumption characteristics of a county and its nationals.

1.2 The progress of brander

In the emergence of a comprehensive brand society in the future, there will eventually be two kinds of branders: one is brand organizer and another one is brand consumer. The creation, service or consumption, that regards brand as the main body, constitutes the comprehensive structure of the global brand economy. Among them, the most important roles are brand builders including the brand founders, brand leaders and brand officers, followed by the employees in brand organization, brand supply chain, brand management network and various types of brand service providers, who get the premium from the brand.

We all clearly know that all products and services in the future will complete the branding stage, all markets will become the brand market and everyone around the world will eventually consume brand in all areas, all fields and all aspects. Brand will accompany each person during birth, growth, learning, work and even life, and every human's brain will have the opportunity to pick some exclusive and strong brands.

The focus of global brander progress is who can become the brand builder and how to become the brand builder. The hope of a country or a nation is concentrated on the breeding and training of brand builders, and there is no doubt that the new generation of creators, who are self-improved, independent, self-innovative and daring to be the pioneers, should be given respect by all the people.

2 Brand quintessence: the pursuit of the brand artistic conception

Human beings always try to find a balance between philosophy and science, the kind of balance that clearly brings a higher understanding of life, career or product, and those understandings are called the brand artistic conception (philosophy process of the brand) and brand reengineering (scientific process of the brand). They have similar impact, so the brand builders are strongly seeking the perfect unity of emotion and ration.

Brand artistic conception is the performance process of brand in the philosophical aspect: the nature's pursuit of aesthetic things, the insight and deep understanding of the life truth and broad-minded thinking of the balance of nature are all integrated. Brand builders make a new breakthrough in several aspects, e.g. brand intelligence, brand business philosophy, brand context, brand design thought, brand aesthetics, etc. in order to create an unprecedented ultimate enjoyment in pioneering ways. This pursuit is groundbreaking, unprecedented and unique.

Brand artistic conception refers to the process in which a brand user perceives a brand in a psychological, visual, tactile, gustatory ways, etc. Human beings have discovered the human sensory

"Feedback" process from scientific research. Reactive organs in humans will take reactions when observing things or organisms will receive stimulus when a nerve impulse is reacting, then transmit a certain nerve impulse, which will return back to the nerve center along the afferent nerve. Brand builders have applied the "nerve impulse" process to build strong impressions on senses in users' brains, ensuring that the brand features are unique, a perfect pleasure of sense and a completely value-added choice.

As the artistic conception itself is a mysterious pursuit, humans make great efforts to achieve the demand of aesthetic and experience the pursuit process of a brand or have fun in the enjoyment of brand, so as to release a large part of pursuit space and premium space for brand.

The international brand can make the users adapt to various characteristics of brand by the feeling adaption, which represents a brand self-learning process. After learning, brand users will establish a stable sense of reliance, trust, glory, ownership, which is a constant stimulus that the international brand gives to the brand users' sensory system for it to adapt to the brand as the time goes by.

The basic conditions for the existence of international brands are that brand builders achieve consumer education through the realization of brand conception. The understanding process is also a very important psychological change and psychological adaptation process for brand users, whose significance is clearly known by the brand builders from the beginning.

Brand builders clearly know that it is necessary to build a series of new sensory habits and using habits for brand users, which is self-learning process carried on by the brand users as well as the entire user brand group. In this process, brand users gain unique knowledge, information and using habits by using and experiencing, and have deep understanding of the brand so that brand will be rooted in the everyone's heart. In the using process, brand users will quickly grasp the main features and advantages of the brand and improve the awareness level of people, things, products, so that brand users unknowingly establish the pursuit of the brand artistic conception, and also establish a series of new exclusive brand using habits.

2.1 Brand artistic conception--The emergence of brand beliefs

Humans can obtain a series of sentiment from nature, civilization, culture and life, which will contribute to the thinking of brand philosophy and constitute brand spirit, brand idea, brand culture and other new brand languages, but obviously it is not the highest realm of brand.

The international brand strives for the perfect interpretation and expression of the brand conception, thus creating unique brand thinking. The expression of these ideas will be defined as a higher level of ultimate pursuit, such as brand management philosophy, brand spirituality, brand context, brand design etc.

Some brand builders explore the realm of the brand by meditation, religion and art; some brand builders design brand ideas by the trend forecast of future science & technology and dreams; some brand builders present the perfect artistic conception that brands intend to express. Expressions should build a new, creative, native and fresh vitality no matter what type they are, and the great and fantastic ideas should be poured into brand, no matter if they start from nature or from mental state.

This is a great process of shaping the soul for brand, therefore, brand gains great vitality which will fit in everyone's life perfectly for it to become the ideal brand of people. These brands are vivacious, unrestrained, pure and quintessential, and brand users can attain surging enthusiasm and ultimate enjoyment from them, including fragrance, happiness, pleasure, joy, etc. The brand can connect with people on an emotional level, it can bring pleasure and cheer people up, thus encouraging people to spread the brand spontaneously and the brand gets connected with everyone's work, life and happiness deeply to become and becomes an integral part in everyone's life.

Implement dreams into business, joy into career, combine perfect enjoyment with pure fun- brand artistic conception eventually forms a strong brand belief that the staff within brand organization are willing to contribute to the brand and are happy to work, and make efforts on ideal brand every day. Besides, brand dealer network is willing to spread the enjoyment of beauty to thousands of households and brand users are willing to spontaneously assemble into a brand users group so as to be the most loyal supporters of a brand.

2.2 The generation of brand spirituality

Brand spirituality is the deep mining of humans for brand artistic conception. As a state of nature and life, spirituality is the direct reflection of a perfect expression of brand's soul. Brand builders are usually very pure; some of them will obtain all the good sentiments from nature and life and express them through the brand work in order to build the brand soul, so that the brand is fantastically and vividly displayed in the world.

Forests, rivers, fields, blue skies, rocks, woods, flowers, birds and beasts bring the pure enjoyment of sense to people, that is why the brand builders, photographers and artists look for inspiration and spirituality in nature to try to connect spirit with nature, integrate perception with ration, and connect all the good things with brand.

All the brands can be modern fashion brands. Only the brand keeping pace with times can be immortalized and as the punch line of brand spirituality endows the brand with the soul, inspiration, elegant design, smooth curve, the perfect arc, fantastic colors, the ornament of science and technology, intricate exquisite expression, the perfect interpretation of the unique sound, all of them deeply integrated with brand, the spiritual enjoyment of brand builders strongly pursued and the elaborate masterpiece thoroughly tempered by brand designers.

As a natural expression, spirituality runs through the perfect creation and design process of the brand. From the inside to the outside, from the outside to the inside, the spiritual design needs to be integrated into the brand. The packaging, shape, feel, texture and core are especially pivotal. The future brand encourages design ideas to express by creating a good feeling and sense for users and also a pure user experience.

Returning to nature and looking for aesthetic artistic conception is the most representative trend pursuit of urban population in modern society, while the younger Y generation (the generation after 80s and 90s) stands for the rise of the most mainstream consumer groups. Therefore, brand spirituality related to youth, fashion, trend and dynamic will become the key trend that the brand organization should study carefully in the future.

2.3 The design of brand users group

In the "fans" economic period, the global trend promotes a trusted brand while reflecting on three economic characteristics: First, the brand premium period of fashion trends and advanced science & technology, sharing radiance between them; Second, a brand safe consuming period based on trusted transaction; Third, a "fans" marketing period characterized as brand attraction.

These three economic characteristics constitute the three basic conditions for the existence of international brands: First, high premium and additional value of brand is generated from its own leading popular features of the brand and is a perfect connection of developed, advanced science & technology and modern aesthetics fashion design; Second, the brand transaction is a very reliable and trusted transaction environment and transaction media, in which people trust the brand without any worries towards the completely safe purchase psychology; Third, the brand sets up a strong brand consumer group supporting long-term brand management by attracting or absorbing a large number of regular customers and followers.

Any international brand will not be there to please the consumer's purpose, or to meet the customer's needs as the goal. The mission of the international brand is to create popular trends, to create the most advanced technology, and to create the latest advancing direction for the world, and that is why they create the latest and unprecedented new demands and establish the storm center for attracting the newly created trend demands, or build the central stage of the world to create new trends that appeal to the tide.

The next step is simple. International brands never need to meet the needs of all the customers, but they only need to hold on a small part of core followers and list a few consumers that meet the purchasing conditions. Only by meeting some harsh conditions can they may become its customers.

International brands list the characteristics of their own customer groups, i.e. they are mainly men and the majority of them are married and have children and are highly educated, so they need products that are able to demonstrate their identity and can give them enough sense of security. For example, "mainly male, 18 to 35 years old, successful people, people in the first-tier and second-tier cities, with the growth of income, strong will and ability of purchasing advanced equipment "or "customers that pay more attention on external image, prefer fashion element design, tend to catch up with the fashion trend, and have a strong dependence on the beginning use."

The success of an international brand depends on the accumulation of a considerable number of brand user groups, which lay the foundation for the considerable sustainable management protection of brand. Brand only deeply plows their favorite part of the user, who constitutes the user group of brand, but the non-relevant user is not target that attracts the brand. Brand advertising and brand communication are strictly defined in their own media and resources and even many of the top international brands consumed by non-professional users or the public are completely unfamiliar and have no public popularity.

2.4 Brand association building

When an international brand appears, it has defined its own level of brand association, making the brand evolve into a unique element of the world, integrating the equal values for goods, environmental or social elements into one in order to constitute an important part of the wonderful multicultural culture in the world.

When a typical new brand gets born, it may be included in the global top fashion symbol system as a new popular fashionable symbol, having both social identity value and emotional value. In the design stage of brand artistic conception, it may be connected with NIKE, Rock, BONO, LV, BMW, GUCCI, OPTAH, Fifth Avenue, Apple for it to build the brand image camp and match or combine them.

In the era of knowledge economy, brand association will have a more profound evolution, and the number of intangible knowledge products will increase substantially, so the new brand may be linked with knowledge system and knowledge brand may be accompanied with world-class research institutions or laboratories(such as the Brookings Institution, Mayo Hospital, the US Army Knowledge Online, Rand Corporation, Bell Labs, Lincoln Laboratory, DuPont Laboratory, etc.) to constitute a new research or technology association system of brand, which is the most important brand development trend of the frontier fusion of the knowledge economy.

Culture brand association has more fantastic colors and themes, the application of modern photoelectric technology, the combination of popular culture and fashion, which will make the ancient or emerging culture derive the new ecological civilization. The cultural fusion between Hollywood, New York Central Park, Harry Potter, The Lord of the Rings, World of Warcraft, Disney, Coca-Cola, McDonald's, Marlboro, Levi's, Palm Beach, Mexico Maya, Maldives, Dubai etc. will quicken the development of the deeper brand imagine and generate the new global brand cultivation.

Section IV Brand Culture

Brand association building derives a series of new changes, such as the association of Nike with the Olympic Games, the association of Billabong with surfing, the association of Google with satellite, the association combination of Microsoft with the futuristic smart city or smart bank, and the association of myopia presbyopia glasses with space material, the association of home appliances with intelligent networks, the association of architecture with green urban landscapes, the association of wearable equipment with modern life, the association of Knight Industrial 3000 in the *Knight Rider* with jet fighters. The modern brand constantly builds the future concept of science and technology, simulates future prospects, pushes the concept of products, and thus creates a new brand association structure.

Brand association building also appears in the brand name and requisite features, such as the combination of Rejoice and soft supple hair, the combination of Safeguard and clearing bacteria, the combination of Head & Shoulders and cleaning dandruff, the combination of Tide and washing the stain, the combination of Ariel and the washing action of washing machine, the combination of Centrino and chip processing speed, the combination of Vienna and music, the combination of Babylon and Hanging Gardens, the combination of Hong Kong and international cities, the combination of Dubai and super buildings, the combination of Wall Street and finance, the combination of Disney and the fairy tale world, the combination of Bermuda Triangle and the mystery, or the combination of road warrior and off-road vehicle, the combination of the future warrior and the coolest wearable technology, the combination of naming of mine king and mining machinery, etc..

2.5 Expression of brand context

Brand context refers to the context in which the brand language is expressed, i.e. expressing the in-depth feelings of the brand through texts and images. Brand, in fact is to create a feeling that can be expressed not only through LOGO and designs but also through texts and images that play a vital role. The context described in commercials and words would arouse direct association to ideas of brand users and provide incredibly immersive experience for audiences, this will initiate a strong sense of inner resonance which is manifested as an ultimate pursuit of the brand that can be completed by desiring and obtaining ownership of the brand.

At this end, the brand context will make a wide range of exploration. Pictures, sound and texts which can highlight the scenes of artistic concept are widely used in brand advertising, copy, manuals and publicity. As for brand advertising and promotional materials, theme will be reflected as: "Brand-new X Series, to drive the world to move forward", "Pure driving pleasure", "Lead the times, never give up", "Gorgeous craft, best taste", "Distinguished style, efficient motivation" and other brilliant feeling enjoyment.

To specifically describe the copy, the brand context intensively uses magnificently artistic language with strong passion and ultimate taste to lead the reader into an artistic sensory experience. Some typical description of the example is as follows:

"Wherever you take a sip of wine, you are destined to leave a long lasting impression on other people around you. From outside to inside, a large area of bright and transparent design not only highlights the essence of the wine, but also represents the virtue of integrity and uprightness. Man with righteous heart will be more tolerant and generous; with magnanimous mind, man achieves more."

"A ray of sunlight has to travel about 100 million miles to reach our planet, therefore, your top-level sedan definitely deserves this privilege. The specially-selected blinds are exclusively designed for you. Only push on the button and you can be in the intimate encountering with clear sky, being free from daily chores and enjoying close contact with natural sunshine."

"Walking through the roof of the world, city subway and cross-sea bridge, modern city, rural scenery and tranquil seascape are all integrated into modern people's life ... In modern times, cultural connotation and modern life enhance beauty of each other and show brilliance."

All successful brands originate in the interpreting concept of vision. Unparalleled brand connotation interprets the language that brand used to communicate with human mind. With the scene of artistic concept and beautiful language of profound sense of immersion into the picture, spreading and advertising every touch point, international brand therefore draws people's attention, infiltrates into people's hearts, upsurges in people's mind and takes root in people's innermost, lingering for a long time.

2.6 Spirituality progress of brand artistic conception

As the unique relationship between man and natural and the spiritual world, spirituality is regarded as the ultimate pursuit of transcending physical senses, time and the material world. Brand founders strive to establish a new set of transcendental beliefs and faiths and qualify brand organization evolving into a new brand-based brand spirit organization.

Social scientists define spirituality as "sacred", and the sacred itself generates worship. From ancient to modern times, spirituality and religion have integrated into one all alongand people define the generating way of spirituality by the confrontation between religion and secularism. At the beginning of twentieth century, the separation of science and religion and the pursuit of spiritual artistic concept together changed the word "spirit". People began to learn in the eastern and western spiritual culture, perceive spiritual insight, make spirituality progress under the guidance of spiritual mentors, seek and comprehend the truth of life.

After the World War II, spirituality and religious completely disconnected and absolutely evolved into an active exploration to human inner world. Through the sincere self-disclosure, self-creation, free expression, people obtain a new meditation and thinking.

In late 20th century, the creation of a new era, the new thinking trend of the self-realization, spiritual and psychological experience of brand and user experience have become important parts of brand design, deduction and development to new generation creators. With people regarding the spirituality choice and consumption choice as a significant feature of brand product instruction complement, brand artistic conception gains a broader field of vision.

As people no longer confined to theism or atheism, they extended the brand spirituality experience to a wider range of thinking practice. Spiritual experience includes the overall thinking of individuals, human society, nature or the universe, or with the divine realm, which aims at realizing a more comprehensive self-expression and self-realization.

The future brand building and reconstruction is bound to increasingly rely on the expression of the brand artistic concept, while expression itself is completed through the self-realization of the brand founder. To complete this process of making progress, brand founders first of all need to be a social person - possess the virtue of being devoted, enthusiastic, kind-hearted and tolerant to society, which is the premise of making brand development, and then self-realization - the creation and devotion of self-worth -- is the great gene of brand progress.

3 Brand concept: the philosophy thinking of brand values

Brand concept: the core value of the brand is to pursue the goal of service, technological innovation and product quality. From the date of creation or undergoing major brand reconstruction, many brands will define the business philosophy of the brand to clarify a certain sense of the brand mission, responsibility, principles, positions, beliefs or style.

A typical brand management philosophy is Konosuke Matsushita's "philosophy of running water".Konosuke Matsushita's corporate responsibility, established in the process of running the business, tends to make things that the public needs, becoming as cheap as tap water. The excellent quality and affordable price make goods be like offering running water to customers. The greatest source of enterprise benefit is to make customers benefit often.

Section IV Brand Culture

Typical brand concept is the old Watson set for IBM's three brand philosophy: we respect each person; we state that the sole goal of company is to serve consumers; we pursue excellence and surpass the others.Brand concept is a kind of advocacy and execution through all aspects: enterprise R & D, production, technology, using people, products, services, marketing, advertising, etc. A brand that hasn't got its own unique concept is not likely to achieve sustainable development. A brand that has its own concept, but hasn't strictly implemented it, has it also difficult to obtain unprecedented development.

To be exact, the brand sells its specific and unique values which make all brand organization staff sparing no effort to melt into a whole and make people struggle together. The top global life insurance event of the elite - the Million Dollar Round Table (MDRT),is yearning and pursuing the global life insurance salesman and is also an excellent life insurance sales and service symbol of spirit brand action.

MDRT encourages all life insurers to maximize their potential in professional development, technical competence, and sales performance, to enhance the professional standards and professional reputation of life insurance salesmen which leads life insurance salesman to the track of reputation, quality, and admiration service profession. It has positive and far-reaching influence on the healthy development of life insurance industry.

Brand concept realizes the carrier of brand unique style through the effort of all brand organization staff transmitting to its consumers. Therefore, various brand organizations are actively developing their own unique brand theory, such as DuPont: for better life to create better chemical products; Electric: progress is our best product; IBM: IBM is the service.

These brands shape their business goals in a powerful way. We find that internationally renowned brands often have a firm belief that they are beyond imagination. They all tend in a globalized, endless way to develop unique value of the transcendent. Such kind of clear, philosophical pursuit is an important guarantee for the success of international brands. Those are all partial financial goals or realistic style of brand concept, because it is often quite difficult to promote the company to achieve success in a faster or more large-scale way, since the brand aging speed is quite fast.

Exercises

1. Multiple-choice Question: In the brand artistic conception, the development of human is divided into _____. ( )

    A. general man, industrial man, social man, brander

    B. general man, economic man, industrial man, social man, brander

    C. general man, economic man, industrial man, social man

    D. economic man, industrial man, social man, brander

2. Discussion: How is brand belief sublimed into brand artistic conception?

Chapter 4

Brand Aesthetics

Brand aesthetics is an important subject to express brand sensory feelings so as to study the feelings and emotion rules of brand in aesthetic point of view. In order to embody design ideas of the brand, brand builders and talented designers fully cooperate with each other to seek and create the latest aesthetic and fashion trend.

1 Design ideas of brand aesthetics

The most typical design idea is the Italian modern design rising after World War II that is known as "Modern Renaissance". And Italian designers incorporate culture and philosophy into designs instead of focusing on theories or practice. From pasta to Ferrari, from furniture to architecture, from product to clothing, they have created a new design idea of "integrating architecture, aesthetics, technology and human relationship together" magically.

Italian furniture occupies a pivotal position in world history for its famous design capability in the world. Being popular all over the world, it is synonymous with high-end luxury because it features authentic classical European style and more importantly regards every piece of furniture as work of art earnestly and romantically and presents a unique design idea well.

To perfectly present future, modernity, concept, trend, technology and art, American designers integrate science technology with art; German designers work to combine exquisite art and modern manufacturing technology closely; French designers perfectly combine romance and modern design fully into fashion; British designers develop product design ideas with strong emphasis and demonstration of their pure local culture; Japanese designers focus on widespread application of practical, dynamic and strict modern project technology in design ideas; Latecomers South Korean designers are devoted to brand innovation process with their excellent creativity and variety.

These countries above take full advantage of pure design ideas, their artistic and imagery enjoyment, thus becoming global modern design centers and making their cultures organically transformed into modern brand design ideas, which has a profound influence on pushing them to be the most important brand-exporting countries around the world. Whenever the culture of a country is evolved into an internationally popular modern cultural symbol after great rejuvenation, its position as a branding superpower will change dramatically, making its brand popular in every corner of the world.

For brand organizations, its brand designers need to keep pace with times; fashion designing enterprises shall be the center of fashion storm for sales miracles new generation's brand. Brand styles that highlight the dream and "Cool" elements will be an important direction of brand design ideas in the 21st century, outgoing the previous brand that focuses on noble style in terms of popularity. Just as safety is no longer the central focus of automobile advertising, concept cars have become the latest people's expectations for car brand design ideas instead.

2 Taste: Psychological distance of brand aesthetics

People always link one's aesthetic manner with the pattern, quality, design and style of the product he buys, so as to identify his taste. And they also believe that whether the product's brand is international will prove one's pursuit of taste in some degree.

Taste is not only the primary premise of brand design ideas but also the reflection of brand premium when people purchase products and pursue brands. The cost of a cup of coffee may only be one dollar, but a cup of Starbucks coffee sells for four US dollars in China. In workdays, many white collars workers in high-end offices have the habit of buying Starbucks coffee back to the workplace, in order to show their consumption ability and taste of life. Starbucks successfully combines the environmental designative the freshly brewed coffee and taste of life of modern urban residents, eliminating psychological distance of brand aesthetics.

People regard international brands as the art of aesthetic pleasure, which constitutes taste. Although people's aesthetic manners and consumption levels varies, the average and broad base majority of them form the brand's target audience and core user groups.

The study of psychological distance (aesthetic distance) dates back to the early 20th century and was developed into the important core of international brand representation in the early 21st century, playing an important role in brand design, marketing, as well as international market management of and expansion of overseas market of transnational corporations. International brands utilize customers' psychological gaps between "self needs and aesthetic feelings" successfully so that design ideas in artistic conception are released in the heart of brand's customers.

At first, psychological distance refers to the distance between "brain and soul", and the gap of aesthetic cognition and feelings between home brands and multinational, trans-cultural and trans-consumption-level brands in global competition. And designs based on psychological distance structure are regarded as the theme of trans-cultural brand design ideas.

An enterprise or a nation, when deciding to put its brands into global market, should pay attention to psychological distance of brand aesthetic ways, which is an important cultural variable. The first reason why a brand or brands of a country are popular and sell well in the world is that the culture is widely accepted in each country. And international brands should make particular efforts to deal with acceptance level of global young consumers so as to settle the issue of psychological aesthetic distance, for the youth represents the future popular ways of brand design ideas and the aesthetic needs of the next generation of consumers determine the future direction of a brand.

3 Brand fluency: consistent requirements

Brand fluency, easy to be neglected previously, refers the smooth process of product R&D(research development), appearance, packaging, kernel, components, quality, delivery and service, and is reflected in brand product design itself and the process of delivery and service management. And it may be disrupted by brand perception, product defects, quality instability, delivery environment and service delay, which would lead to customers 'dissatisfaction and more importantly bad perception and experience. To be specific, brand fluency determines the premium performance of a brand.

Traditional quality view considers that product quality should be examined and requires products to be "qualified". Different from previous quality management, brand quality has a higher requirement that the quality of products must be excellent, which meets requirements of fluency in manufacturing and users' experience.

Brand fluency is felt and experienced by users, and judged by the users according to their perception on the product. For example, the smooth surface of a product will create tactile enjoyment; the streamlined design of a product can enhance its visual stimulation, eventually prompting users to buy it immediately. Quality stability is a comprehensive judgment users make after using the product for a long time and comparing performance and quality of products.

Considering that more high-end, more precious and more expensive brands rely largely on word-of-mouth marketing, thus brand fluency becoming the highest pursuit for brand organizations during brand designing.

There are four ways to improve brand fluency: 1. to pay attention to R&D and manufacturing is particularly important, because professional, advanced, developed and precise R&D and strict manufacturing process will make the fluent presentation of brands in the market possible;2. the enterprise should improve management for strict and scientific management from R&D, delivery and service based on complete brand standardization;3. the comprehensive application of brand aesthetic design contributes to perfect design of brand from entirety to core components, and even to all the components and amazing colors, finally to make brand as charming and dynamic as artworks.

The first three ways work by stimulating the users' sensual pleasure, attracting them to trust the design for the first time and producing smooth purchase experience, and will enhance brand fluency through these ways again and again, which is named "brand fluency design of high sensual pleasure", namely the pro-perception of brand users. And the last one way is to make users use the products, thus transforming brand fluency assumption into highly smooth experience.

Every day everyone is making progress and learning something new. After the design is trusted for the first time, brand fluency will immediately stimulate users to purchase the products, but this action is just brand fluency assumption for users never use it before or consult their friends. The premise of impulsive rational purchase is that users assume the product is satisfying enough and can be tested and consumed for a long time.

It is a long process from brand fluency assumption to brand fluency acquaintance and to trusty brand fluency design. However, during the use of products, quality instability may result in failures of trust, and flaws of user experience may make users unsatisfied. Then such purchasing behavior becomes lessons learned, and users no longer purchase products of the brand and persuade others not to purchase too, in this way, the brand fluency is interrupted. Brand laboratory established by corporations can change the design of fluency by testing and studying frequency of occurrence and link of occurrence of assumed examples in experiment, in order to reach design performance of Grade A brand fluency.

Men's brain waves can record fluent things, recognize the truth-false of brand fluency, identify whether it is a lesson learnt or a reliable fact and know the brand fluency well, which is the common basic experience of human beings in feeling good things and judging the truth, namely the ability of dealing with fluent information. Only when users are increasingly familiar with brand fluency, their positive experience of the brand will be transformed into trustworthy emotional experience. When the behavior of purchasing brand products occurs constantly, this brand enterprise in this way will attract users to purchase its products repeatedly and quickly contribute to brand-specific purchasing with the help of its users.

The economic secret of brand organizations that feature sustainable management is to rely on brand users with strong empathy of brand fluency to purchase products repeatedly and continuously recommend brands to new users. On the contrary, corporations with low brand fluency need to spend more time and cost of marketing on attracting customers and solving problems of frequent interruption of brand fluency among customers and be able to anticipate failure. Brand fluency is the process of self-adaption and interaction between a brand and its products, which is the basic brand theory of successful Grade A brand.

4 Implicit brand philosophy

The perception of brand philosophy needs not to be gained by brand users through specific advertisements of brand organizations, but in the two stages of pre-marketing and post-marketing.

In pre-marketing, brand organizations advertise selling points and performance advantages of their products in various ways (such as advertisements, user experience, brand news, brand observation, comparison of competing goods.) to let potential users compare their products with competing products, so as to deliver products based on pro-perceptions that brand users make.

In fact, most brand philosophy cannot deliver products by pro-perceptions in pre-marketing, because users don't know detailed factors including performance indexes, quality stability and after-sales safety when purchasing products and philosophy ideas of brand designs are developed by users after using products for a long time. The post-marketing is a process of implicit brand philosophy in which consumers will continuously self-discover, surprised by the products and recognizing the correct decision of repeated purchasing.

Implicit brand philosophy brought into reality by actual users' experience is a quite accurate process of perception and experience as well as a process to explore the realization of highly credible brand fluency. And it is a perfect interpretation of brand sensual pleasures, users' experience and quality stability, promoting the brand to be a synonym for pleasure of purchasing, faith in usage, purchasing trust and recommendation as well as release and empathy of ideological design and realm that absorb elements of work, life and society.

Most people judge things based on binary opposition—right or wrong, good or bad, successful or unsuccessful, and positive or negative, which is a quite contradictory way of thinking. As a result, even a negligible flaw in brand quality will lead users to lose faith in the brand or be disgusted with it.

Painters always resort to three-dimensional cone instead of two-dimensional structure to present images on canvas. Aesthetic habits are easy to understand for 3D movies and 3D printing can present three-dimensional pictures or objects. But most people fail to realize that they are interpreting pictures or brand products based on three-dimensional framework. Brand itself in the eyes of users is a balanced and abstract aesthetic concept presented in a three-dimensional way.

Brand builders and designers must make use of the three-dimensional balanced ideas to solve this problem and achieve brand using experience through self-adapting balance of users. Under normal conditions, brand fluency that is both rational and emotional is needs to accomplish the overall design of brand products, and brand organizations should express their design ideas by starting with rational and impulse buying of users, so that users can find beauty, convenience and fun of usage, leading technologies, and the perfect fusion of design ideas and lifestyle. In this way, unnoticeable brand philosophy is the process of self-discovery of users.

5 From brand experimental aesthetics to brand experience aesthetics

Art boasts excellent enjoyment value, but art cannot be directly evolved into aesthetic application of brands. The aesthetic design of art is put into applied aesthetics of brand from artistic conception, abstraction, ideas and concepts. People develop aesthetic design ideas in every daily social application to make aesthetics and brand closely combined. Thus the art design is not showed only in the form of art as museums' collections.

The brand aesthetics is widely applied and plays an extremely important role in various areas such as industrial design, architecture, interior design, fashion design, fashion, film, food, city landscape design, marketing, packaging, entertainment, website design, lighting, music and digital technology. All of these influence each other and create more colorful lifestyle, which makes goods get rid of original forms and evolve into modern brand fashion through primary R&D, production, branding, marketing, so that each brand product is developed into artistic masterpieces like exquisite artworks and greatly enriches artistic conception of the brand.

Brand experimental aesthetics and experience aesthetics have become the core to accomplish product branding. After experimental research and creation, brand organizations acquire the magic power to upgrade brand function from primary products manufacturing to brand creation. Consequently, focus of discussions of people is the brand rather than products, and vice versa.

People will be discussing on product itself and not brand. They will be hypercritical in areas such as price, quality and service, and examine all functions and additional management ability of products in their self-centered viewpoints. With a brand effectively reducing the users' criticism and deriving out the brand premium, people would believe that it is worthwhile to spend more money buying products of the brand, and form a new habit of brand usage by learning and using products according to rules defined by the brand. The powerful and unconsciously influenced brand education would further effectively with stand competitors' market strategy and increase the cost of competing brands.

The purpose of all experiments is to create the best user experience, namely to create new brand experience aesthetics and develop the best standard framework for application of experimental aesthetics in next-step bulk-product manufacturing, quality testing, market operations and sales. By this means, the brand experimental aesthetics is officially moving towards brand experience aesthetics, and brand users obtain the best brand experience by themselves after using the brand products. Finally, brand experience aesthetics created the brand legend.

6 Perfect expression of brand design ideas

Perfect expression of brand design ideas is realized by brand using habit design, performance design, industrial design, packaging design, project management techniques, first-time trust design, delivery design, communication design, network technology, etc.

Ranking the first, using habit design is to teach users how to think, act and form inertial thinking by changing their usage habits. Performance design covers systematic design of physical, chemical and technological performance and functions. It is achieved through intensity, chemical component, purity, power, revolving speed and expression of various structures, materials and techniques. And it is also an independent element brand and technology license brand business pattern, such as audio technology, antilock braking system technology and the independent study of service management technology.

Industrial design plays a vital role in mass production from the point of "conception of industrialization", including production line technology design, mass production process design and industrial external design. But it is not just limited to industrial manufacturing; instead, it can be applied in the field of any possible batch management or service.

Although customized personalized products are an important trend of future manufacturing industry, its premise must be the design of segments for more professional industry. In fact, the link age of instant networked e-commerce orders and factory production data is an efficient manufacturing mode of industrial production. Where there is mass production, there is industrial division of labor.

In external design and the form of industrial products, modern and future manufacturing industry depends on modern creative aesthetics, post-modern aesthetics and spirit, which leads designers to consider aesthetic factors ahead of the time in order to increase sales of products and design perceptual and aesthetic application of surreal factors, such as smoothness, light reflection, texture, pattern, curvature, color, simplicity, usability, speed and symmetry of products, elements of the nature, environmental protection, climate, modernism and future vision.

Brand builders, brand concepts and industrial aesthetics designers should spent energy on the appearance of products and their components. They shall design products according to any possible ways that allow people together products. The cross-society and cross-cultural factors are also important design aspects to consider. Industrial designs aiming at the appearance should focus on researching and educating the sensory forms of users and triggering aesthetic empathy of users at every touch point. In addition, from the view of systematic design, every step and after-sale convenience should be planned as a whole and expressed in detail to make the design match well and contribute to brand users' application.

Packaging design is another key point is to present the brand. The brand's final design is presented through the texture, color, quality and form on the packaging and this first impression will directly stimulate customers' desire of buying the products. Designing ideas on modern packaging are expressed through modern, creative, simple and bright color or low-purity color, and focus on the influence of color sensation on visual aesthetic. For example, simple and bright colors have been the mainstream color patterns on packaging in modern America and South Korean designs. Modern creative packaging design is developing towards the fashion of fantasy. At the same time, grave colors are abandoned in global modern packaging design because of their sense of repression, backwardness and cheapness.

Project management (PM) technology is an important representation in brand standardization. It depends on whether every design parts, management operation process and service process resolved in projects is fluent for seamless management. The advanced and reliable project quality management and systematic projects play an important role in brand premium. Many brands will not become international brands for their shortcomings in basic project management and interruption of process fluency. However, the future customized brand products will mainly rely on accurate division of process, careful management and quick manufacturing. Although project management technology is a subject of brand scientific study, it runs through brand design ideas from the beginning to the end and will ensure efficient and perfect presentation of the brand design ideas.

First-time trust design is a process design that users try to understand, engage with, take interest in and consume a brand as a result of various communication factors (such as finding a brand accidentally, look for a brand, hearing of a brand). Its core is how to deal with the confidence issue that any potential consumer has when purchasing a brand product for the first time consciously or unconsciously. The safety of brand consumption will become very important. With highly-trusted design, brand organizations stimulate consumption desires based on brand aesthetics and create safe purchasing mentality, enhance service and remove consumers' concerns, and finally having the new consumer purchasing the brand for the first time.

Delivery design is are search design for the process of delivering, which includes delivery mentality, delivery process and delivery service. Different from first-time trust design that is for the first time purchase of a brand, delivery design is for long-term coherent delivery and repeated consumption of brand users. Delivery interruption means that companies will lose not only frequent consumer but his recommendation of the brand to more users, the seriousness of which can be observed in the "Golden Triangle" of brand profit.

Communication design is the main mode of modern brand promotion. Brand communication should be carefully designed to make sure that corporations communicate information on brands (such as safety of consumption, selling points of brands) to specific brand user groups and play an important role in consumption education. It does not necessarily refer to advertisement which is only one of the ways in communication, but interpersonal network communication by media, which means that the brand is communicated from people to people, people to information network or media to media. Both interpersonal communication among brand users and diffusion communication from users to media are the core of brand communication.

Modern and future network technology includes dozens of networking technologies, such as management and service network technology, online and offline and mobile internet technology, interpersonal network communication technology, product function networking, next generation of internet technology of brand organizations. In the future, brand e-commerce will definitely be enterprise e-commerce, which is focused on linking the following together, departments of enterprises, management process and supply chain, links service stream, communication network and brand user groups and creates a dynamic knowledge network that is spread at different levels, closely and organically connected. It is the ultimate form of brand organizations in the future.

Modern and future marketing is marketing design, marketing action and systematic sales that needs to further examine the human's mode of thinking, study the mentality of brand users and create new aesthetics experience. The curiosity, desire and aesthetics are the main direction to drive development of a brand in the market.

7 New futures: aesthetics of hyper-modern conceptual brand

Conceptual brand designs a brand that focused on conceptual product creation and represents the global fashion trend. By creating large amount of conceptual products, brand organizations explore future fashion trend, conduct experiments on product concepts, analyze data on market trends, predict design orientation of a brand, select crucial concepts and finally complete the mature product design. In general, brand organizations that mainly engaged in conceptual products can always stand out in all brands and lead the trend.

The formation of concept is actually a type of artistic expression. With ideas of concept of art, creative and innovative ideas are translated into design drawings or a new form of brands product, so as to express their design ideas through concept. The R&D department of Intel developed its next generation of chips by probing into performance and prevalent characteristics of computers in ten years; global auto brands identify customers' preference by presenting conceptual products in international auto shows; and household appliances brands lead the trend by promoting conceptual products. Marketing of brand organizations is transformed through the launch conceptual products by brand reengineering enterprises. Business plans in Japan start with "concept" and then project planning.

It is essential for a conceptual brand organization to figure out the shape of future generations of product that are futuristic, modernization, scientific, fantastic and creative. Conceptual product itself might be completely distinctive from the actual product. Brand organizations can identify the major direction of their next generation of products through experiments on concepts. Therefore, conceptual product itself is all about changing the world. Conceptual brand organizations realize self-fission based on massive designs and developments of conceptual products. Through persistently eliminating outdated design ideas, patterns and ways of representations, they keep challenging themselves, remaining dominant in the fashion world or created a new global fashion trend.

Conceptual brand is completely idealistic and might even not be realized. However, it comes up with new concepts, which provides space that is worth exploring for brand organizations to develop. Besides, it inspires human beings' creations and offers future reference samples for human progress. Moreover, it brings incredibly amazing imagination as well as a better life for human beings.

Conceptual brand also reflects both global technological creativity and aesthetic creativity, inspiring direction of future products. Besides, it provides a new opportunity for R&D, brand aesthetics design and entrepreneurship in the world to reform, create and re-forge.

A market without conceptual brand falls in a state of "suspended animation", and is isolated and outdated without vigorous elements to challenge. Of courses, it is a matter of foresight for conceptual products. Even the market seems emerging or enjoying mature business models and forms nowadays, it will witness rapid ageing for a lack of creativity. And then, the emergence of innovative conceptual brand organizations will definitely profoundly change all business models and forms and reshuffle the existing market.

8 Laws of brand attraction in aesthetics

Brand attraction is a trump card played by brand organizations to win the market and be sustainable, and reveals the unique charm of a brand. It can draw attention from the potential users and convert them into brand users and even followers, so as to form a massive regular customer base.

Brand attraction will be the mainstream approach and core strategic competence in future brand marketing as well as the major way of practicing global marketing. It is related to elements of visual appearance, reliability, interest inspiration and targeted purchase. Brand organizations arouse customers' interests through brand's attractive designs, which makes brand marketing a popular, initiated, systematic and self-suited marketing approach.

Visual attraction is based on customers' acceptance of brand aesthetics. People tend to pursue beautiful things. Thus, as a carrier of consuming desire, brands should be designed to arouse customers' consuming desires and stimulate them to make decision faster through the design of brand aesthetics.

Reliability attraction refers to the credible purchasing environment for customers to guarantee safety of the purchasing behavior. The first-time trust design makes sure that the first purchasing process is trustworthy and safe in terms of purchasing environment and by using and experiencing the brand is a favorable enjoyment. Future brand products, especially e-commerce products, must run in a global framework of high reliability that may be remote, invisible, confidence-oriented and safe consumption. Perception of brand consumption security is the major determinant for users to choose a certain brand instead of others, thus improving the sustained appreciation ability of the brand and the cost of other brands to attract customers will increase in folds in the future.

Interest inspiration for brand means that customers generate strong interests in a spontaneous, self, and natural manner. Thus, the users will display the following physiological actions, discover, understand, sense, rely on and rely greater on a brand more actively than ordinary people. Brand interest, for it enjoys not only the value of scale economy and high appreciation capacity, but also unique initiative and self-publicity, it serves as the key to help brand organizations win the market and sustain their business.

Targeted purchase rate refers to the comprehensive comparison with brand competitors that reflect brand consuming behaviors according to statistics. This means that the higher the rate is; the more market share it would occupy in its business field. In addition, targeted purchase rate of a new brand determines its capacity to influence the market. Targeted purchase rate might be exclusive such that customers with targeted purchasing behaviors will have strong exclusive sentiment towards other similar brands.

SECTION IV BRAND CULTURE

Marketing of brand attraction can be done by means of brand communication and brand discovery. Influential brand communication possesses an extraordinary power that can have strong effects on customers' soul and make them pay more attention to a brand spontaneously and learn its culture. Brand discovery capacity enables new users to discover a brand unintentionally through the surrounding of the environment, brand advertisements and friends' recommendations and subsequently become interested in the brand.

9 Progress of brand aesthetics

With the improvement of aesthetic manner, everyone is improving his aesthetic point of view, which means that brands should outpace their competitors in terms of aesthetics. Higher living standard and faster globalization contribute to changes in aesthetics, and changes in preference for brands aesthetics and consumption are accompanied by rising incomes of people. People expect to live a life that is full of enthusiasm, passion and warmth. Therefore, they are eager to pursue ideal and beautiful things in their lives. In this way, they make fast progress in aesthetic manner of brands.

The application of color is a typical example. Red is regarded as a mainstream color in some countries, but studies show that blue is human's favorite, followed by green. That is why products in red are difficult to sell. With the pursuit of environmental protection and returning back to the nature, green is more likely to attract people's attention than blue, for there are a lot of blue logos and packages, while those in green are much less and tend to be more eye-catching.

Likewise, according to some researches, human's favorites are water, trees, flowers and plants, mankind (especially beautiful women, children and famous historical figures) and animals (especially wildlife and domestic large animals). Human prefer colors that are pleasing to eyes, pure and peaceful and do not like colors that are dull, restless and in a mess. These facts call for principled requirements for designing brand advertisement, website and brochure. To people with high quality taste, beauty is the pursuit of the thoughts of philosophy and living styles. People will spend more time on holidays, their internal soul will have a pleasure sensation towards the beautiful nature and plants. Beauty has become the new requirement for aesthetics improvement; this is especially true for those who are from the urban city and leading a stressful and competitive life.

As the current society is full of monotony, most of the people are nearly worn out by the slings and arrows of daily life. Some of them chose to escape from the reality, especially the Y generation (80's and 90's generations) prefers a surrealistic artistic environment which is full of challenges, technologies, futures, fantasies and novelties. For example, the Celtic Revival will definitely have profound influence on the Y generation and become the important source of inspiration for the next generation in fashion design.

As the fictional, fantasy, emotional and inspirational movies have been the world focus and the mainstream of modern culture, the aesthetic mannerist early 21st century has witnessed profound changes. Aesthetics will move towards futuristic, fashionable, fantastic, digital and surrealistic virtually realistic realm of aesthetics. Human's expectation of the future is far greater than their interests towards ancient history. Nowadays, the younger generation has eliminated the traditional aesthetic manner as they are more concern about the future of themselves and the world.

The aesthetic manner has been drastically changed, so it is crucial for brand organizations to improve their aesthetics fast. The brand organization either improved themselves constantly or be obsolete in the near future.

Exercises

1. Fill in the blanks:_____ can interrupt the brand fluency.

2. True or False Question: Brand aesthetics is an important subject used to express brand sensory feelings so as to study the feelings and emotion rules of brand in aesthetic point of view. (   )

3. Discussion: Briefly describe four ways to improve brand fluency.

Chapter 5

Brand Culture Consumption

Brand-driven consumption, which features culture consumption, represents a high-level development stage of human civilization. The mass production in the aftermath of the Industrial Revolution led to drastic growth of commodities both in terms of variety and quantity. Coupled with the ever-increasing income of the mass population, "brand" eventually came into existence during the 20th century.

After thousands of years of cultural development when commodities were quickly consumed and daily necessities were sufficiently provided, human beings transformed from consuming traditional physical objects to an era of buying products with cultural meanings. After 1950s, the development of consumerism was mainly represented by the growth of non-functional culture consumption, and the essence of the super consumption society was the economy of brand culture consumption.

1 The evolution of social culture

The evolution of social culture is represented by life as a form of human culture that is unique to different social classes, especially when it emerges in upper social class and gradually migrates into lower social classes, and as a result the processes of cultural evolution, cultural enrichment and cultural migration came into being.

The human culture has gone through long historical periods. In early times, representative cultures such as the Celtic aristocratic culture, the Roman European culture, the rites and music culture of China and its humanism have profoundly affected the development of human history. The cultural openness and tolerance during the China's Tang Dynasty in the 7th century, the chivalry and troubadour spirit in Europe in the 11th century, and Renaissance in Italy in the 13th century, the Romanticism of Germany and UK in the 19th century and the cultural prosperity of the US in the 20th century are all but some basic cultural forms of human life.

Culture is the full demonstration of our life styles as it contains elements such as science, art, knowledge, style, custom, faith, religion, politics, morality, law and other factors related to the human's material and spiritual life. With the convergence and evolution of different cultural circles and cultural centers, and with time passing by, the scenario of culture diversity was formed and consolidated throughout history.

Culture is initially formed in royal families and among aristocrats and governmental officials; objects loaded with cultural meanings and different artistic forms were originally built for the spiritual enjoyment of the rich. In the very beginning, culture was used to judge a man's property ownership, indicate his social status and the amount of wealth he possesses. Culture also evolves and changes in styles and forms with the development of human history, and many of the culture forms that used to express the development status of a certain historical period were not only dominant in that particular period, but also well-kept throughout history as a basic cultural form, which obviously embodies the characteristics of that certain period and later showed momentum of long-lasting vitality.

Human beings distinguish the natural environment, space, status, material and geology, etc. with different names, labels, grades and categories, and constantly add elements such as language, literature, painting, music, dance, sacrifice, ceremony, architecture, technology, technique, legends and other expression method such as historical events and historical figures, all of which contributed to the abundance of tangible culture and non-tangible culture of the mankind. With the constant evolution of the upper and middle class and with changes to their wealth and social status, culture is spread to the general public to reflect the life and social conditions of the general public. A good example is that almost all the cultures have rules about what an aristocrat should eat, wear and use, and what etiquette they should follow at various occasions.

The upper class and the rich initially used high culture to distinguish themselves from the folk and low culture which represents the general public and the poor. The same applies to the distinction between civil and barbaric, which, after all, is a habit of human beings to demonstrate the cultural superiority of their social class and level of civilization.

All human beings are connected by various types of interpersonal relationships such as relatives, teachers, students, classmates and trade relations which are formed through communication, transaction and trade during production, delivery, life, business and diplomatic activities. All these relations are nothing but basic relations supporting the mankind to survive and thrive. The abundance of material and spiritual culture was made possible thanks to diverse communications and connections.

Human beings are always creating more diverse cultures. The mainstream culture, popular culture and other diverse cultures, formed in each historical stage, are the result of human activities such as revolution, creation, reviving old traditions, fighting against traditions and consuming activities. These have constantly added to the connotation of brand culture and made cultural characteristics more obvious.

Cultural spectrum and memes have existed since the very beginning. Mature culture forms have been flowing across and came in contact with other culture forms between countries, people and races. Cultures with unique character are migrating on a global scale as a form of cultural meme, which contains a fixed set of culture genes and elements. In this migration process, new cultural memes are formed due to the cultural communication of different memes, eventually forming the grand scenario of cultural diversity.

2 The formation of brand culture

The overall culture landscape of mankind is formed by different cultural circles, cultural centers and cultural sectors. The radius of influence of a culture is often represented by a cultural circle, such as the culture circle of Europe, Asia, Africa, America, India and the Anglo cultural circle to name but a few. A cultural system with fixed culture characteristics is normally represented by a nation, a culturally concentrated area or a cultural center such as the Arabic culture, Chinese culture, Tibetan culture, Silicon Valley culture, Hollywood culture, Thames River culture, etc. Regions filled with abundant material types, life styles and specialty cultures may also lead to a variety of cultural sectors such as jewelry culture, coffee culture, tea culture, sports culture, collection culture, countryside culture, beach culture, port culture, urban culture and tourist resort culture to name but a few. All these have formed the network of the rich, colorful cultural combinations and eventually the culture spectrum of mankind.

Brand culture did not come into being by accident. It consists of three typical forms: a brand that inherits culture, develops culture, and creates new culture. Cultural inheritance is also a form of cultural protection. Some brand places itself in an established culture form and develops itself by protecting such culture form. Brands falling into this category include the Korean Red Ginseng, China's Dragon Well Tea, Sunkist Orange of the US and Beijing's Quan Ju De Roast Duck to name but a few. The development focus of these brands lies in protecting their brand value, maintaining their market position and smoothing their marketing channels so that their brand continues to be an integral part of the cultural circle which they represent.

To seek more market opportunities, some brand re-explores culture from historical cultures or existing cultures so as to make a culture brand with distinct source and market and get new brand opportunities through the development in the present context and market. For example, China's herbal tea brand Wong Lo Kat was developed through cultural exploration from the ancient formula dating back to the year 1828 and established its position in the field of herbal tea culture. Gloria Jean's coffee has its roots in the coffee culture, and has been expanding its market presence through continuous chain-store operations. To create a culture would be much more difficult, but those daring brand founders have exerted tireless effort and established new brand cultures such as Nike Sports and Virgin Airways and have made great steps in market development.

As the sub-culture in various fields of human civilization, brand culture has not only taken on the function of the protection, extension and development of culture, but also obtained its own market position and the supply capacity of cultural consumption. Any kind of brand culture, be it in different development forms, has come into being through the inheritance, development and creation of culture and turned out in different stages according to different development models.

The coffee culture dates back to the 17th century when the cafes sprang up in London and became a trend. Artist, writers and celebrities at that time often gathered in cafes; politicians and scholars also made acquaintances and exchanged new ideas and discoveries there. The coffee culture originally emerged as a social atmosphere, from which come a number of cultural brands such as Gloria Jean's, Peet's, Starbucks, Kirkland, Paula Deen, Nestle, as well as the coffee culture forms such as Irish coffee and Latte. Those brand cultures constitute the major market of the global coffee consumption, where many emerging coffee brands have their outreach in coffee culture. Furthermore, the coffee culture also includes the coffee-related food such as sandwiches, pastry; utensils such as coffee grinders, pots and trays etc. The coffee culture also covers the cultivation, processing and channels of coffee beans.

3 The theory of the development of brand culture

The development of brand culture is to build cultural superiority with a brand as the cultural symbol, through the process of the conception, enrichment, and expansion of brand culture.

The core of brand culture is the emergence of a brand as the cultural symbol. Such symbol may simply be a name or a figure at the very beginning, and becomes concrete through cultural exploration and creation. In some cases, it may be a name or figure with prolonged development and accumulation, or a mature brand with considerable foundation for development, and needs the injection for new cultural connotation of brand by reproduction in brand culture dimension.

Culture, in the form of various symbols as the representation during the process of human development, includes both monotonous manifestation and diversified combination such as descent, tradition, myths of origin, style of dressing, and daily habits etc. When emerging as a culture symbol, the brand must be concretized with cultural connotation. For example, an ancient city has been endowed with cultural characteristics through enrichment, and it further needs exploration, refinement, reshape and reproduction of culture in a brand-oriented manner to develop into a city brand with concrete image, clear-cut features and abundant connotation.

The development of brand culture needs to clarify the brand conception; that is, to analyze, reshape and clarify the definition, description, mission and duty of the brand. A brand needs a very accurate orientation in its initial stage. The orientation of brand development, the strategy and the business model shall all conform to the unity, accuracy and independent description of the brand conception. A brand can usually deal with one thing, and that is to recognize the brand and clarify its direction of development and help build and develop the brand. And when the brand reaches a certain level of development in its structure, it needs to restructure itself, dividing or merging the brand or splitting associated products and businesses to further concretize the brand conception.

The enrichment of culture is to gather around the core of brand symbol and conception, and form the system of interpretation of the brand and the expression of culture. It should develop culture with imagination and creativity, organize the element of a brand, and define a meaning and the expression in the form of the brand that enhances people's understanding of the brand culture. The content of enrichment includes the core connotation including the background and style of the brand; the related history, records, collection of facts and cultural extensions such as picture, video, literature, music, story, legend, movies, and statistics etc.; the tangible and intangible forms such as the product forms, package, service scope of the brand etc.

Section IV Brand Culture

The spread of brand culture mainly involves its trading, exchange and intersection. Culture selects and relocates during the process of trading, exchange and interaction. In this way, the brand has become popular or obscure among people in a meming manner, rendering itself as the major component of human's diversified culture. This will in turn promote the creation of culture, enrich the brand culture and increase the opportunity of culture selection, and finally giving birth to an abundant brand culture and an era of brand culture selection.

Thanks to the development of brand culture, many brands have stood out by developing excellent brand culture. Those brands have brought people with a sense of superiority to enjoy the brand culture, and condensed people's sentiment towards it, so as to convert the superiority and sentiment into products and services carried by the brand, thereby obtaining the outlook of the brands' economic development, economic return, and the form of long-term and stable operation in social and market economy. Finally, a series of human cultures gather to form the connotation of the brand, and become the manifestation of the major operation, business, and brand value of the world's enterprises.

4 The super brand consumptions

Since the 20th century, the purchasing power of the world's population has grown with the increase of people's wealth and disposable income. More and more brands are needed in our daily consumption, and those with cultural component are replacing and eliminating those with the basic commodity forms. Therefore, the products obtain the development and improve its non-functional consumption capacity with the increasing cultural components.

In this way, many countries in the world have become the brand exporters and developed into the creation centers or interaction centers of modern brand consumption culture. The brand culture incorporates cultural expression and value such as national characteristics, ethnic features, lingual context, style, history, traditional, modernism, experience and expectation etc. The brands bring together the worldwide cultures and make them co-exist, and finally becoming the ultimate product representing people's consumption capacity and purchasing power.

As it is known to all, today the brand is a daily consumption that is in search of the beautiful life. It is not only the main power of world economic development, a cultural carrier across country, nation, religion, class and gender, but also the symbol representing the daily lifestyle and consumption capacity of the world's population.

People are entering a super consumption era if not already in it. Super consumption is the consumptions of the brand. The core of consumption is the brand, and the nature of the development of purchasing power is to drive the growth of social demand and economic development with the development of brand. The brand economy is the major development model of the social economic civilization and the symbol of development level in the 21st century and moving forward.

People's understanding of the brand is changing in the process of such consumption. People are getting attached to some brands with their constant consumption and use, thereby deeply affecting people's wide recognition of those brands in the market and the daily life. The brands begin to replace the classification and industry, the category of products, and the name of enterprises, and render the consumption towards a targeted and continuous manner to incur fixed, periodical and permanent consumption. Some brands therefore develop into the century-old ones with continuous selling.

In the 21st century, consumptions has seen an all-round and prosperous development in all marketplaces and life scenes as a typical lifestyle, and quickly became the main structure of social and economic development throughout the world. The development of consumptions has completely released people's passion for shopping as well as the increasing purchasing power. "Buy whatever you want" becomes so popular throughout the world, and shopping is the most typical lifestyle for all the people in the world in the 21st century. People can hardly separate the brands from their life. In the meantime, various magazines featuring popular lifestyle and guidance of brand consumption have developed in a rapid pace. The hottest topics on the Internet, media and social life are the selection of brands and their users' experience.

In the process of the emergence and development of consumptions, brand culture has become an important means of purchasing in the global consumption culture in a meming form. Consumption is not about how the products manage to satisfy different demand for consumption, or how to satisfy the consumption demand of a specific person. Brand culture is directed to a certain kind of brand users with a common cultural demand even if the users are a non- mainstream or a minor group with a very few people.

Big brands will care for the common demand of a massive group in global market so as to create and develop an integrated high-quality product that is fixed, classified and popular whereas small brands take on the model of attracting those minor groups with common culture type and reach their consensus of the brand culture. In spite of the market volume, the nature of both big and small brands is to provide a cultural feature that reflects expectation and common pursuit in the market, and express such cultural feature in the form of a concrete product or service. Even after the increase of custom-made service in the 21st century, enterprises still provide brand culture products that can be customized, assembled and adjusted individually and are subject to mass production. Only the procedure of production and processing are divided; changes are made to the production processes, components, organizations and links as well as the means of delivery in an adjustable, self-adapted and agile manner so that the brands may meet diversified demands.

5 Reform of brand consumption culture

People are still in a rapidly changing era of reform of brand consumption culture. The reform is mainly seen in the aspects of the historical change, the life circle and the free choice of brand culture.

The development of brand culture generally takes on historical changes, where the popular styles in different times clearly distinct with one another. It can be seen from the old photos, pictures, movies, and study on the cultural history that all clothes, hairstyle, electrical appliances, articles about the daily use and social life have a clear time trait. People can easily tell which cultural context belongs to which country from which era. This is an overall meming change of people's cultural pursuit, where a contextual culture trait that is comprised of the fixed-form popular brand culture reflects the collective, centralized and unified change in people's aesthetic standard towards the brands in a certain era.

The historical change of brand culture relates to the significant cultural change and development of human's major culture circles in history, and also relates to the aesthetic standard and spirit of the time as sought by the whole society and its population at that time. Once entering a new era, a series of new memes which symbolize and interprets the culture will come into fashion among each social class, so as to distinguish from the old culture and show the new cultural characteristics. The early history saw the manifestation of material life as the meme while, after the emergence of brand economy, it turned the major popular brands as the meme, therefore constituting the change zone of the brand culture with distinctions featured in each major country in during their history. Furthermore, it also becomes the cultural sign and image of the history of the development of human civilization in the form of dynastic cultural history.

Brand culture has accelerated its development since the 18th century. After that, the demand for luxury culture saw a significant increase, giving birth to a number of brands. The earliest brand culture rose from the demand of the wealthy class, emerging from the origin of some special and high-value commodities, exquisite craftsmanship, cultural empowerment of the rare materials, and handcraft with cultural and artistic creation etc. The brand culture at that time was characterized by its tradable, handmade and rare nature.

New forms of art were also emerging in the creation of intangible cultures such as opera, fine art and performance, which became the main demand for cultural consumption of the aristocrat. Those new forms of art were also an important source to enrich the brand culture, closely linking the form of brand culture with real life. In this era, cultural consumption has seen an increase in the nature such as coffee, sugar, tea, precious metal, clothes, perfume and shoes etc. They have shaped into different forms of culture and deeply developed with the demand for intangible culture into particular forms such as aristocratic spirit, chivalrous spirit, and tea culture etc., forming the brands in the tangible or intangible cultural empowerment.

The development of brand culture was originally the trading, exchange and interaction between the production side and the demand side, which gave brith to the division of labor and the new culture forms. The Industrial Revolution established the massive production and sale of industrial commodities as the major form of the supply of consumer goods. In order to improve people's recognition, impression and memory, brands appeared in the form of logo and obtained a legal nature of property right. The Industry Revolution gave rise to the practical consumption, where daily necessities were produced massively and kept changing people's daily life, with consumer goods as the major consumption.

The fierce competition arose from the rapid growth of purchasing demand, the improved liquidity of commodities, and the sufficiency of competing products finally gave rise to the brand development in the 20th century. After 1950, as the war ended, shopping not only became a popular lifestyle, but its convenience also helped popularize the consumption. It was at that time when the cultural consumption nature of brands was enhanced and soon cast off its function demand and changed from the nature of daily necessities into the joy of living. Consumption for romance began to see a rise; the demand for cultural consumption in the brands soon established; and the era between the brands and the consumers came to life. At this time, the cultural cycle of brand consumption became the periodical consumption featuring brand culture.

6 Cycle of brand culture consumption

Entering the 21st century, the creation of brand culture has accelerated and diversified, changing the historical change of brands into a life cycle of generations. A generation refers to the overall life cycle of a brand featuring the cultural consumption by the increased population in every decade. Many forms of product and service as well as cultural demand and the trait of cultural consumption will change from generation to generation. People's demand for fashion, aesthetics and style of brands are changing all the time.

The accelerated creation of fashion has been an important manifestation of global competition, where on one hand, the brand runners keep accelerating the creation of brand culture; and on the other hand, the consumers keep seeking new and fresh experiences, rendering the brand culture in an ever-changing and growing state. Many fields of brand culture consumption have endured a rapid change of fast brand. The market is moving in high speed; the life cycle of those brands are largely shortened. For example, the electrical products of fashion consumption have only 18 months of life cycle. Among the forefront clothing brands, the new styles launched by the world designers will quickly become outdates, one after another. The life cycle of the brands in the fore end of the market competition only lasts for weeks, whereas the daily consumption brands at the rear end of the market competition will live for one or two years.

The life cycle of brand culture consumption is also an important trait to distinguish the brand economy from commodity economy. The mainstream brands in the global market will properly use the life cycle of brand culture to speed up the elimination of products in the pursuit of popularity. People used to judge commodities by its quality and price, and demanded more for durability and longer life cycle. However, in terms of brand economy, people judge the brand culture consumption by the fashion trend, shortening the period of actual use of the brand products.

The usual life cycle of PC and mobile phone is three to five years, but under the impact of the life cycle of brand culture, the actual life cycle is shortened to one or two years. As people keep buying new products launched by the brands, the brand runners will regard each launch event as a great chance to hit the market and stimulate the culture consumption. It not only expands the market influence and volume for the brand, but also pushes people to change new products while throwing away the old ones.

With every year's launch event, the sales boom is not only a transformation stage of the brand culture and a great chance to promote the brand economy by boosting purchase, but also an important way of competition in an era of excessive supply. The generation switch of brand culture consumption in some of the hottest markets is speeding up with an obsolescence rate from 25% to 50%. That is, the markets and the users are obsoleting the old product forms and cultural structure at a rate of 25% to 50% so as to update to the latest brand products. This is an important business model in the brand and capital market. The percentage of brand users and the amount of new arrivals constitute the major system of profit cycle. To name a few, the mobile phone industry and the movie industry are typical brand markets for brand culture consumption. The life cycle of brand culture in mobile phone market only lasts for months whereas in movie industry the peak of box office only lasts for two or three weeks.

The free choice of brand culture plays an important role here. People may choose their favorite brand for fashion, trend and popularity from the diversified brand culture free willingly, stick to their favorite brand style, or choose a different one from the free brand or individualized culture. The free choice from consumption and diversified culture is consistent. Different brands will adapt themselves to the market and enjoy free development. There are always new brands to join and expand the emerging demand for brand culture consumption, offering an unprecedented chance of development for the abundant brand market, urban popular culture and fast brand projects. The multi-level, diversified market structure with abundant brands is thus established.

7 Improvement of Brand culture

The social classes in the world population will always be there, and will only disappear when people elevate the common prosperity to a considerable level. The brand culture originally came from the aristocrat and was initially established among the wealthy class. The most prominent consumption that comes with the population increase is to buy whichever new expectations. Theory B has revealed such decision-making feature of buying brands.

Under the existing social economic development, brand culture consumption exists in individuals. Brand is both a token of status, representing the purchasing power of everyone, and the manifestation of consuming power. Brand reflects the most typical values such as the symbol of social status, lifestyle and level of purchasing power.

Consumption of the wealthy class is always considered as the part with the most added value for the brand. Brand runners usually regard it as the most attractive market of consumption. It conforms to the cultural taste, lifestyle and habits and likes and dislikes of the wealthy class, which becomes the VIP market for the brand service. The meme of collective selection of brands takes the major market of the global consumption culture. With the increase of income and the upgrading of consumption, the meme of collective selection of brands keeps joining in the consumption demand of the new population among the middle and wealthy class, creates and leads an era where all the daily consumption is made of the brands, an era where products are completely materialized by culture.

The non-wealthy population also desires to pursue brand culture consumption, which is realized by imitating the brands. The non-wealthy population may also buy brands in addition to the daily necessities. This group is imitating the brands by imitating the forms of products, making many alternatives of brand culture available in the market, and increasing the supply of brands in the grass-root consumption market. The alternative brand products reflect people's desire for the brand culture consumption, and keep stimulating people to increase income by working hard to obtain more chances for brand consumption. Therefore, the global market has transformed into a post-materialized era featuring brand culture consumption in accordance with the 21st century.

Brands exist in the global consumption market with its particular attraction. The development of brand market is mainly in the form of brand attraction. Consumers are buying brands when they can

SECTION IV BRAND CULTURE

afford to, and remain doing so even when they are not, rendering brands as an expression of strong demand. People are expressing their attitudes towards experiencing, thinking or desire by getting to know various brand products and services, discussing, buying or by mere looking. Finally, the brands developed into a representation of cognition for a particular consumption culture, level and demand for consumption, as well as the strong desire to satisfy such demand. This is decided by the individual demand for brand culture consumption.

The brand culture consumption satisfies three typical demands, i.e. the demand for others, for oneself or mixed. The demand for others includes the common recognition, token of status, or praise from others, which is the representation of level of consumption and the embodiment of values of personal pursuit in other' eyes. The demand for oneself is the level of consumption power, the joy of brand culture, and the psychological factors such as satisfaction, pleasure and happiness etc. The mixed demand refers to both demands to show off to others and enjoy oneself, such as buying a luxury car, designer clothes, jewellery and food etc.

In addition to the demand for brand culture from the wealthy class, brand is also characterized by the flashy consumption, which means to demonstrate one's economic power and level of consumption. People often show their level of consumption and social status and fashionable pursuit by owing or using a certain culture brand. Some types of brand culture consumption also represent the general level of consumption in some countries. For example, Chinese people regard the possession and use of property, cars, jewellery, and wines brands as a basic social cultural demand when getting married.

In order to closely follow the trend of brand culture, the irrational flashy and vying consumption has become a representative trait in social culture, which largely increased people's consumer debt. Since the instalment and credit card consumption appeared in 1920, the consumer debt has become a major reflection of purchasing power in terms of brand culture consumption. Such consumption is mostly made in the brand market. The addiction of brand consumption is rather common in the society.

Entering the 21st century, the brand economy has finally replaced the commodity economy as the embodiment of possession of material wealth and individual cultural rewarding. When material consumption power becomes a universal value in the society, the brand will not only be the representation of social status and level of consumption, but also the expansion and outreach of brand culture consumption, such as to customize cars and buy custom-made brands.

Exercises

1. Multiple-choice Question: The formation of brand culture is not an incident. It includes the typical types as below: _____.

   A. Brand inherits culture from culture;

   B. Brand develops culture from culture;

   C. Brand creates new culture;

   D. All of the above.

2. Essay Question: Which aspects sees the great reform of brand consumption culture? Describe the process?

3. Discussion: Describe how the brand culture has developed.

Chapter 6

Brand Culture Connotation

The brand-booming period is an inevitable blowout of brand development for any country in the process to become a brand exporter. It indicates the rapid changes of demands, i.e. the enterprises' demand for the long-term management of their brand vs. rising demand for the brand culture connotation, driving a number of brands into the important development stage of brand culture consumption.

Brand culture consumption is mainly directed to the connotation which is established through the development of the genes, memes and the modal of brand culture of the core, connotation and denotation of a brand. It is an extension from the connotation to the denotation through symbolization and derivation after a brand is granted with its name and image; a scientific and philosophical process to develop the cognition for it and finally accomplish it; an in-depth building of foundation which make use of three-order structure to empower the brand culture; and a materialized form of civilization of the brand products.

Most of the brands have only played less than 10% of their cultural function. To demonstrate the materialized extension of cultural connotation, brands must apply its rich and strong cultural connotation to a particular material from internal to external. It is also a process to transfer the meme where the meme of the rich cultural connotation is spread via the brand symbol from the brands to the users and interpreted accurately by the latter. A brand will become genuinely alive after its meme, model, and form are transferred and after the brand realizes the exploration of connotation, derivation and demonstration.

1 Brand-booming period

The brand-booming period refers to the periodical stage in which a large number of brands are emerged during the process of a country's brand development. Initially all the brands are dormant, frozen after they were given a name, logo and VI system. When the emerging brands reach a certain number and enter a considerable level of competition with the upgrading of the domestic consumption, the brands in this country will all enter a booming period in which the competition between brands will transfer intensively onto the ones in respect of the long-term management and the cultural connotation of the brands between enterprises.

In short-term, many enterprises woke up from hibernation and dashed into an in-depth pursuit for brand, driving a country's brand-building demand into an acceleration of development in a quick and collective manner. This is the so-called brand-booming period in which there is a boom of brands just like the "Cambrian Explosion"; brands with genuine lives emerge and a large number of domestic brands collectively began to upgrade simultaneously to cross-border brands and even international brands.

The brand-booming period usually lasted for one or two decades. It is the perfect time for a country to nurture brands and to speed up the restructuring through obsolescence in the related industry chain, so that the rising demands for various brand services are sufficient to go through the brand-booming period. When a country realizes the construction of a stable market structure represented by the national brand economy, the country will become a brand exporter and during when this occurred the brand-booming period has ended.

Originally, any country's brands exist in a dormant status in which the development of brands calls for a significant support from the related industry chain, while a single economic community and market are not sufficient to support a single brand to quickly grow into an international brand, and the consumption market has not shaped a united form of brand culture consumption. Only when the number of dormant brands in a country accumulates and reaches a certain level, and the market demand for brands and the advanced industry chain are developed to a certain level, when all of the four conditions to wake the dormant brands are satisfied, then the brand development in the whole country will enter into the brand-booming period and break into the "Cambrian Explosion" of brand lives. Brands will emerge in a significant scale.

For a non-brand-exporter, its brands will stay dormant from the very beginning. That means all the brands are almost frozen after the initial concretization where a brand is given a name, design of logo and the visual identity. Few brands can move on to explore and demonstrate its cultural connotation, but the brands have not died but only become frozen and dormant and stopped to develop its market relations.

Just as the birth of international brands calls for four conditions, the wake of brands from dormant status also calls for four conditions. Firstly, return the brand to its original aspiration. A brand can change from the pursuit of the existing market value to the pursuit of long-term development, pay attention to the structural development in respect of the brand management, and focus on the exploration of the long-term development and intangible values. Secondly, the improved awareness of brand culture consumption by a country's population will give rise to competitions. Brands no longer stress on the short-term survival but care for the stronger demand for cultural connotation, and switch from the market development to the development of brand culture. Thirdly, national confidence and brand faith are added to the brand culture and become a collective will of all the brands for the competition between civilizations. Fourthly, corporate brands are upgraded to brand organizations. In order to address the long-term development, some coordinating roles such as brand advisor emerged and established a long-term learning mechanism. The era of scientific and philosophical development of brands has come.

Major countries in the world have all experienced the brand-booming period from its initial founding of brands to becoming the influential brand exporter. A large number of cross-border brands were born within a short period of one to two decades, many of which even became international brands, marking a significant, large-scale and explosive transformation. Therefore, the brand economy of a country realizes its restructuring of brand exporter represented by the highly developed brand economy and the active participation into the competition by the brand.

As mentioned in the introduction of brand, the first international brand will not solely emerge in any country. A brand is rooted in a country's civilization and will develop with the overall revival or creation of civilization. It is the competition between civilizations. Therefore, any brands, or the brands of a whole country will experience a long term of dormant status until the country enters into the brand-booming period in which the "Cambrian Explosion" of brand lives will happen.

Corporate brands in a large number of varieties will emerge in a significant scale in this period, and quickly upgrade onto an international competition level. All the brands and the brand economies will also experience a new round of competition of obsolescence after a long time of birth. Through the selection of competition, a group of genuine brands will be born and show the historical trait of social economic culture in which the representative brands of a country is formally established. Those representative brands will complete the important cultural meming process when established in the brand-booming period. It is a historical opportunity of the rise of great brands.

2 Shaping the soul of the core of brand culture

The core of a brand culture is the central component of the operating system of a brand, the core of the cultural genes and the interpretation of the systematic management of a brand. The core of a brand culture must be designed comprehensively. It is a process to shape the soul by exploring, planning and designing the whole core of the brand. However, complicated the managing system is, however huge the market is, the core of a brand culture must be targeted at the long-term management and adopt a centralized operating system designed with good planning and systematic organization, and expand to a complete brand system in different levels.

The development of the core of a brand culture is the creation of genuine vitality for a brand. Brands must be rooted to its source. Source must come before the brand, and brand image will come after source and brand. Any brand element does not come without its historical emergence, its cause, and its record of transformation. The future development of a brand by nature is the historical enrichment, the print and evolution from its very beginning, and the continuation, transformation and evolution based on every stage of development. A brand will have no future without the historical source. To forget the history is to miss the origin, mission and duty which a brand must hold onto, and the brand cannot be inherited. The development of a century-old brand is the inheritance of spirit and history from generation to generation.

The core of a brand culture is the center of its whole image, which cannot be changed easily or need to be renewed in a defined direction. The change to the key element of a brand culture and to the source of expansion for the brand image must be subjected to the decision making of the high level based on the demand for market development. These elements and sources include the renewable such as introduction and chronicle of the original brand, and the non-renewable such as background, description, name, logo and general development of the original brand.

The introduction of the original brand is the content that must be defined on the basis of its history and future for the purpose of the internal and external communication. It can be added with defined content based on the result of each stage of major progress, and the addition or renewal must contain the time and the person involved in it. The brand introduction in various channels must maintain consistency, completion and standardization. A counter example is that the introductions of many brands are different or inaccurate on Wikipedia and Baidu, and the content is rather confusing. The chronicle of a brand is an event records made against timeline and can be added or renewed when necessary.

Once established, the background and description of the original brand cannot be changed easily. The background is the most essential part of a brand. It is the particular source of brand name and the core of logo design and interpretation; a formal document explaining why the brand is called so, what the general requirement for the logo design conception is, and whether the brand comes from a civilization, a legend, a historical allusion, an expression of the founder's thought, an endowment of a historical figure, or an invented word for some reasons.

The name and logo of any brand cannot be invented without a background, or merely by a lead or a designer's free play with groundless imagination and interpretation. As the soul of a brand and the origin of all its cultural connotation, the background of a brand must be taken seriously and be endowed with rich values in historical, scientific and philosophical terms after in-depth exploration, analysis and thought on the brand culture, and combined with the real thought, orientation and outlook by its founder before it is finally established. Since all the elements of brand image must be designed on the basis of the brand itself, the overall design is actually a process to shape its soul, to derive it into a culture, legend, dream, passion, motive, and a civilization that is worth fighting for. It is the truth for a brand life to be interpreted, inherited and developed. Bad design has only form but loses its soul, which will miss the sense of mission and historical continuity which all the employees of the enterprise are fighting for.

The description is the standard label for a brand to summarize its guidelines and formal interpretation for various purposes. Usually the description is a sentence or a brief introduction. The name and logo of a brand include the English, Chinese or Korean versions of the name, the logo of the brand as well as the protection of its intellectual property.

The general development structure is the core of the long-term and structural driving force for a growing brand. It includes the sub-branding plan and related names and logos in the process of present and future development. The portfolio of professional brands to be developed, the division of labor and the protection of the related intellectual property must be clearly added on the agenda. As the resource of brand names and slogans and the registration of intellectual property have increased rapidly, the resource begins to show the sign of exhaustion marked by many repeated names and logos. The future brands will be worried about its naming. Therefore, it is necessary to protect the intellectual property in advance.

The general development structure is the comprehensive, guided, and key management system and strategic decision making for a brand, and it will remain unchanged unless in face of utmost necessity. It is the brain of a brand, the civilization inheritance which is constantly expanding and is strong enough to support a century of development, and the source of vitality to guide a brand to trace its source and keep moving forward.

3 Cultural empowerment

It is a basic condition of the genuine creation of a brand to enable it with labor and empower it with culture. The nature of cultural empowerment is a process to realize brand value by shaping, increasing, and improving the brand value and finally achieving the added value with the power of culture. The cultural empowerment is the result of systematic development through the concretization, symbolization, derivation and cognition on the basis of the brand culture connotation.

Brand culture offers a fundamental recognition of a brand. It is a science to develop brand using the epistemology and a refinement of value to realize the abstract summarization of brand culture using the symbolized act of brand. People's original pursuit for a brand is targeted at the fame and market size. When a brand has been promoting, marketing itself for a long period to the extent that people are so familiar with its logo, they will falsely regard such acts as the natural marketing measures for development. In this stage, the brand will be adjunct to the marketing department with mere presence instead of valuable existence, and does not show any sign or feature of vitality. In strict truth, such brand is yet to be called a brand; it is only a company name and logo which people are aware of and can recognize, a stage where the brand lives on its form without a soul.

A brand must be endowed with particular cultural nature and integrated with culture creatively to symbolize it as a brand culture; representative operators must form a close attachment of public relation with its senior managers, employees and users to establish a typical role like a sign. Only in this way can a brand be established in real term and become a national sign representing a country or a region.

Through the shape of culture with value, mission, meaning, target, history and background, a brand demonstrates its high-level pursuit such as the aspiration and teamwork in its dream, the truth of vitality, and the philosophy of life, etc. and responds to people's rising demand for brand culture consumption. It must be representative, inclusive, typical, and always responsible for all the people to transform from its original form of products and services to a product of market consumption with cultural value. It is the basis for brand awareness in which people get to know a brand in the aspects of consumptions and enterprises.

The cultural empowerment is a systematic, complete and complex process, and a forward-looking decision from the market development of brand in its initial or mid-term development. A series of culture formula must be set up in respect of psychology, behavior and method to enrich a defined culture and transfer to the brand culture model so as to maintain activeness in the market.

4 Premium of brand culture consumption

The development of brand is a thought of human development to conduct systematic study and overall design using semi logy, interpretation, sociology and culturology. The expression of a brand in cultural level is symbolized at the beginning. Pan-brands usually refer to the names and logos that are commonly seen and recognized by people, which are not genuine brands. The genuine ones must contain in-depth and symbolized understanding of the cultural connotation.

The cultural connotation is a highly branding product with which people or users can accurately judge the explicit and implicit cultural values and the way of cognition of a brand. It is a clear recognition and judgment of the artistic and aesthetic pursuits of a brand and the attachments, and is integrated with the individual understanding of culture into a culture meme and model which can be universally understood and emotionally associated by the society.

When people are in different social levels and cultural status, they will form two conflicting cultural judgments regarding any material or phenomenon, such as civilization and savage, delicacy and crudeness, high quality and low quality, likes and dislikes. In particular judgment, people will make different judgments regarding a same material or behavior under the influence of the individual civilized level and accomplishment. For example, the stubbornness in an uncivilized sense is perseverance in civilized sense. This is a direct reflection of the different civilized levels depending on the level of civilization between the judge and the subject. When in low level, the subject is barbarous; when in the same level, acceptable; high level, aesthetic. In different contexts, different people will have different recognition and judgment in cultural perspective and change it into the decision in a cultural nature. It is an important cultural basis to realize the added value of a brand.

People's judgment towards the premium of a country's brand or a company's brand also depends on such system. When the civilization of a country shows an advanced or ancient trait, people will make a high-level judgment. They think that the product of the ancient civilization of this country deserves an added value on the basis of its fair price, and are willing to accept the product by adding value to it. Likewise, when a material with brand culture connotation emerges in the consumption market, people think that it is acceptable when the price is higher than the peers because the thing deserves more.

Such consensus of the premium is based on the universal understanding of different culture forms. The premium presented by the cultural connotation of a brand is the key to build the main body of market competition and the level of premium. This is also a particular empowerment to distinguish the brands from the general products, and an important feature to distinguish the brand economy from the commodity economy. If a country does not contain any cultural connotation in its brands, the products for export will end in a fierce price comparison in commodity form. Consumers will think that those pan-brands commodities do not contain cultural connotation and should be treated like its peers with the same price.

In the modern global economy, the cultural connotation is a universal way to present the brand value, and an inevitable choice by the consumers in any country after the level of consumption is upgraded. Consumption is mainly directed to the culture of brands. With the increase of income, such external effect will be clearer. The competition between brands in global market will ultimately turn on the competition of brand culture.

5 The principle of cultural connotation

The cultural connotation is the process to symbolize and interpret a whole brand and shift its model. It is in nature to make the brand name and logo into memes and conduct systematic derivation in the cultural spectrum. It is the materialization of the external form of cultural connotation, and the result of the scientific development to form an external model with rich connotation. Initially a brand only has a name, logo and a standard visual identity and will not generate any culture. It needs to make candid definition and explanation of its symbol and interpretation and present the resultant meme as a model to realize the shift of model for the whole brand culture.

A brand needs to activate its memory meaning, concept or association with the symbolization such as its name, logo and material, etc. This is because people usually understand the value of a substance through symbols. People's universal response to any name logo or material comes from the symbolized empowerment. For example, gentleman is the symbol of gentleness and courtesy. Diamond used to be a rare natural mineral with the same value of precious metals; when it becomes the symbol of love and faith after the symbolization of cultural connotation, its value increased by a large margin.

Flowers will have different values in different fields. In terms of function, flowers belong to green plant; in terms of connotation, flowers are endowed with different meaning. For example, rose represents love and romance; it is also the national flower of the US representing beauty, fragrant, passion and love. Daisy represents hermit, integrity, good luck, decency and elegance.

Section IV Brand Culture

The connotation of different perception will be shifted in different fields and lead to different judgment in terms of understanding and values. For example, a dog will have different connotations in different fields: it can be called canine (e.g. dog in veterinary science), a close friend (as a cute and friendly pet), a family member (as it is loyal and hospitable), security (as a house guard), a professional trainee (e.g. police dog or hound dog) and puppy (nick name of dog in internet slang and animations). Such shift of connotation results in different judgment of emotion and value regarding the dog. It is an important component in the diversified human culture.

The biggest difference between pan-branding and genuine branding is that the former does not contain any connotation or nature of cultural value. Without the connotation, any word, name or product will be meaningless and will not contain implications, but will only be used to describe the general substances and the distinctive features, such as black hair, search engine, a mobile phone brand, etc., without any extension or change of context and meaning. It is merely a matter-of-fact expression and lacks of emotion, attitude and value judgment which cannot be extended culturally.

The brand culture is realized through the model of connotation plus extension, such as passion + people = passionate people; rose + 11 + online shopping = everlasting love for the beloved; heart shape + pattern = sign of friendship.

To clarify the culture with a particular meaning is to organize the genes of cultural brand in a cultural sense and upgrade the same into a brand culture meme, so as to define the brand with concrete and clear connotation and shift it from the ostensive reference to symbolization or particular reference. Many brand names are generated from an original cultural gene, and many products are memes based on the cultural gene. For example, the winemaking technique on Ireland and Scotland are derived into world-famous wine brands like Hennessy in France, Chivas, Whisky, and Jack Daniel in US; the French chateau culture is derived into Chateau Lafite, Latour, etc., modern jewelry design also gets inspiration from ancient classical patterns, etc.

The connotation of the cultural consensus is the connection between symbols. It is the cultural genes adopted from human cultural spectrum making the value of brand culture multiply. Although many brand names emerge as new phrases, they are quite acceptable as they come from the combination of cultural elements in the spectrum on which people have already reached consensus. For example, many cultures are derived from the custom that the Chinese people stress on the unity of heaven and man; project Apollo adopted the name of the God of Light in Greek mythology; invented civilization like Star Wars helps people to reach a common cultural understanding by creating new roles, clothes and signs.

5.1 Symbolization of brand

Symbolization is a way to concentrate the complex development of a brand into a simple understanding by systematic interpretation. Brand is a symbol that must serve as a representation with deep connotation. People use symbols to represent complex information when they are exchanging messages. It represents the explication and implication of a brand to represent the conceptual understanding of an idea, a way of thinking, a visual image, a behavior or material.

People use symbols to express particular ideology and social structure and represent a particular culture in various aspects. A typical example is the map on which people mark the location, direction and shape of rivers, roads and cities with various symbols. Likewise, human brain is like a map which analyzes different demands for cultural consumption through brand symbols, and by that means obtains the pre- and post- evaluation in the aspects of memory, security and emotion regarding various brands.

Symbols are complex signal system. Every brand symbol contains its own awareness, aspiration and absolute meaning. The symbol guides people's thought and act to form a pursuit and good experience. Although the brand logo is separated from the symbol, it still belongs to the symbol system. Only a symbol with particular connotation and characteristic can guide people to make judgment on various choices and take corresponding actions according to its basis. It is just like the traffic signs which guide people to go forward, turn left or stop.

The brand symbol is added with various representative actions, brand functions and cultural features such as scientific research, advanced products and services. People get to know this world when using those brands and learning various brand symbols. The understanding thus developed further and served as the basis to make judgment, i.e. people determine the class, cultural level and security via the brand symbols.

Human life is endowed with meaning by the usage of large amount of symbols; significant presence is established in society with the creation of various symbols. Brand symbols is a bond connecting people and addressing various consumption demands, based on which people judge their likes and dislikes, preferences, ways and level of consumptions, and what characteristics of cultural demand lying in the consumption.

5.2 Interpretation of brand

The connotation of a brand needs to be interpreted. Interpretation originally comes from philosophical expression and the interpretation of religious scriptures. It is a system of explanation and comment using standard theory, and is characterized by multiple cultural systems such as history, archaeology, historical textual study, philology, sociology, culturology and inheritance, paving the way of prolonged inheritance of many classical works and religions on cultural basis. In terms of brand study, the interpretation is the philosophical understanding of a brand, and a particular derivation of cultural connotation of a brand.

Be it sacred information in religion or the cultural source of a brand, all information needs to be interpreted to ensure that people can understand accurately and improve their knowledge. The information needs to be communicated to uncertain recipients via reasons, stories and philosophy, changed into various daily thoughts and applications by a particular group, and combined with people's thoughts on practical issues. Only in this way will the people establish a real faith and experience regarding the source, version and person involved in the information, and form a daily way of thinking.

For example, Venus is the Goddess of Love and Beauty in Greek mythology in charge of all the romantic love on the earth, and often appears in many brand names. The image processing system of Panasonic camera is named "Venus Engine", expressing a pursuit for the beauty of image. A spot-removing treatment is called "Stainless Venus" and the Venus brand is founded implying that the treatment will make women more beautiful. A professional pencil for drawing and construction design is named "Venus Pencils", borrowing the image of goddess to interpret the cultural connotation of the brand.

Such brand interpretation may appear in any fields. Based on the understanding of various brands, people apply the interpretation to various cultural contexts in the society. But the genuine interpretation is not merely about the names, but also involves a complete interpretation system. It is the cultural connotation presented by the dual development of de-constructivism and constructivism. Culture shall be deconstructed in the first place. The symbolized cultural elements such as name and logo shall be broken down and analyzed and re-created into new memes by means of constructivism. Cultural interpretation without deconstruction and construction can hardly make full use of the brand culture; nor can it be the base for whole brand culture on the genuine understanding of a brand by global consumers so as to develop into a genuine understanding at the consumption end as a new cultural spectrum and the individual application of culture such as personal will, emotion, experience and life.

For example, a mountain commonly seen in the nature has existed for thousands of years on the earth. It may not contain any special meaning; but when endowed with a mythological or sacred meaning and described with much literary and artistic symbolization, it becomes an important historical inheritance and a key component in human cultural spectrum. Endowed with cultural value and defined with cultural basis, the mountain will be upgraded onto a spiritual level and obtain a deeper understanding into a common cultural sense as a famous site with particular cultural memes such as source, symbolization, art, history, legend, etc.

The nature of epistemology is to apply the knowledge and reasonable belief, and interpret a particular, special cultural knowledge into a cultural cognition as human's common sense. It calls for a particular nature of knowledge and uses interpretation to build a complete, self-adaptable and communicable cultural combination as a part of human truth and faith.

In this process, the independent cultural system formed on the basis of reason and faith becomes the focus of development of brand culture in respect of interpretation. Internally, the brand needs to use the special forms of legal interpretation and bible text explanation, repeatedly interpret to the investors and employees in order to establish the brand culture and distinguish itself from the peers. In this way, the structure of the brand culture is built into a spiritual world which people are willing to fight for, inherit and promote. In this way, a brand can live on.

The cultural connotation of a brand formed on the basis that the memes will interpret the brand accurately only when it becomes an independent cultural system of cognition and faith and a structural brand interpretation system. Only with an abundant cultural connotation can brand users distinguish the cultural difference between the competitors and develop it into the trust, reliance and support for a brand. Therefore, users will maintain their continuous power of consumption towards a brand thanks to the brand interpretation and realize the brand runner's aspiration for long-term operation.

Today brand designers also use interpretation to express their inspiration, concept of design and the use of the products in R&D so as to build a comprehensive understanding of the product among people. This is the designer's philosophical thinking and cultural understanding in a user's position towards people and the world. Then the designers transfer such understanding into the soul and spiritual emotion of a brand through symbolization, and establish among the users a faith not to miss or give up the brand.

The interpretation of brand is often explicit and seldom implicit. With the explicit shaping of the cultural connotation, a brand will become an explicit cultural feature and constantly waken the systematic understanding or experience of use involving the symbolization, legend, technique and services of a brand, etc., that are stored in people's memory.

A brand without the interpretation system will not be inherited of its brand awareness. It is a premature model of mind, and a combination of an unexpressed prototype with a yet-to-be described shape of brand. Such brands are frozen and dormant and do not have vitality. They cannot arouse any passion among people, or improve deeper understanding among the users. It happens that a brand without aspiration and cultural connotation will not attract talents, which has nothing to do with the salary but is because people think it unworthy to work for such brand without soul or fun, and it does not have the pursuit and future which people are fighting for.

Only when a brand is added with particular meaning can people regard it as a meaningful job and satisfy their spiritual demand. A brand needs to create its prototype into a common imagination, shared value, burgeoning prospect and pleasant atmosphere if it wants improvement in connotation. Just as two apples changed the world among which one fell on Newton's head while the other was bitten by Steven Jobs, the connotation of apple is rooted in itself and derived into the brand culture.

6 The process of brand culture connotation

The specific process of brand culture connotation includes the naming, imaging, representation, derivation, extension, cognition and realization based on tri-division. Firstly, the division of symbolization and connotation: naming, imaging and representation are the processes of symbolization while derivation, extension and cognition are the processes of connotation. Secondly, the division of meming and modeling: naming, imaging and representation are the processes of meming while derivation, extension and cognition are the processes of modeling. Thirdly, shift of model: realization is the process of shift of model.

Naming: The cultural connotation of naming involves the meaning, voice and context, which are also the source to generate a writing and artistic expression. Meaning: the literal reference, be it ostensive, symbolized or particular. Voice: the dynamic development, situation and characteristics of the name and the associated phrases. Context: What conscious, experience, sense, thought and cognition the name and its supporting description arouse. It is the reflection of vitality of a brand expressed by lingual aesthetics, making people feel the environment.

Imaging: It is the imaging system of a brand logo, including logo, brand image system, application figure system, associated cultural sign and image, which is the process to form an image of a brand and the main body for symbolization. Logo is the major sign, mark and emblem for symbolization. The brand image system mainly includes the corporate identity which is consisted of standard image recognition and dynamic management system such as VI, BI and MI. Application figure system includes mathematical signs, digital mark system, UI system, etc., associated cultural sign and image system includes a series of associated brand images such as signs, photographs, sketches, background to help people expand the understanding of brand image and improve cognition in response to the characteristics of a brand, e.g. sketches in scientific or epic style bearing the brand logo.

Representation: Representation makes particular reference for a brand and tells what a brand represents. It indicates the particular meaning of a brand with specific description of meaning so as to express the true feeling, underlying meaning, symbolized implication and main style of a brand. Representation is the core of cultural connotation.

Derivation: Derivation is to explore the cultural connotation of brand with various historical studies, literature and artistic expression such as historical materials, archaeology, mythology, legend, story, poetry, performance, movie, game, construction, etc., and to express, present and reproduce it. It is a process to discover and develop a brand culture using various techniques, means, and advanced scientific technologies for protection purposes. Its function is to enrich the cultural connotation and demonstrate the brand culture. It is also the major way to present brand culture where people get to know, understand, record and remember a brand, and incorporate their own spirit, emotion and conscious into a brand culture.

Extension: Extension is the specific form of products and services. Any product or service of a brand has to attach to a specific form through the connotation. Neither the material form nor virtual form of a product can exist independently; otherwise, the product does not have the nature of brand and is only a common substance. However, the brand connotation is presented through the substance and the latter will upgrade onto the spiritual level, thereby realizing the extension from the internal connotation to the external materialization to shape a brand.

Cognition: The brand cognition is mainly reflected in the function especially the experience of the brand product. It is the particular form for the users to experience a brand as its products and services using their vision, touch, smell, hearing, body and mental perception. It is a perception, reflection and memory based on experience, and an external expression of culture through the materialized feeling.

Realization: Realization means that the final brand product is culturally empowered after the six processes of naming, imaging, representation, derivation, extension and cognition, thereby accomplished in respect of the final product, market end and the consumer's perception to become a genuine brand and realize various values such as brand culture consumption, investment, collection, recommendation, etc. From this point, a brand begins to present its particular value in capital market. No matter the market is huge or small, a brand will have vitality after realization, and meet the demand of connotation to inherit and develop in the long run.

7 The ternary structure of brand

Generally, brand experts, entrepreneurs, managers and investors regard brand as a binary-market structure, i.e. brand is a development process between the enterprise and consumers. There is a profit demand for a brand and serves as a supply market with a relationship between products and consumers. Only a very few brand researchers and founders see that brand exists in a ternary structure, i.e. brand is a stable and balanced order among the brand aspiration, connotation and users. It is a sustainable system which shifts model with its meming and modeling structure.

As people mainly live in a binary world, their judgment of various issues is determined by the binary opposite natures, which leads to the false conclusion of most brand experts and entrepreneurs and the major faults in brand building efforts.

The common brands and products only finish the imaging of logo and visual identity based on binary expression without establishing any cultural connotation and extension. Later when the specific products bear the brand logo, the brand refers to the specific product. Brand must extend from the external shape to the internal quality; and the product development only changes its function, shape, package and form, while interpretation such as advertisement is only directed to the product and targeted consumers. Such interpretation is directed at the materialized products and in respect of quality, technique and usage, and it is communicated to market the information of brand recognition to indicate which brand the product belongs to. Branding department is often a subsidiary of the marketing department. Enterprises usually focus on the market competition and consumer's purchasing habit, promote the sale of products and collect sales data, and evaluate the performance on the basis of financial figures.

The genuine brand is the product of the ternary world. Brand is presented by ternary factors, and has a ternary order and structure. As a particular information symbol, the understanding of brand symbol is candid. It not only includes the meaning, voice and context as well as the change of different languages in the background of globalization, but also involves the in-depth exploration, analysis and expression in respect of symbolization, meaning and way of derivation. Through the study on human culture spectrum, the signs and impressions involved in a brand symbol are organized by culture and form a dynamic perception in shape. People can feel the vitality of a brand even in a static picture. The spiritual structure presents a philosophical and aesthetic sense.

Brand adds its strong and abundant connotation onto the specific material inside out to realize the external materialization of cultural connotation. The brand product is created in a ternary order and structure out of the free, self-driven and civilized creativity, the understanding of people and world, people and nature, people and consumers, of beautiful things, and the spirit of contribution. Such material production and aesthetic creation in the nature of cultural consensus depend on the understanding and cognition of brand design. Since human civilization and everyone's cultural perception is half-virtual and half-realistic, the brand product is also half-concrete and half-spiritual, half-material and half-cultural, half-materialized and half-inspirational. The structure combines the abstract with concrete, connect and integrate information to create the materialized perception of brand product and spiritual world.

8 Shift of model

Brand is an advanced cultural system to transmit all the connotations in the form of symbols to the users for interpretation through the shift of model of the whole brand. It is a process to shift the brand meme as the whole model to the brand users who consumes brand culture, and a process to move a whole brand to the model of brand culture and keep consistent with the high-speed market activity.

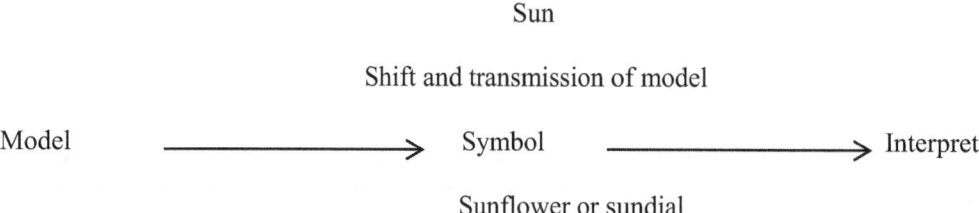

Be it sunflower or sundial, they both reflect the movement of the sun and become the dynamic model. The light synchronizes the process of movement as it connects information and interprets the same. After the analysis, exploration and enrichment, the brand culture will collect the output of complex brand culture information with the symbolized carrier of brand logo and transmit signals to the users. The users will interpret the complex information they received when recognizing the logo, thereby finishing the shift of model of the whole brand culture. They will feel the abundant cultural connotation in multiple dimensions. It is a process of cultural empowerment. The brand culture which is consumed by the users is not confined to the functional demand of a product. The consumption of brand culture gradually replaces and obsoletes the functional consumption of product until the comprehensive upgrading of brand consumption throughout the world is realized.

Celtic: Symbol→Representation (meaning)→Culture (poem, music and movie) ⟶ spread repeatedly

This process realizes the transmission of the brand name and logo into the symbols. That is, after the brand culture is enriched with information, the logo serves as the carrier to send out the information of interpretation. Users activate the information with the help of brand logo, automatically receive and interpret the information, and transmit the abundant information of cultural connotation. Based on the transmission of symbol, people realize the exchange of information. If the advanced brand culture system is not created, the transmission will be impossible. The Celtic civilization is the world recognized origin of modern brand, and has been creating symbols, endowing them with representative meanings, interpreting the same with culture (poem, music and movie), and spreading it to finish the fundamental development of brand.

Brand symbol is rooted from human's social principle and its system is re-designed. It is a cultural expansion of the understanding of people in the world, and an important component of all human symbols. After being interpreted by the abundant cultural connotation, such understanding will leave prints in people's brain and mind, which define the decision making and perception. When touched by symbols, people's mind will show strong responses and activities.

The study of brand culture mainly deals with the intersectional understanding of the ternary order, and studies human's cultural pursuit, especially the nature or cultural background and reference, as well as people's level of perception instead of psychology, linguistics or marketing. A brand is supposed to realize the integration of meaningful cultures with the information endowed and connected to the brand logo. It is supposed to create a set of meaningful icons and consumption indexing system to transfer the cultural memes into visible image as specific as a logo, disseminate the same in the market, and receive the response from the information recipients who are also the recipients of brands. In this way, the brand makes a strong splash in the market in the model of brand attraction.

Any consumers would like a closed system where all the things are regarded as a whole and a complete system. Therefore, a brand calls for a continuous culture. It needs to use the naming element, literal structure and clear relation as well as aesthetics and symbolization to become a self-adaptable body and integrate various information such as vision, touch, smell, action; various signs such as chart, diagram, index; and music, function, advanced scientific study into a modeling perception system with multiple memes and transmit the same to the target recipients, i.e. the brand system users who share a common cognition. When the set of information symbols are presented to the users, the model will be classified and analyzed into a complete cultural connotation.

The transmission and shifting effect of symbols between the brand and users is not there from the beginning. The relationship of symbol transmission between the brand and users' needs to be created, established, strengthened and developed so as to match the symbol to the corresponding users through constant upgrading of cultural connotation, thus the accurate effect of symbol transmission is determined.

The brand promotion is to make clear of the component of the cultural connotation model. It uses the brand logo as the symbol system to make the brand into a meme that can be received, interpreted and shifted into user's own experience, so as to play a positive role and become the choice of brand culture consumption throughout the world.

The ternary cultural relationship of brand deals with the following issues: Firstly, the brand runner: what connotation information can be transmitted effectively by the brand symbol? Secondly, the targeted users: can a brand present a complete and concrete perception of brand extension among its users? Thirdly, nature of the imperishable soul of a brand. Therefore, the ternary relationship of a brand corresponds to the determination between the brand runner and its users. The former shall strive to run

Section IV Brand Culture

its brand well while the latter is pleasant to accept it, thus realizing the sustainable development of the brand in a common environment.

Exercises

Multiple-choice Question: The shape of soul of a brand includes the renewable such as the introduction and chronicle of the original brand, and the un-renewable such as the background, description, name, logo and general development of the original brand. (   )

A. Background, chronicle, story, description, name, logo, and general development plan

B. Introduction, story, description, and name

C. Chronicle, logo, and general development plan

D. Chronicle, story, description, name, and logo

2. True or False Question: The brand-booming period refers to the periodical stage in which a large number of brands are emerged during the process of a country's brand development. Initially all the brands are dormant, frozen after they are given a name, logo and VI system. (   )

3. Essay Question: Describe the cultural empowerment of brand.

Chapter 7

Brand Image Upgrading

The brand image of one enterprise is often not in place with a single try, but goes on periodic upgrade process of brand reengineering by clearing and adjusting redundant brand image in every stage to identify the necessary complete brand image in the next stage of branding development and stand out as the main role in market competition. The brand image design and its implementation process also determine whether a brand capability level attains to Level C, Level B or Level A in the important landmark development stage of brand capability level.

The promotion of brand image involves the effect enhancement of brand image, the overall upgrading of brand image, the design principle of brand image, the standard of brand image and the overall management of brand image, the essence of which is to boost the consensual process related to brand investors, employees, brand consumers and other participators in the brand development by the promotion of brand image so as to achieve the aim of various brand system optimization including the structure governance of brand organizations, the market adjustment of brand, the increase of social public trust, and the increase of economic efficiency.

Brand image upgrading is also the important core of developing brand culture connotation. After the development of brand culture connotation, brand cultural content, brand development prospect and brand cultural consumption value accumulated and precipitated in medium and long term of brand history attain to balance so that brand effect is enhanced comprehensively, brand premium level is improved, longer periodic development result of brand is guaranteed and positive efforts are made to maintain the vitality of brand alive and vigorous.

1 The periodic upgrading of brand reengineering

Brand image upgrading is a systematic project that from the first day of establishment any enterprise in the world start brand preparation including naming the enterprise, through its commercial department to register the legality of the business subject, designing logo pattern, printing business cards, decorating offices, producing printing materials, registering trademark, supplying uniforms for employees and holding the opening ceremony as required. Names and logos of enterprises are always with the whole development of these enterprises for several months or years and even hundreds of years in spite of any enterprise starting initial work of brand from the date of establishment, however, few people recognize that it is brand and 99% of enterprises do not step into the branding road carefully.

When a company decides to develop a brand, it will go through all the stages of branding development, and when a brand runs in the market for many years, it should be given the reengineering every once in a while, when facing development periods, the major adjustment of market structure and brand aging. In fact, the road of brand development is the periodic brand upgrade process completed by the ongoing cycle of brand reengineering. Reviewing the history of every brand that have lasted for centuries or those brands that have lasted for decades, we can find their historical fragment of passing brand reengineering, which is the epitome and precious memories of major process of every brand, and also constitutes and enriches the important historic change records of brand connotation.

When we focus on the future development in a longer term, we will find that the brand image upgrading plays an important role in the historical stage of brand development, and each brand conducted major brand image upgrading project once or several times in its early thirty years of

Section IV Brand Culture

historical development. This cyclical adjustment laid the foundation for the factual foundation of the development for the brand's long-term development from a certain extent.

The construction of brand image is developed through these four stages, "name and logo, effective identification, brand popularity, brand influence" and they correspond to four important effects including "distinguishing market competition sector, market decomposition, professional division of labor, enhancement of brand trust" respectively.

From the beginning, the brand determined name and logo, and the basic development direction of brand, generally composed of the "name + market description" or "name + industry" as the brand name combination for distinguishing the role of market sector in a highly competitive market to explicit the basic identification situation of brand. Then the brand is used to accelerate its market decomposition in the targeted market through the united vision and identification construction to shape the brand image, and through every promotional method and marketing method to strengthen effective identification of brand image.

With the increase in the number of brand users and the spread of brand communication, the main role of brand is being transformed into the professional division stage of brand and is being used to emphasis the profession of brand and consolidate professional market position. With the brand popularity transformed into brand influence, the brand wins the trust of users constantly, and brand name and logo establishes the contractual relationship of public consensus between the market and the users. After interaction between brand and users in the process of delivering products and serving users, the task of brand will focus on enhancing brand trust.

However, as the market changes periodically, when brand or brand image ages, the brand needs to repeat brand reengineering in order to implement complete or progressive brand reform. A typical situation is that the frequent occurrence of brand supplement is common in the expansion of the brand market, mainly because that in order to participate in market competition directly, market expansion stage of brand causes the profession of brand to change, the increase of brand products lead to pan-culture redundancy, brand identity confusion occur in the process of brand investment and merger & acquisition (M&A), and inadequate long-term management of brand image cause brand image confusion according to function and performance of products.

At present, the contents of brand reengineering refer to the structural changes of brand governance level, the overall promotion of brand performance, the update of brand identification methods or the structural adjustment of implementing enterprise brand grouping development so that market can identify brand division of labor more clearly, promote the overall brand image and widen the gap competition between brand products and possible competing products.

Periodic brand image upgrading is the result of enterprise brand awareness update and the method of strengthening brand scientific development and the important processing of the system of brand language transforming into their own brand language, promoting brand professional development through brand technology and brand art. Besides, it is the process that brand is from the expected universal recognition about common sense of internalized identification, self-orientation, competition hope and frontier position to reach the stage of public consciousness and to transform the brand development power into users' expectation, frontier position and decisive competition ultimately, which is the complete embodiment of brand development level and industrial market leadership position.

The developmental requirements of brand image upgrading are: the developmental structure of an enterprise is from short-term cyclical organizational structure into long-term brand governance structure, the brand image is from pan-brand into concrete, and the market structure is from the integrated market into the professional market so that the brand image will show the scientific spirit, condense superb skills, reflect the professional level, present the ultimate style, show detailed aesthetics and other brand philosophy, reflect the overall development pattern of the brand in the new future development stage.

Any brand should go through the brand image upgrading in the development, the important stage of which will be reflected in the brand spanning from regional brand, industrial brand to international brand, or two major historical landmark stages of upgrading to the world brand. Some brands will also become the outstanding representatives of pioneering spirit of brand power shouldering overall image of national brand as brand exporting countries and important parts of global premium capability of national brand. In addition, brand image upgrading is embodied in creating new brand cultural center, consolidating and developing its own brand culture circle and establishes a strong brand culture segment to achieve competitive development level of the thorough brand differentiation.

2 The enhancement of brand image effect

Global market survey reflects that the current consumers have regarded brand image as the first element of the purchase. On the one hand the consumers value brand image most, and on the other hand enterprises are expected to update brand image. The deliberate purchase rate of brand users has been the decisive factors of brand development of global enterprises and brand academia, brand evaluation, brand identification of capital market.

The creation and updating of brand image is not only about giving a name, changing a LOGO, changing product package and redecorating facade, but is to also needing a grand brand-for-mark ceremony held by enterprise in order to complete brand image upgrading.

Actually brand is "between the characters, the infinite is value, between the enclave, its own world", a deep mark left to people composed of several characters, an endless reverie reflected to people with a graphical symbol and surging emotions caused by all the historical enrichment and grand prospects of future development. Besides, all the brand cultural connotation and brand civilization both are spread, stretched and extended in the form of brand signifying symbol as the center, which is not only the high trust brought by consumers and investors, but also thinking frontier and practical wisdom of brand development, and even perfect scientific expression and philosophical thinking of brand.

For consumers and investors, consumers only need to identify a simple brand symbol, and behind the brand symbol there is an integration enriching all the material and non-material culture of a brand organization including spirit, attitude, quality, origin, production, service and so on. Besides, the symbol is also the foundation of all the efforts of enterprises.

Hence, brand has the characteristics of public contract: it is the foundation of public and user's trust, the touch of evoking trust and the best medium of trust transfer; also, it is the center of brand showing its brand products performance, cultural content, development level, market grade, artistic conception and aesthetics interpretation; besides, it is the market value for brand to express its consume safety, welfare transfer, value delivery, rational choice and purchasing results. Brand is the main body to express responsibility, mission, value of enterprise, the extension of brand cultural nature and civilization totem presenting protection, incentives, excitement, and superiority, national consciousness, virtue, social prestige and social prestige— a kind of independent thinking, a kind of doctrine, a kind of civilization or a surreal image.

All rich cultural connotation and surreal perception are ultimately assembled by brand as a symbol, which is a kind of public brand performance of altruistic nature, with a clear property ownership of the high-value assets, which is not only brand strength, but also the specific embodiment of the brand's social value and economic value.

Brand image is the embodiment of the development strength of brand owners, including the brand's professional position, market position and competitive strength; brand is social value embodiment of the brand owners, including the brand symbol, social stratification and cultural choice; the economic value embodiment of the brand owners, including the investment value, premium level and the consensus of the parties.

Brand image is also the effective application of brand classification technology, highlighting the form of the key business organization, namely making the abstract concept clear, the hidden value dominant, the technical characteristics prior and the main function of performance highlighted, so that all value factors concentrate on expressed symbol of brand image as a prerequisite for brand promotion and the main body of brand communication, and brand becomes the key cultural meme to attracting brand users naturally, automatically and self-adaptively. It will not only accelerate the development of the market, but also promote the market synergies, and both represent different competing relationship with the competing goods, but also maintain a good brand user relationship with the brand users.

In the blowout concentrated development period of global brand development, the profound development of brand image, the application of brand effect and enhancement of the brand value will be proved that this is the most valuable investment and is the stage achievement of a brand in its history. In addition, brand image upgrading will also probably be the opportunity of increasing revenue for the brand by improving brand structural efficiency to enhance market supplement of brand products and service capability, promote brand income structure and premium ability and to achieve the transfer of brand consumption level.

It needs to be reminded that: in development history of many brands, there have been the frequent situation that brand image changes in early development period, therefore the fact of the brand image upgrading occurred several times, the reason of which is the brand governance level and the brand strategy pattern is incomplete. Due to lack of vision and the exploring process of future market, the brand may change with market and important leaders changing, frequently carry on brand image upgrading and return to the process of counter-recognizing, recognizing and re-recognizing the brand users and the public on a brand many times, which is the cost of largest strategic design error in brand. When a brand has certain brand influence in the national or international market, the expense of just replacing logo would be a huge cost.

Brand scholars usually believe that: changing logo too frequently is generally considered to be the lack of effective brand governance structure, the lack of enterprise strategic vision, the existence of uncertain growth risk, the existence of brand connotation vacuum, the enterprise is in the unstable, intermittent and abortive development situation and its future historical development track is not a perfect progressive linear, but will present a curve development track after several tortuous.

3 The overall upgrading of brand image

Brand image upgrading must meet three general principles of the brand thinking: the overall design principle of brand, the Lancet principle, the principle of the natural ecologic development, so brand image upgrading must be the overall upgrading of brand image and be the brand image upgrading project under the guidance of the overall brand thinking.

The overall upgrading of the brand image is mainly the stable order structure composed of the formulation of brand rules, brand technology application and brand certification. By the cooperation of global capability, the development of global order science is promoted in the form of ternary order structure, the decisive mistakes are controlled in the brand construction and brand reengineering process of enterprises, the lost of time and economic costs is reduced in the blind practice process of enterprises.

The formulation of brand rules is composed of international rules-making and standardization organization, brand discipline research institution and national brand standardization organization, industry representative and consumer representatives group, etc., mainly for the overall design of brand theory, the formulation of brand standards and the guidance of brand overall technology, and promote the science of brand technology implementation by the means of releasing regular standards, guidelines and other forms. For example, the first national brand standard in China *Evaluation of Business Enterprise Brand and Guide of Enterprise Culture Construction* (GB / T 27925-2011) is broadcasted and implemented in China.

Brand technology application level including enterprise brand and the corresponding brand consultants, brand consulting institutions, brand research institutions, brand management software companies and other brand technology system R & D institutions and brand service providers, implements brand practice voluntarily according to brand rule of system and takes responsibility for the specific technical implementation of the overall design of brand image. Then enterprises can practice by themselves according to their own needs or give the management and implementation rights to the brand consultants in the form of outsourcing.

Brand certification is usually certificated by third-party brand certification implemented by governments or research institutions and with international mutual recognition, and implemented according to the voluntary needs of enterprises on the specific implementation of brand technology and market performance implementation certification and the overall brand management. The third-party brand certification institution approved by CNCA (Certification and Accreditation Administration of the People's Republic of China) is Beijing Sky Certification Center. Brand certification is brought into national brand development policy supporting range practiced Chinese government, such as brand strategic development funds of supporting enterprise, brand construction funds, brand communication funds, brand certification subsidies, tax relief and other policy support as well as the procurement of countries, provinces, cities and the selection of brand products. Apart from the third-party brand certification, international mutual jobs are being implemented at present, such as the U.S. Brand certification.

Similarly, the overall practice of brand image upgrading is also achieved by the brand image design principle, brand image design standards, the ternary order structure of overall management of brand image of the brand management orderly. Among them, as the practical necessary scientific law in process of brand image design, brand image design principle defines a number of specific principle rules in brand image design. Proposing some specific technical requirements should be followed in the process of brand image design; brand image design program is the specific thinking direction, working methods and design requirements in the implementation of brand image design. The overall management of brand image puts forward the theory and methods of overall and holistic complete management of brand image.

The overall design of brand image is different from the formulation of the brand visual image design (VI) manual in the general sense, because VI is just an integral part of the overall design of brand image, on the whole, the overall design of brand image focuses on proposing the requirements of long-term development of brand image with characteristics of the overall design, the overall use and systematic development. Any brand has the opportunity to develop into a century brand, only if the brand image design meets the stable and mature competitiveness for long-term development of enterprise brand, and brand image, brand image focuses on systematic presentation and systematic management in the process of design matching with the further brand culture connotation development, brand art expression, brand value evaluation and every brand technical system referring to the brand management perfectly , and it can achieve the requirements of transforming with the structural design of brand marketing strategy and brand management system of IT.

In the level of global market competition, the main body of brand competition has been transformed from the large and comprehensive pan-brand into the brand components in the enterprise brand clustering system and the independent professional brand in the market, and the focus of brand image development is shifted from the brand image integration effect into the branding professional system effect with brand development structure. From the view of the future long-term development required by brand governance, brand image design should put the first sight on the forward-looking strategic market structural design, and comprehensive branding should focus on the overall image intensification of the parent brand, and optimize a single professional brand.

The overall design concept of the future global brand is the openness of the brand image system, that is, the open system of the brand image, which focuses on three aspects including independent brand development capability, brand focusing business core and synergy and cooperation effect of global brand, to establish a normal fact base for global cooperation of brand market and to provide a normal source base for free networking access by brand communicators in the Internet and mobile Internet, the combined application among brands and so on.

The overall design process of brand image includes four links namely the rule, audition, design and test, and the need to follow certain brand rules and technical requirements. Besides, the analysis of brand is the combing of brand image management, completing the brand design on the basis of opening brand image system and sealing up the actual samples of brand image. According to the theory of brand stretch, stretchy application methods of brand image should be tested. If necessary, we should also pay attention to the cross-cultural attribute research of brand image as the basis of brand design.

The promotion of brand image is a consensus process and is the important process to promote investors, consumers, talents, employees, users, cooperative resources, etc. to attain to the consensus on the future prospects and to develop a general consensus. The overall design of the brand image should also pay attention to the development of emerging brand image design and brand image application including the enhancement of network effect, digital vision, etc.

The brand image upgrading reflects the rise of brand development to attract those people interested in the resources and the public, and to create self-adaptive communication value between the public and the target users group so as to achieve brand leading effect.

4 The shaping of brand image elements

Brand image element is a group of highly branding core components, which not only has the unified normal characteristics, but also has the characteristics of implementation, stretching, openness, cross-media, etc. Moreover, the main elements of the brand image should also have extensible characteristics of components, symbols, interpretation for brand culture connotation and brand artistic expression.

Brand image element is the signifying symbolic structure of the brand, is the core of brand consumers' decision-making identification and perception, is the purchasing power factor of the brand market and the consumption enriching center of the brand culture, the expression form and combination method of which determines whether the brand can present the important economic value of the user's preference, the wiliness of paying higher price, the elimination of price sense, and then is the basic carrier for the realization of the brand value.

Brand image elements include the brand culture core, the brand key image elements and the brand approval image elements. Thus they can form a deep branding management system of brand image including the overall core, the backbone links and normal scopes, bring everything required in the future process of brand development into the scope of operation within the strict order, focus on long-term enterprise branding in the future to achieve dynamic development structure extending on the basis of the actual development needs, and establish high-quality brand image system according to five basic brand rules including the general design, the overall standard, the system opening, the elastic application and the dynamic updating.

The development of brand image needs to be systematically distributed and designed according to the sequence of parent brands and sub-brands. Therefore, the brand elements need to have a clear inheritance relationship, hierarchical relationship and distributed system structure, and must focus on tracing the source. Brand image element itself does not include the parent brand story, the parent brand naming, the parent brand graph and the parent brand development structure in the overall design of brand culture core, which requires a high level of overall design and cultural exploration, so in the general sense, the brand image elements are usually interpreted and extended after the establishment of the parent brand culture core, that is, the overall design of the core is responsible for modeling soul and fixing direction but the design of brand image elements is responsible for modeling shape and extending in detail.

The key image elements of brand are defined for the important image links of brand in the development process in detail mainly on the parent brand, including the specific text standard, color standard, graph standard, brand mission, brand advertising language, brand image spokesperson, brand image experience shop, brand profile, brand story and the key image elements of sub-brand sequence and other structural components.

The home page contents in brand key image elements design manual must be the evolution page of important image elements in brand history ordered according to brand history. Before the presentation of brand important image elements, the historic grand strategic adjustment and the major changes of brand important image elements should be recorded in the form of brand history files in the process of brand development, such as the historic evolution of the brand mission, the change of brand advertising language, the replacement of brand image spokesperson and the historic evolution of every design changes of the brand main image experience shops.

In the history of the brand these current brand image important elements include those brand image element links remaining invariable (5-10) or changed according to the needs of market development by important brand decision and its latest changes should be promptly transformed into brand history files and those changed contents will be updated.

The brand approval image elements are brand image elements fixed or changed dynamically in accordance with the actual development needs and extension, supplement and enrichment of parent brand and brand important image elements, mainly including the design of parent brand name and flexible stretching logo, the design of brand auxiliary language and graphic combination, the design of application, with branding formulation requirements including formatting, formulating, producing, sizing, embedding, etc.

Brand name and logo graph not only need to be used in printing, digital and other technical forms, but also considered comprehensively according to different needs of using and the using habit of characters and graphic size, the general implementation scope of character and graph combination methods with sub-brands and collaborating brands. According to different usual requirements of various possible using environmental, normal design should be done and various possible using environmental and application scene should be considered thoroughly to avoid inconvenient and improper deformation and mistaken application to the detailed implementation process.

Brands auxiliary language and graphic combination design refers to the combination graph of characters (such as parent brand advertising language, branch institutions, etc.) and the parent brand and normal requirements of ordering position design, so auxiliary character format matching with parent brand should be considered and ruled. Application of brand image design have seven styles including brand documents, brand office supplies, brand office environment and brand digital image, brand image packaging, brand image derivatives, brand image communication.

Brand documents are the brand image application contents of strict standard format, including standard file format, file format, press format, brand record form, brand certificate, etc. Brand office supplies are the brand image application contents of strict standard products, including pens, notepads, paper cups, work cards, office furniture, table signs, work uniforms, etc. Brand office environment is the brand image application content of strict standard format, including the door welcoming, front, green plants, building numbers, glass collision bar, office location map, guide card, etc.

Brand digital image includes strict standard format requirements of a variety of digital application interface, digital graphs, digital icons, digital symbols, digital label application, etc. The brand image packaging includes strict standard format making requirements of standard labels, paper packages, box packages, etc. For production, brand image derivatives include strict standard product requirements of badges, atlas, ritual clothing, decorations, gifts and others. Brand image communication materials include normal graphs and requirements (such as the specific size, embedded requirements, angle, etc.) broadcast in news, advertisements, books, photographs, videos, films and so on by presenting brand names, brand logos, scene of brand image according to branding format requirements formulated in the trend of formatting, formulating, products, sizing, embedding, etc.

The related brand image system should be set up for sub-brands and presented in brand approval image elements in detail, with brand image designed independently according to the requirements of brand approval image elements and every sub-brand done special visualization norms, not regardless of strict normal use requirements. As a large number of facts have shown that enterprises usually missed out on this link but these sub-brands are the key of brand promotion and brand marketing during this current period, hence the non-normality of the enterprises puts their brands down to low-level construction stage. After the normal efforts of systematic and overall brand, the brand image in a group brand maintains the development basis of orderly development, scientific rule and systematic opening.

All the brand image elements need to be based on the overall design concept of brand dynamic development, and different brand image elements have long-term and timely standard features as well as format requirements, so some brand image elements remain unchanged for ever or for a long time. Once established, it will be used for a long time, thus some expression of brand image elements will be influenced by history on the basis of tradition, some brand image elements will show advanced design of future, some brand image elements should pace with times and some brand image elements have timely requirements combined with sudden social hot topic. In the process of brand development, many brands should pace with times and constantly add on new brand image elements. In general, brand image elements maintain in dynamic moving opening system and upgraded according to progressive development requirements without any changes, which is the necessary development pattern of brand image development.

5 The principle of brand image design

Brand image design is not brand art design, but brand artistic conception, brand culture connotation and brand artistic expression established on the basis of brand science and brand philosophy with practical aesthetics expression of classical, scientific, fashionable style. The design of brand image must pay attention to public significance and social communication environment, so that it eventually plays a strong brand gravitational role and the value of self-spread from the public.

The design of brand image must follow the principles of normative ethics and cross-culture studies, and pay attention to the requirements of system development, open creation and open use, whereby the essence is to complete and maintain the developing dynamic brand image system development by open and distributed design principle.

The inspiration of brand image design comes from the brand symbol tree (the classic symbol graphs since the birth of the human) and the understanding of things in the natural world, from endless pursuit of the brand dream, from the ideological realm of interpreting brand and from the wisdom essence of mastering knowledge economy in order to complete the perfect creation of brand image, which not only is ideas, realm and pursuit, but also contributes and serves pure heart, sincere feelings and virtue of human society.

The final work of the brand image design should have the characteristics of distributed manual, and the design and production of serial brand image norm manual is completed according to the hierarchy and distribution of the brand development structure. If content structure is complex, it will be presented in the form of fascicles. Any brand design work must meet the requirements of traceability, manageability and development; it will also need to adhere to the principle of regularization, severization, systematization, and completion and is brand image interpretation established on the basis of a broad consensus.

Brand image design has a historical value, because every brand is a precious historical imprint after hundred years, and the stories which occurred in the history, the spirit expressed, the legend interpreted, the responsibility undertaken and the culture presented are the soul that supports brand to interpret, pass and broadcast constantly and also the eternal way of management that a brand tree of life encourages, attracts and inspires people to go on managing the brand, protecting the brand, broadcasting the brand and purchasing the brand spontaneously in the history of hundred and thousand years, so the traceability of brand is continuous development history of a brand being passed one by one like a baton in the race - the future is imminent history .

Once the brand image system is identified, it must be clearly defined, regularly reviewed, and timely updated. The design methods of system should pay attention to and meet the design requirements of ductility, combination, expansibility. Brand culture should pay attention to the principle of complementary, brand collaborative development (such as collaborative test of logo organization with the strategic partners), the use scene development of brand (such as outdoor advertising position and farsighted situation), multicultural culture principle (such as the style of core theme culture), the principle of fitting brand market grading (such as the grading requirements of grape wine), the principle of psychological perception (such as color sense), the principle of brand identification technology change(such as the use of QR code), the expression methods of the characters and graphs (such as common abbreviation names and common names in the news) and cross-cultural principles (such as different cultural conflicts and contradictions between different nations).

After the completion of brand image design, systematic testing should be conducted so that every combination form can be flexibly applied to a variety of environment, scene and market portfolio to maintain high accordance of brand image and show the most beautiful appearance of brand without distortion. Without the system testing program, the brand image is not equal to completion, because it also needs to be tested and adjusted according to different testing situations. After checking design draft, it should be transformed into normal trial stage of brand image products and keep on checking the design draft depended on the completed products after making various brand image design draft.

6 The norm of brand image

The process of normalizing brand image is the exclusive neutral specific process of normalizing brand image that no matter what brand must be developed relied on the exclusive neutral theory of brand design in the development process of enterprise. Among them, the meaning of the exclusive neutral nature is explicating whether the process and result is true or false without any neutral boundary. Also, the process is a series of normal testing process implemented to avoid visual identification errors, visual errors, applied method errors, quality deviation of products and change the environment and done to protect the completion unify, image unify and brand image of overall brand image in quite significant branding process with high-quality perception and high-value recognition of brand users. Besides, the process is the insurmountable and unambiguous strict orderly process, only by the process, a brand has the capability of stepping into the Level A brand in brand image, otherwise it will just remain in Level B brand.

The exclusive neutral theory of brand design emphasizes the details of the global brand and should perfect the completion of branding in the attitude of exclusive neutral nature, identity and non-contradiction standing in the position of heart of the fairness, which is the basic will and mentality of brand and the neutral division and isolation thinking undertaking the order layer in the ternary order thinking.

Exclusive neutral nature requires that any matter in a brand is either right or wrong, there should be no neutral vague boundary and there is no similarity. Identity requires that the essence of any matter of brand should not change because of conditions or environment, it should always be its own and always represent itself forever and nobody can replace you in the competition as long as the efforts have been done for the essence of things. Non-contradiction requires that the same proposition does not have right or wrong, specious, ambiguous and confused conception or answer simultaneously and the things must be judged by accurate languages and accurate conclusions. Brand is a holistic overall expression, which is from the perfect combination and coordinate accordance of brand element components. Every details in the brand image should be separated from it and every component should be stripped and elaborated to be put into the overall design ideas after achieving perfect requirements, and integrated into one with the overall structure of the brand image, and then will not pursue any compromise and harmonic factors.

The norms of brand image will be strict to trial-produce, test, check various application possibility and varied forms of brand image for the quality of products, produced materials, virtual environment of brand and digital form of brand, and will choose suppliers and formulate relative management norms strictly so as to complete the norm stage of brand image, determine the complete checked design draft in the process of norm, do the last preparation stage before the official announcement and should be participated by brand appraisal institutions and natural ecology scholars if necessary.

Brand image norm is a kind of strict mandatory implementation requirement, which is unified and consistent brand image system conform to the long-term brand governance structure, long-term brand development strategy and overall brand image performance, normal socialization identification, systematic brand technology application and sensitive market combination conditions.

Brand image norm should be carried out under the guidance of brand consultants to consider the long-term development structure of the brand order layer, the brand long-term strategic direction methods and bidirectional expressing contents of brand norm in the long-term macroscopic level of brand future development and the implementation guidance level of brand image details. Once determined, the overall image system of brand will play an important overall programmatic role in the long period and maintain in decades or centuries without the change of main structure. In the dynamic adjustment, it should pace with times and the upgrade of brand image elements must be carried on in the form of overall optimization.

Brand image norm process, completed the brand from the brand founding dream, from the individual ideology, the brand idea into the social public service thought profound understanding of the stage, is a non-personal idealized performance, it is the brand organization A great creation, is the brand to achieve public visualization, as a symbol of the times imprinted, interpretation of the interpretation of the brand cultural connotation of the foundation.

On the basis of considering long-term goals and operating characteristics, brand image norm is the process to achieve brand science and brand philosophy in the overall external level of visual appearance and visual perception level and trace the source of brand story by using history sense and future sense of origin and future to mold the aesthetics of the overall brand image and using brand extension theory to extend the scientific methods of the brand sense and three-dimensional sense.

In the process from the creation of the brand image to the maintenance of the brand image, brand image will play a role in creating the level of brand awareness, maintaining customer relationship and accumulating public credibility, which is the capital upgrade process that brand image is separated from traditional brand image identification with original meanings, brand image is enhanced and the brand premium level and the ability of assets accretion is developed. For example, some specific elements of brand creation include the origin, history and culture, technical level and other aspects of the original element shape, and are needed to explore, summarize, lift into the combination of brand image in order to make every brand image element touch the hearts of people through every practice, summary, upgrading so that the brand and brand users are integrated into the culture, the perception culture, the development culture.

Brand image norm includes the work norms before design, the norms in design work process and the design work achievement norms, in which every process of brand image design is embodied as works, is the creation achievement of brand image design. Only by the normal creation and normal design, high-quality brand image on the basis of brand image overall management can be completed and make it the next prerequisite and specific implementation guidelines for brand communication.

In the norm stage before the brand image design, brand learning is necessary for the brand image demanders, the host of overall brand image design and sub-contractors of brand image design, brand image managers to understand the synchronous learning process of the brand image, master the basic rules principles and technical requirements of the brand image, to better integrate into the brand image design process and to create an outstanding brand image design work jointly.

Brand image design process norm should follow the overall design rules, system opening rules, brand image planning and specific quality requirements, accurate definition, visual requirements of printing products and digital products, do multi-circle wide creation and detailed optimization, complete the brand image element design required by the brand in the best general norm methods, and need to make the appropriate normal technical requirements for all the clear links needed to normal expression.

The results of brand image design are the result affirmed and checked for the application scope of various combination elements including language, typeface, graph, etc. Besides, all the design of main stage should record, collate and file the process of creation.

Brand image norms should also focus on principle requirements of autonomy, matching, scalability, flexibility, completeness, system, series, process and intellectual property rights. The result of the brand image norm is to meet the needs of the frontier market development of the brand for a long time in the future, to expand the brand history as the main axis, to achieve perfect brand image expression which includes global expression, universal expression, and expression of full process by expanding brand history as the principle axis.

7 Brand image management

Brand image management is the management process full of stringency, mandatory, historical traceability and normality. Many world famous brands are of high popularity while the real level of brand development is limited. Mismanagement and management disorder happened when enterprises do not follow the scientific laws and technical requirements. Besides, the shortage of cultural prospect and aesthetics can also lead to manage problems.

Non-normal use of brand image too often is the root to the failure of brand image promotion and expression which can be happened through the processes of creation and presentation. Many elements can lead to the brand's variability, such as to recognize a brand while lacking of traceability and not following the scientific methods systematically, lacking of perseverance in brand's expression and presentation and plenty of manage problems as well. Determination is the basic ideological state and attitude in brand promotion, even the behavior of perfectionism. It's also the biggest difference among us which can lead to complete different branding achievements. As for manage problems, they purely are the concrete embodiment of scientific manage level and developing ability of management technical system in actual operations.

Brand image management is to achieve the application of management technology and scientific management ideas including the brand cultural connotation, brand cultural synchronization and the enterprise cultural centripetal force. In the actual operation of brand management, there are four processes of dynamic management: brand image management principle, brand image system research, brand image design process management and brand image application management. The total requirement of brand image management is to normalize processes first. Only by doing this can prevent the mismanagement of the brand image, can achieve effective brand management. Scientific and strict implementation of brand image management is the basis of achieving the maximum of brand effects and brand value. Besides, it is also a kind of high value of contribution to make the brand image reality from an idea.

Brand image management is a vital part of brand development. Firstly, it is necessary to form a fixed brand sequence department and talent groups. Brand sequence department refers to branding committee that is made up of strategic layer, executive layer, operation layer, supply chains, and user layer. The main tasks are brand's general development and brand's organization upgrading. As the vital content of sequence department, brand image management needs the support of third-party brand consultants. If necessary, we also need to cooperate with internal third-party brand management enterprise which has no straight subordinate relationship with it to deal with the daily management of the brand image.

The chief brand officer is one of the management representatives for brand management. Specific brand management works must obtain written authorization from the top leader. Then the corresponding brand image management documents and general image design projects need the chief brand officer to sign. After that, *"the promulgation order"* should be published in the preface part of brand documents such as *Brand Image Management Manual, Brand Image Norm Manual, Brand Visual Image Manual*, etc. Moreover, it must be signed by the top leader or the chief brand officer and so as to be carried out strictly as the official documents.

To avoid serious management errors such as the improper usage, mismanagement and lack of norm of brand image, brand image management must be transformed from the old unwritten files to current strict sense of the highest written documents. To achieve this, the enterprise must put in great efforts. During the design processes, conceptual dislocation and personalized bias due to the over-trust to designers and individual consciousnesses should also be prevented. Therefore, systematic management is necessary within brand sequence structures.

Brand image management is the most important brand assets of an enterprise. It is also a very important kind of capital strength representing the investment value, premium level, brand market value, development level and long-term vitality of the brand. Nobody can underestimate its value. Whether a brand can realize a hundred-year dream, a brand founder or a re-creator can make historical records, a brand can still exist after a hundred years' development is depended on the efforts and funds of the brand image management. This is the most valuable investment in the history of brand development.

Brand image system research is made up of plenty professional research processes for brand image establishment including multiple researches, historical material analysis, archaeological site empirical research, brand founder's dream, brand employees' hope, and users' preference analysis in order to establish the brand's basic form, developing origin and to achieve culture enhancement.

Brand image design process management is a program-formed management to the whole process of brand design including the general design and hierarchical distributed design. Multiple creation and consideration are also necessary. After the brand image design draft has completed, a variety of materialized manufacture, the sample rating, suppliers' selection and identification and products of brand image must be done. Each batch of products should be stored, and brand digital applications should also be tested and be checked.

The reason of why many global brands are unable to achieve the real sense of branding is the neglect of materialization processes so that real products and materials do not match brand design requirements which completely shattered and put down the actual image of the brand. Goods manufacturers are not strictly selected which lead to printed color cast and size variety. Besides, brand image design process and brand materialization process are not docked. Design draft itself has a large number of design defects, and a variety of cross-confusions make the brand image lose its management significance.

During the completion of the brand image design, they simultaneously complete a variety of legal intellectual property protection works such as trademark registration and advertising language registration should be completed at the same time. Moreover, various legal documents such as brand use authorization, brand use normal protocols and brand rights procedures about brand management must be formulated. The main management file systems include the specific use of norms, the division of jurisdiction and conventional norms.

Various brand image normal files and legal documents should be completed by the final confirmation, deliberation and rating, then signed up by the brand manager representative and promulgated. The brand image norm is a field of operational implementation with restrictive usage, and all normal parts (including prints, electronic files and digital files) should always be in place.

In order to achieve the purpose of brand image enhancement, the announcement of brand image also needs to carry out brand ritual press release to make it a major change record in brand's history, and produce further social impacts. Brand communication will be started from the origin, set the launch points, and constantly enhance the brand image from the origin to the terminal of the spontaneous diffusion processes.

The main tasks of the daily management of brand image is the routine verification and monitoring for brand usage including pre-review of brand promotion, brand application expansion records, dynamic usage monitoring and brand competitive defense. Brand monitoring focuses on brand image variants monitoring, such as name changes, the using channel changes, the spontaneous market selling points display changes and the deformation of the customary uses. Some variants can be used to be new brand image elements.

In order to achieve the brand image enhancement, the componentization of the brand image parent marker or subject marker should be finished according to festivals, national or ethnic cultural elements and consumers' personal preferences. And it should be organized by the brand officials or users. The competitiveness of the brand image must match the market self-adaption flexibly to achieve the core unity of the brand image norm, and the diversity, modularity and flexibility of the brand image behaviors.

In addition, during the brand development processes, we should pay attention to satisfy the needs of the brand's response level on market changes, active cycle of brand users, closely related hotspots and diverse interests-combinations, and work hard for the rapid introduction of new products, service brand updating, enterprise brand clustering and scale-up effects enhancement and opening design encouragement.

Brand officer is the professional sequence of the enterprise brand, and is also the strict discipline maintaining force and perfectionist groups. All brand usage models should be incorporated into the scope of brand management, and all changes of brand image steps should be signed up by the corresponding brand officers. Then a complete brand image management records should be made. In addition, brand shows involved in market activities including various exhibition events should implement a serious brand image field management principle, items placed location and direction details should be included, and it should be checked out meticulously by brand officers.

In order to prevent brand image management interruption caused by leadership negligence, personnel changes and other factors, brand image management should contain the application of preventive "interrupt - extended program" and the corresponding rules. When interruption and dormancy happened, the brand can restart reengineering or reasonable continuation timely. In addition, the brand management should have the brand defense measures in market competition including the brand crisis rapid response rules. Therefore, when policy impacts, recall requirements and negative information appears, the enterprises can make rapid change. And when competition changes appear, the enterprises can counterattack timely and quickly.

Exercises

1. Fill in the Blanks: The construction of the brand image is developed through the four stages of "name and logo, effective identification, brand popularity, brand influence", respectively corresponding to four important effects including "_____,_____,_____,_____".

2. Multiple-choice Question: The practical design includes _____ , _____ and other styles。（ ）

A. Brand documents, brand office supplies, brand office environment

B. Brand digital image, brand image decoration, brand image derivatives, brand image communication

C. Brand office environment, brand image decoration, brand image derivatives, brand image communication

D. A B

3. Essay Question: What is the branding professional system effect?

SECTION IV BRAND CULTURE

Chapter 8

Brand Artistic Expression

Brand artistic expression refers to the manifestation of brand philosophy and brand aesthetic design ideas. It is an artistic development process that changes people's basic knowledge through changing their knowledge and ideas with brands as the medium. It is the result of artistic expression of philosophy, aesthetics, ideas, propositions, forms, genres and other memes in the ultimate brand outcomes.

Brand artistic expression interprets international design fashion and pop culture in a way of modern philosophy and aesthetics, presents pleasure of good life and culture with artistic creation and creative sense, stands for the material and spiritual contributions made by all brand officials and designers as perfectionists for human development, and indicates the melody of life played by the language of all global brands.

1 Brand context

Brand language, as the common language of global brands, connects the ecological environment of various brand languages in the global market together. No one can tell what a brand language truly is. Brand language in a true sense should be the real understanding and expression of brand builders in the depth of their hearts and souls, which makes brand language successfully create brand context and give to each brand a real sense and creation of life, and then distil brands into art.

A stone, a piece of paper, a piece of iron, a model, and a packaging …… all these things can reflect the signs of life and shared information of life, and brand builders distil, organize and develop the vigor of brands in order to build the rich and colorful brand world for us all.

Brand is a kind of detached and dynamic brand vitality designed by brand builders using brand language that goes through all the vicissitudes of thousands of years, as the cultural relics or patterns buried deep inside the earth that were discovered in archaeological sites which still tell us the stories that happened thousands of years ago. You can give the eye to meanings and artistic conception that brand builders express materially through material surfaces, textures and other features, and give an ear to brand language expressing thoughts, realization and skills from heart after thousands of years.

The real brand builders understand differences between brand and pan-brand. Through creating brand context, they can trace it to the source of brand, lead the future of brands, link brands with life and connect brands with all things on earth; they can transmit inner understandings of brands when the brand is handed to you by passing a thousand-mile journey; they can make you deeply realize the will, intention and heart of the branders, when you use all kinds of brand products.

Brand language, the world's greatest and subtlest language, comes from the inner feelings and highlights the brand builders' purest pursuit of beauty and most sincerely and in a friendly manner welcomes new brand users. As a result, brand builders can user their brand language to create aesthetic experience in the shape, texture, touch, color, visual image and other aspects of brand products and combine those factors together with the taste by using the environment of brand users to present the attractive ecological structure of aesthetics, for example, brand's actions, shapes, romantic charm, experience and pride in various aspects such as natural scenery, stadiums and family. In this way, brand would arouse psychological needs such as mentality, desire and emotions, and be integrated into the natural world, into thousands of scenes, into daily operation of each person and into everyone's heart and soul.

People may know that brand demonstrates the virtual, substance, psychological and physical perception of fashion, exclusiveness and life enjoyment, but only a few of them would seriously experience or trace the heart of brand builders and pay tribute to them. As the ultimate creators of all brand contexts, brand builders transform all ideas, thinking, and practices from the bottom heart into aesthetic pursuits. For example, the sound of the engine is defined as a pleasant enjoyment of music, and Steve Jobs adheres to round frame specs in iPhone designs. Brand builders around the world apply the common brand language to give rise to the needs for spiritual and emotional ownership and enjoyment of the brand and perceive the fact of the modelled brand context in brand users.

The pursuit of brand builders finally enables brand language to adopt the form of philosophic and aesthetic expression of "inspiration comes from the nature, the idea stems from structure, the form follows the function and aesthetics create artistic conception", and present brand context to the world via brand products and service, and contribute to human beings' wellbeing in the form of brand context that is manifested by brand artistic expression.

2 Brand situation theory

Brand deals with the expression of brand context that is developed from brand language, and the realization of brand context refers to where brand users find themselves in against different backgrounds. Brand design should follow the principle of brand situation theory and rest the soul of aesthetic design on "form artistic conception, visual creation, perceived feelings and experienced aesthetics".

Brand is not art initially, but it transforms the form of brand products into art and pursues better aesthetic interpretation. Brand realization in the 20th century is structure-based (function – behavior – structure) while brand situation in the 21st century corresponds to the order of "performance – situation - perception", that features the bidirectional development of brand builders' pursuit and brand users' expected best performance and experience. Brand builders must answer the following questions: is there any other factor that should be taken into account; in what situation would brand users feel a sense of superiority; and how would brand users experience and perceive the life contained in brand products.

Brand situation theory is about the ternary brand design order ideas with its focus on situation-based environment and realization of the highest mission of brand design of "world prediction, observation and transformation".

Within the world prediction, brand designers' designs are based on expected and assumed world environments that can reveal brand aesthetics, and show the distinctive pursuit of excellence of brands, accented through various service environments.

Within the world observation, brand users in a variety of world environments discover beauty of the brand intentionally and unintentionally, demonstrate the sense of superiority given by the brand, and highlight their classiness, pursuit of life and pleasure of brand users all the time.

Within the world transformation: what is the best, what is perfect, what design can better reveal brand designers' pursuit of brand artistic conception and aesthetics expression. Whenever the brand product is used, how does the product change the world via design style, application and classical degree.

Brand situation theory creates good and unforgettable memories: the brand, based on construction of memory, is rooted in people's hearts and brings profound memory for people, and creates wonderful moments while using the brand. The brand is founded and developed to confirm users' strong conviction of the brand "not to be missed or given up".

Brand situation theory requires the brand to bring users an in-depth cultural enjoyment of pleasure, happiness, glory and appreciation, and design the brand from the perspective of psychological perception and emotions, so the intelligence quotient (IQ) of brand builders is of vital importance. And it is not difficult to explain why successful entrepreneurs are mostly with high intelligence quotient (IQ), who create their brands with sensitivity to perceptions, while brand officials work as perfectionists who carefully review the perfect expression of details of brands for brand users.

3 The art form of brand stratification

Brand stratification refers to the modelled development relationship between society stratification, brand consumption stratification and brand design stratification for social stratified global brand consumption market. Varied brand cultural needs of different social stratum lead to multiple forms of brand art and give rise to the ecological entities of various brands in the global market.

The formation of brands is a transitional meme combination process from needs of upper class to public needs. In the process, brands begin to occupy the global mainstream market and upscale market and have access to high profits, and finally result in global brand economy and play an increasingly important and competitive role in global market development and global consumption upgrading.

Art is at first a cultural system that focuses on high-end cultural needs of the aristocracy, nobility and intellectuals who are well-educated or regularly exposed to high cultural patterns, and widens their gap with the general public in terms of cultural consumption and artistic level for specific changes in art. Demands for art expression and brand from the outset are hierarchical. For example, troubadours in the 12th century, operas and symphonies that are defined as elegant art, and Chinese calligraphy and paintings that are known as hobbies of literatus and gentlemen since ancient times. The brand, in essence, models such hierarchy synchronously.

High culture is part of the culture of gentlemen which then leads to cultural stratification in rituals, manners, clothing, food, traveling and other aspects. Brands therefore develop different forms of artistic expression according to different social stratums. Brand culture is always put into an upward spiral for the rising general consumer demands. The middle class is the group moving towards brand consumption while the upper class is the group of specific brand cultural consumption.

Cultural and artistic products are usually regarded as a part of the upper class and mark the self-adapted brand cultural changes within the long established specific cultural structure and aesthetic framework of the upper class. Such cultural paradigm would automatically absorb the quintessence of art around the world and create high-end artistic brand culture consumption market with specific consumption environment and patterns. During the Renaissance from the 14th century to the 17th century and during China's Song Dynasty from the 11th century to the 13th century, social stratification began to involve cultural consumption stratification, which engendered the typical consumption patterns of the Eastern and Western civilization, making the two periods the early stage for emergence of brand cultural consumption stratification.

Musical art is not the music in the less technical way, but refers to the classical music forms with characteristics of artistic creation. For example, there are some differences between elegant music or folk music and popular music. Especially after the emergence of films, the close combination of music art and film art and the popularity of elegant music in the world illustrates how the music art flourishes.

Differences between high culture and pop culture are mainly reflected in aesthetic social stratification: needs of upper class create the environment necessary for the development of classical music, literary classics and film blockbusters. In addition to high culture and pop culture, there are also the precious metal culture (high price based cultural consumption) and the bronze culture (cultural consumption of ordinary people), proved from the fact that in early ancient Greek classical knowledge became a part of ideals of the nobility and exerted an edifying influence on the upper class. In the service of the public at different hierarchies, art creation tools, techniques, styles and fineness may vary.

Artistic area segregation is quite obvious in the world. For instance, civic culture, including reality shows, escapist novels, kitsch, quarrels, humor and artistic creation that portray the common citizens and families, belongs to popular culture. In the area of low cultural needs, being formulaic, the popularity of culture depends the state policy, people's understanding and social fault and can be divided into positive, negative and neutral culture, and contribute to various pan-brands that are not real brands and do not contain cultural connotation but can be recognized by people who are familiar with their names and products). Pan-brands essentially imitate brands or assume themselves to be brands as a result of the diffusion of the top-down brand meme bandwagon effects.

Not all brands that are familiar to people in the market are true brands. Positive brands are public brands in another sense. After the Second World War, ideas of brand equality, which originated in the United States, promoted overlapping of mass culture, media culture, image culture, consumption culture and cultural and artistic development and artistic consumption. In this way, the US turned into the first center of social popular culture and witnessed a pool of popular brands, which spurred the European culture to be inclined towards the public and to produce many brands for the public. At the same time, venture capital and financial markets strongly facilitated the development of those brands towards popularization.

Brand popularization requires a big investment and has high research and development costs, which make popular brands available to enterprises with much capital, investment value and mass production and service. More brands, owned by private capital, should firmly maintain high prices and their positions in limited markets and not be listed for sustained development.

4 Brand modernism

Development of design patterns of global mainstream brands mainly depends on the modernist philosophical movement. With the development of global culture in the 20th century, the profound reform of modernist ideological design trend was brought about in the West. Modernism leads to dramatic changes in expression of brand designs, lifestyles and aesthetic ideas. "The traditional is the synonym of underdevelopment" is a typical social aesthetic idea while "the western stands for the advanced" is a consensus of the public in global brand consumption market, which creates a brand situation for diversified international universal brands to make innovations and catch up and imitate each other. Emergence of such design ideas is definitely not a coincidence.

The concept of "modern" from the perspective of the eastern civilization is a historical time one, is divided into ancient, modern and contemporary eras according to historical period. It refers to the general philosophy and aesthetic expression of design and consumption culture in the eyes of westerners. As a result of the big difference, Europe and North America are the home to main design centers, development centers, R&D institutions of international brands, while Asia could only be a follower of brand trends for a long period.

In brand science, the term of "modern" is a concept of philosophical idea and design aesthetics that first appeared in the 5th century in order to distinguish it from religious culture and made its literary debut in the 6th century. In the 17th century in Europe, quarrels between people with classical ideas and those with modern ideas would always come to the question of "is modern culture certainly superior to the classical culture". Around 1900, modernism evolved into a global cultural and artistic expression of philosophy and design aesthetic idea.

Modernist philosophy, that appeared around 1900, marks the beginning of changes of the world style. New forms of expression, new art, new theories, new ideas, new markets and new opportunities undergo unprecedented development, and every corner of the world witnesses scientific, cultural and educational movements relevant to new design ideas as well as the emergence of popular pursuit of modernism based on rapid technological progress and social modernization, and various branches of design ideas such as modernist design, post-modernist design, futuristic design and neoclassic design. Specific expression of the brand form hinges on the school of brand design ideas and design styles of the designers, so as to create the diversified popular brand concepts.

Modern brand design style has developed into the basic mode of global brand cultural connotation, which is combined into the transnational and cross-cultural mainstream cultural structure in areas of ideas, meanings, attitudes, viewpoints, images and so on, and is then embodied in the virtual or material, so as to constitute the mainstream lifestyles featuring brand divisions. It is completely different from the historical concepts of "modern" and "contemporary".

Design ideas and brand design styles all over the world, the development of which has been deeply influenced by modernism, would resort to modern designs as the mainstream way of expression. In other words, architecture, industrial design, packaging, garment, shape, language and art are affected by structural trend of the main design styles, and therefore brands of these countries are equipped with brand cultural memes necessary for international popularity and can be transformed into generally accepted culture.

The dominant characteristics of mainstream brand cultures would determine whether a country's civilization and brand culture can be integrated into globalization and become a basic structural form that is generally accepted by the international community in the cultural tide. Brands in the eastern civilization, if failing to express or surpass the philosophical understanding of the brand civilization with modernism, would not the accepted by western civilization, let alone grow into world-renowned international brands.

Modern furniture, architecture, appliances, machine aesthetics and intelligent environment show that modern designs are characterized by material saving, lightness, simplicity, stylization, beauty of lines, sleekness and advanced science and technology in order to get rid of complex decorations, focus on comfort in the rapid pace of life and the beauty of lines, and demonstrate design ideas with the logic from structures and functions. Modern designs, in the search for novelty, creativity and technological innovation, connect modern, future, scientific, technological, classical and brand cultures together, which is the mainstream design trend of constant reforms and the evolution with new concepts and design ideas.

5 Modern neoclassicism

Another main reason for rapid development and general acceptance of modernism is that it properly deals with the relationship between tradition and modernity and is an important part of how the tradition is modelled in modernism with sustainability as the mission. Modernism and traditional culture is clearly opposite, but not contradictory to each other. International modern fashion styles explore and develop the classical culture, so as to make progresses in cultural development and present ancient culture with the form of fashion by utilization of new technologies, materials and design styles.

Most of the world's mainstream brand designers are equipped with aesthetic pursuit of modern design ideas, and all brands are created by modern designers and manufactures who constantly developed forefront designs and create new styles, discover new material, develop unique techniques and pursue simplicity and formalization to accommodate the fast production and transportation mechanism and the point deformation model of contacts of consumption cultures. Brand designers strive to go beyond the known visual experience. With globalization becoming a place of strategic importance for modern international fashion designs, several global cutting-edge design centers emerge, gather and develop into more advanced modern brand design ideas, expressions and combinations of industrial chains, such as Italian furniture design, French fashion design, American Silicon Valley technology design and Seoul's creative design.

At the same time, modernism has also witnessed the emergence of a number of stylized design trends advocating brands, such as minimalism (with a variety of interpretations and distinctive forms of creations) and the Chinese style (presenting classical Chinese culture by means of modern fashion). However, all brand designers avoid mentioning the traditional culture or only promoting traditions, but instead they introduce more in-depth interpretation of traditional culture in their design ideas, but not at the same time.

Some outstanding brand designers believe that the quintessence of civilization, classic cultural symbols and body art should be preserved and brilliant ancient symbols and civilization imprints should be interpreted by means of modern fashion, which can be found in Hong Kong, Singapore, Xi'an Qujiang Culture and many other products of South Korea and Japan that put forward neoclassicism with elements of modernism and international fashion and pop culture by applying the design idea.

Brands also enjoy characteristics of nationalism. In the case of prevalence of nationalism, inheritance and protection of the ancient nations becomes the common consensus of these people, so that a cultural circle with typical national characteristics is created around the world that presents the long popular cultures of nations based on local customs, rituals, ancient legends, natural landscapes, historical sites, totems and symbols. Within the cultural circle, civilization can be preserved, culture can be protected, classics can be developed, brands can be inherited and customs can be respected. As a result, cultural circles for international cultural exchanges and traveling arise, and brands with strong national cultural characteristics become popular within their cultural circles and among a small amount of cultural enthusiasts from other areas, contributing to diversified global cultural brands and human cultural heritage.

6 Modern fashion

Early Western people have found out that there is no fashion change in China, Japan, India and other eastern civilizations. To be more specific, Chinese culture sticks to the tradition for thousands of years and Japanese clothing witnesses no changes for more than a thousand years. In the meanwhile, Europe respects the universal modernist cultural consumption values of intergenerational fashion trend changes, and to put it in other words, it purposely triggers global culture fashion trend changes every once in a while to stimulate repetitiveness consumption. Westerners redefine the term of culture according to the structural changes and facilitate the upcoming world-wide intergenerational brand fashion changes and consumption booms.

Europe is the birthplace of fashion. After the Renaissance, European designers since the 14th century launched periodic fashion design movements, and as a result, the society underwent periodical changes with fashion trends, and then the whole trend of social cultures followed the pace of fashion evolution.

After the development of modernist philosophy in the 20th century, European designers and enterprises discovered the important economic value of fashion in modern cultural consumption: it is a way to create and connect brand markets of repetitive consumption. Since then, fashion has been regarded as an important economic activity, and a variety of fashion magazines and life magazines have appeared, chasing the latest fashion trends and accelerating cyclical fashion obsolescence of products.

The world therefore witnessed the development of a market of dynamic modern society, modern civilization and modern fashion trends that move forward with times in which styles in fashion constitute a fashion circle, and show typical brand cultural consumption characteristics of a fashion generation, styled regions and cyclical changes. It is the mainstream form of modern international fashion and an international language for international brand design and cultural exchanges in varied contexts.

Fashion is the specific practice of brand design style trend and a popular style, especially in clothing, consumer electronics, cosmetics, small appliances, furniture, automobiles and other popular consumption areas, and there are many customary trends of style changes that mainly originate from the latest designer creations. Fashion, cyclical in nature, drives the trend in order to stay fashionable, and makes the world's fashion trends rapidly change. Against the background of global rapid media brand communication, a life span of brand product styles could only be weeks or one to two years.

Brand fashion designs make progress in a way that is rapidly changing fashion trends and drives the development of consumption culture in fashion and brand designers constantly, delivers the latest styles to the global fashion market, which is similar to the venture capitalists' betting on investment projects, so as to shift the fashion trend and lead to overlapping of consumption cultures and changes in levels of the consumption market.

The changing system of fashion plays an important role in the process, and it is featured with deliberate changes in combination of styles and elements and pursuit of the new and fashionable styles. Designers will change consumers' tastes through the use of prediction such as major changes in accessories and upgrading of key components, so that consumers will follow the trend and decisively discard old styles, elements and performance combinations.

From Europe to the United States and then to Korea, many fashion brand entrepreneurs and designers are familiar with it and apply it in all possible market areas, and the most typical fashion changes are utilized in mobile phones, laptops, games and other popular consumer electronics and virtual product areas. Through the structure of changing fashion, technology companies launch generations of new revolutionary brands and contribute to upgrading of fashion consumption by upgrading their products. The popular trend has a bandwagon effect, and people may follow the popular trend even through neglecting the reason for the trend. This marks the information cascade effect of brands in their design and market structure development. Brands are communicated and influence each other through information sources, information triggers and information spontaneity, thus quickly make profits in large-scale brand consumption and begin to prepare for the release of the next generation of fashion brands and products.

Designers with a keen sense of fashion usually work as a team or independently in the name of the design studio. Their design styles, being diversified, frequently change as a result of individual or team work but always stick to a pattern and follow the trend. One company may set up a number of design studios that undertake projects and make designs for days or months. Large brand design project will assign each design studio with specific tasks, and some designs and productions may develop into independent brands and enjoy reputation in the industry with their successful works.

7 Modern mass culture and niche culture

Mass culture is influenced by modernism and fashionism passively, and prevails in regions with vast cultural exchanges and interaction. In regions with closer cultural exchanges and more intensive media, the fashion consumption is more concentrated and the fashion change cycle is shorter, while in regions farther away from the cultural interaction center, the fashion change cycle is longer and periodical changes of fashion are more obvious which means that several fashion trends emerging at different periods may reach out to the market simultaneously. Position in the market and the corresponding development mode of a brand depend on brand leaders' structural design of the brand market and their final decisions.

The future brand is a market where mass culture and niche culture co-exist. Popular brands will maintain its position as mainstream brands for a long time, because true brand development is featured by the consensus of modern brand fashion and requires costly, high-tech and effective research and development and market investments, making it impossible for many brands to become mainstream or to replace the mainstream brands in the market. From competition among windows, e.g. Apple and Luixus in the film system, it can be observed that the development of modern brand is a complex system, and a large mainstream brand needs a large number of specialized operations to continue to be highly competitive.

Brands in the mass market adjust their material and production technology and provide derivatives of fashion products at a low price by reducing costs and components, using alternative materials and imitating other brands. Some enterprises closely following fashion imitate major fashion elements and copy product forms to launch alternative fashion products, so as to enter the middle and low-end consumption market.

Niche brands, the result of development of concepts for a minority of people, create a very small brand market. They are born to demonstrate artistic personality and win cultural recognition from a minority of people. They show the individual pursuit of brand designers, and enjoy brand design and its application. They fully express the intention of the creator through exclusive media and in an exclusive way.

Many contemporary concept artists have become main brand designers of niche brands. In the beginning, they mainly oppose the mainstream art forms and brand styles with free ideas, thus deducing and creating some representative brands with individuality. In this process, many entrepreneurs and designers turn to individual fashion brands to meet the needs of the minority and the non-mainstream aesthetic ideas. Consequently, the "cool" culture is born and quickly becomes popular among a certain population for its novelty, and finally disappears with the reduction of novelty.

Nevertheless, brand stratification has determined that the niche brand is a sub-layer of global brands rather than the mainstream of brands. The development of large brands mainly models the shift of universal public aesthetic ideas. The niche brand is not necessarily the mainstream of the global brand market for the reason that it cannot win a lot of investment because of the risk of cultural exclusion in the mainstream market. To put it in another way, pursuit of individuality and large-scale development cannot coexist, and the niche brand can only flourish in a certain environment and within a scope.

8 Brand industrial design and packaging design

The industrial design comes from artisans' pursuit of aesthetic design in handcrafts who highlight the shape, jewelry, carving and other decorations in artworks while retaining their practical functions so as to improve their worth and aesthetic value. Modern industrial design, a combination of traditional craftsmanship and industrial scale, integrates systematic performance design, product modeling, process aesthetics, user interface design and art design together and manifest modern design aesthetics in areas of interactive design, cross-generation design and sensory design by expressing technical concepts, product shapes and artistic styles

The theory of brand design evolution refers to the gradual transformation of brands based on the needs to create consumption cultures requirement. In 1907 in Munich, a group of artists, designers and manufacturers set up an organization to advocate design and new ideas. The industrial utopia established in the early 20th century inspired modern creative inspiration of artists and designers, and made industrial designs the cornerstone of German modernist designs. The organization, essentially a public opinion group vigorously promoting industrial designs, proposed to "raise the status of industrial labor through education and joint actions on related issues by means of cooperation in art, industry and handicraft." In 1920s, the idea of industrial design was established in Germany, and then rapidly became the European consensus of industrial design.

Many modern design ideas were put forward in the early 20th century and eventually integrated with various design ideas to form universal ideas of modern designs in the world. For example, the principle of "Form follows function", associated with architecture in the 20th century, requires that the shape of an object should be primarily based upon its intended function or purpose. Architecture can be preserved for a hundred years, and its design should be based on future aesthetic ideas in order to always match the future specific aesthetic tastes in the future in spite of changes in aesthetics. The principle believes that designs should set functions as the priority and form and an object should be built on its functions. Such design idea has become an important part of industrial design ideas.

Modern industrial design requires perfect embodiment of beauty perception and focuses on studies of negative experience and design defects to create near-perfect experience through continuous experiments. It presents products in multidimensional design by taking into account the sensory designs (touch, smoothness and accessories) and how the product is used in the context of different actions of people, and demands treating subtle changes in qualities of an object (such as smoothness) from different perspectives. It enhances brand conception with creative philosophy, design aesthetics and aesthetic attitude to reach the soul of aesthetic design of "artistically perceived form, visual creation, perceived feelings and experienced aesthetics".

Packaging is a technique that combines the tasks of loading, storage, transportation, marketing, delivery, handling and collecting in order to pack and protect products. It is also a form of artistic design and creates visual and tactile experience for users by presenting the packaging design pursuit of the brand. Packaging design involves important aesthetic designs and design implementing contents of materials, workmanship, labeling, printing, packaging and extraction.

The earliest packaging was made from natural materials such as wood, pottery and bronze, and natural textures, painted or engraved decorations, emblems, stamps and inscriptions were utilized to indicate the owner, way of delivery and quality of the product. The emergence of large-scale packaging coincided with the development of brands. During the industrial revolution, the soap industry created the formal packaging that was printed with information of brand logos, slogans and places of production in order to make the portable soap, reduce the risk of rain and moisture and highlight the product appearance for brand users to identify and purchase the product, and then expand sales of soap and transport products to more areas.

With the growing demands for brand consumption, brand packaging has also undergone profound changes at multiple levels and in varied forms in the design expression, labeling requirements, storage patterns, printing technology, ways to open packages and environmental needs, and made exploration in the packaging art, making itself an important part of brand art expression and even a challenge issued by the brand in the market to a certain extent.

9 Brand elements of art and creation combination

Art, defined as something used for expression of emotion and exchange of ideas reveals the soul of creators, and artistic creation is a philosophy featuring the interpretation of art in brand connotation and artistic expression of products.

Art is not equal to the brand, but all brand builders are artists in achieving the brand. When pursuing art, brand builders should be able to experience the vigor of the brand and understand how to express emotions, ideas and profound meaning, and the manufacturing and thinking process in order to grasp the sense of capability training. Many products, especially hand-crafted products, require artistic thinking during development and production. Brand builders need to resort to art in the expression of imagination, function of symbolization, ritualization and art inspiration. For example, music bands perform to gradually arouse the audience and finally make them feel relaxed. Brand builders use these artistic techniques in the designs of brand experience.

Art is developed from the oldest visual arts including painting, sculptures, prints, photography and other image-creating skills and techniques and slowly absorbs various forms of expression to eventually evolve into an ideology about beauty, ideas and artist conception, with literature, calligraphy, paintings, sculptures, architecture, music, dance, plays, films and works of folk art included. After the development of global brands, art is quickly integrated into brands and becomes an important component of brand culture.

Art has two forms of realism and imagination, just like Louis Lumière and Georges Méliès in the history of film industry. Art expresses how people think in ways of the real and virtual world, in order to communicate emotions and arouse thinking about all the good things.

Brand art is the art of brand expression and events that brand art participates in. It refers to brand-based artistic expression and activities. Artwork can be any form favorable to communication or expression, which is characterized by communication and interaction between the brand and users.

Brand art aesthetics that aim at the masses are inclined to public expression rather than individual intention, and cannot go beyond people's pursuit of beauty. It is a kind of artistic expression that is based on the universal aesthetic attainment. Brand art stimulates emotional connection between human beings and materials, arouses aesthetic perception and gives rise to changes in emotions, a process of consciousness communication and action triggering, endowing brands with huge appeal.

This brand art, the expansion of practical and applied aesthetics, delivers what is true and beautiful. Developed from naturalism, it is a truth-based way of communication with its inspiration from nature, and creates an original, public and crude language context by materializing the brand. Brand art is different from public art in terms of ways of expression, and the former symbolizes practices of art creation practices and emphasizes brand participation and collaboration. Innovators of brand art lead its ways of expression, and sustain the interactive opportunity of the long-term development of the brand.

Brand art in the niche market does not have to be accepted by the public, because the brand is only responsible for its user groups. Brand art is not necessarily perfect, and needs to match itself with the needs of brand users. As community art aims at grassroots, brand art also has a fixed field of artistic expression. Brand art, as a form of art needs to deliver something to brand user groups, expresses the brand's understanding and care for users in the artistic process, reflect the brand interaction, and turn troubles into opportunities, which touches more upon the designs and art creation that mainly focuses on the connotation of brand culture.

The art in brand culture is composed of various artistic elements such as painting, music, film and plays, but over 75% of brand art comes from paintings visual lay. As a result, knowledge of aesthetics or art designing is pretty crucial for brand art and relates much to work of designing (e.g. the design of VI) and requires an understanding of composition of a picture, of aesthetic ideologies, mainstream schools and forms of creation. Line brand art and digital brand art are the focus of development that can realize interaction between brands and their users with the help of the virtual brand community or digital art forms.

Some brand art would also touch upon artistic performances when communicating with brand users, but it should be noted that actors' performances in brand marketing events are of little relevance to brands. Some forms of art would risk being excluded in its ways of appeal, such as different brand conception of popular music and elegant music audiences. These ways include investment in forms of public art such as sponsorship of TV music programs and support of photography contests, in order to attract art enthusiasts to have an understanding of the brand and win brand users.

Brand art is overall based on social practices, derived from life and developed also in practices. It is committed to apply social practices to achieve the knowledge creation and development of theoretical and systematic knowledge. Sciences are not only studied in universities or laboratories, which is a common rule. Practices involve background research, site management, social observation, group perception, literature research, practice order and so on. Brand learning and service learning in education are accomplished in social practices, and then to serve the practices. Art of social practicing strengthens the understanding of art and approaches its targeted groups with aesthetics, ethics, collaboration, people, news etc. Not only artists, but also business leaders should perceive the form of brand art in the true sense in social practices in order to create clear and accurate objects instead of free and ambiguous ones, so that art can effectively participate in social development of the brand.

10 Surreal conceptual design in the 21st century

Changes of modernism in 1900 had a profound impact on the development of brand culture throughout the century, making brand culture in the 20th century an interaction between the ideal and the reality. Modernism opened a new chapter of modern civilization in which popular culture was regarded as the major reason for social-economic movement. Modernism is a development way of the rapidly changing brand fashion that is facilitated by games, movies and music. Some relevant design ideas are still influencing today's designers in various fields.

The 21st century marks the super-modernism or the reality of neo-futurism that is essential to connect the virtual with reality and history with future in the new millennium. It is also a new era for human civilization to challenge the limit of imagination.

Modernism advocates reasonable changes, while super-modernism esteems hypothetical changes. In the virtual world, everything is possible, and plastic arts, clothing styles and future articles used like never before can suddenly appear. People can set out on their journey to the past, present and future and travel between different civilizations to open up world of the imagination and inspire creation of various forms of culture and art, and lead reforms in science and technology, culture, products and service.

The surreal conceptual design in the 21st century is more of a utopian world, a brand culture world with weakened influence of modernism and coexistence of super-modernism and anti-modernism. The

Section IV Brand Culture

21st century is a new millennium for the brands to flourish, and in which the brands will appear and focus on sufficient imaginative design ideas, pushing themselves to the limits known to people.

Super-modernism, with unprecedented imagination and dreams, connects the future imaginative world with the real environment, and focuses on themed cultural scenes of the space, on the natural ecology of the earth and its context, and on new materials and technology. People can develop imaginary science and conceptual products in areas of the future cities, watches, robots and automobiles, and incorporate brand ideas into everything. It will represent an era of surreal fusion of products and art, an era of rapid progress, and of a masterpiece that integrates brands with life, nature and ecological sustainable development, all together present in imagination, science and technology and cultural development.

Everything belongs to the future, and the world of brands has just opened up.

Exercises

1. Fill in the blanks: Brand language, as the common language of global brands, connects the ecological environment of various brand languages in global market together. The pursuit of brand builders finally enables brand language to adopt the form of philosophic and aesthetic expression of "_____, _____, _____ and _____".

2. True or False Question: Design ideas and brand design styles all over the world, the development of which has been deeply influenced by modernism, would resort to modern designs as the mainstream way of expression. This is not true. (   )

3. Discussion: Briefly describe the system of fashion changes.

Chapter 1

DID Brand Reengineering Principles

We need to discuss the booming of brands. As a unique power, brand reengineering is the source of power for brand development and this power is more comprehensive, powerful and sustainable than any other management powers, such as leadership power, executive power, influence power and charisma.

According to the researches on brand science, in the global economic activities and enterprise development in the past, today and future, the power of brands has more significant influence on the economic production than we have thought.

The researchers from different countries throughout the world have made many meaningful researches on the power of brands, such as the active explorations in terms of popularity, reputation and brand communication. However, we think that these researches are insufficient to reflect the great features and profound bases of the brand development power, and are unable to represent the rules and potentials of the brand reengineering in the global markets. Finally, we have proposed the concept of brand nuclear explosion power to represent the potential of development in brand reengineering.

1 Why brands are nuclear explosion power

Humans are obsessive on--- under what conditions are the international brands popular throughout the world born. Many countries hope to create world-leading international brands in a great number to ensure that brands are no longer created accidentally.

However, international brands are never produced at will. The birth of an international brand shall not only be based on a series of brand science principles but also a brand forging environment with certain conditions.

The birth of any powerful international brand is just like the principle of nuclear bomb exploding: a great quantity of energy is released in several microseconds, and the whole bomb will become plasmas with high temperature and pressure within the reaction areas, it expands outward quickly and generates optical radiation to form intense shock wave. When people are shocked over the nuclear explosion, a new international brand has been created and a global new brand power may be born too.

1.1 Rules of brand nuclear explosion power

International brands are not created under greenhouse conditions. The brands developed under such conditions could not withstand any adverse market situations, and cannot be developed into great brands. A good nurturing environment might not be able to develop an international brand. In contrast, in diversity a brilliant international brand is likely to be born. International brand is usually derived from great dreams, went through a tough journey of brand creation, precise brand strategizing, scientific brand designs and solid branding process to turn a perfect brand into the limelight.

We could divide the brand nuclear explosion into four stages, namely, brand dream stage (potential), brand interpretation stage (nuclear force), brand designing stage (movement) and brand reengineering stage (impact wave). Nuclear explosion power may be produced between any two stages, which means that the brand nuclear explosion power is not released at one go. Instead, it will occur continuously and many international brands benefit from such explosions to make great achievements.

1.2 DID principle of brand nuclear explosion

We have designed the DID principle to explain the operation rules of brand nuclear explosion power at the time of releasing new brands. The principles of brand nuclear explosion could be seen throughout the development of a brand, and scientific movement principles could be used to realize the powerful activities of brands in markets. All members of the brand organization shall understand this process so as to realize the overall organization effect for brand development (See Fig. 1-1).

Fig. 1-1 DID Principle

The brand nuclear explosion power include brand dream (D), brand interpretation (I), brand design (D) and brand reengineering (R). Each stage may generate brand nuclear explosion power, and the brand reengineering (R) is a recycling process (proposed in 2014).

Brand dream (D) – Brand dreaming stage (nuclear potential) -- The impacts from the birth of an international brand and great dreams.

Brand Interpretation (I) – Brand interpretation stage (nuclear force) -- impacts from brand interpretation, brand interpretation system, brand release and brand blue print.

Brand Design (D) – Brand designing stage (nuclear movement) -- The constant impact from the brand activity period.

Brand Reengineering (R) – Brand reengineering stage (nuclear shockwave) -- The powerful impact from the comprehensive reengineering of existing brands in the market.

The four stages of DID have shown the rules of the birth and evolvement of a powerful new brand from its birth to its forceful entry into market, the improvement of the market and the realization of brand achievements.

During the stage R (brand reengineering), the existing brand will be reorganized with new images and scientific flows during the major strategic changes of the brand, so as to enter into the market again with a boom, change the market territory, its market positioning and competitive edges.

The DID-R stage is applicable to all international brands. The R process forms a cycle, showing the miracles in the development of an international brand. The whole DID-R process includes four different brand nuclear explosion development rules.

2 Brand dream stage (nuclear potential)

All of human beings achievements begin from our dreams. Where there is a dream there is nuclear potential. Despite the fact that any new company is established based on dream, not all dreams could give birth to a brand. We could see from the international brands with great achievements, such as IBM, Google, HP, LV, Samsung, Panasonic, and Ferrari··· they are all started from dreams. Some brands, such as Coca-Cola, may have failed to make any achievements based on dreams initially, but during the development, numerous new brand founders joined and created an outstanding legends from brand dream.

It is an important emerging economic strategy for a country to research brand dreams, which could determine if a country could become a brand exporting country or if a country could be able to create a great number of international brands. To describe brand dreams more specifically, we have defined the brand founders as "New Generation Creators", who are the major force producing international brands centrally. The economic activities without such structure can hardly be called as entrepreneurship economy, which means whether the entrepreneurship activities are in the national economic structure of creative destruction.

The brand dreams are established on the large international brand enterprises owing brand industrial clusters. Such enterprise would promote new brands constantly to occupy the professional markets in different fields. Such enterprises include P&G, Coca-Cola, Microsoft, LV and etc. They have many professional brands in many divisions of different markets, which have occupied the leading positions of the markets. These enterprises would promote new brands constantly to accelerate the segmentation of the markets, use the new competitiveness of the new brands to compensate the aging of the old brands and use the emerging brand technologies to accelerate the internal metabolism of the company - brand elimination speed. Such brand dreams are built based on the strategic layout of the enterprise management.

2.1 Birth of great brand countries: new generation creators

Every company and every country is constantly improving and making every effort to become powerful brand or great bran country. We hereby put the focus on the new generation creators - the main force of brand economy should have similar characteristics and use the new generation creators to distinguish the entrepreneurship economic activities and entrepreneurs. Since the new generation creators are emerging and fresh, the owners of new dreams, they will use the original and wild creativity to complete the construction of brand dreams. The independent creation is vital, which is totally in line with the Schumpeter entrepreneurial spirit. We must distinguish and analyze the category of entrepreneurs.

The brand dreams of the new generation creators are not simple, which may be only rough outlines and simple frameworks, but most of the parts are grand. The brand creators are always trying to change something, such as making the fastest car in the world, the best pen in the world, the best cell phone, the calculators of next generation, the most comfortable environment to enjoy coffee or let people experience and adapt to a new lifestyle, or doing every effort to make a new product popular throughout the world.

Product categories are not seen in this process. In contrast, single product has been the first choice made by many brand founders. Even there is no new single product being created, some new business models created independently could become the source of brand dreams.

We will discuss the typical features of brand output countries as below. If the economy, policies, banks, loans, angel investments and finances of a country are made for the unprecedented dreams, the country may become a brand exporting country, otherwise, it will become a brand importing country.

Section V Brand Reengineering

The brands are born in a wild way of creation. This is the starting point of the brand dreams. The supports from brand investors, such as national policy inputs, angel investors or investment financial organizations, to the brand dreams of new generation creators could promote the births of international brands at the Class A brand stage in a central and massive way. Otherwise, it's hard to make international brands or brand countries.

2.2 Formation of brand nuclear potential

Brand nuclear potential is determined by the talented creativity of new generation creators; and the pursuit of the brand creators for brand excellence. Such pursuit may be rigor since the brand must be perfect, the best and unique in the world. Therefore, the new generation creators have amazing dreams and will make great efforts to make their dreams come true. They have used a special way of thinking – framework thinking.

The framework thinking is the overall definition to the brand dreams, and is a perfect picture made for the elements of brands at the strategic level, such as the brand future, brand development structure, brand market layout, brand expansion speed, and the perfect formula of brands. These blueprints will become the key routes for brand development and guide the actual implementation of brand practices in global market.

In brand exporting countries, the process from brand dreams to brand release would be easy, but in brand importing countries, it will be difficult. Improper brand economic environment may hinder the natural development of the international brands of a country.

2.3 How is an international brand born at the beginning?

The birth of an international brand is a difficult process, and the difficulties in this process are hardly known. People always see the glories of an international brand but not the stories behind it. Researching and interpreting the difficult process of brand birth and investigating the scientific rules for new generation creators to create brands will improve the scientific nature of the brand birth and realize the massive scale economic effect.

We have noted that reports and records may neglect the difficulties before the birth of brands. Since there are not any good examples of brand birth and scientific rules as well as any prequel of the brands, the entrepreneurs and emerging brand founders could not obtain valuable information. Therefore, the creation of new international brands is lagged behind. It's hard to see new brands and new dreams in the world. The raises of international brands are always considered as accidental phenomena and treated as individual cases or motivation stories that can hardly be known by people.

Walt Disney went bankrupt for seven times, and he had to wander with his luggage times and times again. Henry Ford also went bankrupt for many times, and was only a daydreaming engineer in the eyes of the others in his 40s. Enzo Ferrari has spent his whole life to make his dream of making the best and fastest race car in the world since 13 years old. The great genes of brands are rooted in the pursuits of the emerging creators to brand dreams. The ambitious brand dreams will never be changed, therefore, the brand legends are created one by one.

2.4 Nuclear explosion principles of band dreams (see Fig. 1-2)

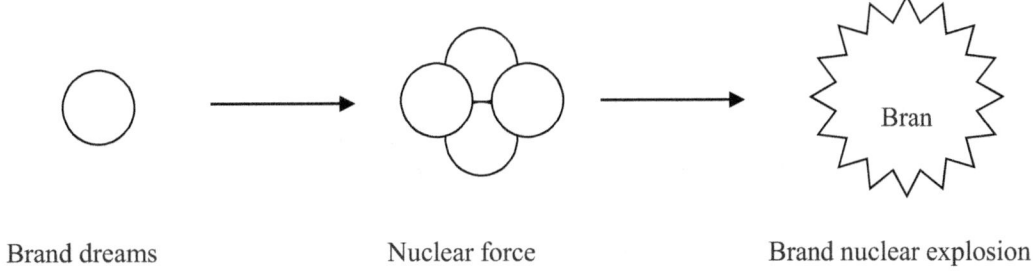

Brand dreams   Nuclear force   Brand nuclear explosion

Fig. 1-2 Nuclear Explosion Power Principles of Brand Dreams

The nuclear potential of brand dreams depends on the special nuclear forces of the brand dreams. Brand dreams will generate powerful nuclear force under certain conditions. Brand dreams will influence peoples through loves, careers, families, friends, colleagues and the society, or form powerful interaction in a group, so as to generate powerful adherence and gather all the strengths into the brand dreams.

When describing the interactions between nucleons, way of success for the interaction of nucleon is to establish a potential cell nucleus to form nucleon source, but not to consider all components of the nucleus. The creation process of a brand is on the contrary to the establishment of a company. Most enterprises will pay attention to the composition of departments and members during the establishment of such enterprises, for example, a trust worthy person shall be assigned to oversee the financial affairs of the company.

Obviously, the nucleon function of a brand is not like this. What has to be established by the brand founders is the nucleon center – nucleon energy source. To realize the rapid explosion effect based on the degree, energy and quality of brand dreams, the brand organization shall establish a backbone team for the brand dreams. The short-term financial performance and composition of departments are not the strategic center in early stages, and the investors are not the key points. The dream brand organizations will focus on the R&D of important technologies, the determination of core products and the powerful impacts of the brands at the time of entrance into the market.

We could understand that: the nuclear explosion power of brand dreams is the powerful energy gathered by absorbing great number of interacted nucleons, so as to generate sufficient explosive power. The brand will be born officially in this process, and the brand nuclear explosion power will be seen throughout the whole development of the brand so as to develop the brands into powerful international brands through evolution fission – evolution fission – re-evolution fission. It is an amazing fission and progressive process from the powerful brand dreams to the outstanding brand achievements.

3 Brand interpretation (nuclear force)

Brand interpretation consists of a standard process: brand interpretation system – brand releasing – brand blueprint.

From the enterprise brands and even the city brands in the market, we could see that most brands do not have any interpretation system, are not officially released and not even have any brand blueprints. This has led to the chaos of the brand and it does not have a uniform interpretation to outside. People do not know the degree to which the brand will develop, the investors will not be confident of the brand, and the company employees are unable to foresee the future of the brand. In such case, the brand is a failure in general, and the brand development route will be trapped in stage C, or may have the opportunity to enter into stage B, but can never enter into stage A.

The employees of many small and medium enterprises will introduce their enterprise by saying that "our company are in the field of certain industry" ... instead of introducing the company brands, since they know that their enterprises do not have any brands, or the impression of the brand is very vague and people does not know about the brands that are being introduced to. In such cases, they can only use the businesses of the companies to make introduction.

In fact, when a new brand has just entered into the market, it is very frail. Even if the company has operated for many years, the public and the market have no idea about the brand, leading to the unwillingness of the employees of the company to talk about the brand.

This is common on the global market. The acceptances to new brands are normally very low, and people will intensely doubt and resist to the brands that they have never heard. It is very hard to make the people or client accept a new brand, and this is fatal to the company in the early stage. However, not all enterprise founders could understand this rule. Therefore, many new companies would not be able to talk about brands or survive in the market and finally will fail after operating for a while.

There is a misconception: brand is a business for large enterprises, which requires a lot of funds, and the newly established small enterprises are not able to build their own brands. Obviously, this is a misunderstanding to brands. Most of the first Top 500 enterprises in the world were established during 1860 and 1921, and most of the next Top 500 enterprises were built after 1975. To our surprise, many world-famous international brands, such as Boeing, Panasonic, IBM, Dupont, HP, Google, Apple, Yahoo and Facebook were born in garages, basements, laboratory, dorms and retail stores. Many NASDAQ companies were established with the funds of less than US$1,000. Brand dreams with reasonable brand interpretation have conveyed the road of flourish and rapid development for international brands.

3.1 Nuclear explosion principles for brand interpretation (See Fig. 1-3)

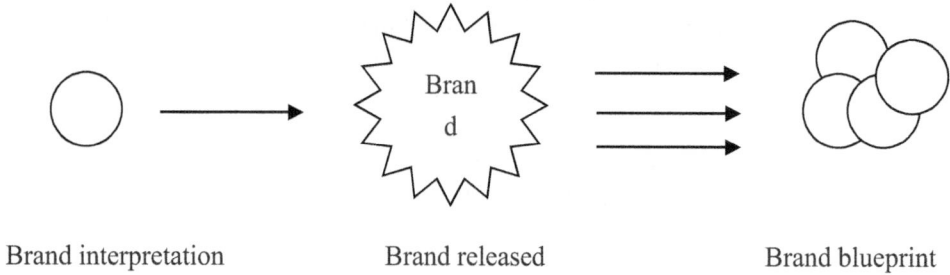

Brand interpretation　　　　Brand released　　　　Brand blueprint

Fig. 1-3 Nuclear Explosion Principles for Brand Releasing

We divide the brand interpretation into the following process "brand interpretation – brand released – brand blueprint" to reflect the impact of brand interpretation on market.

Brand Interpretation System – A rigorous and scientific brand interpretation system is the most important link before the brand releasing. It is also the supreme strategy, guiding thoughts and principles driving the brand development history, and the soul of an enterprise brand.

Brand Released – This is the announcement of the entry of brand into market, the official debut of the brand in the world, the great ceremony to lay a solid foundation for a powerful brand, and the fighting attitude and pledging ceremony of all employees of the brand organization.

Brand Blueprint – This is the major measure to announce the future development of the brand, the new future dream announced to the brand dealers, brand organization backbone members and all employees, and the high confidence level shown to investors, users and the public.

The establishment and practices of the brand interpretation are the key steps during the brand development. Even during the reengineering of an existing, the brand interpretation shall also be conducted. Any brand cluster shall also re-start this process when releasing new brands. Under the conditions of diversified global markets, and violent market competition, brand interpretation has become more important than ever before. We don't believe that a new or reengineered brand without interpretation could be able to withstand the market competition pressures. A newly established enterprise without brand interpretation can hardly convince the development dealers and clients, and the brands without brand interpretation can hardly achieve positive market performance after entering into the market.

3.2 Brand interpretation system determines the whole brand development process

People will deem the IPO of a company as a marking of the company's success. In fact, the releasing of the brand interpretation system is the most important moment of the development of a brand. The future of the brand is started from this moment, the legend of an international brand is founded at this moment, and the supporters of the brands and other entrepreneurs will always talk about this story.

What had happened during brand interpretation? Why so many enterprises in the world failed or why have the initial ambitions and dreams become bubbles or painful memories due to the shortage of brand interpretation system?

Brand interpretation is the official explanation to a brand, or what is this brand, what is the definition of the brand, what is the slogan of the brand, what is the mission of the brand, what is the development target of the brand, what are the most important principles during the brand development, what is the stand of the brand, what is the origin of the brand, what are the brand stories, what is the organization structure of the brand, what is the culture of the brand organization, and what shall be forbidden during brand communication. The structural framework of the brand has determined the future directions of the brand and the development strategies, presentation methods and activities of the brand.

The brand interpretation system is the supreme strategy for the entire brand, and the official interpretation center, thought center, guiding center and principle center leading to the development of the whole brand. During commercial brand planning, people will always pay attention to the application of brand concept, and define a brand by determining the concept of the brand, but neglect the establishment of the whole brand interpretation system. We have found that: many enterprise brands or city brands are established with great efforts and huge funds, but the complete and uniform brand interpretation system is lacking.

In future practices, people will find that the brand interpretation and the brand activities are in chaos, there is no central thought with great potential to guide the development of the brand, the slogans of the brand are constantly changing, and there is no uniform center for the employees of the organization, leading to the losing of cohesion of the brand. If the presentation of a brand is change constantly, unconsciously, people will find that the brand force is dispersed, that the brand dreams have lost their glories, the wills of the leading group of the company will perish, the employees' expectations to the future of the brand will be lost, and the issues related to the brand development could not be solved.

3.3 The irreplaceable functions of the brand interpretation system

We have proposed that the brand interpretation system is the core of the whole development of a brand, and we will further analyze the brand interpretation system hereafter.

The rigorous and scientific brand interpretation system is the most important link before the brand is released, the accurate official information used to interpret the brand internally and externally, the basic strategic keynotes determined for the brand, and the general thought guiding the rapid development of the brand in the future. The brand interpretation system includes the brand definition, brand slogan, brand missions, brand stories, brand spirits and brand cultures. It is the core of the whole brand identification manual, and the guide at the brand strategic and spirit levels, which could not be replaced.

Se should note that the CI (corporate identify system) is not the core of brand interpretation system, and it is only the expansion of brand interpretation, the important part of the brand identification manual, and a standard identification form after establishing the core contents of the brand interpretation system. It is very important to take note of this point. It is very common to use CI to replace the brand interpretation system, and the common methods are to change a name, change a logo or release a CI and it is wrongly being interpreted that this is everything that the brand system has.

In fact, the difference between the brand interpretation system and CI is that the brand interpretation system has defined the general brand thought at the strategic and spiritual levels for the far future, which will be used throughout the life of the brand during a long brand development period. It is defined by the enterprise management and the brand technical experts at the highest level and its height, depth and durability could determine the life of the brand, which shall be strictly implemented by the whole brand organization, since any negligence may lead to the brand failure.

In addition, the brand interpretation system does not need to be the complete brand documents, but only the structural strategic description of the brand initially, and the initial description to the definition, mission and duties of the brand. After releasing the brand, the system could be expanded continuously based on the core of the brand interpretation so as to complete the whole brand interpretation system. The new chief brand officers shall fully responsible for the brand interpretation system, and some bold chief brand officers may develop the brand interpretation system to a higher level and they may further improve the brand interpretation system to provide the brand with more powerful vitality.

3.4 Nuclear explosion power of brand releasing

The brand releasing is not only to hold a press conference to announce the official birth of a new brand to the world. After the birth of the brand (generally, a brand may be born in a small group or scope), a careful preparation shall be made for the official debut of the brand. Even for brands operated by brand clusters or reengineered brands, special attentions shall be paid to the brand releasing process.

The brand releasing is a cautious matter. The official release of a brand marks the official birth of a new brand in the world. Before the official releasing of a brand, many works shall be done to ensure the successful releasing.

Despite the fact that many international brands are born in unknown environments and have become world famous in many years, this situation has changed today and in the future. Especially in the age of modern social media, the silent appearance of a brand means that the brand has lost the best time to enter into the market from its birth date, and in most cases, the silent brands will disappear silently.

By contrast, the new rich persons are always the new generation creators who are ambitious and are not even able to hold brand press conferences but dare to pursue the title of No.1 in the world. The stories of Google whose slogans used to be the "Next Generation Searching Engine" and "Best Image Searching Engine in the World" may motivate the new creator's generation after generation. Those new generation creators who are trying to change the world and have the belief that the world could be changed even there is only one or two persons are using their unique ways to show their ambitions and the vigorous brand future. The brand releasing means profound future to them. Although they would use different brand releasing forms, the brand releasing is significance to them and to the whole world.

3.5 Brand releasing is the first nuclear explosion of the brand organization

If the nuclear explosion power of the brand dream is called nuclear potential, the official releasing of the brand is the nuclear force, which means the first important nuclear fission of the entire brand organization and the brand will enter into the market with faster and more powerful energy. With proper preparation, a great brand press conference will become an active attack to the target market, and the powerful impact wave of the brand will provide sufficient market capacity for the brand. Otherwise, the market will not accept the new brand for a long period, leading to unnecessary workloads and economic losses in the early stage of the operation of the company.

Since all segments of the global market have been saturated, the establishment of the companies with Class C and B brand capacity will face tedious the market issues and the brand benefits could not be achieved in a short term for new brands, so the brand releasing and the following brand blueprint have become more important.

According to our comparisons in many aspects, whether it is the official debut for a brand or the market launching conducted by the domestic brand dealers of the brand organization, brand press conference will be more important and have better effects than any ordinary activities related to the business opening, new product marketing, experience meeting and exhibitions, depending on the news that could make a brand be important based on the concentrated explosion.

No matter isn't the global market, national market or the domestic market, brand press conferences are of great value to the market entry, brand influence, short-term sales and long term brand operation. The effects of the conferences that are supported with music, surroundings and ambience are of significance to sales achievements, which could change the many-to-many market development into the one-to-many sales. In brand releasing experiments, we have found that this method is widely accepted by the brand operators and dealers with long-term sights, who would like to use such ceremonies to solve the marketing lunching issues completely.

3.6 Binding of brand press conferences and market launching

Brand press conferences will generate intense media effects and market reaction, which may be an important opportunity for the centralized experiences for brand channel partners, dealers, strategic partners and brand consumption opinion leaders though voices, texts, important figures, images and ambience. The well-organized brand press conferences could be able to achieve the rapid launching target of the brand after entering into the market. Given the limited brand distribution intentions and mainstream brand consumers, the recognition to new brands is low, and the weight of brand press conferences will be improved constantly. If possible, emerging enterprises and new brands would like to use brand press conferences.

We should note that the brand press conferences must be strictly bonded with the market launching activities. If the salespersons could not understand the significance and functions of brand press conferences, the effects of attracting investments and developing markets for new brands will be compromised greatly. In our brand releasing experiments, we have found that the market sales will be far lower than expectations due to the poor cooperation of the sales team. In such case, the market benefits of brand press conferences have not been totally released. To realize the best sales performance, the most important things to be done include the preparation and training of the conferences, the on-site management and the post-conference following up. All of the enterprise managements and salespersons shall make every effort to achieve great market performances.

From the very beginning of the press conference, the market personnel shall focus on developing the early dealers and clients, and implementing the first wave of impact on the market with invitations to the conference. Especially, at the early stage for a new brand entering into the market, given the low acceptance, weak brand premium and incomplete standardization of the brand management, holding press conference will greatly improve the confidences of the first dealers and partners, so as to complete the impact on the market in a more powerful way.

If it is impossible to hold large-scaled brand press conference, the birth of the new brand shall be announced to the public officially in a simple and low-cost way, such as brand news. We have noticed that, at the early stage of entering into the market, many brands are not well prepared, leading to the low confidences of dealers and clients to the brand, who are reluctant to place orders. Although companies are making every effort to recruit more marketing and sales personnel so as to have more people to generate sales, but the overall sales performance of the company is still not as good as expected.

Section V Brand Reengineering

The new markets in the future will be occupied by powerful brands. The brands that have entered into the market in a powerful way will have the highest capability. Especially, the dealers who are looking for brands will prefer powerful brands, large orders and rapid payments will be the direct benefits of brand press conferences.

3.7 Nuclear explosion effect of brand releasing

Brand releasing is an organization and preparation process which shall be carefully planned, meticulously managed, strategically coordinated, and generally controlled, so as to realize the strongest nuclear force. Therefore, to achieve the best effect of brand releasing, it is necessary to conduct massive media warming up and warming up among the target consumers of the brand during the countdown to release. It is the target of the brand press conference to make the brand popular before releasing, so as to draw attentions and intended orders.

The releasing of Olympic Games is as long as 10 years. Bidding for Olympics could make a city or a country active, and the expectations of the people to the Olympics will become the nuclear potential of the brand. After a city has become the hosting city of Olympics, a series of related activities will be held in the following 8 years at the municipal, national or even international level, so as to motivate the enthusiasm of a country or the world and generate powerful nuclear potential.

Finally, the grand opening ceremony of the Olympics will become the nuclear explosion center for media, public, countries, and societies. The event that only lasted for a couple of weeks will draw all attentions from the world.

Similarly, the holding of brand press conferences is a necessary and important strategic action, it is a grand ceremony that is important during the birth of a brand, marking the official releasing of the brand to the world, and the products bearing the brand will be accepted by the world. The releasing of the *Global Brand Announcement* is the solemn declaration and undertaking of a brand to the world, and the assault horn for the brand to enter into the market. Any company shall not neglect the functions of such ceremony at any time.

3.8 Key strategies for brand releasing

See Fig. 1-4 for the complete brand releasing process

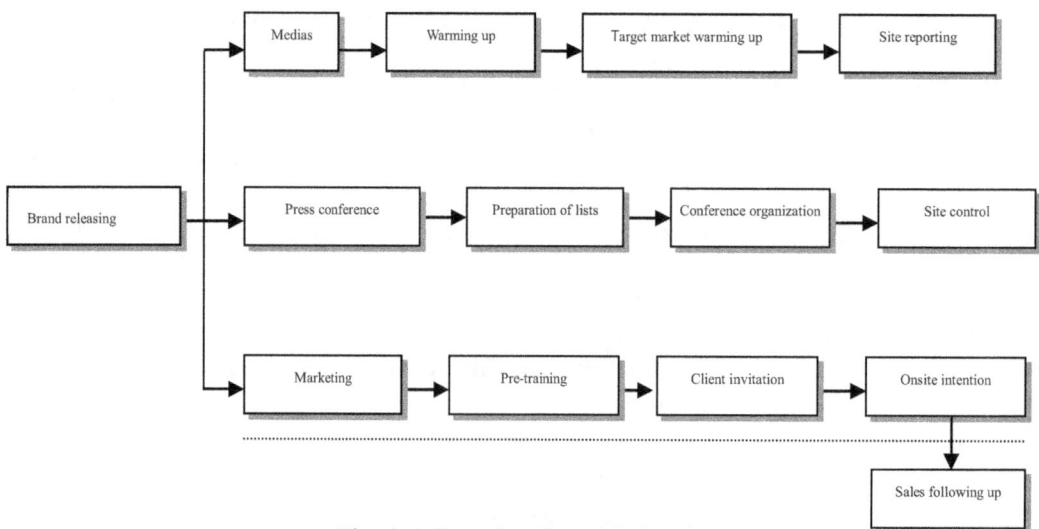

Fig. 1-4 Complete Brand Releasing Process

A complete brand releasing process includes three core aspects: 1. Media; 2. Press conference; and 3. Market sales. The works in these three aspects shall be conducted at the same time. A checklist shall be designed for the brand press conference and the press conference shall be conducted according to these lists which includes all the programs during the conference. The related works shall adhere to these lists strictly to ensure the success of the press conference.

Media: Before holding the brand press conference, the massive media warming up shall be conducted for at least one to three months, including but not limited to online media, print media and mobile media. Then the massive warming up shall be conducted in the targeted markets, including the DM leaflets of the press conference, the brand guessing activities and the countdown advertising of the brand releasing. The key professional targeted markets shall be focused on to conduct accurate and intense promotions.

The onsite media reporting is also an important link. The specific media reporters shall be invited, the media columns shall be opened, news centers shall be established on the site of the conference and the news officer shall be assigned. All of the media interviews shall be diverted to the news officer and the other employees shall not accept any interviews. This is especially important for listed companies. Live broadcasting, onsite reporting or onsite interviews could be used to improve the communication effects of the onsite reporting.

Press conference: The preparation committee of the brand press conference shall be established according to the needs, and corresponding working teams shall be built, such as administrative team, secretary team, security team and logistic team. The tasks and responsible persons of these working teams shall be assigned, and working team meetings shall be held periodically. The conference organization is an important rehearsal, during which the works related to the site investigation, routing map, desk position map, manuscripts of the conference's host, conference protocols and site arrangements shall be completed and the actual duration of such works shall be breakdown into minutes or even seconds.

According to the actual needs, more professional working teams shall be established and the related responsible person shall be assigned, such as the sign-in team, onsite news team, prop team, protocol team, display arrangement team and shooting team. A successful press conference is based on the cooperation among the working teams and the efforts made by the general commander. If the conference is well prepared, the works are clearly defined and the rehearsal is properly conducted, the self-adapt system management could be realized through the orderly engagement of the time points.

3.9 Important marketing strategies for brand releasing

The market sales shall be conducted at the same time with the press conference. All salespersons shall see the press conference as an important sales opportunity, on which sales leads could be mined, the investment attracting and sales tasks could be completed and the enterprise brand could be launched. Any market development or sales personnel missing or neglecting such opportunity shall be eliminated. The persons expressing negative opinions and doubting the releasing effects before and after the conference shall not be allowed to join the sales team. This is very important, since high morale is the only way to guarantee the success of the conference.

The training provided to the marketing and sales personnel before the conference is very important. The training shall focus on the questions that may be asked by dealers and potential partners in terms of the launched products, distribution policies and brand blueprint, so as to be familiarized with the questions and standardized the answers to them. PADS scientific analysis and brand comparison and analysis technologies could be helpful to ensure the effects of the training. The unrelated trainings shall be limited. The marketing and sales personnel shall be able to skillfully answer any questions asked by the visitor onsite and inform the clients of important information according to the brand interpretation system and brand blueprint strictly. This will guide the clients' thinking direction and help the clients to make wise decisions.

SECTION V BRAND REENGINEERING

After completing rigorous training, the important work to be done by marketing and sales personnel shall be inviting potential dealers, clients and brand consumption leaders to participate in the brand press conference; screening for potential clients through online searching, online application and the industrial society lists; send the *Brand Press Conference Invitations* to them; strictly register the invited list; and send out the official *Invitation Card for the Brand Press Conference.*

Another important link is to distribute the electronic or printed *DM Invitation Leaflets for Brand Press Conference* to the distribution organization and the key client groups in the targeted markets, which could be distributed by Miss Etiquettes, temporary employees, online part-time workers and partners through different channels and media in various places. By sending out a few hundred thousand to a few millions of DM leaflets there will be significant brand promotion effect. The brand organization shall register all persons taking part in the press conference by themselves, and determine if such persons shall take part in online press conference or onsite conference. The exquisite electronic or printed invitation cards could show respect to the participants.

3.10 The most important asset in brand releasing

On the site of press conference, there is a very important link – prepare the electronic or printed *Brand Distribution Interest Form* and the first edition of the brand handbook for each participant and pens shall be prepared for the offline press conference. This is very important since it is the core of the press conference. The most important function of brand press conference is to collect a large amount of order intentions, and the most valuable part of the conference is that it could collect a huge number of sales leads. For those that have been signed the contract of interest before the conference, the official signing ceremony may be held on the site of the conference with the brand dealer representatives.

After the press conference, the marketing and sales personnel shall contact or visit the interested dealers (partners or clients) found on the sales leads list to convey these leads into transactions. Generally, the lists will become invalid in two months after the press conference. Therefore, the market progress management is the key point to follow the lists.

In addition, it is important to take photos and videos of the conference, since such videos and photos are the most powerful evidences showing the development of the brand, and the supporting information indicating the great forward-looking capability of the brand. In the future client expansion, these videos; photos and media reports of the press conference are the most important marketing weapon to convince potential clients.

The new enterprises without brand press conferences may not have convincing promotion materials, leading to difficulties in developing markets and low client's confidence. The salespersons of such enterprises will spend a lot of time and money in looking for sales leads or convincing clients. In such cases, the market acceptance is low and most dealers (clients) may feel not confident or unsecure about the brands.

3.11 Brand blueprint: what is the future for the brands

In addition to the announcement of the birth of a new brand, one other important information shall be published by the enterprise during the brand release – the brand blueprint. The purpose of the brand blueprint is to tell everyone who is inside and outside the brand organization, including the employees of the organization, the interested dealers and the future consumers about the future of the brand.

In addition to the brand investors, shareholders and members of director board, all members of the brand organization would like to know the future of the brand, including the employees, brand dealers, brand user groups, news media and everyone that is concern about the development of the brand.

According to the nine-month theory we have proposed, most new companies will see shareholder conflicts, financial problems and leaving of employees in three months after the establishment, which means that the companies have entered into the control-losing stage. However, in most cases, the leaders of such companies will not be aware of such situation, and will not consider it as a serious control-losing, the companies are developing in a negative way. In six months after the establishment of the company, many shareholders and employees will leave the company, and in nine months, more than half of the new enterprises will be shut down and the brand dreams will end.

The major cause of the above situation is that people could not get the answers they want, or the future of the brand. This is because the brand leaders have failed to produce the brand blueprints to tell the stakeholders of the brand organizations about the future of the brand, the prospect of the companies, and the methods to realize the flourishing of the brand, the confidences of dealers, partners and employees will be lost.

When the founders of the brands (or the chief brand officers) are unable to answer this question, the situation will be relatively bad, since the employees will not have targets, could not see the prospects of the brands and could not identify their developments in the brands. Therefore, this terrible condition will obstruct the development of the companies. Potential dealers and clients may have the same attitude, and they will carefully observe the birth of a new brand, since they care more about the long-term benefits from the cooperation with the brand, the prospect of the brand, and the survival rate of the brand. With such concerns, they will not feel safe about the brand and will like to wait and be reluctant to place orders.

3.12 Proposed structure for brand blueprint

Brand blueprint is the overall planning of a brand, which could tell everyone inside and outside the organization, including media, interested dealers, partners, potential clients and future employees about the future of the brand and how to complete the brand construction and realize the dream in a scientific way.

We have designed a set of standard brand blueprint structures (see Fig. 1-5), which are applicable to any organizations or enterprises.

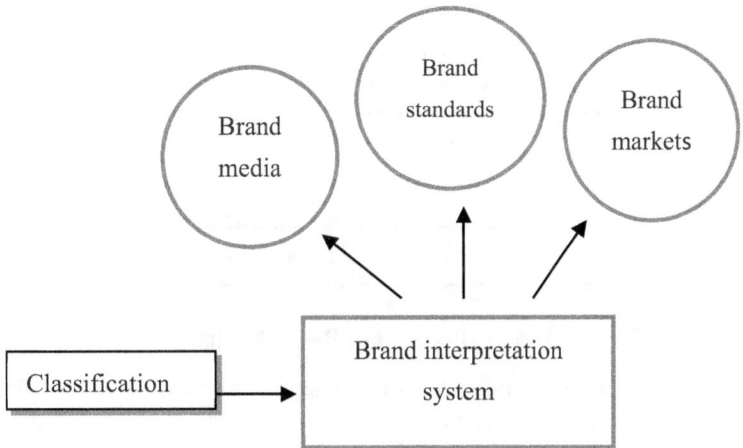

Fig. 1-5 Brand Blueprint Structure Recommended by DID Scientific Principles

The recommended brand blueprint structure with the brand interpretation system as the center to define brand classification has three parts, namely, brand media, brand standards and brand markets.

The brand interpretation system may be a constantly improving dynamic system, which has defined the basic brand interpretation keynotes, and enterprise cultures, brand identification documents, principles documents may be added.

The brand classification is the accurate classification of brands, and the enterprise brands could be distributed into one or more brand classification combinations according to the brand classification techniques. In addition, to identify the brand strategic routes, a more important purpose of brand classification is to identify the category that a brand belongs to, such as professional brands, trustful brands, modern brands or international brands. The clear brand classification could effectively help the enterprise employees, dealers and clients to understand the key strategic development of a brand.

If the leader or employees of a company do not know the category of their brand, the presentations and activities related to the brand will be in chaos. The enterprise and employees will not know which advantages the brand has and shall be developed. The company will have to spend a lot of time and money on searching for the brand development path. It is common to see indecisive brand strategies and ever changing brand planning in the early stage of a company.

To the interested dealers, potential partners and clients, and the new talents and employees in the future, the brand blueprint is the way to arouse everyone's hopes for the future, which could scientifically convey the development road of the brand and provide people with great confidence. Especially, for the brands requiring dealers, clients and investors, the brand blueprint could describe everyone's hopes and expectations for the future.

In the past, Edward Disney made a picture of the Disney Land to tell people how to make his splendid dream came true on a barren land. In the past, a world map is used by CNN to mark the places of its CNN reporter station in the world, and today, CNN has established a news reporting network throughout the world. Today, people will use 3D and 4D technologies to simulate the possible business projects in the future, and the real estate developers and interiors designers could use building models and 3D effect drawings to illustrate the actual image in the future. For any brands, the methods of illustration and realizing the future of the brand is the key to motivate everyone to fight for it, invest in it and make decisions about it.

3.13 Brand media

Brand media are the communication strategy based on the modern media and new media. Brand communication is the major form of the operation of brand media.

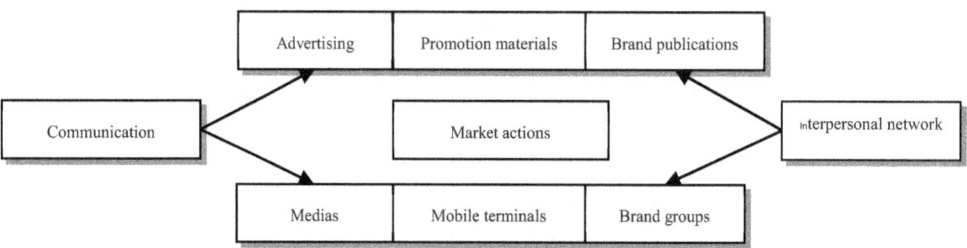

Fig. 1-6 Brand Blueprint of Brand Media

The first key point for brand communication is to make brand market action plans to drive the market with effective market activities (actions) to promote concentrated contract signing. In the early stage of an enterprise, the brand market actions with accurate targets and action powers are of great significance to the entry of the brand into market, or the brand communication shall be targeted, specific, challenging and funny and could be able to influence the market and the potential targeted groups. All brand communications shall be conducted based on brand market actions.

The second key point is the physical communication media: Massive communication in large areas shall be conducted through brand advertising (TV, video, Internet, and newspaper advertisements), brand promotion materials (brand handbook, DM brochures, brand posters and consumer guides), and brand magazines (brand user reports, brand dealer reports and brand employee hierarchy reports). Enterprises shall select communication methods according to costs and other conditions. Making brand magazines is an important communication aspect. Especially, in the early stage of an enterprise, specific personnel shall be assigned to make specific communication contents for all potential dealers, investors and clients to inform them of various dynamic massages, and help the targeted groups to make decisions.

The third key point is the extensive media communication: Enterprises shall assign specific personnel to make and communicate contents for media communication (broadcasting the brand news through Internet, newspapers, TV, websites, syndicated columns and professional investment publications), mobile terminals (official micro medias, micro E-publications, micro interaction, micro leadership communication, micro professional market communication, micro stories, and micro fans management), brand user groups (specific brand interest groups, the intense communication through network and user concentrated areas, and brand consumer education), so as to implement content marketing.

The core of brand communication is in fact, interpersonal communication or establishing intensified interpersonal communication network and promote through words of mouth. According to the three-layer principle of brand communication, the contracted brand communication organizations and the brand communication organization shall conduct the intensified and accurate communication activities around the first level (origin level, including the word origin and planning origin) and the second level (soft chain level, including the soft communication chains and guiding expansion chains), so as to fully activate the effect of the third level (the self-respond, self-adapt and we media expansion communication).

Interpersonal network is the largest and most important communication network in the world. Dealers and clients under certain conditions or backgrounds have their own groups, interests, professional fields and networks. Therefore, the professional media communication conducted on the specific interpersonal network is the best communication method with the highest cost-efficiency. Traditional advertising is to screen possible interested clients among the public without focus, and most of the costs have been wasted on the public who are not interested. In contrast, the modern communication focuses on accurate communication and intensified communication plans to get regular consumers, which double up the effect.

3.14 Brand construction plans in brand standardization

Brand standardization means Brand + Management Standardization, which requires the planning for brand construction period and the guidance on execution methods (see Fig. 1-6).

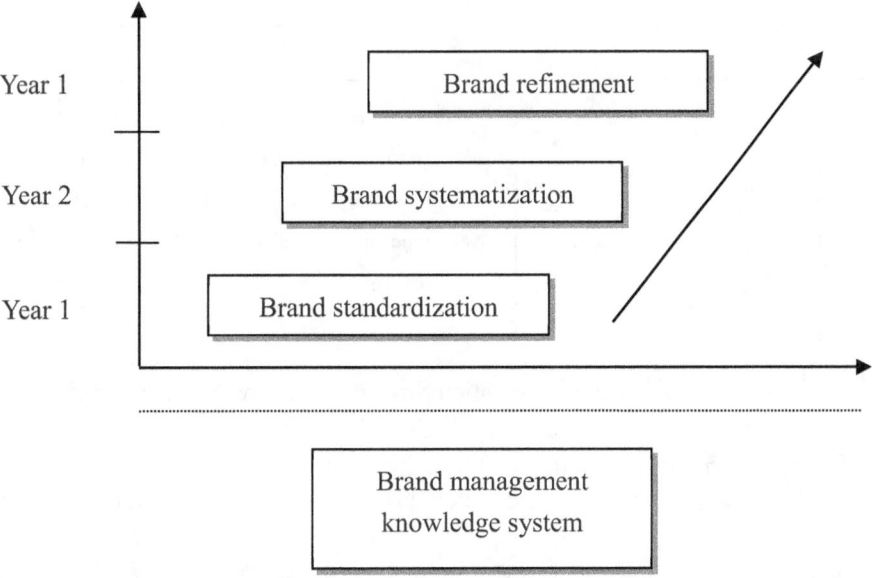

Fig 1-6 Time Blueprint for Brand Standardization

Since a long period is required for a new brand to construct before entering into the market, we set the brand construction period as three years. In the first year, the brand standardization shall be completed (standardize manuals, documents and management of the brand). In the second year, the brand systematization shall be completed (the brand organization shall develop a high-efficiency management system) and in the third year the brand refinement shall be completed (the brand organization shall develop vertically to complete the coverage of the brand in the market).

Three years to complete the brand construction is an ideal brand development process. If this period is too long or too short, it will be hard to complete the overall construction of the brand and the brand can hardly be accepted by people. However, it is reasonable to complete the construction process in three years to focus on different works in each year so as to implement the frameworks and the construction.

Special note: The completion of brand construction is based on the dynamic knowledge system for brand management or the dynamic knowledge management shall be used as the basis for the whole brand system construction. In the age of knowledge economy, knowledge is the most valuable asset. It is a major reform for modern companies and future enterprises to rapidly collect, analyze, and scientifically use the dynamic knowledge inside and outside the brand organization in terms of brand management method. Especially, the future enterprises have only one special management method – only the companies operated with dynamic management knowledge system can survive in the global market.

3.15 Implementation of brand technologies in brand standardization

We have proposed that the brand standardization is Brand + Management Standardization, and a series of brand technologies shall be used, including scientific brand principles, brand technologies and brand document systems.

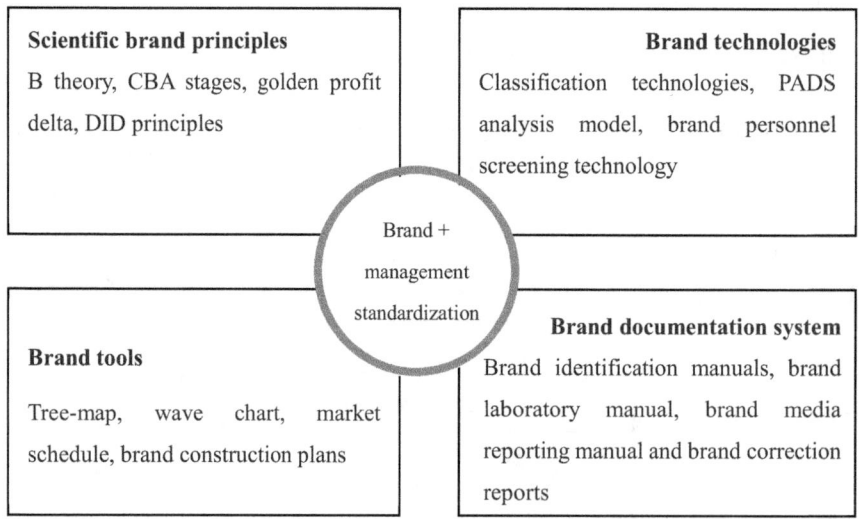

Fig. 1-6 Technology Implementation Structure of Brand Standardization

The scientific brand principles include B theory, the CBA stage division of brand, the golden delta of brand profits, and DID scientific principles, which have formed the basic scientific rules of the brand science.

Brand technologies include brand classification technology, PADS scientific analysis model, brand personnel screening technology, brand training technology, brand construction technology, brand communication technology and brand laboratory technology. We think the development of enterprise brands will fully enter into the age of brand technologies, and the brand technologies will be more important than ever before.

Brand tools include tree maps, weave maps, market schedules, brand construction plans, proposals, and a series of other diagrams, forms and standard copywriting. As a series of open-source procedures, brand tools will be constantly invented and developed.

Brand documentation system is a management system containing various handbooks and documents. Any enterprises with effective brand management shall have clear, detailed and standardized handbooks and documents to specify the details of the brand and guide and supervise the using and management processes of the brand in a scientific way.

The brand documentation system may include all handbooks to be used by a company, including but not limited to brand identity handbooks, brand laboratory handbooks, brand media reporting handbooks, brand channel handbooks, brand terminal handbooks, and brand users' handbooks. Brand correction reports are special management documents, which shall be used for brand supervision and error correction during the brand construction period.

Different from the previous standardization of the ISO standards to various works, the brand standardization is to achieve the optimized result so as to make standards.

During brand standardization, we have designed and used a series new scientific brand principles, technologies and tools. As a new dynamic knowledge management system, many technologies, tools and methods are unprecedented, and the old tools used before, such as PDCM quality cycle could not be used in brand standardization, since such tools may lead to serious management mistakes.

3.16 Blueprint of brand marketization (Fig. 1-7)

The purpose of brand marketization is to establish specific market structure according to the key targets of market construction.

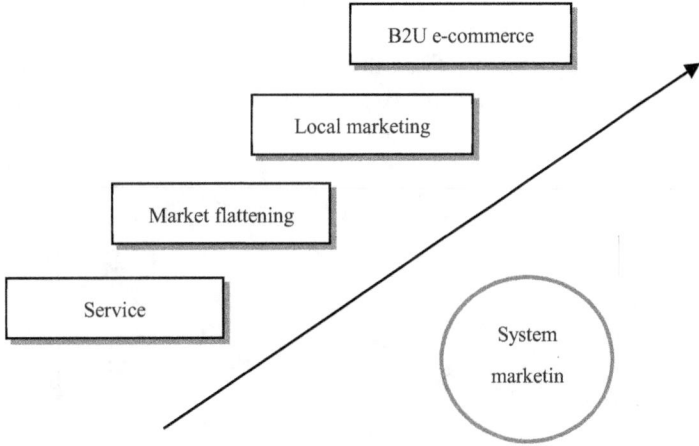

Fig. 1-7 Blueprint of Brand Marketization

The brand marketization includes the market conception model guided by enterprises. The enterprises shall maintain novelty to meet the latest market trend and create new market models to ensure forward-looking and systematic nature.

The typical market models include: service marketing (establishing the marketing flow with the service flows before, during and after sales), market flattening (channel sinking, market management structure with the markets at municipal, and township levels as the center, and prepositioning of market development and services), domestic marketing (marketing network established with the domestic marketing as the main body), B2U e-commerce (brand to user e-commerce). Brand organization shall design a market conception structure suitable to its own advantages according to the industrial features and encourage the creation of new models.

One of the typical methods to create brand is to create new market structures and marketing modes. In the past years, in different market segments, some cutting-edge enterprises or management (market) researchers have created a series of unprecedented emerging models, which have been used as the key methods for brand expansion, such as the chain operation model of Mc Donald's, the no-store retailing model of Dale, the central disk model of the Chinese liquor industry and the online presales model of MI.

The final target of brand marketization is to complete the systematic sales. Today's market will not depend on the sales model focusing on certain salesperson or department. Selling is a complete system, which all employees shall be participate in, brand department, marketing department, sales department and client department.

The typical systematic sales is to carefully arrange the whole network by establishing different task teams for Facebook, Twitter, YouTube, search engine bidding and online games to combine various links organically such as professional labor division, cooperative works, making calls, visiting, activities, donations, news communications and video making, so as to establish a systematic sales network. Each social element and task system will try to promote sales, and we shall not neglect the outstanding contributions made by such working teams. The future sales must be conducted through the cooperation and overall marketing of a team and a brand organization. The systematic sales capability is the most important factor to evaluate the brand sales capability in the future.

4 Brand design (nuclear movement)

Brand design (See Fig. 1-7) is an important stage that may be easily neglected. A common problem is that an enterprise may request the marketing department and sales department to be responsible for the overall brand market action, and the market development of the brand will become the work of one division of the marketing (sales) department. The other departments of the brand organization, such as R&D, quality, production and service departments, will not care about the brand and nobody will contribute to the brand or be responsible for the brand.

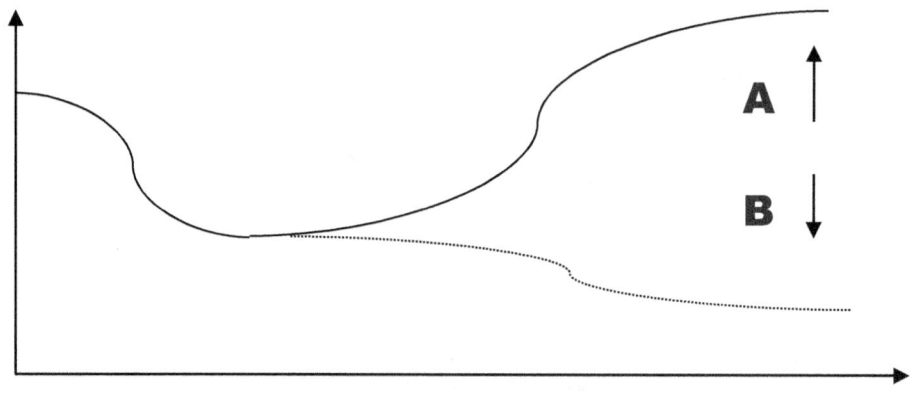

Fig. 1-7 Roles of Brand Design

After holding the brand press conference, the brand will officially enter into the market, but the attention and influence of the brand will see reduction to the end B for a certain period. If the enterprise could not take certain measures to improve the influence of the brand, it will not generate premiums in the market and most brands will not be able to recover after this setback. We have observed many brands and found that, without good brand marketing design, the brand will return to the situation of using performance price ratio, sales promotion activities and discounts to attract clients, and the brand that entered into the market powerfully at the initial stage will start see weakening sales numbers soon. The brand effect will lose its limelight.

In theory B, we emphasize that the harsh requirements of consumers could only be met in the brand enterprises with medium capability, and the brands in Class C or Class B stages will face fierce market competition and could combine various links such as products, services and sales policies to attract clients. In a homogeneous market competition environment, such condition will worsen, and the brand will become meaningless. We have found in the market that most new brands can easily fall into the bottom of B and the brand will become invisible. The emerging enterprises shall pay special attention to this.

The ideal situation is such that the brand could be improved to the bottom of A, through reasonable brand designing after the releasing. This is to constantly appreciate the brand. In the actual brand operation, brand is not only the result of long-term operation. More importantly, the brand is the result of effective design. The brand shall be responsible for long-term development and the short term market actions shall be responsible for short-term businesses. Only when the long term and short term targets are combined, strategies and executions are synchronized, the brand will then have profound influence and promote the achievement of short term sales targets. This is why the brand design nuclear explosion power is proposed.

4.1 Nuclear explosion principles for brand design

The nuclear explosion principles for brand design are expressed with the brand tool – wave chart (See Fig. 1-8).

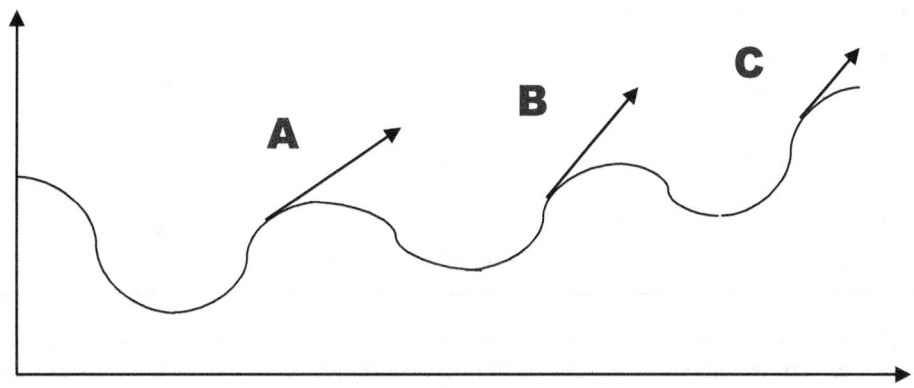

Fig. 1-8 Nuclear Explosion Principles for Brand Design

Sea tide law (wave chart) is a tool we invented and used for brand market design, which could define the multiple market promotion designs after the brand had entered into the market.

After the entry of brand into the market, the promotion strategies have significant functions in the operation. Effective and scientific designs shall be used to take brand market actions to draw staffs, funds, resources and the attentions of the users to the brand. This enables the brand to generate powerful influences from time to time and attract a group of regular users, so as to let the whole market accept the brand as soon as possible.

We call this process as the nuclear explosion power of brand design. In fact, this brand operation process is the reason we promote the brand nuclear explosion. For every three months or a certain period of time, the brand organization shall make every effort to design a major action that is able to influence the whole targeted market. Through massive brand news warm up and projection, gathering all the strengths in the brand organization and executing the nuclear explosion continually to form strong and impactful influence on the market and enter into it rapidly.. This movement is also called nuclear movement, during which the brand organization will rapidly occupy the leading position in the market with its great power.

At the early stage of starting a business, the nuclear explosion of brand design is almost the only correct brand tactics. Therefore, from the moment of the establishment of the brand organization, such nuclear movement shall be clearly defined and the whole organization shall make every effort to realize it. Correspondingly, the whole brand organization shall establish a series of nimble management methods for the rapid market operations and use some special strategies.

4.2 Designing capability of brand market

The brand designing capability is represented by the peak pulling design in the brand wave chart. Massive brand actions with great influences shall be used to draw attentions to the brand. For the market movement process without brand designs, after the release of brand activities, the attentions of the market will decrease in a short period of time. There will also be a drop in the enthusiasm of the company's employees. If the development of a company is too quiet, the users in the market may feel weak and the employees will feel bored.

Therefore, exciting and innovative activities shall be organized at a regular interval to gather the power of everyone. Each peak promotion and the peak pulling in each brand market action could represent high-level brand designs. Such actions could push the brand to a peak with rapid expansion and development. Such active brand organization will be the hot spot in the market and caught the attentions of everyone. The company will surpass the norm and generate huge turn over. We recommend that the interval of market actions shall be 3 months, wave by wave nuclear explosion on the market is the proud and glory moment which everyone will look forward to. The brand will be totally different due to the dream brand action design, it will surpass the norm and the brand will appreciate greatly.

The brand designs are reflected through the designs of market actions and service programs, and the naming of such actions may include: "blue storm", "green shield plan", "quality goods in stores", "ticket gift pack" and "well wishes from far", "golden wrench project" and also for a series of actions that are large in scales, have great influences, huge market impacts and strong appeals. These actions shall reflect the powerful brand styles and executed with huge budgets, lots of verve and large actions. In the past, there might be many market activities, but such activities may not have powerful impacts on the market. This is due to weak influence, boring contents, not able to create a profound influence on the market and the market events could not come together with the company's employees.

We should note that management activities, sales activities and social welfare activities could be comprehensively reflected in brand designs, which requires the implementation by the whole enterprise. As much as possible to include all employees and use the brand market actions with large influences to combine various social resources and develop the brand to a higher development platform. The brand action without the participation of all employees is bound to fail. The brand leaders shall authorize the brand actions fully, emphasize on the efficiency of implementation and effectiveness of executions.

Commercial sponsorship activities shall be separated from the brand market actions. Brand market actions shall focus on brand operations to improve the attention rate, which are the most important key actions in the whole organization. The advertisement shall also match with the market actions, with the market actions as the focus, to generate sufficient stimulation to the market. It is unscientific to only release product advertisement, which will cause competition at the product level, and could not lead to the appreciation of the brand.

5 Brand reengineering (nuclear impact wave)

When an existing brand has begun aging, or a mature brand has determined to reshuffle the market, the brand reengineering actions will play an important role. The brand reengineering actions of the enterprise will once again release the energy of the brand organization andmotivate everyone. The reallocation of market territory will definethe enterprise entering into its' second start up, third start up and fourth start up.

The core of brand reengineering is that the enterprise will decide to implement the DID stage again. Brand reengineering is not as simple as changing the name, the logo, or holding a press conference. The brand reengineering has more a profound meaning and it has to be a major reform of the whole brand organization.

The flow reengineering is the core of the brand reengineering. To meet the new competition needs, the company shall determine to reform the product lines, re-design the organization structure, and re-organize the unreasonable links of the working process. The company shall focus on the long-term future and the management improvement in the next step so as to complete a thorough reform.

The success of brand reengineering is determined by the strength of the reengineering. The largest obstacle in brand reengineering is the brand organization itself. As the brand organization has been around for many years, businesses, positions and works of the brand organization have stabilized and the objecting voices are the largest resistance to brand reengineering. If the enterprise could not perform brand reengineering, it will be aging gradually. The operation system, business model, production and manufacturing and sales will be lower than the overall market efficiency, and be eliminated in the end.

The international brands that can keep its leading positions went through brand reengineering from time to time and resurrect. Such reengineering could be performed any time. In addition to the forward looking judgment and frontier scientific positions, more attention shall be paid to the reorganization of the industrial chain to maintain the latest development. The brand reengineering between the internal organization and projects are constantly improving. It is important to eliminate old technologies, old mind sets and old methods.

After brand reengineering, the brand shall appear in the market with new image, attitude and marketing strategies. With the efforts of all employees, the market territories shall be re-divided and this is the primary target of the brand reengineering of the brand organization. The brand reengineering among products are also still being conducted. The company shall constant research new products to replace the previous generations' and each releasing of new products will mean the reengineering of the brand.

6 Single product is the key point for brand nuclear explosion power

The single product strategy is very important in brand nuclear explosion. Many brands could benefit from the sales miracles created by single products. The enterprises undergoing brand reengineering shall use single products to impact the market. Therefore, the brand organization is called the super factory, which will be famous in the world by making super dream brand products.

Ford T Model is the first single product making sales miracle. On September 27, 1908, the first T model vehicle was born in Piquette factory of Detroit in Michigan on September 27, 1908. That year has become a remarkable milestone in the history of industry. With its budgeted cost, T model vehicles have made automobiles a useful commuting tool in every family. This led the United State to become "a country on wheels". The inventions made by Henry Ford contributed to the legend of the T Model. From 1908 to 1927, the T model occupied half of the vehicle output in the world, contributing to the raising of the automobile industry.

Coca-Cola, Wang Lo Kat, iPhone, AK47, the Star War, the Avatar and Band-Aid are all the legends created by single products. The charm of single products is that the brand organization may consolidate all its energy and strength to research and market on the single product respectively. With the consolidation of resources, this guarantee the highest force is being used to impact the market.

Many enterprises may have been involved in too many fields, have too many products and models or production lines, hence, leading to the over dispersion of resources. The diversified operation strategies which are used to meet the different needs in the market will usually weaken the brand's core competitiveness. This leads to the poor performance of the brand in the market and there is no influential product to impact the market. In such case, the nuclear explosion power of the brand is in serious shortage.

Even for brands that have existed for years, during weak period, the optional strategy is to conduct brand reengineering immediately, sell or stop the non-core businesses, reduce staffs, and consolidate the resources on main business. Through brand reengineering -- strengthening of the capacity of single product -- complete its brand's history with a perfect make over.

7 Execution force of brand practices

The practices of brand organization require great execution forces, which depend on the determination of the leaders of the brand organization, the pursuit of the founders to the brand, and the firm style of the implementation of brand strategies. If the top leader of an enterprise does not have confidence and assertive and the enterprise has not implemented the brand practices strictly, there will be fluctuations, and the brand will eventually become Class C or B brand only.

Spirit is more important than strength. The essence of the brand is the forging of the organization soul to so that the brand will have unprecedented appeals to attract talents to join the organization and the attentions from all user groups. Such spirit has been driving the reengineering of the brand to achieve higher targets.

Management style is the major representation of the execution capability of brand organizations. The type of management style to execute brand practices, the drive that is based on prospects and dreams, the creation environment based on flexibility and freedom, the management method based on strict sciences and the pursuit to perfectionism based on the brand creator…all these may become the typical management styles of a successful brand organization.

The execution capability of brand practices also depends on the deep understanding on scientific management. Whenever the enterprise grows in size, the management standardization does not become the core of the management. When enterprises are small in size, it may depend on marketing to increase the sales. Larger enterprises will depend more on management. Management analysts are the most important force in management. The management system which using systems and IT technologies is the foundation for the unlimited development of the brand organization.

Execution capability does not depend on people but on the orderly operations of the management systems. This is the only way for any company to develop into powerful brand organization. Any brand development without the warranty from scientific management will result in failure due to the low quality management level.

8 Age of powerful brands: powerful market entry

Today is the age of powerful brands, and only powerful or more powerful brands could be able to survive in the market and achieve great success rapidly.

Powerful brand organizations could attract the powerful resources and attentions in the world, and obtain advantages during the brand communication. The consumptions will increase greatly due to the familiarity to the brand. As a brand consumption desire, the powerful brands could increase its attractions in the market greatly. The appreciation of the brand will obtain unprecedented returns for the powerful brands.

For powerful brand organizations to achieve success in the market easier, they could use the media effect actively, project large volume of brand news release, mold the brand repeatedly and withstand the market forces. While reducing the huge advertising cost, such organizations could be able to occupy the commanding heights of the market with the lowest marketing cost. Many companies, such as Google,

Starbucks, Apple, Benz, BMW, LV and Haier, have become successful through powerful brand communication capacity.

The powerful brand organizations will also drive the formation of powerful enterprise culture which could be able to create a good cultural environment for careers, and will play an important role in attracting talents. The turnover rates of powerful brand organizations are very low, since the powerful enterprise culture could release powerful nuclear energy to attract talents, and provide intensified creativity. When the creation desire of everyone is stimulated, the powerful brand organization will become more powerful.

Just develop your organization into a powerful brand organization and make your international brand dreams come true through brand reengineering. Start your brand war with stronger attitude, more confidence and stronger determination. The brand is you -- is the honor of all employees of your organization. Your brand --- the world will be more exciting because of you!

Exercises

1. Multiple-choice Question: Brand releasing is an organization and preparation process which shall be _____, _____, _____ and _____, so as to realize the strongest nuclear force.

    A. carefully managed, strategically coordinated, and generally controlled, with most powerful explosion

    B. carefully planned, carefully managed, strategically coordinated, and prepared in an organized way

    C. carefully planned, carefully managed, strategically coordinated, and generally controlled

    D. carefully planned, strategically coordinated, generally controlled, and prepared in an organized way

2. Essay Question: What is brand reengineering and what are the roles of brand reengineering for enterprise development?

3. Discussion: Describe the sea tide law.

Section V Brand Reengineering

Chapter 2

Brand Organization Reengineering

For a time-honored brand, brand aging will occur at certain interval, and new brands may appear at any time. In the age of diversified competitions, global companies are stimulating the enthusiasm of the whole organization to change the market landscape through brand reengineering. Therefore, brand reengineering is essentially a self-improvement process of a brand organization. When a brand organization has determined to make a reform, a grand brand reengineering movement is started.

1 Brand reengineering: self-improvement of brand organization

Against today's global competition characterized by major crisis, challenges, changes and opportunities, the international brands and countries are competing constantly, and brand reengineering and enterprise reforms could be seen everywhere. Not all brand reengineering activities could be successful. On the contrary, only a few companies could make it in this aspect. Many brands may disappear despite of their efforts to change, not only including small brands, but also the large ones that will also be subject to the risk of bankruptcy.

On the list of failed international brands lie Motorola, Nokia, Compaq, Kodak, Blackberry, Hummer, Saab, Daewoo, Pan American World Airways and Reader's Digest......

To start over again is the most important strategic policy for brand reengineering. A brand organization can only be re-organized with the determination of destructing everything of the organization. Do not be reluctant to leave the mature market, patterns and the reserves obtained in the past, and do not stick to what you have achieved before. A brand could complete its reengineering without repudiating itself totally.

To start it over again is not only a decision, but also an important management method. The launcher industry of China is famous for its low accident rate while Russia always see major accidents or failures in this aspect. This is benefited from the Zeroing Management established by Qian Xuesen, which means that in case of errors or problems by chance during launcher R&D, the whole process shall be started over again until all errors have been corrected. This will be repeated over and over again until all problems and risks are eliminated.

BUG in software development, flaws in automobile designing and manufacturing, and the post-sales service problems of home appliances share the similar problem, that is to promote the products with flaws due to the lack of the best management method and the determination to start over again. The zeroing management is the precondition for zero flaw rate. Starting over again is the improving and growing process of a powerful brand organization.

The reengineering process of brand organization is neither the minor improvement on the previous basis, nor the significant improvement based on the existing strategic basis, let alone the changing of LOGO or product models. No one will order you to start over again, adversely more people will tell you that your efforts are in vain. However, if you do not have the determination to start over again, the reengineering of the brand organization could not be thoroughly completed.

2 Rise of brand: creative destruction

In 1912, Schumpeter proposed the creative destruction – the entrepreneurship. He regards the business starting as the destruction of the old combination of means of production, the old competition order and old production structure by virtue of the original, wild and adventurous creativity to give birth to new economy. Schumpeter pointed out that, entrepreneurs are a fleeting phenomenon. When an entrepreneur is dedicated to creating, he is an entrepreneur, and when he stops creating, no longer can he be called an entrepreneur.

This idea is upheld by all Americans. Therefore, the banks, angel investors, investment companies and financial institutions are built based on new thoughts, and the whole United States on new ideas and dreams. Education in the United States is creativity-based. Nobody will stifle any talent dreams, instead they are willing to encourage and invest in the seemingly unattainable dreams, which turned the American economy of the United States into the number one in the world with their brands, technologies and cultures becoming globally popular.

Most American people are talking about the future rather than the relatively short history because what they are thinking about is the people and the world in the future that they would like to focus on. Therefore, a great number of super imaginations, talent dreams, conceptual products, leading skills and advanced technologies are generated in this country. Everyone in the country is eager to change the world, and everyone believes that his or her dream will lead the world while each enterprise would like to deem itself as an international company with business spanning the global rapidly.

By contrast, there is another theory, the Kerzner theory, which believes that, if there is a benefit, insignificant improvement also abides by the entrepreneurship. Developing countries, such as China and India, are following this theory. The micro innovations based on duplication or minor improvements have become the main feature of the entrepreneurship economy. The insufficient intellectual property protection and worse anti-monopoly competition environment have restricted creativity, and many dreams have collapsed due to realism. People are talking more about the long history and current realities, and the economy is only pushed by the historical knowledge and experiences. Only few people would like to talk about where the future will lead to.

We must treat this problem seriously, or deeply understand the roots of creativity. International brands and the core competitiveness of enterprises in the world are coming from creativity. The power of creative destruction is the great gene that formed the global brand economy and the basic guarantee for successful brand reengineering.

We do not need to pay attention to the cause of the failure of a brand, just like that we do not need to talk about the cause of Qin Dynasty's extinction. We shall focus on the basic points – how does a brand rise. The brand reengineering process is a great fission process. Only quick and complete repudiation of your brand can deliver the brand reengineering. A brand's success comes from the repeated process of reengineering. Only in this way can the brand stay young fresh and dynamic to the world forever.

3 Reengineering of brand organizations

A brand develops in the form of organization but not pure enterprise or company which is only limited to its internal employees. Brand organization includes the brand founders, brand organizers (brand leaders, brand officers, brand consultants, brand backbone employees, and brand organization employees), brand operators (brand dealers and brand service providers), brand supply chains and brand user groups, making it an organization expanding outward without limitation.

Current and future brand organizations will become more and more complicated, abstract and dynamic, covering the traditional channels, personnel communication, Internet, mobile medias and social networks, which could not be controlled by the traditional pyramid-shaped organization structure.

SECTION V BRAND REENGINEERING

During brand development, the enterprise must be aware of the importance of brand organization. Only all employees and resources related to the brand are organized effectively can the effect be maximized. The structure of a brand organization is not a pyramid-like vertical structure, but is more like a football field or target, with the brand founders or leaders as the core, expanding outwardly to from a hierarchy structure composed of strategic layer, executive layer and operation layer.

As a profound topic, histology tends to be more thought provoking than the company system. This is because a brand organization doesn't equal an enterprise. A brand organization is an expanded company structure with the form of company + dealers + supply chain +users. However, the enterprise cultures belong to the organization development science, including the organization cultures and undertaking cultures, which could cover the internal and external of the organization until all stakeholders of the brand could be covered.

Therefore, when talking about brand organization, we mean the brands existing in the form of organization, including all structural networks connected by the internal and external organization chains. Enterprise means the limited company, a specific legal form of enterprise. Obviously, brand organization is far larger than enterprise form, and an enterprise may not be able to represent or own a brand. In most cases, it's improper to regard company or enterprise as brand, since the value and meaning of the brand in the society will be neglected. Brands are an economic form, owned by a collection of enterprises, and could represent the future direction of social and economic development. Thousands of legal representative limited companies may belong to one brand, and brands may be the strategic economic assets of a country, and a special economic form shared by all people in the world. Therefore, the value of brand organization is far larger than that of limited company.

We should also note that the reengineering of brand organization is an important moment for the considerable enhancement of the specialization and movement ability of the enterprise. Given the repeating works, the enthusiasm and creativity of the employees of the brand organization will be reduced rapidly, and the company will risk the withering creativity. Therefore, the brand organization shall focus on fully releasing and stimulating employee's creativity while enterprise shall establish a more scientific agility system to complete the reengineering process.

We believe that each employee is a creator, and the brand organization is the collection of creators. Only constant creation and the creative destruction activities can drive the organization forward from within. The reengineering of organs may improve the reengineering of the whole body. In this way, the brand organization can stay vigorous and keep its global competitive advantages.

3.1 From leadership to leadership level

Previous researches on leadership science mainly focused on the realization of leadership, which means the individual capacity of the brand leader. However, for brand organization, a new concept shall be adopted, which is the leadership level with the relative works as an integral whole.

It's necessary to distinguish leadership from management to investigate the influence of leadership level on brand organization. Leadership is to guide employees through ideology and ideas with leaders providing directions. Management means to use detailed management methods. The company's leadership awareness and style will determine the direction of the whole brand organization. What the leadership level supports, encourages or promotes will become the direction of the whole company. This is not the favor of any leader of the company, but the consist leadership environment of the organization. In organizations established without leadership level, many disagreements, or even conflicts in terms of leadership awareness may emerge, bringing about the informal confrontational organizations within the company, which will be the root cause for the collapse of the company and bad management situation.

We have divided a company into the leadership level, the management level and the operation level. Compared to the past, there may be some changes in the working contents of these levels. Members at the leadership level shall function as leaders with major working contents as leadership methods, including the temporarily appointed organizers of management activities or market activities. Members at the management level shall be responsible for management works, such as dealer management and production material management, who shall focus on detailed management works. Members at the operation level shall be responsible for the detailed procedures or working steps according to the relative requirements.

The company shall focus on the labor divisions of the leadership level and the management level. The leadership works shall be distinguished from the management works, so as to prevent insufficient leadership or excessive management. The focus of leadership shall be placed on guidance and coordination, as well as awareness direction, so as to stimulate the vigor and efficiency of the organization. The focus of management shall be placed on the detailed execution, and works completed according to the relative requirements, so as to complete the division of tasks effectively by a micro method.

The development of the overall awareness of the leadership level of the brand organization and the recognition and implementation of the branding shall be completed through the leadership level. The leadership level is also the backbone power of the brand organization, and the rapid and effective development of the organization mainly depends on the uniform awareness, supports and actions at the leadership level. A leadership level with high uniformity in terms of ideology, awareness and actions is the basic guarantee for the achievement of the brand organization. Otherwise, if the awareness of the leadership level is unorganized, or there are conflicts in the organization, the organization will see the highest risk.

3.2 Brand clusters

The global brand competition pattern features obvious brand clusters. Global brands are professional ones with each cluster including several single brand organizations. Large yet comprehensive cross-discipline brands are quite rare.

To explore different markets or to satisfy consumers' demands at different levels, the organization will be divided into several business groups composed of different product departments, or brand clusters composed of different sub-brands. The reengineering of brand organization mainly focuses on the adjustment of organization structures or brand clusters. Given the specialization of the market in the future, there will be more professional brands, each professional brand will focus on one professional market and occupy the leading position, and there will be more and more large brand organizations with brand clusters.

Professional brands shall focus on professional markets to solve one core problem. For example, on the shampoo market, the Head Shoulders of P&G mainly focuses on scurf problems, while Rejoice on the smooth appearance of hairs. The products of Microsoft include Internet Explorer, Windows, Microsoft Office and Windows Media Player, while the Office include Word, Excel and Powerpoint.

According to the observation of global brands, we could see that Apple, Coca-Cola, P&G, Toyota, Unilever and JNJ are the enterprise brand clusters containing different brands.

The brand clusters of Apple include: iPhone, iPad, iPod and iTunes; the brand clusters of Coca-Cola include: Coca-Cola, Sprite, Smart, Fanta, and Minute Maid; the brand clusters of Google include: Gmail, Blogger, Chrome and Panoramio; the brand clusters of MacDonald's include: Cheeseburgers, Big Mac, Mac Rice, McCafe; the brand clusters of Inter include: Solo, Core, Pentium, Celeron and Atom; the brand clusters of Toyota include: Toyota, Lexus, Daihatsu, Sayn, and Crown; the brand clusters of Benz include: Mercedes-Benz, Maybach, Smart, and AMG; the brand clusters of Gillette include: Fusion 3, super interaction, Vector, Eagle, and Rhinoceros; and the brands under LV include: Hennessy, Givenchy, CD, Ebel, Luxury, Zenith, Dior, Guerlain, Sephora and Zenith.

3.3 Formation of network organization

From the interpersonal network of Amergin, from 5th century B.C to 1st century A.C., there were hundreds of Celtic countries on the Europe continent, covering Ireland, England and Gaul, and each country had a Druid, and all Druids established a order network through the interpersonal network. China established the earliest road network in the world in the 3rd century B.C, which was composed of the Qin mail roads and Qin straight roads. In the 2nd century B.C, a trading network was established from Chang'an to the Europe – the Silk Roads, which is the transnational trading network with the longest history and greatest influence in the global.

During American Civil War, the railway network and telegram network were developed at the highest speed. In 1867, Joseph Glidden invented the barbed wires. The whole United States is established on the thinking mode of networks. Systems and networks are the typical organization thoughts in the scientific and economic development in the United States. With the rapid developments of the broadcasting networks, TV networks, Internet networks, mobile communication networks, social networks, logistic networks and digital networks, we have entered the network age of the 21st century.

The rapid development of network organizations and the profound changes caused by the Internet to human beings will in turn promote the enterprise leaders to focus on the network reforms, to restore the network forms of organizations to the network changes of human beings in early stages, to restore the network organization pattern featuring interpersonal connections and to actively create the new network organizations. Most enterprise leaders are still concentrating on the Internet or mobile networks or logistic networks, who are driven by American network organizations to adopt the network organization thought.

From the order network in the early age to the profound reform of the network organizations, a brand organization must have a powerful brand leadership core to gather and attract all key personnel (those who are keen to and trust the brand), and then attract the brand fans and people who are interested in the brand.

We all know that the internal and external connections of a brand organization are in the form of complicated network organization structure, with a flexible organization pattern and unlimited 3D network connections. Any link of the organization may generate brand premium and may contact with or attract new brand users.

3.4 3D command chain

We shall discuss another deep topic, that is the 3D command chain of a brand organization. The food chain in nature and the modern military command system can prove this.

Food chain is a natural ecological system for mutual predation, parasitism and interdependency. For example, grasses → hares → foxes → wolves; or cereals → pests → birds → eagles; or alga → shrimps (crabs) → fish → birds. More complicated food chains can form the self-adapt ecological order network of the nature. The destruction of food chains, such as killing certain beasts, will be deemed as a criminal of destructing the ecological environment of the nature.

Military command systems are outstanding in modern military, such as land-based missile system, defending missile system, air strike system and 3D combined combat system. The command chain could be used to connect the satellites, radars, surveillance aircrafts, fighters, self-propelled guns, armored personnel carriers, carriers, destroyers and submarines in the air, on the ground and under the ocean, so as to establish an overall combat system with orderly operation and cooperative combats. Each weapon, person, target and combat unit could take independent action according to the fighting commands, and meanwhile they are the integral organic combat units in the whole command system.

From the food chain and military command chain we can see that, a brand organization is not only in the form of network. The backbone network of the brand organization is a highly developed, coordinated and effective brand command chain. Particularly, during the large scale reorganization of a brand, the brand command chain will play an important role of a rapid commander and cooperator.

Brand mobile management system and brand marketing command system are necessary for the high speed operation of modern brand organizations. By commanding and coordinating the branches and management operators in different cities, lands and oceans throughout the world, a brand organization will acquire the rapid mobile fighting capacity. For example, the tracking system based on satellite scanning that is established by express company, the ocean or earthquake monitoring system, the logistic system for oils and hazardous materials, and the hygiene and city management systems have widely used the command chain as the main management method. The large enterprise management and market actions in the future will be deployed with more IT and mobile technical systems.

4 Values and value creation of brand organizations

Values not only stands for the core of the brand organization order, but also the capacities of brand organization and its members to judge various values. The formation of values is based on value creation. The management order of brand organization is superior to the enterprise social order governance. Enterprises stay free from social problems, phenomena or conflicts so as to from independent, meaningful, leading, active, orderly and systematic values.

We could divide the values into three value systems, namely value judgment, value perception and value concepts, which shall be used as the value management order to help the brand organization effectively understand and use the value system. The opinions of the organization on the future, and the education, development, progress and achievements of the members of the organization shall be coordinated. The value system is a management order guiding the working attitudes, responsibilities, moods and pressures of the employees. See Fig. 8-4 for the value system of brand organization.

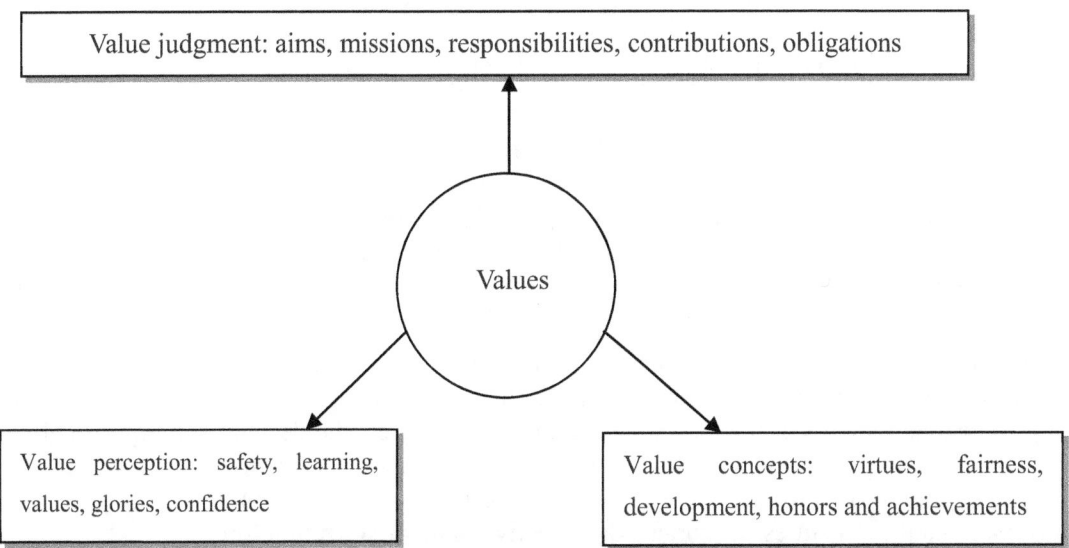

Fig. 8-4 Value system of brand organization

The value system of brand organization shall be expressed as follows:

Value judgment: aims, missions, responsibilities, contributions and obligations;

Value perception: safety, learning, values, glories and confidence;

Value concepts: virtues, fairness, development, honors and achievements.

Value judgment is the requirement about how to clearly judge values, which include the aims and missions of the organization, and these are the main bodies of the value identification of the brand organization; responsibilities, contributions and obligations emphasize on taking obligations, and they are both the spirit quality of the brand organization and the basis for accountability and responsibility determination. Contributions are the important awareness promoted by the brand organization, and the members' contributions must equal their returns within the brand organization. The obligations emphasize the basic obligations to be performed in the brand organization.

Value perception could represent the organization power and the necessary requirement for members of the organization to join in or become backbone personnel. At first, the demands based on psychology and behaviors shall be met, and secondly, the demand for learning and progress shall be satisfied. Values are the method to represent personal values and the logic for the brand organization to judge the values. Glories are the group feeling obtained by the organization members who shall feel the happiness and pride to join the organization. Confidences are the wills and mental experience provided by the brand organization, which are the perfect combination of self-confidence and the organization confidence.

Value concepts are the major awareness root and the organization environment to be achieved by the brand organization. The brand organization shall uphold and guide its members to obtain certain virtues, and establish a fair competition environment to reflect fairness in all aspects. If the individual development could match with that of the organization, what motivations could be provided to every member in the organization, and what actual progresses will be encouraged, what honors could be obtained by the members, and how is the honor system of the brand organization designed shall be considered. When a member is participating in a brand organization, he should think about how to realize success and achievements. Success is a sense of joy when completing each work or project, and achievement is the material performance obtained by individual through participating in the organization. What achievement making methods or results would be encouraged by the brand organization?

The creation of values is the result of order and moral senses, and the group interaction between brand organization and individuals. The brand organization order created with reasonable and complete value system can enable the enterprise to develop into a more perfect, reasonable and attractive brand organize and release the powerful brand organization force.

5 Management order of brand organization

The management order system of a brand organization is composed of management order structure, group policy making system, management progress system, management reporting system, committee establishment, brand announcement, management site, organization deeds, learning progress schedule, development and promotion plans, and organization alliances.

Quite different from the organization structure, management order structure is neither the straight line management structure based on positions and obligations. Management order structure includes the roles, positions and honors of the backbones and members, sizes, the design of interpersonal network chains, covering all official and non-official uniform structures related to the brand organization inside or outside the enterprise, which is the result of the effective management order body of the brand organization and the structures with organization activity and organization force.

Brand group policy making system is a systematic scheme based on management order structure and the action guidance emphasizing group participation, group policy making and group actions in various links. In brand organization, the participation scales, quantities and degrees of group policy making are the key to solving the group splitting problem. In terms of product models, colors, future thoughts, post-sales service system and brand activity designs, only more related or unrelated brand fans' participation can turn their opinions, suggestions, and voices into our common fruit of labor – this product is jointly made by us, this plan is jointly designed by us. The group policy making could translate all possible social population into firm supporters of the brand organization.

Brand management progress system is the core structure for the brand organization to promote various management items, management activities, market benefits and market activities. The brand organization shall subdivide the management tasks into project teams, indicators and examination plans and establish progress offices and the progress officers at all levels so as to coordinate the work progresses in all aspects. Progress management is an effective method to promote important businesses and performances of the brand organization.

The brand management reporting system mainly concentrates on research reports, fact reports and management site reports, which has defined the receiver of the reports, the way of reporting and the focuses of the management, as well as the way to improve management level and efficiency. And reporting systems including the brand standardization correction reporting system may play a role in correcting the organization development.

The committee establishment occupies an important position in the brand organization. Different professional committees shall be established to design, coordinate and supervise the management contents so as to effectively improve the management level of the organization, and prevent mismanagement mistakes, uncontrollable management and losses management. For example, high-level quality review committee could be established to review the working and purchasing quality, improve the working quality and efficiency and prevent the unnecessary economic losses that may occur during purchasing.

Brand announcement is an important announcement made during brand releasing and global promotion, and also the important document for companies to show the organization aims, missions, and outlines to the supply chain and the public. At least, the members at the brand strategic level, brand technical level and brand executive level must make declaration and vow to the brand at their own wills. Making declaration is an important ceremony and the important will power, self-control and ethic guarantee to the performance of brand obligations and responsibilities.

Managing the management site constitutes an important management aspect of the brand organization. All management problems occur on the management site. Factories, offices, sales stores and post-sales sites shall be deemed as management sites. Brand organization shall pay attention to the scientific management researches of the management site. The management site reports are an important method to improve management.

Organization deeds is a contractual relationship between the organization and its members, including the document contract and consciousness contract. The former one is the legal document or written document such as contract, agreement, announcement and rule while the later one belongs to the ethic and value contract formed by consciousness and ideologies.

6 Cultural causes of brand organizations

Different from the past enterprise cultures, the enterprise culture of brand organization is a branded organization cultural cause.

At first, the most important thing is branding. This is the brand culture with the brand as the center, which is nothing of the simple enterprise culture. Brand culture will generate huge and active cultural influence within and out of the company. The value system of the brand organization management order and the management order system shall be deemed as the main body to establish unique brand consciousness culture and even the powerful brand civilization.

Secondly, the enterprise culture of the brand organization is a clear brand organization culture. It is a kind of organized culture strength, and a collective, overall, systematic, complete and unique culture. The purpose of organization works is to establish, form, reconstruct and expand new orders.

Finally, it is an undertaking culture and a cultural pattern eyeing on the formation, expansion and development of undertakings, which feature clear, active, positive, sunny, achieving and honor cultural perception. It represents people's dream and hope of long-term undertakings, and could gather the spirits, enthusiasm, wills, strength and contributions of everyone.

In general, the enterprise culture of brand organization has risen above the old enterprise culture, forming a unique cultural pattern that could stimulate the development of the brand organization, or even a totally new brand civilization. The charms, infectivity, transmission capacity and influence of brand civilization could push the development of the brand organization to a historical height in the world.

6.1 Damages to brand organization caused by enterprise culture resistance

For the enterprise culture of a brand organization, the key research point is the culture resistance, or what is the specific culture that will be accepted by a particular group of people. Never force all people to accept one culture, since this is extremely wrong. There are different religions, social awareness and personal tastes in the world. Generally, one brand culture may be embraced by some people and objected by others.

This also implies to the internal culture of a company. Culture resistance commonly occurs, such as slacking at work, accountability resistance, and adverse opinions. The resistance may prevent the enterprise culture from realizing the cultural effect expected by the enterprise management, or from being upgraded into the enterprise of a brand organization or even the culture of a brand organization.

A brand organization entails the research of culture resistance in real terms to identify the cultural attributes of the brand user groups and employees. This is an important factor enabling the brand to become popular among certain groups and maximizing the vitality of the employees of the organization.

As in physics, friction could significantly reduce the effects of forces. The enterprise culture resistance is the huge friction in the enterprise culture. Strengthening the researches on culture resistance is helpful to release the brand organization capacity to form the unique culture of a brand organization.

6.2 From constraint theory to motivation theory

The constraint theory means the management method designed based on constraints. However, when it comes to enterprise culture, constraints may lead to the management style featuring imposed awareness or behaviors, such as spurring management and punishment management. Such words as "forbidden" or "disallowed" could be seen in the management rules and documents.

Different from the previous situation, the Y century generation (those who were born in 1980s and 1990s) may pay more attention to freedom, idealization, pressure releasing, and virtual reality. They will try to protect themselves from pressures, and look for better lifestyles. In such case, if the constraint theory is still used as the enterprise culture management method, there will be culture resistance and even serious management accidents.

Learning progress plans, promotion stimulation plans and brand honor system are the major measures to establish effective incentives, which could respectively meet the demands of learning, practicing and development, providing opportunities for fair competition, reasonable promotion, salary increase and positive energy, and representing, proving and admitting the values of individuals and groups through the brand honor system.

The reasonable design of the incentive system is the basic culture management capacity of the enterprise culture. Only the complete and systematic system can realize the important functions of the individual members in the brand organization. It's the important cultural reform direction for enterprises in the 21st century to match the value representation and value creation with value acknowledge and value return.

7 Practitioner network of brand organizations

Practitioner network is an important pillar to form and expand brand cultural effect in the brand organization, which is the dynamic, moving, active and positive action and supporting network, and the comprehensive collection of various backbone supporting forces within and beyond the enterprise.

The brand organization shall vigorously carry out actions, and effectively manage such actions so as to realize the rapid development, expansion and achievement of the brand organization by mobilizing the key brand personnel and active practitioners within and beyond the enterprise.

The brand practitioner network is the important pillar in the modern interpersonal network social relationship. In addition to the social network pattern in the Internet, there is also large scale interpersonal social network in the real world. The interactions, encourages, recommendations and value transmissions among people could generate an active, live and constant environment and atmosphere for the brand organization in terms of action supports.

Brand practitioner network is the modern management method that could fully make use of the network organization structure and social relations of the organization members to achieve the brand organization effects, which shall be integrated into the research direction and management implementation direction of the brand organization, to ensure the high-degree interaction among the parties relative to the brand, and this is the important purpose to establish and develop the brand practitioner network.

The brand practitioner network shall be directed by the brand organization, which bears the strategic commanding and coordination functions in the network, and can use new medias such as Internet, mobile internet and e-commerce to realize the wide transmission of the brand, the establishment of the user groups and the systematic sales.

8 Reengineering of brand agility organization

Agility organization is a special form adopted by the initially established enterprise, which is significantly different from the mature and stable brand organization structure. The agility organization requires all members to make quick response to the market. All the objectives of the organization are focusing on the rapid market organization at the early stage of its establishment.

The agility organization is just like a fast-moving force, which include a command and coordination department, a fast-moving department and the rapid respond members. The leaders and key members of the agility organization shall be highly capable to eliminate all complicated processes and unnecessary links, and the members shall be reduced to those from few departments, such as the brand transmission center, R&D department, market department and sales department.

The brand department shall be responsible for the brand designs with the task to complete the early market standardization and massive brand transmission. This department may be an independent or an outsourcing department, superior to the other departments in terms of structure to ensure its independent operation features. It's better to be led by the top management of the company, or report to the top leaders.

The company shall also have a special market progress control office and corresponding position to direct and adjust the market targets in its early stage, subdivide and implement the working tasks according to the item system, control, collect and supervise the progresses of all programs, and accelerate the market promotion speed.

After having entered the market, the enterprise may need to accelerate the market sales business in the early stage. Therefore, the management over salespersons will become a key point. The massive recruitment and rolling elimination method shall be adopted to weed out the salespersons with poor market development capacities and recruit new employees on the monthly basis so as to maintain a highly-efficient market development team and develop outstanding talents as the future market sales backbone.

At the early stage of an enterprise, it's necessary to assign the chief training officer since the training focusing on brand standardization is very important in this stage. The poor performance in market development in early stage is caused by improper training. If the salespersons do not have good market development methods, the management persons of the departments do not have deep understanding of standardization, and the new employees lack enthusiasm of the brand, the business performance of the enterprise will be poor in the early stage.

SECTION V BRAND REENGINEERING

9 Brand civilization forms

Outstanding brand organizations will finally evolve into a special, powerful and fixed brand culture form, and its brand images, elements and features will become a unique trending culture.

Since the 20th century, many brands have established unique culture forms with special and identifiable features through brand culture creation and reconstruction, generating the rapidly developing cultural creative industry in the 21st century.

It's common to see the cultures or culture creations exist as brand in the 21st century. Brand civilization has become one of the mainstream civilization expression of diversified civilizations in the history of human beings.

The concrete brand civilization is to create a lifestyle, working style and funs, so as to form a series of civilization patterns and fashions through such styles and funs.

The brand civilization in the 21st century will form another special virtual reality civilization – another earth, or the civilization form that is totally different from the actual lifestyle. The ceremonies, buildings, participants, specific image elements, appearances, living environment, lifestyles, and awareness are creative, and this may be a new civilization that has never existed on the earth.

Movies, cartoons, novels, games and theme parks as well as cultural creative products will produce large quantities of such new civilization forms. The original physical brands will absorb such cultural elements to create new brand civilization. The virtual reality produced by the combination of "virtual + reality" will become a major method to generate new brand civilization forms in the 21st century, and the common demands of a new generation of brand user groups – they would like to flee from the pressures of actual lives and find their existences in the virtual world.

Exercises

1. Multiple-choice Question: The internal and external connections of a brand organization are in the form of complicated_____, with _____ and _____. Any link of the organization may generate brand premium and contact with or attract new brand users. ( )

A. network organization structure, a flexible organization pattern, unlimited 3D network connections

B. unlimited 3D network connections, network organization structure, a flexible organization pattern

C. a flexible organization pattern, unlimited 3D network connections, network organization structure

D. The above choices are not correct.

2. True or False Question: The enterprise culture of a brand organization is a branding organization undertaking culture, and the research key point of the enterprise culture of the brand organization is the culture resistance. ( )

3. Discussion: how could we understand the destruction of the brand organization caused by the enterprise culture resistance?

Chapter 3

Reengineering of Brand Management System

A brand is a complicated systematic project requiring general designing. The systematic reengineering of brand management is the breakthrough of the organizing of a brand in terms of management technologies. The brand shall use system management to update the brand to an ecological organization status, use the ternary order layer structure to develop the brand in a stable and mature way, and ensure the sustainable development of the brand.

1 The management reengineering of brand strategic updating

The reengineering at the strategic level of the brand is based on the long-term governance thought and structure using mid- and long-term development strategies, which could ensure that the brand management system could support the strategic structure required for the brand operation for a long term in the future. The brand strategic reengineering depends on three important thoughts: promotion of core inspirational products; powerful brand confidence; and dedication to dreams and R&D.

The foresight period of entrepreneurs is normally 10-30 years. Similarly, the brand reengineering period is about 10-30 years. This doesn't mean, however, that a brand must be reengineered after being developed for 10–30 years. The brand reengineering period means that the 10-30 years is a projected estimate of what is hoped for, or in the case that the core products promoted next could gain popularity earlier than similar products by 10 to 30 years, so as to promote the next generation of core inspirational products and could thereby overturn the whole industrial and product patterns.

Steve Jobs, the founder of Apple, told investors at the time of launching computer products that what they were promoting was the next craze, and what they were considering was how to change the computer industry. After the promotion of smart phones by Jobs, the mobile communication giants fell down, such as Motorola and Nokia. Motorola and Nokia, who opened the mobile communication industry, did have creativities. When any brand has promoted core inspirational products, the powerful destructive creative force will make the original industrial ecology instantly collapse.

Kodak dissembled because of a wrong judgment involving sticking to film technology during the age of digital photos. The annual output of China's Shaanxi Automobile Group used to be 3,000 heavy trucks. After brand reengineering, and the creation of the golden supply chain, the group promoted the F3000 heavy truck through an intensified sales activity, increased the annual output to 100,000 heavy trucks and entered into the leading group of heavy trucks in China.

Powerful brand confidence is from the dreams of brand founders to change the world. The strategic layouts of brand founders have determined the final achievements of the brands. The powerful confidence is making miracles for brand reengineering. Many international brands with great achievements firmly believe that they are No.1 in the world, making the most advanced and best products.

Rashid bin Saeed Al Maktoum, the founder of Dubai, believes that people would only remember the first man that stepped on the moon, and made the dreaming city with his crazy mind – Dubai.

At the beginning, Google used a white bed sheet to make a slogan on the top of a two-storey building, writing "Google——The Next Generation of Search Engines" and "Grand Opening", which was mocked by the industry. When Mark Zuckerberg, the founder of Facebook, delivered a speech at an event, he said, "We are going to change the world, and we are going to change the universe".

The dreams of Howard Hughes were to make the most profound movie in the world, the fastest plane in the world and the largest plane in the world. His company used creative research technologies to send unpiloted spacecraft to the moon in 1966, opening the grand plan of landing on the moon. At the beginning of IBM, Thomas J. Watson named the company International Business Machines, defining the world pattern of IBM.

When we were researching international brands with great achievements, we found that their successes are not made occasionally. Such brands tend to always focus on dreams and R&D, and would use scientific management and scientific thoughts to conduct brand reengineering again and again so as to research the most advanced and best management technologies, as well as use such technologies for the rapid and massive developments of those brands.

International brands will always make R&D the priority by establishing laboratories and research centers. Many international brands, such as DuPont, Dolby, Philips, JNJ, and Bell Labs, would make R&D the core of the whole brand development by focusing on problem solving and R&D of various core technologies. To research the next generation of electric vehicles, the automobile cell researchers from the automobile companies throughout Japan have been gathered to research the next generation of automobile cell technologies and share the research information.

In the age of knowledge economy, the creativity of knowledge is the largest fortune. R&D will generate a more powerful creative destructive force than ever before. By contrast, the business models preferred by investors in the past will become insignificant in the future. The enterprises or industries without independent R&D core technologies will be pushed out from the world leading group. The global R&D centers established by international brands will be divided into four classes, class I and II R&D would only be conducted in the original countries of the brands, and Class III and IV research centers will be established in other places in the world to conduct local difference studies or periphery studies.

In the future, enterprises will exist in the form of collaborative enterprises. Each international brand caring about R&D will focus on its own core research and their own fields. For example, many core parts are researched and made by the most professional companies in the world. The technologies of mobile phones and home appliances may come from different professional R&D companies. Various professional companies will participate in joint competition through collaborative management in the form of a collaborative enterprise. The comprehensive enterprises without collaboration will be eliminated due to the weak core technology capacities.

In the global competition of the future, each industry may have Top 1000 enterprises, or 1000 professional and breakdown enterprises will develop into top international brands focusing on different professional markets. The large yet comprehensive enterprises will fail due to too many product lines and weak R&D capacities. Only when a professional market has no professional brands, such companies may survive.

1.1 Power for management improvement: management professionalization

The future of management is the age of credentials in management, which will be an important advancement incentive for the development of the science of management in the world.

The science of management has witnessed significant changes today. Modern management is the perfect combination of science and management. The role of art in management is insignificant, and management science is a future-oriented science. The purpose of management science is not to solve the leftover or current issues, but to establish self-adaptable management rules that focus on the long-term future of conducting scientific designing, and to overturn creation and professional implementation, so as to improve the management level according to the estimates to management development and market competition to adapt to management improvement over a longer term.

In the modern and future management methods, the management method and contents are being changed by artificial intelligence, human engineering, consciousness upload, new material invention, space exploration, unmanned systems, industrial extraction, service intelligence, agile manufacturing, computer systems, interstellar Internet, future logistic network, trustful e-commerce, digital network and sensing network.

Management professionalization includes management sciences, management systems, management knowledge, management networks and management professions. It involves scientific studies, flow design, dynamic knowledge management, network organization development, and talent and resource construction of management science. In addition, higher foresight requirements have been proposed, and the improvement of the management of global companies will more and more depend on the rapid improvement of management professionalization.

Brand standardization is Brand + Management Standardization. We will discuss the five aspects of management professionalization and brand science, brand systems, brand knowledge, brand networks and brand talents (the five aspects of management professionalization) hereafter, which are important management pillars for a brand organization, representing management improvement and the enterprise management reform direction led by brands.

1.2 Management professionalization: the future of the brand science

The issues to be solved through management professionalization are: what is the most advanced? what is the most perfect? what is the most different? what could represent the management level?

A brand is started from an amazing dream. When a brand is born from a dream, it shall be created or reengineered through a solid management professionalization process so as to make the journey to Brand Achievement. Otherwise, great dreams, good expectations and investments will be in vain and become a bad memory.

What is the most advanced? This is the first issue to be considered for brand management. To realize the rapid expansion and development of the brand organization, and manage the ever growing brand organization, the enterprise shall make the scale management priority, making development outlines and to design the management system in advance so as to prepare for the upcoming scale expansion management. Only the advanced, scientific and well-developed management base could meet the development needs and become the carrier for global expansion and rapid operation of the company.

What is the most perfect? The difference between a brand organization and ordinary companies is that the pursuits of a brand organization is that branding and organization management are equally important. To create a perfect management method, the brand organization shall recruit many management consultants, provide management training and develop management analysis to keep the leading edge of the management team in terms of management tendency. In addition, the brand organization shall create and use the most advanced management concepts, and invent or introduce the most advanced management systems, so as to reduce the management flaws and loopholes of the organization, and reduce management accidents. The brand organization shall deem itself as a highly developed learning organization, with management improvement occupying an important position in the organization. The purpose of all of these is to improve all aspects of the management.

What is the most different? The key management point of a brand organization is to be distinct. For example, how to be distinct in terms of management and marketing. The differentiation strategies of international brand organizations are the major strategies used to obtain competition advantages. This is a totally different management attitude with the brand followers. The brand followers will make every effort to imitate the management methods and product advantages of the brand organizations. The brand organization shall conduct new researches and create actively and passively to maintain the leading competition advantage. However, the active creation is better than a passive creation.

What can represent the management level? Management is an important advanced productivity itself. Large enterprises may pay attention to systematic management capacity while small enterprises only care about marketing. This is an essential difference between them. Because of this, companies are divided into different types. However, enterprises focusing on management will develop into large enterprises more rapidly. The large brand organizations maintaining competition advantages will pay more attention to management quality and would try to convey advanced management thoughts, advanced management methods and management operation capacities in every management link. The comprehensive and highly efficient improvement of management quality is always the target of all large enterprises. The brand organization should deeply understand the importance of management quality in enterprise operation so as to show a more powerful, and more systematic management capacity.

2 Scientific branding

The creation of a brand is a process of invention: inventing a feeling or method, such as taste, texture, appearance, manufacturing technologies, chemicals, and physical methods. For example, the Heidelberg printers, PDF and fried onion rings.

Another key point of scientific branding is the scientization of management, which is to realize the comprehensive development of the brand by systematically inventing management methods. Management scientization has been established as early as the Qin Dynasty in China, the age of the Taylor system in the United States and the time of Deming in Japan. Scientific management has always been the method for improvement of modern management science. Management without scientific methods will not be successful.

Firstly, the leading position of scientific thoughts should be determined by management science. The management of a company must be based on the improvement of scientific thoughts, as well as scientific methods and studies. Secondly, the scientific experiments of management science must be the most important link in enterprise management. For brand standardization, the scientific experiments of management methods shall be deemed as the core. The management methods established without experiments will not withstand tests. Finally, the most important thing is order, or the establishment of management rules. Order is the eventual target of management improvement. Enterprises shall establish a self-adaptation scheme for workflow management in order to realize the automatic operation of all management effectiveness so as to get rid of the influence of man-made factors. The thought of person-oriented management styles is wrong and not scientific.

2.1 Brand experiment technologies

Brand organizations will generate new products and management methods under scientific experiment conditions. The United States has listed researchers for green cards into the highest EB-1 level (Extraordinary Ability Visa), who can apply for the green cards in their home language and without an employer required, which is a much higher offer than applications made by persons with higher educational backgrounds. The latter being required to have employers and to register with the Ministry of Labor. In addition, students in the United States shall have to write a thesis, and the scientific research capacities and the future-oriented scientific quality have the leading positions in the education of the United States. These have proved the importance of scientific studies and researchers to the development of national economy and competitiveness.

Brand experiment is an important research process, a strict invention process and a repeating process, which requires sufficient foresight, certain investments and sufficient research capacities. Such investments are absolutely wise. The enterprises in developing countries may neglect this key link, leading to the low brand premium capacity and the reduced overall competitiveness of the brand on the global market.

The method of using empiricism to complete brand research has been abandoned for a long time. Strict scientific experiments are used to test, investigate and research the changes to the appearances and applications of brand products caused by different lights, colors and shapes. For example, the influence of vehicle shapes and air flow on speed, the changes related to product shapes and consumption impulsion, and new popular foods determined through experiments on food taste and appearance. These brand experiments have been broken down into different research items according to certain topics, which shall be completed by different scientists and artists through cooperation. The aesthetic experiments of a brand are conducted through sensibility studies, and rationality experiments of the brand are made against the physical conditions or features of the brand. The brand laboratory will conduct various comparison experiments through a combination of sensibility research and rationality research.

The experiments of modern brands are mainly based on natural sciences, especially on psychological cognition, behaviors and neurosciences, as well as sensing judgments, rational judgments and behaviors generated by the brand users. The pair comparison, sequence method, production method, appearance tests, group statistic comparison and reaction time measurements may be used. More complicated methods may also be used, such as human engineering experiments, eye movement tracking, EEG and functional magnetic resonance imaging.

2.2 Scientific experiments of management methods

Another focus of brand experiment is the scientific experiments of management methods. This can be seen in the weapon making of the Qin Dynasty of China and the scientific management experiments conducted by Taylor and his followers, such as pig iron handling experiments, metal cutting experiments and movement experiments. These scientific management experiments have not only changed an era, but will become the management improvement method to be noticed by enterprises today and in the future.

Using scientific experiment methods to obtain advanced management technologies and systematic management methods is an important management improvement process. The Hawthorne studies, which were conducted at the Western Electric Company Inc. in Chicago, United States from 1924 to 1932 is the last management science experiment with great influence today. Afterward, no experiment with similar influence has been conducted in the field of management science. Management experiments at the globally integrated enterprise level are also rare. This should be noted by managers of global enterprises. Scientific management experiments are the integral parts in the management improvement process. Only management methods obtained through scientific experiments can have profound influence on the management processes of global enterprises.

We believe that management science institutes and the management teams of any enterprise should make great efforts to conduct scientific research in the field of management science, so as to realize management improvement through scientific experiments, comparison analysis, data collection and onsite tests. Scientific research and experiments are the results of the joint efforts of researchers throughout the world. The conclusions of these experiments are very important to the improvement of global management. We propose to conduct scientific experiments for management, and share the experiment conclusions at a global level, and encourage the far-sighted management research institutions and universities to jointly research the scientific experiments for management methods and promote the study of scientific management.

Scientific management experiments are as important as chemical and physical experiments. The experiment researchers in the field of management science are the major force leading the improvement of management science. Each invention and application of achievements of such management experiments are a milestone for management improvement of the human beings. Any enterprise hoping to accelerate management improvement shall actively conduct scientific experiments of management, and the inventions of systematic management methods. We believe that enterprises that cannot be integrated into management scientific experiments and management inventions will eventually be eliminated during management improvement.

3 Brand systematization

The old management codes, systems and information will be finally updated to management systems at higher levels, or management systems with brands as core.

The brand management systems are a result of management scientization. Management is existing in the form of systems, or a series of self-adaptable management rules shall be made to complete the designing of the system and the self-adaptable operation of management. The management production of today is completed through many intensified and developed management systems, such as aircrafts on Mars, launching of rockets and satellites, the automatic operation of unmanned factories, the working of robots, the electrical and signaling systems of high-speed rail trains, the automatic ticket checkers, which are the results of management systematization. The management systems have eliminated many positions requiring personnel in the past, such as machine operators, automobile assembly operators, ticket sellers, ticket inspectors and inspectors.

The future is the age of management systems. The management workflow of enterprises has been changed to systematic management styles based on IT, mobile, systematic and network technologies due to the management systems. The administrative management, production management, manufacturing management, equipment management, quality management, storage management and market management have been subject to large scale reform and elimination in the form of management systems. The management systems valued by enterprises in the past are being eliminated in a faster way, and the reengineering of management systems will rise. All of the management links and nodes will be organized organically to operate in a modern way. The works of each person are the processes of the nodes. The works will not be changed due to persons and the persons are the control points of the nodes.

In fact, there is no position for persons in enterprise management. Persons shall complete the creation jobs as the creators. Only if there is no order, a great number of persons will be seen in an enterprise. The traffic lights are the best example. Traffic lights are used to guide traffics according to self-adaptable rules. Only in case of traffic controls or accidents, will the traffic police arrive at the site to guide traffic. Only when the creative works could not be done by machines, or when the enterprise has no high level automatic production conditions, persons will replace the machines to complete basic works. Eventually, many manned jobs will be eliminated. It's only a matter of time. Many more complicated and intelligent management systems will be built.

3.1 Inventions of management systems

System management technologies could be represented with profound reforms of the management technologies in Japan after Deming was invited to the country. The typical examples of system management technologies include the 5S site management, TQC all-employee quality management, Toyota onsite management, Honda 4S store management, lean management thought, fishbone diagram, the 6sigma management in the United States, P&G brand management system, SA8000 enterprise social responsibilities, ISO management standards and the CMM software mature degree of Carnegie Mellon University.

With the rapid development of modern computer software technologies, the system management technologies of the United States have witnessed unprecedented development, and the software programs, such as EPR (enterprise plan of resources), CRM (client relationship management) and SCM (supply chain management) have become the new typical examples of system management technologies. Enterprises in the world have noticed a positive influence of the development of management software for the modern management development.

However, the system management technologies in the age of software have some faults. For example, the management levels vary from company to company. There may be many faults in management flow. Therefore, the management software programs developed or introduced by companies are not mature. In addition, as the representatives of the IT industry, software companies are not the experts of management technologies. Such conflicts have led to the fact that the whole management software industry is in the non-professional management age. It's common to see the repeating development and revising of management software, and outstanding and mature system management software programs are rare.

The national informatization and military informatization of the United States have witnessed a long setback period, during which a lot of IT investments were lost. The initial informatization works were done by different units individually with different management methods, parameters and interfaces, leading to the chaos of the management information system, and the cooperative works could not be conducted. Finally, the system had to be designed from top to bottom to solve the cooperative issues, and the whole management system was standardized.

Some typical management technology inventions have promoted management improvement, such as the electric data interface (EDI) of Wal-Mart, the effective customer reflection (ECR) and quick respond system (QR). Hilton designed its booking system in 1977, and the Hilton network in 1985. The two systems have realized synchronized reservations and reporting services at the hotels, operation department and booking center. McDonald's has designed the operation standardization and participating financing management method to solve the fund expansion issues.

Modern management requires more system management technology inventions. The management technologies in different professional management fields have been made into systems, which have significant functions for the optimization of the managements in more links. The inventions of mature management system technologies are an urgent problem. It's important to pay great attention to intellectual properties (especially the invention patents), the investments in inventions of management system technologies, and the applications of the management system technologies. The leaders in the frontier of top management technology inventions will be an important improvement force needed for the management improvement in the world for a long time.

We have to say that management technologies are not only the individually advanced management methods in local enterprises. Good management technology inventions shall be applicable to the enterprise management advances of the enterprises of the world. Enterprises shall increase investments, make inventions, conduct research and promote the advanced management technologies. The learning and sharing of the management technologies globally will promote the fast improvement of management levels of enterprises of the world. Various emerging management technology inventions will generate more system management technology inventions on a larger scale. The enterprises will obtain more invention ideas and use better management technologies to provide better products and services to society and improve the welfare of all human beings.

3.2 Advances of brand management technologies

A complete brand management technology system has four aspects, including the brand principles, brand technologies, brand tools and brand documentation system. The designing of the technical system is not closed, it shall be an open source knowledge system which could be used to invent, supplement and derive new systems.

The brand principles are an open source system used to define the basic scientific rules of brand science, and research the interactions and mechanisms between the brands and various applications, which could be developed as an independent subject. The study objectives of the brand principles are brand design and management site. The former has defined the basic scientific laws to be followed for brand design, and the later has studied the basic scientific rules that may be seen in various management site links such as R&D, production, marketing, consumer contacts and consumer feedbacks. These studies shall be done with brand terms, brand scientific models and brand capacity rating.

Brand technologies are about the research regarding management methods at the technical level, and is the systematic knowledge used to guide or implement brand management, focusing on detailed working trainings and operations. Brand technologies have been divided into details, including general technologies, such as brand classification technology, brand construction technology, brand transmission technology and brand cooperative technology; and the detailed operation technologies, such as PADS scientific analysis models, brand laboratory technologies and brand talent screening technologies. Researches and applications of brand technologies represent that the brand organization is able to implement the brand management in detail, and are the detailed practices to improve brand capacities.

Brand tools are the practical methods used for brand management, which could be used to simplify operations in a repeating way and improve the operation capacity of the brand works. The researched and invented brand tools could be used for brand design, brand analysis and another detailed management links. Using brand tools could significantly improve the brand management efficiency, featuring convenience, guidance, operation ability and accuracy. Typical tools include tree-shape diagrams, wave diagrams and ternary diagrams.

The brand documentation system includes standard documents, manuals and other written materials, records and reports, featuring standardization, guidance and convenience. The brand documentation system includes guidance documents (brand global announcement, brand construction plans and brand plans), brand manuals (media manuals, transmission manuals and brand activity manuals), and brand works (brand operation guides, brand records and brand correction reports).

Brand principles, brand technologies, brand tools and brand documentation systems are a basic guarantee to an effective brand management, which could make the brand management into an organic body to realize a self-adaptable management, enrich the brand research and ensure the effectiveness of the development of each enterprise brand. The inventions and applications of brand management technologies are important improvements of the global brand science and brand practices, marking that the brands have fully entered into the laboratory state of the brand management technologies, and that the technical supports have become the core pillars for brand development of the enterprises in the world.

4 Brand knowledge

The management improvement issues that can be easily neglected is the brand knowledge. Since the old management over depends on the experience of the managers, the management experience has substituted most management contents in most cases. People may over depend on the management experience of one person, pay attention to what he or she did in the past and learn the experiences from other enterprises or persons to change their own management methods. People will also pay attention to the management methods used by successful entrepreneurs. People will pursue their management secrets and only a few of them will become popular management methods. However, this is not the essence of management and not the method for management improvement.

The improvement of the management science of the future will highly depend on the operation of the developed dynamic knowledge management system. At first, we should distinguish the experience management, static management and dynamic management. At present, the mainstream learning methods are still experience management and static management.

Experience management is to use the working experiences and management experiences accumulated in the past, which are from the knowledge or skills handled by individuals through practices. During the talent recruitment and selection, companies may pay too much attention to the experiences and achievements of the candidates and will limit the persons with unrelated backgrounds from entering into the organization. Static management believes that the management will not change, and the contents of the management are the experiences and rules that have been recognized. In such case, the knowledge application capacity shall be improved by analyzing existing management cases. The university education and books mainly focus on static management. Companies may pay too much attention to the knowledge system in higher education and continuous education, which may lead to serious flaws of the brand management knowledge system.

The knowledge economy age of the 21st century is an age with rapid development of dynamic management. The age of the experience management and static management of the 20th century has long gone. If the knowledge management systems of companies and individuals could not keep pace with time, they will be eliminated rapidly, and the aging of knowledge will be accelerated.

In dynamic management, we assume that the knowledge will change at any time, and that the society, organizations and persons are in rapid change, so as to deal with the rapid knowledge updating system in the knowledge changes with dynamic agility respond system. The companies in the frontier of global competition will use the creation of dynamic knowledge, dynamic researches, dynamic updating and dynamic applications as the core contents of the enterprise knowledge management system.

In the 21st century and far future, since the management and working contents of enterprises and individuals may change at any time; new sciences, tendencies, management methods and marketing activities will occur; the contents and styles of working of everyone may be subject to profound changes due to the new contents of management, market and marketing; and new management issues may occur every day, the only way to deal with rapid changes is to change rapidly, so as to deal with the ever-changing world in a faster way.

Enterprises shall focus on foresight judgment to adjust the management of the enterprises in a fast way. The leadership of an enterprise shall maintain the most acute judgment to handle the changes of the knowledge in frontier, understand new knowledge, thoughts and tendencies rapidly, and use the latest thoughts and knowledge to make the organization faster.

4.1 Dynamic management knowledge system

Dynamic management is very important in the age of knowledge economy. The management of enterprises shall be within the dynamic knowledge management and operation framework, and the universities, research institutes and the future management talents receiving training and education shall use the rapid operation of the dynamic knowledge management system as the mainstream management learning and application method.

Knowledge management system is an integrated system to be established by modern companies for the collection, treatment and sharing of all knowledge of the organization. The knowledge bank of the company shall be established to update the knowledge of the company and to be used as the main learning method. The dynamic management knowledge system is built based on the dynamic management operation, emphasizing the collection, analysis, research and application of the dynamic management knowledge.

In developed countries, the knowledge networks are operated with the modern dynamic management knowledge systems, such as AMO, the agricultural specialist system, evidence-based medicine Cochrane cooperation websites. The contents of knowledge management are not limited to the collection and using rate of knowledge, but will focus on the fastest knowledge collection, analysis, production, abstracting, distribution and application. It will be a continuous knowledge updating cycle from knowledge application to knowledge collection.

In the global competition in the future, the core competitiveness will no longer depend on economic strength. It will be common to see small enterprises defeating large companies. The core competitiveness will depend on the more comprehensive, effective, powerful and faster knowledge advantages. Knowledge shall become the core advantage guiding the policy making of enterprises. This is the management advantage to be learned and applied by all members of the brand organization.

A developed dynamic management knowledge system will be the focus for the reform of the organization in the future, and the precondition to keep the best brand activities of the company. The transfer from information to knowledge is a necessary road for the transmission and development for any company. A knowledge-oriented brand organization is the driving force for active learning, active competition and self-optimization. It's the target for all leading enterprises to release the high speed market competition energy based on the dynamic knowledge management system.

4.2 Global brand knowledge system

In researching the brand standardization, I think there should be four models for global brand knowledge systems, including: the brand knowledge management system at the enterprise level, PADS brand open source knowledge system, international brand league match system and international brand index system. In addition, a global brand technical committee shall be established. I think these will make great contributions to the development of global brand technologies and the improvement of enterprise management technologies.

The key point of the brand knowledge management system at the enterprise level is to establish a knowledge system at the brand organization level, which will be used for the brand dynamic knowledge management inside and outside the company, with the cooperation of the management departments and upstream and downstream knowledge cooperation, and the external expansion of supply chain and brand operation network, emphasizing the collection, production, processing and distribution of knowledge.

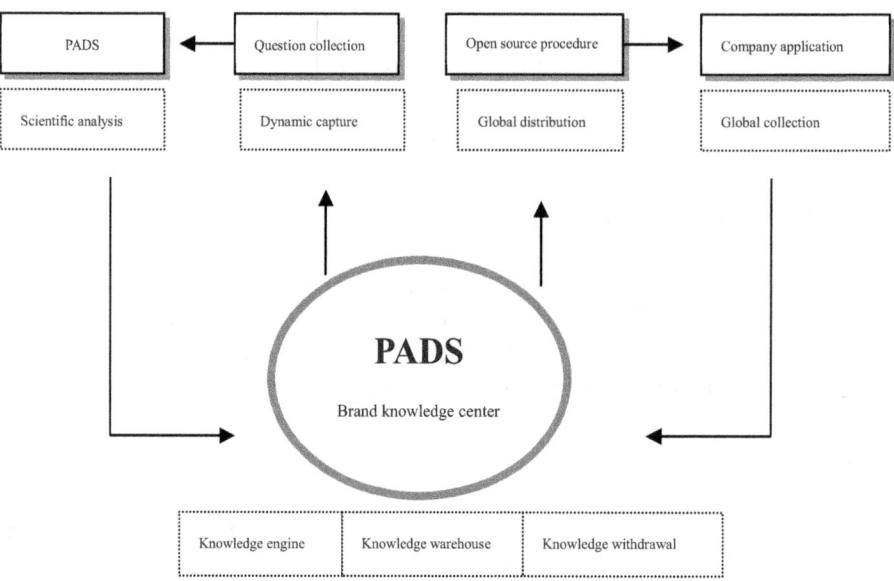

Fig. 3-1 Model of PADS brand knowledge center

PADS brand open source knowledge system is to form knowledge engine, knowledge warehouse and knowledge withdrawal system by establishing global brand dynamic management knowledge center. Through the operation of the system: 1. Collect the brand issues asked by the brand organization, brand graduates and brand officers that are willing to participate in brand knowledge cooperation to conduct the massive scientific analysis for PADS dynamic knowledge management, and backflow the knowledge to the global brand knowledge center; 2. establish the open source procedures of the brand knowledge and documents based on the results of PADS scientific analysis to distribute the knowledge on a larger scale and collect the dynamic brand knowledge generated through the applications by enterprises. The PADS brand open source knowledge system shall be subject to two-way distribution and two-way collection so as to accelerate the improvement of brand knowledge globally.

The international brand league match system is a joint competition participated in by the brand organization, brand officers, brand suppliers, and brand graduates. The items include brand knowledge application, brand advertising designing, brand construction plans, brand transmission plans, brand plans, and brand manuals, and the comprehensive and specific brand indexes will be displayed through BRP (brand capacity rating).

The international brand index system can provide guidance to the global brand consumers for brand selection and for the brand organizations as a reference according to the performances of brand organizations, and the comprehensive and specific brand indexes. The indexes include brand performance, brand quality, brand customer satisfaction, brand purchasing rate, and brand competitiveness. The international brand indexes will be released through periodical reports. The system is an objective and fair capacity estimation method for brands.

As a blueprint, we think the objective, fair and pure academic and market best brand research and knowledge actions shall be established for the development of the global brands so as to deeply influence the management improvement of the brand organizations of the world. This is a scientific form for the orderly development of the global brands. The knowledge of global brands depends on the mutual support and cooperation of the brand organizations in the world.

Exercises

1. Multiple-choice Question: A complete brand management technology system has four aspects, including_____. The designing of the technical system is not closed, it shall be an open source knowledge system which could be used to invent, supplement and derive new systems. (   )

   A. the brand principles, brand technologies, and brand tools

   B. the brand principles, brand technologies, brand tools and brand documentation system

   C. brand technologies, brand tools and brand documentation system

   D. the brand principles, brand tools and brand documentation system

2. Essay Question: What are brand experiment technologies?

3. Discussion: Describe the brand dynamic management knowledge system

Questions for Review & Answers

I. Fill in the blanks:

1. Brand science is a subject focusing on development objects, its characters are: brand science as_____.

2. The brand user groups are realized through three stages, namely, _____, _____, and _____.

3. Brand perception performance is established through the brand users' _____, _____, _____, _____, _____, data analysis and reporting process based on the brand feedback model.

4. The frontier exploration is to provide enterprise brand with_____, _____, _____, _____, and _____.

5. The deciding competiveness factors are, including seven typical competition strengths, namely, _____, _____, _____, _____, _____, _____ and _____.

6. The three major forms of brand civilization are: _____, _____, and _____.

7. Class B (exploration class): _____, _____, and _____ stages of brand, which are actually in mature.

8. Brand _____, brand _____ and brand _____ are the three key basic subjects of brand science.

9. The three development stages of the overall design ideas of brand products: _____, _____, and _____. In addition, the new _____, _____ and _____ shall also be followed.

10. The brand experience facilities developed by brand organizations include typical brand experience forms, such as _____, _____, _____ and _____.

11. Global management technical systems are composed of four technical system links, _____, _____, _____ and _____. Framework systems are the marco-long-term outlook for _____, _____, _____, _____ and _____ in the future, centering upon the frontier exploration and conceptions that may occur in the next 10 to 30 years.

12. A high-quality *Brand Construction Project* should meet the following four elements: _____, _____, _____, and _____.

13. Brand recognition system includes: _____, _____, and _____.

14. There are many brand strategic collaboration forms, mainly including: _____, _____, _____, _____ and _____.

15. Brand artistic conception means brand users' perception process gained through _____, _____, _____ and _____.

16. Brand culture consumption has met three typical demands: _____, _____ and _____.

INTRODUCTION TO BRANDS

17. The soul-shaping of a brand culture is a complete process to _____, _____ and _____ the brand culture core in a cultural way.

18. The brand nuclear explosion power is composed of _____, _____, _____ and _____, and each stage may have brand nuclear explosion. The brand reengineering stage (R) is a repeatable cycling process.

19. Global brand competition pattern has the clear feature of _____. All Global brands are professional brands, and each _____ is composed of several _____. The large and complete interdisciplinary brands are quite rare.

20. The creation of a brand is a process of invention: inventing a feeling or method. For example: _____, _____, manufacturing technology, _____, _____, and _____.

II. Multiple-choice Questions

1. Brands are the core capacity for human beings to develop social economy, the supreme pursuit of _____ instinct and the symbol of human civilization development level.

   A. Social and economic development;   B. mental and physical creation;

   C. scientific and cultural development;   D. product and service creation;

2. The main certification reference is the *Evaluation of Business Enterprise Brand and Guide of Enterprise Culture Construction* (GB/T 27925-2011). The certified enterprises could obtain the brand ratings of _____.

   A. One-star, two-star, three-star and four-star;   B. Two-star, three-star, four-star and five-star

   C. Three-star, four-star, five-star and six-star;   D. Four-star, five-star, six-star and seven-star

3. The shortages of the old brand management centering on the brand positioning include: _____.

   A. Brand is managed only by the marketing department

   B. Brand management is unrelated to all employees

   C. Employees other than those of the sales & marketing department will not participate in brand contribution

   D. A, B and C.

   _____ theory is rapidly weeding out the _____ theory, and will finally become a stable self-adaptable brand ecological chain with mature operation in the super brand ecological chain network. ( )

   A. Brand consumer   producer   B. Producer   brand consumer

   C. A B

5. Service flow management is the scientific service development organization patter based on _____, which will be ultimately updated to the Service Flow. ( )

   A. high flexibility and cross-network nature   B. integrated development

   C. A B   D. A B C

6. People tend to directly judge the value of a brand based on its reputation created by the brand news and make the corresponding decisions, be they_____. ( )

A. employees, talents, investors, competitors or third party analyzers

B. investors, competitors or third party analyzers

C. third party analyzers, employees, or talents

D. third party analyzers or competitors

7. The brand classification technical structure is divided according to the tree structure, which is divided into Class I, II and III. The Class I is _____, Class II is _____ and Class III is _____. ( )

A. brand construction speed/key brand capacity/important brand capacity

B. brand construction speed/key brand capacity/brand capacity elements

C. key brand capacity/important brand capacity/brand capacity elements

8. The systematic brand sales is to treat the sales of an enterprise as a complete system composed of _____, so as to apply integrated marketing to specific sales projects. ( )

A. market subsystem and transmission subsystem

B. transmission subsystem and sales subsystem

C. market subsystem, transmission subsystem and sales subsystem

D. market subsystem and sales subsystem

9. World brand market positions can be divided, according to the brand market positions classification method, into _____, _____, _____, domestic brands, local brands and minority brands. ( )

A. world brands, international brands, national brands, local brands

B. world brands, international brands, national brands,

C. international brands, national brands, nationwide brands

D. B C

10. Brand attraction includes such attraction elements as _____, and it is the mainstream method and core strategic capacity for future brand marketing. ( )

A. Visual attraction, reliable attraction

B. Reliable attraction, brand interesting attraction and designation purchasing rate

C. Visual attraction, reliable attraction and designation purchasing rate

D. Visual attraction, reliable attraction, brand interesting attraction and designation purchasing rate

11. Brand situation and principles for brand designing are the brand situation theory, with the _____ as the soul of brand aesthetic designing. The brand situation in the 21st century is _____, and its core is to realize the ultimate brand design mission of _____ according to the situation structure. ( )

A. Artistic conception of situation, visualization of ideas, perception of experiences and realization of aesthetics.

B. Performance – situation – perception

C. Estimate the world – investigate the world – change the world

D. A, B and C.

III. True or False Questions

1. The development history of brand definition is the development from identification theory, function theory, economy theory and value theory to social theory, and is the development process strengthening impression and understanding of brands through social and economic activities. ( )

2. Theory A of brand thought power emphasizes: the formation of the thinking power of brand is a great creation process with the wisdoms of human beings, the thinking power of brand is the basis for the creation of everything, the thinking power of brand has created the demands of human beings, the thinking power of brand is the inevitable result of the highly coordinated development of brand consciousness, brand organization power and brand attraction, the thinking power of brands is the important milestone of the social and economic development of human beings. the thinking power of brand is a precious mental pursuit of human beings, and the thinking power of brand is the rare core development power for human beings. ( )

3. The brand presentation performance could determine the brand value performance retroactively. The most important problem of the brand value performance is to present the brand value directly in the best way and from the best angle. ( )

4. Brand sensing network is the indispensable detection arrangement for new brands to enter market. The duration for arranging the brand sensing network is 3 to 6 months generally. With the completion of brand sensing function, the brand sensing network will be updated to a higher stage – brand interpersonal relationship network. ( )

5. The brand performance is represented through: good brands, good products, good ideas, good raw materials, good images, high quality, more safety, internationalization and good tastes. ( )

6. The abnormal conditions of brand development are manifested by various management problems, which may be mainly reflected by brand mistakes. ( )

7. The perfect expression of brand quality could be realized through the brand stretching theory of general designing, quality pursuit and overall improvement. ( )

8. The brand planning with modern rationality is within the development scope of the operational research serving brand governance and brand strategies. ( )

9. Tomorrow Management must be composed of the management technology structures at the industry and enterprise levels. All industries during the high-speed market development will form their own brand with decisive competitiveness to occupy the leading position in market. ( )

10. Brand technology preparation shall follow: general brand designing principle, lancet principle and natural ecological development principle. ( )

11. Professional brand definition: a brand shall devote to one thing diligently and eliminate unnecessary links. ( )

12. The global management advances in the future must highly depend on complete development of management subjects, progress of management technologies, discoveries made by management experiments and inventions of mature management systems. ( )

13. Instead of reporting major events, the brand self-media shall focus on brand news and brand users, and shall have a strong sense of belonging. ( )

14. The synergy of brand users is mainly reflected through brand participation and brand interaction. Brand will highly depend on synergy to establish a long-term brand future based on the development of synergetic technology. ( )

15. The cultural transmission process could be divided into three levels: brand culture, enterprise culture and brand user. ( )

16. The brand artistic conception reveals three key points: pursuit of the aestheticism of nature; philosophical thinking of the truth of life and comprehension of the ternary order balance. ( )

17. Brand culture enrichment is a combination with the brand symbol and brand concept as the center and brand culture representation method as content. ( )

18. Brand officers are the occupational sequence of enterprise brands, a self-disciplined investigation team and a group of perfectionists. ( )

19. The single-product strategy is very important in brand nuclear explosion power. Many brands have benefited from the sales miracles created by single product when entering market. ( )

20. Based on the dynamic management operation, the dynamic management knowledge system is emphasizes the analysis and application of dynamic management knowledge. ( )

IV. Essay Questions

1. What is the doubt principle of brand users?

2. What are the reasons that the brand development level fails to reach the value network level in which brand matches with users?

3. What are the expressions and causes of the fact that brand science failed to grow into a complete subject in the past?

4. What's the motivation of brand organization?

5. What are the development structures of brand products?

6. What are the forms of brand products experience?

7. Why does brand construction may turn out to be a failure?

8. Brand development has entered a watershed, and what are the different development patterns of it?

9. What is the core of the brand process reengineering?

10. What are the aspects scientifically expressing brand culture?

11. How to determine if an individual has good tastes?

12. How to understand the brand symbolization?

13. What is surreal designing in the 21st century?

14. What is the brand organization reengineering? What's its meaning to enterprise development?

15. What is brand systematization?

V. Discussion:

1. How many propositions are there in brand B theory, and what are the brief contents of these propositions?
2. How to understand the re-definition of new media?
3. Please discuss the lays of enterprise brand strategy.
4. How to understand brand development power?
5. How to understand the roles of brand quality system design and brand officers in enterprise brand development?
6. How do the strategies and tactics of brand planning function in market?
7. How to interpret the value of brand news?
8. Please briefly describe the purpose of brand technical preparation.
9. What are the major methods for brand marketing?
10. Briefly describe the three-level of brand transmission.
11. Briefly describe the social value of brands amid great cultural change.
12. Briefly describe the shaping of brand image and conditions needed.

Answers

I. Fill in the blanks:

1. Frontier science

2. Brand communities, foundation of brand, brand user groups

3. Perception level, perception degree, perception method, research of perception respond, perception measurement

4. Frontier thoughts, frontier discoveries, frontier experiments, frontier R&D, frontier drive

5. Victory determination, knowledge system, management design, concept route, brand performance advantage, full-scale operation and real-time response

6. The brand civilization based on image; the brand civilization based on reality; the brand civilization based on artistic expression such as pictographic and abstract image, picture composition, plane, three dimensional image, and decoration

7. Construction stage, intermediate stage, the brand seems mature

8. Brand principles, brand pathology and brand organization

9. Overall design ideas of brand products, design ideas of typical products, and design ideas of brand product development; brand product development mechanism, brand product development structure and brand product-oriented development process design

10. Brand experience pavilion, brand virtual scene, online brand experience technology, development of brand experience activities

11. Framework order, actions, technology implementation; competitive environment, industry transformation, operation mode, market design and market exploration.

12. (1) When; (2) What; (3) Who ; (4) what quality.

13. Brand idea recognition, brand image recognition, brand impression recognition

14. Industrial value chain collaboration, core competitiveness collaboration, product core value collaboration, united competition collaboration and diversified collaboration

15. Psychology, vision, touch and gustation

16. Demands for others, self-demands or mixed demands

17. Cultural exploration, planning and designing

18. Brand dream stage (D), brand interpretation stage (I), brand designing stage (D) and brand reengineering stage (R)

19. Brand cluster, cluster brand and single product brand

20. Tastes, texture, appearance feelings, chemicals, physical methods

II. Multiple-choice Questions

    1. B
    2. B
    3. D
    4. A
    5. C
    6. A
    7. C
    8. C
    9. B
    10. D
11. D

III. True of False Questions

    1. √
    2. √
    3. √
    4. ×
    5. √
    6. ×
    7. ×
    8. √
    9. ×
    10. √
    11. √
    12. √
    13. √
    14. ×
    15. ×
    16. √
    17. ×
    18. √
    19. √
20. ×

IV. Essay Questions

1. Users will see the new brands with a strong sense of resistance. The instinct for sense of security during brand consumption will form a natural protection for human beings. People will be wary of all unknown matters. Even tiny risk will stop them from moving forward. Therefore, people throughout the world may adopt a defense attitude to new brands in general.

2. There are three key points: (1) the output party of the brand value has good feel. There is brand value chain without brand value identification system at clients; (2) the brand value chain and the brand value identification system are not in consistency; the value output information is in chaos with less output or more output exceeding the committed scope, resulting in low quality and efficiency of brand value output power; and (3) the brand value identification based on multiple Internets is not well developed with insufficient designing capacities and low development level.

3. Major expressions: as a basic subject for human beings, brand science could not make an important subject in knowledge fields of human beings officially given the lack of systematic researches and theories. Brand science is still short of basic scientific theories, research spirits and sufficient researchers, leading to the fact that the previous application of brand science mainly focused on business patterns.

4. Organization motivation is the initial motivation for people to decide to establish or participate in a brand organization. Meanwhile, it could be used to identify the overall motivation of the existence and development of the whole brand organization. Positive motivation can accelerate the brand organization development while negative motivation will produce damages of different degrees to brand organization.

5. Six, which are systemized products, functional products, industrial ecological products, morphological products, cross-generation products and N-generation products.

6. Brand experience design (BXD), brand participated marketing (BPM), brand experience management (BXM) and interactive perception enhancement (IPE).

Brand experience design (BXD) mainly appears in user feeling and use during the entire process of brand product; Brand participated marketing (BPM) is a kind of interactive development mode encouraging users to participate in brand experience design, service and application process.; Brand experience management (BXM) is a management mode with ceaseless upgrading, optimization and dynamic development based on brand experience process; and interactive perception enhancement (IPE) mainly focuses on touch point deployment, value finding way, brand value expression method and brand consumption education method during direct or indirect interaction between brands and user

7. In most cases, brand construction cannot meet its initial goal, which is caused by knowledge discrepancies. The promoters of *Brand Construction Project* are usually the managers in relatively lower level, or other brand PR (planning or consulting) companies, which aren't part of the enterprises' top management level. Thus, these people have insufficient understanding towards the enterprises' long-term brand strategy, which directly leads to an ineffective *Brand Construction Project* without strategic vision.

8. The development of brands has entered a watershed now, or the development form of heavy and light brands. The heavy brands are those developed through huge advertising input such as TV advertising, outdoor advertising, magazine advertising and TV program sponsorship whereas the light brands are those developed through the Internet, mobile facilities and person-to-person transmissions, and people can hardly see any light brand advertisements on TV.

9. The core of brand process reengineering is to create clients' expectations. It's a reengineering action with the brand value chain as the core. Instead of treating business as the

only core, the reengineering focuses on the overall management, all employees and all processes. The core of the new brand process engineering is the value importance in the whole brand process. The value could be represented through core value propositions, enterprise responsibilities, working values and service values. The formation of the value chain has defined the value contribution and output of all departments, processes, works and individuals in the brand organization. The value output is the realization of brand profits, and is the profit chain that determines the final brand premium.

10. Brand culture expressions are represented by important functional values in three aspects. (1) ecological development life value of brand culture; (2) brand culture is essentially higher than all cultural forms of enterprises; (3) the monetary value of brand culture as asset.

11. People always link one's aesthetic manner with the pattern, quality, design and style of the product he buys, so as to identify his taste. And they also believe that whether the product's brand is international will prove one's pursuit of taste in some degree. Taste is not only the primary premise of brand design ideas but also the reflection of brand premium when people purchase products and pursue brands.

12. Symbols are a way to translate the complicated development pattern of a brand in a simple way through concentrated system. Brands are symbols with profound symbolic meaning. People use symbols to transmit various complicated information. Symbols are the conceptualized recognition representing a brand or (in an explicit or an inexplicit way) a thought, way of thinking, visual image, activity or physical matters.

13. The surreal conceptual design in the 21st century is more of a utopian world, a brand culture world with weakened influence of modernism and coexistence of super-modernism and anti-modernism. The 21st century is a new millennium for the brands to flourish, and in which the brands will appear and focus on sufficient imaginative design ideas, pushing themselves to the limits known to people. Modernism, with unprecedented imagination and dreams, connects the future imaginative world with the real environment, and focuses on themed cultural scenes of the space, on the natural ecology of the earth and its context, and on new materials and technology. People can develop imaginary science and conceptual products in areas of the future cities, watches, robots and automobiles, and incorporate brand ideas into everything. It will represent an era of surreal fusion of products and art, an era of rapid progress, and of a masterpiece that integrates brands with life, nature and ecological sustainable development, all together present in imagination, science and technology and cultural development.

14. The reengineering of brand organization is an important moment for the considerable enhancement of the specialization and movement ability of the enterprise. Given the repeating works, the enthusiasm and creativity of the employees of the brand organization will be reduced rapidly, and the company will risk the withering creativity. Therefore, the brand organization shall focus on fully releasing and stimulating employee's creativity while enterprise shall establish a more scientific agility system to complete the reengineering process. Each employee is a creator, and the brand organization is the collection of creators. Only constant creation and the creative destruction activities can drive the organization forward from within. The reengineering of organs may improve the reengineering of the whole body. In this way, the brand organization can stay vigorous and keep its global competitive advantages.

15. The brand management systems are a result of management scientization. Management is existing in the form of systems, or a series of self-adaptable management rules shall be made to complete the designing of the system and the self-adaptable operation of management. The management production of today are completed through many intensified and developed management systems, such as aircrafts on Mars, launching of rockets and satellites, the automatic operation of unmanned factories, the working of robots, the electrical and signaling systems of high-speed rail trains, the automatic ticket checkers, which are the results of management systematization. The management systems have eliminated much manpower. The future is the age of management system which will transform the management processes of enterprises into the

system management of IT, mobile, system and network technologies. The administration, production management, manufacturing management, equipment management, quality management, warehouse management and market management are witnessing large-scale reform or experiencing obsolescence in the form of management system. The management system as the old management method cherished by enterprises is undergoing accelerated elimination. And the management system reengineering will come to prominence. All management links and nodes will be organized in an organic way and operated in a modern manner where the work of each person will be the process of the node. Work will not change due to people, on the contrary people will be control points on numerous nodes.

V. Discussions

1. See section 2 of *Brand Power*
2. See section 1.2 of *Internet + Brand*
3. See section 1 of *Brand Strategy*
4. See section 3 of *Brand Consumption*
5. See section 6 of *Brand Quality*
6. See section 3.2 of *Brand Planning*
7. See section 1 of *Brand News*
8. See section 4 of *Brand Technology Preparation*
9. See section 1.5 of *Brand Marketing Technology*
10. See section 1.2 of *Brand Communication Technology*
11. See section 1.3 of *World Brand Pattern*
12. See section 4 of *Brand Image Upgrading*

Answers to the Exercises in Section I

Chapter 1 Brand Introduction

1. Brand economy of human beings, brand ecological organization
2. ×
3. Refer to section 3.2 of the Brand Introduction

Chapter 2 Brand Definition

1. Identification theory, function theory, economy theory, value theory and society theory
2. Ability, quality, value, reputation, influence and enterprise culture, name, symbol and image design
3. Economic awareness, product awareness, marketing awareness, service awareness, social awareness, organization awareness, nation awareness, global awareness and human awareness.

Chapter 3 Brand Standardization

1. Industrial persons, handicraft persons, industrial persons, individualized industrial person
2. √
3. Standardization focusing on orders, Standardization focusing on optimization, Standardization focusing on codes, Standardization focusing on rating, Standardization focusing on system networks.

Chapter 4 Brand Power

1. Brand consciousness (height), brand organization capacity (depth), brand attraction (width – the common name of brand attraction)
2. Brands, consumption, enterprises
3. (1) Brands are the safe consumption activities for certain desires, (2) People will pay more for brands, (3) The desires met by brands are special demands, (4) Brands have consumption levels, and people will do every effort to complete such consumption process, (5) People rely on brands and will resist other brands, (6) Consumers will not recognize the business types of the brands nor the enterprises, (7) Consumers will rarely purchase new brands and only accept the recommendations from reliable sources, (8) Consumers may only make trail purchasing for new brands with strong consumption prevention consciousness, (9) Violent brand consumption could only be seen in the enterprises with mid-brand capacities. The lower the consumption power is, the higher the consumption requirement will be.

Chapter 5 Brand User Groups

1. Early development, market expansion, long-term and stable sustainable operation
2. B
3. Refer to section 3.2 of Brand User Groups

Chapter 6 Brand Performance

1. Brand perception performance, brand presentation performance, brand value performance, brand essence performance and brand utility performance, the brand performance in the global synergic network.
2. B

3. Refer to section 6 of Brand Performance

Chapter 7 Leading Position

1. Creation or reengineering, development directions, future prospects

2. B

3. Primary brands are the important strategic selections made by enterprise brands to obtain leading position, or a series of market preparations and actions assuming that the brands could become the primary brands in some fields. The primary brand is also an important epitome for a brand organization to establish its leading position. From the first day of brand creation or reengineering, the strategic target of primary brand has been determined. Next, a series of massive reforms shall be conducted to define the primary brands in the minds of consumers, and the physiological effect shall be rooted among consumers from the very beginning, so as to use market actions to complete the great changes from imagination to implementation. When the press conferences are held to release such brands, the revolutions with huge influence on the market have started. Sufficient preparation and strategic arrangement are always conducted before the sun rises.

Chapter 8 Deciding Competitiveness

1. B

2. The concept system is a series of effective competition strategies designed by the brand organization using the frontier thoughts. Such strategies include the imagination of the future, the determination for the current challenges, and the strategies for market divisions, which shall be used as the guiding thoughts for each stage and each period to complete the thought and activity support for the long term development of the brand. Concepts are a series of ideological forms which could be used to guide the central thoughts and action routes of the brand organization actions.

3. Refer to section 3.1 of Deciding Competitiveness

Chapter 9 Internet + Brands

1. Information, time, communication, usage, knowledge, ecology

Information sources, time cluster, usage method, knowledge system, brand ecological organization.

2. √

3. For enterprise brand development on network, the specific development rule is slope development mode; the attraction is from content marketing including brand news, brand advertising text, channel operation, micro-video and machine intelligence. The brands extremely active on internet can develop to a network brand with large influence only by sustainably implementing and rapidly upgrading brand content marketing strategy. The impetus is comprised of various internet solutions, including statistical analysis, tendering system, WeChat business system, payment system, CRM and product placement in film and TV.

Answers to the Exercises in Section II

Chapter 1 Brand History

1. Global reach, global premium, imprint owned, place of origin, quality grade, and quality stability

2. √

3. Refer to Section 1 of Brand History

Chapter 2 Brand Principles

1. Users, customers, regulars; from users to customers, and then to regulars

2. √

3. Refer to Section 5 of Brand Principles

Chapter 3 Brand Pathology

1. Reason and mechanism of occurrence, development rules, and pathological state

2. Universality, centrality, and concurrent occurrence

Firstly, enterprise brand development lacks the systematic and scientific development route and the summary of scientific management and development rules; the brand management is seriously unscientific; secondly, the long-standing case management teaching makes teachers handle management problem as a typical case or an individual case, and development ability of scientific management is insufficient; thirdly, the practical management ability on site is seriously insufficient; enterprises lack scientific diagnosis ability to frequently and rapidly handle various dynamic management problems on management site, and the management problems of enterprises are multiple and concurrent.

3. Refer to Section 5 of Brand Pathology

Chapter 4 Brand Strategy

1. Thinking of structure, anticipation, order, leadership, science, creation, themed topics or route, and operation

2. √

3. The strategic thinking of brand is used to guide basic brand behavior of enterprise. The strategic thinking will govern the overall situations, and guide strategic layout and deployment. It is the key ideological soul and value creation way of enterprise brand strategy.

Strengthening the country by famous brands, strengthening the enterprise by famous brand, brand economy, brand cluster, brand internationalization, brand professional, brand feeling, making particular brand strong, brand capacity, lean brand, brand security, brand learning, brand naming rate, brand profit chain, and brand user groups, etc.

Answers to the Exercises

Chapter 5   Brand Organization

    1. Enterprise, brand, brand organizations, and brand ecological organizations

    2. √

    3. Refer to 1.1 of Brand Organization

Chapter 6   Brand Consumption

    1. Producer, operator, and consumer

    2. √

    3. Brand consumption demands develop into five main forms: the development of survival conditions (natural environment enjoyment level for food, residence and travel), development of brand basic demands (brand performance development level, service life, quality stability and performance elements), development of special brand demands (personality, identity, honor, nutrition, health, happiness and relaxation), development of brand user group demand (sense of belonging, sense of achievements, sense of identity, sense of value, sense of participation acceptance, emotion, and long-term demand), and development of brand consumption safety (food safety system, purchase channel, reliable e-business, new brand perception mode and primary trust design of brand).

Chapter 7   Brand Products

    1. D

    2. √

    3. Refer to Section 6 of Brand Products

Chapter 8   Brand Service

    1. Brand service demand chain, brand service supply chain, brand service profit chain

    2. √

    3. The idea of brand after-sales service specially refers to the strategic ideas for long-term service that brands should establish, including the extension of producer's responsibility, rethinking of service objective, service-oriented ideas, leading edge detection, service profit chain, service upgrade and service marketing. It is the source of main competitive thought for a brand to set up the service value chain and carry out systematic design of brand service flow. Brand after-sales service appears as a typeof a service idea. Such idea is based on the service profit chain development structure of the "after-sales service reselling".

Chapter 9   Brand Quality

    1. Better state, optimal experience and quality stability

    2. B

    3. Brand quality cannot be assured by promise or guarantee, or recognized by detection, or improved by PDCA quality link. However, it is completed by structural design as overall structure of a brand, and it completes staged brand quality advancement by overall design, quality pursuit and overall improvement; it is the global progress of brand quality reliability, stability, advancement and development quality system; it is the fundamental development idea and structure to guarantee long-term future development of a brand, ability to guarantee overall prospective pre-design and

cutting-edge position and systematically solve any possible quality problems in future brand development, and the key factual basis for decisive competitiveness development ability.

Chapter 10 Brand Experience

    1. D

    2. √

    3. Refer to Section 3 of Brand Experience

Chapter 11 Brand Planning

    1. Brand proposal, proposal on key points of brand strategy, and brand plan

    2. D

    3. It comprises three parts, respectively (1) the brand planning is the overall brand governance of ideas aiming to create a long-term stable development strategy, and can only solve problems of short-term market expansion and growth; (2) the brand development in the 21st century mainly depends on the process of making the brand scientific. Brand planning follows artistic ideas, just as military, which is deemed as both a scientific development and an art application; (3) the brand development has no shortcut or isn't based on a certain occasional lucky opportunity, but needs progressive and systematic development and self-adaptive expansion through practical, diligent and stabile approaches.

Chapter 12 Brand News

    1. Brand impression– brand reputation – brand emotion – brand credibility

    2. √

    3. Different from the common news, the brand related news is a pattern generated jointly by the brand party, media, and brand related party, and a special communication pattern jointly generated with the cross-spreading and interactive ecological chain influence in the multi-net interconnected media medium. It is also a fundamental ability to review a brand from its enterprise brand upgrading all the way to the brand organization status. Moreover, the purpose of brand news development is to set up and maintain the brand image, develop brand reputation, and acquire brand effect, brand premium ability and brand assets value, with the speed of the process being incremented due to increasingly improving brand influence.

ANSWERS TO THE EXERCISES

Answers to the Exercises in Section III

Chapter 1　Brand Technical System

1. A

2. The brand Technical system is the most important reengineering technologycentered on the brand in the whole management. The brand technology has firstly established the leading position of the brand management in the future enterprise development. Centered on the brand, it develops the other managementtechnology and then forms the systematic "management integration" for the future enterprises.

3. Refer to Section 4.4 of Brand Technical System

Chapter 2　Brand Technology Preparation

1. Brand dream, brand conception, brand general design and brand technology preparation

2. D

3. Any enterprise shall, whenever deciding to develop a brand, go through a branding process with complete system and scientificrules and brand technological requirements. For the purpose of developing brand in the future, an enterprise shall make full preparation in capacity and resources for the brand technology construction and a state shall do well in the systematic engineering for the brand technology preparation to fully carry out brandfor domestic companies. The brand strategic resources include brand technological resources reserve, brand talent resources reserve, brand capital reserve, brand cooperation resources reserve and brand emergency strategic resources reserve.

Chapter 3　Brand Construction Technology

1. D

2. ×

3. Refer to Section 6 of Brand Construction Technology

Chapter 4　Brand Classification Technology

1. Professional brand, trusted brand, premium brand, tide brand, leading brand and international brand

2. The invention of brand classification technology mainly depends on the following five factors: (1) Being similar with the periodic table of chemical element. (2) Carrying out benchmarking management. (3) Selecting brand strategic routes. (4) Rapidly conducting brand diagnosis. (5) Establishing the basis for brand rating, evaluation and index.

3. Refer to Section 1 of Brand Classification Technology

Chapter 5　Brand Recognition Technology

1. C

2. √

3. Refer to Section 3.10 of Brand RecognitionTechnology

Chapter 6   Brand Management Technology

1. Establishing management rules, conducting management experiments, formulating management brochures and SOPs (Standard Operation Procedure), managing brand recording documents and finishing brand reports.

2. B

3. Refer to Section 5.4 of Brand Management Technology

Chapter 7   Brand Marketing Technology

1. Promoting stage, hard-selling stage, marketing stage and brand attracting stage

2. √

3. Please refer to Section 2.1 of Brand Marketing Technology

Chapter 8   Brand Communication Technology

1. Brand news communication, word-of-mouth communication, warming-up communication, thematic communication, topic communication

2. D

3. The brand knowledge system is a modern knowledge library consisting of a whole set of knowledge tree, knowledge points, knowledge materials, etc. set up for brand identification and brand communication. The knowledge system should be dynamic and constantly record different knowledge such as the latest R&D and product application. It should be able to upgrade; access and apply the collection and communication mode. What is more important for brand knowledge system is that it consists of knowledge such as brand history, the market field which the brand is in, product usage method, and product application cases. The brand knowledge in these systems is extremely effective in communicating brand.

Chapter 9   Brand Collaboration Technology

1. D

2. To establish a collaborative enterprise, the parties participating in establishment of collaborative company shall set up a collaborative committee or office to be responsible for the joint affairs and coordination of collaborative company. The collaborative committee (office) shall include the senior representatives and officers appointed by the participating companies. It might also require the collaborative technology experts, industrial study experts, management consultants and management analysis,etc. The collaboration could be mainly divided into connection technology and data integration collaboration, production plan collaboration, agile manufacturing synchronized collaboration and brand market collaboration, etc.

3. Refer to Section 2 of Brand Collaboration Technology

Answers to the Exercises in Section IV

Chapter 1 World Brand Pattern

1. Functionality– culture –realm
2. √
3. The main brand creators and responsible world corporations have the consistent development target: change the world and live a better life.(1) the development of mass culture demanded mainly by the common people; (2) pursuit of universal cultural state for people to live a better life; (3) the social value contribution consciousness for the people to demonstrate more advanced science, more refined technologies, more perfect brand, better products and better services; (4) the development force thought of friendship, peaceful coexistence, mutual progress and shared development achievements among the people.

Chapter 2 Brand and Enterprise Culture

1. Tracing, integration, extraction, development, implementation, commanding and coordination
2. A
3. Refer to Section 3 of Brand and Enterprise Culture

Chapter 3 Brand Artistic Conception

1. B
2. Brand context refers to the context in which the brand language is expressed, i.e. expressing the in-depth feelings of the brand through texts and images. Brand, in fact is to create a feeling that can be expressed not only through LOGO and designs but also through texts and images that play a vital role. The context described in commercials and words would arouse direct association to ideas of brand users and provide incredibly immersive experience for audiences, this will initiate a strong sense of inner resonance which is manifested as an ultimate pursuit of the brand that can be completed by desiring and obtaining ownership of the brand.
3. Refer to Section 2.1 of Brand Artistic Conception

Chapter 4 Brand Aesthetics

1. Brand perception, product defects, quality instability, delivery environment and service delay
2. √
3. Refer to Section 3 of Brand Aesthetics

Chapter 5 Brand Culture Consumption

1. D
2. The reform is mainly seen in the aspects of the historical change, the life circle and the free choice of brand culture. The development of brand culture generally takes on historical changes, where the popular styles in different times clearly distinct with one another. It can be seen from the old photos, pictures, movies, and study on the cultural history that all clothes, hairstyle, electrical appliances, articles

about the daily use and social life have a clear time trait. People can easily tell which cultural context belongs to which country from which era. This is an overall meming change of people's cultural pursuit, where a contextual culture trait that is comprised of the fixed-form popular brand culture reflects the collective, centralized and unified change in people's aesthetic standard towards the brands in a certain era.

3. Refer to Section 3 in Brand Culture Consumption

Chapter 6 Brand Culture Connotation

1. A

2. √

3. Refer to Section 3 of Brand Culture Connotation

Chapter 7 Brand Image Upgrading

1. Distinguishing market competition sector, market decomposition, professional division of labor, enhancement of brand trust

2. D

3. In the level of global market competition, the main body of brand competition has been transformed from the large and comprehensive pan-brand into the brand components in the enterprise brand clustering system and the independent professional brand in the market, and the focus of brand image development is shifted from the brand image integration effect into the branding professional system effect with brand development structure.

Chapter 8 Brand Artistic Expression

1. Inspiration comes from the nature, the idea stems from structure, the form follows the function and aesthetics create artistic conception

2. ×

3. Refer to Section 6 of Brand Artistic Expression

Answers to the Exercises in Section V

Chapter 1 DID Brand Reengineering Principles

1. C

2. The core of brand reengineering is that the enterprise will decide to re-implement the DID stage. Brand reengineering is not only changing name or LOGO, or holding a press conference. The brand reengineering has more profound meaning which is a deep reform of the whole brand organization from top to bottom. When an existing brand has begun aging, or a mature brand has determined to reshuffle the market, the brand reengineering actions will play important roles. The brand reengineering actions of the enterprise will release the energy of the brand organization again, re-motivate the confidence of all persons, and redefine the patterns of the market. During this process, the enterprise will announce its second, third or forth business starting. After brand reengineering, the brand shall appear in the market with new images, postures, and market attacks. With the efforts of all employees, the market landscape shall be re-divided, and this is the primary target of the brand reengineering of the brand organization. The brand reengineering among brands are still being conducted. The company shall constantly research new products to replace with the old ones, and each releasing of new products means the reengineering of the brand.

3. Refer to section 4.1 of the DID Brand Reengineering Principles

Chapter 2 Brand Organization Reengineering

1. A

2. √

3. Refer to section 6.1 of the Brand Organization Reengineering

Chapter 3 Reengineering of Brand Management System

1. B

2. Brand experiment is an important research process, a strict invention process and a repeating process, which requires sufficient foresight, certain investments and sufficient research capacities. Such investments are absolutely wise. The enterprises in developing countries may neglect this key link, leading to the low brand premium capacity and the reduced overall competitiveness of the brand on the global market.

3. Refer to section 4.1 of the Reengineering of Brand Management System

Learning Methods for *Introduction to Brands*

In general, at least 2 or 3 years are required to thoroughly understand the study and application of theories in *Introduction to Brands*. As a major research achievement representing global brand thought and theory, *Introduction to Brands* is an open systematic theory applicable to the United States, developed countries in Europe as well as developing countries, such as China.

Learning Methods for Introduction to Brands

Introduction to Brands is a subject with great practicality that can with stand the history test of human beings. Time and the wide applications will prove its advancement. There are six methods to learn *Introduction to Brands*, and learners can arrange their study schedule according to actual conditions.

Method 1: systematic learning, or learning the contents gradually according to the distribution system of the theoretical structure. Method 2: principal line learning, focusing on solving brand problems in one aspect based on application subjects. Method 3: real-time learning, flexible and immediately applicable, one can select the chapters at will. Method 4: direction learning, directly using corresponding brand science principles, rules and technologies according to brands' development direction. Method 5: question learning, learning the book for specific questions, explaining the difficulties with notes, similar to referring to classics. Method 6: problem-solving learning, using theories in the book to resolve actual brand problems, or checking brand problems and cases according to the brand principles to verify actual application values of the theories and the authority of the answers.

Major Problems Systematically Resolved by *Introduction to Brands*

When learners have to solve brand development problems in one aspect, they can organically combin in grelated chapters of the book. Good scientific theories can predicate any possible brand problems, causes, processes and consequences so as to settle direction and scientific routes for brand applications and solve various problems. *Introduction to Brands* lists seven hot spot problems that may occur in enterprises and designs a branch structure for theoretical learning. When learners want to solve any problems, they can learn corresponding chapters according to tips and sequences with the bold words as important contents.

1 To solve brand development direction problem systematically:

To master the basic rules of brand science, one should learn: **Brand Introduction, Brand Definition, Brand Power**, Brand History, **Brand Principles, Brand Pathology**, and World Brand Pattern.

2 To solve the three major problems blocking the brand development of Chinese enterprises:

To solve brand governance structure problems: **Leading Position, Deciding Competitiveness, Brand Technical System, Brand Strategy,** Brand Products, Brand Service, **Brand Quality, Brand Experience, Brand Planning as well as Brand and Enterprise Culture.**

To solve brand cultural connotation problems: Brand Artistic Conception, Brand Aesthetics, **Brand Culture Consumption, and Brand Culture Connotation.**

To solve brand image up grading problems: **Brand Culture Connotation, Brand Image Upgrading and Brand Artistic Expression.**

3 Solve brand development method problems:

To solve the brand performance problems (future brand competitions based on Internet): **Brand Performance, Internet + Brand, Brand Consumption, Brand User Groups, Brand Culture Connotation**, Brand News, Brand Communication Technology, Brand Management Technology, and Brand Collaboration Technology.

To solve brand construction method problems: **Brand Technology Preparation, Brand Construction Technology, Brand Classification Technology**, Brand Standardization, Brand Management Technology and Brand Communication Technology.

To solve brand reengineering problems: **DID Brand Reengineering Principles, Brand Organizations Reengineering, Reengineering of Brand Management System**, Brand Standardization, and Brand Management Technology.

Postscript:
Heading for brand subjects theory studies at higher levels

After more than a decade, the systematic research and theoretical designing of Introduction to Brands have achieved periodical accomplishments, but this represented a new starting point rather than an end. We all know that brand subjects are a newly established subject, and extensive theoretical thoughts, development directions and practices entail our further researches so that brand theories achievements in different stages can be shared by readers throughout the world.

1 Ten sub-theories of *Introduction to Brands*

The sub-theories of *Introduction to Brands* are the continuous research and systematic expansion of brand theories, and the proposed ten sub-theories include *Brand Evaluation Method Theory*, *Brand Construction Activity Theory*, *Brand Education Theory*, *Brand Communication Theory*, *Brand Expansion Theory*, *National Brand Strategy Theory*, *Brand Standard Strategy Theory*, *Social Organization Brand Strategy Theory*, *City Brand Strategy Theory*, *Enterprise Brand Strategy Theory*, and *Brand Feng Shui Theory* which is an independently attached theory.

With its 10 sub-theories, *Introduction to Brands* aims to propose systematic structural theory designing against overall development. These researches have displayed important development functions, economic values and subjects' directions with regard to social economy, brand evaluation and brand strategies, aiming at providing a wider view for theoretical analysis, research discoveries and actual applications of brand science researchers and practitioners throughout the world.

The purpose of the ten sub-theories of *Introduction to Brands* is to define detailed directions, ways and methods with regard to general brand competition in social and economic development of all countries by taking a full account of a series of important issues concerning man's future advancement, such as human beings' progress, fair competition in global markets, competition between brand output countries and brand input countries, brand position in social system and economic constructions of a country, the third party brand evaluation at national and social levels, brand and national education structure, economic supporting potentials of brands in industries and cities, brand strategic economic roles and the guiding competitiveness of implementing brands at enterprise competition level.

If *Introduction to Brands* have answered the three major questions, namely "what are brands", "how to establish brand subjects systematically", and "how could the enterprises develop practical brands in the future", the ten sub-theories have resolved the four problems such as "evaluation technologies of brands", "formation of brand society", "development of brand economy" and "view of the brand strategies". The topic of "Brands as the Total Intangible Assets" will be the focus leading the frontier exploration of new brand theories.

POSTSCRIPTS

2 Further development of brand thoughts

We are heading for a highly developed brand economy. The competition body of such economy is the emerging social economic development structure underpinned by brands, whose essence is to fundamentally and profoundly reform current commercial economic activities of human beings from three aspects:

Brand industry was formed as one of the basic industries of human beings. The forming of brand industry structure and its developing as one of the basic construction industries have profoundly changed the existing economic subject structure and the practicing methods of enterprise brands like railway industry and power industry did. Therefore, contents of the commercial science such as advertising, products, marketing and commodities can be integrated into general development structures of the brand theory to form systematic brand service industry, brand service business and brand service mechanism.

Brand develops as a core asset value. It will change the existing GNP development pattern, stock exchange and financial stock market structures. The key point of the changes is the identification of the brand value as the gross national intangible assets, which is an economic result of the comprehensive weighing of the virtual economic and actual economic elements. The total intangible assets of the country, cities, industries or enterprises will greatly improve contents of the brand management level and brand premium level in the intangible asset value of national economic development, so as to make future economic development structure more reasonable. The second key point is the economic value identification of the long-term operation of quality brand assets. Quality brand assets will realize the stable, huge and sustainable investment and holding values so as to suppress large stock price fluctuations brought by speculative transactions in the existing stock market. The stability, reliable transaction value and the asset holding method of quality brand assets will profoundly change a series of economic concepts such as finance, investment, stocks and transaction methods.

Brand brings huge economic development potential for national prosperity. The largest brands are not the best, but specific brands are better. The national brands or enterprise brands can achieve better development only by complying with the scientific brand principle of "being large yet specific and small yet beautiful". The brands essentially exist in the form of clusters. The development of any multinational economies or one core economy of a country falls into the panel, structural and cluster form, and is the economic development result by combining several industrial brand clusters, which has a vertical distribution structure. All enterprises will have various group cluster structures with multiple brands like main-sub brands and dominant-secondary brands after developed to a certain scale. The industrial brand clusters and group brand clusters are the main structures of the future global brand economies, and the important economic powers for a country, an area or an enterprise to participate in global market competition. Small brands have great economic potentials in family prosperity and increase of per-capita income, which could realize the economic development values of the handicrafts, diversified and individualized freelance jobs, smart business startups, creative enterprises, personal enterprises, family enterprise, farmer companies, craftsman brands, and other small entities, so as to release their economic potentials to make each family richer. Many small and beautiful brands can also last for hundreds of years to continuously generate income for generations. The brand economic development structure following the principle of "being large yet specific and small yet beautiful" will become not only eternal basic foundations for social and economic development of brands in different countries, but also strategic direction guiding the transmission from the employment economy, business starting economy and large enterprise economy to the highly developed brand service economic structure.

3 Further establishment of brand science principles and brand rules

The completion of *Introduction to Brands* has officially confirmed the scientific research values of brand science and scientific management science, and is the development results of significantly improving the scientific content of brand science to make it like the physics, modern medicine and other basic subjects of human beings.

Introduction to Brands is based on the nature of brand subjects. Its essence is the contributions to theoretical brand science, corresponding to the roles and values of the theoretical physics. It is an emerging brand science subject's structure established based on the systematic researches, discoveries and inventions of the scientific theories by exploring the development methods of tens of subjects such as sociology, network science and pathology.

The theoretical brand science has integrated all brand societies, economies, phenomena, direction and practices that appeared since the birth of human beings into scientific theories. It determines the important research methods by referring to scientific principles, subject structures, system technologies, rules and standards. It designs brand science with scientific structure, interprets brand science with scientific theories, promotes and guides brand practices with system rules and standards. And it translates brand applications into actual technologies for enterprises with the mature brand technology so as to integrate the vertical economic development value of brand society in terms of brand scientific tests, brand practice application and brand industrialization.

The theoretical brand science explains general phenomena with scientific denomination, scientific power and scientific principles, and guides the practical scientific value with theories, which is the emerging development direction of brand science, and has specified that the brand learning or application in global economy, countries, large families or enterprises shall be carried out based on the brand science. Continuous researches will produce more brand scientific principles, subject's structures and brand rules, utilization methods and tools. We can see that research entails painstaking effort, into which we must devote dozens of years or even the whole lifetime. But we will never regret having chosen this course. We wish a more prosperous future of brands and a better off life of all families.

Dreams make human beings great and brands eternal!

Authors Postscript

The study on *Introduction to Brands* started 15 years ago. The three authors, Tan Xinzheng, Zhu Zerong and Yang Jinfei started exploring the brand theory from different professional fields, and have successively written articles with over three million words.

Only a few researchers have systematically and deeply studied the historical development of the world brands. Through long-term practice, we have finished this book, the *"Introduction to Brands"*, after spending thousands of days and nights working on the research. Before this book is finished, the first national standard for brand evaluation in China that we have researched and drafted will come into being.

Evaluation of Business Enterprise Brand and Guide of Enterprise Culture Construction (GB/T27925-2011) was issued in 2011 and it is the first national standard in China regarding brand evaluation. Its evaluation models are the core elements of brand construction. Evaluation is carried out from multiple aspects including the "brand strategy management", "commodity quality", "service quality", "enterprise culture", "user loyalty", "integrity", "social responsibilities" and "influence" of enterprises. The viewpoints are completely different from that in the *Brand Value Evaluation* that was formulated by ISO. It is the first national standard in the world for evaluation of brand construction.

This national standard, which is of historical significance, was established due to thanks our own researches. Tan Xinzheng, Zhu Zerong and Yang Jinfei, respectively as drafter and writer of the "*Evaluation of Business Enterprise Brand and Guide of Enterprise Culture Construction*", have made significant contributions to the standard. At present, Beijing Sky Certification Center is carrying out in China the third party brand certification pursuant to this standard and upon approval of the Certification and Accreditation Administration of PRC. A batch of Chinese top enterprises has up till now passed the brand certification.

Brand research in the world is still "young". An integrated brand theory system cannot be expressed neither by one book nor by one standard. We kept deepening our research and we have found out that brand is not the only element for enterprise development; the size of the total intangible assets value is the core competitiveness for the sustainable development of an enterprise. In the near future, readers will gain more insight about us researches and books.

Authors
October 2016

Seven categories of brand

- ❖ Craftsman Brand: Does brand develop by the pursuit of pure craftsmanship?
- ❖ Professional Brand: Does brand occupy a certain professional market field?
- ❖ Trusted Brand: Is brand trustful and can be consumed by the consumers in a safe and reliable way?
- ❖ Premium Brand: Does brand have high profits that people are willing to purchase with more money?
- ❖ Tide Brand: Could brand meet requirements of certain specific fashion or cultural elements?
- ❖ Leading Brand: Does brand show the leading status in a certain market?
- ❖ International Brand: Is brand international enough to spread all over the world?

Enterprises focus on developing one or more combinations of key brand abilities.

The classification method of international brand is applicable to professional division of global brands.

Signification of the Mark
OF
Sino-American Multicultural Alliance

    Multiculture means the combination of multi-nation, different classes, different life styles, different habits, different interests and the like, namely the aggregation of habits, rules and inward purification.
    Both China and America own superior geographical condition, had experienced cruel war, possess profound historical background, face frequent population change, rapid economic development and powerful strength. Both countries were, are and will be the leaders in the whole world and enrich global multiculture constantly.
    The mark of Sino-American Multicultural Alliance covers the representative elements of China (the Great Wall and the Five-Star Red Flag) and America (The Eagle and the Star-Spangled Banner). The mark takes the main tones of two national flags as main line (red and blue), and takes the Great Wall and the Eagle as outline. The wings (red) letters S&A is the English abbreviation of "Sino-American Multicultural Alliance ". The image of the mark is integrated and elegant, and represents rich connotation with concise content, which is proper and clear with powerful visual impact. The culture exchange between China and America and the mutual tolerance and cooperation of the two countries will surely promote the development and open a new era.

BYLAWS

OF

SINO-AMERICAN MULTICULTURAL ALLIANCE INC.

ARTICLE I - MEMBERS

Sino-American Multicultural Alliance Inc. (the "Company") shall have no members.

ARTICLE II - OFFICES

The principal office of the Company shall be 136-20 38th Avenue, Suite 3A1, Flushing, County of Queens, State of New York. The Company may also have offices at such other places as the Board of Directors (the "Board") may from time to time determine or the business of the Company may require.

ARTICLE III - BOARD OF DIRECTORS

Section 1. Powers and Duties. The Board shall have general power to control and manage the affairs and property of the Company, subject to applicable law and in accordance with the purposes and limitations set forth in the Certificate of Incorporation and herein.

Section 2. Number. The number of Directors constituting the entire Board shall be not less than three and not more than ten. Subject to the foregoing, the number of Directors may be increased or decreased from time to time, by resolution of a majority of the entire Board, and no decrease shall shorten the term of any incumbent Director. As used in these bylaws, the term "entire Board" shall consist of the number of Directors that were elected as of the most recently held election of directors.

Section 3. Election and Term of Office. The initial Directors shall be the persons named in the Certificate of Incorporation and shall serve until the first meeting of the Board. The Directors shall hold office for one year terms; provided, however, that any Director elected to fill an unexpired term (whether resulting from the death, resignation or removal or created by an increase in the number of Directors) shall hold office until the next annual meeting at which the election of Directors is in the regular order of business and until his or her successor is elected or appointed and qualified. Directors may be elected to any number of consecutive terms. To become a Director, a person shall be nominated by a Director and elected by a majority of the Board.

Section 4. Qualification for Directors. Each Director shall be at least 18 years of age.

Section 5. Removal. Any Director may be removed at any time for cause by a vote of Directors then in office at a regular meeting or special meeting of the Board called for that purpose.

Section 6. Resignation. Any Director may resign from the Board at any time. Such resignation shall be made in writing, and shall take effect at the time specified therein, and if no time be specified, at the time of its receipt by the Company. The acceptance of a resignation by the Board shall not be necessary to make it effective, but no resignation shall discharge any accrued obligation or duty of a Director.

Section 7. Vacancies and Newly Created Directorships. Any newly created Directorships and any vacancies on the Board arising at any time and from any cause may be filled at any meeting of the Board by a majority of the entire Board. The Directors so elected shall serve until the next annual meeting at which the election of Directors is the regular order of business and his or her successor is elected or appointed and qualified. A vacancy in the Board shall be deemed to exist on the occurrence of any of the following:

(a) the death, resignation or removal of any Director;

(b) an increase in the authorized number of Directors by resolution of the Board; or

(c) the failure of the Directors, at any annual or other meeting of Directors at which any one or more Directors are to be elected, to elect the full authorized number of Directors to be voted for at that meeting.

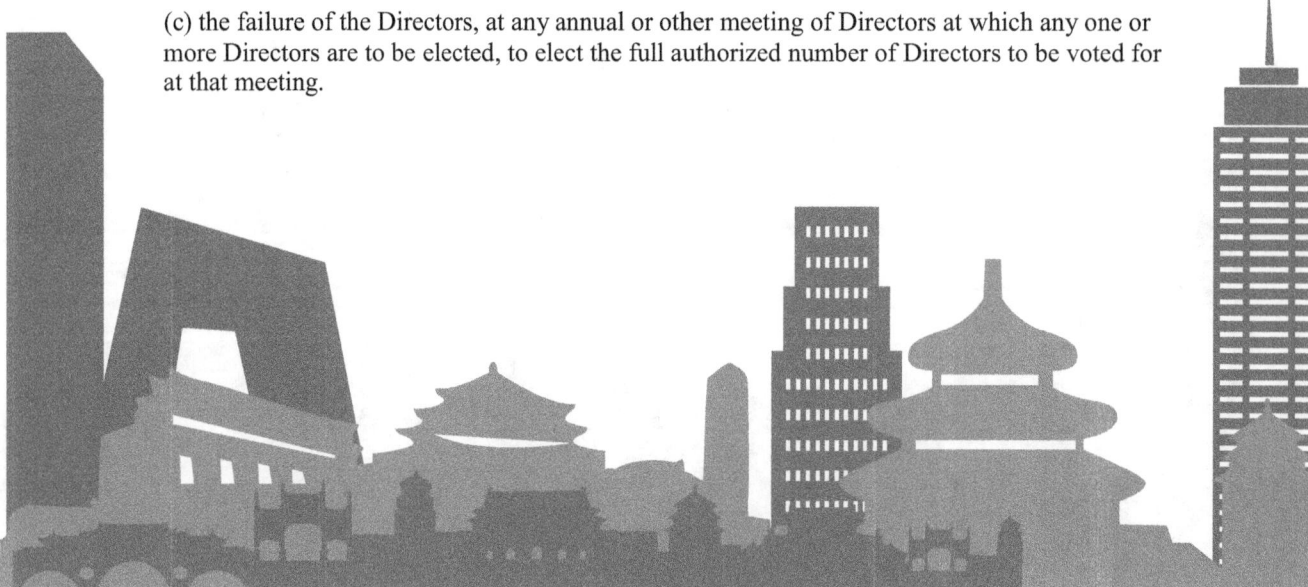

Section 8. Meetings. Meetings of the Board may be held at any place as the Board may from time to time fix. The annual meeting of the Board shall be held on the third Monday in April of each year, or at such other date, time and place as fixed by the Board. Other regular meetings of the Board shall be held no less than once per year at a time and place fixed by the Board. Special meetings of the Board shall be held whenever called by any Director.

Section 9. Notice of Meetings. Regular meetings may be held without notice of the time and place if such meetings are fixed by the Board. Notice of the time and place of the annual meeting, each regular meeting not fixed by the Board and each special meeting of the Board shall be (i) delivered to each Director by email or facsimile at least five (5) days before the day on which the meeting is to be held; or (ii) mailed to each Director, postage prepaid, addressed to him or her at his or her residence or usual place of business (or at such other address as he or she may have designated in a written request filed with the Secretary at least seven (7) days before the day on which the meeting is to be held). To discuss matters requiring prompt action, notice of special meetings may be sent to each Director by email, facsimile, or telephone, or given personally, no less than forty-eight hours before the time at which such meeting is to be held. Notice of a meeting need not be given to any Director who submits a signed waiver of notice whether before or after the meeting, or who attends the meeting without protesting, prior thereto or at its commencement, the lack of notice to him or her. Waivers of notice sent by email must be able to be reasonably determined to be sent by the Director. No notice need be given of any adjourned meeting.

Section 10. Quorum. Unless a greater proportion is required by law, the quorum shall be a majority of the entire Board.

Section 11. Voting. Except as otherwise provided by law or these Bylaws, at any meeting of the Board at which a quorum is present, the affirmative vote of a majority of the Directors present at the time of the vote shall be the act of the Board. If at any meeting of the Board there shall be less than a quorum present, the Directors present may adjourn the meeting until a quorum is obtained. Any one or more Directors of the Board or any committee thereof may participate in a meeting of the Board or committee by means of telephone, video conference or similar communications equipment provided that all persons participating in the meeting can hear each other at the same time and can participate in all matters before the board. Participation by such means shall constitute presence in person at a meeting.

Section 12. Action by the Board. Any action required or permitted to be taken by the Board or any committee thereof may be taken without a meeting if all Directors of the Board or the committee consent in writing to the adoption of a resolution authorizing the action. Such consent may be written or electronic. If the consent is written, it must be signed by the Director. If the consent is electronic it must be able to be reasonably determined to be sent by the board member. The resolution and the written consents thereto by the Board or committee shall be filed with the minutes of the proceedings of the Board.

Section 13. Compensation. No compensation of any kind shall be paid to any Director for the performance of his or her duties as Director. Subject to Article XI below (Related Party Transactions), provided that there is full disclosure of the terms of such compensation and the arrangement has been determined to be fair and reasonable and approved by the Independent Directors of the Board, this shall not in any way limit payment for services provided to the Company by the Director in any capacity separate from his or her responsibilities as a Director.

ARTICLE IV - OFFICERS, EMPLOYEES AND AGENTS

Section 1. Number and Qualifications. The Officers of the Company shall be a President, a Secretary, a Treasurer and such other Officers, if any, including one or more Vice Presidents, as the Board may from time to time appoint. One person may hold more than one office in the Company except that no one person may hold the offices of President and Secretary. No instrument required to be signed by more than one Officer may be signed by one person in more than one capacity.

Section 2. Election and Term of Office. The Officers of the Company shall be elected for a one-year term at the annual meeting of the Board, and each shall continue in office until his or her successor shall have been elected and qualified, or until his or her death, resignation or removal.

Section 3. Employees and Other Agents. The Board may from time to time appoint such employees and other agents as it shall deem necessary, each of whom shall hold office at the pleasure of the Board, and shall have such authority and perform such duties and shall receive such reasonable compensation, if any, as the Board may from time to time determine. To the fullest extent allowed by law, the Board may delegate to any employee or agent any powers possessed by the Board and may prescribe their respective title, terms of office, authorities and duties.

Section 4. Removal and Vacancies. Any Officer, employee or agent of the Company may be removed with or without cause by a vote of the majority of the entire Board. In case of any vacancy in any office, a successor to fill the unexpired portion of the term may be elected by the Board.

Section 5. Chairman: Powers and Duties. The Board may appoint a Chairman of the Board, who shall be a member of the Board and, if present, preside at meetings of the Board and exercise and perform such other powers and duties as may from time to time be assigned to him or her by the Board or as may be prescribed by these bylaws. The Chairman shall not be a paid employee of the Company.

Section 6. President: Powers and Duties. If no Chairman of the Board is appointed, or if one is appointed, in his or her absence, the President shall preside at all meetings of the Board. The President shall have general supervision of the affairs of the Company and shall keep the Board fully informed about the activities of the Company. He or she has the power to sign and execute alone in the name of the Company all contracts authorized either generally or specifically by the Board, unless the Board shall specifically require an additional signature. The President shall perform all the duties usually incident to the office of the President and shall perform such other duties as from time to time may be assigned by the Board.

Section 7. Vice-President/CEO: Powers and Duties. A Vice President shall have such powers and duties as may be assigned to him or her by the Board. In the absence of the President, the Vice President(s), in the order designated by the Board, shall perform the duties of the President.

Section 8. Secretary: Powers and Duties. The Secretary shall keep the minutes of the annual meeting and all meetings of the Board in books provided for that purpose. He or she shall be responsible for the giving and serving of all notices of the Company, receiving the annual Conflict of Interest disclosure statements and shall perform all the duties customarily incidental to the office of the Secretary, subject to the control of the Board, and shall perform such other duties as shall from time to time be assigned by the Board.

Section 9. Treasurer: Powers and Duties. The Treasurer shall keep or cause to be kept full and accurate accounts of receipts and disbursements of the Company, and shall deposit or cause to be deposited all moneys, evidences of indebtedness and other valuable documents of the Company in the name and to the credit of the Company in such banks or depositories as the Board may designate. The Treasurer shall, at all reasonable times, exhibit the Company's books and accounts to any Officer or Director of the Company, and whenever required by the Board, render a statement of the Company's accounts and perform all duties incident to the position of Treasurer, subject to the control of the Board.

ARTICLE V - COMMITTEES

The Board, by resolution adopted by a majority of the entire Board, may establish and appoint committees of the Board consisting of at least three Directors with such powers and duties as the Board may prescribe. The members of such committees shall be appointed by the Board. Such board committees shall have all the authority of the Board, except as to the following matters:

(i) the filling of vacancies on the Board or on any committee;

(ii) the amendment or repeal of the Bylaws or the adoption of new Bylaws;

(iii) the amendment or repeal of any resolution of the Board which by its terms shall not be so amendable or repealable; and

(iv) the fixing of compensation of the Directors for serving on the Board or any committee.

ARTICLE VI - CONTRACTS, CHECKS, BANK ACCOUNTS AND INVESTMENTS

The Board is authorized to select the banks or depositories it deems proper for the funds of the Company and shall determine who shall be authorized on the Company's behalf to sign checks, drafts or other orders for the payment of money, acceptances, notes or other evidences of indebtedness, to enter into contracts or to execute and deliver other documents and instruments.

ARTICLE VII - BOOKS

There shall be kept at the office of the Company correct books of account of the activities and transactions of the Company including the minute book, which shall contain a copy of the Certificate of Incorporation, a copy of these Bylaws, and all minutes of meetings of the Board.

ARTICLE VIII - FISCAL YEAR

The fiscal year of the Company shall be determined by the Board.

ARTICLE IX - INDEMNIFICATION AND INSURANCE

Section 1. Indemnification. The Company may, to the fullest extent now or hereafter permitted by law, indemnify any person made, or threatened to be made, a party to any action or proceeding by reason of the fact that he or she or his or her testator was a Director, officer, employee or agent of the Company, against judgments, fines, amounts paid in settlement and reasonable expenses, including attorney fees. No indemnification may be made to or on behalf of any such person if (a) his or her acts were committed in bad faith or were the result of his or her active and deliberate dishonesty and were material to such action or proceeding or (b) he or she personally gained in fact a financial profit or other advantage to which he or she was not legally entitled in the transaction or matter in which indemnification is sought.

Section 2. Insurance. The Company shall have the power to purchase and maintain all insurance policies deemed to be in the best interest of the Company, including insurance to indemnify the Company for any obligation which it incurs as a result of its indemnification of Directors, Officers and employees pursuant to Section 1 above, or to indemnify such persons in instances in which they may be indemnified pursuant to Section 1 above.

ARTICLE X – AMENDMENTS

These Bylaws may be amended or repealed by the affirmative majority vote of the entire Board.

ARTICLE XI – RELATED PARTY TRANSACTIONS

Section 1. Purpose. The purpose of this policy (the "Policy") is to protect the interests of the Company when it is contemplating entering into a transaction or arrangement that might benefit the private interest of a Director, Officer, or Key Employee of the Company. The Company will not enter into any such transaction or arrangement unless it is determined by the Board in the manner described below to be fair, reasonable and in the best interests of the Company at the time of such determination. This Policy is intended to supplement, but not replace, any applicable state and federal laws governing conflicts of interest applicable to non-for-profit and charitable organizations.

Section 2. Definitions.
(a) Affiliate. An affiliate of the Company is a person or entity that is directly or indirectly through one or more intermediaries, controlled by, in control of, or under common control with the Company.
(b) Financial Interest. A person has a Financial Interest if such person would receive an economic benefit, directly or indirectly, from any transaction, agreement, compensation agreement, including direct or indirect remuneration as well as gifts or favors that are not insubstantial or other arrangement involving the Company.
(c) Independent Director. A member of the Board who:

(i) Has not been an employee of the Company or an Affiliate of the Company within the last three years;

(ii) Does not have a Relative who has been a Key Employee of the Company or an Affiliate of the Company within the last three years;

(iii) Has not received and does not have a Relative who has received more than $10,000 in compensation directly from the Company or an Affiliate of the Company in any of the last three years (not including reimbursement for services as a Director);

(iv) Does not have a substantial Financial Interest in and has not been an employee of, and does not have a Relative who has a substantial Financial Interest in or was an Officer of, any entity that has made payments to or received payments from, the Company or an Affiliate of the Company in excess of the lesser of: (a) $25,000 or (b) 2% of the Company's consolidated gross revenue over the last three years (payment does not include charitable contribution);

(v) Is not in an employment relationship under control or direction of any Related Party and does not receive payments subject to approval of a Related Party;

(vi) Does not approve a transaction providing economic benefits to any Related Party who in turn has approved or will approve a transaction providing economic benefits to the Director.

(d) Key Employee. A Key Employee is a person who is, or has within the last five years, been in a position to exercise substantial influence over the affairs of the Company.

(e) Officer. A person who has the authority to bind the Company as designated in the Bylaws of the Company.

(f) Related Party. Persons who may be considered a Related Party of the Company or an Affiliate of the Company under this Policy include:

(i) Directors, Officers, or Key Employees of the Company or an Affiliate of the Company;
(ii) Relatives of Directors, Officers, or Key Employees;
(iii) any entity in which a person in (i) or (ii) has a 35% or greater ownership or beneficial interest or, in the case of a partnership or professional company, a direct or indirect ownership interest in excess of 5%;
(iv) Founders of the Company;
(v) Substantial contributors to the Company (within the current fiscal year or the past five fiscal years);
(vi) Persons owning a controlling interest (through votes or value) in the Company;

(g) Related Party Transaction. Any transaction, agreement or any other arrangement with the Company or an Affiliate of the Company in which a Related Party has a Financial Interest. Any Related Party Transaction will be considered a conflict of interest for purposes of this Policy.

(h) Relative. A Relative is a spouse, ancestor, child (whether natural or adopted), grandchild, great grandchild, sibling (whether whole or half blood), or spouse of a child (whether natural or adopted), grandchild, great grandchild or sibling (whether whole or half blood), or a domestic partner as defined in section 2994-A of the New York Public Health Law.

Section 3. Related Party Transactions and Duty to Disclose: A Related Party Transaction is not necessarily a prohibited transaction. If the Company contemplates entering into a Related Party Transaction, the Independent Directors of the Board must determine if the transaction is fair, reasonable, and in the best interests of the Company at the time of such determination. If at any time during his or her term of service a Related Party acquires any Financial Interest or when any matter for decision or approval comes before the Board in which a Related Party has a Financial Interest, the material facts of that Financial Interest or potential Related Party Transaction must be promptly disclosed in writing by the Related Party to each member of the Board. The Board will then follow the procedures in Section 4 of this Policy. Any failure by a Related Party to disclose to the Board a known Financial Interest or a known potential Related Party Transaction may be grounds for removal of such person from the Board and/or his or her termination from the Company.

Section 4. Review and Voting.

(a) Non-Participation and Review. All transactions, agreements or any other arrangements between the Company and a Related Party, and any other transactions which may involve a potential conflict of interest, shall be reviewed by the Independent Directors. All Related Parties with a Financial Interest shall leave the room in which such deliberations are conducted. The Independent Directors will then determine whether the contemplated Related Party Transaction is fair, reasonable, and in the best interests of the Company at the time of such determination. The Company will not enter into any Related Party Transaction unless it is determined to be fair, reasonable and in the best interest of the Company at the time of such determination.

(b) Consideration of Alternate Transactions and Comparability Data. If the contemplated Related Party Transaction pertains to compensation for services or the transfer of property or other benefit to a Related Party, the Independent Directors must determine that the value of the economic benefit provided by the Company to the Related Party does not exceed the value of the consideration received in exchange by obtaining and reviewing appropriate comparable data prior to entering the transaction. In those instances where the contemplated Related Party Transaction does not involve compensation, transfer of property or benefits to a Related Party, the Independent Directors must consider alternative transactions to the extent possible, prior to entering into such transaction.

(c) Comparability Data. When considering the comparability of compensation, for example, the relevant Comparability Data which the Independent Directors may consider includes, but is not limited to (1) compensation levels paid by similarly situated organizations, both exempt and non-exempt; (2) the availability of similar services within the same geographic area; (3) current compensation surveys compiled by independent firms; and (4) written offers from similar institutions competing for the same person's services. When the transaction involves the transfer of real property as compensation, the relevant factors include, but are not limited to (i) current independent appraisals of the property, and (ii) offers received in a competitive bidding process.

(d) Voting. The Independent Directors after considering alternate transactions and/or comparability data shall determine in good faith whether the transaction or arrangement is fair, reasonable, and in the best interest of the Company at the time of such decision. Any such transaction shall be approved by not less than a majority vote of the Independent Directors present at the meeting. The Independent Directors shall make their decision as to whether to enter into the transaction or arrangement and shall contemporaneously document the meeting under Article 6 of this Policy. All Related Parties with a Financial Interest must not be present for deliberations and voting on the transaction or arrangement in which he or she has a Financial Interest. Only Independent Directors shall vote on Related Party Transactions. No Related Party shall vote, act, or attempt to influence improperly the deliberations on any matter in which he or she has been determined by the Board to have a Financial Interest. Any attempt to vote, act, or improperly influence deliberations by a Related Party on any matter with which such person has a Financial Interest may be grounds for such person's removal from the Board or termination from the Company.

(e) Compensation. A voting member of the Board or an Officer who receives compensation directly or indirectly from the Company for services or a Director serving as a voting member of any Committee whose jurisdiction includes compensation matters is precluded from voting or acting on matters pertaining to that Director's or Officer's compensation. No voting member of the Board or any committee thereof whose jurisdiction includes compensation matters and who receives compensation, directly or indirectly, from the Company, either individually or collectively, is prohibited from providing information to the Board or any committee thereof regarding compensation.

Section 5. Records of Proceedings. The minutes of all meetings of the Board at which a Related Party Transaction is considered shall contain:

(a) The names of the persons who disclosed or otherwise were determined to have a potential or actual Financial Interest and/or conflict of interest, the nature of the potential or actual Financial Interest and/or conflict of interest, any action taken to determine whether a Financial Interest or conflict of interest exists, and the Board's decision as to whether a Financial Interest and/or conflict of interest exists.

(b) The names of the persons who were present for discussions and votes relating to any determinations under Article 6(a) above, including whether the Related Party and any Board members not considered to be Independent Directors, left the room during any such discussions, the content of such discussions, including discussion of alternative transactions, and whether or not the transaction with the Related Party was approved by the Board.

(c) The minutes shall be documented contemporaneously to the decision and discussion regarding the Financial Interest or conflict of interest.

Section 6. Initial and Annual Written Disclosures. Prior to a Director's initial election to the Board, or an Officer or Key Employee's employment at the Company, and thereafter on an annual basis, all Directors, Officers, and Key Employees shall disclose in writing to the Secretary of the Company:

(a) Any entity of which such person or a Relative of such person is an officer, director, trustee, member, owner, or employee and with which the Company has a relationship,

(b) Any Financial Interest such person may have in any company, organization, partnership or other entity which provides professional or other goods or services to Company for a fee or other compensation, and

(c) Any position or other material relationship such Director, Officer, Key Employee, or Relative of such person, may have with any not-for-profit company with which the Company has a business relationship.

A copy of each disclosure statement shall be kept in the Company's files and made available to any Director, Officer, or Key Employee upon request.

Section 7. Annual Statements. Each Director, Officer, and Key Employee shall annually sign and submit to the Secretary of the Company a statement which affirms such person: (a) has received a copy of this Policy, (b) has read and understands the Policy, and (c) has agreed to comply with the Policy.

ARTICLE XII - NON-DISCRIMINATION

In all of its dealings, neither the Company nor its duly authorized agents shall discriminate against any individual or group for reasons of race, color, creed, sex, age, ethnicity, national origin, marital status, sexual preference, mental or physical disability or any category protected by state or federal law.

ARTICLE XIII - REFERENCE TO CERTIFICATE OF INCORPORATION

References in these Bylaws to the Certificate of Incorporation shall include all amendments thereto or changes thereof unless specifically excepted by these Bylaws. In the event of a conflict between the Certificate of Incorporation and these Bylaws, the Certificate of Incorporation shall govern.

ADOPTED the 22nd day of April, 2016.

Address: 139-01 Main Street Suite 403, Flushing NY 11354

Tell: +1 (917) 285-5064   +1 (929) 426-9039

www.ingramcontent.com/pod-product-compliance
Lightning Source LLC
Chambersburg PA
CBHW080632230426

43663CB00016B/2839